KT-142-348

91
TAS
(D23)

Event Management

A Professional and Developmental Approach

Greg Damster, Peter de Tolly, Wren Dry, Jürgen Gasche, Debbie Johnson, John Knocker,
Nicola Lloyd, David Maralack, Nancy Nuntsu, Howard Pell, Nimish Shukla, Kamilla Swart,
Debbie van Oudtshoorn, Jo-Ansie van Wyk, Tom Wanklin
and
Dimitri Tassiopoulos (editor)

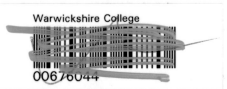

Event Management
A Professional and Developmental Approach
Second edition

First published in 2000
Second Edition 2005
Reprinted 2006

ISBN 0 7021 6658 8

© Juta Academic 2005
P O Box 24309, Lansdowne, 7779

Project Manager: Fiona Wakelin

Subediting: Pat Hanekom

Proofreading: Ken McGillivray

Layout and typography: Martingraphix

Cover design: Pumphaus Design Studio cc

Printed and bound by: Paarl Print, Oosterland Street, Paarl, South Africa

Key to Icons

 Aim of the chapter

 Important information

 Definitions

 Examples

 Case studies

While every attempt was made to contact copyright holders the publishers regret that this was not always possible. Any errors or ommissions in this regards will be redressed in future editions if brought to the attention of the publishers.

About the Authors

Greg Damster (Chapter 15): Greg is the Special Events and Competitions Manager of the Community Chest Western Cape. He has been with the Community Chest since 1993 having served as a volunteer for the carnival since 1973. One of the main fundraising events on the Community Chest calendar is the annual carnival held at Maynardville – an annual event for the past 49 years. Greg has been instrumental in raising the standard and income of the carnival which at present takes in a net profit of more than R1,5 million over the four trading days.

Peter de Tolly (Chapter 4): Peter holds degrees in Architecture (BArch, University of Cape Town, 1963) and Urban Design (MArch, University of Toronto, 1970). Between 1995 and 1997 he was seconded to the Cape Town 2004 Olympic Bid Company. As part of the bid's management team, he was Director of Planning and Environment. His main responsibility was the preparation of the Olympic Plan. As one of the five finalists, the plan was the first explicitly developmental bid in the history of the Olympic movement and the first to undertake a strategic environmental assessment (SEA) as part of its comprehensive environmental planning and analysis. Peter has consulted in the United States (the University of Minnesota, 1970 to 1972) and has coordinated waterfront planning for the City of Toronto and three other levels of government (1970 to 1979). Peter has retired and is now a consultant. He is the former Director: Special Projects of the City of Cape Town.

Wren Dry (Chapter 15): Wren is the assistant to Greg Damster at the Community Chest. Her main portfolio is creating new fundraising events (for example music concerts, both local and international) as well as ensuring the smooth running of the present events. She has been with the Community Chest since 1997.

Jürgen Gasche (Chapter 12): Jürgen is a qualified chef and patissier who has worked through the ranks of kitchen brigades in Germany, the Bahamas, Kuwait and South Africa. Before joining Walter Sisulu University (formerly known as Border Technikon) as a lecturer in Culinary Studies and Techniques, he worked as Executive Chef for Sun International. In this capacity he regularly planned and managed large catering events. He is also a registered trainer with the UK-based Hotel and Catering Training Company. He is currently a lecturer at the Centre of Excellence in Leisure and Tourism at Walter Sisulu University.

Debbie Johnson (Chapter 14): Debbie is a Lecturer at the Cape Peninsula University of Technology (formerly known as Cape Technikon), Department of Tourism Management. She holds a Masters Degree in Post School Education and a National Diploma in Travel and Tourism. She has worked for SATOUR, 1987–1996, involved with marketing, tourism development and conference organising. Debbie has been involved with the conference industry for the last 13 years and also served on the founding council of SAACI (Western Cape). She joined the Cape Technikon in 1996 – current and lectures tourism development and has developed all the event management training programmes offered at the Cape Technikon.

John Knocker (Chapter 17): John has been employed at Specialised Exhibitions (Pty) Ltd. since 1985 and has been a director for the last 15 years. During his period with the company, he has held the overall responsibility for all of the exhibitions organised by the company. This was accomplished through a team of sales personnel, each being responsibile for sales for their own events.

Nicola Lloyd (Chapter 3): Nicola holds a Masters degree in Urban and Regional Planning and spent eight years with the City of Cape Town before being seconded to the Cape Town 2004 Olympic Bid Company. There she assisted with the preparation of the Olympic Bid Candidature File and was responsible for the coordination of the 270-strong South African delegation which visited Switzerland for the final decision by the IOC. In 1998 she established an event management company in Cape Town – QED (Quality Event Design) – with her partner Laura Steed. QED specialises in the organisation and management of conferences, exhibitions, sports events, corporate launches and productions. She is currently employed in the private sector.

David Maralack (Chapter 3): David is a Deputy Director in the Western Cape Department of Cultural Affairs, Sport and Recreation, responsible for sport promotion and development. He has been involved in numerous bid processes, such as the Cape Town 2004 Olympic Bid Committee and on the Cape Town organising committee of the Soccer World Cup Bid 2006 and 2010. He has been project manager for numerous major sport events including the Cape Town leg of the Olympic Torch Relay 2004. He is the author of the *Bidding and Hosting Manual for Sport and Recreation Events* on behalf of the South African Sports Commission.

Nancy Nuntsu (Chapters 8 & 11): Nancy holds a PhD degree from the University of the North. She is currently employed as the Head of the Centre of Excellence in Leisure and Tourism Research Unit (CELTRU) at Walter Sisulu University and has published several articles in peer-reviewed journals.

Howard Pell (Chapter 17): In 1970 Howard was appointed Managing Director of Specialised Exhibitions (a company in the Hortors Group). In 1973 he returned to the Kalamazoo Division and took over as Managing Director. He remained in this position until his retirement in 1990. Specialised Exhibitions is the largest exhibition organiser in South Africa and mounts between ten and fifteen exhibitions each year. Howard also served on the Executive Committee of the Exhibition Association of South Africa (EXSA) and was the chair for two years.

Nimish Shukla (Chapters 8 & 11): Nimish is a senior lecturer at the Centre of Excellence in Leisure and Tourism at Walter Sisulu University. He has a Masters degree in Commerce and has been involved in this field for the past 12 years, both within the industry and academia. Nimish specialises in the field of tourism marketing and promotion.

Kamilla Swart (Chapters 13 & 16): Kamilla is a senior lecturer/ researcher at the Cape Peninsula University of Technology (formerly known as Cape Technikon), Department of Tourism Management. Her interest in sport tourism, and specifically events, ignited as a result of her work at the Olympic Bid Company. Kamilla completed her doctoral degree in sport tourism and graduated from Illinois State University (ISU) in December 2001. She worked at Octagon SA from 2000–2003 specifically consulting to the Durban Events Corporation, amongst other corporate clients. Kamilla was the lead consultant for the Department of Environmental Affairs and Tourism and South African Tourism who commissioned a study, 'Towards a National Events Strategy for South Africa'. She has co-authored the first U.S. text on sport tourism in 2002. Her manuscripts have been published in the *Journal of Sport Tourism* and *Visions in Leisure and Business*. Kamilla has also been chosen as one of the 10 Outstanding Persons in Sport Tourism in the 1990s by the Sport Tourism International Council.

Dimitri Tassiopoulos (Chapters 1 & 2): Dimitri holds a Masters degree in Business Administration and a BA (Hons.) in Political Science from the University of Stellenbosch. He is currently reading for his doctorate. Since 1993, he has been involved in various national and international research projects, of a multidisciplinary and multi-institutional nature, concerning agri-, event, cultural and wine tourism, amongst others. He specialises in entrepreneurship and strategic management and is currently an Associate Director at the Centre of Excellence in Leisure and Tourism, Walter Sisulu University. Dimitri volunteered his services to the Athens 2004 Olympic Games.

Debbie van Oudtshoorn (Chapter 7): Debbie was born in Port Elizabeth and graduated from the University of Port Elizabeth (UPE) with a B.Com. majoring in Business Economics and Economics. She has five years' experience in the hotel industry. Previously employed at Walter Sisulu University, where she lectured in Financial Management to the Tourism Management and Hospitality Management students, she is currently employed in the private sector.

Jo-Ansie van Wyk (Chapter 18): Jo-Ansie van Wyk lectures in the Department of Political Sciences, University of South Africa (UNISA), Pretoria. She holds an MA (Political Sciences) from the University of Stellenbosch. She is a Research Associate of the Institute of Security Studies (ISS), Pretoria, and the African Water Issues Research Unit (AWIRU), Pretoria. Jo-Ansie has received various awards, amongst others the New South Africa Security Policy Fellowship from King's College and a Fellowship of the Venice Commission of the Council of Europe. She is a member of council of the South African Political Studies Association (SAPSA) and vice-chairperson of the Pretoria branch of the South African Institute of International Affairs (SAIIA).

Tom Wanklin (Chapters 5, 6, 9, 10): Tom holds a BSc (Hons) in Town and Regional Planning from the University of the Witwatersrand and has extensive experience as a development planner. After lecturing in Tourism Development and Event Management in the Centre of Excellence in Leisure and Tourism at Walter Sisulu University he returned to full-time private practice; with tourism consulting and project implementation as an additional offering.

Contents

CHAPTER 4 Event Impact Assessment 74

Peter de Tolly

CHAPTER 5 Event Planning 96

Tom Wanklin

CHAPTER 9 Event Programming   205

Tom Wanklin

CHAPTER 10 Risk Management   228

Tom Wanklin

Please note: Appendices, Glossary, Further Readings, Tables, Figures and Diagrams may be accessed on the web site www.jutaacademic.co.za

Acknowledgements

As is the case with all literary ventures, we could not have produced all this work without the assistance, guidance and support of many individuals. Initial ideas and suggestions were provided to us from round-table discussions with various event management practitioners and academics.

We are delighted that Dr Joe Goldblatt (CSEP, Professor & Executive Director of the School of Tourism & Hospitality Management, Temple University Philadelphia, Pennsylvania) was willing to write the Foreword. He is a highly respected professor and scholar in event management and these qualities make him an ideal candidate to comment on this work.

We wish to thank the following:
- Beryl Douglas, SAACI (Head office)/Contact Publications (Pty) Ltd
- Deidré Cloete, Conferences Et Al
- Don Bell, Marketing Director, Gate 7 Consulting Services (Pty) Ltd
- Henriette Greef, Conference Division of SA Tourism
- Janet Landey, Ex-President of ISES (South Africa)
- Louise Roberts, Walter Sisulu University
- Sandra Hustwick, Cape Town City Council
- Tersia van Tonder, Marketing Consultant, Gate 7 Consulting Services (Pty) Ltd
- The Exhibition Association of South Africa – EXSA

We are also especially grateful to Tim Brophy and Al Karaki, of SA Tourism's Information Technology Department, for their assistance in providing access to the SA Tourism national events database (2003–2004). Our appreciation is extended to the production staff of Juta & Company for their excellent handling of our manuscript and to their commissioning editor, Ute Spath, for her support in seeing this work to its completion.

Special gratitude is extended to Thandiswa George and Sonwabile Sepoko for their assistance with the data processing aspects of this manuscript. Finally, there are, of course, other people in our lives about whom we care deeply and who have made enormous sacrifices while we wrote this book.

Preface

Event management is an exciting new medium and a sector of the South African tourism industry which has become a positive force. It is now widely accepted by most tourism stakeholders as a development and marketing strategy by which destinations can gain from the economic benefits of tourism.

Event tourism is a particular form of tourism which has seen considerable growth in recent years. In contrast with permanent tourism attractions, events are temporary occurrences, usually with a particular theme, which aim to attract people to the focal point of a short-lived, organised activity in which visitors may participate, watch, view, learn and enjoy.

Event organisers have a number of goals and objectives. Events can extend the tourist season or they can spread demand over a season. Events can be designed as marketing tools to publicise and promote a destination or attractions. They can also be used to stimulate demand by attracting *extra*, *new* or *repeat* visitors. Events can be intended to generate additional revenue for a destination (Light, 1996: 183).

When this book was first prepared in 1999, no one knew how large the event management field would become and few envisioned the profound potential of such an evolution both in education and in the event industry. The first edition became established as the authoritative text on event management for a developing country context. The second edition remains the first multidisciplinary book of its kind written for a developing country context, however, based upon international best practice in events management. It comes to you as a collaborative approach between experienced event practitioners and academics from a number of academic institutions.

This book is intended as an academic and 'how to' professional text. Although there are many books on event planning, sponsorship and management, there is a dearth of books that provide the theoretical and methodological knowledge base which is a prerequisite for establishing events in a developing country context. Further, the need to develop adaptable problem-solving skills, foster professionalism and stimulate event research is seen as an overall outcome of this book.

Event Management: A Professional and Developmental Approach is about the actual process of understanding what events are, and ultimately planning and managing events for the sustainable economic benefit of tourism destinations.

The book consists of three parts. Part A provides an introduction to the background of events and the main participating stakeholders. Chapter 1 looks at event history, the current event situation in South Africa, and introduces a code of ethics and professionalism for events. Chapter 2 is concerned with the issue of the activities of the various stakeholders of events. Part B provides readers with an insight into best practice in management and planning and is based on current international theory and practice. Chapter 3 covers with the process of securing and hosting an event. This is seen in the light of evaluating the cost and benefits of hosting an event and the process whereby some sought-after international events are subject to international bidding, as required by some event owners. Chapter 4 provides an in-depth impact assessment of events on destinations in terms of socio-economic and environmental factors. The event planning process is discussed in chapter 5. Chapter 6 investigates establishing best practice in event organising and coordination. Chapter 7 is concerned with one of the least-liked but most crucial activities of event management — accounting and financial management. Event sponsorship, discussed in chapter 8, is one of the most critical lifelines of organising events, especially in the light of ever-tightening public sector purse strings. Event programming, the subject of chapter 9, is a critical skill all event organisers need to master in order to increase the retention of visitors at a destination for longer than one day. Chapter 10 outlines the reasons why event organisers need to be aware of the benefits of putting in place a proper risk management plan. Chapter 11 is concerned with ensuring that the event is properly marketed and communicated to all the stakeholders in a culturally diverse context.

Should stakeholders be excluded from the communication process, this could result in questions about the event's future sustainability. One of the main activities at most events is the exposure of event participants to the activities of food and beverage professionals, as discussed in chapter 12. The proper planning of such an activity is critical for the success of any event.

Part C is concerned with applying and focusing the theory on some of the better known segments of the events sector. The overall purpose of this part is to assist the reader with developing the necessary skills and knowledge to be able to organise any such form of event. The MICE (meetings, incentives, conferences and exhibitions) segment is examined in some detail in separate chapters. Chapter 13 aims to assist readers with understanding the bidding and planning process which must be followed when organising a mega-event. Meeting management is discussed in chapter 14. Festival management and organisation is discussed in chapter 15 to ensure an in-depth understanding of how to put together such an event successfully. In chapter 16, the process of organising sports events, is discussed. Exhibition management, one of the most easily experienced forms of a business event, is discussed in chapter 17. And, finally, chapter 18 exposes the reader to the techniques and skills required to successfully organise various forms of political, civic and government events.

NOTE: Internet sites have been provided for further information and are presented in good faith and believed to be correct, the authors, editor and publisher make no representations or warranties as to the completeness or accuracy of the information and make no commitment to update or correct any Internet information.

Foreword

The isiZulu word *imbizo* means 'a gathering'. In the summer of 2004 a group of researchers gathered in the South African veld near the magnificent God's Window to advance the field of event management. It was appropriate that this group of distinguished international researchers would hold their gathering in a land where many believe the potential for human celebration was born.

As these scholars worked to advance the field of event management on a global scale, Dimitri Tassiopoulos, the editor of South Africa's first text book in the field of event management studies, was completing the second edition of this work. He and the team of contributing authors have once again made a significant contribution to the field of event management not only in the country of South Africa but on a global basis as well. Throughout this book, the authors have chronicled the history of the field and connected this history to the historic struggles of South Africa. Furthermore, they have provided a significant number of models and charts that enable the reader to readily understand and effectively use the principles of event management.

The recent award to South Africa of the 2010 Soccer World Cup demonstrates that South Africa is poised to become a world leader in event management and marketing. That is just one of the many reasons why this book is so important, as the event leaders of this country seek to influence others worldwide through their commitment to quality and innovation.

Perhaps most importantly, this team of authors has demonstrated how a land and people that has experienced tremendous turmoil through the ages, connect their historic positive evolution to milestones in the form of events that are historic, ceremonial, and meaningful for millions of people. Readers will greatly benefit from careful research, easy-to-use examples, and inspiring wisdom.

Although this book is primarily directed to the South African reader, scholars and practicioners throughout the world will also benefit from the global examples provided. I will keep this book within easy reach as I continue to explore the future of the field while remaining devoted to its historic roots in the continent of Africa.

Therefore, you too are invited to this *imbizo* convened by Dimitri Tassiopoulos and company. At this gathering of great ideas, you will help advance a profession born in the land of Africa and now rapidly advancing toward a great new future just as the country of South Africa will also enjoy as a result of the most important book.

Dr Joe Goldblatt, CSEP
Professor of Tourism & Hospitality Management; Executive Director for Professional Development & Strategic Partnerships; Event Tourism Specialist; E-mail: joe.goldblatt@temple.edu

Third Draft, May 8, 1998
The Future of Event Management
Charter
Researched and Submitted by Leaders in the Special Events Industry
Columbia University's Biosphere 2
May 3, 1998

Introduction

The event industry is one of the world's largest employers and contributes major positive economic impact. The event industry is not only our profession but also a personal mission through which we are able to make a positive contribution to the lives of millions of people. Through events, human beings mark important milestones. As event professionals we are responsible for positively impacting people and the environment in which we live. We are humbled by this responsibility and share a reverence for this mission. We give thanks for the heritage that we have received from past generations and embrace our responsibilities to present and future generations of event professionals.

The event industry stands at a defining moment. A fundamental understanding and commitment to economic, technological, and environmental challenges is needed to ensure a sustainable future for this industry and the professions it represents. Foresight and positive use of knowledge and power are the foundations for a successful future of the event industry. We must advance the event industry, finding new ways to balance self and community, diversity and unity, short-term and strategic by using and nurturing, preserving and expanding.

In the midst of all of our diversity as a special events industry, we are one humanity and one family with a shared destiny. The economic, technological, and environmental challenges before us require an inclusive ethical vision. Alliances must be forged and cooperation fostered at every level, in every profession, and in every community on earth. In solidarity with one another and the community of life, we the stewards of this profession commit ourselves to action guided by the following interrelated principles.

Mission

To anticipate environmental, technological, and economic change in order to ensure a successful and enduring industry we must:

1. **Serve** as responsible custodians of the natural environment and educate others to understand this value and financial benefit.
2. **Improve** our technological capabilities to simultaneously reduce cost and improve quality.
3. **Establish** strong mutually beneficial strategic alliances for educational, social, and economic benefits worldwide.

Responsibility and Accountability

We believe that in order to achieve long-term sustainability for this profession it is essential that we continually monitor, evaluate, analyze, and correct these goals as needed to ensure proper accountability.

1. **Serve as responsible custodians of the natural environment and educate others to follow our example.**
   a. Begin to commit ourselves to do well by doing good.
   b. Use pre-cycling and other pre-planning strategies to reduce negative impacts on the environment.

c. Develop written environmental policies for our businesses, professional organizations, and industry.
d. Reduce and re-use event materials to promote positive impacts on the environment.
e. Continually monitor environmental changes in order to develop new strategies to lessen negative impacts.
f. Promote positive environmental practices within our businesses and industry to encourage others and newcomers to share this responsibility.
g. Utilize green achievements as a selling tool and positive public relations opportunity for current and future clients.

2. ***Improve our technological capabilities to simultaneously reduce cost and improve quality.***
a. Utilize technology as applicable for every facet of the event industry.
b. Invest in the research and development of software that will improve efficiency, quality, and financial yield.
c. Encourage the development and use of technology (i.e. World Wide Web, Internet 2) for the production and marketing of events.
d. Reduce technological cost through cooperative agreements.
e. Improve communication and collaboration through encouraging the use of electronic systems by internal and external publics.
f. Provide training for ourselves and those we supervise to ensure educational parity with these emerging technologies.

3. ***Establish strong beneficial global strategic alliances and cooperate with one another for mutual economic benefit.***
a. Encourage organizations to increasingly utilize events to convey their mission, or,
    Provide competitive compensation schemes to attract the highest qualified employees.
b. Encourage inclusiveness among all peoples for maximum participation in and benefit from the events industry.
c. Identify systems that determine the actual economic return on each event/investment.
d. Balance the need for qualified employees, economic expansion, with realistic forecasting to ensure financial growth.
e. Share, invest, and utilize initially quality re-usable goods, emerging technologies, and environmental awareness to reduce cost and increase financial yield.
f. Create cooperative buying opportunities with industry partners.
g. Seek out and encourage suppliers who use green practices.
h. Encourage organizations to utilize events to increasingly communicate their mission or cause.

Covenant

Embracing the values in this Charter, we can grow into a sustainable profession that allows the potential of all persons to fully develop in harmony with the events industry. We must preserve a strong faith in the possibilities of the human spirit and a deep sense of belonging to the universal family of event professionals. Our best actions will embody the integration of knowledge with compassion for our fellow human beings.

In order to develop and implement the principles in this Charter, the members of the special events industry should adopt as a first step an integrated ethical framework for lasting and future sustainable policies. This framework should serve as an irrevocable covenant that will remove all previous and future barriers in order to achieve the principles set forth in this Charter.

Adopted by acclamation the 3rd of May 1998 by the event industry leaders.
United States of America

Part A

CHAPTER 1

Events – An Introduction

Dimitri Tassiopoulos

AIM OF THE CHAPTER

This chapter aims to evoke an understanding of the basic concepts and definitions of the events sector and to offer a way of thinking about event tourism, thus providing a framework of knowledge for readers approaching this sector of the tourism industry.

LEARNING OBJECTIVES

After having studied this chapter, you should be able to:

- understand the definitions, history, type and different forms of event;
- understand the trends and dynamics of events;
- explain why destinations bother with events;
- understand why the study of events needs to go beyond a developed country concept;
- comprehend why the hosting of events in a developing country context needs to be understood;
- describe the current situation of the events industry in South Africa;
- explain the concepts of ethics and professionalism in event management.

1.1 THE WORLD OF EVENTS

Although increased publicity has been given to the events industry as we have come to know it over the past few years, the phenomenon of events can hardly be described as a new one. Throughout history, events have been an important feature of people's lives. The first Olympic Games were held in Ancient Greece in 776 BC and countless religious events and festivals have been held throughout the ages (Jago & Shaw, 1998: 21; Trigg, 1995: 136). One can only speculate about what procedures, problems and techniques event organisers of the time might have faced and used.

A survey of the oldest South African event organisations, most of which were meeting organisations (or conference organisations), indicates that these started operating on a small scale in the 1960s and early 1970s. The South African exhibition sub-sector of the events industry began in the mid-nineteenth century. The South African event management sector has, however, shown a marked growth since 1994 as the tourism industry has reoriented itself towards reaping the benefits of inbound tourism to the country.

South Africa's recent apartheid political history, however, has left the country with developmental challenges that require a holistic approach if they are to be addressed. Event management could be seen as one of a number of strategies that destination managers could use to overcome these challenges and it is widely accepted that events contribute significantly toward increasing tourist traffic and driving economic development in a region. If managed and coordinated effectively, a well-designed event strategy has the potential to deliver the following benefits and achieve the following objectives for a destination:

- provide a means by which to reinforce a destination's benefits and attributes and generate a favourable image for the destination as a tourist destination;
- establish a destination as a major tourist attraction by attracting high yield visitors, especially repeat visitors;
- enhance a destination's competitive position within a country and place it on the global tourist map;
- generate an increased rate of tourist growth;
- truly bring a destination to life, showcasing its brand personality and instilling confidence and pride in its local community;
- maximise the use of, and revenue for, existing facilities;
- increase favourable incidental media coverage through the event platform that extends the normal communication reach;
- improve the organisational marketing and bidding capability of the community;
- increase community support for events (SA Tourism & DEAT, 2002: 17).

As Janet Landey (1999), past-president of the International Special Events Society (ISES) (South Africa), maintains:

> The greatest challenge we have in South Africa is to ensure the successful transfer of skills in our industry, through education, experience and example. Striving for excellence in all aspects of our profession by performing consistently at or above acceptable industry standards – continually expanding our own spheres of knowledge and passing it on.

The aim of this chapter is to equip prospective entrants into the events sector with a better understanding of this exciting new field of the tourism industry. The youthfulness of the event industry however does mean that event industry does not have some of the characteristics of more established industries, such as well-developed professional standards which reflect well-defined terminology, adequate market intelligence, appropriate education and training structures, and clear entry routes (Rogers, 1998: 1). This chapter forms a basis for the subsequent chapters in this book and consequently seeks to develop a framework to ensure that the planning and management of events is focused, coordinated and aligned with other areas of tourism development and urban management.

1.2   INTRODUCTION

The events sector of the tourism industry is young, dynamic, and growing and maturing at a rapid rate. From its origins in North America and Europe, it is now a truly global sector of the tourism industry. The benefits of event management and event tourism are increasingly being realised by many developing countries such as South Africa.

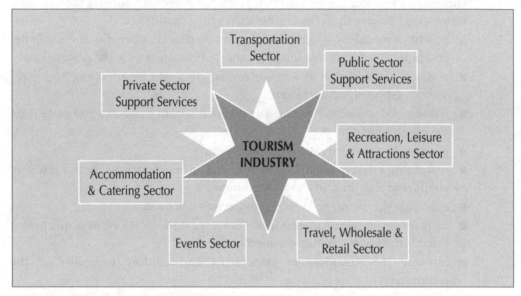

FIGURE 1.1 *Graph of the tourism industry (adapted from Jordaan, 1994: 6 and Cooper, Fletcher, Gilbert, Shepherd & Wanhill, 1999: 321–339)*

1.3   THE EVENT DESCRIBED (Refer to Figure 1.2)
1.3.1 Event tourism

Events are becoming established as an integral and major part of tourism development and marketing strategies. *Event tourism* could be used to describe this phenomenon and this could be defined as the 'systematic development, planning, marketing and holding of events as tourist attractions'. The goals of event tourism could be:

- to create a favourable image for a destination;
- to expand the traditional tourist season;
- to spread tourist demand more evenly through an area, and
- to attract foreign and domestic visitors.

Statistics indicate, for instance, that in the exhibition segment of the events sector there is a strong international presence of between 15 and 20%. This also benefits other tourism sectors such as hospitality and transport. Many such event delegates turn these business trips into mini holidays (*Sunday Times*, 28 February 1999: 16).

Events can become the most common channel through which visitors satisfy their desire to sample local foods and traditions, participate in games, or are entertained. Local and regional events can have the added advantage of keeping the domestic tourism market active. Smaller local events have the advantage that they can make event tourists believe that they are participating in an authentically indigenous activity (Getz, 1991: 127).

Event tourists or visitors can be defined as those who travel away from home for business, pleasure, personal affairs or any other purpose (except to commute to work) and who stay overnight at an event destination. A same-day event visitor does not stay overnight but may visit another destination or return home; such a visitor consequently makes a more a limited contribution toward the event tourism multiplier (Masberg, 1998: 67).

1.3.2 The tangible product

Events can be described by referring to their tangible components. Getz (1991: 123) proposes that the tangible products of an event are actually presented to the public as a 'façade': these are the mechanisms by which a visitor experience is partially created. There is a synergistic process involving these products and many intangibles to create the atmosphere that makes the event. Further, events are usually produced as a means of achieving some greater goal. Even in cases where events have not been planned with tourism objectives in mind, tourism tends to becomes a strategic factor once the destination managers begin to market, promote or package the event as part of the attraction mix of a destination.

1.3.3 Visitor experience

Events present the visitor with a unique perspective of ordinary everyday life with an opportunity to participate in a collective experience where novelty is assured because events occur infrequently or at different times.

1.3.3.1 Targeted benefits

Targeted benefits are those which position the event differently and provide a competitive advantage. Event visitors are attracted to particular events that offer something extra, in addition to the basic services provided and the general benefits derived from all events. The event theme is therefore critical in sending the message to potential visitors about the benefits that they could gain from attending. The name of the event alone, however, is not enough; neither are the activities. The presentation of the theme should be such that the unique benefits offered by the event are clear. Each element of the tangible product can provide a competitive advantage – for example, ethnic food and activities.

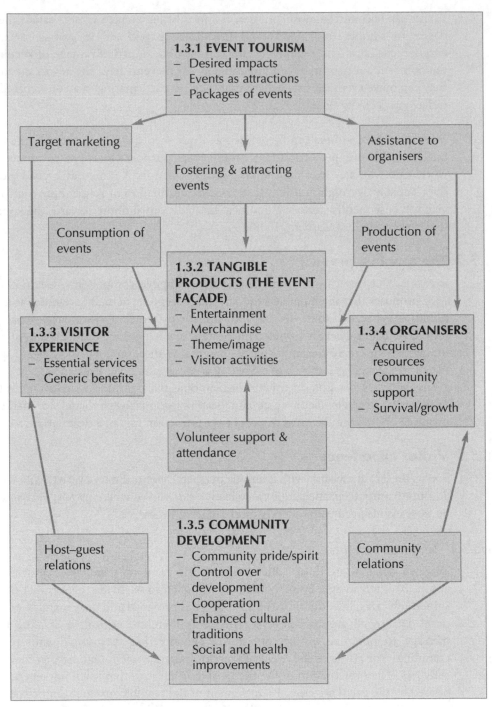

FIGURE 1.2 *Special event perspectives (from Getz, 1991: 122)*

1.3.3.2 Generic benefits

Generic benefits are those which distinguish events from permanent attractions. Such benefits are likely to be expected by a visitor regardless of the tangible event programme. The relative importance of each of these benefits varies from event to event. According to Getz (1991: 124–125), generic benefits fall into the following categories:

- *The spectacle.* The spectacle element of events, especially media-oriented events, has universal appeal. Raw spectacle can, however, overpower the fundamentals of festivity, ritual and games that the events could embody. Spectacles play an important role in any event by focusing on visual, larger-than-life displays and performances. Events oriented towards television, however, run the risk of having the event programme being subject to the demands of television programming.

- *Ritual.* This is at the heart of most traditional events, such as festivals, either in secular or religious form. Symbols and themes that may invoke community or national pride and loyalty, often found in parades, are closely linked to ritualistic activities.

- *Games.* Event visitors and volunteers expect to have fun at events. Such expectations can be fostered through a general atmosphere of festivity and through the opportunity to participate in, or witness, various event activities.

- *Sense of belonging.* The sharing of experiences with others in a public celebration or display can be seen as a major leisure motivator. This emotional benefit is usually the main reason why many people participate in events, either as volunteers or visitors.

- *Authenticity.* This subject is much debated in the literature with no clear conclusion as to its significance and is an issue for continued research and clarification. From an event tourism perspective, the real issue is ensuring visitor satisfaction and community support. Tourism developers should be sensitive to the goal of protecting events that are primarily cultural and local in nature.

1.3.4 Organiser's perspectives

Once event organisation becomes established, producing the event might over time become secondary to the survival of the group, or totally different goals may replace the original goals. Getz (1991: 125–126) outlines three key processes requiring analysis.

- *The environment and the organisation.* The environment for events comprises both the physical and community setting. Most events have a community impact because they are dependent on community volunteer participation and attendance. The physical impact tends to be less for most events, unless major construction occurs. Event organisers should view the community and physical environments as resources and therefore worry about negative impact.

- *Transforming process*. Most organisational energies should be directed at converting resources, including volunteers, into the event and event outcomes. The outcome of the event should not be the event itself but what the event can do towards achieving its broader goals. This leads to the consideration of a whole range of possible outcomes that define event products in terms of their effects on the host community.
- *Internal management processes*. Events differ from most attractions in that they rely on volunteers. This makes management more 'challenging', notably because of the lack of professional expertise, difficulty in recruiting and retaining volunteers for long periods, and diffuse goal setting and decision making. Further, the volunteers may not view the event product as equally important as the prestige, community involvement or socialisation considerations of the event.

1.3.5 Community development

This concerns the enhancement of the host population's way of life, economy and environment. Events can be expected to reflect the needs of the host community, but this cannot be taken for granted. Problems can occur when the event is imposed on the host population and is controlled by a narrow interest group.

Events can create linkages between people and groups within communities, and between the community and the world. Research on the socio-cultural impact of events reveals both positive and negative forces; the costs and benefits of events must therefore be carefully considered, with an emphasis on the host community's perspective.

Community development can benefit from events if the following objectives are satisfied.

- The community must have *control* over the event.
- Event *planning* must be *comprehensive*, taking into account the social, cultural and environmental impacts.
- *Local leadership* and inter-organisational networks must be fostered.
- The event must be directed at meeting *community needs* (Getz, 1991: 122–128).

Research by Ritchie (1996: 117–126) has shown that an understanding of visitor motivation, activity and attraction participation is needed if a destination is to be economically and socially acceptable. Events have been shown to tail off seasonally through the winter months and to peak in the summer months if used strategically and operated effectively.

1.4 TOWARDS DEFINING EVENTS

The world of events covers a spectrum of planned cultural, sporting, political and business occasions. Refer to figure 1.3 for a diagrammatic representation of the event sector and its various segments.

Events, according to Getz (1991: 122), are a unique form of tourist attraction, ranging in scale from mega-events such as the Olympics and World Cup Rugby, through community festivals to programmes of recreational events at parks.

Events are increasingly being viewed as an integral part of tourism development and marketing planning, even though the majority of events have most probably arisen for non-touristic reasons, such as competitions, cultural celebrations or the need to raise funds for charity.

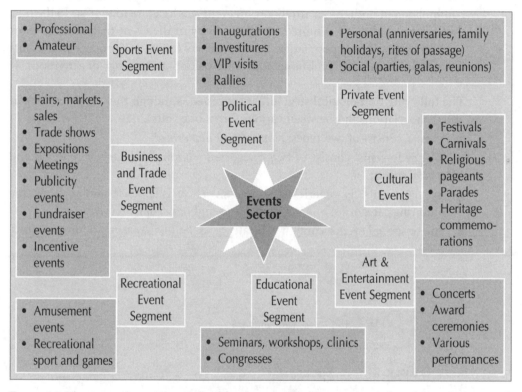

FIGURE 1.3 *Diagrammatic representations of the event sector and its segments (adapted from Getz, 1997: 7)*

Despite the outcomes of events being well recognised, there appears to be a lack of a clear, all-embracing definition for events. Much literature seems to focus on the various characteristics of special events and some of the reasons why they are organised. The literature does not, however, detail what types of events there are that would enable one to determine the range of events that would be classified as special, versus those that are not. Jago and Shaw (1998: 23) testify that 'it is a measure of the adolescence of research on these tourist events that terminology utilised by researchers … has not yet been standardised' and that events 'lack unified terminology'. A typology of clear definitions of the various forms of events is clearly needed if there is to be any chance of research being able to make a contribution towards establishing this sector of the tourism industry as a strategic and developmental tool. An additional complication is that events are not static and that both the *meaning* and *significance* of events could change with changes in society.

A further dilemma that needs to be resolved is whether events should be regarded as part of the leisure field in general, or restricted to the tourism industry. A review of published research indicates that most research and publication on events in recent years comes from researchers associated with the tourism industry. Despite this, an event should be regarded primarily as providing a leisure activity that has the potential to attract tourists (Jago & Shaw, 1998: 24).

Another issue is whether events should be classed as attractions, activities, or a combination of both. As an attraction, an event acts as a lure to tourists to the host destination, whereas it is more often the activity of the event that acts as a draw card for the local host population. Jago and Shaw (1998: 24) propose that events be regarded as hybrid, combining both an attraction and a range of activities.

The following nomological structure is suggested, although there is no consensus about the relationships between various forms of events:

- 'events' consist of two types: *planned* and *unplanned*;
- 'planned events' consist of two categories: *routine, ordinary or common* and *special events*;
- 'special events' is generic term used in a touristic sense and includes the following categories: *minor special events* and *major special events*;
- 'major special events' contain two categories: *hallmark events* and *mega-events*.

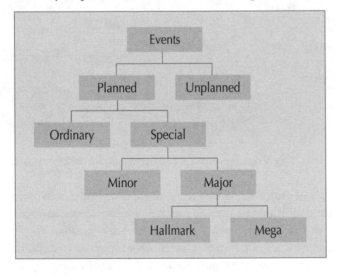

FIGURE 1.4 *Event nomological structure (adapted from Jago & Shaw, 1998: 25 and Getz, 1997: 4)*

1.4.1 A definitional framework

An extensive literature review by Jago and Shaw (1998: 29) confirms that it is unlikely that a single, all-embracing definition of events can be developed as such phenomena include a vast array of types and perspectives of an event can differ when viewed from a national, international or local level.

Events, according to Getz (1997: 4–11), are temporary occurrences, either planned or unplanned, with a finite length of time. *Planned events* have a length of time that is usually fixed and publicised.

Events can be described as transient, and every event is a unique blending of its duration, setting, management and people.

Special events can be described as one-off or infrequently occurring occasions outside the normal programme of the sponsoring or organising body. To the event visitor, a special event is an opportunity to relax or to engage in a social or cultural experience outside the normal range of everyday activities. Special events are always planned, arouse expectations and motivate by providing reasons for celebration. Jago and Shaw (1998: 28) list the most important core attributes of special events as:

- being out of the ordinary or unique;
- having a significant economic impact;
- attracting media attention;
- raising awareness of a region or enhancing its image or profile;
- being one-off or infrequent occurrences;
- being of limited duration;
- offering a social experience;
- attracting tourists or tourism development.

Major events, according to Jago and Shaw (1998: 29–30), are large-scale (usually national or international) special events which are high in status or prestige and which attract large crowds and media attention. They may be expensive to stage, may involve tradition or symbolism, attract funds to the region, lead to demand for associated services, and leave behind legacies or result in urban renewal.

Hallmark events can be referred to as those events that mark an important historical anniversary and can be defined as:

'Major one-time or recurring events of limited duration developed primarily to enhance the awareness, appeal and profitability of a tourist destination in the short and or long term. Such events rely on their success or uniqueness, status or timely significance to create interest and attract attention' (Hall, 1992a: 2).

An example hereof is the '10 Years of Democracy Celebrations' of South Africa, celebrated during 2004, as indicated in figure 1.5 hereunder.

2004 was the 10th anniversary of South Africa's freedom. It was a time for celebration, thanksgiving and renewed commitment. The government adopted a multi-sectoral approach to this milestone in the history of our country in order to ensure that all South Africans and the international community joined in celebrating our democracy. The celebrations were aimed at uniting the country, marking our achievements as a nation and consolidating our democracy. They also provided an opportunity to work on our national identity and to position the country internationally.

The theme for the celebrations was 'a people united for a better South Africa and a better world'. This message emphasised the need for all sectors of our society to look back and take stock of what had happened in the past 10 years. As we celebrated our achievements, we also acknowledged where things did not go as well as we would have wanted, and learn from such lessons as we proudly enter the second decade of our democracy.

FIGURE 1.5 *Celebrating 10 years of democracy (DAC, 2004: Internet)*

In their research, Jago and Shaw (1998: 28) were able to isolate the following attributes as most representative of hallmark events. Hallmark events:

- are large in scale in a relative sense only;
- can be held on an international or national scale;
- are tied to a specific place;
- attract funds to the region;
- attract large crowds;
- are of infrequent occurrence;
- incorporate festivals or other events;
- stimulate demand for related services;
- incur large costs;
- involve prestige and status;
- involve tradition or symbolism;
- leave behind legacies or result in urban renewal;
- result in the event and destination becoming synonymous.

Mega-events can be described as events that can attract very large numbers of event visitors or have a large cost or psychological effect.

Mega-events, by way of their size or significance, are those that yield extraordinarily high levels of tourism, media coverage, prestige or economic impact for the host destination. Examples hereof are the Olympic Games and the 2010 Soccer World Cup. Spilling (1998: 102) views the concept of mega-events as identical to that of hallmark events, a mega-event being seen as a major one-off or recurring event of limited duration which serves to stimulate awareness of a destination and to enhance its appeal and profitability in the short and/or long term. The concept of a hallmark event is related to tradition, attractiveness, image or publicity and provides the host destination with a competitive advantage.

Research undertaken by Jago and Shaw (1998: 30) has indicated the qualifying attributes of mega-events as:

- leaving behind legacies or resulting in urban renewal;
- involving tradition or symbolism;
- involving prestige and status, usually a political approval process;
- incurring large costs;
- stimulating demand for related services;
- incorporating festivals or other events;
- attracting large crowds (usually over a million visitors);
- attracting funds to the region;
- being of international scale;
- being large scale;
- being one-off occurrences;
- having the reputation of a 'must-see' event.

There are no clear, absolute boundaries between the different categories of events as proposed in figures 1.3 and 1.4. It is suggested that the definition of an event depends on one's perspective. For instance, an event held on an annual basis may be regarded initially as a special event because it is so different; however, in subsequent years it may be viewed as a routine occurrence (Jago & Shaw, 1998: 28).

Any event can be categorised as 'special' in terms of the previously mentioned criteria; however, *mega* and *hallmark* are concepts that can only be applied to public events. These categories of planned events, as in the typology, can be found in virtually every culture and community.

1.4.1.1 Cultural events

The most common form of celebrating this type of event is through a festival. Festivals are mostly traditional with long histories. The majority of festivals, though, have been created in recent decades. Heritage events, according to Getz (1994: 321), are a class of events which have historical themes or which celebrate some dimension of a community's or cultural group's heritage.

Parades and processions are often found in festivals. Festivals can thus be defined as celebrations with a public theme where the social and symbolic meaning of the events is closely related to a series of overt values that the community recognises as essential to its ideology and world-view, to its social identity, historical continuity and to its physical survival. This is, in effect, what the festivals ultimately celebrate (Falassi, quoted in Hall, 1992a: 4). Heritage events can be viewed as tools for interpreting community life by bringing people into direct contact with historical facts, objects or ways of life, thereby increasing knowledge and appreciation of traditions. Interpretation, according to Getz (1994a: 321), is an educational activity which aims to reveal meanings and relationships through the use of original objects, by first-hand experience and by illustrative media. Heritage interpretation can make the heritage of a destination come to life for both visitor and resident. This, however, requires a real and authenticated first-hand sensory interaction with the resources of that destination. The term *staged authenticity* is used to describe events which are created with the intention of fooling observers.

Many of the other major events – especially art and entertainment – are frequently found within, or as the theme of, the festival. Sport and recreation are also important festival elements.

1.4.1.2 Business or trade events

Fairs have a long tradition as periodic exhibitions and markets. Although they were often associated with early religious celebrations and usually contained entertainment and amusements, fairs have to do with productivity and business and not themed public celebration. Some fairs are called *exhibitions*, thus reflecting their educational orientation. Many fairs are operated by independent boards or agricultural societies, most having close links with the municipality. Typical elements of such fairs are: agricultural demonstrations and contests, sales and trade shows, amusements, eating and drinking, parades and a variety of entertainment.

The term exposition or *expo* is also applied to trade and consumer shows which generally fall into two types:
- *trade shows*: these are targeted towards industries or specific professions, some incorporating educational components, and to which the general public may have access;
- *consumer shows*: these are held for the general public and can cover virtually any topic (Getz, 1997: 8–9).

1.4.1.3 Meetings and educational events

'Meeting' is a generic term applicable to a group of people assembled for any purpose, and usually refers to a small private business event. *Conclave* is used to describe a very private or secret meeting. When meetings are focused on education, *seminar*, *clinic* or *workshop* are the terms used. *Retreat* describes a meeting that gets people away from their normal environment.

Conference describes a group of people (small enough to facilitate interaction) meeting for the purpose of conferring and discussing. *Conventions* are large assembles of people from associations, political parties or religious groups. A *symposium* or *forum* is a meeting at which speakers or delegates present papers and is generally used instead of convention, which can also denote an international meeting (Getz, 1997: 9).

1.4.1.4 Sports events

The field of sports event management has evolved into a genre of its own. Most types of sport today are organised and competitive, although some games are still played purely for recreation. In the light of the large variety of sports played worldwide, sports events are now big business. It can be argued that sports events have many commonalties with other events, which include their service orientation, a celebration and drama element, media coverage, and similarities in organising and operations.

The term *meet* is used to describe a sports event or meeting that is organised for the purpose of competition. *Tournament* describes a meet organised to select a winner from teams or participating players. *Championships* are meets within leagues to select a winning team; they can be athlete-focused, designed to select the best performer from members in a sport (Getz, 1997: 10).

1.4.1.5 Art events

Art events have their own terminology and associations. Art events are universal, and display considerable diversity in the forms and types of art featured. Art events are classified into the following categories:
- *participatory* events, where there is no separation of audience and performer;
- *performing* events, usually involving performers in front of audiences (for example, drama, dance and music);
- *visual* events, including painting, sculpture and handcraft.

The following criteria are used for the classification of art events:
- temporary versus permanent events;
- regularly scheduled, periodic, or one-off events;
- professionals versus amateur artists;
- paid or free performance;
- mixed or single genre (for example a music festival versus a jazz festival);
- competitive versus festive events (Getz, 1997: 11).

1.5 AN INSIGHT INTO TRENDS AND DYNAMICS IN THE EVENTS SECTOR

Knowledge of trends helps event organisers to develop products that are suited to the current needs of the destination and its market. The most crucial issues in this regard are summarised below and are partly based on the definitive work by Getz (1997: 23–38):

1.5.1 Major trends

1.5.1.1 Strategic event growth

The importance of staging events has increased in a number of destinations around South Africa; more and more destinations are beginning to realise the potential benefit of using events as a strategic development tool. Destinations such as Johannesburg, Cape Town and Durban have, for instance, created permanent posts for this purpose, while other destinations have created posts contingent on being able to prove sustainability. City event strategies for Cape Town, Durban, Johannesburg and Port Elizabeth, according to SA Tourism *et al* (2002: 112), show that differentiation exists in relation to the capacity for bidding for events, ability to attract major events, infrastructural capacity and institutional arrangement. Specific events dominate certain destinations – it could be indicative of certain destinations developing event niches as well as clear branding and positioning. Some destinations have given themselves event-related titles to accentuate their tourism strategy; Buffalo City (consisting of East London, Berlin, Bisho, Butterworth, King William's Town and Stutterheim), for example, has sought to position itself as the 'Sports Event City'. Some level of competition between destination cities is also evident, for instance, Durban and Port Elizabeth both use watersports to position themselves. Attempts are also being made to utilise events to flatten seasonality or to boost tourism in a destination. More recently, municipalities, such as the Cape Town Metropolitan Council, have created event units or bureaux. The proliferation of event products has created exciting possibilities for public–private partnerships among the arts, environmental and sponsoring organisations. This means that events need to be managed as businesses to an ever-increasing extent. Events are beginning to play an important role in destination marketing, the aim being to attract investment, tourism and even desirable residents.

1.5.1.2 Sponsorship

Event sponsorship, accompanied by the professionalisation of event marketing, has grown dramatically. Many events have become dependent on sponsorship revenue to be viable. Corporations are increasingly seeking to market their products and image through appropriate events, such as Standard Bank's sponsorship of the annual Grahamstown Arts Festival. Events offering public participation (for example in sport) are becoming increasingly popular with event sponsors. A trend is for sponsors to target smaller market segments and to aggressively market the niche through relationship marketing. In developing countries, such as South Africa, sponsorships are becoming increasingly difficult to come by. Large cash sponsorships are becoming harder to obtain. This could be because of prevailing economic conditions, but also could be the result of increased competition among event products. It is highlighted by SA Tourism *et al* (2002: 95) that, until recently, sponsorship effectiveness studies were uncommon and a range of sponsorship techniques are now used in order to secure future sponsorships for events.

1.5.1.3 Special purpose event venues

Destinations require appropriate facilities should they wish to bid competitively for some events (for example Cape Town's 2004 Olympic Games Bid). Cape Town used the bid to fast-track the construction of sports facilities around the city. Figure 1.6 further illustrates this concerning the 2010 Soccer World Cup.

EAST LONDON – Buffalo City will participate in South Africa's 2010 World Cup Soccer spectacular. This was confirmed here last night by Buffalo City's deputy executive mayor, Des Halley, at the launch of the 2004/2005 edition of *Focus on Buffalo City*, a glossy niche review of the city's socio-economic position.

Addressing the who's who of the local business community, including the new MEC for Economic Affairs, Tourism and the Environment, Andre de Wet, Halley said he had personally spoken to South Africa's Mr Football, Danny Jordaan.

According to Halley, Jordaan was upbeat that Buffalo City – if it could provide an adequate venue – would be in the national line-up to host matches in 2010.

'We are looking seriously at building a 45 000-seater multi-purpose stadium in Amalinda which will provide easy road and rail access from East London, Mdantsane, King William's Town and centres even further afield. You could say it will be a "regional stadium",' Halley added.

With the MEC in the captive audience, Halley said: 'We are going to come knocking at your door soon for assistance in raising funds.

We will have to work together on this one to ensure it happens.'

'We have the experience of having just recently staged the successful SA Games 2004. More than R20m was poured into that effort. We have the sporting momentum here and need to keep it moving to ensure we realise our dreams for 2010. I expect an early start to the stadium project,' Halley said.

De Wet said he was totally committed to ensuring open and transparent growth and development. 'I have dreams ... others have dreams ... we need to talk and be realistic in what we tackle.'

'But above all, we need to be positive about the future of our region. If we do not promote it positively ourselves, there is little hope of someone else doing it for us,' De Wet said.

He said a number of deals were going to be struck and investments made in the province soon.

'We can't be part of this city, province or the country if we don't address poverty and do what we can to eliminate it,' he said, adding that the next five years could make a difference and that the region needed people with enthusiasm to make it a success. – DDC

FIGURE 1.6 *BC in line for Cup stadium (press article extract, Van der Merwe, 2004: Internet)*

There seems to be an increasing trend toward building mega-event venues such as convention centres and exhibition facilities, festival markets and sports stadia. Destinations are building such facilities to gain prestige or enter into public-private partnerships in order to gain facilities which the destination would otherwise not have obtained. Good examples of such venues are the International Convention Centre (ICC) in Durban, the Cape Town International Convention Centre (CTICC)] and the MTN Sundome in Johannesburg.

1.5.1.4 Risk management and accountability

Donors, sponsors and tourism development organisations are increasingly expecting greater accountability. Due to their importance and to the huge costs involved, events usually do not escape scrutiny. This scrutiny is often accompanied by controversy, with concern being focused on the social and economic impact of the events. A case in point is Cape Town's 2004 Olympic Bid: much controversy resulted from the social and economic impact of this mega-event on the city. Most of the scrutiny in event accountability tends to focus on the tendency to exaggerate event benefits and to underplay hidden costs. Many impact studies tend to gloss over the outcomes and real costs by indiscriminately using multipliers and unreliable data on visitor numbers, motives and expenditures. There is an increasing trend to require event organisers to undertake complete impact and feasibility studies and to report all event impacts.

1.5.1.5 Legal issues

In 1999 and 2000, Draft Regulations and proposals to amend the SA Copyright Act 98 of 1978 were published by the Department of Trade and Industry. As a result of objections and submissions, the Draft Regulations were withdrawn, and the aforementioned proposed amendments to the Act were excluded from the Copyright Amendment Act 9 of 2002.

The negotiations with regard to the SA Customs Union (SACU)/US Free Trade Agreement are scheduled to be completed by the end of 2004. Various organisations and consumer bodies have expressed their concern about inclusion of the Intellectual Property (IP) clauses (i.e. adoption of the US copyright regime) in the Free Trade Agreement, and have made submissions to the National Economic Development and Labour Council (Nedlac).

There has been some confusion as to whether South Africa is a 'developed' or 'developing' country with regard to copyright, as it signed the Berne Convention as a 'developed' country (whilst under British rule) and elected to keep this status when signing the TRIPS Agreement.

The World Intellectual Property Organisation (WIPO) has clarified this matter as follows:

'As far as WIPO's activities are concerned, South Africa is, in all respects, treated as a Developing Country. In particular, it benefits from WIPO's cooperation programme for Developing Countries, part of which is assistance in drafting IP legislation as appropriately as possibly to support their economic, social and cultural development. The WIPO Secretariat is fully available in these respects to the competent government authorities, if and when they so request.'

Also, there has been debate as to whether the South African copyright laws are in compliance with international agreements. In the March 2004 issue of *De Rebus*, the SA Institute of Intellectual Property Law (SAIIPL) President, Stephan Ferreira, stated that 'South Africa has been seen as a leading country in the IP area on the African continent. South Africa has IP laws in line with international norms and compliant with TRIPS – the WTO's Agreement on Trade-related aspects of Intellectual Property Rights – and an IP profession with practitioners qualified in accordance with international standards'.

There are various local and international organisations and consumer bodies that are currently addressing copyright issues in developing countries, including South Africa. Research is being done on what maximum limitations and exceptions are permitted in international agreements and what would be applicable for inclusion in South Africa's copyright laws. For example, the US, Australia, the UK and EU all have exceptions for the disabled, but South Africa and many other developing countries do not have them, although they could (and should) have them in their laws.

FIGURE 1.7 *Copyright in South Africa (Nicholson, 2004: e-mail extract)*

The Copyright Act 98 of 1978 (as amended), referred to in figure 1.7, protects the following inclusive list of categories:

Artistic works
It refers to, irrespective of the artistic quality thereof paintings, sculptures, drawings, engravings, photographs, works of architecture, being either buildings or models of buildings or works of craftsmanship.

Broadcasts
It refers to a telecommunication service of transmissions consisting of sounds, images, signs or signals which takes place by means of electromagnetic waves and is intended for reception by the public or sections of the public (eg. distance education).

Cinematographic films
It refers to any fixation or storage by any means whatsoever on film or any other material of data, signals or a sequence of images capable, when used in conjunction with any other mechanical, electronic or other device, of being seen as a moving picture and of reproduction, and includes the sounds embodied in a sound-track associated with the film, but shall not include a computer program

Computer programs
It refers to a set of instructions fixed or stored in any manner and which, when used directly or indirectly in a computer, directs its operation to bring about a result. Certain categories of computer software programs can also be patented.

Literary works
It includes, irrespective of the artistic quality thereof: novels, stories, poetical works, dramatic works, stage directions, cinematograph film scenarios, broadcasting scripts, textbooks, treatises, histories, biographies, essays, articles, encyclopaedias, dictionaries, letters, reports, memoranda, lectures, speeches, sermons, tables, compilations, including tables and compilations of data stored or embodied in a computer or a medium used in conjunction with a computer, but shall not include a computer program. Literary works shall not be eligible for copyright unless the work has been written down, recorded, represented in digital data or signals or otherwise reduced to a material form.

Musical works
It refers to a work consisting of music, exclusive of any words or action intended to be sung, spoken or performed with the music.
Programme-carrying signal
It refers to a signal embodying a program which is emitted and passes through a satellite.

Published editions
It refers to the first print by whatever process of a particular typographical arrangement of a literary or musical work. The effect of this protection is that there can be more than one claim for copyright protection for one work. The one claim will be that of the author while the publisher company will also have a claim on copyright protection.

Sound recordings
It refers to any fixation or storage of sounds, or data or signals representing sounds, capable of being reproduced, but does not include a sound-track associated with a cinematograph film.

Event products need to protect their brand, programme or theme concepts, celebrity relationships, and logos. This is due to the fact that event organisers are increasingly beginning to view their events as businesses and as community resources that need to be protected with legal mechanisms. Watertight partnership agreements, copyright and trademark protection of names, logos and themes are some such mechanisms that are increasingly forming part of comprehensive risk management programmes of event organisations.

1.5.1.6 Continued growth

International indicators show that over the past few decades there has been a substantial growth in events; all indications are that this growth will continue. Countries with developing economies have much to gain from this trend if they participate in the development of event products. Unfortunately, there are few reliable statistics and research findings available. Few destinations have attempted to monitor the trends and classifications necessary to quantify event growth. In developing marketplaces (countries such as South Africa which are becoming more competitive in the tourism industry), there is a greater interest in issues such as the life cycle of events and the possibility of saturation of events within a destination.

It seems unlikely that there is an upper limit to the number of events that can be organised, given the diversity and benefits of events; however, within a given event, type or destination saturation could occur. New event products entering a mature event marketplace would have to be innovative. Research evidence seems to indicate that event products can continue to grow as attendance and budget sizes have been increasing in many categories of events.

1.5.2 Forces

1.5.2.1 Economic forces

Most people living in developed economies have sufficient disposable income for a variety of leisure activities, including one or more annual vacations. Developing countries have much to gain from this, provided that they produce the right tourism and event products. The rapid growth and diversification of the international event sector corresponds with the economic expansion throughout the postwar era, especially in the 1970s and 1980s. South Africa, however, did not derive any economic benefit from events during this period, as it had been systematically isolated because of the previous government's apartheid policies.

In some newly developing market economies, destination managers find events to be a very cost-effective means of developing tourism. Their events prove to be popular with tourists eager to discover new cultures. Until the time when the incomes of the host populations have increased substantially, events may be the only leisure and cultural opportunities in which residents can partake.

There seems to be a trend towards polarisation between events for the rich and for the poor – some events, even with government subsidies, are priced beyond the reach of the lower- and middle-income groups. Arts events are particularly susceptible to escalating operational and production costs. Government departments are critical role players in creating an enabling legislative environment and free and inexpensive events for the general public. The challenge is to mix the best of free, public celebration with the best of professional event activities without excluding certain sectors of society by reason of income alone. Cutbacks in government subsidies have increasingly required event organisers to compete with other event organisations for the attention of corporate sponsorships, resulting in an aggressive and more efficient form of event management.

1.5.2.2 Discretionary time

In the international arena, improved productivity has resulted in households experiencing an overall increase in discretionary time. Economic upturns and downturns have in many cases created increased unemployment and not shorter working hours; as a result, the long-awaited 'age of leisure' has not materialised. Research indicates that time is valued more. More is expected of free time; in two-job and single-parent families there is less time for family-oriented leisure and the demand for leisure is spreading more evenly over the day, week and year (although the weekends and summer season are still the most popular periods). In a country such as South Africa, these issues are pertinent as households struggle to meet basic economic needs.

1.5.2.3 Population and demographic interests

Socio-demographic forces have a significant impact on leisure travel and event tourism. Factors such as life-stage responsibility, wealth, tastes and physical ability have a critical influence in explaining event preferences and demand preferences. Developing economies are usually characterised by very young and growing populations, while the most developed economies are characterised by their growing aged populations. Industrialised nations are also experiencing growth from immigration and higher birth rates among minorities.

1.5.2.4 Urban conditions

The majority of people in developed countries live in urbanised environments which are negatively impacted by congestion, pollution, crime, social tensions and a declining sense of community. On the positive side, they experience greater art, cultural, leisure and entertainment opportunities. The majority of neighbourhood events are celebrations intended to strengthen community pride or a sense of place; others may be linked to ethnicity and special interests. These events present an insight into the lifestyles of the host populations and can be classified as potential tourist attractions. City-wide events usually serve multiple purposes as they are flourishing in cities active in urban renewal and redevelopment schemes.

1.5.2.5 Political forces

Government departments in developed economies usually support the development and growth of events as policy tools. Government agencies in developing countries such as South Africa have yet to prove their consistent support in this regard. The late commitment of financial guarantees by the national government to the Cape Town 2004 Olympic Bid is a case in point. Sometimes events can be manipulated for party-political purposes: a government might support an event to provide economic stimulation for a depressed area with the aim of re-election. In other cases, major political celebrations and anniversaries can lead to programmes of chauvinistic display by the government. Sometimes events can be used to sidestep normal planning and consultative processes should the political powers wish to remove undesirable groups – especially from the inner-urban areas.

1.5.2.6 Technological forces

Technology has permeated every facet of event organisation. Consumers are increasingly expecting ticketing and packaging to be available over a large area through commercial booking services such as Computicket® and TicketWeb®. Ticketing at events is becoming computerised to an ever-increasing extent, thus enabling better control and detailed accounting of sales.

One of South Africa's premier annual sports events, the Comrades Marathon, held in KwaZulu-Natal, now utilises microchip technology requiring participants to place a microchip in the heels of their running shoes. Scanners along the route read the individual participant's details and relay this back to the event centre for information and control purposes.

Increasingly technology is also being used for special effects through a combination of lasers, sound systems and other techniques to attract attention to events.

1.5.2.7 Values

Prevailing values now require all events to be environmentally friendly and proactive about green management and operations. Sponsors want to be associated with 'green' event products and provide funds to improve environmental practices. Government and business downsizing has resulted in a shift towards self-sufficiency and market-driven decision-making. This value shift in society fosters more private sector events with improved accountability.

Event organisations are increasingly expected to be proactive so as to meet the needs of the economically and physically disadvantaged and to ensure racial and cultural equality, thus avoiding all forms of discrimination.

1.5.2.8 Cultural diversity

The marketplace cannot be assumed to be uniform. The black population, for instance, cannot be assumed to be a single segment in racial or cultural terms. This argument holds for the other racial groupings in South Africa as well. The black market is seen to hold the greatest potential growth for event tourism in the new millennium. The biggest challenge for South African event organisers is to organise culturally inclusive event products where various cultural groupings can feel that a particular event product meets their needs. South Africa needs to cultivate multiculturalism where unity and diversity are valued; this will lead to successful ethnic, multicultural and all-encompassing events.

1.6 WHY DESTINATION MANAGERS SHOULD BOTHER WITH EVENTS

It appears that few developing destinations have focused on events in their tourism strategies, even though many such destinations may have staged successful events in the past. As the need increases to develop distinct competencies in order to achieve a competitive advantage, it is inevitable that developing destinations will look more to their natural or cultural resources. According to Getz (1995: 151–154), developing destinations must take the following into account:

- *Support services*. Developing destinations find it difficult to undertake the necessary research and evaluations to successfully capitalise on event tourism. Intelligence and marketing support systems such as marketing partnerships may have to be shared with other destinations.

- *Quality*. Providing services and products that are of a world standard is a challenge that all destinations face and this can be exacerbated when there is little experience in event production. Training is necessary, as is careful planning of the event portfolio and evaluation research. Stressing event authenticity and spontaneity rather than sophisticated event structures could be an effective strategy for creating quality tourist experiences. Minor events can be packaged with high-quality products such as shopping, dining, sports and nature-based tourist products. Developing at least one good quality hallmark event should be the goal of every destination.

- *Organisation and leadership*. The leadership necessary for bidding and for producing indigenous events is usually a weakness in developing destinations. Management training will be necessary, with an emphasis on building capacity from existing groups. A volunteer recruitment and training programme is essential. It is, of course, possible to develop multi-destination events, thereby attracting tourists into an event tourism cluster; however, this requires the establishment of an event development entity or a strategic partnership.

- *Marketing management*. Many developing destinations are usually overdependent on a single tourism product such as nature-based tourism and should therefore diversify. It is suggested that market segments travelling with the sole purpose of participating in events be targeted. The high cost of long-haul tourism requires careful niche marketing by destination managers; event tourism can be one such niche which provides greater value-added experiences for all visitors.

- *Destination attractiveness*. It is usually more expensive to travel to developing destinations; a special effort is therefore needed to create a positive image and to provide added value. Events can be used to stress unique resources and themes that make the destination worth the cost and effort.

- *Capacity.* In addition to accessibility and transport limitations, developing destinations often lack the physical space, services and basic resources necessary to host major events. Accordingly, minor events with strong image enhancement potential might have to substitute for major events. This is reinforced by the fear of the negative impact that major events could have on sensitive environments and communities. In other words, because of a low carrying capacity in many developing destinations, it is important that events be carefully planned and managed. Destination managers should develop a portfolio of attractions and events that reflect national values, cultures, institutions and history with dignity and authenticity when developing the destination's distinctive competency.

1.7 UNDERSTANDING WHY THE STUDY OF EVENTS SHOULD GO BEYOND A DEVELOPED COUNTRY CONCEPT

In the past, bidding for events has been restricted to cities in developed economies. Such cities usually possess the necessary resources, skills, expertise, facilities and infrastructure to bid for and stage events and have previous experience in this regard. Consequently, event owners trust the capacity of these cities to host events as they have successful track records.

Developing cities should learn to bid and win the right to host events in order that they may also take advantage of the multiple direct and indirect benefits. They should study the past experiences of other cities, both successful and unsuccessful, and learn to become more internationally competitive. Refer to chapter 3 for further information in this regard.

Destinations in developing countries must also broaden the concept of legacy from that of mere physical infrastructure to the benefits experienced in preparation of a new vision for a destination city or town. In the case of Cape Town, the legacy left to this city's authorities in terms of moving towards implementing the vision for the city's future and proposing frameworks for the future development of strategically located land is rich indeed: the establishment of new partnerships between local authorities, the private sector and communities; skills training and development of the city's human resources. Cape Town also held a number of smaller international sports events during its bid which improved the management experience of local firms and the communities' willingness to find practical solutions, encouraging the fast-tracking of development applications, and the development of a lasting database for the future. This mass of information could become an invaluable resource, if maintained and updated, for other developing destinations wishing to host an event.

1.8 AN OVERVIEW OF THE CURRENT SITUATION OF THE EVENT INDUSTRY IN SOUTH AFRICA

The events sector of the tourism industry represents a major untapped source and everything should be done to develop this segment of the tourism market in South Africa. The challenge facing every regional and local tourism organisation is to determine to what extent this market segment can be developed to the benefit of the region and the country at large. Local authorities have a major role to play in attracting and developing event products for their destinations.

South Africa's six major cities (the seventh city being under consideration at the time of writing) have joined forces in a strategy envisaged to boost South Africa's share of the international meetings market, currently estimated to be worth almost R1 billion. The Southern African Federation of Convention Cities (SAFCC) – made up of Cape Town, Johannesburg, Durban, Pretoria, Port Elizabeth, Bloemfontein and the most recent applicant, East London — aim to position the cities as icons for international leisure tourism, conventions and sporting events. The concept is based on a theme of diverse cities and aims to effectively market South Africa as the preferred destination worldwide through joint partnerships between the cities. SAFCC envisages that the three stronger cities (Cape Town, Durban and Johannesburg) will cooperate to raise the awareness and profiles of the less well-resourced, in respect of events, Bloemfontein, East London, Port Elizabeth and Pretoria as business tourism destinations. It is hoped that the formation of the joint marketing initiative – for which a founding protocol is already in place – will go some way toward counteracting the fragmented nature of much of South Africa's international meeting and general tourism marketing, which has often seen provinces and cities competing for the same market. The individual cities will remain competitive in their own right, but will act together as a lobbying mechanism for South Africa and will exchange information and research data. This campaign draws on the success of the German city experience, in which Germany markets its leading cities as driving forces in their own right – 'The Magic 10'. (*Sunday Times*, 28 February 1999: 18; SA Tourism, 2004: brochure; and, *SA Conference, Exhibition and Events Guide*, 2004: 20)

Event tourism in South Africa is in its infancy – due to our political legacy – but is estimated to expand even faster than the 10 to 15% annual growth rate predicted for the tourism industry. It is emphasised that at this stage pre- and post-meeting tourism is a feature of most international meetings. Anything from 500 to 700 people, or more, visiting South Africa for a single meeting are normally in the A or B income group level. These meeting delegates sometimes bring their spouses and families and stay up to a week within the country.

Typically, event organising skills are concentrated in the hands of white-owned businesses and there is now a concerted effort to transfer skills across the broader spectrum of the population and to create entrepreneurs in disadvantaged population groups.

The arts and culture sector, frequently regarded as a soft sector and a drain on the economy, has been recognised as contributing imagination and creativity, the root of innovation which plays a vital role in moving business forward. With this in mind, Business and Arts South Africa (BASA) was launched in February 1997 as a joint initiative between government and the business sector to stimulate the development of arts in South Africa. Under this scheme, a sponsoring business or an arts organisation with one or more private sector sponsors can approach BASA for additional funding for a particular project, event or organisation. This is a matching grant programme which ensures that both sponsor and recipient are clear on their relative responsibilities before entering into a relationship and that the sponsor derives appropriate benefit from the sponsorship (*Business Day*, 25 May 1999: 29).

1.8.1 Event statistics

The gathering and analysis of event statistics in South Africa is in its formative stage. At the time of writing, there was no single entity that undertook to collate, do comprehensive research and analysis of all events in South Africa. South African Tourism (SA Tourism) has been in the process of institutional transformation, for some time, and currently sees its mandate as being to market South Africa as a preferred international tourism destination. To this end, SA Tourism promotes South Africa as a destination for international meeting and incentive events. Currently, SA Tourism is building limited capacity in respect of research and analysis of the aforementioned sub-sectors of the events industry. SA Tourism currently compiles an annual national calendar, or database, of all South African events (raw statistics), that largely exclude meetings and exhibitions, and, for the purpose of this study are termed 'generic events'.

Contact Publications, a commercial venture that includes an event data-gathering initiative, collates raw data (date and place) of international and national events (meetings and exhibitions) that are taking place in South Africa, and publishes this database, in the form of the annual *SA Conferences and Exhibitions Calendar*.

Currently, the entry of event details into both of the aforementioned databases by event organisations is voluntary and inconsistent, which makes it difficult to derive an accurate analysis of the events sector in South Africa, especially from a strategic and long-term perspective. The strategic and long-term significance of both databases, at the time of writing, remains unclear.

Case study 1.1:

The New Zealand Tourism Board's event management database, forming part of NZ-HOST, compiles a database of events to provide strategic and marketing services to both tourists and the formal structures of tourism organisation (Ryan, Smee, Murphy & Getz, 1998: 71–83). The event database commits the regional tourism organisations (RTOs) and local tourism organisations (LTOs) to perform the primary data collection, coordination and promotional functions of events within their regions.

It is accepted, as a point of departure, that the two aforementioned databases are representative of the total number of events taking place in South Africa. Namely, Contact Publication's *1999–2004 Calendars of Events* (almost exclusively meeting and exhibition type of events) and SA Tourism's *2001–2004 Calendar of Events* (or so-called 'generic events'). These databases are analysed in 1.8.1.1 and 1.8.1.2, respectively.

1.8.1.1 Contact Publication's 1999–2004 Calendars of Events

The overall provincial distribution of meeting and exhibition events in South Africa for the period 1999 to 2004 is depicted in figure 1.8.1. Analysis of the results suggest that 1999 was an exceptional year for events being staged in South Africa and may be indicative of the end of the post-1994 boom period that the country experienced in respect of being able to attract international events. Analysis of these event statistics, however, excluding 1999, suggests that the provinces can be grouped into three clusters in terms of event distribution: *high, medium,* and *low:*

- *High cluster*: this cluster is led by Gauteng and the Western Cape with the leadership role seemingly taken by the Western Cape Province in 2004. The Western Cape appears to have become the preferred destination for the hosting of events with the opening of the Cape Town International Convention Centre (CTICC) in 2003. The third province in this cluster is KwaZulu-Natal, which has been a consistent performer concerning hosting world-class events. Analysis of the statistics, however, suggests that currently the event market has 'plateaued'.
- *Medium cluster*: this grouping is led by the Eastern Cape Province, by a narrow margin. The other members of this cluster are the Free State and North West. In all cases, the event market in this cluster is seemingly 'flat' or declining.
- *Low cluster*: the members of this grouping are Mpumalanga, Northern Cape and Limpopo. Event activity amongst the members of this cluster has been consistently low for the duration of this period. The event statistics even suggest a downward trend.

A more in-depth analysis of the event distribution data indicates that the provincial event distribution is polarised according to the availability of event venues. Most events in Gauteng, for instance, take place in the Greater Johannesburg region; in the Western Cape they are mostly organised in and around the Greater Cape Town Metropolitan Area; in KwaZulu-Natal they are found largely in Durban; in the Eastern Cape they take place for the most part in and around Port Elizabeth, and so forth.

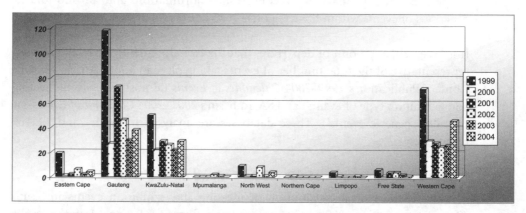

FIGURE 1.8.1 *Provincial event frequencies in South Africa, 1999–2004 (Contact Publications: 1998, 1999, 2000, 2001, 2002, 2003, 2004)*

There is seemingly a need for the implementation of an effective national event development strategy that will focus on improving the capacity for bidding and hosting by the 'moderate cluster', and to fundamentally improve the event hosting ability of the 'low cluster'.

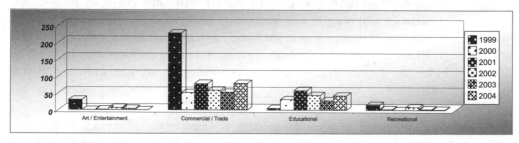

FIGURE 1.8.2 *Event types in South Africa, 1999–2004 (Contact Publications: 1998, 1999, 2000, 2001, 2002, 2003, 2004)*

An analysis by types of events (largely meetings and exhibitions), as depicted in figure 1.8.2, indicates that the commercial/trade event segment dominates the current event market in South Africa. This is followed by the education type event segment. The art/entertainment event segment and the recreational segments occupy distant third and fourth positions, respectively.

An analysis of the data of the monthly national event distribution, for the period 1999 to 2004, is indicated in figure 1.8.3. The study suggests that the national meeting and exhibition event season in South Africa is characterised by two peak seasons: May and September. September is the leading event month by a narrow margin. There is a general downward trend in event activity after September as business traditionally prepares for the end-of-year Festive Season. The large volunteer and entry-level employee base that becomes traditionally unavailable during this time further accentuates this trend. The months of January and February are considered to be 'slow' event months. The event sector only shows an upward trend as from March, and peaks in May. The period June to August is seen as a 'flat' but moderate period for event frequency, with a slight decline toward the month of August.

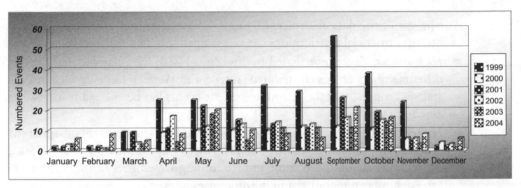

FIGURE 1.8.3 *Event monthly frequencies in South Africa, 1999–2004 (Contact Publications: 1998, 1999, 2000, 2001, 2002, 2003, 2004)*

1.8.1.2 SA Tourism's Calendars of Events

The SA Tourism's *Calendars of Events* (all types – but excluding the event data compiled by Contact Publications) have been compiled as from 2001. It needs to be noted that this database was originally paper-based but has become Internet-based as from 2003. Since 2004, the inclusion of generic events taking place around the country has been actively pursued by SA Tourism for inclusion in this database, whereas in the past, event data was included in the SA Tourism database largely at the discretion of the event organiser, or owner.

The analysis of SA Tourism's *2001–2004 Calendar of Events* provides an alternative but important perspective on the state of affairs in regard to the staging of generic events in South Africa.

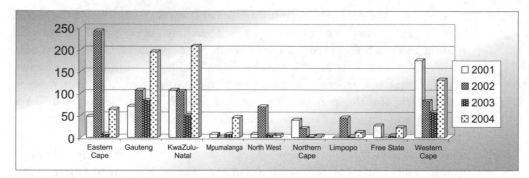

FIGURE 1.9.1 *Provincial event frequency in South Africa, 2001–2004 (SA Tourism: 2001, 2002, 2003, 2004)*

An analysis of the data as depicted figure 1.9.1 suggests that, concerning generic events, the provincial distributions can be grouped into two clusters: *high* and *low*:

- *High cluster*: this cluster is led by KwaZulu-Natal, by a narrow margin. The other members of this cluster are Gauteng and Western Cape. In all cases, the statistics suggest that the growth in generic events has been steadily increasing, albeit at a small rate.

- *Low cluster*: this cluster is led by the Eastern Cape. The other members of this group are Mpumalanga, North West, Northern Cape, Limpopo and Free State. Although there has been some growth amongst members of this cluster, the growth has been marginal and in some cases uneven.

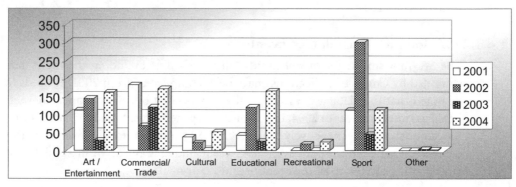

FIGURE 1.9.2 *Event distribution by type in South Africa, 2001–2004 (SA Tourism: 2001, 2002, 2003, 2004)*

The analysis of figure 1.9.2 suggests that trade, educational, sport and art/entertainment types of events remain the most popular types of generic event staged by event owners and coordinators. Analysis further suggests that, though cultural and recreational event types have been showing an increasing growth trend, there is a requirement for additional developmental support for such generic events to reach their full potential.

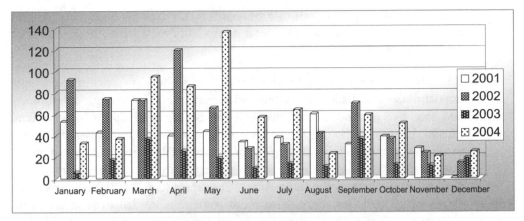

FIGURE 1.9.3 *Event monthly frequencies in South Africa, 2001–2004 (SA Tourism: 2001, 2002, 2003, 2004)*

Figure 1.9.3 suggests that the period of March to May remains the most popular for the hosting of generic events. May is seen as the peak season month for generic events. The period from June to August is a relatively 'slow' but stable period for the staging of events. The results show that September has a marginal increase in events being hosted and thereafter there is a downward trend towards December. January and February, it is suggested by the findings, is a marginally more popular period to stage generic events, as apposed to trade and educational events, in South Africa.

A comparison between figures 1.8 (1, 2, 3) and 1.9 (1, 2, 3) suggests that there are similarities between the top event-hosting provincial destinations, and types of events. Membership of the leading cluster of provinces, the analysis suggests, is similar because the event-hosting ability and quality of the event infrastructure is the most developed amongst the members of this cluster. The analysis further suggests that trade and educational events have a particular preference for hosting their events during certain times of the year, with peak seasons in May and September. There seem to be no strong preference for when to host generic events. The research suggest that the periods January to May is the most popular period for hosting generic events.

FIGURE 1.10 *Combined total of all events in South Africa, 2001–2004 (SA Tourism and Contact Publications)*

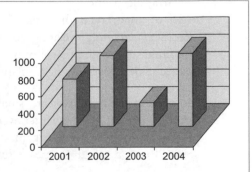

An analysis for the period 2001 to 2004 reveals that, except for 2003, there has been a small but upward growth in the total number of events staged in South Africa. This is illustrated in figure 1.10.

Consequently, an analysis of the South African event sector reveals both opportunities and challenges for destination managers. The strategic development and use of event products and offerings can benefit destinations by identifying gaps in the event market and proactively developing event products and offerings to fill this gap. In October 2002, SA Tourism and DEAT received and approved final draft of a commissioned research report regarding the development of a national events strategy for South Africa. The report (2002: 112) concludes that 'a clearly articulated and coordinated event strategy is needed to ensure that the opportunities are maximised and potential pitfalls are minimised. The lack of synergy among various stakeholders, both in the public and private sector, hinders South Africa's ability to become a major player in the global event tourism industry'.

1.9 THE NEED TO DEVELOP PROFESSIONAL EDUCATION FOR EVENT MANAGEMENT AND A CODE OF ETHICS

Event management and the event tourism field are increasingly attaining professional status; this is accompanied by a growth in related professional associations and educational programmes. Along with this trend comes the realisation that events need to be managed like businesses.

A needs analysis of the Australian event industry undertaken by Perry, Foley and Rumpf (1996: 85–93) distinguishes the seven most important attributes of an event manager as: vision, leadership, adaptability, high organisation skills, good communication skills, marketing skills and people management skills. These attributes are seen as similar to the quality management skills required to build an enterprising nation. Perry *et al* state that event managers need to develop the following competencies: qualifications, entrepreneurship, global orientation, people and communication (soft) skills, strategic skills, teamwork skills, networking skills, customer focus, innovation, multidisciplinary skills, the ability to learn quickly and the ability to sustain high pressure. The survey also ranks, in order of importance, the type of knowledge required by event managers to be effective: marketing; relating to the media; project management; budgeting, attaining sponsorship; economic impact analysis; business planning; market research; local government regulations; and contingency planning.

Most event organisations are small and have few, if any, paid staff. There is, however, a trend towards larger events and bigger budgets and it is possible that a greater number of event organisations may in time become employers. There seems to be a trend to create fully professional events, complete with staff, sponsors and venues. As competition increases amongst the event organisations for resources and tourists, more events will be organised professionally, leading to an increased demand for skilled event personnel.

Exposure to international standards and competition since the ending of South Africa's political isolation has spurred on local event organisers to greater levels of professionalism. Previously, there were no standards within the event marketplace to define the ideal professional event organiser. Furthermore, there was no professional organisation which could be approached to put forward the names of individuals qualified to manage events (such as meetings) in South Africa. Many event sector associations now have in place, or are in the process of establishing, professional codes of conduct that will deal with issues such as member–supplier and member–client relationships.

Most people who call themselves 'professionals' in fact fail to meet the criteria which epitomise professionalism. These criteria are: government sanction (normally through licensing); self-regulation (normally through certification); accreditation by the professional governing body of education delivery programmes; and, a sound theoretical knowledge (Getz, 1997: 17). Wright (1988: 7) highlights the following requisites for professionalism:

- compliance with predetermined standards of professional conduct;
- educational criteria encompassing basic, advanced and continuing education;
- an examination of knowledge and experience leading to some form of certification.

Thus, the responsibilities and authority that go with the position form the image of professionalism; these are the parameters that determine status and, consequently, salary. In the United States, the *National Directory of Occupational Titles and Codes* lists meeting (read *event*) management as an 'official' profession. According to this directory, an event manager 'is an individual whose job description is to organise, plan and execute for individuals who meet for common cause, whether educational, recreational, motivational or as an incentive to achieve objectives' (Polivka, 1998: 708).

The following are listed by the International Special Events Society (ISES) (1996: 49) and Getz (1997: 18) as generic ethical standards: truthfulness, integrity, competence, conformity to the highest standards, accuracy, loyalty, fairness, concern, confidentiality, responsibility to uphold all laws and regulations, striving for excellence, honest business practices, commitment to growth through education, providing the highest level of service and treating employees with respect and courtesy.

The mission of the International Special Events Society (ISES) is to educate, advance and promote the special events industry and its network of professionals, along with related industries. To this end, ISES strives to uphold the integrity of the special events profession in the eyes of the general public through its 'Principles of Professional Conduct and Ethics', to which each member agrees to adhere. These principles are to:

- 'Promote and encourage the highest level of ethics within the profession while maintaining the highest standards of professional conduct.
- Strive for excellence in all aspects of our profession by performing consistently at or above acceptable industry standards.
- Use only legal and ethical means in all industry negotiations and activities.
- Protect the public against fraud and unfair practices and promote all practices that bring respect and credit to the profession.
- Provide truthful and accurate information with respect to performance of duties. Use a written contract clearly stating all charges, services, products, performance expectations and other essential information.
- Maintain industry-accepted standards of safety and situation.
- Maintain adequate and appropriate insurance coverage for all business activities.
- Commit to increase professional growth and knowledge, to attend educational programmes and to personally contribute expertise to meetings and journals.
- Strive to cooperate with colleagues, suppliers, employees, employers and all persons supervised to provide the highest quality service at every level.
- Subscribe to the ISES Principles of Professional Conduct and Ethics and abide by the ISES Bylaws and policies.' (ISES, 1996: 49)

As professionals in an industry which is still growing (as a formal industry), it is important to authenticate event practitioners as well as the industry so that practitioners can be looked upon as professionals in a viable, thriving industry, complete with diversified intricate careers (ISES, 1996: 50).

An essential element of professionalism is that of ethics. The reason for having these standards and enforcing them through certification is to:

- make provision for disciplining members who violate these standards;
- ensure that all members understand the meaning of professionalism;
- ensure better quality events and effective organisations;
- ensure that members practise their profession uniformly and avoid unfair competition, and
- raise credibility with customers, stakeholders and the public (Getz, 1997: 18).

Ethics can be defined as a moral philosophy or set of principles; *moral* concerns the goodness or badness of human character, or what is wrong or right in conduct (ISES, 1996: 49).

Business ethics and a business code of ethics are described as:

© Juta & Co Ltd

'Business ethics can be defined as principles of conduct within organisations that guide decision-making and behaviour. A business code of ethics can provide a basis on which policies can be devised to guide daily behaviour and decisions at the work site' (David, in Van Aardt & Van Aardt, 1997: 200).

Janet Landey, CSEP (Certified Special Events Professional), former president of the South African Chapter of ISES and co-owner of Party Design cc, shares the following case study on ethics.

Case study 1.2:

'Some years ago we submitted a proposal to an event manager for an outdoor event – the design of which included a complicated layout of pot-plants. The event manager passed our quotation directly to her client who declined the offer – no problem. However, imagine my reaction when I received a phone call from an 'irate' venue manager demanding that I come and sort out the thousands of plants that had been dumped at his facility. When I explained that I was not doing the job, he replied: 'Well, these are your drawings with all your details and specifications on them!' So, what does one do? I immediately phoned the event manager, who was mortified and distraught – mutual decision was taken to invoice the client for a design fee. The result? Within 24 hours the design fee cheque was in our hands.' How does one stop this kind of thing happening?

The events industry is highly networked. The last thing one wants is to be known for accepting (or demanding) free gifts, abusing FAM (familiarisation)/site inspection trips or taking advantage of free perks at the hotels and airlines' expense. Reputations are the most valued possessions – something that can be destroyed with unethical demands (Polivka, 1998: 401).

Social responsibilities are directly linked to business ethics and the former is described by Griffcn (quoted in Van Aardt & Van Aardt, 1997: 203) as: *'the obligation of an organisation to protect and enhance the societal context in which it functions'*. In 2002, DEAT (2003: 4–5, 40) developed South Africa's Responsible Tourism Guidelines. These guidelines provide encouragement to event managers (among others) to grow their businesses while providing social and economic benefits to local communities and to respect the environment. The main points can be summarised as follows:

- *economic guidelines:*
    - assess economic impacts before developing event tourism;
    - maximise local economic benefits by increasing linkages and reducing leakages;
    - ensure communities are involved in and benefit from event tourism;
    - assist with local marketing and event product development;
    - promote equitable event business and pay fair prices.

- *social guidelines:*
  - involve local communities in planning and decision making;
  - assess local impacts and cultural diversity;
  - be sensitive to the host culture.
- *environmental guidelines:*
  - reduce environmental impacts when developing event tourism;
  - use natural resources sustainably;
  - maintain biodiversity.

In conclusion, event operations are asked to subscribe to the principles and practices of responsible event tourism in conducting their operations and to strive to minimise the impact on the environment, spread the benefits throughout the local economy and promote community well-being.

Browse these Internet sites

www.businesstourismpartnership.com
www.capetownevents.co.za/
www.exsa.co.za
www.fairtourismsa.org.za
www.ifea.com
www.ises.co.za/

www.juliasilvers.com/embok/
www.risa.org.za
www.saaci.co.za
www.safact.co.za
www.southafrica.net

QUESTIONS FOR SELF-EVALUATION

1 Discuss what ethical issues could influence the operation of an event company.
2 Can you think of arguments for or against social responsibility in event management? If so, what are they?
3 An event manager has a reputation for demanding special amenities, not called for in the contract, for the organisation's officers and for personal use. The supplier is aware of this situation, but reluctant to challenge the event manager at contract time for fear of losing the event. Discuss the situation.
4 Identify the ideal personality characteristics of an event manager. In your opinion, why are these characteristics more prominent in event management than in the general population?
5 Discuss the skills required of an event professional.
6 Relate the relevance of the Global Code of Tourism Ethics to the event professional.
7 Why is thorough research of the needs of your prospective event visitors important?
8 How can the choices an event manager makes impact on the environment?
19 Analyse the differences between a mega- and hallmark event.
10 Discuss the implications of the various trends and forces influencing the event sector.

CHAPTER 2

Event Role Players

Dimitri Tassiopoulos

AIM OF THE CHAPTER

This chapter focuses on the various event role players (for example corporate and association) and intends to equip the reader with the necessary knowledge to identify the various service and product clients and providers when organising an event.

LEARNING OBJECTIVES

After having studied this chapter, you should be able to:

- understand the event triangle (the event with its management and performers, the audience and sponsors);
- distinguish between the various suppliers and buyers of events;
- show that you have a basic knowledge of the agencies, intermediaries and other important organisations (domestic and international) involved in events.

2.1 INTRODUCTION

The event industry is highly complex, comprising a multiplicity of buyer and supplier organisational role players, sponsors and event audiences. For many event organisers – the so-called 'buyers' – the organisation of events is only part of their function. On the other hand, the 'suppliers' include the providers of meeting venues, destinations and accommodation, transport companies, agencies and specialist contractors. The suppliers and buyers are linked together and supported by national and international associations and bodies, the trade press, educational institutions, each making a contribution to this industry.

2.2 THE EVENT TRIANGLE

No event takes place in isolation and each event involves a set of interdependent and interacting elements within a system: the event product with event participants, the audience or customer, and the sponsors. Events benefit from administrative support, planning and marketing, indicating a financial link between the event, its audience and its sponsors. This interdependent relationship is illustrated in figure 2.1.

Schaaf (1995: 53) identifies three underlying principles that interact in the event triangle model:

- Event management requires sponsors for financial subsidy and publicity.

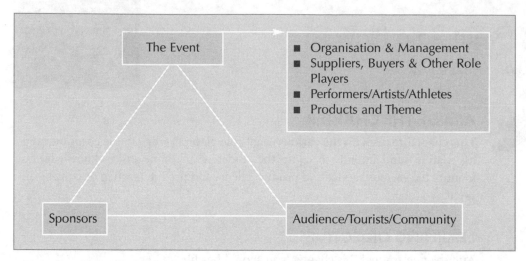

FIGURE 2.1 *Diagrammatic representation of key event role players (adapted from Schaaf, 1995: 46)*

- Event performers solicit compensation for their time and talents.
- Sponsors need events for promotional exposure and opportunities in their target market.

The financial success of events lies within the framework of this triangle. Each event, performer, audience and sponsor has goals that are satisfied by the other groups. If events maintain their audience, sponsors invest billions to communicate through them (Schaaf, 1995: 71).

The event audience or tourists, according to Schaaf (1995: 49), can have a physical presence at the event venue and an electronic presence via radio and television. The event audience can also be represented through the print media such as newspapers, magazines and journals. Sponsorships provide companies access to a variety of promotional packages, including all forms of media advertising, licensing rights, event promotions featuring giveaways, sampling, signage, billboards, VIP receptions, and merchandising sales opportunities (Schaaf, 1995: 50).

The organisation of an event and the event itself provide a vehicle for attaining certain goals and have the task of creating certain outcomes such as economic and social benefits. These outcomes can include unintended and negative impacts, which need to be identified through research (Getz, 1997: 14).

'Event management could be viewed as the planning, organising, directing and controlling of event resources for a relatively short-term objective that has been established to complete specific goals and objectives. Furthermore, event management utilises the systems approach to management by functional personnel (the vertical hierarchy) assigned to a specific event project (horizontal hierarchy).' (Kerzner, 1998: 4)

Thus, event management is designed to manage or control event resources on a given activity, within time, cost and performance requirements. Event management, according to Rutherford Silvers (2004: Internet), as with any other form of management, 'encompasses the assessment, definition, acquisition, allocation, direction, control, and analysis of time, finances, people, products, services, and other resources to achieve objectives. An event manager's job is to oversee and arrange every aspect of an event, including researching, planning, organising, implementing, controlling, and evaluating an event's design, activities, and production'. Event management is 'an intricate weaving of the process and the scope of management functions', illustrated in figure 2.2, and are 'the functional units (grouped by domain) forming the warp fibres – the foundation threads of the fabric of the event. The processes – or weft threads – are interwoven through these foundations for each event, with the evaluation thread from one event forming the research thread for the next event. If you eliminate one of the threads, the fabric of the event is weakened, leaving holes or places where it may unravel'.

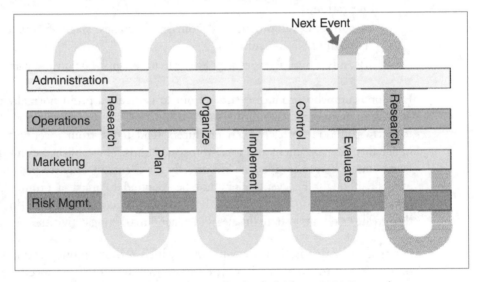

FIGURE 2.2 *The event management process (Rutherford Silvers, 2004: Internet)*

Appendices 2.1 and 2.2 include graphical representation of the EMBOK (Event Management Body Of Knowledge) Taxonomy representing a selection of disciplines required for the successful implementation of events. The Taxonomy 'illustrates the scope and complexity of the event management profession to internal and external constituents and stakeholders, current and future practitioners, and allied and supplier industries' (Rutherford Silvers, 2004: Internet).

In order to gain community support, attract grants and sponsorships, and achieve sustainability, events need to successfully meet a multiplicity of goals. Events are produced by organisations for a variety of reasons. Governments and non-profit-making and community organisations are producing festivals to an ever-increasing extent. Increasingly, profit-motivated organisations are organising events for clients who require economic development through event tourism, such as tourism agencies, resorts and facility managers. Getz (1997: 43) provides a three-sector classification of events:

- *Private, for-profit organisations:*
  - organisations producing events for profit under contract or individually;
  - corporations creating events for marketing and sales purposes;
  - hotels, resorts and facilities using events as attractions and image makers.
- *Non-profit-making or voluntary:*
  - charities and causes use events to attract revenue and support;
  - community-based societies and informal groups stage events for multiple community benefits.
- *Government agencies or public–private groups:*
  - leisure and social agencies organise events to foster sports, health or social integration;
  - economic development and tourism agencies stage events to create employment and income;
  - arts and cultural agencies stage events to foster appreciation and participation.

Entrepreneurs who produce events set out to generate a profit normally through admission charges, merchandising, sponsorship, media revenue and rental of service to participants. Historically such producers tend to be from meeting planning, hospitality, entertainment and tourism backgrounds. In established event markets, event entrepreneurs compete or bid directly for clients in order to produce many events. Although the event might not be required to make a profit, the event organiser has to do so. Corporations that sponsor events are another business entity that create or obtain a share in sales and general marketing activities.

Sponsors are organisations or companies which provide money, services or any other support to events and event organisations in return for specific benefits. Many sponsorship agreements are of a short-term nature, although longer-term relations are desirable. It is usually only with longer-term agreements that a true partnership can evolve, as the partners get to know and understand their mutual goals without sacrificing their individual principles (Getz, 1997: 44).

Clients and audiences may also be called *tourists, guests, customers* and *visitors* – these are the customers who have purchased the event service. A marketing orientation requires that we think of them as having paid a price for a product or service delivered. Event attendance is predominantly purchased or undertaken by the host destination's residents, with travellers forming an important segment of the event visitor market. In some cases, travellers from outside the host destination may form the larger group at certain planned events such as meetings (Getz, 1997: 44).

2.3 THE EVENT SUPPLIERS AND EVENT BUYERS

As is common in other industries, the event sector comprises 'buyers' and 'suppliers'. For the purpose of this chapter, *suppliers* and *buyers* refer to those role players who play an intimate role in researching and producing the event for consumption by an audience. In the case of the meeting industry, the buyers are the meeting organisers and planners who buy or hire venues and related services in order to stage their event.

2.3.1 The buyers

Within the meeting industry, writers such as Rogers (1998: 24) refer to two broad types of buyer: *corporate* and *association. Government buyers* are a further category of buyer. All three types of buyer may employ the services of various agencies to assist in the staging of their event.

2.3.1.1 The corporate buyer

Shock and Stefanelli (1992: 27) refer alternatively to the corporate buyer as the business market. They point out that this market can be divided into three segments: *shallow, mid-level* and *deep:*

- The *shallow* segment refers to low-budget events with short lead times. For instance, a caterer (the supplier) might only be required to deliver a few deli platters and salads within a day to a local tourism workshop event organised by a local tourism organisation (the buyer). Clients within this segment shop around for the best price. They are, however, conscious of quality and service, but they are normally on a limited budget and cannot afford the best. The shallow client of today can become a potential good (mid or deep level) buyer of the future.

- The *mid-level* segment is usually planned well in advance. Price is important; clients will not quibble over small amounts of money. It is important that the event (for instance, the Eastern Cape Tourism Board's Annual Woman Entrepreneur Gala) be memorable and consistent with the status of the executives in the business community. This segment can quickly lead to repeat business, as events can become a regular occurrence. An event organiser who provides excellent value will be the favoured event provider for the clients. Business executives are trained to shop around for the best value, but will remain loyal when it comes to their personal pleasures and benefits.

- The *deep* segment involves upmarket events that are expensive and where cost is a secondary consideration. Events such as the annual SA Tourism's Tourism Indaba can represent repeat business for the Durban ICC. While most large meeting events tend to move around a country, many tend to patronise the same destinations on a regularly scheduled basis. Even though most large event clients are booked years in advance, the event organiser should be prepared to serve at short notice as the loyal client expects this.

Rogers (1998: 25) describes corporate buyers as event organisers who work for corporations which are established primarily to generate an income and provide a financial return for their owners. These can be manufacturing or service organisations and are found in all sectors of industry.

Very few organisations have dedicated event management departments. In fact, during a recession corporations often opt to make savings by closing down or downsizing their event management departments and outsourcing this function to event organising agencies. In some cases, employees from former event management departments are re-employed on a freelance basis.

Staff involvement in organising events varies widely. On the one hand their function may be to collate information on potential event venues, while on the other they may be given complete responsibility for planning and running an event. Rogers (1998: 25) estimates that about 80% of corporate organisers have received little training in event planning and organising; such activities account for just part of their overall responsibilities.

Identifying the corporate buyer is therefore a major challenge for organisations wishing to market and promote their facilities and services to these role players. The transient role of such corporate event organisers makes it difficult to provide an effective education and training framework, to develop their expertise and increase their professionalism. The lack of such support systems hinders proper recognition being given to the role of the corporate event organiser as a component of an organisation's communication strategy.

Corporate events vary in size and type; Rogers (1998: 27) lists them as:
- annual general meetings, board meetings;
- exhibitions;
- incentive travel events;
- product launches;
- team-building events;
- technical and sales conferences;
- training courses and seminars.

The majority of corporate events are held in hotels. Some events may take place in purpose-built event venues; however, few corporate events are attracted to civic venues and town halls because they could be perceived as staid and simple. The same may be said of academic venues, unless these comprise dedicated meeting and event venues with high-quality facilities.

Corporate events usually have a relatively short lead time in contrast to association events, with just a few weeks or months in which to plan and stage the event. The majority of corporate events usually involve small delegate numbers of no more than 100 delegates. Frequently delegate participation in such events is not voluntary as participation is part of daily operations. The budget for corporate events, expressed in terms of expenditure per delegate, is usually higher than many association events, as the organisation – and not the individual delegate – pays for the delegates' attendance.

Corporate events are now more intensive business-related events than was the case in the past when they were viewed as a 'getaway'. Return on investment (ROI) is now a catch phrase across the event industry, emphasising the need to measure the effectiveness of all investments in all activities – including those made in an organisation's workforce. Despite this, research by Rogers (1998: 27) shows that around one-third of corporate event organisers do not evaluate their events after they have taken place. This calls into question the professionalism of the organisers and the organisations' investment in them as staff.

2.3.1.2 The association buyer

Association event organisers or 'buyers' represent a wide range of organisations that include:
- voluntary associations and societies (to further interests or hobbies, for example Rotary International);
- trade unions;
- religious organisations;
- professional and trade associations;
- political parties;
- charities;
- civic groups.

Shock and Stefanelli (1992: 31) refer to this market as the SMERF market, SMERF being an acronym for the social, military, education, religious and fraternal markets. It is also sometimes referred to as the 'Grunt' market.

One of the largest segments of this market is the fraternal market which is made up of organisations such as Rotary International, Lions, Round Table and other similar organisations. These represent a good, steady source of business because they meet at the same location each month and do not move around.

The military segment also represents a prime source of steady business, especially for those cities that have a major military base, for instance Bloemfontein. There are many awards, parades, armed-forces days and birthday events. Most local hotels can expect to attract their fair share of this market segment as they represent a welcome change of pace and offer more space.

The education segment generates a steady amount of revenue as there are many ongoing seminars, symposia and other events. There are also many high school functions.

The SMERF market is not as profitable as the corporate market; however, the event organiser can use this market to fill events during the off-peak event season between lucrative events. Many of the attendees probably are also bona fide corporate clients and their exposure to the event service may convince them to use the same services for a corporate event.

The SMERF market is similar to the corporate market in terms of the types of events required. These markets have meetings, attend sponsor training sessions and have educational functions.

Few association events are established mainly to generate a financial return as they are of a non-profit-making nature and exist to provide a service to their members and the community. Association events must, however, be run professionally because often they are in the public domain through media exposure. While association organisations themselves are non-profit-making, the planned events must cover their costs and in some cases generate a profit which is used in the administrative and promotional costs of planning and organising future events (Rogers, 1998: 29).

Delegates attending association events usually share a number of common characteristics:
- They usually choose to attend the event voluntarily.
- The accommodation range varies from bed-and-breakfast establishments to 5-star hotels.
- They often have to pay their own expenses, which require the event organiser to keep the costs as low as possible.
- The number of delegates attending a major annual event will typically be higher than for corporate events.

Association decision-making processes are different from those of corporate organisations, even though many of the larger associations have dedicated event organisers or units. The decision when and where to hold the event is usually taken by a committee elected by membership. An event organiser is expected to do much of the research and related work, producing a list of venues and services from which the committee chooses and makes recommendations.

Destinations produce detailed bid proposals outlining how they could help the association stage a successful event (similarly with corporate buyers). Such bid documents contain formal invitations (signed by the mayor or an important dignitary), provide a full description of the destination, highlighting its attractions, access and communication infrastructure, information on support services available at the destination and a list of services provided by the event venue, details of accommodation facilities and full details of the venue being proposed to stage the event. The local tourist office (LTO), acting on behalf of the destination, may be required, or invited, to make a formal presentation to the selection committee of the association, in competition with other destinations that have been short-listed.

Before a final decision is made, the selection committee may undertake an inspection visit to assess the destination first hand. The selection process can be very protracted. Lead times for association events are usually much longer than for corporate events. It is not unusual for association organisers to book venues several years in advance. The reasons for this may be a limited range of suitable venues and the organisational requirements of large events.

Many association events have may both the delegate and his or her spouse attending; this occurs much less frequently with corporate events, unless they include an incentive element. Partner (or spouse) programmes are designed to entertain the delegates' partners while the event is in progress. Often destinations work with the event organisers to help in the planning of the spouse programmes, as well as the coordination of tours and activities both before and after the event. Because of their large size, association events are often held in purpose-built public venues. Some use town hall and civic venues while others book university and college venues. Hotels are booked over the weekend as the rates then are cheaper (Rogers, 1998: 30–33).

2.3.1.3 The government buyer

Government buyers are very similar to association buyers. Local authorities, central government departments and agencies, educational bodies and health services are included here. This form of buyer is also non-profit-making and is accountable for the spending of public funds. Delegates for government events are normally not expected to pay their own expenses to participate in the event. It is likely, though, that the event will be run on a tight budget, using less expensive venues and facilities.

There is a trend for public organisations to book more up-market facilities. Such trends help to account for the major investments which tertiary institutions are making in their venue and accommodation stock to enable them to compete in a highly competitive marketplace (Rogers, 1998: 33).

2.3.1.4 Market subgroups

A *market sub-group* is the term used to describe an ancillary or auxiliary market that piggybacks on another market (Shock & Stefanelli, 1992: 37). For instance, guests at one large event may also take the opportunity to celebrate a reunion. Hence, it piggybacks the larger event. Event organisers should be trained to be aware of such auxiliary events and to capitalise on them. Most hotels generally make a conscious effort to court the market sub-groups forming part of large event audiences.

2.3.2 The suppliers

Event suppliers refer to those who make available for external hire the destinations, venues and specialist services. Relatively few of these suppliers are, however, dedicated exclusively to the event industry.

2.3.2.1 Venues

It is impossible at this stage to give an exact number of venues available for external hire in South Africa. There is no clear and uniform national classification system for event venues yet in place. Research by Rogers (1998: 33) has highlighted the fact that hotels make up the majority of all event venues and are particularly important to the corporate market. The main types of hotels active in the meeting market are city centre hotels, hotels near to national and international communications infrastructure such as airports, and game ranch venues. In addition, hotels that are located close to large event venues also benefit as providers of accommodation when a major event is organised at the venue. Larger association events frequently choose one hotel as their headquarters and this can hold a distinct public relations advantage with the hotel being featured in national and even international media coverage. The Tourism Grading Council of South Africa (TGCSA) in 2004 launched a grading scheme for venues used by the meetings and incentive sub-sectors. South Africa, according to Mackenzie (2004: 33), is seen as one of the first countries in the world to have a venue national grading scheme for the meetings and incentive sub-sectors. The grading of event venues is seen to assist event buyers in making informed decisions. In addition, it is seen to assist South Africa in showcasing world-class venues internationally, and assist marketers and operators in attracting additional international events. The demand for events, according to SA Tourism *et al* (2002: 60–61), is influenced by facility provision. This relates to the event infrastructure as well as the tourism-related services. It is required to constantly improve and maintain facilities. While events can tend to be hosted in destinations with the best facilities, it is also necessary to use events to kick-start developments in other regions.

Apart from hotel facilities, other principal types of venues include the following.

- **Civic centres.** These include town halls, council chambers and committee rooms that are available for hire.
- **College, university and other academic venues.** Many of these venues are available for residential conferences during student holidays; some can stage non-residential events during term times. Increasingly, academic institutions are investing in venues which are available throughout the year, such as Port Elizabeth Technikon's Conference Centre.
- **Purpose-built centres (residential and non-residential).** These are designed to host various types of events, ranging from very large events with hundreds or thousands of event delegates to smaller, day or residential events (for instance, Durban's International Conference Centre).
- **Unusual venues.** This describes a wide range of venues available for the staging of events. The attraction of an unusual venue can give the event a special appeal. Some venues may have high-quality facilities, others may be quite limited. Possible venue options include sports venues, cultural and entertainment centres such as museums and theatres, tourist attractions such as theme parks, and transport venues such as steam trains (Rogers, 1998: 39).

2.3.2.2 Destinations

Event organisers place more importance on the location than on any other single criterion when selecting the event site. The location (destination) may be expressed in terms of town, city or region of a country, or even a whole country, and the atmosphere or ambience it creates for the event. Each event destination must contain a range of venues, facilities, attractions, support services and infrastructure to assist in attracting event business. Cooper, Fletcher, Gilbert, Shepherd and Wanhill (1999: 103) indicate that most destinations comprise a core of the following components:

- *attractions*;
- *amenities* – accommodation, entertainment, and food and beverage outlets;
- *access* – local transport infrastructure;
- *ancillary services* – local service organisations.

The amalgamation of the destination components, the amalgam, comes together to form the destination. The quality of the destination components and service delivery system will ultimately determine how an event organiser perceives the suitability of a particular destination for event business. Destination management organisations frequently provide a one-stop service to the event organiser on what their destination has to offer. They should also be involved in product development: identifying weaknesses in venues and facilities and general infrastructure, and working towards eliminating these (Rogers, 1998: 40).

2.4 EVENT AGENCIES, INTERMEDIARIES AND OTHER IMPORTANT DOMESTIC AND INTERNATIONAL ORGANISATIONS

2.4.1 Event agencies

'Agencies' is a generic term used to describe a range of different organisations supplying services to event organisers. They act as both suppliers and buyers: they undertake a buying role on behalf of their clients, who may be corporations or associations, and they may act as intermediaries contracted to assist in the planning and running of events. According to Shock and Stefanelli (1992: 301), such intermediaries are sometimes referred at as '10-percenters'. This derives from the fact that their fees are generally 10% of the total bill. If the event is large, the fee may be reduced.

Clients frequently use intermediaries when the event is large and represents a major undertaking. For instance, it may be multi-functioned, multi-venued, and have many outside contractors. Intermediaries are often used in civic and political fundraising events where it is necessary to solicit financial support and to sell tickets. Fundraising fashion events, theme events, charity auctions and art events are also mostly organised and implemented by professional intermediaries.

Intermediaries tend to be more astute buyers than the average event buyer and tend to drive hard bargains. They sometimes want more control over the event than the typical event service provider wants to surrender.

Communicating event proposals through a third party such as an intermediary can be difficult and inefficient. It may prove difficult for the event service provider to determine if the proposals are consistent with the wishes of the client, as some intermediaries do not allow contact with the client concerned.

Problems can also occur if the client decides to approach the service provider direct instead of the intermediary. If discussion involves prices, the service provider faces an ethical dilemma if the intermediary was marking up the prices and rebilling the client. In such a case, before talking to the client the service provider should meet both to avoid potentially troublesome occurrences.

Agencies have a variety of forms and names and this can be confusing. The principal types of event intermediaries within the event sector are outlined below.

- **Business travel agencies.** These agencies seek to cater for the needs of business clients rather than the general public. They also are involved in sourcing venues for various business events and may contribute to the planning and organising of such events (Rogers, 1998: 49). A recent trend in the industry has been the merging of travel agencies and professional conference organisers (PCOs). The former have the transportation expertise and the latter the meeting management know-how. This gives the buyer a one-stop service (Shock & Stefanelli, 1992: 305).

- **_Convention and visitor bureaux (CVB)._** The International Association of Convention and Visitor Bureaux (IACVB) was founded in 1914 to promote good professional practices in the solicitation and servicing of events. This organisation has more than 400 member bureaux worldwide (Polivka, 1996: 213–215). The CVB are non-profit-making umbrella organisations that represent a destination in the solicitation, servicing and marketing of the destination to all types of travellers to the area. These bureaux do not actually organise events but serve to:
  - encourage groups to hold events in the destination they represent;
  - encourage visitors to enjoy their visits and the historic, cultural and recreational opportunities that the city or destination provides;
  - assist groups with event preparations and implementation.

  Convention and visitor bureaux generally provide very specific information and services for the following activities:
  - promoting and building event attendance;
  - event housing services, especially in the case of multi-property events;
  - on-site registration and information; and
  - on-site registration staffing (Polivka, 1996: 221–223).

The local CVB can provide some of the services provided by other intermediaries free of charge. The CVB provides useful information about the destination that can be used by the client to evaluate the destination's suitability for an event and can be a useful one-stop shopping source. The most tangible benefit for clients is the time saved. In addition, these bureaux can also provide suitable alternative selections for the client and logistical support at the local level (Shock & Stefanelli, 1992: 307).

Most CVB operate on a lead system, whereby the sales manager circulates meeting specifications to facilities and lodging entities that can accommodate the requirements. Basic information required by the CVB is usually indicated on the event lead sheet. Event lead sheets will customarily be distributed to all lodging members capable of handling the event. The event manager may decide to limit the lead distribution and may establish certain parameters. Specifying a particular location or proximity to a major transportation node such as an airport may effectively limit the distribution of the lead. Some event managers who may be familiar with the destination's properties may indicate certain facilities by name; in this case only these facilities should receive the lead, unless otherwise indicated (Polivka, 1996: 217–218).

Once the event is concluded, the relationship between the CVB and the event manager should continue. The CVB will request registration statistics and a critique of the event experience to evaluate the manner in which the facilities and communities responded to the event organisation's needs. The post-event evaluation assists the destination, improving the destination facilities and services for the next event. The final housing report provides critical information obtained from the hotels on actual pick-up, cancellation and no-show percentages (Polivka, 1996: 224).

- *Corporate hospitality companies (CHCs).* Corporate hospitality and entertainment often involve the exploitation of major sports and cultural events to improve links between the organisation and its clients or potential clients. Frequently events are arranged specially for the company and involve drinks reception, dinners and banquets, dances and discos. Formal presentations or short speeches are often included in the event to ensure that the company gets the message across. Corporate hospitality companies are often involved in corporate team-building exercises aimed at clients and/or employees. Such activities can include golf days, off-road driving or 'paint ball' games (Rogers, 1998: 48).

- *Destination management companies (DMCs).* Destination management companies range from those which provide very specialised services to full-service firms capable of handling all group logistics.

Some organisations may only act as specialised ground handlers operating in the incentive market. They have a specialised knowledge of the specific destination (city, town, region or even country). They may also have access to unusual venues such as private houses that may not normally be open to the public. They have considerable buying power and this makes them very useful to incentive houses that may not be from the specific destination. There is a very close relationship between DMCs and incentive travel houses. It can be seen that there is an overlap between the work of a PCO and a DMC, as well as the work of a convention and visitor bureau. Destination management companies are employed by the client to locate a venue, handle accommodation, assist with transport arrangements, and to put together itineraries and programme arrangements. Most DMCs earn a commission (Rogers, 1998: 48).

Other DMC organisations provide only ground transportation such as buses, limo and van services, while others can subcontract or handle personally everything a client needs. For instance, full-service firms book entertainment, plan themed events and coordinate spouse and tour programmes. Full-service firms may also provide staff, for example to exhibitors who require local models to work exhibition booths or who need trained registration personnel. The DMCs are often used to secure props for themed events; this may include appropriate balloon art and pyrotechnic displays.

Many out-of-town clients are willing to pay local DMCs to provide guidance in an unfamiliar destination as it is difficult to judge the quality of services available if the client has never visited the destination before. Client events that are held in different destinations every time prefer to work with DMCs (Shock & Stefanelli, 1992: 306).

- **Event production houses.** These organisations specialise in the actual staging of the event: designing and building event sets, providing lighting, sound systems and special effects. They have creative and theatrical skills that are used to produce professionally stage-managed events that should be a memorable experience for the delegates (Rogers, 1998: 46).
- **Exhibition organisers.** Many exhibitions have a conference programme as a way of adding value to the exhibition and making it more worthwhile for companies to attend. Some conference organisers organise the exhibitions themselves. Others prefer to employ the services of specialist exhibition organisations (Rogers, 1998: 50).
- **Ground transportation.** A typical ground transportation company handles primarily guest baggage. The company can be hired by the event client to pick up guest luggage and bring it to the hotel and to return the luggage to the airport at the end of the event. Some ground transportation firms specialise in transporting clients' personal property. A local transport operator may pick up event material such as equipment and product samples and deliver them to the event venue.

Some ground transportation firms specialise in providing limousine services for picking up and dropping off guests. They can also be on call for personal needs during events. This type of service is often used, as it is in many cases a cheaper alternative to using taxis. Some ground transportation companies specialise primarily in entertainment. Some trips, such as charter boat rides and trail rides, are planned strictly for the entertainment value (Shock & Stefanelli, 1992: 305).

- **Incentive travel houses.** Incentive travel is an international management tool that uses travel to motivate and/or recognise staff for increased levels of performance in support of organisational goals. This has given rise to incentive travel houses or agencies. Incentive travel programmes often involve travel to overseas destinations and there is a need to continually discover new destinations and create programmes that are more memorable. Incentive travel houses charge a fee to their clients for the work done on their behalf (Rogers, 1998: 47–48). In South Africa, they are represented by the Society of Incentive and Travel Executives (SITE).
- **Professional conference organisers (PCOs).** Professional conference organisers are alternatively known as contract planners, meeting organisers and multiple management companies. Sometimes PCOs are erroneously described as event managers. The PCO is employed to assist in the organisation of *meetings,* researching and recommending a suitable venue, helping to plan meeting programmes, booking accommodation for delegates, handling financial arrangements and the registration of delegates. The PCO is

normally paid a fee by the client organisation and may charge the venue a commission. Commission may also be charged on accommodation bookings and other services provided (Rogers, 1998: 45). In South Africa, PCOs are represented by the Association of Professional Conference Organisers of South Africa (APCOSA).

- *Special event planners.* These agents are sometimes commissioned by corporations to plan and implement company events. They usually have a select client list that is contacted on a periodic, predictable basis. Professional sports teams use special event planners to coordinate after-game parties, half-time events, parades, etc (Shock & Stefanelli, 1992: 303). Major events such as the Olympics and presidential inaugurations usually use special event planners. If several such planners are used, one of them may be responsible for overseeing and coordinating all the other planners through drawing up a master plan for the event and deciding how each planner will be utilised. In South Africa, these professionals are represented by the International Special Events Society (ISES) – see Appendix 2.1 on the web site.

- *Venue finding agencies.* Such agencies offer a limited service restricted to researching and recommending suitable venues for events. They normally present a short list of three potential venues to their client and usually receive a commission on the value of the bookings from the venue. Venue finding agencies may also get involved in booking accommodation for delegates and can expect to charge the accommodation providers a commission. The services of the agency are provided free of charge to the client (Rogers, 1998: 46).

- *Other agencies.* Some organisations may play a role in organising part of an event for their clients, although this may not normally fall under their day-to-day activities. Such organisations are public relations and advertising consultancies, management consultants and training companies (Rogers, 1998: 50). In a developing country such as South Africa, these role players often do more than all the others listed above.

2.4.2 Other important organisations

As the events industry matures it requires other organisations to function professionally and establish a code of practice. Below is a list of various organisations that play a supporting role within the events industry.

- *Consultants.* They undertake projects on a fee-paying basis for clients who normally operate on the supply side of the event industry. Such consultants may be involved in determining the potential market for a proposed new venue, the specification of a new event venue or the major renovation of an existing venue; advising on marketing strategies for a venue or destination; and, undertaking feasibility studies to establish and operate new venues (Rogers, 1998: 52).

- *Educational institutions.* The education and training of the event industry's future workforce is critical for the future growth and development of the industry. Tertiary institutions are increasingly devoting attention to the events industry in their syllabi (Rogers, 1998: 52).

- *National, regional and local tourism organisations*. Most countries now have national tourism organisations (NTOs) which have been established to promote the country internationally. A number of countries have established national event bureaux to specifically research, market and promote this sector. There is no standard format for such national bureaux: each operates differently (Rogers, 1998: 51). In South Africa the regions or provinces have established regional tourism organisations (RTOs) and, with varying degrees of success, are promoting the regions as event destinations. Similarly, various cities, towns and villages, the local tourism organisations (LTOs), are attempting to position themselves as desirable and ideal event destinations. South Africa's six major cities (Cape Town, Johannesburg, Durban, Pretoria, Port Elizabeth and Bloemfontein) have joined forces as the Southern African Federation of Convention Cities (SAFCC) in a promotional strategy to increase South Africa's share of the international meetings market. Refer to chapter 1 for a more detailed discussion on this issue.

- *Trade associations*. These organisations are formed to serve the interests of the members and their activities include lobbying and representation, establishing codes of practice, marketing and promotion, education and training, research and information.

- *Trade media*. The event industry trade media are primarily magazines, such as the *Southern Africa Conference, Exhibition & Events Guide*, published on a regular basis, and may contain articles on new developments and ways to improve the quality of event management. The Internet is increasingly playing an important role in this regard. The trade media fulfil the role of keeping the industry informed of the latest developments taking place. Their circulation also provides an advertising and PR medium for suppliers wishing to promote their services and facilities to potential buyers.

Browse these Internet sites

http://www.aime.com.au/
http://www.bestcities.net/
http://www.efct.com/
http://www.eibtm.ch/
http://www.ettfa.org/
http://www.eventguru.co.za/
http://www.globalmedianetwork.co.uk/
http://www.iacvb.org/

http://www.iccaworld.com/
http://www.imex-frankfurt.com/
http://www.i-mi.com/
http://www.juliasilvers.com/embok
http://www.olympic.org/
http://www.tourismgrading.co.za/
http://www.wtmlondon.com/

QUESTIONS FOR SELF-EVALUATION

1 Discuss the prime responsibility of a CVB.
2 Explain the purpose the leads process serves during site selection.
3 Explore how a CVB can assist with on-site registration and information dissemination.
4 Contrast the difference between association and corporate buyers.
5 Explain why an event organiser should consider dealing with the SMERF market.
6 As an employee of a large trade association that holds an annual event for about 1 000 delegates, with an exhibition alongside the conference ('CONFEX'), you have been tasked to contract out the planning of this event. Describe the types of agencies you would approach. Provide reasons for your choices.
7 Assess the various market segments within the corporate market and suggest how the event manager should manage these.
8 Discuss the role of the main actors within the event system. Explain their relevance to a prospective event organiser.
9 Discuss the role of event intermediaries.
10 Explain why event managers should take cognisance of the auxiliary event market.
11 Event suppliers play a vital role in the production of events. Use examples to illustrate your response.

Note: Appendices 2.1 and 2.2 can be found on the Juta Academic web site: www.jutaacademic.co.za

Appendix 2.1 *Graphic Representations Using the Rutherford Silvers EMBOK Taxonomy (Source: Rutherford Silvers, Internet)*
Appendix 2.2 *Graphic representation by Janet Landey, CSEP, illustrating the application of the EMBOK Taxonomy to industry disciplines (Source: Rutherford Silvers, 2004: Internet)*

Part B

CHAPTER 3

Bidding for Major Events

David Maralack and Nicola Lloyd

AIM OF THE CHAPTER

This chapter describes the process that any organisation should follow when considering whether or not to participate in bidding to host a major event.

LEARNING OBJECTIVES

After having studied this chapter, you should be able to:

- understand that bidding for an event is a competitive process;
- identify the critical questions to be answered before deciding to bid for an event;
- understand the critical phases of a bidding timetable;
- identify the planning and organising activities which are indispensable to the bidding process;
- identify the critical aspects of a bid document.

3.1 INTRODUCTION

The process of bidding for a major event (sport, cultural or conferencing) begins with an idea or a concept that forms the basis of a bid. The concept could be based on an event with standardised features such as the Olympic Games or Soccer World Cup event or it could be a new idea to procure the rights to host an event, such as the North Sea Jazz Festival in Cape Town, South Africa (see case study 3.1). For both standardised and new events, the organisers must develop a concept that will be attractive and where the plan is technically sound.

Case study 3.1: The North Sea Jazz Festival

The North Sea Jazz Festival is a mega-event originally based in Holland. Through a lobbying and procurement process, members of the music fraternity in Cape Town bid to host a similar event there. This has subsequently become an event of international proportions and profile. It is now being suggested that the event has developed a character of its own and may now be able to be branded independently of the original festival.

3.2 CALL FOR BIDS

A group of organisations or individuals usually owns the commercial and legal rights to an event ('event owner'). The event owners look for the most appropriate location and event management team to implement their event. Owners of events which take place annually or every few years look for different venues or destinations around the country or internationally. The process of bidding for these events is established by the event owners and may vary in complexity, depending on the scale and frequency of the event.

Unless an event is independently conceived of and owned by an organisation, which then proceeds to organise it, a tendering process is usually put in motion, which allows any number of competitors to submit their proposals for consideration by the event owners. As this scale and frequency grows, the benefits and commercial returns are perceived to increase and the process also becomes more and more competitive. In the first instance, a decision must be made as to whether or not to bid for an event. For this decision to be made responsibly, and in order to compete successfully to host an event, a thorough understanding of the event requirements, the bidding timetable, the competitors and the benefits and risks, which may arise, is essential.

The bid process commences when the event owners invite, either by public announcement or nomination, a number of associations, cities or countries to submit a proposal. The event owner predetermines a set process for bidding and the timetable by which time-critical information or documentation must be lodged. There may be a pre-application process determined by the event owner. This may include an expression of interest from all interested parties. The event owners may then develop a shortlist and preferred bidders will then be requested to present formal and detailed bids for consideration.

It is imperative to note that the bidding process tests the ability of the prospective host to meet all the event owner's requirements and to host a successful event. Therefore, the bidding process includes preliminary planning for all aspects of hosting the event. The contents of the bid book, or plan, is detailed below (also see section 3.6).

3.3 DECIDING TO BID FOR A MAJOR EVENT

When deciding whether or not to submit a bid for an event, there are a number of questions that require consideration before any decision is made. Many of these questions relate to bidding for larger-scale events, but should be considered in any bidding process. Table 3.1 details a list of preliminary questions that will inform a bid strategy. These should form the departure point for bidding and inform the decision to bid.

TABLE 3.1 *Framework for a bid strategy*

The following questions may be used to structure a bidding strategy for an event:

- How does one make the event attractive for the event owners, the participants and visitors?
- What does this destination have to offer the event?
  - participants, family, friends
- How to attract visitors that are not competitors or family?
- Why will they come here and not go somewhere else?
- What attractive packages can we provide?
- Can we afford to host the event?
- Will other critical role players such as national, provincial and local government be able to support the event?
- What is the direct economic benefit to the organiser, city and country?
- Does the event act as a marketing platform?
- How can the tourism market around the event be maximised?
- What image can be portrayed for the location?
- What media will cover the event?
- What will be the major international media spin-offs?
- What business opportunities will result?
- What impact on trade relations will result?
- Is there a potential to attract associated events, conferences and annual meetings?
- How may community interests, through competition and entertainment, be promoted?
- How may youth development – schools education programmes – be created to increase interest?
- Who are the stakeholders and how do you intend to formalise the relationships with decision-makers?

Very few cities and organisations will find themselves in the fortunate position of being able to answer each of these questions positively. This does not mean that they should decide not to bid, but rather that they should be pragmatic about all the realities of bidding. It may be a matter of weighing up the risks and benefits and developing a pragmatic plan to ensure a successful bid and event. What might apply and work within one context may not necessarily be applicable in another time or place. There is, therefore, no guaranteed formula for success. Ultimately the decision to bid should depend on the views of a number of people who will have weighed up the risks and benefits in terms of their particular interests.

Key questions to be considered when deciding to bid for a major event include the following.

3.3.1 Does the deadline set by the event owners for the submission of a proposal allow for preparation and submission of the documentation required to present the bid?

Timetables for bidding are established by the event owners and are strict and usually very demanding. They should be considered and well understood before any decision to bid is made, as there can be no extensions to the due dates.

It is essential to consider what trade-offs and compromises will have to be made and to be absolutely realistic about the implications of meeting the deadlines. In many instances, for example, timetables for bidding leave little if no time for consultation with the many role players who would be involved in hosting the event.

If the undertaking is an international event of large scale, the timetable should be assessed to determine whether any opportunity exists to host test events in the facilities to be used beforehand. This is particularly applicable to large sporting events.

It is also important to consider the timing of the bid politically, geographically and historically in terms of the event owner's requirements. Event owners are sensitive to the geographical spread of cities in which their event is hosted. They aim for a degree of diversity and may avoid awarding the rights to the event to a city or region for a host of reasons, which include geographical location and political stability and ideology. The event owner will also consider the occurrence of other major events during the same period or in a similar geographical location. It is therefore important to assess these implications when deciding to bid.

The technical expertise available to prepare a bid proposal should then be carefully considered. This is particularly relevant in a developing city context where there is usually little or no experience available at the beginning of a bid for a major event. Time must be sufficient to allow for assessments of other previous bids in order for lessons to be learned, procedures to be understood and the strengths and weaknesses of the bid to be identified and addressed.

We shall see that the responses to the event owner's requirements contained in the bidding proposal should be informed by and respond to already existing local legal and planning policies and frameworks. To the extent that these are missing or deficient, it may make preparation of responses in the time available impossible. On the other hand, if time is plentiful, then it may be possible to use the energy unleashed by the bidding process to help establish the most critically needed local policy frameworks.

3.3.2 Will the bid meet the event owner's macro geopolitical requirements?

As previously stated, it is important to consider the timing of a bid politically, geographically and historically in terms of the event owner's requirements. Event owners may be sensitive to the geographical spread of their event. An analysis of what other events are occurring over the same period should be considered.

This applies especially to cities bidding to host international or national events that are held annually in different locations around the country or world. For instance, large sporting events such as World Championships move around the world each year. If the International Athletics World Championships were held in Johannesburg this year, there is little chance that South Africa or even Africa will hold them next year. The same applies to large annual exhibitions and conferences.

3.3.3 Are the (First World) requirements of the event owner reconcilable with the socio-economic and political realities facing a developing city?

The technical requirements for some major events are usually provided in documents made available to bidding entities by the organisation holding the rights to the event and are used to a large extent to standardise and facilitate their evaluation of different bidding cities.

The technical requirements for a major event will cover the need for financial deposits, technical aspects, the degree of local support for hosting the event, and the provision of letters of support for the bid. In cases where event owners do not outline detailed descriptions of the technical requirements to be provided, a bidding entity should carefully analyse the submissions by other cities for previous events to ascertain the level of detail provided.

For a bidding entity to compete effectively in the bidding process for a major event it must demonstrate a substantial appreciation of the event owner's requirements, a sympathetic attitude towards the needs of all the participants, an in-depth knowledge of the sophisticated specifications of the media and a good grasp of the lessons learned from past efforts at hosting the event.

Those involved in the preparation of the bid must also gain a rapid understanding of how providing these requirements will impact on their local context in the short and long term. They must understand how specific or flexible the instructions are from the event owner as to the way in which infrastructure and facilities are to be provided. In addition, an understanding of the more specific requirements which other organisations may have will be necessary (such as the end users and managers of facilities, individual sports federations specifications, local community needs). The bidding proposal will offer proposals to the event owner, which will demand involvement from both public and private organisations. The capacity of the public and private sectors to deliver what is required within the stipulated time frame must be assessed.

The lessons learned from other events held previously are, therefore, invaluable. A bid entity should seek tutors from the organisers of previous events staged by other organisations/cities. Once an understanding of the requirements of the event has been gained, sufficient time in the process should be set aside to allow for the strengths and weaknesses of other competitors which are bidding for the same event to be carefully assessed. In this way, it will be possible to determine the particular strength of the bid and what possibility there is of succeeding.

The evaluation should include assessments of the technical capability of the city, its political context, public and media sentiments, the sentiment which might be felt towards it by the event owners, and its preparedness in terms of the facilities, infrastructure and accommodation required to host the event. Evaluating the technical attributes of the competition may entail visits to other bidding organisations or cities. The documentation from other bids, which have been either successful and/or unsuccessful in the past, should be obtained to gain an understanding of the event owner's preferences and dislikes. It is also useful as a guide to product quality and organisation.

Developing cities face considerable disadvantages compared with developed cities in bidding for events. They normally lack capacity in infrastructure and organisational skills. A bid by a developing city for the right to host a major event will probably be made within a context of rapid growth and change and serious local deprivation experienced by the majority of the city's residents. The underlying approach of a bid must, therefore, seek to achieve some improvement to the lives of the most deprived inhabitants of a city.

In a developing context, hosting an event must address the priority development needs of the poorest sectors of the population. The bidding entities have to ensure that infrastructure necessary for the event serves a vital purpose after the event in providing the most deprived of communities with critical facilities and services. A crucial question asked by an event owner will be whether the governance of the city is sufficiently established, and administratively competent, to provide the essential foundation for the bid if required.

For a developing city bidding for a major event, the challenge will always be to assess whether it can offer the event owners an event that achieves more than one objective.

3.3.4 Is the bid able to deliver a sufficiently saleable product to attract the private sector sponsors that will be essential?

The hosting of a major event entails the securing of both public and private sector sponsorships to fund its organisation. Sponsor support will depend on whether there is sufficient unequivocal, upfront political, private sector and public support for bidding for the event and on the degree of media and public exposure offered in return. The degree of popular local and international interest that may be created for the event requires upfront consideration.

3.3.5 What will be the benefits of bidding for and hosting the event – locally, regionally and nationally – and to whom would they accrue?

The benefits to a city and its region of hosting an event may be measured in a number of ways and feasibility studies to determine the impacts of the event should be conducted before proceeding to bid for an event. Determining the number of jobs created (part-time, full-time/skilled, unskilled/permanent or temporary) and the area and nature of land and facilities improved or redeveloped in a city as a result of event-related activity are two means of assessing this impact. There may also be a number of potential negative impacts and costs which have to be mitigated against in the management of the event. These should be investigated and considered before deciding to bid for an event and monitored during the hosting phase if the bid proposal is successful. Chapter 4 deals extensively with this process.

3.3.6 Does the city in which the event would take place have the required transport infrastructure, facilities and accommodation?

Air, sea, regional road and rail access to a venue/city in which the event may take place from elsewhere in the country or abroad must be addressed. A safe, reliable and efficient transport system providing movement between hotels and venues is a prerequisite. The event owners will assess the state of the venues and infrastructure to be used and in most cases will look more favourably on bids showing that all of these are in place and have hosted or been utilised for similar events in the past. If all or any of the required venues and infrastructure do not exist, as may be the case in developing contexts, the bidding entity must assess whether or not it will be practically and financially feasible to build them in time for the event and, more importantly, for what purpose they will be used after the event.

3.3.7 How much public and private investment will be required, and will this be affordable in the light of other possible competing requirements?

The bidding process will be costly and its funding should be provided on a shared basis between public and private sectors. The financial costs of bidding need to be understood in advance and once the bid process is underway the required resources must be forthcoming timeously. Sponsorships and municipal facilities and services will be needed. A consideration will be how much outright funding from the private sector will be needed to prepare the bid proposal and how much value-in-kind assistance will be asked of the public sector.

3.3.8 Has the bid the blessing of any federations, associations or institutes whose active and ongoing support and involvement will be essential?

The technical preparation of an event plan, the technology and communication proposals, the transport plan, the environmental proposals and preparation of cost estimates for infrastructure that will be required by the event owners will all require the involvement – and often approval – of a variety of stakeholders and authorities. The complexity and time required to obtain these commitments and approvals should not be underestimated when considering the submission of a proposal to host an event.

3.3.9 Is there the human capacity and skill to draw from in order to bid for and host the event?

Of all the considerations in deciding to bid, this is the most fundamental. While support is the critical starting point, without capacity and capability it is meaningless. It is essential to assess the capacity and capability of the key responsible stakeholders – public and private sectors and communities – to sustain and deliver on a bid for an event. The bid entity will need to assess its needs for public sector capacity vis à vis the negotiated contributions of the private sectors. The evaluation of capacity must look ahead to the possibility that the bid will be successful and a crucial capacity question at the outset is the availability of the right kind of people to lead and direct the bid.

Table 3.2 provides a checklist of questions on 'Deciding to Bid' (Source: South African Sports Commission, 2003: 16).

TABLE 3.2 *Summary issues on deciding to bid*

- Are the First World requirements of the event owner reconcilable with the socio-economic opportunities and limitations that we may offer?
- Would we be sufficiently prepared to deliver a good quality bid in the time frames required?
- Are the event and the bid a sufficient product that could be sold to potential private sector sponsors?
- What would be the benefits of hosting the event for the local, regional and national area?
- Who would benefit and how?

- What sorts of measures are to be put in place to maximise the benefits and minimise the risks?
- Does the city have the required infrastructure, facilities and accommodation?
- If not, what would be the costs of providing these to a level that would be financially and practically feasible?
- How much public and private investment would be required to ensure that the infrastructure is brought up to speed?
- Is there sufficient support from local government?
- Is the human capacity available that would ensure a successful bid and hosting of the event?
- Does the bid have sufficient support from critical stakeholders such as the federation, who will provide ongoing support?
- Is there sufficient public, private and political support for the bid?

3.4 TYPICAL PHASES IN THE BIDDING PROCESS

As we have said, the bidding process for an event depends to a large extent on the nature of the event. The typical phases in any bid process are as follows:

- *Research and development*. In this phase organisations consider the merits and risks of bidding before formally announcing their intention to bid. Prospective bidding organisations must adequately assess whether to bid for an event and then to understand the nature of demands that may be placed on them when staging it. Depending on the scale or importance of the event, this phase may entail the election of a city by a country to bid for an event on its behalf, and the appointment of the necessary consultants to undertake cost-benefit analyses.
- *Official invitation to bid*. The event owner officially invites organisations or cities to bid and provide a detailed timetable for submission of proposals.
- *Confirmation of the bid*. Bidding organisations formally confirm and announce their intention to bid for an event. This announcement is usually supported by the necessary political and financial endorsements and may include the provision of a deposit to the event owners in the case of a major event such as the Olympic Games.
- *Bid preparation*. The bidding entity begins the preparation of a 'candidature file', bid document or proposal, either through the assistance of consultants or the formation of a legal bidding company.
- *Presentation of the bid*. The bidding entities submit and present their proposals to the event owner by a stipulated date.
- *Lobby and evaluation phase*. In the case of international events where the stakes are high, the event owners begin an evaluation of each bid submitted and the bidding entities, in turn, begin to lobby individual members of the event owners' organisation of the merits of their proposal and for votes in their favour.

- *Final announcement.* The event owners gather all the candidates and announce the successful bidding entity. In the case of a large-scale or major event, the host city will be announced and a contract signed immediately after the announcement.
- *Hosting phase.* The successful bidding entity enters into a contract with the event owners and begins the preparation for the event.

Guidance for bidding for events

The professionalisation of bidding for events is in a nascent stage in South Africa at present. Depending on the nature of the event to be bid for, guidance may be sought from:

- The South African Sport Commission, which has published a bid manual and set of protocols
- The South African Department of Environmental Affairs and Tourism
- The MICE Sector of South African Tourism
- The Destination Marketing Organisation in the Western Cape Tourism office, which has an events strategy and has assisted with numerous bids
- United Kingdom Sport, which has published a guide for bids (advice is given on preparation of bids; business plan templates, economic impacts; checklists; etc).

It must be noted that events related to tourism are business driven and must fall in line with the respective national or provincial events strategy.

3.5   PLANNING AND ORGANISING

It has been said 'we need to know where we would like to go before we can plan the best way of getting there'. A bidding entity's event plan should be based on a vision, which derives from broader long- and short-term visions for the future. This vision should guide decisions that are made and reflect the concerns, aspirations and values of all the people involved.

While the hosting of an event may only take place over a few days, the actual preparations may take much longer – even years in the case of a major event. In bidding for a major event, goals, objectives and principles should be formulated which balance candidature and societal requirements. These will derive from the philosophy that has been developed by the bid and should form the basis of the manner in which the bid entity proposes to host the event if successful.

The broad spatial implications of meeting an event owner's requirements must be established as early as possible. A spatial plan should be prepared which meets the event owner's requirements as well as impacting positively on the city in which the event is planned.

Explicit approaches should be prepared and adopted with respect to the operational and infrastructural aspects of hosting the event. The location of facilities (both competition and training), the location of specific uses, the provision of any required housing and other accommodation (for example hotels), the use of improvements to transport infrastructure, the identification of projects for immediate implementation and the achievement of environmental sustainability all require explicit approaches to be formulated.

Once the principles and a spatial plan have been agreed to, the next step in developing the event plan is to test the applicability of various venues and infrastructure to defined event owner's requirements. This may be done in terms of ownership, proximity to public transport, relationship to other facilities like accommodation and tourist attractions, and environmental impact.

The bidding process for an event is usually tight, extremely demanding, conducted by individuals from wide backgrounds/professions and does not allow for anything less than 'getting it right first time round'. The complex and time-limited nature of the proceedings will necessitate a strict, professional and ruthless management process prioritising all work requirements according to a work breakdown and leaving little room for mistakes. Precise and competent identification of what is required and how this work should be scheduled is imperative to avoid doing anything that is not absolutely necessary. Effective project management will, therefore, be at the heart of all the activities of a bid.

The design, provision and management of systems (that is, information storage, handling and communication, financial management, procedures, technology, etc) will either facilitate or hinder the work of the bid. They will establish the patterns of work and communication within the bid and between the bid and outside; they will provide the mechanisms that enable people to work together effectively and can be a main contributor to the culture of the organisation.

Critical systems focus areas include:

- information storage, retrieval, developing, processing, dissemination;
- document management;
- financial management: budget forecasting, cost controlling, creditor payment;
- procedures that guide communication within and outside the bid: verbal, written, formal, informal;
- choice of computer and telecommunications technology: hardware and software and its interlinking internally and externally (this is an important consideration for bidding cities in a developing context which do not have well-developed communication networks);
- control of the nature and flow of the work and its products;
- employment and dismissal procedures, performance appraisal and remuneration;

- employee development and human relations;
- quality assurance.

The work breakdown should be prepared according to the event requirements – always making provision for prioritising work and formulating contingency plans for unexpected situations. Schedules for detailed planning, community consultation, design, construction, site making, and test events must be prepared timeously, so that the event owners can be guaranteed of delivery on time and the local authorities and other groups involved in the planning and development of the sites can have a clear understanding of where they fit into the process and, therefore, the implications of delay on their part.

A job scheduling system such as a computerised project management package is useful in forcing individual managers to define their work responsibilities, products needed, resource requirements and deadlines.

3.6 CONTENTS OF A BID PLAN

As indicated above, the bidding process is fundamentally about displaying the ability to host the event and therefore should include evidence of planning for aspects of hosting the event. A potential bid book or plan will require the following contents:

- candidate characteristics
- legal aspects
- finance
- environment
- security
- medical and health
- transport and traffic
- event requirements
- accommodation
- telecommunications.

3.6.1 Candidate characteristics

Required is information on the political, economic and social structures within which the event hosts will work. Of particular relevance would be the responsibilities of various levels of government that will be involved in hosting the event and will ultimately provide guarantees.

3.6.2 Legal aspects

The Bid Committee should conform to the legal requirements of the event owner, in particular:

- use of symbols
- revenue raising and distribution
- customs and immigration.

3.6.3 Finance

The financial cost of hosting must be clearly identified and should include:
- capital expenditure on facilities, infrastructure and venues
- operational expenditure for hosting.

3.6.4 Environment

Often event owners require information on location of the city, altitude – as it may affect performance of athletes – temperature and humidity, precipitation, and so forth.

3.6.5 Security

This is often the most critical aspect of a bid document, as the event owner needs to be assured that the event will proceed without any security breaches. Security issues to consider:
- crime prevention plans in the host city
- security plan for venues and accommodation
- emergency and evacuation plans
- access control for vehicles and people
- security plan for high profile or high risk groups.

3.6.6 Medical and health services

Description of the availability of medical care in and around the venues and accommodation should be provided.

3.6.7 Transport and traffic

These would include:
- travel to the host city
- travelling in and around the host city
- travel to and from venues
- transport for people with disabilities.

3.6.8 Event requirements

Whether the nature of the event is sport, cultural or a conference, the host has specific requirements to ensure that the event is well run and will conclude successfully. The event owner usually identifies and determines these specifications and special emphasis must be given to this aspect.

3.6.9 Accommodation

Information must be given on availability of accommodation and its proximity to the venue and places of interest. Often special requirements are laid down for various levels of competitors, officials and dignitaries.

3.6.10 Telecommunications infrastructure

Mega events most often depend on media and broadcast coverage. The event owner must therefore be assured that proceedings will be available for broadcasting in the various forms and not be limited by lack of infrastructure.

In preparing for the bid process, it is advisable to establish a checklist no matter how large or small or simple or complicated the event. A checklist of issues to consider follows this section.

3.7   CHECKLIST

A checklist needs to be drawn up for each significant event, milestone or requirement in the bid process. No list can ever be exhaustive as each event is unique and conditions that may apply vary. The master checklist must therefore be adapted to the particular circumstances of the event. However, some of the key questions that will form part of the checklist are listed in table 3.3.

TABLE 3.3 *Checklist of questions for a bid process (Source: South African Sports Commission, 2003: 57–58 and UKSport, 2003: Internet)*

1 THE EVENT	What is the name, nature and scale of the event?
	How often is the event held and where has it previously been hosted?
	Where will the event take place, with respect to geographical area, city and suburb?
	Why does your organisation wish to bid to host the event?
	When will the event take place and over what period?
	Is there a forecast of impacts and attendance numbers from previous events?
	What potential linked events may be organised?
	Is there enough infrastructure or do we need to provide new infrastructure?
	Will the human resource requirements of the event be met?
	Is there clarity on the financial implications of the bid and the event?
2 THE BIDDING PROCESS	What organisation owns the rights to the event?
	Is there a critical path for the bid? If so what are the critical milestones?
	What other organisations are bidding to host the event?
	Is there a formal lobbying period?
	Will an evaluation team visit to assess your potential?
	Are there potential competing events occurring over the same period?

	Where would the bid headquarters be located?
	What are the strengths of your bid?
	What are the obvious weaknesses of your bid?
	Is there support from the national federation, SASC, and all levels of government?
3 MEETING THE BIDDING	What are the bidding and hosting requirements?
	Is there a specific bidding manual?
	Do you have enough time to meet the bidding requirements?
	Are there sufficient resources to meet the requirements?
	Is there adequate infrastructure to host the event?
	If not, what improvements and/or temporary facilities are needed?
	Do you have the technical infrastructure to host the event?
	Are dedicated training facilities required?
	What special transport arrangements will be required?
	What additional accommodation arrangements will be required?
	What media and IT infrastructure is required?
	What accreditation and security measures will be needed?
	What specialised equipment will be needed to which you do not presently have access?
	Are all venues and modes of transport accessible to disabled people?
	What guarantees does the event owner in the bidding process require?
4 ORGANISATIONAL STRUCTURE & CAPACITIES	What is the nature of your bidding committee?
	Who will lead your bid?
	Who are the decision makers in your bid?
	What is the composition of your committee or board?
	Is there sufficient organisational expertise to compete?
	Who are the stakeholders in the event at all levels?
	What will be expected of them in the bidding process?
	Do they have the capacity to assist within the time frames set?
	What systems are currently in place to run the bid?
	How much public sector input will be required from national, regional and local government level?
	What potential is there for South African participants to excel at the event?
5 FINANCIAL IMPLICATIONS	What budget is required to submit your bid?
	What upfront finances exist to compete effectively in the bidding process?
	Is there an initial inflow of capital from the event owner?
	What funding arrangements are in place or are needed?
	Is there private sector interest in the bid and the event?
	How marketable is your event in terms of media coverage?
	What marketing and sponsorship restrictions apply to the bidding process and event?

What sponsorship arrangements have been secured?
Do you have financial assurance and insurance cover for the bidding process?
Is the event financially and economically viable?
Have you conducted a feasibility study? If so, please provide the documentation.
What are the potential positive and negative impacts resulting from bidding and hosting the event?
Please provide relevant documentation on the impact of the event. This includes environmental, social, economic and infrastructural impacts.
What legacies will be derived from bidding and hosting the event?
Which geographical area and who in particular will benefit?
Will a post-event evaluation be completed?
What monitoring and evaluation mechanisms will be established during the bidding process?
How will the event fit into national and regional sports and tourism strategies?
Why will participants and spectators want to come to your destination as opposed to any other?
Are the human resources sufficient to meet the requirements for the event?
If not, indicate the measures in place to meet this need.

3.8 SCHEDULING CRITICAL STEPS IN A BID PROCESS

Preparing for a bid may be a daunting task, as indicated by the checklist in table 3.3. However, it may be useful to start off with the key practical questions that have been detailed in tables 3.1 and 3.2. The answers to these questions are a guide to developing an effective assessment of whether to bid for an event or not. While answers are being developed for the practical questions, critical points in the process also need to be considered of when critical information and processes need to be complete.

It is important to remember, *'there is never enough time in bidding'*; therefore, scheduling tasks (even in a rudimentary way) and setting priorities is important to meet the deadlines set by the event owners. Usually event owners do not compromise on deadlines set for lodging bid documents. To assist with meeting the deadlines or milestones in the project, it is important to stick to the schedule. One way of determining your critical delivery dates can be conceptualising scheduling. This process is illustrated in figure 3.1.

Figure 3.1 identifies the broad tasks such as the initial concept, detailed conceptualisation, strategy, feasibility and the formal bid document. Each of these tasks will have a number of sub-tasks and different requirements. An event owner, supporter or government department may require that certain information be detailed and forwarded at specific steps in the process. Scheduling is a tool to assist the successful completion of a project and connects the shortest possible time sequence between the various interrelated activities. Table 3.4 contains some of the key issues to be considered.

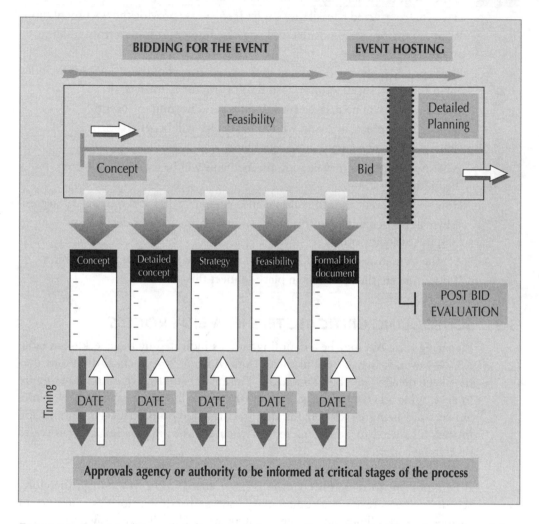

FIGURE 3.1 *Conceptualising scheduling in a bid process (Source: South African Sports Commission, 2003: 56)*

TABLE 3.4 *Key issues for scheduling tasks*

- What are the critical tasks that need to be completed?
- What is the nature of work required to complete the task successfully?
- Determine the relationships between the various tasks, i.e. can one task be started only when another task is completed?
- Prioritise these tasks in order of importance.
- Determine the timelines for the completion of each task:

- How long does each task take to complete?
- By when MUST it be completed?
- Determine clear responsibilities on who must complete the task
- Determine the critical path of tasks, i.e. in what sequence must tasks be completed and what is the shortest possible time period connecting the critical tasks

(Source: 'Bidding to Host an International Sport and Recreation Event in South Africa: A Guide for Sport and Recreation Organisations' : South African Sports Commission 2003)

For example, in the Call for Bids stage (section 3.2 of this chapter), an event owner or government department may require a pre-application concept to be approved prior to detailed conceptualisation of the bid. This task will probably have very specific requirements and timelines, which may be very different to the other stages of the bid process. It is, therefore, important that this task and all its requirements be detailed on the critical path of the bid process. A similar exercise needs to be followed for each of the other stages in the bid process. Even though this exercise may be regarded as time consuming initially, it will be valuable in ensuring that all milestones are achieved and that the correct information is forwarded at the correct time. As bidding for major events has become so competitive internationally, event owners will disqualify a bid if all information is not received in the correct format and at the required time.

Besides providing relevant information, it is important to remember that the bidding process tests the ability of the prospective host to meet all the event owner's requirements and to host a successful event. Therefore, detailing the critical path of the bid process as early as possible will enable the bid organisers to meet exact standards and timelines.

Browse these Internet sites
www.sasc.org.za
www.uksport.gov.uk
www.southafrica.net
www.capetourism.org
www.sportsdestination.christchurch.org.nz

QUESTIONS FOR SELF-EVALUATION

1 What does an event owner look for in a successful bid document/proposal?
2 What questions should be considered when deciding whether or not to bid for an event?
3 What are the typical phases in any bidding process?
4 What difficulties are inherent in a bid from a developing country?

Note: Appendix 3.1 can be found on the Juta Academic web site:
www.jutaacademic.co.za
Appendix 3.1 *Some definitions*

CHAPTER 4

Event Impact Assessment

Peter de Tolly

AIM OF THE CHAPTER

This chapter introduces the concept of identifying and assessing the key impacts of bidding for and hosting an event, so as to determine possible benefits and costs. Costs (that is, negative impacts) pose risks and uncertainties for the event proponents, the authorities, the society and ecology in which the event will take place.

LEARNING OBJECTIVES

After having studied this chapter, you should be able to:

- determine whether your event is in keeping with the principles of sustainable development;
- know when your proposal requires an environmental impact assessment (EIA)[1] or a heritage impact assessment (HIA), or a combination of both;
- define the key impacts that need to be assessed in bidding for an event;
- understand their implications;
- display a broad understanding of a number of impact assessment tools which might be used and which must be appropriate to the scale – from the national to the local – and to the purpose;
- explain some of the possible mitigating measures for potential adverse impacts;
- start to develop an appropriate response.

4.1　INTRODUCTION

While there are potential benefits to be derived from hosting an event, in the form of visitors attracted, city image enhancement, needed facilities and infrastructure, new jobs, both short and long term, and profit for the event organisers and promoters, there will also be costs – financial, social and environmental. The costs are risks and uncertainties that need to be anticipated, assessed and quantified, responded to and, if it is possible, managed. It is not only the bidders who will need to understand and assess potential risks: there will be many others who will need to be satisfied with the affordability and feasibility of preparing for and hosting the event and with its possible after effects.

For large events, which will require intensive capital investment in facilities, infrastructure and in organisation, risk assessment and impact assessment will be essential. Bidding for a large or mega-event will almost certainly require the approval of various authorities and the provision of guarantees of performance. Provision of financing for infrastructure and facilities may also be required. These will only be provided if the authorities and financiers are satisfied that the likely outcome of hosting the event will be positive.

In bidding for a mega-event, care should be taken to ensure that the planning process accommodates people's constitutional rights with regard to the environment. The South African Constitution, for instance, gives everyone the right to an environment that is not harmful to their health or well-being, and the right to have the environment protected, for the benefit of present and future generations, through reasonable legislative and other measures that:

■ prevent pollution and ecological degradation;
■ promote conservation, and
■ secure ecologically sustainable development and use of natural resources while promoting justifiable economic and social development.

In bidding and planning for an event, check that the principles of sustainable development which underpin citizens' constitutional rights are adhered to in the planning process:

■ Have you ensured that social, economic, cultural heritage, ecological and institutional factors have been integrated?
■ Have you involved all sectors of the community in a multi-sectoral approach to the planning of your event?
■ In weighing up the costs and benefits, have you shown concern for the future, i.e. taken a longer-term view?
■ Have you worked within the ecological and cultural heritage limits of the environment?
■ Have you developed partnerships with the local authorities and civil society?
■ Have you linked local issues to global impacts?
■ Does your proposal align with the principles of equity, justice and accountability?

The National Environmental Management Act 107 of 1998 (NEMA), provides a list of principles that should be referred to frequently in the bidding process as a checklist for ensuring that the process and outcomes are sustainable.

The National Heritage Resources Act 25 of 1999 (NHRA), aims to promote good management of the national estate. In bidding for events, heritage resources need to be protected, maintained, and preserved and heritage places or objects are to be preserved and sustainably used so as to safeguard their cultural significance. Cultural significance is defined as 'aesthetic, architectural, historical, scientific, social, spiritual, linguistic or technological value or significance'.

The chapter concludes with an outline of environmental impact assessment and heritage impact assessment requirements. Where an event requires new facilities and infrastructure, these processes will play an important part in determining whether and how these will be provided. An understanding of the Environment Conservation Act 73 of 1989, as amended, NEMA, and NHRA, and their application is essential in South Africa when seeking approvals to hold an event. Risk and its management in the hosting of an event are covered in detail in chapter 10.

4.2   IMPACT AREAS TO BE INVESTIGATED

There are three major types of impacts: environmental, socio-economic and cultural heritages, which are all interlinked. Therefore they need to be examined concurrently for benefits and costs – both short and long term, tangible and intangible. This will require assessing economic parameters such as affordability and profitability, social and environmental impacts on people's health and well being, establishing just who will benefit and how, and establishing whether there will be degradation and will destruction of natural and cultural heritage resources.

One of the objectives of Integrated Environmental Management (as contained in section 23 of NEMA) is to 'identify, predict and evaluate the actual and potential impact on the environment, socio-economic conditions and cultural heritage, the risks and consequences and alternatives and options for mitigation of activities, with a view to minimising negative impacts, maximising benefits, and promoting compliance with the principles of environmental management set out in section 2'.

In addition to EIAs and HIAs, which will be covered later, NEMA also makes provision for impacts, not provided for specifically under this legislation, to be assessed. Section 24(1) of NEMA states, 'In order to give effect to the general objectives of integrated environmental management ... the potential impact on the environment, socio-economic conditions, and the cultural heritage of activities that require authorisation or permission by law and which may significantly affect the environment, must be considered, investigated and assessed prior to their implementation and reported to the organ of state charged by law with authorising, permitting, or otherwise allowing the implementation of an activity.' Generally speaking, a fairly low-order approval such as those mentioned above requires the authorisation of the local authority. The local authority will be able to advise whether or not an environmental assessment or heritage impact assessment is required.

The aspects to be covered by this type of assessment, in terms of section 24(1) are covered in section 24(7) of NEMA.

Scale is important. Whether impacts will need to be assessed nationally and regionally, as well as locally, will depend on the scale and nature of the event. For small events that are local in nature, project-level assessment will probably suffice. Large-scale events that require new facilities and infrastructure and may take place in more than one city will require a macro-assessment approach that assesses risks holistically and on different geographic scales – perhaps nationally, regionally and locally. This chapter examines both macro-assessment and local-scale assessment. The need for concurrent risk assessment is covered later in this book in chapter 10, subsection 10.1.3.

Clearly, when deciding whether to compete for the hosting of an event, it is essential to define and explore benefits, costs and impacts in order to determine whether the event will be affordable, feasible and desirable – economically, socially, politically and environmentally.

If analysis shows that the event will be profitable and affordable, but that there will be negative social and/or environmental impacts, then the scale of these will determine whether to proceed. If analysis shows that the negative impacts are not serious and are manageable, then the authorities and the public will have to be convinced of the mitigating measures proposed and of their affordability and likely effectiveness. If the negative impacts appear not to be affordable and/or manageable, then other event opportunities should be sought.

In a developing context, there are specific issues in relation to bidding for and hosting any large-scale event that should be considered. These are listed in the text that follows. They are based on a study of a number of cities that have either hosted or competed for an Olympic Games (Roaf, Van Deventer & Houston, 1996: 31).

- *Benefits will not necessarily accrue to all of those who pay for the bidding and hosting of an event.* There can be an uneven distribution of liabilities and benefits. In other words, the benefits usually accrue to the established and well off, rather than society as a whole (particularly the historically disadvantaged). Benefit analysis must be sufficiently broad-based to cover all sectors of society.
- *The poor are vulnerable.* The demand for accommodation for an event may lead to rent hikes and the dislocation of people. The new development that was created might be unaffordable to those most in need, and might not be sustainable after the event.
- *Benefits do not automatically trickle down to the poor.* Suppliers, contractors, consultants, operational and administrative staffs usually represent the more skilled sectors of the population and the expenditures needed to host the event will directly benefit them. Any profits made will go to the suppliers of goods and services, the event promoters and organisers, possibly to sports federations (in the case of sporting events) and to the authorities in the form of taxes.
- *Time is not on anyone's side.* The decision to bid is usually made late and the timetable for bidding and then preparing for hosting is likely to be highly

compressed. This merely exacerbates the skewing of involvement in the preparation and management of the event to the skilled and well organised.

- ***The public sector must play a major role***. If social and environmental objectives are to be met and the disadvantaged in society protected, then it is inevitable that the public sector will have to be a major player.
- ***There is often a gap between social promises and delivery***. The bidding phase is characterised by often-extravagant promises designed to secure the event, and the period of preparation for hosting by insufficient funding and broken promises. Social and environmental improvement programmes will be the first to suffer.

Undertaking impact/risk assessment at an early stage of the bidding process will not only assist the key decision makers (financiers and authorities) in deciding whether or not to proceed with the bid, but will provide a core to the involvement of the public in developing a bid. The larger the event, the more certain it is that the public will have to be involved in key decisions. Human nature being what it is, the public will primarily be concerned with risks rather than with benefits – particularly those who enjoy a good quality of life and are concerned about anything which they perceive has the potential to threaten it.

Assessing impacts and risks and establishing benefits/costs should not be a one-off study, but an ongoing process of evaluation that is set up at the outset of considering whether to bid. One danger of not doing this is that once the decision has been made to bid and the resources have been found and the bid organisation created, it is difficult to 'stop the ship', even if evidence is to hand that to proceed would be unwise. Another danger is that the bid will have no way of answering its critics. Detailed risk assessment and acceptance is more readily handled in a climate of substantial political and public commitment to the bid. Until that has been achieved, every party will be more concerned with self-protection and scepticism. All of these risks can be minimised or averted by careful or appropriate planning.

4.3 ASSESSMENT ON A NATIONAL AND REGIONAL SCALE

The Environment Conservation Act 73 of 1989 requires that an applicant assess the likely scales of impact, from the local to the regional, national and international levels. Macro-scale assessment will apply to the hosting of large-scale events such as the Olympic Games, Commonwealth Games, International Exposition and Football World Cup. The event may require to be held in a number of venues, in more than one city. Simple project-level assessment will not suffice.

4.3.1 Economic assessment

There are numerous techniques for assessing risks and benefits/costs. Macro-economic simulation and forecasting is one. International consultants and the Development Bank of Southern Africa, on behalf of national government, used this cross-sector macro-evaluation of the impacts of hosting the 2004 Summer Olympic Games in Cape Town. This was a real and monetary sector macro-model with implicit multipliers and dynamic interaction. Another possible technique is a static, input–output approach with rule of thumb multipliers. A third is to do a thorough comparative analysis of past experience by cities that have hosted large-scale events. If you do this, you will need to take into account the specific structural characteristics of the city and regional economies and the national macro-economy. A weakness of the risk assessment exercise may be that it focuses largely on the macro-risk and benefit and pays little attention to the micro-effect on a specific area and its people.

This is a highly complex field, the details of which are beyond the scope of this publication. Determining the respective merits of the differing approaches is for each bidding organisation to decide, together with the authority finance bureaucrats with whom it is dealing. Whatever it decides, it must set up a process and methodology that is capable of withstanding scrutiny by publics, academics and non-governmental organisations. Part of this methodology is the need to market and adequately explain the risks and benefits within the local area. If an event proposal is not seen to be credible by the organisations mentioned, then the results will be disputed. Irrespective of the outcome, the bid will receive bad publicity and this is likely to affect the bid negatively.

4.3.2 Cost-benefit analysis

Who will benefit and how? Will the event ameliorate long-term socio-economic inequalities and inequities? Will it stimulate the local, regional and national economies and, if so, how?

Cost-benefit analysis is one technique that is used to assess these questions. It compares both the tangible and intangible costs and revenues of a particular project. Costs and benefits may include public and/or private expenditures as well as individual, community, corporate or environmental gains or losses. The technique offers the advantage of neutrality: the numbers used can lead to an exact determination of the alternative which is best, and there can be no inference made that the evaluation process has been interfered with for personal or political reasons.

In this light, the technique has the potential to be extremely valuable in that, if the theory behind it is acceptable to everyone, the outputs which come from it, must also be accepted. As Dickey (1975: 325) points out: 'In general, it gives the appearance of a certain mathematical purity – a purity that cannot be tampered with and is instrumental in providing the decision maker with results unbiased by emotional factors.' The problem with event assessment is that you can be quite sure that emotional factors will be paramount. The problem with the cost-benefit approach is its failure to take into account many so-called 'human factors'.

These human factors can be outlined as follows (headings and basic argument drawn from Dickey (1975: 325)).

- **System effects.** In the real world, proposed alternatives do not stand alone: they tend to form part of larger wholes or systems.
- **Unequal alternatives.** Cost-benefit ratios developed for evaluating alternative courses of action rarely compare 'equal' situations because the problem under study is usually modified by the alternatives proposed.
- **Risk and uncertainty.** A distinction needs to be made between the terms. Dickey (1975: 236) distinguishes between them in the following way.
  - Problems of risk are those in which the future outcomes or consequences have a known probability of occurrence; thus, while the chances of a particular outcome may be known, no assurance can be given about which particular outcome will take place.
  - Problems of uncertainty are those in which even the probabilities of the future outcomes or consequences are unknown and in which the probabilities can be determined subjectively.
- **Inclusion of various costs and benefits.** The costs and benefits need to be defined explicitly; this leads to the problem of defining and accounting for all costs and benefits. This is likely to be a difficult task which, in any event, will require an identification of cause-and-effect relationships.
- **Measurement of benefit factors.** In the measurement of a given alternative, a major difficulty will be that of defining and measuring the factors. Some will be tangible, others less so or intangible.
- **Commensuration.** This is the problem of mixing apples and oranges, of putting benefits in monetary terms. Assigning a 'value' can be problematic, yet if all benefits or costs are not made commensurate, you can run the risk of assigning a value way out of line with its real worth.
- **Perceived versus actual costs and benefits.** The issue is whether you use actual costs and benefits which accrue or the ones perceived by the people affected.
- **Discounting of costs and benefits.** How do you compare correctly the different time sequences and differing streams of costs and benefits? Today's money is worth more than tomorrow's, similarly with today's benefits. The unevenness over time of the streams of costs and benefits causes accounting difficulties.
- **Double counting of costs and benefits.** You need to guard against counting any cost or benefit until it has been shown to be a distinct entity separate from any of the others under consideration.
- **Determining who benefits.** Cost-benefit analysis does not indicate just who will receive the calculated benefits. The problems are ones of scale and values. Just who gains and who loses has great social significance. It will be key to the

event being sanctioned by authorities and publics. Clearly, this is an extremely critical consideration when choosing an evaluative technique.

- **Transfer of costs and benefits.** This deals with the problem of how you ensure that any group will, in fact, land up being the desired beneficiary or being the necessary payer.
- **Multiplier effects.** The transfer of benefits allows for the multiplication of benefits. As Getz (1997: 341) points out: 'Economic Impact assessments often include a "multiplier" calculation to demonstrate that incremental tourism expenditure has "direct", "indirect", and "induced" benefits for the local economy. The idea is that "new" money ripples through the economy, changing hands many times, thereby having a cumulative impact greater than the initial amount of tourist expenditure. Unfortunately, it is not that simple.'

The problems cited are that there are different types of multipliers and different ways of expressing them, and that there is often little empirically based evidence for them. They are also used or misused to exaggerate the benefits.

For a fuller discussion of these topics, the reader should consult Getz (1997). His chapter 14 deals with event evaluation and impact assessment. Part of this is a thoughtful discussion of cost-benefit analysis, including 'how-to' examples. This is essential reading.

4.3.3 A linkages assessment model for mega-events

Harry Hiller (1998) has recognised the imperfections of traditional cost-benefit analysis and has developed what he calls a *linkage model*. He describes it as follows:

Mega-events are usually assessed in terms of the economic impact of the event itself with little attention given to the event as part of a broader process that can be investigated longitudinally. An adapted political economy model is proposed (because the mega-event is seen as essentially an economic initiative) that distinguishes three kinds of linkages. Forward linkages refer to the effects caused by the event itself. Backward linkages refer to the powerful background objectives which justify or rationalise the event. Parallel linkages are side-effects which are residual to the event itself and not directly under the control of the event organisers. This longitudinal approach also distinguishes between pre-event, event and post-event impacts so that unintended and unanticipated consequences can be identified.

Hiller concludes his introduction with the statement that 'Impact assessment ought to be part of every mega-event plan, and that impact equity and a mitigation plan to control adverse effects ought to be in place.'

This article should be essential reading for any aspirant impact assessor. Of interest to local readers is the fact that part of Hiller's experience is grounded in the time he spent in Cape Town during Cape Town's bid for the Olympics in 2004.

4.3.4 Strategic environmental assessment

While there exists a well-developed body of knowledge about how to undertake cost-benefit analysis, a state-of-the-art tool for undertaking risk–benefit assessment – known as strategic environmental assessment (SEA) – has only recently been developed. The approach adopted is holistic – encompassing economic, social, physical and environmental sectors. In revising impact assessment regulations in terms of NEMA, strategic environmental assessments will be included as an essential tool for evaluating the cumulative impacts of several development proposals in a given area, which may be within a city, region or a country. Because the use of this method is somewhat in its infancy, the following text describes its underlying principles.

Strategic environmental assessment can be described as a process of anticipating and addressing the potential socio-economic and environmental consequences of proposed initiatives at higher levels of decision making. It aims at integrating these considerations into the earliest phase of policy, plan or programme development, so that environmental, social and economic considerations are put on a par.

A SEA focuses on the national and regional levels (providing a helicopter overview), complementing the local project-level (site-specific) environmental impact assessments (EIAs). Benefits and costs need to be established at different scales, from the national, provincial, regional, metro and local levels and sectors: socio-economic, environmental and political. Cumulative impacts need to be assessed, which is not possible through individual EIAs.

A SEA will not necessarily give a simple *yes* or *no* as to whether or not to bid for or host an event. The SEA should aim to identify and assess the issues of strategic importance and the interrelationships between them. It should inform public debate and help the public and authorities to judge whether the potential benefits of preparing for and hosting the event will outweigh the potential costs. The SEA will also identify the critical conditions which are likely to determine whether the event will achieve its bidding and hosting objectives.

In order to be strategic, the SEA must:

- examine the event proposal as a whole rather than on a project-by-project or sector-by-sector basis;
- understand how the different components of the bid for the event relate to each other;

- establish which aspects of the bid are relevant to public policy;
- identify and address the most important questions and issues that arise from the bid proposal;
- anticipate the likely consequences of implementing the various aspects of the bid proposal (including intended and unintended, positive and negative, short-term and long-term consequences);
- evaluate which of the predicted consequences are likely to be more important than others on the basis of society's core values and policy objectives;
- determine how decisions affecting one aspect can influence others, and
- assist people in making informed decisions and choices about the proposed bid.

The SEA should be undertaken independently of the bid team, and be driven by a publicly agreed-upon value framework. It should be holistic and interdisciplinary, but strategically focused; it should be professional and focused, but open and accountable.

A SEA should be linked where possible to Local Agenda 21 initiatives (the international plan of action to achieve sustainable development). Among its many dimensions are integrating environment and development in decision making. This should be a goal of any attempt to bid for and to host a large-scale event. Further, Local Agenda 21 recognises the importance of strategic urban management in achieving its goals. This is of equal importance to developing and sustaining a bid and then hosting the event.

4.3.4.1 Socio-political issues

It has previously been observed that developing countries have their own particular socio-economic realities. In developing countries the problems deriving from poverty will be pre-eminent, whether these concern water or sewage or disease or waste, or population growth. All of these are products of poverty. In developing cities, as in Cape Town, affluence is contrasted with poverty, lack of access to resources with over consumption of resources; in sum, all of the issues that were raised at the Rio Earth Summit and the subsequent World Summit on Sustainable Development (WSSD) held in Johannesburg in 2002. These realities will require a broader interpretation of environment to encompass quality of life – of the historically disadvantaged in particular.

Consequently, environmental problems are rooted in the distribution of assets, income, rights and power over the use of resources. The challenge in creating a sustainable future for a developing city lies, therefore, in bringing into a positive relationship three key elements: the environment, poverty and development. Developmental precedent shows that a positive relationship can come about only if civil society and the state are brought together creatively and productively in partnerships which are part of a strategic urban management approach (see diagram below).

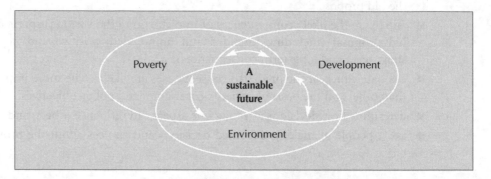

A bid for a large-scale event in a developing country will find itself at the epicentre of debate about resource allocation and development priorities. The bid and its public sector sponsors will have to deal with a dichotomy of the First World norms and requirements of the event owners and the Third World realities of the developing country. These will have to be reconciled for the bid to succeed.

Developing countries also have political realities. One of these realities is that local government may be the weak partner among the various levels of government in the country, lacking both the political and financial power to act. Trained public service personnel may be lacking, due to historic imbalances of power. There may be local service failures and deficiencies; local government may have the authority to deliver services to a future event site, but lack the finance to do so.

4.3.4.2 Environmental impact assessment

Planning and hosting a large-scale event must be done in a manner that is environmentally responsible. While what this entails will vary from country to country and from city to city, there are international protocols and specifications that will apply. The owners of large-scale events will certainly be committed to the principles of sustainable development and will look to their event to foster them. Given the high profile that environmental issues enjoy internationally, it behoves a bidding organisation to look to being proactive in this regard in order to develop a winning bid.

Environment must be seen in its broadest definition to include biophysical and socio-economic criteria.

Respect for the environment is now one of the principal elements in the organisation of any sizeable event. The nature and form of that respect will be specified in the guidance manuals of event owners. All will be based on protocols arising from summits such as that in Rio in 1992 and enshrined in principles and specifications. These, in turn, have informed the actions of the World Bank, the International Monetary Fund, and the environmental and planning legislation of countries around the world.

There are a number of important principles:
- Both NGOs and CBOs must be actively and meaningfully involved in the bidding process.
- As developmental issues are central to the environment, so is improving the quality of life in disadvantaged areas.
- Principles of sustainable development should be applied within the bidding organisation in dealing with use of energy, water and with waste management.
- Opportunities to link environmental projects to economic growth and job creation must be explored and implemented.
- Solutions to environmental problems must be appropriate to the country's context.

The outcome of these concerns is:
- the need to carry out environmental impact assessments for all sites and facilities where there may be a significant detrimental effect on the environment;
- reuse and upgrade of existing facilities whenever and wherever possible;
- ensure ongoing use and maintenance of new facilities built for specific events
- restoration of run-down areas;
- avoidance of unnecessary destruction of land, protection of natural habitats and biodiversity;
- minimisation of pollution and consumption of non-renewable resources, and
- the need to increase environmental awareness among the general population.

The following paragraphs describe the differences between strategic environmental assessment (SEA) and environmental impact assessment (EIA).

A SEA addresses the effects of key sectors constituting the biophysical environment – economic, social, ecological and physical – on planning and development. A SEA will provide a helicopter overview, at the metro, regional and national scales. The SEA is central to achieving sustainable development and is therefore aimed at understanding the consequences of policies or major projects in an integrated, holistic way. By contrast, local-level assessment will usually be done on a project-by-project basis, often in the form of environmental impact assessments (EIAs).

The following is a table from the publication entitled *Strategic Environmental Assessment: A Primer*, prepared by the CSIR (1996), modified by the author on the basis of the Cape Town 2004 experience.

EIA	SEA
Is reactive to a development proposal	Is proactive and informs development processes and proposals
Assesses the effect of a proposed development on the environment	Assesses the effect of the social, economic and ecological development needs and opportunities
Addresses a specific project	Addresses areas, regions or sectors of development
Has a well-defined beginning and end	Is a continuing process aimed at providing information at the right time
Assesses direct impacts and benefits	Assesses cumulative impacts and identifies implications and issues for sustainable development
Focuses on the mitigation of impacts	Focuses on maintaining a chosen level of environmental quality
Narrow perspective and a high level of detail	Wide perspective and a low level of detail to provide a vision and overall framework to guide future planning, development and management
Focus on project-specific impacts	Creates a framework against which ongoing impacts and benefits can be measured

The holistic nature of the SEA process makes it an approach particularly well-suited to provide the overall methodological framework for all the benefit, risk and impact assessment studies that will be needed in deciding whether to compete for a large-scale event.

A bid should look to using the SEA as a basis for the social and environmental policies and performance criteria that will need to be developed for the management of the hosting phase. This is a very challenging concept, and it will have to be negotiated with the responsible authorities in order to be effective. But, if undertaken during the bid phase, it could be a major time saver later.

Case study 4.1: Strategic environmental assessment: Cape Town 2004 as a case study

One of the major contributions of bidding for the 2004 Summer Olympic Games in Cape Town was the commissioning by the Bid Company of an independently undertaken SEA. This was arguably the single largest such study undertaken at that time (certainly a first among bidding cities up until that time) and constitutes an important methodological precedent. The following text is drawn from Volume One of its main report (Olympics Assessment Team, 1997).

© Juta & Co Ltd

The terms of reference were as follows.

- To identify and evaluate the potential systemic impacts of preparing for and hosting the 2004 Olympic Games in Cape Town on specific economic, social and biophysical processes. Particular emphasis was placed on those longer-term impacts which could affect the development of the Cape Metropolitan Region and South Africa as a whole.
- To identify specific proposals in the current (Olympic) plan, which might need to be reconsidered if the bid were successful.

The study approach

The study was organised into four phases. In *Phase 1* of the study, the proposed approach was considered and endorsed by a wide range of interested and affected parties and an extensive listing of issues relating to the bid was prepared. An assessment of the values and goals outlined in relevant legislation and public policy documents indicated which of these issues should be considered as *strategic issues*. These issues were:

- Economic performance
- Small business opportunities
- Public finance
- Job creation
- Price effects
- Institutional capacity
- Population growth effects
- Public involvement
- Transport
- Nation-building
- Housing
- Sports needs
- Promoting sustainability

In *Phase 2* of the study, the strategic issues identified in *Phase 1* were examined in more detail through a comprehensive series of specialist investigations. These were:

- Public Participation and the Cape Town 2004 Olympic Bid.
- The Cape Town 2004 Olympic Bid and Nation-building.
- The Cape Town 2004 Olympic Bid and Sustainability.
- Population Growth analysis for the Cape Town 2004 Olympic Bid SEA.
- Assessment of the Institutional Capacity of Cape Town to host the Olympic Games in 2004.
- A critical analysis of the DBSA Macro-economic Predictions for the Cape Town 2004 Olympic Games.
- Public Finances Analysis for the Cape Town 2004 Olympic Bid.
- The impact of the Olympics on the Construction Industry.
- The Tourism Economic Effects of the Olympic Games.
- Housing and Accommodation Cape Town 2004 Olympic Bid.
- Cape Town Olympic Bid Transportation Assessment.

- A critical assessment of Sports and Recreation Planning and Management for the hosting of the Cape Town Olympic Games.
- Urban Development Dynamics Cape Town 2004 Olympic Bid.
- Assessment of the potential impacts of the Cape Town Olympic Games on the Natural–Urban System Dynamics.

The titles give a very clear indication of the wide scope of investigation.

In *Phase 3*, the findings of the specialist studies were summarised, synthesised and analysed so as to provide a holistic assessment of the potential systemic effects of bidding for and hosting the games in Cape Town in 2004.

In *Phase 4* of the SEA, which followed the release of the draft Strategic Environmental Assessment Report, interested and affected parties had an opportunity to review the draft report and to make suggested changes, before the Olympics Assessment Team prepared its Final Report.

For a more complete understanding of the methodology used for Cape Town 2004, reference will have to be made to the full documentation.

4.4 ASSESSMENT AT THE LOCAL LEVEL: EIAs AND HIAs

This will usually be site-specific, as the event will take place either in an existing facility (either as-is or upgraded) or in a new facility. If the latter, the location is likely to be determined by planning undertaken by the responsible local authority. Provisions for access and servicing will be determined jointly with the authorities and the form of the facility also designed with them. Each region and city has its own planning legislation and the event proponents will need to be familiar with the technical and approval requirements.

In South Africa, environmental impact assessment is regulated nationally through sections 21, 22 and 26 of the Environment Conservation Act, while heritage impact assessments are provided for in terms of section 38 of NHRA. Frequently, HIAs are included as a component of the EIA rather than as a separate study requiring a separate public participation process. Attempts are being made to integrate both EIAs and HIAs with planning applications, which may be required, for example, when a facility is to be built on public open space.

Environmental impact assessments (EIAs)[1]
EIAs are applied regionally by each provincial authority. It is to these sections that the bid will have to turn for guidance as to what is required procedurally. As the EIA regulation procedures are in the process of review at the time of writing, it will be best to approach the provincial authority as to what authorisations are

required, and what procedures should be followed. It is prudent to do this early on in the bidding process as the first step will be to determine what, if any, aspect of bidding for and hosting the event will require to be assessed, and at what level. For developments that may have a significant detrimental impact on an environment that has/may potentially have national significance or status, such as a National Heritage Site or a National Park, application must be made to DEAT, and/or to the SAHRA. Whereas, if a development may have an impact on a site of provincial significance, such as a Protected National Environment, or a Provincial Heritage Site, application must be made to the Department of Environmental Affairs, Development & Planning (DEADP) and/or to Heritage Western Cape (PHRA). One of the principles of this legislation is early application. The EIA regulations state: 'This legislative process should be applied as early in the proposed activity's planning stages as practicable and before irrevocable decisions are made, in order to ensure that environmental considerations are incorporated proactively into decisions taken.'

The existing legislation describes the application procedure to be followed to obtain authorisation to commence with a listed or desired activity. However, it is vital to find out from the competent authority if a 'scoping checklist' (which is a brief 40-page questionnaire) will suffice, or if a Scoping Report and a public participation process is required, which can be a two- to three-year process if the application is particularly complicated, controversial or on a sensitive site. The key component of this is the preparation and submission of a 'scoping' report, the results of which will determine whether a full-scale EIA will be required. Both the process for its production and its required contents will need careful consideration by the event technical team.

The following is a brief outline of the contents of an *environmental impact report* (EIR), as required by the legislation.

- *A description of each feasible alternative*, including
  - the extent and significance of each identified environmental impact; and
  - the possibility for mitigation of each identified environmental impact.
- *Assessment of impacts*, according to a synthesis of the following criteria:
  - nature of the impact;
  - extent (whether local, regional, national or international);
  - duration (short, medium or long term or permanent);
  - intensity (low, medium or high);
  - probability, the likelihood of the impact actually occurring (indicated as improbable, probable or definite).
- *Determination of significance*, through a synthesis of the aspects produced in terms of their nature, duration, intensity, extent and probability, described as *low, medium* or *high*.

- *Mitigation*, seeking to find better ways of doing things, minimising or eliminating negative impacts, enhancing project benefits and protecting public and individual rights to compensation. Mitigation options include:
  - alternative ways of meeting the need;
  - changes in planning and design;
  - improving monitoring and compensation, and
  - replacing, by relocating and constructing an alternative resource.
- Addressing *key issues*.
- *A comparative assessment of the feasible alternatives*.

The relevant authority, interested parties and the public review the environmental impact report. The Act specifies the following procedural review criteria:
- legal requirements;
- quality of scoping;
- quality of impact prediction;
- quality of determining impact significance;
- assessments of alternatives;
- quality of mitigation proposed, and
- public participation process.

The Act sets out the following as the basis for reviewing the technical information:
- *Effectiveness*
  - enhance environmental protection
  - efficient use of resources.
- *Efficiency*
  - consider cost implications for developer and others.
- *Equity*
  - impact on the poor, the developer and the authorities.
- *Administrative implications*
  - capital implications, legal implications, technical implications and capacity implications.
- *Acceptability*
  - to the public, NGOs, CBOs, labour, industry, consultants, Department of Environmental Affairs and Tourism, and other authorities.
- *Cost implications*
  - to a broad range of bodies.
- *Macro-economic impact*
  - contribution to economic growth
  - provision of employment
  - inflationary effects
  - regional development.

The Guideline Document concludes with a description of the appeal procedures contained in the Act.

Heritage impact assessments (HIAs)

When is a heritage impact assessment required? An HIA (in terms of section 38 of NHRA) may be required when any person intends to undertake a development categorised as:

(a) the construction of a road, wall, powerline, pipeline, canal or other similar form of linear development or barrier exceeding 300 m in length – racetracks, rowing facilities, Olympic villages, etc. would fall into this category;

(b) the construction of a bridge or similar structure exceeding 50 m in length;

(c) any development or other activity which will change the character of a site
  - exceeding 5 000 m^2 in extent, or
  - involving three or more existing erven or subdivisions thereof, or
  - involving three or more erven or divisions thereof which have been consolidated within the past five years, or
  - the costs of which will exceed a sum set in terms of regulations by SAHRA or a provincial heritage resource authority;
  - the rezoning of a site exceeding 10 000 m^2 in extent, or
  - any other category of development provided for in regulations by SAHRA or a provincial heritage resource authority.

The other categories of 'development' would include any physical intervention, excavation, or action, other than those caused by natural forces, which may in the opinion of a heritage authority in any way result in a change to the nature, appearance or physical nature of a place, or influence its stability and future well-being, including:

(a) construction, alteration, demolition, removal or change of use of a place or a structure at a place;

(b) carrying out any works on or over or under a place;

(c) subdivision or consolidation of land comprising a place, including the structures or airspace of a place;

(d) constructing or putting up for display signs or hoardings;

(e) any change to the natural or existing condition or topography of land, and

(f) any removal or destruction of trees, or removal of vegetation or topsoil.

If the event falls into one of these categories, the responsible heritage resource authority must be notified at the very earliest stages of initiating such a development and furnished with details regarding the location, nature and extent of the proposed development. They may then require a heritage impact assessment report.

The heritage authority will specify the information to be provided in a report, which will include:

- the identification and mapping of all heritage resources in the area affected;
- an assessment of the significance of such resources;
- an assessment of the impact of the development on such heritage resources;
- an evaluation of the impact of the development on heritage resources relative to the sustainable social and economic benefits to be derived from the development;
- the results of consultation with communities affected by the proposed development and other interested parties regarding the impact of the development on heritage resources;
- if heritage resources will be adversely affected by the proposed development, the consideration of alternatives, and
- plans for mitigation of any adverse effects during and after the completion of the proposed development.

The report will be considered by the heritage authority and they will advise on the following:

(a) whether or not the development may proceed;
(b) any limitations or conditions to be applied to the development;
(c) what general protections in terms of the National Heritage Resources Act apply, and what formal protections may be applied, to such heritage resources, and
(d) whether compensatory action is required in respect of any heritage resources damaged or destroyed as a result of the development, and
(e) whether the appointment of specialists is required as a condition of approval of the proposal.

Developments impacting on a heritage resource protected at national level will be referred to SAHRA by the provincial heritage authority. The applicant may appeal against the decision of the provincial heritage resource authority to the MEC (the member of the executive council of a province responsible for cultural matters).

4.5   AN OUTLINE OF SOME POSSIBLE MITIGATING MEASURES

Roaf, Van Deventer and Houston's publication (1996), previously cited, contains a chapter entitled 'Practical Suggestions'. This introduces the concept of mitigating measures. It also contains an Appendix (A (ii)) which summarises mitigating and compensatory measures recommended or implemented for the hallmark events it used as case studies.

4.5.1 Socio-economic measures

Roaf *et al* argue that any mitigating measures should arise from socio-economic impact assessment. This assessment should focus on the central question: *who benefits?* In a developing country, how the historically disadvantaged will benefit, if at all, in the form of jobs, economic advancement and the amelioration of socio-economic inequities, will be the central concerns. The impact assessment should result in a Social Impact Management Plan, which should form part of a broader-based Environmental Management Plan. (This topic forms the last part of this chapter.)

The Appendix in Roaf *et al* briefly describes mitigating socio-economic measures. The following is a précis of their text:

- Economic and social strategic plan, one of whose components was the establishment of a 'Social Foundation' to fund locally based projects aimed at reducing inequality (Barcelona Olympics 1992).
- Housing Impact Monitoring Committee (Melbourne Olympics 1996).
- Social Development Fund, designed to capture rate and tax benefits accruing from hosting the event (Melbourne Olympics 1996).
- Olympic Accommodation strategy, designed to protect low-income owner-occupiers and tenants and to provide an accommodation database, especially for lower priced tourist accommodation (Fremantle America's Cup 1987; Melbourne Olympics 1996).
- Development control, regulating the conversion of boarding houses to tourist accommodation and other changes of use.
- Amendments to Residential Tenancies Act, designed to tighten eviction and rent increase procedures and to implement Fair Rent provisions (Fremantle; Brisbane Expo 1988; Melbourne).
- Rent control, controlling rents in key locations, setting hotel rates (Fremantle; Brisbane; Melbourne).
- Compensation, providing emergency funds for displaced tenants, and relocation payments to tenants by developers (Fremantle; Sydney Bicentennial 1988; Melbourne).
- Housing referral and advice services, providing housing assistance to displaced tenants and community liaison officers in the most affected areas (Fremantle; Brisbane; Sydney Bicentennial; Melbourne).
- Affordable housing, by designating a proportion of housing in the Olympic Village and Media centre as affordable housing, providing compensatory projects to increase the supply of affordable housing for rent or purchase (Fremantle; Atlanta Olympics 1996; Melbourne).
- Emergency housing, to increase the stock of emergency housing from surplus government properties (Melbourne).

- Olympic ombudsperson, to adjudicate on cases of losses incurred as a result of the Olympics (Melbourne).

4.5.2 Environmental measures

The key focus areas will revolve around the (minimisation of) use of water resources, sewerage, energy and wastes.

4.6 INTEGRATED ENVIRONMENTAL MANAGEMENT

A winning bid will, in all of its aspects of planning, development and management, want and need to be proactive. It will want to ensure that whatever regional and/or metro-scale plan is to form the context of the bid is based on environmental capability and suitability analysis. In so far as assessment is concerned, it will need to go beyond project level and site-specific environmental assessment to looking at macro impact assessment, as part of an environmental management system. We previously introduced strategic environmental assessment (SEA) as the recommended risk/impact assessment tool. This is only one of its assets. It can also form the underpinning of an environmental management system.

Any bid for a large-scale event should, therefore, seek to develop an environmental management system (EMS) for all event-related activities. This system should be designed and developed to take the event from the bidding stage, through to the hosting of the event, and beyond. To plan solely for the bidding stage would be short-sighted; after all, one bids to win the event and therefore maximum continuity with minimum disruption should be the objective.

There are minimum requirements for an EMS to be effective. All actions should be based on helping to achieve sustainable development. This means starting with appropriate planning: responding to and incorporating into the preparation of the event plan key environmental principles, policies and proposals developed by authorities in their regional, metro and local plans. Environmental impact assessments will have to be undertaken at whatever scales are shown to be necessary during the scoping process. At the site and facility levels, environmental principles will need to be prepared for all the briefs at the design stage of the event projects. In addition, environmental performance criteria for construction projects will need to be identified. Where possible, environmental projects should be linked to economic growth and job creation. An environmental awareness programme should be created and partnerships sought with community-based organisations, nongovernmental organisations and authorities to achieve short-term upgrading and improvements in needy areas.

Browse these Internet sites

http://travel.utah.gov/Olympic_TTRA.pdf
http://users.iafrica.com/s/sh/shandler/exec1.htm
http://www.aef2004.org/
http://www.gamesinfo.com.au/pi/ARPICOE.html
http://www.iiiee.lu.se/ercp/workshops/docs/02_large_scale_events.pdf
//www.uea.ac.uk/env/all/teaching/eiaams/PDF_dissertations/Harris_Michael.pdf

QUESTIONS FOR SELF-EVALUATION

1   What would lead you to decide that a strategic environmental assessment (SEA) was necessary rather than an environmental impact assessment (EIA)?
2   What factors would determine whether hosting an event should be aborted or whether mitigating measures would suffice?
3   How would you define an environmental management system (EMS)?
4   What do you think differentiates achieving sustainability in a developing country as opposed to a developed country?

[1]At the time of revising this chapter for the 2nd edition, the Department of Environmental Affairs and Tourism published draft new environmental impact assessment (EIA) regulations for public comment. As there has been no finality on these at time of publication, the reader will have to contact the department to check the present status and applicability of these draft regulations.

CHAPTER 5

Event Planning

Tom Wanklin

AIM OF THE CHAPTER

This chapter aims to provide insight into the activities involved in the planning process, how events are planned and the role players involved. The different planning tools and various elements in the environment are described. This chapter is accordingly aimed at providing a broad understanding of planning activities enabling interaction with event planners during the event planning process.

LEARNING OBJECTIVES

After having studied this chapter, you should be able to:

- understand how planning fits into the events management process;
- describe the different forms of planning and how to carry out the planning process;
- understand the systematic and integrated planning processes and how events can be achieved using these approaches;
- identify who is responsible for planning and the various planning tools that are available;
- discuss the event environment and various components such as parking, security and landscaping;
- understand the critical success factors in event planning;
- display a basic knowledge of the likely impacts of event planning and an awareness of the consequences of events.

5.1　WHAT CHOICES DO WE HAVE?

Experience has shown that we have certain choices relating to planning:

- We can just let things happen.
- We can control so that certain things are prevented from happening.
- We can force things to happen.
- We can plan, manage and encourage things to happen.

In an increasingly complex environment with more individual thought and activities, the use of control or force is no longer achieving satisfactory results. Unless we plan and manage the events we are responsible for, the event activities will not take place when they are intended or preferred to occur. In addition, the ongoing management and sustained quality of an event or events will not easily be maintained.

5.2 THE EVENT MANAGEMENT PROCESS

In trying to contextualise where the planning process fits into event management, it is appropriate to consider the various steps by which an event (or set of events) is brought into being, planned, organised and completed. This process is summarised in:

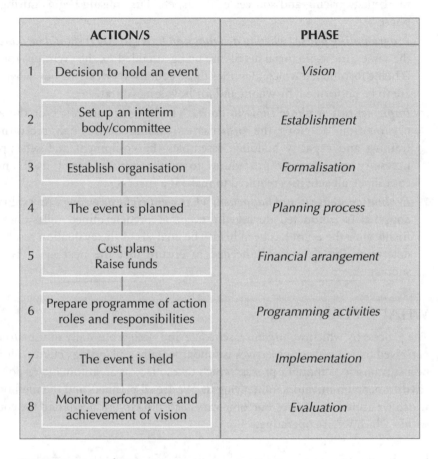

ACTION/S	PHASE
1 Decision to hold an event	*Vision*
2 Set up an interim body/committee	*Establishment*
3 Establish organisation	*Formalisation*
4 The event is planned	*Planning process*
5 Cost plans Raise funds	*Financial arrangement*
6 Prepare programme of action roles and responsibilities	*Programming activities*
7 The event is held	*Implementation*
8 Monitor performance and achievement of vision	*Evaluation*

FIGURE 5.1 *Event planning process*

The activities and phases are now discussed in more detail.

1 **Visionary phase (what).** An authority, group of persons, 'champion', or a charitable institution makes a decision or forms the intention to hold an event.

2 **Organisation establishment phase (who).** Set up an interim body, steering committee, convening organisation or association of interested and affected parties to begin the process of establishment. Arrangements are made, the constitution of the organisation drawn up, articles of association/ memorandum are prepared and stakeholder organisations identified and commitments made.

3 *Planning phase (what is to be done)*. The vision is transformed into goals and objectives, planning commences and the planning process proceeds, including impact studies.

4 *Financial phase (how much)*. Draft plans are costed and a business plan is prepared, evaluating financial viability, funding requirements, sponsorship, marketing, pricing and sources of funds, etc. Fundraising begins during this phase.

5 *Programming phase (when to do what and how quickly it should be done)*. At the same time as financial details are being attended to, the event programme is being formulated which identifies those actions to be carried out, when they are to be performed, by whom and for how long (duration).

6 *Implementation phase (how to do it)*. The interim committee or the event organisation develops the organisation resources through recruitment, training and capacity building, assembles the equipment and sets up the necessary management procedures to administer the event itself and to coordinate all activities required to make it a success.

7 *Evaluation phase (what happened; what went right or wrong)*. An evaluation appraisal is conducted during the event at predetermined milestones and finally after the event has been held. The analysis of the evaluation results will determine the refinements needed to ensure that the next event is more successful.

5.3 WHAT IS PLANNING?

The process by which we organise, schedule and design our daily routine to meet perceived basic needs or objectives is fundamentally a planning activity. This can be a subconscious thought process which takes place as an automatic response to environmental motivators influencing us. We are all planners and the methods by which we achieve a planned outcome vary according to our needs and the context within which we are operating.

Planning through a rational and deliberate set of actions can encompass a variety of contexts ranging from day-to-day living, working and leisure, to numerous technical planning activities involving financial planning, economic planning, human resource planning, town and regional planning, etc. Planning can also vary according to levels of detail, ranging from national, regional and local, to detailed site layout planning and architectural planning.

 Planning can thus be broadly defined as the process by which we design various suitable actions, in order to achieve a set of objectives. The planning process necessitates that the existing situation be continually evaluated and a choice made between different decisions for future actions, based on changing circumstances.

© Juta & Co Ltd

Accordingly, in the context of event management, *event planning is the process by which we design our events and shape various actions in order to achieve successful events (of a certain type, size, financial return, employment impact, and so on).* During the planning process we need to continually monitor the existing situation and compare it with the plan, so as to ensure that the plan does not become outdated or redundant due to changing circumstances. Amendments to the plan are accordingly made to ensure that it helps us to achieve our objectives.

All planning procedures tend to follow a systematic process:

- identifying a problem;
- studying the problem;
- formulating proposals to solve the problem;
- implementing the proposals;
- waiting and watching to see if the problem is solved, and
- starting the process again.

The need to plan generally relates to an effort to achieve order in events, coordination of actions and programmes to achieve a desired end state. Planning is essential to manage time, prevent waste and achieve efficient economics in the development process. Without planning, there would be chaos and a breakdown in elementary systems and infrastructure.

5.4 STYLES OF PLANNING

Over time a variety of planning styles have been developed to suit the circumstances of particular needs and objectives or a specific planning exercise. These planning styles or methodologies have tended also to be in response to the failure of arbitrary subconscious planning activities to achieve a satisfactory result. The different styles of planning are highlighted below.

- *Laissez faire*. This involves a reticent approach to problem solving, whereby planning is only conducted when a problem occurs. As a result, this methodology tends to be reactive and biased towards a benign philosophy: maybe if we do nothing the problem might go away!
- *Interactive/incremental*. In short, random planning activities are carried out. A problem is addressed in bits and pieces, rather like a bee finding honey in a field of flowers. Most planning activities in our daily lives fit this planning style.
- *Systematic*. The conscious, deliberate and rational planning process which is utilised in most technical activities (including event planning) fits into this planning methodology. The science of rational thought has identified a series of steps which are followed in order to achieve a satisfactory plan which will fulfil the needs, vision and objectives which are defined at the outset.

- **Comprehensive.** This style of planning sets out to achieve a holistic plan which addresses each and every aspect of the setting or environment which is being planned. This planning methodology presupposes that the planner/s are capable of analysing and formulating plans for all components of the environment, thereby being capable of producing a comprehensive plan. This method has not been as successful as expected because comprehensivity is limited according to the information and knowledge available at the time.
- **Integrated.** In an effort to achieve synergy between interacting components of an environment, an integrated planning approach has been formulated. This style of planning has adapted the systematic approach to achieve horizontal linkages between project components and to plan for integration between sectors rather than separate sectoral solutions (which tend to be isolated or insular in nature).

5.5 EVENT PLANNING

In the context of planning for an event (as a one-off project) or a series of events on a sustainable basis, the different planning styles most suited to this activity would be systematic and integrated planning. While it is important to strive for as comprehensive a plan as possible, it is accepted that total knowledge about an environment is not always available and therefore comprehensivity is not achievable.

5.5.1 Systematic planning approach

First, it is necessary to consider the systematic planning process and the way it can help event planners. There are basically eight simple steps in a systems approach which are depicted in figure 5.2.

Definition of terms:
- *Goal* – what you want to achieve.
- *Objective* – what you want to achieve by quantity, within a time frame. Objectives need to be specific, measurable, achievable and time based (SMART)
- *Policy* – a set of statements which set out the approach to guide decision making ('rules of the game').
- *Strategy* – the actions required to implement the plan within the stated policies.

In systematic event planning, a conceptual proposal to organise and hold an event would include the goals and objectives which define the nature of the proposed event. A feasibility study (as outlined by Getz, 1997: 77) would take the form of a study designed to assess the existing situation, examine factors which are able to support the event and those which may act as a hindrance to the event, study the potential market and strengths, weaknesses, threats and opportunities which may exist. Having determined whether or not an event appears feasible, the organisers and sponsors are able to make an informed decision as to whether to proceed with preparing a preliminary plan or to abandon the project.

At such a point, the event organisers should also be in a position to submit a bid for an event (in case a tendering bid is envisaged). An example of a bidding process is the Olympic Games bid process where countries compete for the rights to hold the event every four years (refer to chapter 3). Having won the bid or having prepared a preliminary plan, the detailed plan can be prepared. This would comprise a large number of detailed designs of the proposed event facilities, the activities to be held and the requirements for equipment, materials, resources and facilities.

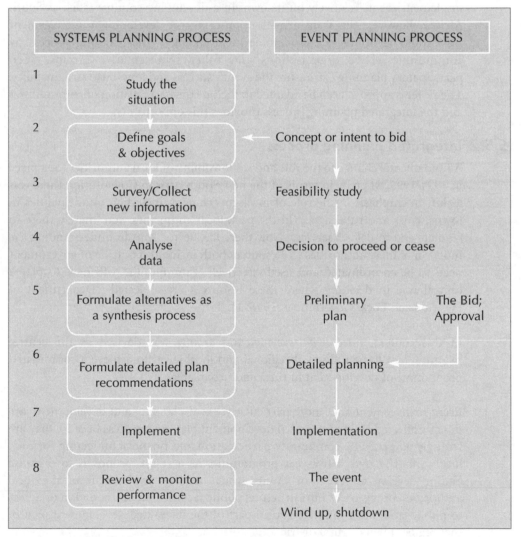

FIGURE 5.2 *Relationship between systematic and event planning processes (adapted from Getz, 1997: 76, figure 4.1)*

Following the detailed planning stage would be implementation and (if it is a single event) the organisation would carry out its final event evaluations, wind up its affairs and shut down. (Refer to chapter 9: Event Programming.) If the event is to be held regularly, the planning cycle would start up again as part of the continual process.

The systems approach to planning envisages a continual process of review and monitoring the plan and the event itself during and after its implementation.

The systems approach outlined above tends to be most effectively used in an environment where the local authority or an events organisation is in an independent setting (for example, a private company) and can plan, organise and implement events relatively on its own. In a developing country (such as South Africa), however, the transformation process and development management institutions recommend considerable involvement in the planning process by communities, civic organisations and other representative groups. Such participatory planning can ensure the event's success and long-term sustainability. The systems approach can be adapted to include the participation of communities and the integrated planning process provides this opportunity.

5.5.2 Integrated planning process

A fundamental change to the role and responsibility of local authorities took place in 1994/1995, whereby in terms of the new South African Constitution there was a shift in emphasis in the role of local government, including municipalities in towns, cities and rural areas. 'In the past, local authorities were merely there to regulate and to deliver services. Now there has been a shift in understanding the function of these authorities … Resources both inside and outside of government need to be co-ordinated and used effectively. Communities will have to play a central role in deciding where these resources are allocated' (Department of Housing and Local Government, 1998: 1).

In this context, *integrated development planning* was devised as the central planning tool to be utilised at regional and local levels to achieve a coordinated programme of development in rural and urban areas.

Event management and, more particularly, event planning and development, are directly affected by the integrated development planning process because they are strongly governed by community participation and financial budgeting for each local authority over a five-year programme. As a result, proposals to organise and/or develop an event or events which require involvement of the local authorities, provision of infrastructure, public facilities, accommodation or access to public land, must ultimately form part of the integrated development plan of that region, town or rural district.

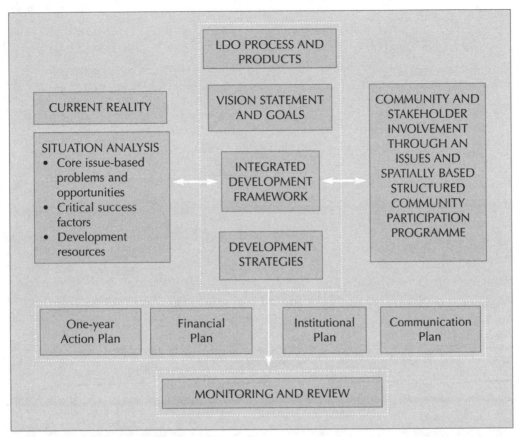

FIGURE 5.3 *Integrated development planning process (adapted from Department of Housing and Local Government, 1998)*

Integrated development planning (see figure 5.3) follows a logical process, which is outlined below.

- As a result of a study of the current situation and the identification of needs, a vision and mission statement is formulated to meet the defined needs. (For example, various communities, stakeholders and role players may determine that certain events are needed to develop the tourism product in their area.)
- A strategic framework is then prepared which identifies those strategies which need to be implemented and those detailed objectives, actions, programmes and budgets which are required.
- Detailed proposals are prepared which in the development planning context are termed land development objectives (LDOs).
- In order to implement these proposals and strategies effectively, an integrated set of plans is prepared involving finance, human resources/institutional and communication components. In an event context these plans could include sponsorship, operation, funding sources, staffing needs, marketing and promotional proposals.

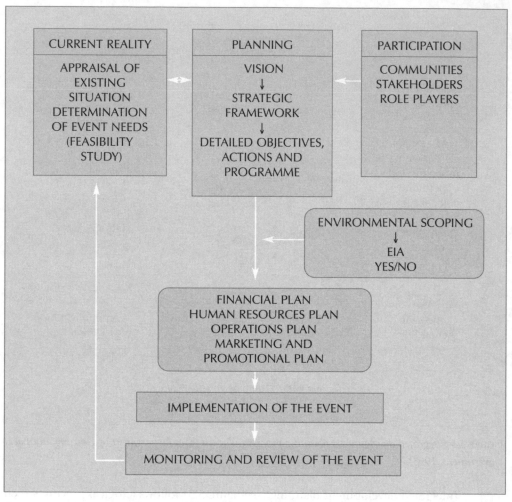

FIGURE 5.4 *Integrated event planning process*

In a developing country such as South Africa, the integrated planning process could be adapted for the event planning process as set out in figure 5.4.

It will be noted that this process diagram includes provision for input from an environmental scoping exercise and allows for an environmental impact assessment to be conducted if required. Environmental scoping involves a preliminary assessment of the proposed project and the key impacts it could generate. For example, a proposed adventure challenge event involving mountain-bike trails, rock climbing and motor-cycle racing through the countryside needs assessment concerning possible environmental impact and the actions necessary to prevent or reduce such impact. Environmental scoping also involves consultation of interested and affected parties in a public meeting. It determines whether or not a more detailed environmental impact assessment needs to be conducted, or whether or not the project is able to proceed under certain conditions, without an environmental impact assessment.

5.6 WHO IS RESPONSIBLE FOR PLANNING?

The planning process can be the responsibility of a number of different role players, including:

- national, provincial and/or local spheres of government;
- parastatal institutions such as tourism boards;
- community groups, associations, civic organisations, political parties – such as welfare groups, arts and craft clubs, SANCO, ANC;
- professional event management teams – such as the Cape Town Olympic Bid organisation, SA World Cup Soccer Bid, etc.

As mentioned previously (refer to 5.5.2), the integrated development planning process requires an integrated approach between those organisations responsible for event planning and the local authorities which are responsible for the overall development planning of the area or region within which the event is to take place. A considerable number of institutions and event planning specialists have stressed the importance of community participation in the tourism and event planning process. The marginalisation of local communities is a direct result of poor community consultation and is precisely the reason behind the current thrust towards 'people-centred planning and development' through the Reconstruction and Development Programme in South Africa since 1994. The responsibility for planning in the South African context is now intended to be in the hands of the integrated development planning committee, with each local authority as chairperson and convenor. Event planning becomes one of the sectoral components of the integrated planning process and through this planning committee it is intended that all stakeholders be consulted.

In many instances, however, event planning is a specialist function and community consultation or 'partnership' need not necessarily mean control or management involvement. Communities do, however, require that they are in support of the vision, goals and objectives involved in the event because of the benefits it could offer them and also the possible negative impact or costs that could result. Very often, mega-events or hallmark events are nationally driven and the local community is not given much of an idea of the costs such events can have on their quality of life in the short and long term. The marketing hype associated with major events can often overshadow negative impacts to the detriment of the local host community, and consultation will assist in reducing problems in this regard.

5.7 PLANNING TOOLS

There are a few tools which planners use to assist in their work in various planning procedures. The advance in computers and information technology is obviously an important component. However, there will always be important thought processes which aid the planning activity. These include the following:

- exchange of views;
- mindmapping;
- technical tools.

5.7.1 Exchange of views

The exchange of views between planners, participants, stakeholder organisations, representatives of communities and interested and affected persons is a critical component of successful planning. This is achieved through 'one-on-one' discussions and group sessions (or workshops as they are often termed). For any of these meetings to be effective they need to be structured with an agenda (which is prepared through group consensus) and a clear understanding of the outcomes expected from each session.

Group meetings or workshops require facilitation by an experienced person (usually on the planning team) who can help all participants to express their views without domination or manipulation by certain individuals. Tools to assist in this process include the use of participatory cards (where each person expresses his or her own view on individual cards and these are displayed, grouped and analysed in full view of the participants), flipchart sheets, overhead slides and digital powerpoint projectors.

For the sessions to be successful, the protocol involved in inviting participation by various representatives of communities has to be carefully observed to avoid political sabotage, embarrassing boycotts and arguments.

5.7.2 Mindmapping

In a more intensive process than an exchange of views in a meeting, the planning process can also utilise the technique known as 'mindmapping'. This technique was developed by Tony Buzan and is defined as 'a whole brain, visually interesting version of outlining' (Wycoff, 1991: 31). The technique involves an individual or group of people brainstorming a set of issues, ideas and proposals in such a way that they are drawn in an informal picture with linkages shown to a central theme. Mindmaps have the following characteristics:

- The main issue or focus problem is drawn or written in the centre of the page.
- Ideas are represented by key words and are linked to the central focus issue by lines.
- One word is printed per line.

- Subsidiary ideas are linked to the matching key ideas by lines, creating a collection of ideas in themes.
- Linkages and integrated connections can be highlighted by colours and diagrams.
- Mindmaps are colourful and fun, involving the creative free flow of ideas from each participant in the planning process.

Mindmapping techniques are useful planning tools because they allow uninhibited contributions of ideas by members of a group and display the ideas and their interrelationships visibly in an interesting and pleasing way.

'Mindmapping and brainstorming work together to further encourage creativity and idea generation' (Wycoff, 1991: 99). However, brainstorming differs from mindmapping because it generally results in random lists of ideas rather than the collective, linked approach of mindmapping.

5.7.3 Technical tools

Apart from 'hands-on' drawings and maps, plans, designs and sketches, computer technology provides various tools such as CAD (computer-aided draughting) drawing/publishing software and GIS (geographical information systems) which can be used in the drawing, design and graphic aspects.

Data analysis uses GIS, mathematical modelling, matrix analysis techniques and simple spreadsheets for planning procedures.

5.8 HOW DO WE PLAN?

Adopting the recommended integrated events planning process discussed in paragraph 5.5.2 (refer to figure 5.4), there are several steps which can be followed to prepare a plan. These include:
- the establishment of an interim committee/event organisation;
- situation analysis;
- environmental appraisal;
- vision;
- strategies;
- actions and programmes;
- participation by stakeholders and community;
- environmental impact assessment;
- financial planning;
- institutional planning;
- communications marketing/promotions planning;
- implementation;
- monitoring and review.

5.8.1 Establishment

It is understood that an event organisation or interim committee (refer to chapter 6) will have been formed. This organisation will be responsible for the management of the planning process and will formulate a planning brief.

The planning brief is an essential guide to the planning team because it sets out the details of the focus of the project, the issues to be addressed and guides the limits of the data collection exercise to be undertaken. In addition, the brief provides a clear instruction on how the work is to be done, the time to be used and the target dates for achieving various milestones.

Any planning exercise which does not have a brief setting out the parameters of the project to be undertaken is doomed to failure or, at the very least, a wastage of time and funds.

5.8.2 Situation analysis

An appraisal of the existing situation is usually carried out to gain an understanding of what is happening in the area, town, city or region concerned. The study can assist in reaching a better understanding of the issues, problems or needs that exist. This understanding is crucial because it ensures that the plan is relevant and deals effectively with the identified needs. The activities include the following steps:

- *Data collection focused on the nature of the problem/s being appraised (for example – is there a need for sporting events in the city?)* Collection of information can include conducting interviews with interested and affected persons, leaders, organisations and participants in the events industry. This new information would be called *primary data*. Information can also be collected from existing sources including libraries, museums, local authorities, events organisations, etc. This available information is called *secondary data*.

  Data collection can be very expensive and care should be taken to focus the research on collecting information which is relevant and useful.

- *Feasibility*. Prior to preparing a detailed plan, it is often useful to undertake preliminary feasibility studies which can guide the decision-makers (the centre-event organisers) as to whether or not it is appropriate to continue with the planning exercise. Analysis of the data should enable a preliminary assessment of feasibility to be undertaken at an early stage, before large sums of money or time are expended.

- *Participation*. The data collection and analysis stage of the project is a key point where the community, interested and affected parties and relevant stakeholders have an opportunity to participate. This can involve individual contributions and group meetings or workshops. Effective consultation with all affected parties is critical because, if any groups or individuals are left out of the process, their input might be lost and/or the exercise will be discredited because it is considered exclusive rather than inclusive.

5.8.3 Vision

Having successfully obtained a good understanding of current realities and needs, and having been reassured by the positive outcome of a feasibility study, it is possible to formulate a vision for the event. A vision statement involves a broad outline of what it is hoped will be achieved in the long term. It is a desired end state and does not include details of quantity, size or cost.

The vision statement is often also called a *goal* and it is essential to the planning exercise because it gives the organisation something to work for and a means to measure performance or the product in future.

5.8.4 Strategic framework

Having formulated a vision (or ideal goal), it is necessary to formulate the strategies by means of which you intend to achieve that vision. A strategy is often defined in the context of military action which relates to the manoeuvres, actions or activities required to achieve an objective or goal (such as to conquer a fortress). In a similar way, a strategic framework sets out how you intend to work and the methods you intend to adopt to achieve a vision. An example could involve a music festival event and your strategy could be to engage the services of a professional musical festival company to organise the event. An alternative strategy could perhaps be to organise such an event utilising 'in-house expertise' but to confine it to a certain market through narrowing down the selection of music.

The use of various strategies in a careful way can set the tone of an event and have a very important influence on how it is structured and designed.

5.8.5 Objectives and actions programme

Having formulated the vision and strategic framework, it is possible to formulate objectives. These are detailed statements of what it is hoped to achieve, by what particular date and target amount. Coupled with these objectives are also the action plans regarding who has to perform an activity, how they are to work and the programme they will need to follow.

The ability of a planning team to set meaningful objectives is emphasised by Bell and Vazquez-Illa (1996: 555) who state that 'Successful planning requires that management have a clear understanding of where it wants to go and how it plans to get there, in both the short and long term. Without a clear set of goals and objectives, the organisation could become paralyzed.'

An integrated plan will require that all the objectives, actions and programmes are linked together so that the event works successfully and no one section operates exclusively and without reference to the others. For example, the event plan needs to synchronise the transportation proposals with suitable site access, parking and traffic management measures, which at the same time take into account the human resources capacity of the traffic management department within the local authority.

5.8.6 Participation

As explained in the data collection and appraisal stage, effective participation of community representatives and interested and affected parties in the planning process is essential. This can be achieved by holding meetings and workshops and/or by including nominated representatives on a planning committee.

Care should be taken not to allow the formation of a large committee (in excess of 12 to 15 persons) because large groups can be difficult to manage and tend to give poor individual input. It is also a problem ensuring that representatives of stakeholders and communities refer back to their constituencies and keep them well informed. If the planning process is over an extended period, large committees tend to dwindle in size, and the members lose their mandate through loss of confidence or trust from their constituency.

5.8.7 Environmental impact assessment

An important component of the planning process is the environmental impact assessment of the proposed event. The first step in the process is an environmental scoping report which examines the impact of the event at a broad and preliminary level. After the completion of the scoping report, the findings have to be submitted to the Department of Economic Affairs, Environment and Tourism for appraisal by environmental specialists. It is at this point that it will be decided whether or not a full environmental impact assessment is required.

It should be noted that the environmental assessment work has to be done by designated specialists, who are registered with the Department, usually in the Nature Conservation division. In order to achieve a sustainable event which is sensitive to the environment within which it is situated, an appropriate environmental consultant on the planning team is recommended. The environmental impact assessment process is discussed in detail in chapter 4.

5.8.8 Financial planning

Chapter 7 devotes considerable attention to financial planning and management. This component of the planning process is crucial to the realism of the plan because it sets out the costs, budgets, sources of funding, cash-flow projections and accounting arrangements necessary to achieve a successful event.

5.8.9 Institutional/human resource planning

Chapter 6 provides input on organisational aspects, human resource planning, skills transfer, training and management elements. It is not possible to implement the plan if there are insufficient, inadequately trained and poorly managed personnel. In addition, the institutional arrangements relating to the organisation, accountability, line of command, troubleshooting and backup plans are an essential component of an event plan.

5.8.10 Communications/marketing and promotions planning

Chapter 11 provides details on these aspects. For any plan to be effectively implemented it requires widespread information distribution and communications so as to ensure inclusivity and effective participation of all affected parties. Often it is a tendency for event organisations to complete the preparation of a plan and quietly work away at implementation. The organisation fails to continue communicating with communities and role players while the project proceeds and this can result in discontent, misunderstandings and confusion when building actually commences or an event is held.

5.8.11 Implementation

Implementation of the plan requires organisational input and project management (refer to chapters 6 and 10). Often it is found that the plan requires modification due to changed circumstances while implementation takes place.

5.8.12 Monitoring and review

An essential component of event planning is the monitoring and review of the performance of the event during implementation and after the event has been held. For this process to be effective and valuable, it is desirable that it be carefully designed and structured, using key performance indicators to measure the various components of the event. For example, key performance indicators can be based on the original objectives set out in the plan which determine the size of the event, the projected market expected to attend, the budgeted expenditure and income, vehicles accommodated, etc. Monitoring an event can also be achieved by conducting an opinion survey of participants before, during and after the event, utilising questions which can be compared and statistically analysed. A review of media coverage, reports on radio, television and in-industry journals can also give added review input.

Monitoring an event can provide the event organisers with important information which enables them to improve the plans and ensure a better, more competitive event in future. Monitoring is also extremely important for feedback to the event sponsors and financiers because it helps them to determine the extent of exposure they received and the value gained by their involvement.

5.9 PLANNING THE EVENT ENVIRONMENT

A critical component of the event is the environmental character, setting, layout and image associated with its design, construction, materials, facade, appearance of signs, buildings and vegetation. All these components contribute to the event 'experience' and determine the context within which all the activities operate. 'You can have the best publicized, programmed and sponsored event – however, if your site is not well laid out, and visually pleasing, the event will not be perceived as successful … Ideal site layout should combine artistry and practicality into a design that stimulates revenue' (Citrine, 1997: 17). Considerable scientific and technical expertise comes to play in the planning, design and construction of various event facilities. Such expertise includes urban designers, landscape architects, quantity surveyors, architects, civil and structural engineers, traffic engineers, interior designers, sound engineers, graphic designers and artists. Certain fundamental planning hints are recommended for consideration below; however, readers are referred to specialist planning and design manuals and expertise for more detail should it be required.

Perhaps the most critical component in the planning of any event is to find a locality which ensures that the event has a high profile, maintains a good image and is easily seen by prospective participants. This important issue is described as the 'technique of interpretation' (Cooper *et al*, 1999: 225) and means that events and destinations should maximise the opportunity to be noticed. This can be done by the use of imaginative and visible signs, buildings, towers and audiovisual media. In addition, themes can be a potent tool which will make an event more visible and more appealing in an ever-growing and competitive environment.

5.9.1 Locality

There is a wide variety of events, all of which have unique features. Some events generate high noise levels (such as motor racing), necessitating a remote locality, others require specialist localities due to the nature of the event (for example, an ice skating championship), and some events are limited to the use of certain specialist buildings or parcels of land.

Regardless of the unique locality requirements of each event, the fundamental consideration in choosing a particular locality is access to the market (namely the participants). These participants would include the people and organisations participating in the events, the spectators and the service organisations supporting the event.

Accessibility needs to be considered in terms of the following features:

■ proximity to major transport corridors or at least primary routes including road and rail;

- integration of modes of transport (that is, types of transport) which enables easy, efficient and economic movement through common destinations (for example, arrivals and departures of taxis, trains and buses);
- availability of bulk infrastructure including sewerage, water, electricity, telecommunications and roads;
- ease of access to airports, railway stations and, if appropriate, harbours;
- relationship to other events, accommodation, facilities and service activities which could help to achieve a successful cluster of event and tourism products.

High accessibility does not necessarily mean 'close to' in terms of distance and a well-chosen location for an event can utilise efficient transport to enhance accessibility. Often the selection of different localities for an event can be assisted by consulting the local authority which is responsible for the area at an early stage. These organisations have structure plans and integrated development plans which usually reserve areas for events, sports activities, leisure and entertainment.

After having chosen a selection of alternative localities which suit the proposed event from an accessibility point of view, it is necessary to refine the alternative localities in terms of additional features.

The various localities should be assessed in terms of:
- ease of acquisition of the land and/or buildings (either by rental or purchase);
- the likely comparative cost of acquiring land at different localities (for example, privately owned land can often be highly priced);
- the alternative costs of connecting to bulk infrastructure and the capacity of the infrastructure to accommodate the event;
- the current zoning and land use development restrictions pertaining to the land and, if these restrictions are not supportive of the event, the likely time period to change the restrictions (and possibly the likelihood of the local authority supporting such changes); it should be noted that title deed restrictions can require Supreme Court judgment and take up to two years to achieve;
- the findings of a preliminary environmental scoping analysis which provides comparative appraisal on the suitability of each locality (a strategic environmental appraisal (SEA) in effect).

The above-mentioned technical evaluation of alternate localities would need to be finalised by a rigorous consultation process to ascertain the feelings of all interested and affected parties. This process would involve 'one-on-one' meetings with the various stakeholders and should culminate in a well-publicised public hearing in the area of the proposed event (when once a short list has been achieved).

Ideally, a site analysis of the alternative localities would have been conducted (refer to 5.9.2 below) so that the public hearing will be able to give support or opposition on the basis of informed decisions.

The critical importance of consultation with interested and affected parties (IAPs) cannot be stressed strongly enough and in South Africa (for example) this is a legal requirement of the environmental appraisal process.

5.9.2 Site analysis

Having succeeded in choosing at least two localities which appear to be suitable for the intended event, it is necessary to carry out a site analysis of each. A considerable number of technical requirements are involved in this process and usually a team of specialists, including physical planners, engineers, architects and environmentalists, would perform this activity.

Any suitable site should possess the following attributes:

- sufficient land and flexibility to accommodate the event/s, vehicle parking and future expansion needs;
- readily available infrastructure;
- an absence of conflicting adjacent land uses or communities which may be detrimentally affected by the event (or alternatively may affect the event);
- suitable slopes and orientation of the site to take advantage of views, vistas, prevailing winds and to avoid conflict with sun (as sports activities) and poor weather conditions;
- the site should preferably be able to be secured to control access and also prevent external vantage points from overlooking the event;
- depending on the locality of the site, any sensitive fauna and flora needs to be identified and protected; similarly, the natural drainage areas across the site need to be protected and development of these areas avoided to prevent flooding and environmental degradation;
- appraisal of potential risks associated with the site needs to be conducted (for example, flooding, pollution from adjacent areas, etc).

5.9.3 Securing the site

Having acquired the rights to the selected site through acquisition or rental, it is essential that the property in question be securely bounded by fencing, walling or any other suitable barrier. This is not only necessary to prevent unauthorised entry to the event in future but, more importantly perhaps, to prevent invasion of the site by 'homeless' families who may take the initiative on identifying a vacant area of land, close to amenities, which is suitable for residential settlement. In the event that such an invasion should take place, and informal dwellings erected, current legislation requires the landowner to establish in court that the families need to be relocated and alternative accommodation be provided. This could take a year or longer to resolve and thereby incur considerable expense.

5.9.4 Transport

The importance of integrated transport to support an event cannot be overemphasised. The dispersed and segregated nature of most of the towns and cities in developing countries often results in a poor public transport system. Railway and bus services are generally declining due to the absence of public transport subsidies by the state. As a result, the vast majority of the public are dependent on private motor vehicles and taxis to move between home and the event. Two events in East London in 1999, namely the Harbour Festival and the Agricultural Trade Show, are recent cases in point. The locality at which these events were staged is situated away from taxi and train termini. Attendance by at least 50% of the population of the city was drastically inhibited because of poor public transport to and from the event.

Perhaps the only event in East London where a substantial deviation from the normal taxi routes occurs is the celebration of New Year's day when thousands of revellers demand transport to the beach in the coastal cities and towns. The substantial movement of people for these activities would suggest that future events could benefit from a similar mobilisation of taxi facilities.

Carefully planned transport linkages and the active involvement of taxi associations and bus transport owners could substantially transform the attendance at events and thereby impact positively on entertainment, cross-cultural exchanges and event viability.

5.9.5 Parking

There is a need to ensure adequate parking for spectators, loading/ unloading areas for suppliers, access and parking for emergency vehicles, and parking for buses and taxis. Most events are characterised by peak parking demands which result because of certain activities which may attract a high attendance for a specific period. Parking capacity should ideally be geared to meet the peak demand.

A variety of parking provision standards are available in technical manuals which provide a guide as to how many parking spaces to provide per number of seats in the auditorium/stadium or premises. Parking demand for festivals, fairs, processions and parades is extremely difficult to ascertain because the attendance potential is impossible to calculate beforehand. Invariably, parking will occur on an informal basis outside the venue and close liaison and planning with the traffic management authorities will be necessary to accommodate this.

Most urban areas have a labour-intensive 'car-guard' service in business centres. These guards are a potential security service for parking areas and employment spin-off would be the benefit of such an arrangement. However, caution needs to be observed with informal groups offering such a service when they are unidentifiable or not accountable for their performance. On the other hand, a considerable number of formal security organisations are available to perform such a service for a fee.

Most local authorities require on-site parking for events and have regulations regarding standards of access, type of road surface, signage, and size and number of spaces. Invariably, the local authority's permission to hold the event will hinge on parking formalities. Traffic congestion due to inadequate parking facilities can be highly disruptive and dangerous; accordingly realistic and practical measures are required to address this component.

5.9.6 Event spaces

The wide variety of events and their activities demand a similar diversity of spaces, buildings and facilities. Getz (1997: 82) highlights how 'Most events have a special physical dimension' or 'setting'. These can be aggregated into six basic types:

- **Assemblies**. These include concerts, conferences, conventions, spectator sports, religious or education ceremonies.
- **Processions**. These concern the linear passage of people, vehicles and/or mobile exhibits in a hall, stadium or a street.
- **Circuit or track**. These involve racing activities where spectators are accommodated along the route or at strategic points (such as the start and finish).
- **Public places**. These are open spaces which are often used for events and can include parks, playgrounds, sports fields, plazas, closed-off streets (for example, the Grahamstown National Arts Festival).
- **Exhibitions/fairs**. These are situated in warehouses and on large tracts of land which can accommodate a variety of stalls, equipment trade exhibits, activities and entertainment.
- **Specialised facilities**. Specific and custom-built facilities are required for sport and for certain specialist activities.

All the above event spaces require fundamental facilities and support services which ensure that the event can be successfully managed.

Basic requirements include the following:
- vehicular access, parking, loading/unloading areas;
- emergency vehicle access and parking;
- emergency first-aid facility;
- administration office;
- information/customer care/enquiries;
- entrance/exit/fire escapes/reception/waiting rooms;

- change rooms and ablutions;
- breakaway rooms/preparation and rehearsal facilities;
- toilets, ablutions and powder rooms;
- communication room/media facilities;
- designated seating or parking for spectators;
- refreshment and dining facilities;
- catering, kitchens, storage, repair and maintenance facilities;
- security booths and accommodation;
- solid waste storage and management;
- accommodation, ramps and parking for physically challenged participants and spectators. (After Getz, 1997: 83)

The arrangement of the above components needs to follow the style or character of the event, for example: a circuit or track event as distinct from an assembly or an exhibition. Each site is different and it is difficult to prescribe how best to achieve the most suitable layout of functional areas. Kevin Lynch (quoted by Getz, 1997: 87) highlights the necessary organisational tools to set out an event space so that people do not get lost, crowds are channelled to follow a logical route and various functional areas are clearly demarcated by signage.

The following are a few examples of the various techniques which can be used in site planning to make the event unique and to 'dazzle' the public:
- The venue or site can be made inviting with clearly demarcated entrances and pathways. Signs and other methods of demarcating main routes such as focal points, towers, banners and archways can direct the movement of people.
- Attractive walkways can be created using trees, grass and booths.
- Decorations can make an area attractive and special effects lighting can turn an average venue into an exciting event.
- Citrine (1997: 17) suggests that one could 'use the environment … It is much less expensive to use the natural environment than to create one.' These measures could include using outdoor breakaway venues and dining arrangements near an attractive garden feature, and so on.

Site planning needs to take into account the fact that people appreciate a convenient venue which is easy to move about in, with a smooth, integrated flow. The most attractive venues and events should be in the outlying areas so that people are lured past the smaller venues or exhibits (Citrine, 1997: 18).

Continued growth in the event industry is resulting in the construction of massive facilities in certain city centres such as Durban (the ICC), Sandton City (Convention Centre) and Cape Town (Conference Centre). This is resulting in multiple events taking place in the same venue and increasing management complexity due to larger crowds, overlap of venues/facilities and catering demands.

The industry will benefit from such growth, but there are certain essential measures which must be taken to reduce conflict, confusion and a decline in the quality of the experience. Lenhardt (1998: 61) lists these as follows:

- '*Easy access* – The building should provide a separate entrance and registration area for each group.
- *Lots of signage* – Banners and signs with the name of the association or show create a sense of personal space.
- *Contiguous space* – Make sure all the areas you would be using are in close proximity to one another. Attendees should not have to race from one end of the center to the other or pass through another group's space.'

5.9.7 Landscaping issues

Emphasis needs to be placed on enhancing the environment of the site through landscaping, the establishment of gardens and vegetation features. Enhanced visual effects can also be achieved by using strategically placed lighting in and around vegetated areas.

Various other landscaping tools can be used to reduce noise from adjacent major transport routes (for example, grassed earth embankments), wind intrusion (for example, trees and shrub belts), and other degradation problems (for example, pathways to prevent soil erosion, dust and crowd damage).

Case study 5.1: SA Games Buffalo City 2004

Background to the plan

The SA Games held in Buffalo City was the second SA Games event held in South Africa, the first having been held in Gauteng two years previously. Planning for the event is predominantly carried out by the SA Sports Commission and the National Ministry of Sport and Recreation. This planning process sets out the overall vision of the games, the goals, objectives and detailed strategies.

The SA Games is designed to be a national nurturing event every two years with the objective of making sure the national sports talent prepares for, and makes a contribution towards the All Africa Games, the Commonwealth Games of Nations and ultimately, the Olympic Games.

It is interesting to learn that there will be a third SA Games event in 2005, to be held in KwaZulu-Natal. This will enable the SA Games to then be a regular event every two years in the odd numbered years, so that athletes have more time to prepare for the Olympic Games (which are held every four years in the even numbered years).

(Source: M.L. Makanda: Project Manager for SA Games, 2004).

5.10 CRITICAL SUCCESS FACTORS IN PLANNING

There are several factors which will determine whether or not the event is planned effectively and held successfully.

Factors which must be taken into account to ensure success include:
- community participation;
- a clear and detailed planning brief which is systematic and effective;
- an established organisation or organisation committee with leadership;
- a multidisciplinary planning team with a principal agent who is responsible for overall coordination and performance;
- a well-balanced and realistic planning programme, with milestones, targets and outputs;
- contingency planning ('what if' scenarios);
- an adequate planning budget.

5.11 PLANNING IMPACTS

The planning process can result either directly or indirectly in various positive and negative impacts as a result of an event being held. These can include impacts in the following sectors:
- economic;
- physical/environmental;
- socio-cultural;
- political/administrative.

The planning and development process by its very nature is at the core of generating benefits or causing problems for the host communities and the environment within which the event is to be held. A mega-event can stimulate or act as a catalyst for a period of time through the improvement of infrastructure, the establishment of sports and cultural facilities and opportunities for competitive advantage. In addition, events can result in greater skills in the community with regard to the holding of future events, an awareness in the region of the opportunities provided by an event and entrepreneurial stimulation. Spilling (1998: 105) describes three scenarios involving impacts from an event:

- *Intermezzo* – where an event is planned, organised and shut down (little impact in the long term – normal development).
- *New level of activity* – where an event can create a new plateau for tourism growth and a new level of activity as a result.
- *Change in growth pattern* – where an event can result in permanent change and a new growth pattern.'

The planning process needs to continually evaluate the likely impacts generated by the event and intervene in areas where spin-off benefits and perhaps a new growth stimulus can be achieved which will benefit the area.

Events can have a variety of negative impacts relating to environmental degradation, unfair competition, unviability (resulting in the host community having to foot the bill afterwards), wasteful infrastructure expenditure (Smith & Jenner, 1998). In the planning of events flexibility is paramount to ensure that maximum benefits can accrue without creating negative impacts. Hall (1992: 29) lists nine factors which determine the impact of hallmark or mega-events:

- **Goals**. What are the goals and how they can be incorporated in the planning process?
- **Size**. Can the event be accommodated by the area and its capacity?
- **Length of event**. The longer the event, the more social disruption can result.
- **Frequency**. One-off events can cause a fast-track planning activity which is more disruptive. Regular events are usually handled in normal planning processes.
- **Location**. Carrying capacity characteristics must be determined.
- **Transport**. How will people be transported to and from the event?
- **Market segment**. What market will attend?
- **Administrative capacity**. What government/local authority structures exist or can be enhanced to administer and coordinate?
- **Infrastructure**. What infrastructure is needed and how can it be used afterwards?

In order to ensure that the planning process takes into account all the above factors, Hiller (1998: 47) recommends that 'impact assessment ought to be part of every mega-event plan, and that impact equity and a mitigation plan to control adverse effects ought to be in place'.

Browse these Internet sites
http://www.personal.usyd.edu.au/~wotoole/epmspage1.html#EPMS_Schema
http://www.esrc.ac.uk/commstoolkit/events/topten.asp
http://www.davislogic.com/event_management.htm
http://www.event-planning.com/
http://www.blackbaud.com/solutions/eventplanning.asp

QUESTIONS FOR SELF-EVALUATION

1 Discuss where the planning process fits into the event management process.
2 Considering the various styles of planning, in your opinion which appear more appropriate for events and why?
3 The South African planning milieu demands a more community-driven and integrated planning process. How does this influence the involvement of local authorities and communities in event planning?
4 Describe the twelve steps to be followed in the planning procedure.
5 There are several key elements involved in creating an effective, interesting and appropriate event environment. Describe these elements.
6 Discuss the factors which determine the locality (or site) of an event.
7 In considering the six basic types of event settings, how does each create demands for special land parcels and infrastructure resources?
8 Three essential measures relate to access, signage and contiguous space. Explain why these should be given special attention.
9 There are seven critical success factors in events planning; discuss these.
10 Planning an event can give rise to four main impacts on the environment; describe these impacts and provide an example of each in your local events industry.

CHAPTER 6

Organisations and Organising Events

Tom Wanklin

AIM OF THE CHAPTER

This chapter provides an overview of event organisations, how they are established, their different characteristics and their working relationships with other organisations. The chapter reviews the organisational aspects of management, service quality, human resource organising, recruitment and training of event workers. Finally, the various operational elements to achieve a successful event using special effects, equipment facilities, space, sound, fireworks and other elements are considered.

LEARNING OBJECTIVES

After having studied this chapter, you should be able to:

- understand the different types of organisations, how they operate and how they are managed;
- understand the meaning of service quality and the methods of achieving this in the events industry;
- explain the recruitment, training and organisational aspects of event workers (permanent, temporary and voluntary);
- broadly describe the different techniques employed to manage queues;
- describe the different types of equipment available for events and understand their operational requirements;
- identify the critical success factors which can influence event organising.

6.1 THE EVENT ORGANISATION

6.1.1 Introduction

Every event has an organisation which is behind it: managing activities, organising funding, administering staff and voluntary personnel, undertaking marketing and public relations, organising security, printing leaflets and tickets, hiring performers, arranging decorations, sorting out parking, and many, many other activities. Each event organisation is unique to the event and the characteristics of the people and environment within which it exists. An organisation 'encompasses the creation, structuring and internal co-ordination of the management system, all with the purpose of fulfilling the organisation's mandate' (Getz, 1997: 131).

6.1.2 Organisation design

The event organisation's structure and key personnel are fundamental to the successful outcome of an event. This aspect is called 'organisational design': the structure of the organisation and its organisational design need to be carefully devised to provide the correct kind of authority, responsibility and accountability relationships for its managers, staff and service contractors (Cleland, 1999: 136). Further to this, the organisation structure and type of organisation can fundamentally influence the philosophies and policies by which it functions. For example, a charitable institution which is raising revenue for a worthwhile cause may operate with different monetary policies from a profit-oriented company which is privately owned and which is accountable to its shareholders.

There are two distinct types of events: the single event which is held once and for which an event organisation is established specifically to organise that event (almost like a one-off project), and a regularly held event which is held each month or each year (for example sports events, beauty pageants, etc). The types of organisations which organise these different events can differ as a result of their short-term or long-term nature. For example, a single event could be organised by a voluntary association or committee, whereas a regular event could be organised by a more established formal company or institution.

The trend in management today is towards more flexible organisational designs due to the establishment of more temporary organisations which have 'modified the traditional concept of organisational design' (Cleland, 1999: 209). Cleland indicates further that 'many organisations of all kinds are starting to abandon the revered "chain of command" where authority and responsibility were placed, in favour of empowering employees to manage themselves ...' and the role of supervisors has changed to that of 'teachers, mentors, facilitators, coaches and the like, where they work with the teams rather than supervising them in the traditional sense.'

Events are very often project based in their nature and make-up. Accordingly the changing management approach towards empowering employees to manage themselves in 'alternative teams' (Cleland, 1999: 210) and project-focused teams under a dedicated project/event manager will affect the event industry and organisational design of the future. Organisations are likely to be smaller, more flexible and less bureaucratic in future.

6.1.3 Different types of organisations

According to Getz (1997: 132), 'determining what type of organisation is appropriate, and getting it formally organised, is a matter of forward planning, consultation with experts and possibly trial and error'. There is also no doubt that most events start with a small, core voluntary group of organisers (a committee or association) and, as the event process takes off, the organisation evolves into a larger structure, with more formal characteristics.

There are seven basic types of organisations (refer to figure 6.1) which are usually found in the events industry.

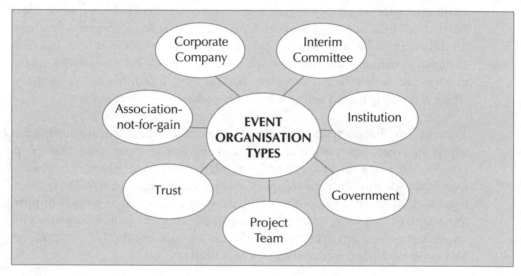

FIGURE 6.1 *Types of event organisations*

6.1.3.1 Organisational structures

Typical organisational structures are usually based on departmental, functional or programme-based approaches. For example, the functional structure usually results in different departments or committees being established to perform a particular function or activity (refer to figure 6.2). (These can also involve different departments responsible for different products or activities.)

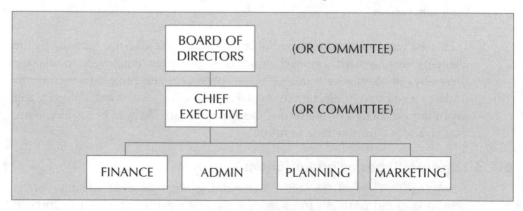

FIGURE 6.2 *Functional organisation (adapted from Getz, 1997: 137)*

On the other hand, event organisations can be arranged on the basis of projects or programmes. This is particularly suited to one-off events and the project team approach, and enables a variety of events to receive programme input (refer to figure 6.3). This is also referred to as a *matrix structure* (Getz, 1997: 38).

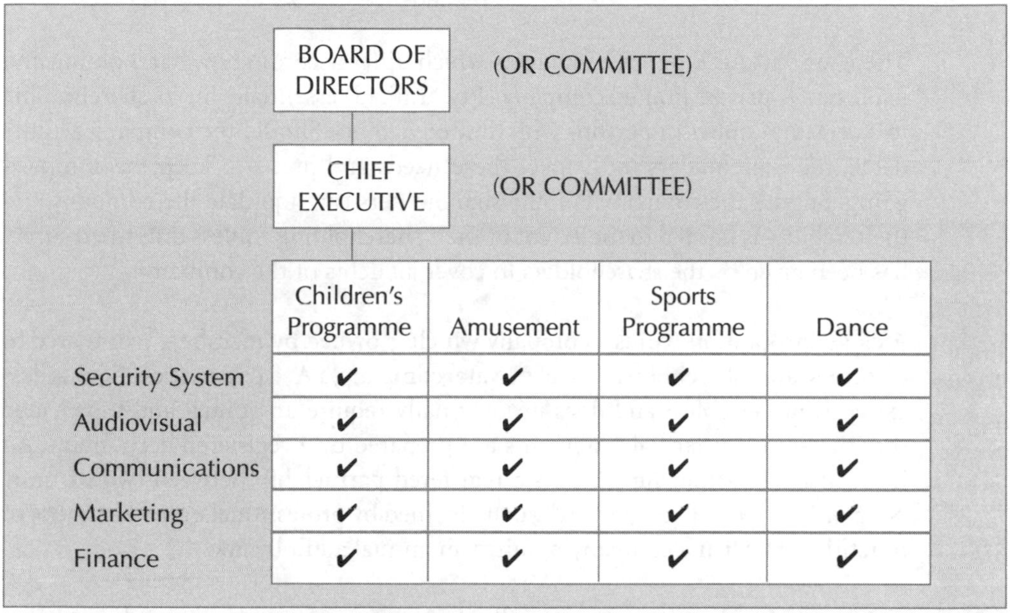

	Children's Programme	Amusement	Sports Programme	Dance
BOARD OF DIRECTORS (OR COMMITTEE)				
CHIEF EXECUTIVE (OR COMMITTEE)				
Security System	✔	✔	✔	✔
Audiovisual	✔	✔	✔	✔
Communications	✔	✔	✔	✔
Marketing	✔	✔	✔	✔
Finance	✔	✔	✔	✔

FIGURE 6.3 *Programme-based or matrix structure (adapted from Getz, 1997: 138)*

The matrix organisation offers the greatest flexibility because there is easier interaction between programmes and the various support services can give more efficient input. This enables greater productivity and keeps the size of the organisation to an optimum level. The functional organisation can result in duplication of services and less interactive management between the different parts of the organisation.

6.1.3.2 Corporate company

The decreasing involvement of government in the events industry generally has sponsored the involvement of the private business sector in the organisation and ownership of events. The private sector often collaborates to set up an event through the establishment of a temporary partnership of organisations, subcontracting of different companies or, thirdly, through several events (each with its own management structure) joining together to create a larger event comprising several smaller events (Getz, 1997: 132).

In the corporate company model, the organisations are formal structures which are created in terms of the Companies Act and have established management boards with senior management, employees and shareholders. The shareholders elect a board of directors at each annual general meeting and the board is responsible for engaging the services of a chief executive officer and employees. Such organisations are driven by profit and tend accordingly to be business-like, efficient and very focused. Each company is governed by its memorandum and articles of association which are the formal rules and procedures by which it must work.

There are various types of companies which differ according to shareholding and liabilities. A private limited company (Pty Limited) essentially limits shareholding to a certain number of persons with limited liability. Should the company acquire debts, the shareholders must meet these needs and invest to keep the company going. Should the company fail, the shareholders can liquidate the company and their liability is limited to the extent of their shareholding (unless unlimited surety has been given by the shareholders to cover all debts of the company).

A close corporation (cc) is a company which is owned by members (compared to directors and shareholders in a private company). A close corporation is less expensive to establish and does not normally require an annual audit, provided that the annual financial statements are prepared by a registered accountant. An incorporated partnership (Inc) is a registered partnership between two or more people. This type of company is usually formed by professional event operators or practitioners. Such a company requires an annual audit by law.

An unregistered partnership usually has an agreement (even a handshake) between people who agree to cooperate together. Sometimes these organisations can be called a *consortium*, which can cooperate for the duration of one or more projects. A sole proprietor is the other type of company, where an individual operates a business in his or her own capacity without partners or a formalised structure involving shareholders.

A public company involves the same type of company except that its shareholders are not restricted to specific people or organisations. The general public can own shares in such a company. A company can be sold to (or bought by) another company or group of shareholders. In addition, a company can be listed on the Stock Exchange to secure investment funding through selling shares to the general public.

6.1.3.3 Association-not-for-gain

These organisations are often called *non-profit-making* or *utility companies* and are established in terms of section 21 of the Companies Act. This type of company was originally formed in the United States of America for the primary purpose of providing utilities (such as electricity, telephones, water, etc) where the local authorities were unable or not prepared to provide such services. In the context of South Africa, these companies have also been formed to manage the delivery of subeconomic services and houses for the disadvantaged poor communities.

A number of events are organised by associations-not-for-gain because they involve a very effective organisational structure for different people and groups working together in association to achieve a common purpose. For example, a local authority, civic structure, church organisation, arts and culture society, and volunteer charity workers could establish an association-not-for-gain. This will be formally registered, have its own bank account, a dedicated set of audited accounts and an event programme under the joint management of a board of directors representing all the associated organisations.

The 'non-profit-making' aspect of these companies is related to the fact that there are no shareholders in a section 21 company. Any person or organisation working for the company may receive payment for work done, but any revenue (profit) generated by the event must be reinvested in the work of the association. Revenue (or profit) cannot be distributed among the association members or employees.

The members of the association-not-for-gain are responsible for electing a board of directors (minimum of seven) at the annual general meeting. The board is responsible for administering the affairs of the company during the year and each board member is accountable for the performance of the company.

A section 21 company cannot be listed on the Stock Exchange and its memorandum and articles of association usually limit the circumstances by which it could change hands. Usually, if an association-not-for-gain has completed its work, it is wound up and closed. However, the articles could also provide that the company and its reserves be donated to a similar organisation having the same intentions and objectives.

6.1.3.4 Trusts

Most organisations which are established as trusts usually work in education, training and charity fields. Trusts are registered in terms of the Trust Act and each trust has a trust deed which sets out the objects of the trust, its organisational structure, working arrangements and procedures. A trust is administered by a board of trustees which must comprise at least three people (usually an accountant or attorney and at least two others).

Traditionally the credibility of trusts is carried by the standing of its trustees, who are usually prominent, respected members of the community. Trusts also establish a high level of community support because they are not 'driven' for the sole benefit of shareholders, but rather by the needs of the community itself.

A trust cannot be listed on the Stock Exchange or bought and sold like a private or public company.

6.1.3.5 Project team

Usually a specific team of people is assembled for the purposes of getting an event off the ground. A one-off event can be organised by a formal company using its own full-time staff or it can engage the services of part-time workers, specialists and/or volunteers.

Maintaining control and accountability are often difficult within project team organisations, especially for large-scale projects such as the Olympics. There is also a difference between establishing an event and running or organising the event itself (that is, the development and operational stages). Quite often the development stage involves a project team which is disbanded on completion of the task. The operational phase is usually conducted by the event organisation which ensures continuity, especially in financing and marketing (Getz, 1997: 135).

6.1.3.6 Government

There are a number of instances where events are developed and organised by government, particularly in high-profile situations such as the Non-aligned Movement Conference held in Durban in 1998, SADC (Southern African Development Countries) meetings and Organisation of African Unity conventions. Government departments have also participated in local events, for example the Department of Arts and Culture (Eastern Cape Province) actively supports the Grahamstown Festival and also supported the Millennium Celebrations 1999/2000. Shortages of funds within government are resulting in less active involvement and recently government has worked more closely with non-government organisations and the private sector to provide support for events.

Local authorities are perhaps the most proactive governments which organise events. City and town councils are often involved in festivals and sports events in partnership with local clubs and societies. The City of East London, for example, is actively pursuing the holding of regular sports festivals in the city in cooperation with the various sports codes and the business sector.

6.1.3.7 Institutions

A variety of institutions organise events, ranging from:
- schools;
- colleges;
- churches;
- technikons;
- universities;
- hospitals;
- welfare groups;
- charitable clubs;

- houses for disabled children, the elderly and homeless;
- environmental pressure groups;
- clubs and societies.

These institutions are often structured as trusts, section 21 associations, welfare organisations and informal associations of members. They are usually comprised of a board of directors or trustees with a number of committees comprising voluntary workers.

6.1.3.8 Interim committees

The final type of event organisation is perhaps the most common – the interim committee. Such a body is usually established to organise and run the event, whereafter it disbands. Although similar to a project team, it differs in that its membership is of a voluntary nature – such committees do not usually receive payment for services rendered and usually do not comprise paid specialists.

6.2 SETTING UP THE ORGANISATION

6.2.1 Founding members

Having considered the organisational design and chosen the particular organisation model which suits the event to be organised, it is necessary to take appropriate steps to establish the organisation. Schmader (1997: 7) states that 'a successful event is no different from a successful business and will function best if treated as such … the most successful events are usually independent, with a clear chain of command, strong leadership and a clearly defined mission statement, just as a successful business'.

In establishing an event organisation, it is vital to select a founding group (or interim committee) of people who have credibility and high regard in the community. This group needs to have a 'champion' or 'champions' who will pilot the development and organisational process through all the ups and downs along the way. Very often, the founding members will comprise the first members of the board and it is vital that they all have a common vision and purpose.

The founding members also have an important role in deciding whether other people become involved, why they are needed and the extent to which they should contribute to the event. Founders also influence the way the organisation is structured, how power is controlled, and the way in which the organisation is constituted. In a step-by-step process (or evolution) an event organisation grows and gathers members, staff and facilities (Getz, 1997: 131). (Refer to figure 6.4.)

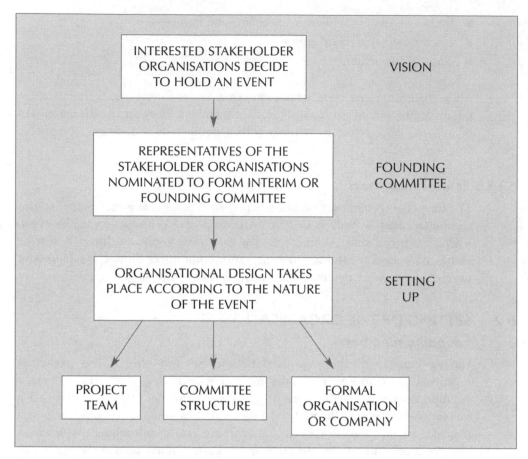

FIGURE 6.4 *Setting-up process*

6.2.2 Organisation articles

All organisations (even informal committees) are best structured on a set of articles which explain the characteristics of the organisation, what it is to do, and how it intends to operate. Formal companies have sets of documents called the *memorandum* and *articles of association*. Trusts have a trust deed and voluntary committees usually have a memorandum or association agreement. These documents are usually prepared by attorneys or accountants who can assist in arranging for the registration of the organisation with the Registrar of Companies or the Supreme Court (in the case of trusts). The memorandum usually covers the following details:

- the vision of the organisation;
- the main purpose of its activities;
- the structure, size, composition and terms of election of directors and trustees;
- membership requirements;
- procedural rules, including the meetings to be held, quorum for voting and decision-making;

© Juta & Co Ltd

- how vacancies are filled, resignations and retirements;
- responsibilities and liability of members;
- management of finance and auditing requirements;
- the financial year and appointment of auditors;
- procedure for amending the articles;
- procedure for winding up the organisation and the distribution of assets and funds.

6.2.3 Organisational accountability

For a successful business or event to occur, there needs to be clear definition of accountability, responsibility and authority. Cleland (1999: 254) indicates that failure to perform can often be ascribed to the following factors:

- 'Failure to define and specify authority and responsibility with people who are solely and jointly responsible.
- Failure to overcome negative attitudes in the organisation.
- Inadequate documentation setting out procedures.
- Inadequate team development.
- Failure to introduce flexible interactive management procedures.
- "Failure to promote synergy and unity … so that resources, results and rewards can be shared". '

A responsible person can be defined as '… one who is legally and ethically answerable for the care or welfare of people and organisations' (Cleland, 1999: 261). This does not mean that the responsible person necessarily does all the work in an organisation: the responsible person sees to it that the work is done through delegation, effective management and following up. Responsibility relates to being able to make decisions, being trusted to make those decisions and being held liable for them.

The matter of accountability is an extension of responsibility whereby managers 'are held accountable for the effectiveness and efficiency of people who report to them' (Cleland, 1999: 262). Successful event organisations need to have responsible people, clearly understood authority and accountability so as to ensure that efficient management is achieved.

One of the most severe problems in developing countries is the shortage of skills capacity and experienced personnel. As a result, it is difficult to engender a culture of responsibility and accountability among management staff. Lack of experience and skill often results in managers denying responsibility and assigning blame to co-workers or subordinates and outside organisations. Event organisations accordingly can benefit from introducing a skills transfer and/or mentorship programme, using experienced managers to uplift and advise emerging event managers.

6.3 ORGANISATIONAL CHARACTERISTICS

6.3.1 Role players

There are several fundamental role players in most organisations, including the board of directors or trustees, managers and employees. These various role players (see figure 6.5) all have a function to perform and must interact effectively to do their work.

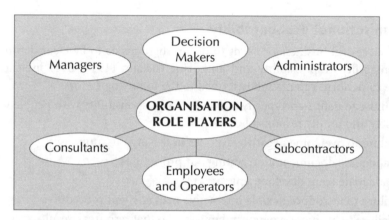

FIGURE 6.5 *Organisational role players*

Usually, the management of an organisation is responsible for ensuring efficiency and productivity in order to fulfil the policies, objectives and vision of the board of directors. The board is also responsible for ensuring that a suitable environment is made available for the functioning of the organisation, including premises, facilities, resources, equipment and personnel.

Large organisations are usually structured in a hierarchy which places the board of directors at the top of a pyramid (refer to figure 6.6).

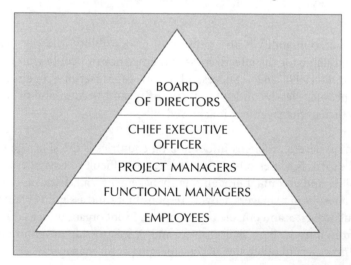

FIGURE 6.6 *Large organisation: hierarchical structure (adapted from Cleland, 1999: 263)*

Smaller organisations, project teams and committees are usually less complex and have fewer tiers in their structure (refer to figure 6.7).

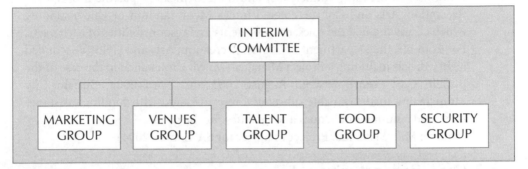

FIGURE 6.7 *Smaller organisation structure*

Case study 6.1: The organisation behind the SA Games

The SA Games organisational structure has been an effective vehicle for organising and co-ordinating a multiple event using numerous venues and facilities in Buffalo City. The structure has three main tiers (see diagram below) an "Executive", the Local Organising Committee (LOC) and four functional committees (Game Services, Sport Services, Support Services and Relationship Services).

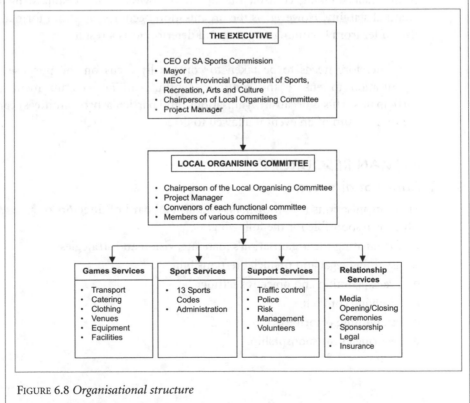

FIGURE 6.8 *Organisational structure*

The three main stakeholders of the SA Games, namely the SA Games Commission, the local municipality and the Provincial Department of Sports, Recreation, Arts and Culture entered into a Memorandum of Understanding which clearly defined the roles, commitments and responsibilities of each party. For example, the Department of Sports, Recreation, Arts and Culture seconded eight officials including a Project Manager (Mr M. L. Makanda in the case of the Buffalo City event) between August 2003 and April 2004. Buffalo City Municipality made available substantial resources and with funding assistance upgraded a number of venues and facilities for the games.
(Source: M.L. Makanda: Project Manager for SA Games, 2004)

6.3.2 Organisational culture

The process by which an event organisation becomes established is gradual and dependent on the ability of the participants to work together for a common vision. As the event process gathers momentum, the event organisation grows from an interim committee of volunteers to a more formal, registered organisation and, finally, an established or professional institution (Getz, 1997: 144). This process has been described as the change process in developing the cultural characteristics of an organisation. Getz (1997: 145) relates this process to the social process of group development, ranging from founders organising the event, leaders taking control, the ups and downs of leadership struggles, to eventual stability. However, as the organisation becomes large and formal, it can also suffer from becoming stagnant and deteriorate as a result.

Care therefore needs to be taken to continually focus on the purpose of the organisation to ensure the continued enthusiasm and commitment of the participants. This is because organisations (and particularly committees) can stifle the momentum of an event if allowed to do so.

6.4   HUMAN RESOURCES

6.4.1 Board of directors

Most organisations (event owners) establish a board of directors or an executive which is responsible for the following:
- formulating the organisation's mandate, vision and strategies;
- assuming legal and financial responsibility;
- event planning and objective setting;
- resolving conflict;
- establishing priorities;
- securing event sponsorship.

These directors are expected to interface very closely with event projects (for example the Olympic Games or Standard Bank Arts Festival) at the initiation and planning stages, but to remain at a distance during execution unless needed for setting priorities and resolving conflict. The achievement of success in event management is based on the successful integration of three role players: the event manager, event line managers and the senior management of the event organisation. It is believed that the reason why event executives often meddle during event execution is that they do not get accurate information from the event manager as to the status of the event project. Accordingly, it is important that the stakeholders be informed on a continual basis.

The most critical node is the relationship between the event manager and the event line manager. These two need to view each other as equals and be willing to share authority, responsibility and accountability (Kerzner, 1998: 16–19).

As a result of the overriding importance of the board of directors in assuring the creditability of an event, the selection of members is a vitally important process, sometimes involving consultation with stakeholders, national, provincial and local authorities, politicians, community leaders, business and labour. The lack of credibility of members can result in an event being delayed or even prevented from taking place.

6.4.2 Chief executive officer (event administrator)

Some event practitioners prefer to be known as event administrators or leaders. However, according to Kerzner (1998: 103), the use of such terminology lies in the traditional hierarchical management style which ill equips event practitioners to deal with making quick decisions. This type of organisation results in no one individual being responsible for the entire event project, leading to a failure to provide the necessary emphasis to complete the project as coordination is complex and conflicts arise when activities need to be coordinated in more than one department. Further, decision-making favours the stronger functional groups and there is no focal point for customers as response to customer needs is slow. Finally, event ideas tend to be functionally oriented with little regard for ongoing projects.

Because of these problems in the past, event practitioners began searching for methods to coordinate the flow of work between the functional event units. The coordination of events was achieved through several integrated mechanisms such as:

- rules and procedures;
- planning processes;
- hierarchical referral;
- direct contact.

The need for event coordinators or managers soon became apparent as it was realised that the control of a project needs to be given to personnel whose loyalties lie in the completion of the project. Managers from the classical management school seriously questioned the amount of authority given to a project manager.

Out of this was born the matrix event organisational form. According to Kerzner (1998: 110), each event project manager reports directly to the event owner and each such project represents a potential profit centre. The event manager in this case has total responsibility and accountability for the success of the event project. The functional departments have functional responsibility to maintain technical excellence on the event project. Thus, while event project management is a coordinative function, matrix management is a collaborative functional division of event project management. In project coordination, work is assigned to specific people or units. In matrix organisations, information is shared and several people may be required for the same piece of work to ensure adequate capacity and expertise.

A successful event is dependent upon the character, calibre and leadership of the chief executive officer of the event organisation, the chairperson of the interim event committee and/or the project team leader. Watt (1998: 28) stresses that 'it is impossible to overemphasize the crucial need for an effective, charismatic leader for any successful event'. The leader/s of the event organisation must possess several leadership qualities and must be:

- motivating;
- enthusiastic;
- analytical;
- well organised;
- diplomatic;
- democratic;
- opportunistic;
- inspirational, and
- decisive.

The chief executive officer and/or team leader needs to be capable of choosing an appropriate leadership style commensurate with the situation, taking into account the ability and input of the rest of the team. Watt (1998: 29) suggests that 'the key leader will also be required to provide vision, direction and an awareness of the external environment to ensure success'.

6.4.3 Employees

A one-off special event will invariably depend on the goodwill and services of volunteer workers. However, a recurring event, hallmark or mega-event will necessitate the employment of key full-time personnel.

It is most important to ensure that the recruitment of key full-time staff be conducted professionally and according to systematic procedures of advertisement, short listing, interviews and appointment. Advertisements need to state clearly the nature of the position, work involved and qualifications/expertise required. This will help the committee to short list applicants and invite them to attend an interview.

In certain instances, it may be felt appropriate to engage the services of a professional personnel recruitment company to find the appropriate member of staff for your organisation. This is often necessary for senior management and specialist staff, such as accountants, project managers, sound engineers and security personnel. The personnel consulting business is most efficient and can fast-track the recruitment process. However, it must be remembered that the consultants require payment of commission based on the member of staff's salary, payable on appointment of that person. In addition, the use of personnel consultants for the recruitment of employees for a charitable or public events association is not always popular in the public's view because 'transparency' and open advertising are seen to be preferable and in the interests of giving everybody a fair chance of gaining employment.

South Africa has an acute unemployment problem and events offer the opportunity to provide a certain number of jobs for the unemployed. Affirmative action in the employment process is a national policy and the employment of previously disadvantaged people (PDPs) and disabled people has to be actively accommodated. The Labour Equity Act requires appropriate affirmative employment for all organisations having 50 or more employees. However, research indicates that the employment benefits of events are overstated because they are reliant mostly on short-term and volunteer workers.

6.4.4 Volunteers

By far the vast majority of special events are organised by committees and volunteer workers. Recruitment often involves a process of 'word of mouth' within the ranks of the member organisations involved on the committee. Often the volunteer workers have just as much responsibility as full-time employees. Accordingly, it is just as important to have clearly defined job descriptions for these workers as for the staff.

The important difference between a volunteer and an employee is the fact that a volunteer's commitment to the event is on a charitable level. An employee is getting paid and has contractual obligations. Volunteers do not have a contract of employment and their interests end immediately the event is over or when they are no longer involved. Accordingly, working with volunteers requires that their special contribution to the success of the event be acknowledged and shared. (The

Basic Conditions of Employment Act 75 of 1997 excludes volunteer or charitable workers.)

Working with volunteers requires consideration, flexibility and enthusiasm because volunteers often work for the 'fun of it' or for charitable purposes. Crayton (1997: 47) explains that 'you will find that the majority of volunteers come back year after year if they have specific assignments, direction and appreciation'.

Volunteers require just as much management and coordination as employees. Crayton (1997: 47) adds that 'all it takes is a little imagination, organisation and a lot of enthusiasm'.

> ## Case study 6.2: Lessons from managing volunteers at the SA Games 2004
>
> Over four hundred volunteers contributed to the success of the SA Games. Despite the success of the event, it was sometimes found that there were duplications of effort and occasions when inadequate use was made of available resources. However, there were certain valuable lessons learned.
>
> - There needs to be a careful 'needs analysis' concerning the number of volunteers to be recruited, and the activities they are required to perform;
> - use of volunteers needs to be thoroughly worked out and managed to avoid duplication;
> - volunteers need to be committed to the event and must understand what is means to be a volunteer, and
> - monitoring of volunteers is essential.
>
> (Source: M.L. Makanda: Project Manager for SA Games, 2004)

6.4.5 Training

The employment of volunteers often means that the people involved are unskilled or perhaps lack sufficient experience for the work to be carried out. It is advisable to conduct a skills audit among the volunteers and to allocate them responsibilities closely allied to their interests or skills. It also helps to assign a coordinator or mentor to a group of volunteers to provide training and guidance. In situations where full-time, skilled employees are not available and the event has to depend on volunteer workers, it is advisable to introduce a training programme to ensure that all personnel are capable of executing their duties during the event. Watt (1998: 29) suggests that there should be two different levels of training, namely:

- *desirable* training – improving skills (catering, bookkeeping, etc);
- *essential* training – ensuring awareness (such as legal rules and requirements; health and safety).

Training can involve routine duties, such as ushering and ticket selling, to more specialist responsibilities, such as crowd management and first aid. There is no doubt that training is time-consuming and costly. However, adequate preparation and the use of older, more experienced volunteers to train younger recruits can assist in keeping costs down. There are also a number of associations and charitable institutions which can provide training free of charge (for example the disaster management department of the local authority, the Red Cross Society and non-government organisations).

6.4.6 Unions

In terms of the South African Basic Conditions of Employment Act 75 of 1997, each organisation needs to have a workers' forum which enables the employees to communicate their needs on a collective basis to management. In many areas of industry, transport and commerce there are well-established union organisations representing the rights of permanent employees.

The events industry is, by its very nature, multisectoral. Accordingly, every event depends on the services of a variety of service industries such as caterers, transport, security, accommodation, maintenance, etc, and as a result many unions will be indirectly and directly involved in an event.

In a situation of subcontracting it is possible to think that the caterer's employees are the responsibility of the catering contractor and not your problem (as events manager or organiser). However, any union difficulties within the subcontractor organisations will have a domino effect on the outcome of the event. It is accordingly essential to have a good working relationship with the unions associated with the event that is being organised. Unions are a good source of large numbers of labourers for big projects and when working with a union it is necessary to have the proper foundation for a successful worker–employer relationship. A successful event depends on the effective involvement and cooperation of all role players (Sivek, 1996: 123).

The event can only benefit from a constructive and cordial relationship with all unions that come into contact or work with that event. After all, any special event is a team effort. Should it happen, however, that a conflict situation arises, Sivek (1996: 124) advises that you 'discuss the situation with the proper representatives. A calm dispassionate discussion of the details should resolve any problems.' In a situation where a subcontracting organisation encounters problems with a work stoppage or dispute, it is essential that the event organisers play an active, supporting role to facilitate a solution to such problems, without necessarily getting directly involved between the employer (the subcontractor) and the employee.

6.5 OPERATIONAL ELEMENTS

6.5.1 Queue management

A major organisational element of events is queue management. While the sale of tickets in advance of the event at other retail outlets in the area can help to reduce queues, the management of entry points is crucial to the success of the event from the points of view of collecting revenue and/or making sure that safety and security norms are observed (for example, in the case of firearms, bottles, alcohol, etc). Getz (1997: 86) maintains that 'queuing (or lining up) should be managed, partly to avoid problems and partly to create a better visitor experience'. The psychological needs and processes of people waiting in line offer significant challenges in queue management. Time can seem to go very slowly when people are waiting; accordingly, entertainment for people in the queue can reduce the boredom and offer organisers the opportunity to include the participants in the event entertainment even before they enter the premises. This entertainment stimulates interest and creates a good impression early on. In addition, people waiting in line can benefit from receiving timeous information about delays and/or the reason for the queue and what is being done about managing the delay through additional staffing measures, thereby helping to reduce frustration, boredom and negative emotional effects. It is further recommended that facilities for the waiting public be provided, including 'water fountains and the supply of occasional benches or seats moulded into the corners of queues' (Pearce, 1991: 21, 215, 217).

Queuing theory, and the quantitative analysis of people waiting in lines, commenced in 1909 (Render & Stair, 1982: 630) and it is stated that there are three basic components of queues:

- arrival of people;
- service facilities and staff;
- the waiting line itself.

The study of queues indicates that there are several basic queue arrangements which can be utilised (Render & Stair: 1982: 37).

- Single channel, single phase system
- Single channel, multiphase system
  (Note: This system can also include a queue which is arranged in an S. This saves space and enables the queue to be better informed as to progress.)
- Multichannel, multiphase system

Pearce (1991: 22) holds the view that 'queues do not have to be a bleak introduction to a tourist attraction. Instead they can be integrated into the design of a facility, they can provide an opportunity to orientate people towards that facility with questions and display panels ... The critical issue to be addressed at tourist attractions is the need to attend to the visitor at all times and people in queues should not be exempt from this attentive service.'

6.5.2 Catering for the physically challenged

Perhaps the greatest omission in event management in South Africa is catering for those who are physically challenged due to disablement and visual or hearing impairment. A number of essential features for every facility where an event is to be held need to be at the top of the check list for the organisers' attention. These include the following:

- reserved parking spaces immediately outside the entrance (such spaces need to be under the management of designated personnel to prevent selfish, able-bodied people from using them);
- appropriately designed toilets, particularly allowing access to wheelchairs;
- provision of ramps instead of stairs;
- availability of wheelchairs for the elderly;
- audio facilities for hearing impaired (such as an assisted listening system);
- reserved seating for people with impaired vision;
- trained personnel to assist the deaf and wheelchair-bound public.

There are also a number of measures which can be put in place to help the physically challenged enjoy the event:

- the provision of a bell at the entrance where wheelchair participants could summon assistance;
- the provision in advance of facilities to accommodate guide dogs, should they not be able to accompany their owners into the event itself, and
- the need to enhance awareness of the provisions made for the disabled.

In this way the organisers will earn support and promotion of the event from all sectors (Richards, 1992: 99).

There is a need to arrange qualified sign language interpreters for meetings and conferences which are being attended by the hearing impaired. In addition, 'guest rooms should have telephones equipped with a flashing light and doors with a vibrating knock signal' (Sturken, 1997: 48).

6.5.3 Facilities

Organising an event can involve an enormous amount of work in terms of the assembly of facilities to ensure success. Various fundamental requirements need to be taken into account, whether the event is a meeting or rock concert, small or large. These include the following (Moxley, 1995: 25):

- an event map or model showing the distribution of activities and key facilities such as toilets, information and customer assistance, entrances and exits to main attractions (this can also involve a computer-generated service – refer to section 6.5.4);

■ facilities for television cameras, including lighting, camera positions and control room (usually an external mobile room), radio and television broadcast/commentators;

■ telephones for general public, media and the organisation (such facilities should allow for fax and modem linkage as separate direct lines);

■ parking, taxi and bus drop-off zones and separate taxi/bus waiting areas;

■ loading/unloading areas separate from general public access and general parking areas;

■ event venue facilities, including changing facilities, stage and performing areas, seating auditorium, assembly areas, catering, dining and toilet facilities, equipment storage, refuse storage areas, maintenance rooms and security facilities.

Case study 6.3: Telkom geared up for festival

'Visitors are being kept in closer touch with family, friends and colleagues than ever before at the Standard Bank National Arts Festival this year.

In order to meet increasing demand over the festival period, Telkom has revamped the public telephone network in town. Nineteen new telephones have been installed at different venues throughout the city, bringing to 455 the total number of public phones in the city – of this total, 250 are card phones.

Telkom has assigned three technical officers to oversee the effective functioning of the public telephone network in Grahamstown, and each phone is checked at least three times daily, said Mandla Tyala, Telkom's senior manager: corporate communications.'

(*Grocotts Mail*, 130(53), Tuesday, 6 July 1999)

Most events involve audiovisual presentations, ranging from simple presentations using an overhead slide projector and a microphone, or a digital projector linked to a computer, or a video conferencing facility, to full sound mixing requirements. Event managers are urged to 'compile a list of the audio visual needs of each presenter', equipment needs and facility requirements, including the capacity of the room, dimensions, availability of electrical power, nature of the sound system, adequate lighting and preparation areas (Sturken, 1997: 39).

Event organising requires that the various facilities be utilised as efficiently and economically as possible to achieve a safe and vibrant event experience. This can be made easier by clever design and décor. Very often the use of décor can add to the event theme and change a fairly boring or uninteresting space into an exciting venue.

Before designing the décor for an event, it is advisable to find out if there are any rules or guidelines about the use of the space, fixing of items to walls, hanging objects from ceilings, and so on. This will have a profound influence on the nature of the décor that is used. The theme or purpose of the event directly influences the type and style of décor, materials and objects used in developing the décor. Care should also be taken to measure the entrances so as to ensure that any décor displays which may be constructed outside the venue can be moved inside without a problem. Daly (1996: 139) also stresses the value of working to a budget and the need to take into account the costs of taking the décor down and storing it after the event.

Modern décor also utilises inflatable sculptures to create an image, interest and excitement. Goldman (1996: 143) distinguishes five types of inflatable sculpture:
■ hot-air balloon;
■ helium-filled aerostats;
■ inflatable costumes;
■ cold-air or pneumatic inflatable, and
■ interactive or technologically enhanced inflatables.

Inflatable sculptures can be used for a variety of purposes, including hot-air balloons for parades, festivals and races, as stationary 'promotional tools and brand presence/awareness' displays, to elevated photography of an event (Goldman, 1996: 143). Helium-filled aerostats, on the other hand, are designed to fly in the wind (manned or unmanned) and include helium-filled airships or 'blimps'. Cold-air inflatables 'use forced air from a blower as an inflatable source'. These can be used as tents and large-scale building backdrops.

Balloons, either used indirectly or in clusters, can also be an effective element in event décor. Yaffe (1999: 151) indicates that the use of balloons as decorations is a growing trend, also involving the use of lighting and special effects. Balloons are regarded as an affordable decoration medium in the events industry.

6.5.4 Computer equipment and information technology

The computer equipment available to assist event organisers is substantial. There is a wide variety of computers and software available to choose from and these must all be governed by your needs and budget. Information technology for the attractions and entertainment sector can be categorised into three areas:
■ monitoring and controlling the use of the attraction (including electronic ticketing and entrance control);
■ applications to help create or enhance the experience (including multimedia and themed entertainment), and
■ marketing and management activities.

The use of computer technology for reservations and ticketing is a widespread activity in the main urban areas of South Africa. The less developed centres, however, still depend on manual systems and conventional printed tickets. Computer-linked systems offer the opportunity to develop very useful databases of event attendance statistics. Information technology is used in bar-code readers in admission entrances, smart cards for season tickets and computer-controlled signs and event maps. 'Audio visual electronic media which can easily be changed as necessary. Kiosks or information pillars with CD-ROM players inside have a significant contribution to make to help guide visitors around the attraction. They are also used to give the visitor multimedia information exhibits' (Sheldon, 1997: 141).

Events are making growing use of computer-generated effects, including virtual reality experiences, audio and visual effects, computer-generated motion simulators, computer-generated waves and computer-generated exhibits.

Finally, the wide variety of software available for word processing, spreadsheets and database purposes facilitates the management of events (in all its aspects). Mummaw (1996: 201) describes the variety of computer-aided design (CAD) software which can assist event management: 'For any proposed venue, the events designer can compose layouts from subfloor to catwalk … CAD represents a labour-saving, efficient-enhancing design aid for the special events industry.'

6.5.5 Special effects

The level of uniqueness and excitement of an event can be greatly influenced by the special effects used to entertain and create a particular atmosphere. These special effects include the following:

- smoke;
- sound;
- lighting;
- fog;
- pyrotechnics (indoors);
- fireworks (outdoors);
- laser lights and laser video projection;
- fibre optics;
- water fountains;
- motorised robots;
- moving/rotating stages;
- confetti canons;
- bubble machines;
- water screens.

The events industry is taking advantage of technological innovation to achieve exceptional exhibitions and experiences. 'Special effects are created electrically and electronically with gases and gun powder, steam, chemicals, water, textures and film. Their transforming catalysts are fiber optics, pyrotechnics, dozens of forms of lighting, including laser lights of many types and intensities' (Surbeck, 1991: 213). The wide variety of special effects and their growing complexity makes it essential to engage experts in the field to ensure a safe and successful show.

When involved in holding special events with fireworks, it is important to consider the effect the show has on animals. Accordingly, the choice of venue needs to be carefully considered. In addition, crowd management in a fireworks show is of utmost importance and one must involve the disaster management authorities and traffic police in the event planning and management of such an occasion.

Certain cities and towns in South Africa will only permit firework displays under special circumstances and with special permits. Accordingly, it is advisable to contact the local authority at an early stage in the event planning process.

6.6　CRITICAL SUCCESS FACTORS

Event organising is a challenging activity which is dependent upon several critical success factors:

- an appropriate organisational structure which is suited to the nature of the event;
- support of the stakeholders in the area, including the politicians, local authority, community, local leadership (champions) and event sponsors;
- an experienced, proactive and committed event organiser (manager, chief executive, etc) with the support of an organised and able group of staff and volunteer workers;
- a well-balanced event programme with attractive elements and at least one unique, outstanding main attraction, and
- a distinctive décor which establishes a theme and enables the use of special effects to enhance the experience of participants.

Browse these Internet sites
http://www.personal.usyd.edu.au/~wotoole/epmspage1.html#EPMS_Schema
http://www.blackbaud.com/solutions/raisersedgemodules.asp
http://www.silicon-trust.com/pdf/secure_8/34_acg.pdf
http://www.rushmans.com/accreditation.htm
http://www.crowdsafe.com/taskrpt/toc.html#TOC
http://www.smithbucklin.com/about/history.cfm

QUESTIONS FOR SELF-EVALUATION

1 Describe the various types of organisations and indicate those which are more suited to charitable and welfare event activities.

2 The process of setting up an organisation follows a number of steps. Explain these steps.

3 There are functional and project-based organisational structures. Explain the difference between these structures and describe how they work.

4 What would be the difference between accountability and authority?

5 The recruitment of personnel is a crucial element in building an organisation. Indicate the differences between full-time employees and volunteer workers and explain how the recruitment process may differ as a result.

6 The management of volunteers requires careful consideration of workers' needs. Explain why this is so.

7 Describe the various elements of a successful event programme.

8 There are various queue management techniques which can be employed. Explain these and indicate which ones are more appropriate in your opinion.

9 Catering for the physically challenged requires that certain features of the event facilities and equipment be appropriately designed. Explain these provisions.

10 Describe what is meant by décor and indicate how it could enhance a particular event setting.

11 Inflatable sculpture is suggested as an additional décor element. Describe the different types of sculptures.

12 Various aspects of computer technology and special effects can be used to add a very special image or experience to an event. Giving examples of these aids, describe how computer technology can assist the event manager.

CHAPTER 7

Accounting and Financial Management

Debbie van Oudtshoorn

AIM OF THE CHAPTER

The aim of this chapter is to enable the reader to prepare and maintain a complete set of accounting books for an event enterprise, as well as to understand the financial implications of such an event.

LEARNING OBJECTIVES

After having studied this chapter, you should be able to:
- distinguish between accounting and finance;
- explain what is meant by accounting;
- explain what is meant by financial management;
- list the reasons why budgeting is of importance to events;
- list the different kinds of costs for events;
- prepare a cash flow;
- prepare an income statement and balance sheet.

7.1   INTRODUCTION

All event enterprises need to know how they are performing. They need to answer the following questions:
- How much money do we own?
- Who owes us money and how much?
- How much money do we owe and to whom?
- What items of property (assets) do we own?
- Are we making a profit or a loss?

Event managers need to be professional about accounting, especially when large budgets are involved. Financial accounting involves the preparation and presentation of the financial statements (income statement and balance sheet) as required by law or other external parties. Generally accepted accounting practices (GAAP) are used by accountants to compile and present the reports. Management accounting involves preparing and internally using the financial reports to assist in management decision-making (Getz, 1997: 234).

An essential system must contain an audit trail that means that it must be possible to trace the transaction using dates and transaction numbers. All the relevant source documentation must be available where necessary.

Transactions are recorded using the principle of double entry. This means that for every debit there must be a corresponding credit. The value of the debits must equal the value of the credits. There are five categories into which an account may belong: assets, expenses, revenue, owner's equity and liabilities. Assets and expenses are basic debits, while revenue, owner's equity and liabilities are basic credits.

Most events are of a one-off nature and it might appear that sound accounting principles are not required or that they may be lax. Big events, such as the Grahamstown Festival, may employ professional accountants, while a smaller event may be quite tempted to ignore proper accounting and control systems.

It is essential that event managers at all levels understand the financial aspects of their business. Such managers will have a better chance of succeeding in their business venture than those managers who have no financial knowledge. This financial knowledge embraces budget preparation, producing accounting records, analysing financial reports, implementing cost control measures, dealing with finance houses or banks, limiting tax liabilities and understanding how computers and their software programs can be of assistance (Hansen, 1995: 197).

Financial planning and the control thereof are critical in event businesses as the cash outflows *precede* the cash inflows – that is, expenses are incurred before any revenue is generated from the event.

7.2   ACCOUNTING TERMS INTRODUCED

The following are a few terms which event managers need to know:

- *Expenses* are the day-to-day running costs of the event.
- *Profit* is the result when revenue is greater than costs and expenses.
- *Revenue* is the money which the event earns.
- *Solvency* is the ability of the event to settle its debts. If an event is solvent, it means that it is able to meet its obligations.
- *Gross profit* is revenue less cost of sales.
- *Net profit* is revenue less total expenses.
- Cutting costs to a minimum is extremely critical in an event organisation. Revenue must be maximised while costs must be kept to a minimum.
- *Fixed expenses* are those expenses which must be paid for irrespective of whether the event is held or not.
- *Variable expenses* are those expenses which increase or decrease with a corresponding increase or decrease in event revenue. Event revenue is dependent on attendance.

7.3 THE ACCOUNTING CYCLE IN AN EVENT ENTERPRISE

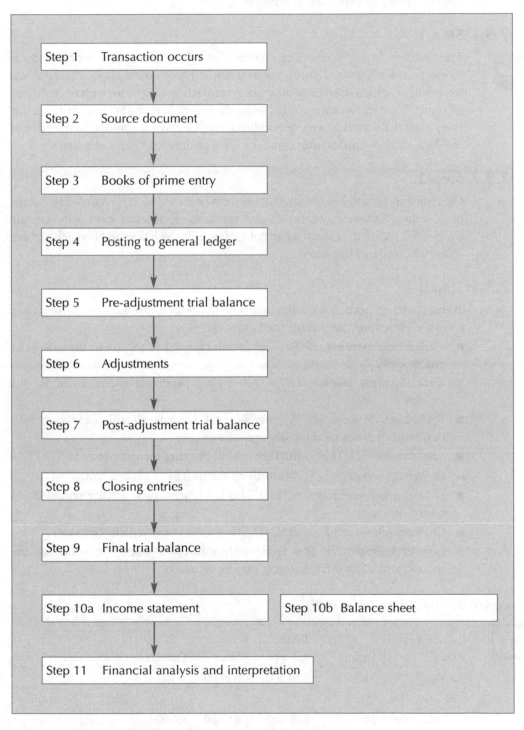

FIGURE 7.1 *Event accounting cycle*

The different steps of the accounting cycle in an event enterprise, as illustrated in figure 7.1, may be explained as follows.

7.3.1 Step 1

The first step in any accounting cycle is that of the transaction taking place. *A transaction may be defined as an agreement between two or more people where one sells something or renders a service to the other.* A transaction may be for cash or credit (on account). Transactions are recorded using the principle of double entry (that is, for every debit there must be a corresponding credit). What is meant is that the value of the debit entry or entries must equal the value of the credit entry or entries.

7.3.2 Step 2

Once the transaction has occurred, it needs to be recorded. It is recorded by means of a *source document*; examples are tax invoice, receipt, cash slip, cheque counterfoil, etc. In the case of a journal entry for depreciation and bad debts, there will not be a source document.

7.3.3 Step 3

Transactions are recorded for the first time in books of *prime entry* or *subsidiary journals*. These journals include the following:

- *Cash Receipts Journal (CRJ)*. This journal is used to record all the cash sales and receipts.
- *Cash Payments Journal (CPJ)*. All cheque payments are recorded in this journal.
- *Petty Cash Journal (PCJ)*. This journal records all miscellaneous cash payments. It is not used for large purchases.
- *Sales Journal (SJ)*. This journal records all the sales on account.
- *Purchases Journal (PJ)*. This records all the purchases on account.
- *Debtors Allowances Journal (DAJ)*. This is a journal in which are recorded any returns inwards.
- *Creditors Allowances Journal (CAJ)*. This records any returns outwards.
- *General Journal (GJ)*. This is the only subsidiary journal in which all the transactions of an event business may be recorded.

EXAMPLE 7.1 *Cash Receipts Journal (CRJ)*

Date	Details	Total receipts	Sales	Debtors	Other	Description
2 May 1999	Mr A	R20 000	R20 000			
26 May 1999	Mrs B	R500			R500	Equipment
30 May 1999	Mr C	R12 000	R8 000	R4 000		
	TOTAL	R32 500	R28 000	R4 000	R500	

On 2 May 1999, R20 000 was received from Mr A in respect of sales; on 26 May 1999 Mrs B paid R500 to the event enterprise for old equipment she bought, while on 30 May 1999, Mr C paid R12 000 to the event enterprise which consisted of sales worth R8 000 and R4 000 towards his account.

From example 7.1 the following will be entered in the general ledger:
Bank will be debited with R32 500; *Sales* will be credited with R28 000; *Debtors* will be credited with R4 000 and *Equipment* will be credited with R500.

EXAMPLE 7.2 *Cash Payments Journal (CPJ)*

Date	Cheque No	Payee	Total payment	Other	Description	VAT
2 May 1999	123	FNB	R5 000	R5 000	Rent paid	
6 May 1999	124	Telkom	R2 280	R2 000	Tel account	R280
12 May 1999	125–129	Staff	R5 000	R5 000	Salaries	
20 May 1999	130	Cancelled	R0	R0		
	TOTAL		R12 280	R12 000		R280

Cheque numbers need to be in sequence so that there is better control of payments made. Cheque number 123 was paid by the event enterprise for rent of R5 000; cheque number 124 was for a total of R2 280 which was made up of R2 000 telephone expense and R280 VAT (value added tax). Cheque numbers 125 to 129, amounting to R5 000, were made out for staff salaries, while cheque number 130 was cancelled.

Example 7.2 will be posted to the general ledger as follows:
Bank will be credited with the total payments of R12 280; *Rent paid* will be debited with R5 000; *Telephone expenses* will be debited with R2 000; *Salaries expenses* will be debited with R5 000; and *VAT (Input)* will be debited with R280.

EXAMPLE 7.3 *Petty Cash Journal (PCJ)*

Date	Voucher No	Total voucher	Food	Beverage	Other	Description
3 May 1999	12	R57	R57			
18 May 1999	13	R100		R40	R60	Casuals
25 May 1999	14	R114		R100	R14	Input VAT
31 May 1999	15	R171	R150		R21	Input VAT
	TOTAL	R442	R207	R140	R95	

Most event enterprises have a petty-cash system in operation to satisfy the need for small purchases for which it is not viable to make out a cheque. Each time petty cash is advanced, the money is signed for and a voucher number is given. These voucher numbers need to be in sequence. In the above example 7.3, a total of R442 was advanced for the month of May 1999. A cheque will need to be drawn for R442 so that petty cash can be reimbursed. (Refer to cheque number 131 in example 7.2.)

Example 7.3 above will be posted to the general ledger as detailed below:
Petty cash control will be credited with R442; *Food expenses* will be debited with R207; *Beverage expenses* will be debited with R140; *Casuals expenses* will be debited with R60; and *VAT (Input)* will be debited with R35 (R14 + R21).

EXAMPLE 7.4 *Sales Journal (SJ)*

Date	Debtor	Invoice No	Total sales	Food	Beverage	Other	Details
1 May 1999	Mr C	1322	R10 000	R5 000	R4 000	R1 000	Old equipment
5 May 1999	Mrs D	133	R500	R350	R150		
9 May 1999	Mrs E	1324	R1 500	R1 200	R300		
	TOTAL		R12 000	R6 550	R4 450	R1 000	

From the above, it can be seen that Mr C, Mrs D and Mrs E purchased goods from an event enterprise on account (that is, they did not pay cash for their purchases). They therefore owe the event enterprise this money which is reflected above. When selling on account, an invoice is made out. These invoices need to follow in sequence.

The following will be entered in the general ledger from the information provided by example 7.4:
Food sales will be credited with R6 550; *Beverage sales* credited with R4 450; *Old equipment* credited with an amount of R1 000; and *Debtors* will be debited with R12 000.

EXAMPLE 7.5 *Purchases Journal (PJ)*

Date	Creditor	Invoice	Total	Food	Beverage	Other	Details
5 May 1999	Company A	F430926	R1 200	R800	R150	R250	Equipment
7 May 1999	Company B	T226650	R6 000	R4 900	R1 100		
9 May 1999	Company A	F431297	R2 500	R1 200	R1 300		
	TOTAL		R9 700	R6 900	R2 550	250	

From example 7.5, which reflects purchases the event enterprise has not paid cash for (that is, it has purchased on account), you will note that the invoice numbers are not in sequence. This is due to the event enterprise purchasing from different suppliers, all of which have different invoice sequences. This invoice number relates to the invoice received from the company from whom the event enterprise has purchased.

The purchases journal for the month as shown in example 7.5 will be posted to the general ledger:
Food expenses to be debited with R6 900; *Beverage expenses* will also be debited with an amount of R2 550; *Equipment* will be debited with R250 while *Creditors* will be credited with the total amount of R9 700.

EXAMPLE 7.6 *Debtors Allowances Journal (DAJ)*

Date	Debtor	Credit note	Total credit	Other	Description
2 May 1999	Mr C	M1	R500	R500	Beverage
20 May 1999	Mrs E	M2	R50	R50	Beverage
	TOTAL		R550	R550	

When debtors (people or companies who have purchased from us, the event enterprise, on account) return goods, the information is recorded in the above-mentioned journal. The credit notes, issued by the event enterprise in favour of the debtors, will be in sequence.

The general ledger entries for the transactions from example 7.6 will be posted as follows:
Debtors will be credited with the total of R550; *Beverage sales* will be debited with R550.

EXAMPLE 7.7 *Creditors Allowances Journal (CAJ)*

Date	Creditor	Debit note	Total debit	Other	Description
5 May 1999	Company A	CN1567811	R 50	R50	Beverage
20 May 1999	Company B	00012444	R900	R900	Food
	TOTAL		R950	R950	

When an event enterprise buys goods on account and the goods are no longer required, are damaged or unsuitable, the event enterprise returns them to the creditor. The creditor will provide the event enterprise with documentation recording the goods returned. This information needs to be recorded in the books of the event enterprise. Example 7.7 depicts this. Because the documentation originates from the creditor, the debit note numbers will not be in sequence.

The creditors allowances journal (example 7.7) will be posted from this subsidiary journal to the general ledger as follows:

Creditors will be debited with the total value of the returns which is R950, while *Beverage expenses* will be credited with R50 and *Food expenses* credited with R900. All these books of prime entry (refer to examples 7.1 to 7.7) which have been explained above, plus example 7.8 which follows, show how the event enterprise will record these different transactions in their set of books. What must be noted is that it is not necessary to have all these different types of prime entry books in which to record all the necessary information. The simplest way of recording all transactions is by making use of only the general journal (refer to example 7.8).

EXAMPLE 7.8 *General Journal (GJ)*

Date	Description	General ledger account number	Debit	Credit
31 May 1999	Salaries	GL21	R2 500	
	Salary control	GL110		R2 500
Being gross salary per payroll				
31 May 1999	UIF company contribution	GL31	R25	
	UIF control	GL145		R25
Being company contribution to UIF				
31 May 1999	Depreciation: equipment	GL16	R18	
	Accumulated depreciation: equipment	GL102		R18
Being depreciation on equipment at 10% per annum				

7.3.4 Step 4

This information as it appears in these subsidiary journals is meaningless, so it is posted to the general ledger. The general ledger is a book consisting of accounts in the shape of the letter T. There is one such T account for every account that is required. This account has a debit side (left-hand side) and a credit side (right-hand side) and information is posted on one or both sides of the account. Thus a transaction is recorded for the second time in the general ledger.

The following is a list of possible accounts that may appear in the general ledger.

Revenue	Costs
Food	Food cost of sales
Beverage	Beverage cost of sales
Vendor	Vendor cost of sales
Music/Entertainment	Music/Entertainment cost of sales
Equipment	Equipment cost of sales
Décor	Décor cost of sales
Advertising	Salaries
Concession	Wages
Donation/Gifts	UIF
Exhibit booth rentals	Medical aid
Interest from Investments	Pension or provident
Merchandise	Leave pay
Registration fees	Bonus
Special event tickets	Advertising and promotions
Sponsorship fees	Audit fees
Vendor commissions	Bank charges
Other revenue	Credit card commission
	Commission paid
	Data Processing
	General expenses
	Insurance
	Judges fees
	Legal fees
	Licences and permits
	Printing and stationery
	Professional fees
	Repairs and maintenance
	Subscriptions
	Depreciation
	Rates and taxes
	Rent paid
	Other cost of sales

7.3.4.1 Revenue terms explained

- *Food revenue* means all sales of food.
- *Beverage revenue* refers to all sales of beverages, including mixers and alcoholic beverages.
- *Vendor revenue* is income from all sales received from vendors, such as vendor rentals.
- *Music/entertainment revenue* means all sales (income) from the charges made for the services which are provided.
- *Equipment revenue* refers to all sales from the charges made for equipment rental and other equipment provided.
- *Décor revenue* is income from all sales from the charges made for this service which is provided.
- *Other revenue* means income from any other sales for services provided.

7.3.4.2 Cost of sales terms explained

- *Food cost of sales* means all costs for food purchases.
- *Beverage cost of sales* refers to all costs for beverage purchases, including garnishes, ice, juices and fruit.
- *Vendor cost of sales* means all costs incurred in respect of vendors.
- *Music/entertainment cost of sales* refers to all costs for engaging musicians.
- *Equipment cost of sales* relates to all costs for renting equipment from equipment rental firms.
- *Décor cost of sales* means all costs for engaging floral designers, as well as the purchase of flowers and items used to decorate parties, functions and events.
- *Other cost of sales* refers to any other costs incurred for which there will be a revenue.

7.3.4.3 Payroll costs explained

- *Salaries.* This means all gross salaries paid to permanent employees.
- *Wages.* This means all gross wages paid to temporary or casual employees.
- *UIF.* This is the employer's contribution towards the Unemployment Insurance Fund (UIF). At present it is 1% of gross salaries and wages. This company contribution is equal to the amount deducted from the employee's salary or wage while he or she is in employment.
- *Medical aid.* This is the employer's contribution towards the medical aid contribution of the employee. Businesses normally pay 50% of the employee's monthly medical aid contribution.
- *Pension or provident.* This refers to the employer's contribution towards a pension or provident fund. It is normal for big companies to contribute an amount equal to that which has been deducted from the employee's salary towards a pension or provident fund.

- *Leave pay.* A schedule is completed on a monthly basis which calculates how many days leave the employee is due at that particular date. It also shows the rand equivalent. When the employee takes leave, the number of days leave is subtracted from the days owing. Should the employee resign from the business, and there is any leave owing to him or her, it must be paid out to the employee. This leave pay expense represents the increase or decrease in the movement from last month to this month.

- *Bonus.* A schedule is completed on a monthly basis which calculates the value of the provision for December bonuses or thirteenth cheques for each employee. Should thirteenth cheques be paid out in December, the balance on the provision account must be nil. The same procedure is started again in January. This bonus expense in the general ledger represents the increase or decrease in the movement from last month to this month. Should an employee resign from the business during the year, it is normal practice for that employee to forfeit his or her share. The employee must be in the employ of the business in December to be able to receive his or her share of the bonus or thirteenth cheque.

- *Staffing costs.* Not all staff involved in events are employed on a permanent or casual basis. They may be volunteers. It is important that all staff involved in an event go through a careful selection process and training procedure. Management needs to be aware that not all staff will be willing to do extra work outside of their normal duties should the organisation want to stage an event for the first time. These feelings need to be respected and management should only involve those members of staff who are willing to get involved (Youell, 1995: 506).

  Certain event managers can employ one or more employees on a permanent basis. These employees are paid regardless of the volume of sales. These people are salaried employees and their costs are fixed. The problem with salaried employees is that when business volume decreases, these employees are still paid. These costs quickly erode profit and create big losses.

  Every event manager should aim to keep payroll costs in check by keeping permanent employees to a minimum. This is achieved by using part-time casual workers who work only when needed.

  Salaries and payroll burden costs such as UIF (Unemployment Insurance Fund), bonus, leave pay, medical aid, pension or provident funds vary from event to event. Payroll costs have components which are fixed and components which are variable, unlike cost of sales which are more variable in nature as they are based on sales volume (Hansen, 1995: 299–300).

- *Volunteers.* Many events rely on volunteers and if it wasn't for the help of volunteers, events would not succeed at all. Volunteers are not paid for their services. Rather they are given vouchers or some other package. These may take the form of T-shirts, name badges, food and beverage vouchers, free transportation from the event to parking areas, tog bags and peak caps.

7.3.4.4 Administration and general costs explained

- *Advertising and promotions.* This refers to all costs for newspaper advertisements, magazine advertising, brochures and menus, direct mail, signage, donations, client entertaining costs, complimentary food or other services, and any other expense related to promoting or creating sales.
- *Audit fees.* These fees are provided for on a monthly basis (that is, every month an amount is expensed). They relate to accountants' fees for the year-end audit.
- *Bank charges.* This means all the service fees, transaction costs and transaction duties as charged by the bank per the bank statements received.
- *Credit card commission.* This includes all costs for fees paid to Visa, Mastercard, American Express and other credit card companies.
- *Commission paid.* This means all the costs relating to referrals.
- *Data processing.* This represents the actual expense for computer processing, such as the payroll preparation, checks, reports and mailing lists.
- *General expenses.* This refers to all costs for sundry items.
- *Insurance.* This means all costs for business insurance.
- *Judges' fees.* This includes all costs relating to judges and sundry items that the judges require.
- *Legal fees.* This means all costs for legal fees.
- *Licences and permits.* This refers to costs for state and municipal licences and permits required to operate the business and also includes special permits and inspection fees.
- *Printing and stationery.* This includes all costs for printed matter not relating to advertising and promotions, such as account forms, stationery forms, catering invoices, office supplies.
- *Professional fees.* This means all costs relating to consultants and engineering firm fees.
- *Repairs and maintenance.* These are all costs for painting and decorating, and repairs to all equipment and maintenance of grounds and gardens. Other costs include alterations and maintenance of buildings, electricity, water and sewerage.
- *Subscriptions.* These include all costs for membership of business organisations, as well as costs for subscriptions to papers and magazines.

7.3.4.5 Capital charges explained

- *Depreciation* refers to all costs relating to the monthly wear and tear of fixed assets, such as equipment and vehicles.
- *Rates and taxes* include all costs for wastage removal.
- *Rent paid* means the interest portion of the costs relating to the finance house or lessor for the business premises used (Hansen, 1995: 314–317).

7.3.5 Step 5

A pre-adjustment trial balance is prepared using information obtained from the general ledger. It is important to note that these general ledger accounts need to be balanced first. It is this brought-down balance from each account that is recorded in the trial balance to check whether the value of the debits equals the value of the credits. This trial balance is called a *pre-adjustment* trial balance, as there may be errors which need to be adjusted. Even though this trial balance may balance, it may contain errors.

7.3.6 Step 6

Should any errors be noticed in the pre-adjustment trial balance, they are corrected by means of a journal entry. Thus this step entails adjustments where necessary.

7.3.7 Step 7

Once adjustments have been posted, a post-adjustment trial balance is prepared. It consists of the pre-adjustment trial balance plus any adjustments.

7.3.8 Step 8

Closing entries is the next step. This involves income and expense accounts being transferred to the profit and loss account. A profit occurs when revenue is greater than expenses and a loss occurs when revenue is less than expenses.

7.3.9 Step 9

The final trial balance will reflect whether the event business has made a profit or a loss. The net result of the final trial balance will be either a profit or a loss.

7.3.10 Income statements and balance sheets

Step 10a

An income statement is prepared to show the financial result of the business. This will show whether the event has made a profit or a loss.

Step 10b

A balance sheet is prepared using the accounting equation, namely $A = OE + L$ where A equals *assets*, OE equals *owner's equity* and L equals *liabilities*. The balance sheet shows the financial position of the event business. It therefore shows what is owned (assets) is equal to what is owed (owner's equity and liabilities). As the name implies, the balance sheet must balance!

7.3.11 Step 11

The financial statements (income statement and balance sheets) are analysed and interpreted. Ratios are calculated and the event is compared with a similar event held last year or an event held by a competitor.

7.4   BUDGETING

Budgets are management tools and plans that involve process and control and are indicators of performance. Thus budgets are performance management tools, their purpose being to allocate limited resources to unlimited needs. Budgets are financial indicators of activities for the year ahead and indicate strategic priorities for the period.

Thus, budgets lead us to *prioritise*. In addition, budgets demonstrate the vision of the organisation and mobilise it in that direction.

According to Goldblatt (1997: 106), budgets are based on:
- the financial history of previous identical or similar events;
- the general economy and forecasts for the future;
- the income and expenses you reasonably believe can be expected with the resources available.

A budget is a financial plan as it is expressed in monetary terms; it is used as a guide for operating an event. The budget is based on available information and consists of revenue and expenses. Before any event is considered, a budget should be prepared in order to determine whether the event is going to be feasible or not. The bottom line of any event is profitability and there has been plenty of money lost and even bankruptcy due to budgets not being prepared. Conditions do change and the budget needs to be flexible in order to accommodate these changes in conditions. What all event managers and staff must strive for is for expenses to be kept to a minimum. Revenue cannot be predicted exactly, but expenses may be controlled and kept to a minimum (Getz, 1997: 230–232).

Event managers use budgets to plan for the future. There are many different kinds of budgets that may be prepared. Examples of budgets are the *capex budget, cash-flow budget* and the *personnel budget*.

The capital expenditure (CAPEX) budget shows the months in which capital expenditure (purchasing of assets) is to occur, while the cash-flow budget plans for the incoming (receipts) and outgoing (payments) cash. The personnel budget shows the expenses associated with employing staff on a permanent and casual basis.

It often happens that the actual results from an event vary considerably from budgeted results. This is quite prevalent as regards revenue. The economy may be in a recession or a boom and this will definitely have an effect on the revenue of an event.

Actual results from an event held this year will be used to prepare the budget for the following year. By using historic information, event managers will be able to prepare a more realistic budget than if no historic information is available. Historic information will not be available for an event to be held for the first time.

EXAMPLE 7.9 *The Weekend Getaway: Budgeted income statement*

Background

You have been contracted by a local company as a Professional Conference Organiser (PCO). You have been requested to organise a one-day weekend function on the 11 January 2005 for 20 delegates.

The following must be assumed.
- You are responsible for organising a one day week-end function.
- There will be 20 delegates, staying one night in twin rooms.
- Three meals, tea and coffee and beverages to be provided on Saturday.
- All equipment (including OHP, computer, microphone, flipcharts).
- Function on Saturday night including music.
- Breakfast on Sunday.

The following would need to be budgeted for:

Conference room hire	R1 000
Equipment hire	R500
Accommodation per delegate	R200
Breakfast per delegate	R50
Lunch per delegate	R70
Dinner per delegate	R100
Tea, coffee per delegate	R10
Beverages for the function	R400
Saturday night function music	R600

The cost for the weekend conference can be calculated as follows:

Quantity		Amount
Conference room hire		R1 000
Equipment hire		R500
Accommodation per delegate	20	R4 000
Breakfast	40	R2 000
Lunch	20	R1 400
Dinner	20	R2 000
Tea, coffee	40	R400
Beverages		R400
Saturday night function music		R600
TOTAL COST		R12 300

The cost per delegate can be calculated as follows:
Total cost divided by number of delegates = R12 300 divided by 20 = R615

Budgeted Income Statement of The Weekend Getaway for the day ended 11 January 2005
Total Sales: R 0,00
Less expenses   R12 300,00
Loss: R12 300,00

7.5   CONTROLLING EXPENSES

Controlling expenses is extremely critical. While expenses must be kept to a minimum, revenue must be maximised. There are different types of expenses associated with events. There are fixed expenses, variable expenses, direct expenses and indirect expenses or overheads. Fixed expenses must be paid for irrespective of whether the event is held or not. Examples are capital expenses associated with equipment and buildings (rent), insurance, salaries for permanent staff and telephone equipment and line rental. Variable expenses are those expenses which increase or decrease with a corresponding increase or decrease in event revenue. Event revenue depends on attendance. An example of a variable expense would be cost of sales, casual wages, postage, decorations and telephone calls. Direct expenses are those expenses which are associated with a specific event. Overheads or indirect expenses are those such as the office rent and general manager's salary (Getz, 1997: 233).

7.6   MANAGEMENT OF CASH FLOW

An event manager must be able to monitor cash flow. Cash flow is the net result of cash inflows and cash outflows, where cash inflows deal with *receipts* and cash outflows with *payments*. The cash budget is thus important. The revenue from events is received on the day of the event while expenses have been incurred prior to receiving this income. The cash outflows will exceed the cash inflows prior to the event being held. This is called a *negative cash flow* or a *deficit*. Once the event has been held, the cash inflows will be received which will exceed the cash outflows. This is called a *positive cash flow* or a *surplus*.

The cash flow is a forecast of monthly expenses and revenue. Danger months will be identified. By being able to identify such months, the event manager will be able to make necessary arrangements, if possible, with the bank manager and suppliers. It might be arranged that the bank account may go into overdraft while the suppliers might extend their credit terms until the event is over. This is known as *back-ending*. Sponsors and donors might advance money to help alleviate the negative cash flow.

When the cash flow is drawn up, it is important to get the timing of the expenses and revenue correct as this has an impact on the available cash. Are all expenses going to be incurred before the event, or most before and a few after? Have grants been applied for? When can the funds be expected to be received? (Getz, 1997: 233).

EXAMPLE 7.10 *The Weekend Getaway: Budgeted cash flow*

Budgeted cash flow of *The Weekend Getaway* for January 2005		
	Dec 2004	**Jan 2005**
Opening balance:	R 0,00	(R12 300,00)
Cash inflows:		
Cash sales	0,00	
Cash from debtors		
Other receipts		
Total cash inflows	0,00	
Cash outflows:		
Cost of sales		
Salaries and wages		
Promotions		
Judges' fees		
Equipment rental		
Other payments		12 300,00
Total cash outflows		12 300,00
Closing balance		(12 300,00)

The cash flow for The Weekend Getaway (example 7.10) can be explained as follows.

Cash inflows concern the ways in which incoming cash is received. Cash inflow thus represents all the receipts.

- *Cash sales* are when money is received at the time of purchase.
- Some sales may be made on account or on credit. This means that although an item or items have been sold, no cash payment is received at the time of purchase. Rather a payment is made at a later date. This payment that is received from someone who purchased on credit, called a *debtor*, is therefore called *cash from debtors*.
- *Other receipts* represents all other forms of cash received that do not form part of the main business.
- *Total cash inflows* is the total of the above-mentioned cash receipts for the month.

Cash outflows consist of all the reasons why cash is paid out of the event.

- The cost that is incurred when we purchase the items needed is called *cost of sales*. The cost of sales represents the cost to us for the items we have sold. If we have consumed these items, then it means that we don't have them. We have therefore sold them.
- *Salaries and wages* represents the salaries and casual wages paid to staff who are employed on a permanent and casual basis.
- Any promotional expenses are reflected here.
- There might be judges for certain events, and the fees to be paid to them are shown under this heading.
- Any equipment that is rented needs to be paid for.
- *Other payments* reflects any other payments that do not fit into one of the above-mentioned cash outflow headings.
- *Total cash outflows* represents the total cash paid out in a particular month.

The closing balance is equal to (R12 300). This closing balance can be either positive or negative. This closing balance for the month of January 2005 will be the opening balance for February 2005.

7.7   AUDITING

Auditing is the process whereby an external auditor will check the financial records. An event enterprise will make use of an external auditor to give his or her opinion whether the books have been recorded using GAAP. Audited financial statements are required when financing or additional financing is required by an event enterprise. Should an event not be audited, there might be the suspicion that the event is trying to hide something (Getz, 1997: 234).

7.8 FINANCIAL ACCOUNTING STATEMENTS

The income statement and the balance sheet make up the financial accounting statements.

7.8.1 Income statement

This shows the financial result of the event. Financiers, sponsors and directors are able to see from this financial accounting statement how well management performed. Did it make a profit or a loss? The bottom line for any event is profitability and it is the income statement which is going to reflect this. Income statements can be prepared after the event has taken place and/or after the audit has been completed. Only revenue and expense accounts are taken into account when drawing up the income statement.

$$\boxed{\text{Profit} = \text{Revenue} - \text{Expenses}}$$

Revenue is obtained from normal selling at the event. Expenses are those which are incurred in the day-to-day running of the event. Expenses are not bought with the intention of reselling. Purchases are the only expense that you buy with the intention of reselling.

Example 7.11, which follows, represents the actual sales and expenses of The Weekend Getaway, while example 7.9 reflected the budgeted sales and expenses. The only difference between examples 7.9 and 7.11 is that in the latter taxation at 30% has been allowed for.

EXAMPLE 7.11 *The Weekend Getaway: income statement*

Income statement of *Weekend Getaway* for the day ended 11 January 2005
Revenue:
Food and beverage	R0
Less expenses:	
Cost of sales	R12 300
Net income before taxation	(R12 300)
Less taxation at 30%	R3 690
Net income after taxation	(R8 610)

Note that this income statement does not take capital repayments, debt or finance charges into account.

7.8.1.1 Retained income

Should the management of an event decide to hold back income made from the event for expansion purposes or for any other reason, such income is called *retained income*. This income which is made from the event is added to the opening balance of the retained income at the beginning of the year. The total retained income at year end will thus represent what was made in total from the lifespan of the event so far.

Sometimes it is these retained profits that have ensured the solvency of an event.

7.8.2 Balance sheet

The balance sheet shows how all the assets have been or are being paid for; it shows the financial position of the event. The balance sheet is drawn up according to the accounting equation, that is:

> $A = OE + L$
> Where: A equals assets
> OE equals owner's equity
> L equals liabilities

There are three categories of assets, namely *fixed assets, investments* and *current assets*. Assets are something of value to us. *Fixed assets* consist of land, buildings, motor vehicles and equipment. Assets depreciate due to wear and tear. This loss in value is called *depreciation*. Assets are shown in the balance sheet at their net book value that is equal to their original cost price less accumulated depreciation. *Investments* represent money that has been deposited for a fixed period of time. *Current assets* are those which are also of value to us, but the difference between fixed assets and current assets is that the value of current assets changes during the year. They are more variable in nature. Examples of current assets are stock, debtors and bank.

The money, cash, assets or whatever he or she has contributed towards the event business represents *owner's equity*. Owner's equity thus represents the owner's interest in the event business. Owner's equity may be increased by further contributions and is regarded as the permanent investment by the owner.

> Owner's equity may be broken into:
>
> capital + profit – loss – drawings

Drawings represent what the owner has taken from the event business for his or her own use; they may be in the form of cash or stock.

Total liabilities are made up of owner's equity, long-term liabilities and current liabilities. Liabilities show the creditors of the event enterprise – that is, owner, finance houses and suppliers. *Long-term liabilities* are creditors of the event enterprise, their debt being settled over a period of time (anything from five years and more). *Current liabilities* represent the shorter-term creditors of the enterprise. These creditors need to be repaid within the year.

EXAMPLE 7.12 *The Weekend Getaway: Actual balance sheet*

Balance sheet of *The Weekend Getaway* as at 11 January 2005

Employment of Capital		Capital Employed	
Fixed assets:		Owner's equity:	
		Capital:	
Current assets:		Loss	(R8 610)
SARS	R3 690	Current liabilities:	
		Creditors	
		Bank overdraft	R12 300
	R3 690		R3 690

Example 7.12 may be explained as follows:
The loss of R8 610 can be obtained from example 7.11. There are no sales, therefore no funds can be deposited into the bank account. The function was paid for by cheque, therefore bank has an overdraft of R12 300. R3 690 represents the liability in favour of the company by the SA Revenue Service for taxation of 30% of the loss.

7.9   MEASURING FINANCIAL PERFORMANCE

7.9.1 Solvency

Many small event enterprises have a cash-flow problem. The reason for this is due to expenses being incurred prior to any revenue being generated. There is therefore the need to calculate the solvency (the ability to settle its debts or obligations) of the event enterprise. Solvency is calculated by means of the current ratio.

$$\text{Current ratio} = \frac{\text{Current assets}}{\text{Current liabilities}}$$

Current assets represent those assets that can be converted into cash within one year, while current liabilities represent those liabilities that need to be settled within one year. It is a measure of solvency, alternatively referred to as the *liquidity* or *quick ratio*.

This ratio calculates that for every R1 the event organisation owns, it owes Rx. A ratio of 2 is normally desired, as this would represent R2 owned for every R1 owed (Getz, 1997: 237).

The acid-test ratio is also a solvency ratio. It is calculated as follows:

$$\text{Acid-test ratio} = \frac{\text{Current assets} - \text{stock}}{\text{Current liabilities}}$$

The difference between the current and the acid-test ratio is stock because stock is excluded from the total of the current assets when calculating the acid-test ratio. By comparing the current and acid-test ratios, we will be able to calculate how much the value of the stock contributes towards the solvency of the event organisation. If the stock holding is very high, then the current ratio will be much higher than the acid-test ratio.

7.9.2 Return on investment (ROI)

This ratio calculates whether the owner is getting value from the event, his or her business. The formula is as follows:

$$\text{ROI} = \frac{\text{Revenue}}{\text{Total investment}}$$

Revenue is represented by the total revenue of the event. Total investment consists of capital plus any further contributions such as retained income plus any debt that was incurred. The objective is to achieve a high ratio of revenue to investment. The owner of an event organisation will want to be able to calculate whether he or she is receiving a good return on any investment he or she has made in the business. If a good return on the investment is not being made, then why not take the financial resources and place them with a bank?

7.9.3 Yield management

Yield management is fundamentally about supply and demand. It is a pricing strategy, aimed at maximising revenue. It achieves this by manipulating demand. For example, during the peak season, event managers want to maximise revenue, so prices charged will be high. This is because demand during the peak season is higher than during the low season. During the off-season the prices charged will be much lower as the event manager will wish to maximise revenue from limited available demand (Polivka, 1998: 632).

Yield management aims to maximise revenue by allocating the right product to the right kind of customer at the right price. In the case of events, for example, gate fees can be increased or decreased according to the demand.

7.10 INTRODUCTION TO FINANCIAL CONTROLS

7.10.1 Cash control/signatories

It is very easy for cash to disappear, so there needs to be a control system in place. A manager or supervisor needs to check the deposit slip for banking. Floats should be checked regularly as there is temptation when they are not checked at all. Should there be a petty-cash float, it should have all the necessary backup documentation supporting the petty-cash vouchers for any petty cash paid out. The person who is being reimbursed from petty cash needs to sign the voucher on receipt of the cash. There need to be at least two signatories on cheques written out. This ensures that there is a control system in place as two people has to give the approval on a payment being made. The receipt book needs to be numbered and it needs to run in sequence. A receipt sequence that is used for this month cannot be the same sequence for next month. For example, if the receipt books are numbered from 1 to 100, perhaps the first book could be A1 to A100, the second book, B1 to B100, etc. This would alleviate the problem of having receipts issued with the same numbers. Should a large volume of cash be handled on the premises, a safe could be installed or use could be made of cash pickups by a security company.

When goods are delivered, a tax invoice (if the supplier is registered as a VAT vendor) is supplied, or in the case of a non-vendor, it would be an invoice. The person who receives these goods onto the business premises must sign either the delivery note or the invoice to indicate that he or she has received them. This is what is termed *proof of delivery (POD)*. Should there be a number of items on the invoice, it must be clearly marked what *has* and *has not* been received.

7.10.2 Stock control

Stock can go missing rather easily if it is not monitored properly. Stock needs to be counted on a regular basis in order to check whether there are any variances between what is in the books of the event and what is actually there.

7.10.3 Asset control

What applies to stock control, applies to asset control. Assets need to be numbered for identification purposes. Assets need to be counted on a regular basis to check whether they can all be accounted for. Should any equipment be borrowed, this must be noted somewhere. Somebody needs to be given the responsibility for controlling assets.

7.10.4 Paid-outs

Paid-outs or disbursements refer to any small payments made. There should be a policy as to what expenses can be claimed and what expenses cannot be claimed.

The person receiving the payment must sign that he or she has received payment. The necessary supporting documentation needs to be attached to the paid-out voucher.

7.10.5 Credit

Suppliers want to be paid within 30 to 60 days of supplying goods and/ or services. Some services require COD (cash on delivery). Supplies that are paid for in cash on delivery will affect the cash flow of the event. It would be advisable for the event manager to arrange credit facilities with the supplier. A relationship can be established with the supplier if it is based on honesty, fairness and frankness.

7.10.6 Tickets

Some events require tickets to be sold and the counterfoil or stub of the ticket must have the same number sequence as the ticket itself. These tickets and stubs need to be numbered for there to be a control system in place. Any complimentary tickets given out should be noted. There might also be unsold tickets of which there needs to be a record.

7.11 COMPUTERS

Personal computers have resulted in financial records, budgeting and reports being more accurate. There is a variety of software available from basic to complex systems. For a small event, it need not be a financial software package that is required, but merely software that would enable a spreadsheet to be drawn up. This spreadsheet could be made a bit more detailed so that it could generate the financial statements and even a cash flow. It is possible to generate a lot of 'what if' spreadsheets showing different situations that could occur.

Financial control in event enterprises starts with bookkeeping or keeping the books, while adhering to GAAP (generally accepted accounting principles). Bookkeeping may be processed manually or use may be made of a computer and its software. The advantage of computerisation is that it is time and cost saving.

7.12 FINANCIAL RISK MANAGEMENT

Risk management is the process of anticipating, preventing or minimising potential costs, losses or problems for the event, organisation, guests and partners. Risks occur in terms of finance, viability of the event, safety and health. Risks cannot be ignored as they occur naturally.

A risk can be thought of as a potential hazard or threat, such as bad weather, dangerous equipment, overcrowding, poorly trained staff. The potential losses associated with bad weather may be cancellation and the consequent financial loss; unhappy customers; potential of electrical shock from unprotected cables and the resulting lawsuits.

Risks associated with events may be of an internal or an external nature. Management may disagree on which risks are important and which are unimportant. It is advisable to get consensus or agreement on this.

Many events carry some degree of financial risk. Risk management deals with identifying and preventing losses, as well as with planning how to deal with such losses when they occur (Getz, 1997: 241–243).

7.13 BREAK EVEN

According to Paige (1977: 168–169), all event managers must be aware what level of turnover is necessary to cover all costs, and at what point a profit will start being made. This is called the *break-even point* and can be illustrated by means of a tabular statement or by presenting the information in the form of a graph. To construct a break-even chart or statement for an event, the following information is required:

- the number of customers per week – this can be calculated from the cashier's analysis sheet which shows the total number of covers as extracted from the customers' bills;
- the average spending power of the customer – this is calculated by dividing the total sales by the number of customers served;
- fixed costs – expenses such as rent, rates, insurance, depreciation, wages, salaries can be divided by 52 to calculate the average fixed costs per week;
- variable costs – this can be calculated as a percentage of the turnover figure.

EXAMPLE 7.13 *Candyfloss Girl: Break-even analysis*

A candyfloss stall serves between 60 and 100 customers per week. The average amount spent per customer is R2,50. Variable costs are estimated at 38% of turnover, while fixed costs amount to R99 per week, including the average labour cost per week.

- The turnover figure is calculated by multiplying the average spending power by the number of customers.
- The variable costs are calculated by finding 38% of the turnover figure.
- The fixed costs of R99 remain constant.

Number of customers	Total turnover	Variable costs	Fixed costs	Total costs	Net profit (+)	Net Loss (−)
60	R150,00	R57,00	R99,00	R156,00		R6
70	R175,00	R66,50	R99,00	R165,50	R9,50	
80	R200,00	R76,00	R99,00	R175,00	R25,00	
90	R225,00	R85,50	R99,00	R184,50	R40,50	
100	R250,00	R95,00	R99,00	R194,00	R56,00	

7.14 GENERAL GUIDELINES

Guidelines for managing money and dealing with banks and bankers:

- *Pay all bills on time.* Never pay bills before they are due unless there is a discount offered for early settlement. There is a disadvantage to paying early if no discount is earned – interest could be earned on your money.
- *Deposit excess cash into interest-bearing accounts.* Take every opportunity to place extra cash in institutions where interest rates are favourable. This is more advantageous than having the cash just sitting in the petty-cash tin.
- *It is rarely advisable to extend credit to clients.* Provide large organisations with a pro forma invoice before the date of the event, so that the necessary arrangements may be made regarding settlement of the account.
- *Do not issue cheques when it is possible that there are insufficient funds in your account.* Approach creditors if there could be a problem with settling their bills. Rather make another arrangement than issue a cheque that could be returned to drawer by your bankers.
- *Establish a personal trusting relationship with the banker.*
- *Reconcile all cheque accounts once a month, as soon as the bank statements have been received.* One of the worst things to do is to let these bank statements accumulate, and then try to reconcile many months.
- *Make deposits on a daily basis.* Money should be deposited as soon as it is received. Accounts should rather be settled by cheque or petty cash than by cash deposit money. This allows for a better audit trail (Hansen, 1995: 334–335).

Browse these Internet sites
http://leoisaac.com/sportman/evt/evt005a/
http://projectware.objectwareinc.com/art/event-management/
http://www.a2zshow.com/
http://www.blackbaud.com/solutions/acctg.asp
http://www.ungerboeck.com/Products/WhitePapers/prod_whitepapers.htm

QUESTIONS FOR SELF-EVALUATION

1 Explain how balance sheets may be used to better manage an event.
2 Management needs to be aware of the different risks associated with an event. Discuss in detail.
3 Explain how an income statement may be used to better manage an event.
4 What is the importance of budgeting?
5 Explain why the flow of incoming and outgoing cash needs to be monitored.
6 Why must revenue be maximised and costs minimised?

Note: Appendix 7.1 can be found on the Juta Academic web site: www.jutaacademic.co.za
Appendix 7.1 *Detailed example of a projected event budget*

CHAPTER 8

Event Sponsorship

Nancy Nuntsu and Nimish Shukla

AIM OF THE CHAPTER

The aim of this chapter is to discuss various issues relating to event sponsorship.

LEARNING OBJECTIVES

After having studied this chapter, you should be able to:

- define sponsorship and its characteristics;
- name the essential elements of sponsorship;
- distinguish between the different types of sponsors;
- identify the main objectives of sponsorship;
- know how to approach potential sponsors;
- describe what is to be included in a proposal and a sponsorship arrangement;
- list potential blocks to a successful sponsorship;
- understand the potential costs and benefits of sponsorship to event organisers and sponsors;
- analyse some of the reasons why companies provide sponsorships;
- draw up selection criteria to judge sponsorships;
- write a sponsorship proposal and a sponsorship report;
- know why you evaluate (what the dividends are), techniques you can use and what to do with the results.

8.1 INTRODUCTION

This chapter is to some extent based on Rossouw (2000: 185–207). A successful event cannot happen without adequate financial support (Watt, 1998: 44). Watt maintains that the biggest, and perhaps the commonest error in committing to an event is to do so without securing the necessary funding at a very early stage. Insufficient funding will have a negative impact on an event from start to finish: it may cause the event to be presented in a poor manner and quite possibly doom it to failure; indeed, it may have to be aborted at some stage, leaving bad feeling all around. Sponsorship is, therefore, critical when organising an event.

Just about every part of our lives is touched by sponsorship: sports events; performance venues; movie premières; concerts; art exhibits; videos; fairs and festivals; car, boat and home shows; individual athletes; trade shows; parades; special anniversaries; city celebrations; fireworks; museums; amusement parks; and cause-related fundraisers. The list goes on and on (Schmader & Jackson, 1997: 61).

Over R2 billion is now being spent by a whole host of companies in South Africa in the lucrative sponsorship market (Skinner, Von Essen & Mesham, 2001: 235)

8.2   WHAT IS SPONSORSHIP, THEN?

Polonsky and Speed (2001: 1361) maintain that although various definitions of sponsorship have been proposed, they all recognise that sponsorship is first and foremost a commercial activity. The definitions below all identify that in return for support, the sponsoring firm acquires the right to promote an association with the recipient.

Sponsorship refers to the use of financial or in-kind support of an on-business activity by a commercial organisation to achieve specified business goals – it has become the foundation of today's event industry (Schmader & Jackson, 1997: 61).

George (2002: 266) *defines sponsorship as the provision of financial or material support by a company for some independent activity (usually related to sport or art) not usually directly linked to the company's normal business, but support from which the sponsoring company would hope to benefit.*

Event sponsorship refers to supporting various types of event ranging from local little league teams, educational partnerships and health fairs, to college basketball teams, around-the-world sail boat races, professional auto racing, and even to the Olympic Games (Mack, 1999: 25). Many events would not exist without sponsorship support.

Sponsorship is a cash and/or in kind fee paid to a property (typically in sports, arts, entertainment or causes) in return for access to the exploitable commercial potential associated with that property (IEG, 1996: 1)

Sponsorship varies widely in a number of aspects including event type, rand expenditure, extent of professional planning and objectives, number and type of participants, media exposure and geographic context (Mack, 1999: 25).

To the event manager, a *sponsor* is any individual, agency or group that provides resources in exchange for specified benefits or performance. Sponsorship is quite different from money given to events out of charity or purely for public relations. The sponsor will view the exercise as an investment and expect something in return for their support – and sometimes it can be difficult to deliver. In effect, sponsorship should properly be regarded as a mutual marketing exercise.

Sponsorship is a cash and/or in-kind fee paid to a property (such as an event) in return for access to the exploitable commercial potential associated with that property (Getz, 1997: 216). Sponsorship, patronage and grants-in-aid can be crucial elements in achieving and developing marketing objectives, but it is important to understand the differences and the responsibilities that are associated with these various forms of support. Sponsorship is not simply an easy way to get somebody else to pay for or underwrite the costs of producing and executing the promotion or event (Richards, 1992: 40).

Patronage usually means financial support or the ability to use and associate the name of known, established and respected organisations, VIPs, nobility or royalty in promotional material including letterheads. In the case of financial support a patron would not expect to dictate other than in the broadest terms how the contribution should be spent (Richards, 1992: 40).

Grants are available from a wide range of sources for all manner of enterprises but it requires a significant amount of research time to identify those which might be applicable to a particular cause or event and then to follow it up.

For many other events, sponsorship spells the difference between quality, size, outreach and success. Sponsorship is seen by many as the panacea to all funding problems; but we all know that there is no such thing as a panacea, or cure-all, and this is certainly true where sponsorship is concerned.

Skinner *et al* (2001: 235) identify the following essential elements for sponsorship:
- A sponsor makes a contribution in cash or kind to an activity which is in some measure a leisure pursuit, either sport or within the broad definition of arts.
- The sponsored activity does not form part of the main commercial function of the sponsorship body.
- The sponsor expects a return in terms of publicity.

Sponsorship is essentially a business deal, which is intended to be to the advantage of both the sponsor and the sponsored. If successfully designed and carried out, with properly defined objectives, sponsorship arrangements can be of real benefit to the community in providing events and facilities which would otherwise not be affordable (Skinner *et al*, 2001: 236).

8.3 WHY IS SPONSORSHIP THE FASTEST GROWING MARKETING MEDIUM?

Changes in economy, demographic shifts and the fragmentation of media have all contributed to sponsorship's growth. Some of the main factors behind the increasing importance of sponsorship are:
- ***Decreasing efficiency of measured media***. Costs for traditional advertising continue to increase, while ratings and readership decline. On top of that is an even more basic problem: consumers are not paying attention to adverts. The bad news for measured media only promises to get worse, as the digital future

puts more power into consumer's hands. Sponsorship on the other hand, provides opportunities for embedded advertising; a fail-safe delivery system where messages are incorporated right into the action.

- *Changing social priorities*. As issues such as poverty, the environment and HIV/Aids loom larger, there is a growing realisation that the needs for society and the interests of business overlap. Sponsorship, which allies companies with community responsibility and improved quality of life, is precisely the kind of statement consumers will respond to.
- *Shifting personal values*. Conspicuous consumption has been replaced by cashing out. Shopping for shopping's sake has become déclassé. Tapping into today's consumers' elusive will to spend requires turning the buying experience into something larger than just accusation. Sponsorship provides companies this opportunity. It says to the potential customer: 'Buy this product not to indulge yourself, but to help make the world better place'.
- *Increasing need for two-ways communication*. In response to the fragmentation of the mass market and mass media, companies are looking for alternative methods to communicate sales messages and deepen their relationships with customers. Sponsorship, which is the most direct channel of communication, is tailor made for this environment. It reaches people in an environment that matches their lifestyle rather than intrudes upon it.
- *High consumer acceptance*. While traditional media is less effective than ever, much of the new media alienates consumers. On the other hand, public response to sponsorship has been overwhelmingly positive. Sponsorship is viewed favourably because it is seen as a form of advertising that gives something back; that benefits someone else in addition to the marketer. (*IEG Complete Guide to Sponsorship*, 1996: 5)

8.4 CHARACTERISTICS OF SPONSORSHIP

Skinner *et al* (2001: 236–237), mention the following characteristics of sponsorship:

- a supplement to, but not a substitute for, already operative direct advertising;
- a means of reaching certain specialised markets directly or indirectly associated with the activity;
- a novel promotional and marketing medium;
- a means of influencing public corporate image and of increasing awareness of product and corporate identity, logos, and symbols;
- an association for fostering relationships, through entertainment, with business associates and the press;
- a beneficial influence on staff relations and morale;
- a means of involving industry in its surrounding community for specific reasons, such as attracting staff and forestalling adverse criticism;

■ a vehicle for 'hard sell' promotions, for example personal appearances by sports people in their sporting gear selling the sponsor's products.

8.5 CORPORATE OBJECTIVES FOR SPONSORSHIP

Event sponsorship is a crucial component of many organisations' communications mix. Companies realise that in sponsorship, the interests of business and society overlap. Event sponsorship allows organisations to reach their target market with less clutter than other communications methods, exposes the product/service directly to the market and provides an excellent mechanism for the organisation to give back to the community by which it is supported (Mack, 1999: 25).

Polonsky and Speed (2001: 1364) suggest that sponsorship can be used to:
■ provide community involvement;
■ counter adverse publicity;
■ build goodwill among staff;
■ increase company, product and brand awareness;
■ reinforce or alter perceptions of product or brand;
■ identify a product or brand with a particular market segment.

8.6 TYPES OF SPONSOR

According to Schmader and Jackson (1997: 65–66), there are several different forms of sponsorship to be aware of before beginning the search. Sponsors may fall into more than one category, and these multiple categories provide opportunities for a variety of sponsors to participate in the event at varying levels of financial commitment.

Exclusive or title sponsor. Title sponsors pay a premium fee to have their name as part of the event itself (for example, the MTN Gladiators). Exclusive sponsors pay extra to close out potential sponsorships by competitive or similar sponsors/products (for example, Powerade the official sports drink of the Olympic Games). Title sponsors are usually exclusive.

Presenting sponsor. Sponsors at this level are usually the major sponsor of a predetermined portion of the entire event.

Co-sponsor. Co-sponsors, as implied, share event sponsorship with one or more other sponsors. There can be co-sponsors at all levels (for example, Coca-Cola), but title sponsorship is usually exclusive.

Media sponsor. Media sponsors usually provide a predetermined amount of advertising support for the event. They may also provide some cash support and publicity. *Note:* selection of a media sponsor may negate support from other similar media. Be sure the advertising provided is worth that. A new event, especially, should be careful about locking into only one medium, as support will be needed from all sources.

In-kind sponsor. Sponsorship on this level is provided through the donation of products or services. While cash does not trade hands, in-kind support helps to lower event expenses.

For some local events, the biggest in-kind supplier may become the principal sponsor and there may in fact be no transfer of money, but a supply of goods or services which are a large cost of the event. It is common for the local authority to be a major sponsor, helping through providing facilities, catering or organisational assistance free of charge (Watt, 1998: 56).

Equally, beverage companies, communication companies, transport companies, computer companies and confectionery suppliers can often become major sponsors without any money actually changing hands.

It is a very good idea to identify all the requirements for a project and then to draw up a corresponding list of possible suppliers to approach for in-kind support. Approach everyone and try to convince them of the benefits of supporting the event. Never leave any stone unturned or any potential source untapped. For many events, this type of sponsorship is all that is required, and in most cases it is undoubtedly easier to obtain than cash.

As an event organiser, normally running on a very limited budget, it is advisable to adopt the slogan, 'never pay for anything you can get for nothing'. In truth, you get nothing for nothing, but at least you can get something from a sponsor instead of paying for it in cash.

Whether the type of sponsorship is financial, media or in-kind support, the list of company benefits derived from it can range from publicity, to product sales, image enhancement, or even improved employee morale.

8.7　WHO TO APPROACH

Choosing who to approach can often be the most difficult, but perhaps the most crucial decision. Often you can totally misdirect the approach and so fail to find a sponsor for what is a very worthwhile competition, exhibition or conference. There is very little point in a mailshot to sponsors. A great deal of careful thinking and research must go into who may be interested in sponsoring a project and why it would be appropriate for their company. Meticulous market research is vital; know the potential companies, their policies and the key individuals to approach (Watt, 1998: 54).

Start by compiling a list of categories and companies that would most likely be interested in sponsoring your event. 'Most likely' can be established by responding 'yes' to all or most of the following questions about each candidate/category (Schmader & Jackson, 1997: 66):

- Does the prospective sponsor sell or operate in the event's host community?
- Does the prospective sponsor's history include past or present sponsorship? If so, what kind?
- Does the prospective sponsor advertise in the host community?
- Does the prospective sponsor maintain a high profile in the host community?
- Is the prospective sponsor's name mentioned with some frequency in the news media? (Is it mentioned for positive or negative reasons?)
- Does the prospective sponsor provide a commercial function that is customer- or client-driven?
- Is the prospective sponsor noted for the support of at least some altruistic or community betterment efforts?

Don't stop with the initial list. Explore new areas. Network with other people. Get introductions. Sometimes the obvious escapes those closest to it. Sources to network through may include (Schmader & Jackson, 1997: 66):
- past and current sponsors;
- associates and peers;
- group ownership counterparts;
- professional association members.

From the 'most likely' list, develop an accurate prospect or candidate list. Call and check names and titles of those who handle sponsorship for each company. Names and positions change frequently – proposals have been sent to dead people! Better to check now than be embarrassed later.

It is common knowledge that a number of companies are interested in sponsorship targeted at specific community groups. For example, it is likely that banks will be happy to sponsor events for young people (aged 15 to 21) since they will be keen to have their name associated with this age group; they are potentially lifelong customers – a very valuable commodity.

Many banks and financial institutions sponsor the arts, believing that it gives them a positive identity with influential business people. Local companies tend to support local events. Consumers in different income groups will support different events, and the events will therefore attract different sponsors. Companies have target markets. It is likely that soft drink companies will be keen to be associated with marathons or major sporting manifestations, for example the constant Coca-Cola and Pepsi battle to be involved in the world's major sporting events.

The key is to approach a relevant company with your proposition. It is unlikely that a company with a fast-car, modern and up-market image will sponsor a seminar on issues affecting elderly people. The problem is to keep very aware of companies and their current target markets. Both of them can change; nowadays some retired people have considerable spending power.

Sponsorship of almost anything can be a very cost-effective public relations exercise; often much cheaper than many other forms of marketing, especially advertising. This can be an effective argument to use on potential sponsors.

8.8 SEEKING SPONSORSHIP AND APPROACHING POTENTIAL SPONSORS

Sponsorship will not always be obtained cheaply. With many events and causes seeking sponsors, the cost of research, preparing proposals, administering contracts, and serving sponsors – including accountability reports – can be substantial. Larger events will increasingly have full-time staff working on sponsorship.

Sponsorship can be extremely difficult to find and a lot of work is required to service it. Remember that sponsorship must be seen as a mutually beneficial business arrangement between sponsor and sponsored, to achieve agreed objectives. Finding sponsors is never easy and relying on finding them is always dangerous. If it is to be more than a one-off event, there is also a danger of losing sponsors at some time; very few support events or promotions indefinitely. It is always worth remembering that they may withdraw at any time for any reason, for example, the fallout from a government ban on tobacco sponsorship in sport. Be aware of the implications of sponsorship; people have said, perhaps with some justification, that sponsors can be more trouble than they are worth. To obtain a demanding sponsor for a very small amount of money and for a small event could prove to be a waste of time for an event organiser. Significant time must be spent in servicing sponsorship and sometimes this time would be more useful to the event if it were devoted to other forms of support (Watt, 1998: 52).

It is very important when you are seeking sponsorship to look at the project from the sponsor's viewpoint. After all, if you can't convince yourself that the project is going to be worthwhile, and that a mutually beneficial package can be worked out, it's unlikely that you'll convince a potential sponsor. A sponsorship seeker has to believe in the event to convince anyone else of its worth (Schmader & Jackson, 1997: 66).

There are no magic numbers to guide managers in pricing their event's sponsorship products. Obviously, the more successful the event in meeting sponsor goals, the more that can and should be received in exchange. The balance between cash and in-kind fees must also be considered, along with the competitive situation.

As a rule of thumb, it is probably wise to value your products high, then negotiate downward. Offering a range of opportunities by price will help match sponsors' abilities with your own needs. Costs should be considered when setting the price of sponsorship products. The time of paid staff is a factor, plus office overheads and direct costs from preparing and distributing sponsorship proposals (Getz, 1997: 223).

8.8.1 Guidelines in approaching a potential sponsor

Before approaching a potential sponsor, use research to learn about their business. Put yourself in their shoes. Sponsors are hit with thousands of messages daily. One must therefore do everything possible to beat the odds, target their approach, and keep from getting lost in the clutter.

If possible, ask current or potential sponsors if you might spend some time with them to get a better handle on their problems or needs. Think about how you can help fulfil their corporate goals in terms of seven basic objectives (Schmader & Jackson, 1997: 67):

- image enhancement;
- driving sales;
- positive publicity;
- differentiating product from competitors;
- good corporate citizen;
- community economic development;
- customer/VIP relations.

Look at what they currently do and where they want to go, and think of how to translate that into what there is to sell. Consider their perspective and ask, 'How will this benefit me?'

Based upon research, ask yourself, 'What does this company need?' Now, what programme or benefits can be created to meet their needs by way of the event? A targeted and personalised approach to any potential sponsor indicates that homework has been done. This increases the likelihood of being given serious consideration (Schmader & Jackson, 1997: 67).

To consider the event from a sponsor's viewpoint, ask yourself these questions (Watt, 1998: 53–54):

- Does the event match their image?
- How much media exposure will they get?
- How much advertising can they get in and around the event?
- Can the company name be incorporated in the title of the event?
- Will there be a possibility of corporate hospitality?
- Will the sponsor meet famous people?
- Are there other promotional opportunities?
- Will the name be synonymous with the event?
- Does the event match up to their target audience?
- Is it value for money?

8.8.2 Other guidelines

8.8.2.1 Be creative

A bright, new idea is much more likely to persuade someone to spend their money, than a hackneyed, old project that has been staged often by many people in the past. An approach to a new company is also worthwhile, as the novelty may interest them. There is a definite line that separates trendsetters and trend followers, and that line is *creativity*. A creative person looks at the same thing as everyone else and thinks something different. This ability is especially valuable in the special events industry. Use creativity to provide something unique. Most events tend to be annual 'reproductions' rather than annual productions. A truly unique event will draw sponsors out of the woodwork (Schmader & Jackson, 1997: 62).

8.8.2.2 Expand the creative horizon

Invite outside sources in for brainstorming sessions. Representatives from sponsor, patron and media groups (supporters and critics) may offer many worthwhile suggestions; and don't ignore the ideas and talents of in-house staff. There is no shortage of ideas, but these ideas need to be used in order to make a difference. In many cases, something as simple as a new paint job, different graphics, improved maintenance, or better costumes can make a world of difference to an event.

8.8.2.3 Put in the marketing effort

Ensure that the product and price are correct and that everyone knows about the quality of the event. If the project is widely known, there is much more chance of attracting interest from potential sponsors. It is important to promote the organisation's and/or the agency's image and good practice. Lifestyle marketing stresses the linking of business to the attitudes and preferred lifestyles of customers. Events present a particularly effective way to reach people while at leisure, engaging in their preferred activities with friends and family, and in their home community or leisure environment (Getz, 1997: 216).

Relationship marketing links companies with communities or customers through causes of mutual interest. Companies and other sponsors working with events can position themselves as being proponents of popular causes. People in general think more positively of sponsors associated with causes and popular events (Getz, 1997: 216).

8.8.2.4 Clearly define the type of market

Sponsors like to know the types of market that may be created. If the participants are affluent middle-aged people, then credit card companies might be quite keen to work with the event organisers (Watt, 1998: 53).

8.8.2.5 Look at the strengths of the event and, rather than be satisfied, make them stronger

Survey the audience or look to ticket sales and other predictors of satisfaction. Once strengths have been identified, build on them. Consider adding more of the cements that are popular. Findings may warrant expanding (or reducing) the length of run. Whatever increases your audience attendance and satisfaction makes the event more valuable to potential sponsors. Similarly, discard or replace weaknesses once they have become apparent (Schmader & Jackson, 1997: 62).

8.8.2.6 Consider changing the nature of your activity, event or promotion

Adapt the event to suit a sponsor's idea rather than just repeating your old unsuccessful methods, or persisting with something that may not specifically suit their desires. The project and the organisers should be flexible enough to adapt to a reasonable sponsor's requirements (Watt, 1998: 53).

8.8.2.7 Analyse the competition and similar events in other locations

Note what competitors are doing that might add to your event. Change for the sake of change is not good, but change to keep an event fresh and growing is essential (Schmader & Jackson, 1997: 62). Competitors are a tremendous source of information. Ask for proposals, materials, and fee structures. Know and be a slave to the competition. Take their best ideas and make them better. (*Improve on ideas, don't just steal them.*) If there is no direct competition, research similar events in other cities.

8.8.2.8 Try to access your sponsors through local business groups

Approach sponsors through local business groups, as well as through the media and in person. These groups can provide ideas as well as contacts. Assess respective images: Check that any images are compatible and try to work with groups where there is an obvious tie-up or correspondence. Sponsors need to be compatible with the event and its participants. Approach unlikely targets: there may be somebody who has never been approached before and who would like to sponsor an event. Perhaps yours can provide the ideal opportunity. Until recently nobody had ever thought of legal practices advertising and sponsoring events, but now it has become quite common (Watt, 1998: 54).

Are your prospective sponsors experienced or inexperienced when it comes to event marketing? This will affect your approach. Does the person you're approaching have the authority to make decisions? To answer this question, simply ask when making the appointment. Don't let a subordinate present your plan to a superior if possible. You are your own best salesperson.

8.8.2.9 Do the necessary research

The 'fit' between events and sponsors is an important consideration. The best sponsors are not just those that provide the most resources but those that ensure harmony, or a close fit, between the goals, images and programmes of each (Getz, 1997: 220).

Researching and targeting sponsors is probably the most overlooked and undervalued step in the sponsorship solicitation process. While it requires some up-front time, the rewards down the road include higher quality sponsorships and fewer rejections. Research and targeting mean carefully sighted, predetermined rifle shots as opposed to the scattergun approach ('Just mail out as many sponsorship proposals and computerised cover letters as you can, and you're bound to get some sponsors') (Schmader & Jackson, 1997: 65).

The purpose of research is to assimilate useful information, regarding the potential sponsor(s) or sponsor category, that can then be incorporated into a targeted sales strategy that best meets the sponsor's needs. The closer the event skews to the sponsor's positioning, the easier the sale.

Examine the markets in which companies seem to be operating and assess whether their target age group is the same as yours. Doing detailed research using newspapers and other media, and in the local library, will pay dividends in the long run. You will come over as a knowledgeable sponsorship seeker and make a good impact on potential sponsors (Watt, 1998: 54).

8.8.2.10 Check existing sponsors

Find out what active companies are already sponsoring; this will indicate the fields that interest them. Banks often look for young secondary school pupils on the verge of opening their first account, potential customers reputedly for life. But this does not mean that companies will ignore other areas; if they already sponsor one sort of event, they may still be interested in a different sort (Watt, 1998: 54). Try to start with media support: If two or three papers, local or national, or perhaps a radio station will work with organisers and give some constructive plugs at an early stage, then sponsorship may be more easily attracted. The support of the media will be crucial to both the organiser and the sponsor throughout the project; getting their support and enthusiasm early on will be very advantageous (Watt, 1998: 54).

8.8.2.11 Next, determine what the impact area is

This refers to the media reach from which the event draws. To determine if the event is international (for example, the Olympics); national (for example, the South African championships); regional (for example, the Comrades Marathon); or local (for example, a marathon in your town) (Schmader & Jackson, 1997: 63).

8.8.2.12 Be honest when determining the impact area

There is a new trend in sponsorship today to market more on a regional or targeted local level, eliminating the pressure to be nationally-oriented and increasing the value of smaller, quality events (Schmader & Jackson, 1997: 63).

Skinner *et al* (2001: 237) identify ten elements which form the framework on which a company can build a systematic approach. They are the following:

1. 'the sponsoring company's aims and objectives;
2. the direct and indirect costs of the sponsorship;
3. the type and character of the sponsorship and its arrangements;
4. the structure, both nationally and provincially, of the administrative controlling body;
5. the participants in the sponsorship;
6. the officials in charge of the sponsored event;
7. the venue controllers, where the sponsored event is staged;
8. the degree of interest by the media in the sponsored event;
9. the audience attracted by the sponsored event, both live and through the media;
10. the government's involvement.'

Each of these elements should be viewed on its own and collectively in relation to the form and stature of the event. The sponsor must also appreciate that any change occurring in one element will cause a reaction in one or more of the others.

8.9 PRACTICAL SPONSORSHIP

Some practical issues can help the whole process and ensure a good corporate image for both parties, leading to a successful sponsorship deal. Not all of them apply on every occasion, but here are some ideas that are worth considering (Watt, 1998: 58–59):

1. An accurate budget breakdown must be given to potential sponsors, so that they are aware of what their contribution means.
2. Potential sponsors should be invited to hospitality at current events, thereby selling future events.
3. The sponsorship price should not be pitched too high or too low.
4. The correct organisations, people and agencies must be targeted; image and resources must be appropriate.
5. The chances of success will be maximised by using all the available market information.
6. All contacts, including social contacts, must be followed for a lead to possible sponsors.
7. A professional approach must be adopted at all times.

8. The price must be right and the package well prepared.
9. The initial approach may be in writing, but it must be followed up quickly with personal contact.
10. Sponsors must be kept informed at all times, even about failures.
11. Honesty at all times is crucial to developing a partnership.
12. Care for your sponsors; attend to all their (reasonable) requirements as soon as they are identified.
13. Good advance planning will help fit into potential sponsors' budgeting plans.
14. Hard work will maximise your sponsor's return.
15. Be creative, flexible and innovative in sponsorship delivery ideas.
16. Be aware of developments in the business world and possible 'opponents' in seeking sponsorship.
17. Joint debriefing and appraisal sessions are essential.

To attract sponsorship the event must be right for the sponsor. A poor event will be potentially disastrous for everyone involved. The organiser's technical skills and knowledge must be used to get the event right in planning and delivery, so making the sponsor's support justified.

In summary, sponsorship with all the allied hard work can be very worthwhile. Both parties must work to make it effective and at no time must the event organisers promise what they cannot deliver. On the other hand, there is a tendency among event organisers to undersell their product, especially when they are seeking support from sponsors or agencies like tourist authorities or enterprise councils. Remember that events can be a phenomenal boost to an area. The returns can be enormous to the local economy. The Comrades Marathon, for example, has a profound effect on the local area in terms of morale, financial return, tourism and commercial return.

Don't be afraid to quote successful examples, but avoid any grandiose or unrealistic claims for your event. If you have something to sell, sell it hard then deliver the goods. A possible sequence could be the following (Watt, 1998: 58):
■ prepare the approach;
■ explore the opportunities;
■ select the businesses;
■ time the approach;
■ present the package;
■ never give up;
■ follow it up;
■ audit the organisation.

It is also essential to conclude the sponsorship arrangement with a comprehensive report on the event, detailing the successes of the deal. Prepared for the sponsor and the event management team, it should contain the following items.

- *Marketing success*. Based on meaningful research during and after the event, it will be necessary to state what impact the project has had on the image of the sponsor and what it has done for them in other ways, for example commercial benefit, corporate hospitality and market penetration. This needs to be based on concrete facts and figures, not some perceived or imaginary benefits.
- *Press coverage*. Copies of all appropriate cuttings, photographs or even audiotapes from radio should be part of the report, giving a clear indication of the level of publicity the sponsor gained.
- *Promotional materials*. Copies of all posters, tickets, brochures or other promotional items should be part of the report, to indicate the image and exposure the sponsor gained.
- *Event analysis*. Comprehensive and clear facts and figures, as well as stated opinions of key individuals, should be presented in any final report, to give the sponsor an accurate indication of information such as attendance figures and performance levels.
- *Gratitude*. A clear statement of thanks should explain all the sponsor has done and the crucial nature of their support. It is best when it comes from participants and spectators as well as organisers.
- *The future*. Proposals for future relationships should accompany the conclusion and thanks. Obviously, everybody hopes that the sponsorship will continue.

George (2002: 268) writes that a report should be sent to prospective sponsors, consisting of the following:
- details of the sponsored event
- evidence of its reputability
- actual or projected audiences (including demographics)
- expected media coverage
- facilities offered to top sponsors, e.g. catering, marquee, seating.

Furthermore, according to George, sponsors need to know exactly what they will get for their expenses and agreements should be drawn up. Agreements generally include:
- entertainment and publicity facilities
- sales outlets at the event
- whether the sponsorship is exclusive or will be shared with other sponsors
- the duration of the agreement (George, 2002: 268).

Giving such professional feedback will be a key factor in retaining a sponsor, or even attracting a new one. Any sponsor will be interested to see how past events have been achieved and reported.

8.10 POTENTIAL RISKS AND BENEFITS

8.10.1 Potential risks

There are potential risks, not the least of which is the possibility that organisers' goals get 'displaced' by those of major sponsors, or that a commercial orientation will alter the event in subtle but profound ways. Event managers should systematically audit their organisation and event(s) to identify and value platforms and potential benefits to offer, then target them to either general types of sponsors or to specific companies. It will help to rank your platforms and 'offers' in order of value to your key targets. In addition, event managers must have a sponsorship plan, know exactly what is needed and what can be exchanged for sponsorship, and be skilled in managing the process.

Both parties could face image problems arising from sponsorship, either through unforeseen incidents or a poor fit. Event failure, such as poor attendance or poor quality, might reflect badly on the sponsor's image. Media criticism or neglect is a risk to both parties. Conflict over policy, programme, and operations can occur, and the unexpected termination of a partnership can hurt.

8.10.2 Potential sponsorship benefits for the event

Assuming that you have contacted a likely company, the next step is to prepare an attractive, realistic and deliverable package of benefits. In return for their support, the sponsoring agency must be assured of some payback. It is also beneficial to approach sponsors at the concept stage, giving them an opportunity to make suggestions instead of presenting something cut and dried. Sponsors like their say in the detail of what is delivered, so early consultation is helpful. The detail and the presentation of this pack are crucial, and only if it matches up to the expectations of the audience will you have any chance of success. It is equally essential that the package is well thought out and is genuinely achievable. If an offer is an overtly unrealistic package, the sponsor will notice and will be frightened off right away.

Sponsorship can provide an event with a number of potential benefits. Whether the type of sponsorship is financial, media, or in-kind (Mack, 1999: 26), the range of benefits derived from it can range from publicity to product sales, image enhancement, or even improved employee morale (1999: 25). George (2002: 267) states that sponsorship benefits include publicity, image boosting, sales and merchandising opportunities. Event sponsorship, according to Rosenberg, Michael, Woods and Kimberly (1995: 13), when carefully planned can enhance a company's presence in the marketplace and add value to its overall image. According to Getz (1997: 218), sponsorship:

- generates necessary revenue for administration and operations;
- increases marketing scope and reach through use of collateral promotions by the sponsor;

- can result in professional and human resource gains, through use of the sponsor's staff and expertise;
- enlarges the event's constituencies (that is, supporters and contracts);
- can enhance the image of the event through association with a positive corporate image.

8.10.3 Potential benefits for sponsors

Coughlan and Mules (2001: 1–9) state that a significant proportion of the literature on sponsorship and many event management texts (Getz, 1997: 218) place emphasis on the means to achieve success in attracting sponsors to an event. This literature is clearly aimed at event organisers rather than the sponsors. The question of how sponsorship helps the sponsoring organisation further its own aims has not received a lot of attention. Companies are looking for various commercial outcomes from their sponsorship. Coughlan and Mules (2001: 1–9) state that sponsors seek image enhancement, market positioning and 'a good marketing return for their dollar'. Arthur, Scott, Woods and Booker in Coughlan and Mules (2001: 1–9) provide a more comprehensive list:

- access to a particular market segment, lifestyle group
- association with large, successful events
- association with health and fitness
- development of sales opportunities such as exclusivity at venues
- relationship building with key customers
- prestige
- development of new markets.

Getz (1997: 218) lists the following benefits that a sponsor may hope to achieve. Heightened visibility (through various media):

- enhancement of the image of the corporation or product through association with a popular event;
- direct safe outlets at the event;
- relationships with customers and target segments;
- enhanced awareness of the corporation and its products/services;
- opportunities for entertaining the sponsor's business associates, staff, VIPs, etc;
- involvement of staff in worthwhile events (team building, morale boosting);
- profitable linkages with other sponsors, suppliers, government officials, institutions, etc;
- differentiation of the company or product from competitors;
- demonstration of a commitment to a particular market niche, such as an ethnic group or gay consumers;
- enhancement of the company's reputation for being community-oriented or socially responsible;

- highlighting product benefits or otherwise reinforcing the public's perception of a product;
- testing new products through sampling;
- providing executive and key clients with entertainment or the opportunity to meet celebrities at the festival;
- providing opportunities for firm-to-firm marketing through festival operations.

8.10.4 Potential benefits to community

Event sponsorship may offer benefits to the communities. Today, as communities increasingly depend upon business organisations' assistance, mutually beneficial partnerships may enhance the quality of the communities as well as the firms involved. Partnerships between corporates and communities are more crucial when corporate support is required for sponsorship of major events that will benefit communities (Mack, 1999: 29). This is illustrated in the following two case studies.

Case study 8.1: The Port Festival

The annual Port Festival co-sponsored by the Ports Authority of South Africa held in East London benefits the local communities in various ways. 'We are still going to sit down and discuss it further but we are happy that we have managed to exceed our fundraising target,' says festival chairman Terry Taylor. About 15 charity organisations benefited from the proceeds of the Port Festival held in March 2004. Also the local entrepreneurs had an opportunity to display and sell their products directly to the public (*Daily Dispatch*, 2004: 17).

Case study 8.2: Arts Carnival Umbhiyozo

The second Arts Carnival Umbhiyozo funded by the Department of Arts Culture Science and Technology held in Kei Mouth and Morgan Bay in the Eastern Cape was able to bridge cultural diversity among its communities. The ideology behind the carnival is freedom of expression be it cultural, religious or supernatural, but, most importantly, humanity and our co-existence. The local schools benefited the most as they have received enormous exposure to arts. 'We as a community have shown how passionate we are about our area, and that we can work together in the spirit of ubuntu,' said Shreez Gallant, carnival production manager (*Daily Dispatch*, Indabazethu, 2004: 3).

8.11 POTENTIAL BARRIERS TO SUCCESSFUL SPONSORSHIP

A major concern of event marketers is the ambush – competitors attempting to grab media attention or other benefits away from an official sponsor. Organisers will increasingly be asked to provide a defence against ambush marketing. The Olympics have been particularly hard hit by ambushers and have become aggressive in fighting them off. This is a high priority because of the enormous fees paid by the 'top' global sponsors (Getz, 1997: 219).

Case study 8.3: ICC's 'Deep Concern' with Samsung ambush marketing

The ICC today expressed its deep concern that it has been forced to disturb the ICC Cricket World Cup preparations of the Indian team because of the ambush marketing activities carried out by electronics company Samsung.

ICC Chief Executive Malcolm Speed said that there is clearly documented evidence that Samsung is deliberately and blatantly flouting the contractual agreements that exist between IDI and the BCCI. 'This is a premeditated campaign designed to infringe and devalue the rights secured by IDI's commercial partners. It cannot and will not be tolerated,' he said.

Advertising campaigns featuring images of Indian players sponsored by Samsung are appearing in India and infringements have also been identified in South Africa. IDI lawyers delivered letters to the Indian management and players on 13 February 2003, in an attempt to secure their support in curtailing Samsung's activities. Earlier today, Indian team management advised the ICC that the Indian players were unaware of Samsung's actions and that they would provide further written undertakings to the ICC about stopping the ambush marketing activity.

If no resolution is reached immediately, the matter is likely to be referred to the ICC Technical Committee for further action. *(Source: International Cricket Council, 2002: Internet)*

Many things can upset a sponsor relationship, but it is important that the organisers don't cause them and that they look at all the issues carefully to ensure that there are no unnecessary blocks on their part. Here are a few items which can cause problems if not handled properly (Watt, 1998: 58–59):

■ *No clearly stated goals.* If there is a lack of clarity and purpose for the event, it will be harder to attract sponsors.

■ *Lack of strategic approach.* If there is no clearly thought-out strategy for attracting sponsors, any work will be ad hoc and probably less successful.

■ *Are the needs satisfied?* In providing a service, it is important to look at satisfying somebody's needs, and if we want sponsorship, we have to look at satisfying the sponsor's needs. If they are not going to be satisfied, they are not likely to support us in the venture.

■ *Publicity.* Throughout the project, publicity needs to be interesting and the right measures need to be taken to obtain it; publicity is the lifeblood of sponsorship.

■ *Reputation.* The combined reputation of the sponsor and organiser must be credible and support a worthwhile project. If either has a reputation that somehow endangers the project, then perhaps no partnership should be entered into.

- *Targeting.* The necessary steps must be taken to ensure that the event audience is clearly identified and potential sponsors are properly targeted. Potential sponsors will expect to receive a clear proposal.
- *Effort.* A significant effort must be put in to gain sponsorship and thereafter to service it. If staff are not willing to put in the time and effort, the search for sponsorship is futile.
- *Staff time.* It is going to take a significant amount of time to find sponsorship and ultimately service it. This needs to be worthwhile and efficient. If not, perhaps other ways of raising the money can be found, methods requiring lower long-term effort.
- *Expertise.* The organisation must have enough expertise to find the sponsorship, deliver the goods and service the sponsorship throughout the project – and indeed the expertise to lay down the proposal for sponsors in advance. A shortage of expertise will be damaging, if not fatal, although expertise can sometimes be bought in.

Despite this apparently negative final list, there is a significant and growing amount of money available for the right events, properly presented.

8.12 FUNDRAISING

Many projects, especially smaller ones, will require some type of fundraising. This can take many forms but, chosen carefully, it can produce quite significant amounts; novel ideas are especially successful. Here are some suggestions (Watt, 1998: 52):

- sponsored runs, swims, cycles;
- dances, discos;
- marathon swims, silences, digs;
- lotteries, raffles;
- car washes;
- gambling evenings, for example race nights and casino nights.

8.12.1 Creating sponsorship platforms

Events must be viewed and managed as marketable products in order to succeed at sponsorship. To the extent that it does not detract from meeting the organisation's mandate and goals, the management should maximise sales by increasing potential benefits to sponsors. This principle also covers events created solely as sponsorship vehicles, for-profit events that won't be profitable without major sponsors, and events that can only grow if they offer the right sponsorship opportunities (Getz, 1997: 221).

Many events use a simple-to-develop hierarchical approach to sponsorship, each with fees and benefits differentiated (for example title sponsor, gold sponsor, silver and bronze).

Many potential sponsors would rather purchase tangible products. For them the following system might work better (Getz, 1997: 223).

- Title sponsor (only one, cost negotiable). Benefits:
- Seven 'presenting sponsors' for programme elements (cost for each to be uniform). Benefits:
- Five product exclusivity sponsors. Benefits:
- Three exclusive media sponsors. Benefits:
- Donors: any number. Benefits:

Potential sponsors will know how many sponsors there are in each major category, at what cost, and with what benefits.

8.13 SPONSORSHIP PROPOSAL

Any proposal should be as bright and eye-catching as possible; here are some items to include (Watt, 1998: 55):

- market research;
- benefits on offer;
- background of the event and the organisers;
- marketing opportunities;
- level of involvement requested.

An appointment should ideally be arranged with the key person in the organisation of the potential sponsor. This should be arranged by telephone, followed up by written confirmation and delivery of the sponsorship package several days before the meeting, giving them an opportunity to study the document. Sometimes a meeting may be impossible, so the project director may be totally reliant on a letter or the package eliciting an answer from the potential sponsor (Watt, 1998: 55).

It is still advisable to set deadlines and say that they will be contacted by phone on a set date to assess their reaction to the package, to discuss details and to consider possible changes to make the proposal more suitable. It is vital to keep your promises about letters, meetings and phone calls; otherwise the proposal will end up in the bin. Getting to the stage of a meeting means there is a 70% chance of finalising a deal, as long as there is a sound case and it is presented with commitment and enthusiasm.

8.13.1 Sponsorship proposal format

Executive summary

The executive summary can be sent with the full proposal or on its own with a covering letter. The summary should be a maximum of two pages in length and should represent a condensed proposal. It should include important aspects such as Introduction, Opportunities/Benefits, Investment, and Deadline of the sponsorship.

Situation appraisal

This covers a brief explanation of why the event exists, using 'subliminal ties' to the interests, goals and objectives of the potential sponsor – that is, quotes and terminology taken from their annual report.

Event background and track record

This includes a brief history of the event, along with information about its successful involvement with similar sponsors.

Proposal and benefits

This is what the event is proposing the sponsor provide and what the benefits will be in return.

Investment

This is just another word for 'cost', but it sounds much better. This section will detail the company's expenditures for the project.

Deadline for decision

The date for the company's final response should be stated explicitly herein.

Addenda

Support materials, press clippings that include the names of sponsors, letters of recommendation, and other indications of success can be included in this section. (Schmader & Jackson, 1997: 85)

8.13.2 Agreement or contract

It is essential that a sponsorship agreement, short or long, be laid out in writing and signed by both parties, detailing exactly what is to be given in sponsorship and exactly what is expected in return. It may also be necessary to include penalties if either party fails to reach the specified levels indicated in the contract or agreement. This may seem a little draconian, but it is based on experience and is certainly the best way to proceed; it solves any problem, either from the sponsor trying to withdraw at the last minute or looking later for benefits which were never previously requested. Such disputes can lead to dissatisfaction. It is always sensible to have an agreement to refer back to, in order to clarify any possible sources of disagreement before or during the event (Watt, 1998: 56). With many sponsors, large amounts of money, and more impersonal relationships between events and corporations, most events and sponsors will prefer a contract specifying:

- purpose: term of the contract;
- schedule of actions and payments by both parties;

- definitions or explanations of actions required from both parties;
- specification and clarification of rights, such as whether or not the sponsor obtains exclusivity;
- liability (who is responsible, insurance requirements);
- use of trademarks, logos, patented processes – if applicable, ownership of broadcast rights;
- specification of retained rights (the event does not give up any permanent rights to its programme, broadcast rights, etc);
- future options (for example, for renewal);
- termination and amendment procedures;
- assignments and subcontracting rights;
- what is *not* covered;
- compliance with appropriate laws;
- penalties for nonfulfilment;
- authority of the signatories.

8.13.3 Do everything you can

If you are lucky enough to get a sponsor, especially a good, firm but fair one, then work hard to keep them. Perhaps this is the area in which most organisers, particularly voluntary ones, fall down. They fail to recognise the commercial agreement they have entered into and the importance of carrying out their side of it and, if possible, bettering it. They feel they can take the money and not produce the goods. This is not the case, and a sponsor will always expect the details of the promised package to materialise. If there is any doubt about what is to be done, it should be resolved in the sponsor's favour (Watt, 1998: 56).

It is a good idea to sign a sponsor on a two-year or three-year agreement; often they will want at least a trial year to see whether they will commit themselves further. It is well worthwhile to keep that sponsor happy (assuming you are happy with them) because this will save a massive amount of work in seeking a new sponsor for your next event. Remember, always deliver what you said you would deliver. Be accountable.

As Getz (1997: 226) advises:
- give more than was promised;
- make sponsors look good at all times;
- communicate regularly;
- make it easy for them to sign up, get most out of the event, enjoy themselves, and re-enlist.

8.14 MAKING SPONSORSHIP WORK

As an event organiser it will often be hard to make the sponsorship deal work as effectively as it could. Everyone must make every effort to do so, but it is often useful to delegate people just to ease the relationship and become the internal PR or sponsor liaison person.

It is also very important to emphasise to the sponsor from the beginning that for their organisation to get the very best out of the sponsorship, they should be looking to invest in other ways in the deal. It is often said that the sponsor putting R5 000 into an event should set aside another R5 000 to maximise their PR benefit from the event. For example, they could benefit from related advertising, corporate hospitality, logo identity, promotional items such as T-shirts, and additional decorating touches for the event venue to highlight their involvement. All these additional inputs will maximise the sponsorship benefits for the company involved. A little innovative thinking in this area can be enormously helpful (Watt, 1998: 57).

McCarville, Flood and Froats (1998: 5) reported on the issue of return on investment by monitoring reaction to a sponsor's promotional efforts in an experimental setting. In the context offered by a hypothetical non-profit-making sporting event, participants were randomly assigned to groups who received (*a*) basic information about the sponsor, (*b*) discount coupons offered by the sponsor, and (*c*) trial samples of the sponsor's products (pizza). Those who received the product trial responded most positively to the sponsorship message. They rated the sponsor's product within the next month. Conversely, promotions that presented only logos, sponsor's telephone numbers, slogans or coupons generally failed to alter perceptions of the sponsor's product.

In a mail survey of Canadian corporations with advertising budgets in excess of CAD$50 000 they were asked about the length and nature of their sport sponsorship involvements, the criteria used to select events, post-event evaluation methods, and reasons for discontinuing past sponsorships (Copeland & Frisby, 1996: 32). The results revealed that these companies valued sport sponsorship as an important form of marketing communication but supplemented sponsorship initiatives with a variety of other communication measures. None viewed sponsorship as a philanthropic exercise. Respondents repeatedly noted the importance of return on investment in making sponsorship decisions. They valued exclusivity, public awareness and positive image above other criteria when selecting sponsorship opportunities. Most of the sponsors had discontinued a sponsorship relationship in the past. Furthermore, only one-third of the sponsors felt that the benefits exchanged with sport organisers were fair and equitable.

Having been successfully awarded a sponsorship, the first action is to announce it. How you do this depends on how important the event will appear to the press, but part of your job is to make it have importance. The most common, simple and straightforward method is to issue a press release. The aim of the announcement is to alert the press about your event. Every press release should answer the questions: Who? What? Why? Where? When? And How? And it should answer them as early as possible.

8.15 EXAMPLE OF SPONSORSHIP APPLICATION FORM

Organisations such as Eskom and the National Ports Authority (NPA) provide services to a large community that has a wide range of interests. Sponsors such as these usually look at various options before investing in a sponsorship opportunity. A sponsorship application form, such as the one provided in figure 8.1, would be typically used to assess a potential sponsorship opportunity.

Company XYZ	
Sponsorship & Event Programme	
Application Form	
Name of organisation:	
Sponsorship contact name:	
Position:	
Contact number:	
Name of event/organisation/programme seeking sponsorship:	
Dates of event/programme:	
1. Sponsorship Details *if insufficient space an additional page may be attached*	
Background on the project/event you wish Company XYZ to support Please provide information as to how long the event is being held for, dates and timings of the event.	
Background information on your organisation Please include information on your mission/vision statement, long-term goals of your organisation	
Your audience *Size of audience, demographic information, membership information*	
Contribution sought from Company XYZ *Amount required in cash; product requirements, payment details*	

2. **Please indicate in the table below** how Company XYZ's contribution will be acknowledged.	
TYPE OF ACKNOWLEDGEMENT	**DETAILS OF ACKNOWLEDGEMENT**
Naming Right Opportunities *Ownership, exclusive*	
Signage *Acknowledging Company XYZ; Company XYZ signage; around venue; indoors/outdoors, banners*	
Additional marketing & promotional tie-ins	
Opportunities for Company XYZ to promote its programmes	
Opportunities to meet with business leaders/colleagues	
Ticketing *Number of complimentary tickets, passes, invitations for Company XYZ.*	
Opportunities for Company XYZ to distribute promotional and educational material	
Media marketing exposure: how the event will be promoted; acknowledgement of Company XYZ received in advertising, etc.	
Other	

3. **Has Company XYZ supported the event/organisation in the past**

☐ Yes ☐ No

(a) **Please indicate in the table below** the past level of support provided by Company XYZ.

TYPE OF SUPPORT	
(Please tick relevant box)	**DETAILS OF SUPPORT**
☐ Financial support ☐ In-kind support, e.g. water bottles ☐ Other	

FIGURE 8.1 SAMPLE *Sponsorship Application Form (adapted from SRS Consulting, 2001: Internet)*

8.16 EVALUATION AND SELECTION CRITERIA

Companies will view sponsorship in a number of ways, including the following:

- Can the company afford to fulfil the obligation? The sponsorship fee is just the starting point. Count on doubling it to provide an adequate total event budget.
- Is the event compatible with the company's values and mission statement?
- Does the event reach the company's target audience?
- Is there enough time before the event to maximise the company's use of sponsorship?
- Are the organisers of the event experienced and professional?
- Is the event newsworthy enough to provide the company with opportunities for publicity?
- Will the event be televised?
- Will the sales force support the event and use it to increase sales?
- Does the event give the company the chance to develop new contacts and create new business opportunities?
- Can the company commit to this event on a long-term basis?
- Is there an opportunity for employee involvement? Corporate sponsorships can promote employee goodwill and teamwork. Employee involvement can also contribute to the success of the event.
- Is the event compatible with the identity of the company's products?
- Is it possible to reduce the cash outlay for the company and enhance the marketing appeal of the event by trading off products and in-kind services?
- Will management support the event? If the answer is 'yes' to all the previous questions, the likelihood of management support of the sponsorship is fairly high. (Skinner *et al*, 2001: 238)

8.17 PREPARING A SPONSORSHIP CONTRACT

The essence of sponsorship documentation is agreement. Try to avoid using the word 'contract' or 'contracting' because by using such terminology, insecurity can be inferred and a written agreement with formal endorsements may be requested. The writing or 'documentation' of agreement is merely the visible, outward statement of the parties' underlying agreement. In essence, the initial basis of agreement is the intent and understanding (whether written or not) of the parties. There are three basic types of sponsorship documentation one can choose from:

- *The confirmation letter*. This is not, in and of itself a contract. Without the signature and written commitment of both parties it is merely one party's statement of what oral contract involves.
- *Oral agreement*. This is valid particularly where one party has acted to its detriment, or relied on the word or oral promise of another. The confirming letter (when not disavowed in timely fashion) provides evidence of the parties intent and is often relied upon in cases of dispute.

- **The formal contract.**: Usually more detailed and more intimidating, is no more enforceable than the letter agreement. It does, however, elevate the parties to a higher level of attention.

Sponsorships are often the heart of the events and they should be pursued and documented carefully. (IFEA Guide, 1997b: 49)

8.18 SPONSORSHIP EVALUATION

According to Cameron (2002: Internet), as a sponsor it is necessary to measure the impact of a commercial sponsorship investment. After all, how many of us believe that sponsorship is sufficiently tangible to be measured at all? If we do not provide fair and objective estimates of the effects of sponsorship, there may be less sponsorship funds and perhaps those funds will be allocated to the marketing areas that can demonstrate effectiveness.

According to *Sportsmatch* (2004: Internet), many events are completed without any attempt to evaluate how well they did because it is thought of as a business activity that is best left to the sponsor. But many sponsors do not evaluate the event; nor try to assess their return on investment. However, we must hasten to add that some sponsors are very professional about evaluations. Self-evaluation is an excellent way of marketing when approaching future sponsors. It tells you how well your event went and identifies the areas of improvement. It also reminds you of the important differences between a sponsored and a non-sponsored event and demonstrates to your sponsor that you value their sponsorship. The self-evaluation technique provides you with information and data to help sell future sponsorships.

Sponsorship evaluation improves your own performance for future events. It makes you more aware of the need to set and meet your objectives. It impresses your sponsors and encourages them to return and re-invest in the future. Sponsorship evaluation is an excellent way of selling yourself when approaching a future sponsor for another event.

8.18.1 Evaluation principles

An evaluation should be based on answers to these questions: What were your objectives for this event, and, what were you trying to achieve? Examples of these objectives could be:
- increasing participation
- improving skills and standards of performance
- providing equipment and facilities
- expanding your geographical coverage
- improving sport in your local community
- ensuring your sponsor is satisfied with their investment

■ targeting government priority groups.

Any evaluation of an event must be measured by how your event performed; and comparing this performance with your objectives.

8.18.2 Planning your evaluation

Planning is essential to a well-managed evaluation. Start thinking about evaluation before the event starts and depending on the event and the requirements of the sponsor decide which evaluation techniques you will use. A range of techniques to conduct sponsorship evaluations exists which can be effectively used to secure future sponsorships. One may use some of the evaluation techniques that are mentioned in figure 8.2.

Measuring participation	Accurately count the number of who participates; if appropriate, at each venue or at each session. Keep a detailed record of participation. Collect this data by age (estimate if necessary), sex and ethnic origin. If relevant to your event compare this participation with data collected from previous events of identical or similar structure.
Measuring skills and performance	Achievement of sporting objectives can be measured by noting before and after performance levels of participants. The sponsor needs to know this and the performance data will aid the search for future sponsorship contracts.
Photographic evidence	You cannot beat a picture. It can be worth a thousand words. Take photos of everything that happens, particularly at the launch. Make sure you photograph any commercial activity by the sponsor: posters, banners, other event signage, sampling, VIP attendees, etc. Photograph participants in action. Also get some shots of participants together with your sponsor's logo or advertising.
Monitoring the media	The role of the media is usually a very important aspect in the success of a sponsored event, particularly if a launch event is involved. Here are some guidelines one could follow: • Keep a record of how many members of the media attend your event or activity. • Collect press clippings – measure the column inches of coverage, count the number of pictures and count the number of mentions of your sponsor. • In the case of TV and radio, find out: what time of day a report was broadcast, how many mentions of your sponsor and how many times was it broadcast. • If advertising time or space was bought: did the advertising appear as requested; if in the press, what paper and what page was it on; and if broadcast, what time of day, what channel and in what programme did it appear.

FIGURE 8.2 *Sponsorship Evaluation Techniques (Sportsmatch, 2004: Internet)*

8.18.3 Make a record of other activities

- Collect all the evidence of branding for your sponsor. This might include leaflets, programmes, T-shirts, kit, stickers, posters, etc.
- Some sponsors will be as interested in spectator/audience attendance as in participation. This can particularly apply to school sponsorship where the parents could be a sponsor's target group.
- If a printed programme is involved, keep data on how many were produced and how many were sold or given away. Your sponsor may advertise in it, and should be featured anyway.
- Note special VIP attendees such as the mayor, local government officials, politicians, high-profile athletes, etc. Sponsors often like to know of VIPs who attend an event to which their name is attached.

8.18.4 Your own research

It is possible that your sponsor is doing market research into your event. This can be expensive, and should be left to the professionals in this field. However, there is a useful research technique that you can introduce to the benefit of yourself and your sponsor. Hand out a questionnaire to all participants asking them a few questions about the event:

- How did they hear about it?
- Who sponsored it?
- How well was it organised?
- What did they get out of it?
- Would they participate again?
- Remember to collect the completed questionnaires before participants leave; otherwise, you are unlikely to see the questionnaires again.

Types of research that may be conducted during sponsorship evaluation may include: audience research (on-site mailed interviews, phone interviews); attitude/image change studies (longitudinal tracking survey instruments); feedback from trade (employee response); market-share data (compare effectiveness of marketing strategies to determine which works best); sales data; and measured media coverage (SA Tourism and Department of Environment Affairs and Tourism, 2002: 100).

8.18.5 The evaluation report

Include the following when writing a detailed evaluation report:

- objectives of the event
- participation data
- measurement of skills and performance
- photographic evidence

- media coverage, with supporting material
- any personal research you may have carried out.

But remember you want facts and truth, even if it shows up errors and shortcomings. This is the way to improve. So be honest and be as accurate as you can.

8.18.6 **What to do with the results** (Sportsmatch, 2004: Internet)

- review them with your colleagues for future events;
- give them to your sponsor to show that:
  - you value their sponsorship
  - you are professional
  - you are worth sponsoring in the future;
- when you solicit new sponsors show them the report as an example of what you can do for them.

8.19 EVALUATING SPONSORSHIP RESULTS

According to IEG (1996: 25), sponsorship results can be measured through using the three broad schools of evaluation:

- ***Measuring awareness levels achieved or attitudes changed.*** The company needs to determine awareness levels, attitudes and image perception among their target and set goals they expect the sponsorship to achieve. During the sponsorship, companies should ask themselves, 'are we on the right path? Are there any strong positive or negative indicators to adjust or change?'. Following the sponsorship, they should ask, 'did we meet our goals?'. Awareness related to name of the company; if the public is aware that the company is a sponsor of the event and their attitude towards the sponsorship should be considered.

- ***Quantifying sponsorship in terms of sales results.*** To justify expenditure to shareholders and employees, sponsors must show that sponsorship makes an impact on the bottom line. They must show that associating with the 'sponsored group or team' will fair position their products and services in the market. Some of the indicators showing positive change in sales are: increase in sales of product or service to customers; increase in distribution outlets; generating more product displays at point of sale; and boost in retail traffic.

- ***Comparing the value of sponsorship-generated media coverage to the cost of equivalent advertising space or time.*** This approach calls for placing a currency, e.g. rand or dollar value on publicity. First, document the number of seconds of television and radio coverage, as well as column inches in print. Then determine the cost to purchase a like amount of advertising. In assigning values; some sponsors use the rate card, while others use qualitative objectives (IEG, 1996). All media coverage received during the sponsorship period featuring the sponsor should be analysed for: number of mentions, the transmission of sponsor's messages, television coverage in minutes (supply a VHS copy if available), copies of articles that demonstrate the value of the property to the sponsor, i.e. featuring their name (NSW, 2002: Internet).

Sponsorships are evaluated in terms of the media exposure they are likely to bring. 'Most sponsors work on a 3 : 1 basis. If there is a potential of getting R15 m in media coverage, they will pay R5 m for the sponsorship. But there is really no norm. The models are difficult to apply and there is a lot of subjectivity involved. It's not like advertising, where audience sizes and circulation are subject to objective scientific measurement. But evaluation is getting more professional' (Koenderman, 2000).

Browse these Internet sites

http://www.dsr.nsw.gov.au/industry/ra-zspeval.asp
http://www.sponsorship.com
http://ifea.com/about/sponsor.asp
http://www.isisa.co.za/isisa/sponsor/sponsor.htm
http://sponsorwise.com/
http://www.sa2010bid.co.za

QUESTIONS FOR SELF-EVALUATION

1 You are to act as fundraiser for the local Youth Day celebration (16 June), which will feature largely young people of school age. Suggest who you might approach for financial support and why.

2 For the celebration mentioned in question 1, prepare a budgeted estimate, giving the anticipated income and expenditure. Also give a two-paragraph report which you would present to the committee on the most important items in the budget. Suggest the structure and mechanisms you would like to see for financial control.

3 Naturally sponsors will be required for this celebration. Identify possible companies, individuals or agencies to target; suggest what benefits could be offered and how the presentation would be made to each of them.

4 Briefly distinguish between the different types of sponsors.

5 List potential blocks to a successful sponsorship.

6 What benefits are sponsors looking for?

CHAPTER 9

Event Programming

Tom Wanklin

AIM OF THE CHAPTER

This chapter provides an insight into the way in which the events development process is managed, so that an event can be set up successfully, within its budget and time frame. The various techniques which could be used to assist event project management are explained and the critical factors for success are outlined.

LEARNING OBJECTIVES

After having studied this chapter, you should be able to:

- understand the nature of event programming and prepare a schedule of activities, objectives and time frames;
- identify the role players in event programming;
- understand the different deviations, cycles and characteristics of event development programmes;
- describe the various programming tools and techniques and understand how they are used;
- explain the various project management activities, the role of a project manager and how project management is achieved;
- understand the monitoring and review of events and how this is done;
- identify the critical success factors in event programming.

9.1 WHAT IS EVENT PROGRAMMING?

Having formulated a plan for the event (refer to chapter 5), it is necessary to put that plan into action and to stage the event. This will require event programming, because each event comprises a large number of individual activities which need to be carried out successfully, at the correct time and in the correct order. Many of these activities are dependent upon other actions being taken beforehand or at the same time. Should this process not take place smoothly, there could be delays and such delays could be costly to the event organisers, the host community and the sponsors.

Event programming, or *project scheduling*, involves three main activities: first, management of the development of the event; secondly, the event programme itself (when the event is held); and thirdly, the shutdown or decommissioning activities which come about after the event has been held. The first activity simply involves the process of setting out in detail those actions which need to be implemented, determining who should take those actions, and then detailing the timing of such actions to achieve the objectives, targets and milestones during the event development process. These time and action programmes form an essential part of the successful management of an event development process. This management process is usually called project management and there are a variety of techniques which are utilised to manage implementation activities. This chapter provides an overview of these methods.

The second activity, the event itself, requires a detailed programme which will enable the event participants, support services, operators and performers to carry out their required actions and duties in harmony, thereby achieving a successful event. The third and final programming activity involves the decommissioning process, whereby the facilities and venue are either closed down or renovated in preparation for the next event.

9.2 EVENT DEVELOPMENT PROGRAMMING

There are six basic steps or activities involved in event development programming; these are set out in figure 9.1.

Even in a developing country, such as South Africa, the process of rapid change and the increasing complexity of activities has a growing influence on the management of events. Event organisers are experiencing an environment of ever-increasing competition, rising costs, funding constraints, and greater diversity of thought and objectives in both individuals and organisations. An event manager has to be highly skilled and professional to draw every component of a plan together in as short a time as possible to reduce risk, retain financial viability and manage a complex situation.

The growing importance of the events industry is also leading to greater significance in the financial impact of events and increasing complexity of their activities. Accordingly, event programming and project management plays an increasingly crucial role in achieving a successful event, within budget and time constraints.

With regard to major events, it is important to stress the huge odds at stake and how 'large, often one time projects (such as mega events) are difficult challenges to operations managers. The stakes are high. Millions of dollars in cost overruns have been wasted due to poor planning of projects. Unnecessary delays have occurred due to poor scheduling and companies have gone bankrupt due to poor controls' (Render & Heizer, 1997: 480).

9.2.1 Role players in programming

The technical team which is responsible for formulating the plan in consultation with the community and event stakeholders would invariably comprise a

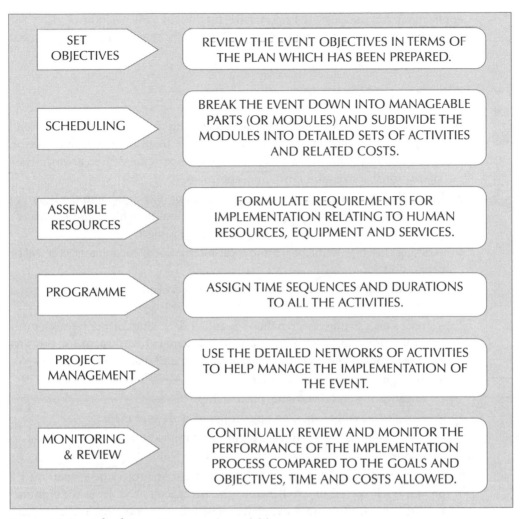

FIGURE 9.1 *Event development programming activities*

professional project manager or managers with experience in programming and implementation. A number of professions have developed project management expertise including physical planners, engineers and quantity surveyors. In South Africa, the availability of trained and experienced project managers is growing and the Professional Institute of Project Managers can supply details of its members should these be required.

The larger the event, the more complex the programme management process and the higher the risks. Accordingly, event organisers are urged to use competent expertise in this process. Project managers require special qualities to handle complex and stressful work situations. Below is an example of the typical requirements and responsibilities of such a person taken from an advertisement in the *Weekend Argus* (12/13 June 1999). This advertisement called for applications for the post of Project Director for the construction of the Cape Town International Convention Centre. The main body of the advertisement stated the following:

EXAMPLE 9.1 *Project manager: job description*

> ■ 'Key stakeholders in the Western Cape, including the Provincial Government, the Cape Metropolitan Council, the City of Cape Town and the business sector, have recently established a Development Company to deliver a world-class international convention centre in Cape Town.
>
> ■ In this flexible contract appointment, you will be accountable to the Board of Directors for recommending strategy and action to achieve the company's goal, as well as for effectively implementing the project.
>
> ■ Working closely with the board and local/international consultants, you will be responsible for:
>   - identifying and agreeing upon the Centre's objective target market(s) and site
>   - reviewing existing research findings and undertaking further research prior to the preparation of a business plan, a detailed work plan for the first project phase, the design brief, construction and marketing plans, etc.
>   - arranging the necessary finance
>   - investigating and developing partnerships
>   - advising on and facilitating operating policy development
>   - maximising opportunities for economic empowerment
>   - resourcing, etc.
>
> ■ Consequently you will need to be an experienced project developer with a proven track record of excellence in the management of large-scale, multi-faceted projects. You are a dynamic, incisive leader and decision taker with proven business, marketing, financial management, negotiation, interpersonal and communication skills. You can provide ample evidence of your ability to facilitate good working relations between disparate stakeholders and of your sound understanding of the international convention business.'
>
> (*Weekend Argus*, 12/13 June 1999)

Such expertise would be responsible for drawing together the other role players identified in the plan, so as to ensure that all activities are taken into account and controlled effectively.

9.2.2 Duration of event programmes

All events have a life cycle which varies according to their unique characteristics. Obviously, those events which take place only once have a programme duration which lasts over a short period.

- Conception of the idea to hold an event
- Feasibility study
- Detailed planning
- Implementation
- Shut down.

The following diagram (figure 9.2) depicts the above process in a time-related manner.

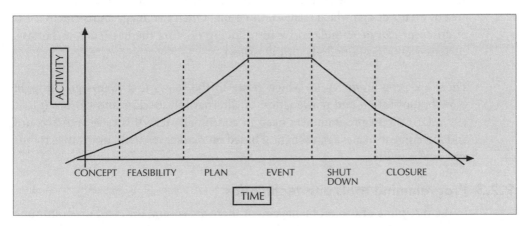

FIGURE 9.2 *Single event duration cycle*

Events which are held on a regular basis (for example perennial or annual events) have a cyclical programme and these are much more difficult to sustain. The regularly held events can often suffer from repetition within their event programme, which can ultimately affect their viability. In addition, the programme cycle needs to take into account the requirements of maintenance of equipment and facilities, marketing, promotion and development of new activities in order to ensure that the event remains fashionable and exciting. Figure 9.3 depicts this process in a conceptual form.

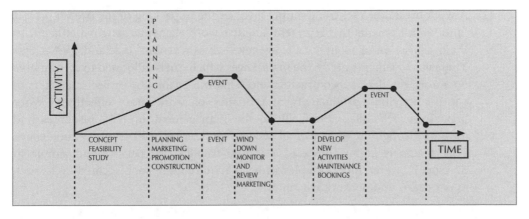

FIGURE 9.3 *Cycle of perennial events*

Getz (1997: 170) points out that 'Programmes should be planned to have a life expectancy and if it is not a planned process there is a risk that the event will lose popularity or money.'

Continual reappraisal of the fashionability of the event, its image and relevance in the context of trends and current events is a crucial component of sustainability. In a number of towns in the Eastern Cape, for example, the events tend to exhibit similar (or the same) craft stalls every year. This fails to achieve a sustainable attendance because the market becomes saturated or at worst bored. This is an area of events design which relates to theming. Often the image and attractiveness of an event can be stimulated by introducing exciting themes (such as fantasy, current events, fashions and cultural issues).

There are programme cycles which relate to the stages that events go through: growth, motivation and rejuvenation or, alternatively, decline and closure (Getz, 1997: 170). Event programmers need to continually take this cycle into account and intervene to achieve rejuvenation based on market research, innovative trends and new activities.

9.2.3 Programming tools and techniques

In the discipline of project management there are several different programming tools or techniques which are used, ranging from simple lists of work to be done, to complex computer project management software. The most common tools are:

- work breakdown schedules (WBS);
- bar charts (such as the Gantt chart);
- network schedules (showing events and activities and times);
- critical path analysis (CPA);
- PERT;
- time/cost analysis.

9.2.3.1 Work breakdown schedules (WBS)

A work breakdown schedule simply involves the unpacking of the overall project 'into work elements that represent singular work elements, assigned either with the organisation or to an outside agency such as a vendor' (Cleland, 1999: 286). These work elements need to be in packages which can be allocated to accountable operators, builders, subcontractors, etc. This will enable the project managers to control activities, productivity and quality of work more effectively. Work breakdown schedules also facilitate the management of risk, resources and outputs through the display of all tasks to be performed in sequence on a chart. This system is popular because it is user-friendly, inexpensive and simple to develop. However, more complex projects require more sophisticated tools, such as bar charts and network schedules.

9.2.3.2 Bar charts

One way of displaying activities and events in sequence is in the form of bar charts, which are linear pictures representing the various activities which have to be performed over time. A bar chart for a typical carnival development is provided in example 9.2 below.

EXAMPLE 9.2 *Bar chart for a typical carnival development*

XYZ PROJECT

TASK NAME	Jan	Feb	Mar	Apr	May	Jun	Jul	Aug	Sept	Oct	Nov
Carnival start	▓										
Stall bookings	▓	▓	▓	▓							
Confirm vehicles	▓										
Landscaping			▓	▓							
Official launch				▓							
Press release				▓							
Stall construction						▓	▓				
Event HQ								▓			
Event wrap up										▓	

These bar charts are sometimes referred to as Gantt charts (after Henry Gantt) and are a widely used 'non-mathematical technique' (Render & Heizer, 1997: 481), simple, user-friendly and inexpensive. The bar chart is useful but cannot adequately show the relationship between activities and time.

9.2.3.3 Network scheduling

In order to be able to effectively control the implementation process, it is essential to have a detailed breakdown of all the activities that need to be carried out and the time that each should take to be completed. Project or network scheduling involves determining the project's activities in the time sequence in which they have to be performed (Render & Heizer, 1997: 480). One can also devise schedules of the human resources needed, equipment and materials required to fulfil those tasks.

Scheduling charts, which combine the list of activities to be performed, the time sequence of the implementation of tasks, and the manpower, money and materials, are used to help manage the project development process. The scheduling activity is very simple and merely requires every single element of the project to be identified. Then the actions or activities required to achieve these elements must also be listed in detail.

After listing all the elements and activities, it is helpful to write them up in a chart which shows the sequence of activities and the way in which they relate to each other. In scheduling jargon, the elements are usually called *events* and they are usually represented by a number in a circle. This number would correspond to the detailed list referred to earlier. These should not be confused with the special events which are the subject of this text.

The activities which are required to achieve the 'events' are shown as an arrow or a line, which links the events (for example: Event 1 to Event 2).

Hildreth (1990: 64) describes each event as an objective and 'the work necessary to accomplish an objective is called an activity'. It is also customary for there to be only one activity between each element or 'event'. As the list of elements (events) and activities is transformed into a chart, it can become a very detailed and complex diagram, full of arrows and circles with numbers.

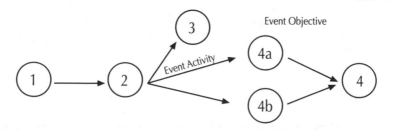

It has been found useful to include the estimated completion time for each activity in these charts. By doing this, the performance of the implementing team, the builders or carpenters, etc can be monitored. More importantly, the implementing team can be informed of the expected duration of each task, so that they can ensure that their productivity is enhanced accordingly.

The length of time to be taken for an activity is usually shown in numbers (days, hours, months, etc) above the activity time, between the events:

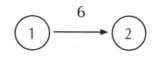

The use of time in a scheduling chart is beneficial because it is possible to calculate the likely date by which the project can be completed. In certain situations, it may be necessary to calculate backwards from the date when the event is to commence, because the commencement date of the event has been decided beforehand and cannot be changed. This will mean that the implementing team needs to produce a scheduling chart which allows for all the elements and activities to be achieved within a predetermined time frame. Examples of this would be the Olympic Games or the World Cup Soccer Tournament. In such situations, the scheduling charts will highlight those activities which need to be carried out simultaneously, to save time and achieve better productivity. Also, the chart would highlight instances where additional resources would be required: double shifts, overtime and additional equipment could help the process to be 'fast-tracked' to achieve fixed deadlines.

The availability of computer technology has greatly enhanced the ability of scheduling and, as a result, also project management. There are a variety of different techniques which are useful tools in this regard.

9.2.3.4 Critical path analysis (CPA)

This network schedule technique was devised in 1957 by Kelly and Walker in the United States to 'assist in the building and maintenance of chemical plants' (Render & Heizer, 1997: 483). It is different from the network scheduling description above, because it identifies those activities which have a critical effect on the event implementation process. These critical activities are represented as the 'longest time path through the network', referred to as the critical path (Render & Heizer, 1997: 483). Critical path analysis has enhanced project management by enabling more strategic monitoring of the project process. It also allows for an implementing team to intervene at critical moments to avoid delays. Such critical elements and activities are not easily identified with the use of bar charts.

9.2.3.5 Programme evaluation review technique (PERT)

The programme evaluation review technique (PERT) is a similar system to critical path analysis and was invented by the United States Navy in 1958 (Render & Heizer, 1997: 483). This technique differs from CPA because it uses different terms and three time estimates for each activity, namely:

- *optimistic* time – the shortest duration likely;
- *most likely* time – the average expectation of the majority of people;
- *pessimistic* time – the most conservative estimate, taking into account the likelihood of setbacks and restarting the project (Hildreth, 1990: 66).

These three estimates of time for an activity can be aggregated statistically to achieve an expected time, which is effectively an average of the optimistic, most likely and pessimistic times. Hildreth (1990: 66) describes the equation for this calculation as follows:

$$te = \frac{a + 4m + b}{6}$$
(expected time)

where a = optimistic time
m = most likely time
b = pessimistic time

The calculation of expected time enables the critical path analysis network to be more informed and realistic. This is because the estimated time has been modified by influences of both a positive and negative nature and the event management team has a more realistic idea of the likely duration of the implementation process.

9.2.3.6 Time/cost analysis

Management of resources can have a profound influence on project implementation; for example, additional construction teams could be brought onto site, or a 24-hour construction programme could be introduced. Sometimes the introduction of certain equipment, rather than using labour-based methods, can result in the construction programme being compressed or 'crashed' (Render & Heizer, 1997: 495). This simply means that the implementation process is executed more quickly by using more people and/or equipment to speed up production. Activity crashing can be a useful technique if there are penalties payable for late completion of a project. It may be more efficient or economical to pay for more labour, rather than suffer penalties.

Render and Heizer (1997: 496) explain that 'the objective of crashing is to reduce the project completion time at least cost'. Careful analysis of the critical path of a project schedule can reveal areas where additional resources could reduce the path and project deviation. However, it needs to be acknowledged that undue 'crashing' can place the project at greater risk should unforeseen events or delays occur.

Both CPA and PERT are totally dependent upon the clarity of project activities, timing and precedence. Time estimates are usually subjective and forecast on the basis of the expectations of clients, managers and event owners. Sometimes overoptimistic estimates can result in failure in the performance of network programmes. Caution is also suggested with regard to 'too much emphasis being placed on the longest, or critical path. Near critical paths need to be monitored as well' (Render & Heizer, 1997: 500).

9.2.3.7 Project management activities

The process by which the implementation of a plan and the development of an event are managed is called *project management*. This can be defined as 'a philosophy and a process for the management of ad hoc activities in organisations, characterised by a distinct life cycle and a management system that uses a matrix organisational design' (Cleland, 1999: xiv). In the context of project management, a project can be defined as 'a combination of organisational resources pulled together to create something that did not previously exist …' (Cleland, 1999: 5).

The process of project management aims to achieve the development of a particular event within the budget and time frames available. This is often displayed in a diagrammatic form as follows:

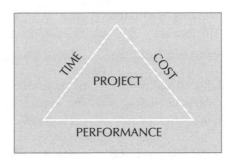

The main person usually responsible for the coordination of the event programming and implementation process is a project manager (or, if it is a mega-event, several project managers).

Any project generally has six characteristics and a project manager needs to facilitate the implementation process on this basis:
- a start and a finish date;
- a time frame;
- a unique operating period;
- the involvement of several organisations and/or individuals;
- a prescribed set of resources;
- a scheduled number of activities and phases setting out their sequence of occurrence (Harris, 1998: 26).

The major intention of project management is to meet set targets, within budgets and within the time frames that have been agreed. In order to achieve this, it is essential to undertake the following activities.
- Establish a clear project goal.
- Determine the project objectives.
- Establish milestones and tasks to be undertaken, the relationship between tasks and time frames.
- Prepare a diagram of the project programme.
- Direct people individually and as part of a team.
- Support the commitment and enthusiasm of the team.

- Distribute information to all role players.
- Motivate and build a project team.
- Empower the team to perform effectively.
- Manage the risks and encourage creativity to find new solutions and ideas (Harris, 1998: 29–30).

Project management teams are usually different from conventional organisations in that they are usually multidisciplinary, small and highly focused. The team requires a stable working environment, with clear lines of reporting to senior decision makers, efficient and high-quality equipment and adequate budgets to get the work done.

It is the responsibility of the project manager to effectively manage the project implementation process, including planning, organisation, motivation, directing and controlling all the activities, role players and stakeholders involved.

Case study 9.1: 'Bravo Africa' Concert – Pretoria, 18 April 1999

A case study in successful event management was the Bravo Africa Concert held by the Three Tenors, Luciano Pavarotti, Placido Domingo and Jose Carreras. The May edition of *Project Pro* (1999: 39) interviewed the Technical Project Manager for Showtime International (Mark Ransom) and reported how the show had been assembled in seventeen days and dismantled in seven days. The biggest concern was the possibility of rain – a 30% probability.

The details of the show give an idea of the complexity and size of the undertaking, including 'setting up a stage (110 m wide × 40 m deep × 32 m high) that could accommodate the three stars (Domingo, Carreras and Pavarotti), the 120-piece National Symphony orchestra and a 300-strong choir ... hospitality marquees and other facilities for artists were catered for. Then there are the public areas – grandstands, three kilometres of rubber turf, 70 hospitality marquees and 700 toilets for an expected audience of 40 000 people.'

The project manager conceded that 'basic project management principles' were used, with planning starting 13 months prior to the event, and a survey being conducted around the Union Buildings to map every tree and plan the placement of grandstands and stage. Nothing had been left to chance.

There are several areas which require careful management and expertise, including stakeholder involvement (particularly a host community), risk management and evaluating performance. In addition, it is useful to be aware of factors which can result in project failure. Cleland (1999: 200) lists these as follows:

1   Lack of understanding of the project complexity.
2   Lack of access and internal communication.
3   Failure to integrate the key elements.
4   Inadequate control.
5   Subtle change in requirement.
6   Ineffective execution strategy.
7   Too much dependence on software.
8   Contractor/customer with different expectations.
19 No shared "win–win" attitudes.
10 Inadequate education/training.
11 Lack of leadership commitment and sponsorship.
12 Not viewed as a start-up business.'
(Cleland, after John Gioia – '*Twelve reasons why programs fail*', PM Network, November 1996, 16–19)

9.3   ORGANISING THE EVENT PROGRAMME

There is a considerable difference between project management programming and scheduling (9.2.3.3) and organising the event programme. The former enables the sequential arrangement of activities in the construction and/or establishment of an event. The latter process involves arranging the various elements, shows, displays and activities during the event itself, in such a way that the event programme is enjoyable and successful. An event programme is vital for several additional reasons:

- the event can be more effectively marketed because the public will be able to choose the time and event component they wish to attend;
- the event organisation will be able to coordinate the activities of the participants and performers, and
- the employees and volunteer workers will be informed as to what work needs to be done, in time and sequence.

The preparation of an event programme involves a similar activity to network scheduling because it is necessary to identify all the activities, resources and requirements for the entire event in check lists. Such a process can be defined as operational planning (Getz, 1997: 89). These check lists can include details such as the following:

- accommodation and facilities for disabled, physically challenged participants;
- facilities, settings, accommodation and seating arrangements;
- services, including water, electricity, telecommunications and sewerage;
- equipment, machinery, vehicles and tools;
- operational needs, including ticketing, customer services, public relations and information;

- crowd management measures, safety and security, disaster management;
- communications and media facilities;
- food and beverage requirements;
- special effects, lighting, sound translation services, signage and advertising.

Having detailed check lists on all the resource needs, arrangements and activities assists greatly in the next organisational step, which is that of designing the programme or agenda for the event. Getz (1997: 159) emphasises the need to 'develop an attractive programme of activities using the key elements of style'. This can be related to creating an experience which will remain a pleasurable memory for those who attended for a long time after the event.

Creating a favourable image of the event through an attractive programme relates to the arrangement and organisation of the activities according to imaginative themes with the use of logos, mascots and various symbols to enhance the excitement and experience of the event. The event can also be enhanced by the use of ritual, emotional stimulation, great spectacles, entertainment, commercial merchandising and side shows (such as buskers, street performers and animateurs).

Finally, the sequence of activities during the event needs to be organised in such a way that the participants are entertained and want to return the next time it is held. In this regard, it is beneficial to have supporting events ahead of the main attraction, so that the event experience rises in excitement to a 'grand finale'. In a similar way, exhibitions and festivals need to arrange their programme to attract attendance over an extended period rather than over a short interval. This can be achieved by having key attractions interspersed with support activities to keep the participants entertained on a regular basis.

It needs to be remembered that long delays between activities can frustrate crowds and, as a result, crowd management can become a problem. Accordingly, event programmes need to be prompt and activities evaluated on the basis of their relevance (in the case of a theme), performance and professionalism. Unrehearsed activities or incomplete exhibits must be taken off as quickly as possible to avoid creating a poor image.

Allowance should be made for food breaks, rest and recuperation. Crowds cannot sustain high levels of excitement for long periods and peak entertainment needs to be interspersed with alternative acts to extend the experience. Programmes for meetings and conferences differ greatly from programmes for jazz festivals, sports meetings and opera. In most cases the formulation of a programme is basic common sense, and organisers need to use the 'core' or main attraction element as the anchor around which other activities can be clustered.

In order to manage the development of an event, the programming process is critical for the project to meet the deadlines, budgetary constraints and performance requirements during construction/ preparation. The second programming activity is that of devising a suitable programme for the event itself, taking into account several key factors such as:

■ dates when it is to be held;
■ duration of the event;
■ agenda or format for the proceedings.

9.3.1 Date for the event

Selection of the date for the event is crucial because it can mean a difference between success or failure. In all cases, whether a regular event or one-off event, it is important to consider the factors which will affect attendance (Whale, 1997: 25), including:

■ public holidays;
■ major sporting events;
■ academic calendars;
■ political activities;
■ days of the week;
■ periods of the month;

- seasons;
- setup time required;
- shutdown time required;
- arrival and departure times of participants.

Public holidays may be an advantage for the attendance of local residents and even tourists from other regions; however, such holidays can result in service industries, volunteers and local authorities being unavailable. In addition, public holidays often result in large-scale travel to other parts of the country which would seriously reduce attendance at events (the Easter holiday is a case in point). Other major events taking place in the same area or even country can have a significant impact on attendance. Academic calendars determine the availability of young people should they be part of the market segment being targeted.

Generally it has been found that political activities, such as an election, will have an effect on attendance at events. This applies to the period leading up to the election and during the voting period. The days of the week chosen for a particular event can have an influence, with Mondays usually being the worst day for attendance. In some areas of South Africa, particularly in the rural regions, Saturdays are preferred to Sunday because of religions activities. However, funerals on a Saturday can result in poor attendance. In certain rural communities, meetings and conferences are preferred during the week and in working hours because of the availability of transport. Poor public transport after hours and on weekends prevents attendance by members of the community from outlying settlements.

The period during the month can similarly have an impact on the success of an event. Payment of salaries towards the end of a working month can result in a 'window' when affordability is higher than usual.

Events which depend on outdoor venues or which require particular weather conditions (such as winter sports) have to be held at times determined by the seasons. The advance weather forecasting techniques available can provide trend data which will help determine the most favourable period to hold the event.

In selecting the dates for an event it is important to consider the timing in relation to popular television programmes which can influence attendance figures (Richards, 1992: 109). Finally, the availability of broadcasting time on various media can influence both sponsorship interest and viewership support. International events also need to consider international time variations and select optimum time slots to achieve maximum exposure.

In order to ensure that the event is held at the correct time and on the correct date, it is essential to liaise with the project management team who are responsible for programming the development (setup) process. The critical path in the development schedule will indicate the shortest possible time for construction and therefore the most likely completion date of the construction or preparation phase. It is always prudent to allow some time for unforeseen delays or, if this is not possible, 'project crashing' may need to be considered to speed up the setting-up process.

9.3.2 Duration of the event

The length of time over which an event is held can sometimes be determined by the nature of the event itself. For example, a sports event would be played according to the rules and time allowed by the referee. Other events, such as a festival, can, however, be more flexible, and their duration could be determined by the capacity of the venue to accommodate the activities over a period of time or by the perceived duration of interest which is expected of the attendees.

The length of an event can also be influenced by the comfort of the participants. For example, it is well known that the average span of attention is approximately 30 to 40 minutes. As a result, it is important to have a varied programme which allows for breaks when people can stretch and visit the ablution facilities. Also, a varied programme prevents monotony and helps to keep the audience entertained. Care should also be taken to build the programme of events towards the main attraction of the event. This holds the attendance figures up and serves to foster a successful outcome.

According to Richards (1992: 108), 'maintaining awareness and excitement at fever pitch over long periods can require substantial stamina and financial resources. A conservative view has to be taken of the actual levels of programming and awareness that can be maintained to attract a target audience over a period of days or weeks.' Care must be taken not to overextend an event beyond its maximum exposure, particularly when the cost of rental of premises and/or payment of artists and performers could bring about a loss of profit. It is often the case that audiences reach saturation and attendance tails off before the main event/attraction is held.

9.3.3 Event format

The agenda of an event needs to be prepared at an early stage in order that all role players have a clear understanding of the sequence of events. This ranges from the organisers knowing which activity is to start and finish where and when, to the local authority traffic policemen knowing the likely traffic congestion periods due to event programmes and, finally, the mayor knowing when to arrive and perform the appropriate civic duties.

Whale (1997: 30) suggests several useful tips to be followed when preparing a suitable events agenda.

- 'Determine what is the main attraction; the reason why the attendees will be attending this event – this becomes the pivot for the design of the programme.
- What refreshments will need to be served, whether these are at mealtimes.
- When will entertainment be necessary.
- If you have an event that attracts attendees from out of town – then you may have to consider their transport limitations ...'

Generally, an event programme is influenced by the scheduled arrival of special dignitaries, key performers or speakers. In the case of a conference or meeting, allowance needs to be made for the registration of guests or participants and for a welcoming procedure. The opening event sets the tone for the remainder of the event (Whale, 1997: 29) and the closing event also can influence the level of experience and enjoyment.

As part of setting an agenda, provision needs to be made for the rehearsal of participants so as to ensure that equipment works correctly and performers know what is required of them.

Case study 9.2b: Grahamstown Festival

Festival fever building up

'While some people feel the opening of the 25th annual arts festival has been "quietish", others point out that the organisers are better prepared than ever before, and that Grahamstown is coping better.

Rita Larisma of ECN reported on Tuesday: With a great gust of wind, hundreds of red, green and blue balloons filled the sky as locals and visitors turned out en masse to welcome this year's patron of the Standard Bank National Arts Festival, former president, Nelson Mandela.

Strong winds blew away most of Mandela's words, but the crowds were jubilant and unconcerned.

What they heard, they liked: "I welcome you to the festival if you are poor or rich, if you are black or white, if you are local or foreign."

Standing in front of the historic Cathedral of St Michael and St George dressed in a blazing gold shirt, Madiba jived to the jazzy sounds of Viva Madiba, played live, while young African dancers in bright orange skirts and beaded bikini tops moved their little hips and arms – dancing in an intimate space facing Mandela and smiling from ear to ear.

Upbeat crowds stood on every available raised area to catch a glimpse of their hero and people even politely took turns on trees and ladders and chairs so that they could spread the joy. "Mandela, you must see each and every one of us," was a call from my left field, while on the right an old woman said: "It is like seeing God. It is like seeing God" – ECN.'

(*Grocott's Mail*, Friday, 2 July 1999)

9.4   PROGRAMMING EVENT SHUTDOWN

In the case of a one-off event which has to be wound up, or should it be decided to close down a regularly held event, care should be taken to programme this winding-down process in a deliberate way. Often this aspect of the programme can be handled poorly because the organisers have lost interest or energy. A poorly managed closure process can result in wastage of resources (through poor controls, theft, mismanagement and delays). Events can also be closed down (with as much fanfare as the launch (Getz, 1997: 173)) to avoid costly overheads and allow reduction of resources (people and funding) to other events or new activities. Alternatively, it may be appropriate to shut down an event and phase in a new event to replace it.

To avoid confusion and antagonism in those communities which may be dependent on a regular event for employment or charity, the organisers may decide to close down an event on a phased basis, over time. However, very tight controls are needed at all times to prevent rising costs and wastage. There are several termination strategies which need to be followed:

- Ensure that all work has been completed.
- Make a review of all contracts to ensure that all their clauses have been fulfilled.
- Monitor the shutdown process to ensure that all activities are being conducted satisfactorily.
- Advise all stakeholders that the event is shutting down.
- Make sure that all financial commitments are fulfilled.
- If appropriate, help employees to secure alternative employment.
- Prepare a project history report so that a record is available for future events of a similar nature.
- As a final component of the project history report, conduct an audit to highlight strengths and weaknesses and to show how mistakes could be avoided in future.

When events are brought to a close, it needs to be remembered that certain activities must be carried out (either in expectation of future events or the revival of the event in the forthcoming year). Such activities can include maintenance of services and facilities, revamping the products and activities, and rejuvenating the marketing process.

9.5   MONITORING AND REVIEW

Effective implementation of the event programme requires a methodical evaluation and review of several components of the event. These would include systematic evaluation procedures before the event is held (that is, during the establishment/development phase), during the event itself and, finally, after the event has been held.

A key element in event monitoring and review is project auditing. Cleland (1999: 337) describes this as ' … a formal independent evaluation of the effectiveness with which the project is being managed'.

Project auditing can involve the following elements:

- identifying those activities that are performing correctly, and why;
- identifying what is going wrong, and why;
- determining those factors affecting the achievement of the objectives;
- evaluating the efficiency of the project management team, organisers and participants (Cleland, 1999: 336).

Monitoring and review not only seeks to check how the event is doing in terms of expenditure, budget and performance, but it also needs to canvas visitor and participant views regarding how well the event meets with their expectations. Such information is vital for planning future events and is also essential for report backs to sponsors and financial institutions, in order to establish the extent to which the event was a success and value for money.

9.5.1 Pre-event monitoring and evaluation

These processes are normally conducted by the project management team which is responsible for the planning, programming and development phase.

The monitoring process seeks to achieve an understanding of the following:

- monitoring of expenditure against the budget during construction;
- monitoring of quality in terms of the specifications and expectations of the organisation;
- monitoring of progress in terms of time, meeting expected milestones on time and the impact of any delays on the critical elements of the event itself.

9.5.2 During the event

The organisers of an event need to take the opportunity of monitoring the achievements of the event.

Monitoring event achievements involves:

- monitoring and evaluating the performance of the activities in terms of budget, expectations and quality specifications;
- monitoring visitor perceptions, attendance statistics and expectations;
- monitoring the extent and nature of media reports and promotional exposure given during the event.

An example of a simple questionnaire used for monitoring visitor perceptions is provided in example 9.3 on page 226.

It will be noted that the questionnaire uses the opportunity of monitoring to obtain various statistics about the visitors. These statistics can include origin, destination, accommodation type, number of attendees, age characteristics, expenditure, length of stay, success of marketing and perception of enjoyment of the event. Not only are the statistics useful for future planning, but they also provide a useful basis for ongoing event planning research – of which there is a limited amount in developing countries such as South Africa.

Case study 9.3: Monitoring the SA Games

During the SA Games 2004, every team held a report back meeting in the evening, after the day's events were completed. The team managers in turn, met with the convenors of their relevant committee to report on the day's activities. The following morning, a monitoring meeting (Local Organising Committee) involving the Project Manager and the four functional committee convenors was held between 07:00 and 09:00. This enabled members to report on progress, problems not adequately solved and matters to be dealt with.

It is interesting to note that during the games, the organisational structure required participants to work through their committees to their convenor. If the problem could not be solved at committee level, then the convenor would liaise with the Project Manager for assistance. One significant lesson learned was the need to locate the 'nerve centre' (administration) away from the venue where the main activities take place. This would reduce the amount of interference by people not willing to observe protocol and the correct lines of communication. In addition, the nerve centre should have very strict security to keep non essential people out of the centre.

(Source: M.L. Makanda: Project Manager SA Games, 2004)

9.5.3 After the event

Monitoring and review at the end of an event is becoming increasingly important (Cleland, 1999: 339) because it enables project outcomes to be evaluated relative to the actual costs incurred. This evaluation stage can be difficult to execute if it involves participants, because at the end of the event people are usually in a hurry to leave, perhaps have a distorted perception of the event (due to excitement, fatigue or emotion) and lack the time to answer a questionnaire (Hildreth, 1990: 146). One possibility is to mail questionnaires to a sample of the visitors to obtain their views after the event. This can improve the quality of the response (because people will have been able to reflect on the event at leisure) but could also be difficult to execute as there is usually a low response rate to mailed questionnaires.

Monitoring and review after an event would accordingly seek to consider the following issues:

SAMPLE FESTIVAL QUESTIONNAIRE

VISITORS ATTENDING 3–DAY FESTIVAL IN TOWN XYZ

Day .... Time .... am/pm

1. Where is your residence?

    Town/City .... Region/Province ....

2. (a) Are you staying overnight in the XYZ area? Yes/No

    (b) If so, what accommodation are you using?

    ☐   ☐   ☐   ☐   ☐

    Hotel/   Bed &   Friends/   Camp-   Flat/
    Motel   Brkfst   Relatives   ground   Timeshare

3. Number of people in your group

    Adults ☐   Children 12 years & under ☐

4. How much do you plan to spend at the festival (excluding
    accommodation and travelling costs)? R ....

5. How much do you plan to spend in areas other than on the festival site?
    R ....

6. How long do you plan to stay at the festival? .... days

7. How did you hear about the festival? (Mark as many as apply)

    ☐   ☐   ☐   ☐   ☐   ☐

    Newspaper   Radio   TV   Brochure   Poster   Magazine

    ☐   ☐

    Word of mouth   Other: Describe ....
    ....

8. Please rate how well the festival met your expectations.

    ☐   ☐   ☐   ☐   ☐

    Excellent   Good   Average   Below   Poor
                                          average

9. Please give your comments or suggestions (to improve the Festival):
    ....
    ....

THANK YOU

EXAMPLE 9.3 *Sample festival questionnaire (adapted from Leibold, 1990, Appendix D)*

- the actual cost incurred for the event;
- the level of enjoyment, perceptions and views of participants in the event (for example the exhibitors, sportsmen/women, actors, etc);
- the views of people who attended;
- the perceptions of the organisers regarding the attainment of the objectives;
- what went well and why;
- what went wrong and why;
- what amendments should be made to the plan, programme and event itself.

9.6   CRITICAL SUCCESS FACTORS

Event programming requires attention to detail and careful project management to ensure success. There are several critical factors which need to be accommodated in the programming phase:

- commitment from the organisation and its management;
- a realistic, achievable and firm schedule of activities;
- clearly defined decision-making lines of communication and authority;
- a well-motivated and cooperative team;
- flexibility in the organisation to accommodate unforeseen change;
- involvement of the project management component as early as possible (preferably in the formulation and planning stage);
- continual review and monitoring of performance, quality and budget;
- involvement of stakeholders with effective distribution of information.

Browse these Internet sites

http://www.webex.com/services/event-center-features.html
http://www.paconsulting.com/industries/travel_tourism/services/private/event+planning/
http://www.premiers.qld.gov.au/library/office/Event%20management%20plan.doc
http://www.strategicevents.com/services.htm
http://specialevents.com/
http://www.shoalhaven.nsw.gov.au/council/forms/CEIK/Part7.pdf
http://www.juliasilvers.com/embok

QUESTIONS FOR SELF-EVALUATION

1   Explain how the life cycle of single events differs from perennial events and describe the various measures needed to sustain the life of events.

2   Describe the scheduling process and the steps involved.

3   Project programming seeks to achieve a successful project with three parameters; name these and explain how you can assist in meeting these objectives.

4   There are various network scheduling methods; name these and describe how they differ from each other.

5   What are the main responsibilities of a project manager?

6   Discuss the skills required by a project manager in developing an event.

7   Discuss the various factors which can result in project failure and indicate how these can be avoided.

8   The monitoring and review process has specific components. Describe these.

9   Monitoring activities should take place before, during and after an event. Why is this the case and how should these activities be performed?

10 What are the critical success factors of event programming?

CHAPTER 10

Risk Management

Tom Wanklin

AIM OF THE CHAPTER

The management of the various risks associated with an event is a crucial component of the events tourism industry. The aim of this chapter is to identify the risks involved and to explain the measures that could be taken to plan for risk and to manage events so as to prevent risks from occurring. The chapter also provides guidance in policy issues, legal arrangements and insurance matters.

LEARNING OBJECTIVES

After having studied this chapter, you should be able to:

- define and understand the different types and various forms of risk;
- identify the causes of risk and the type of environment which enhances risk;
- understand how to analyse risk;
- explain how to plan to prevent risk;
- understand the various management techniques employed to reduce or prevent the likelihood of risk;
- briefly describe the various policies, legal arrangements and insurance options which cater for risk;
- discuss the measures employed to manage the financial consequences of risk.

10.1 THE RISK ENVIRONMENT

10.1.1 Introduction

The growing events tourism industry is just as vulnerable to something going wrong as any commercial activity, construction project or manufacturing process. The combination of people, products, building and activities creates a mixture or recipe which is likely to experience problems, difficulties or setbacks. Such occurrences can result in a loss of rights, life, money, assets and satisfaction – all of which could cause the unfortunate demise of an event, whether a conference, sporting activity, festival or performance.

The key strategic issue, therefore, is what management techniques, plans and actions are necessary to prevent a loss from occurring. To achieve this, it is necessary, first to understand the risk involved and the likelihood of such losses taking place.

10.1.2 Definitions of risk

Perhaps one of the most important factors to be taken into account when holding an event is the uncertainty whether or not it will attract an audience or participants and be regarded as a success. Huffadine (1993: 43) refers to this as 'future uncertainty' rather than a risk. Risk is held to be 'an actual possibility of loss or exposure to loss', where 'loss can refer to any accident or occurrence that will result in injuries, deaths, property damage and destruction, damage to public image or reputation, claims or lawsuits' (Berlonghi, 1990: 19).

10.1.3 Types of risk

There are, however, many types of risk; these can be grouped into four main categories: *economic, performance, physical* and *psychological* (refer to figure 10.1).

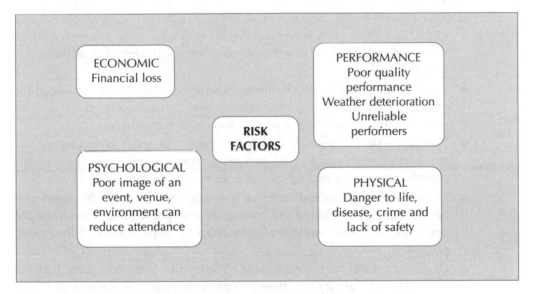

FIGURE 10.1 *Major types of risk (adapted from Cooper et al, 1999: 34)*

Perhaps one of the most interesting features about events is the fact that, like most tourism products, events are service products which are intangible (not easy to measure or evaluate the experience), perishable (they cannot be stored or reused, being time-related), and inseparable from the venue or environment in which they have to be experienced (Cooper *et al*, 1999: 34). These features expose the events industry to a broad range of risks and uncertainties.

The various types of risks are outlined below.

■ *Financial risks.* These include insufficient sponsorship to sustain a bid, insufficient funding to construct the needed infrastructure and facilities, inaccurate (that is, underestimating) capital and operating cost estimates, inaccurate estimating (that is, overestimating) of possible revenue flows; lack of public money needed to make good shortfalls in private sector revenue generation and through underestimating.

- *Political risks.* These include official support and guarantees promised that do not materialise, the use of the event as a political 'football' between parties in order to garner votes, takeovers of a privately run bid by authorities when political gain seems likely.
- *Minority or majority exclusion risks.* These are derived from a need to provide for empowerment, skills training and capacity building, affirmative action dictating the selection of key personnel, and procurement procedures that may lead to increases in the price of supplies and in cost of construction.
- *'White elephant' risks.* These are incurred through the building of inappropriate, overscaled structures necessary for the event but unsustainable after it.
- *After-the-ball-is-over 'hangover' risks.* These are incurred when people wake up to the fact that the party is over and that life as usual must be resumed, coupled with the ongoing need to manage many new and upgraded facilities and infrastructure.
- *Environmental impact risks.* Problems experienced include overloading of the capacity of infrastructure and bulk services, water, waste, air and noise pollution, and despoliation of natural and cultural resources.
- *Transport system/infrastructure risks.* The event may result in development of new infrastructure and demand management systems that cannot be managed after the event when staffing levels will go back to normal.
- *Unnecessary/unaffordable diversion of corporate resources risks.* The money and people required for the bid and hosting the event have to be drawn from the pool that otherwise would feed into other perhaps more socially needed projects.
- *Overly optimistic time horizon risks.* These arise from assuming that the resources and capacity are there to timeously create all the infrastructure, facilities, organisation, systems and procedures that are necessary for hosting the event.
- *Development context risks.* These involve the displacement of tenants, loss of security of tenure, rent hikes, gentrification of housing stock used by the poor and overstretching of construction capacity (that is, the lack of project management capacity, insufficient building materials and inadequately skilled labour).

Risk can also be differentiated into objective and subjective types. The former relate to those risks measured through statistical research, while subjective risk relates to the opinions or perceptions that different people may have about an event (Berlonghi, 1990: 19).

10.1.4 Risk factors

In the event environment there are a number of factors that play a role in determining the likelihood of loss occurring. These factors can be grouped into four main categories (figure 10.2): *perils, hazards, threats* and *vulnerabilities.*

PERILS	HAZARDS
Causes of risk, eg fires, floods and earthquake	Contributing factors, eg loaded guns, bottles and cans, certain buildings and structures
THREATS	**VULNERABILITIES**
Anything that could adversely affect the event or assets of the event, eg somebody acting in a harmful way or saying something harmful	Weaknesses, flaws, holes or anything that could be exploited by a threat, eg somebody or something is vulnerable to someone's threat

FIGURE 10.2 *Risk factors (adapted from Berlonghi, 1990: 19)*

The distinction between these different factors relates primarily to the ability of the event organisers to plan for and manage these risk factors. Obviously the magnitude of perils which affect an event is determined by natural forces; however, the risk of fire and flooding can usually be accommodated. Hazards, threats and vulnerabilities can be addressed through planning, management and policy approaches, which are discussed in greater detail below.

Unique risks can be generated by events as opposed to normal business activities, due to the presence of large crowds, high visibility (and therefore exposure to criminal elements), cultural conflicts and revelry, inexperienced management and volunteers, security, alcohol, drugs, unpredictable weather and quality control (for example, where dissatisfied customers result from poor performance) (Getz, 1997: 241).

10.1.5 Causes of loss

There are six principal causes of loss which relate to poor planning, inadequate management, errors by individuals, unsafe conditions, 'out-of-control energy' and the 'domino effect'. This is illustrated in figure 10.3.

In general terms, a poorly planned event and underprepared team could result in activities taking place, or not taking place, which could cause loss to occur. An example of this could be an event where the event planners fail to give sufficient attention to the time taken for a structure to be built. A hurried programme could result in the concrete structure failing to cure in time before a crowd takes occupancy, leading to structural collapse.

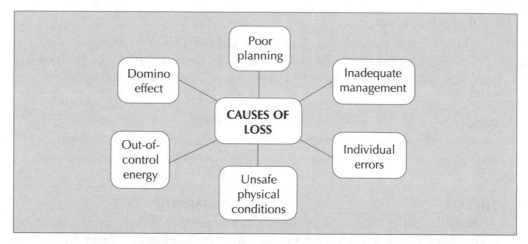

FIGURE 10.3 *Different causes of loss (adapted from Berlonghi, 1990: 12)*

Inadequate management can include poor or unsuitable policies, procedures, supervision, training and communication and it also occurs when resources are not used appropriately and there is a lack of accountability. Individual members of a team can cause a loss to occur through poor attention to detail, improper procedures, poor attitudes and work ethics. Such problems can arise due to poor .training and supervision, but can also be related to personal problems outside the workplace, such as illness and marital discord (Berlonghi, 1990: 12).

Many environments are potentially unsafe and this 'can generally be identified through analysis and common sense, but there is a subjective element as well. Some managers or stakeholders might have quite different perspectives on which risks are important' (Getz, 1997: 241). The risks or losses which can be precipitated through 'out-of-control energy' can include natural disasters, people problems through crowd disorder and lack of control, animal disorder and 'man-made buildings (water pressure, bombs, fireworks, speeding automobiles, etc)'. Finally, Berlonghi refers to the 'domino effect', which relates to the ripple effect as a result of one thing going wrong and causing a chain of problems or failures. The integrated dependency of 'cause and effect' comes into play; for example, 'if those controlling access into restricted areas do not do their jobs then serious security problems can threaten the whole event' (Berlonghi, 1990: 13).

10.2 PLANNING FOR POTENTIAL RISK

10.2.1 How do we analyse risk?

When considering the forthcoming event from the point of view of risk, it is necessary to consider several general attributes within risk analysis before getting down to detailed event-specific issues. The common steps in risk analysis involve eight basic activities (Berlonghi, 1990: 21), as shown in figure 10.4.

© Juta & Co Ltd

The risk analysis report invariably serves as valuable input to a risk management plan.

10.2.2 Risk management planning

The planning process adopted in the management of risk factors follows very much the same procedural steps as those outlined in chapter 5.

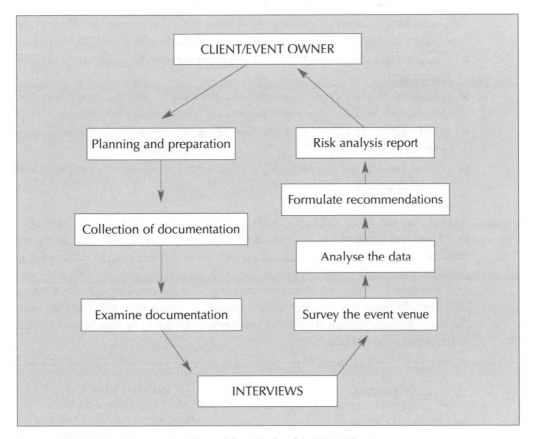

FIGURE 10.4 *Risk analysis process (adapted from Berlonghi, 1990: 22)*

However, certain characteristics of the event must first be assessed by visiting the event venue; the potential risk factors must then be considered in accordance with the following check list:

- assessment of the nature of the event and its setting;
- consideration of time influences (the time of day or night, duration and days in the week or month);
- nature of the target market and attendance (for example, youth groups as opposed to the elderly or disabled);
- location of the event venue and adjacent uses/activities;
- consideration of the weather and environmental factors;

- associated events, before and after (these may impact, for example, on parking congestion);
- various event characteristics which differ according to the type of activities and special equipment needed (for example, automobile racing compared to a conference) (Berlonghi, 1990: 25).

Having given consideration to these factors, it is necessary to rank the anticipated risks according to degree of probability, whether high, medium or low. This can be made easier by grouping the various risks into 'risk fields' (Getz, 1997: 244), such as:

- financial risks (loss of profit, theft, excess cost, unexpected expenditure and/or legal action);
- management risks (poor management, personal problems, interference by stakeholders, and problems with sponsors, suppliers and performers);
- health and safety risks (accidents, health, crime, terrorism, social unrest and emergencies);
- environmental risks (impact on the community, economy, environment, and natural disasters).

By grouping identified risks into 'fields', it is easier to formulate specific strategies to address the problems in a cohesive and orderly manner. Having achieved an understanding of perceived risks, it is advisable to attempt to estimate the potential magnitude of the impact of any risk occurrence (Getz, 1997: 244) and feed this data into the risk management plan. The expected magnitude analysis will also help the event manager to decide on the allocation of priorities between the various risks. Obviously the highest potential degree of loss would receive greatest planning attention.

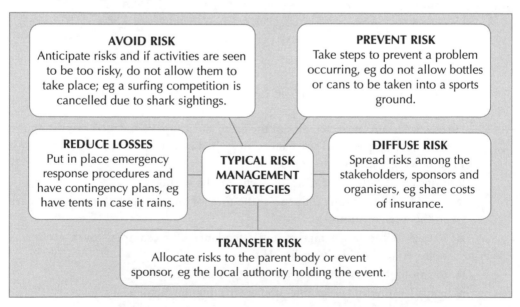

FIGURE 10.5 *Examples of strategies to manage risk (Berlonghi, 1990: 14; Getz, 1997: 245)*

The final aspect of the risk management plan is the proposals section which contains recommendations on the strategies to be adopted to reduce risk, prevent loss and ensure that the event is a success. Such recommendations will define the actions to be taken, responsibilities (by whom), when these actions are to be taken, and clear lines of decision-making and accountability. Both Berlonghi (1990: 14) and Getz (1997: 245) provide guidance on the different strategies which could be applied in a risk management plan (see figure 10.5). However, all events have unique characteristics which necessitate specific strategies in each instance.

10.2.3 Communication

A crucial component of risk management and planning is to foster effective communication between the event personnel. This includes the organisers, role players, stakeholders, volunteer workers and employees. The intention of communication is not to sound an unnecessary alarm or to appear negative, but rather to ensure that all people concerned with the event clearly understand the risks involved and the measures proposed to manage them. Very often, people have different levels of tolerance to risks and their perceptions of risk differ due to attitude, capability and understanding. 'What is a risk to one person is not so to another. The way one person would communicate a risk may not be understood by another' (Berlonghi, 1990: 15).

In attempting to achieve effective communication in a team of people, it is necessary to ensure that they understand the views being expressed in the risk analysis report. Time should be taken to listen to the concerns of the team members and encourage a collective, inclusive approach to solving potential problems. In the process of communicating risk factors, care needs to be taken to reduce anxiety, resolve any disagreements in a positive way and ensure that actions will be the outcome of the planning process.

Finally, effective communication strategies must involve the local community. 'There is less likelihood of a serious public disturbance occurring … when the citizens, businesses, local government and festival organisers work together as a team …' (McCreedy, 1992: 40).

10.3 HOW DO WE MANAGE RISK?

10.3.1 Introduction

The risk management process is broad and addresses every aspect of an event, including pre-event and post-event activities. There are, however, six main management sectors (see figure 10.6) which address the requirements of general risk management. Each event is, however, unique and requires specific attention to meet its varied characteristics.

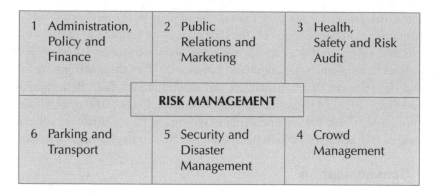

1 Administration, Policy and Finance	2 Public Relations and Marketing	3 Health, Safety and Risk Audit
	RISK MANAGEMENT	
6 Parking and Transport	5 Security and Disaster Management	4 Crowd Management

FIGURE 10.6 *Main risk management sectors (Berlonghi, 1990: 49)*

10.3.2 Administration, policy and finance

10.3.2.1 Administration

The administrative and organisational attributes of an event organisation are discussed in detail in chapter 6; however, with regard to risk management, there are several crucial matters which must be taken into account.

- An important consideration is whether or not the event organisation is experienced or inexperienced in events. If it is inexperienced, it needs to obtain advisers who can build capacity.

- Another relevant factor is the nature of the company and whether it is a private limited company, incorporated partnership, association-not-for-gain, sole proprietor, voluntary association or partnership. All these types of companies have different liability characteristics as far as risk is involved. In South Africa, the first three types of company have limited liability unless the owners act unprofessionally or fraudulently. The remaining types of company (sole proprietor, voluntary associations or partnership) have no liability limitations and the individuals involved could be found personally responsible for losses and for the costs arising from these.

- The organisation which is ultimately accountable for costs, claims, settlements and lawsuits needs to be identified.

- It must be determined whether the management and staff have a clear understanding of their mandate and limits of authority.

- The person/s in the organisation who is designated as the official spokesperson for the event needs to be identified and made known to all staff.

- An administrative procedure for the event, setting out job descriptions, responsibilities and activities for all personnel (voluntary and employed), must be available.

- Key personnel who are strategically important to the event must be identified and a backup plan formulated in case such persons become incapacitated before or during the event itself.

10.3.2.2 Policy

Sound management of an event requires that there be documented policies which the organisation will follow. Policy is defined as 'written or unwritten statements that form the accepted behaviour of an organisation and of the individuals representing the organisation. These policy statements will assist any individual with recognising an issue and state the appropriate accepted reaction' (McCreedy, 1992: 5). It is further emphasised that policies are the most powerful risk management tool in that 'they give substance to your goals and objectives and give your organisation the ethical and moral guidelines to assist in the making of fundamental decisions that affect the direction of the organisation' (McCreedy, 1992: 5).

Each local authority in South Africa has policy regarding events in the area of their jurisdiction. Most policy is contained in local regulations and bylaws. However, in addition to these general rules, each event needs specific guidelines, including:

- alcohol management;
- firearms management;
- first aid;
- cash management;
- lost possessions and property;
- important guest hosting arrangements;
- media relations and representation;
- security arrangements (number of keys in the hands of staff);
- backup of information;
- visitor screening and access rules;
- mail and delivery procedures;
- telephone operations and responses.

10.3.2.3 Legal arrangements

There are several areas where legal contracts become necessary, namely (Martin, 1992: 4):

- sponsorship;
- local authority permits;
- venue/land leases;
- television broadcast rights and fees;
- equipment leases for sound, lighting, communications and signage;
- service industry support, such as waste collection, sanitation, construction and security;
- participants in areas of honorariums and liability;
- volunteer workers in employment terms and liability, and
- recording and performing music, in terms of licensing and copyright.

In appraising whether or not to enter into legal agreements, it is suggested that if an agreement is necessary in order to hold an event or if a loss should occur which could result in liability and an award of costs, an appropriate legal agreement should be entered into.

There are areas of liability and lawsuit in the meetings and conference event industry, particularly where cancellation of a booking occurs. Price (1997: 37) adds that 'the standard hotel contract binds the co-ordinators to meet certain criteria and binds the hotel to very few, beyond a certain number of sleeping and meeting rooms at a specified rate'. Accordingly, the negotiation stage prior to signing any agreements, contracts or orders is seen to be extremely important and a time when attention to detail is essential.

One can never eliminate risk and accordingly 'today's world focuses not on the elimination of risk, but instead on its reduction. The emphasis of all festivals should be on professionalism, safety, risk management, safety, transfer of liability, safety, indemnification and safety' (Martin, 1992: 20). In addition to the emphasis on the need for safety at all times is the fact that indemnities, waivers of liability and consent agreements should be entered into with all performers, participants and any other person who may be at risk or who could place the organisers at risk for liability should anything go wrong.

10.3.2.4 Insurance

Areas where there are risks from administrative or operational matters in events management include:

- discrimination;
- wrongful dismissal;
- acting beyond authority permitted in bylaws;
- violation of state law, and
- failure to properly manage financial affairs.

It is recommended that insurance cover be arranged to cover such claims. Van Meter (1999: 22) recommends cover for directors and event officers to mitigate against 'employment practices liability'.

Outside the administration arena, there are numerous areas which require adequate insurance cover from injury, loss of life, loss of limbs, damage to property or vehicles, and so on. Rae (1999: 20) suggests that 'parade producers can face lawsuits from both participants and bystanders'. In this regard Rae recommends that all independent contractors, vendors and security companies have insurance and provide certification to the event organisers. Similarly, 'every unit in the parade should provide you with a certificate of insurance ... at minimum you should obtain a signed waiver'. Finally, the exclusion listed by the insurance company providing cover needs to be carefully examined to ensure that the cover that is being sought is not being watered down or excluded under certain circumstances.

There are generally three types of insurance coverage:
- general liability insurance;
- property insurance;
- financial loss insurance (against bad weather, cancellation or interruption of business).

Depending on the type of event, certain special cases will require specific insurance such as:
- specific hazards (including bad weather and cancellation, third party liquor liability);
- specified property (on site and off);
- specified persons and groups (e.g. staff, volunteers, participants, audience, bystanders);
- specified venues;
- bonding key employees (against the possibility of loss or theft);
- errors and omissions (for directors and professional staff)' (Getz, 1997: 246).

10.3.3 Financial risk

The financing and financial management of events is dealt with in chapter 7. Particular financial risk management issues are elaborated on in this section because of their relationship to the topic of risk generally as well as to broad administrative issues. Financial planning and budgetary controls are crucial to all business ventures and 'risk management is essential to the modern event manager, both to protect the organisation in financial terms and to ensure a safe and pleasant experience for the guests' (Getz, 1997: 229).

The event industry has many non-profit-making or voluntary associations that aim to hold an event in order to break even. Should profit be generated, this is often passed on to charities. There is a growing trend towards private sector investment in events (particularly with sponsorship companies), with profit being a driving force. This is due to the fact that government departments are reducing monetary involvement in events throughout the world. Accordingly, the risk of financial loss is one which needs to be constantly in the mind of event owners, organisers and managers.

There is a need for professionalism in the events industry and the following principles should be adhered to:
- 'Events are businesses and should be managed as such.

- Event organisations should aim to make a profit (i.e. surplus revenue) to ensure financial self sufficiency; without a surplus there will be no reserve fund and little possibility of capital investment for expansion.
- Events must establish a comprehensive financial planning and control system, including full cost revenue management, budgeting and standardised accounting and reporting' (Getz, 1997: 230).

By adopting the above principles, all event organisations should be able to continually review their position in relation to net worth, solvency and the return on investment (ROI) of each event.

Financial risk management should involve the introduction of strict control policies and procedures on the following matters:
- cash management and receipting;
- signing authorities for bank accounts;
- stock control and stocktaking;
- authorisation for drawing of stores and equipment;
- expense perks, complimentary tickets and credit facility policies;
- ticket numbering and security;
- charitable donations and associated receipting;
- written contracts to be financially and legally sound.

10.3.4 Public relations and marketing

A successful event has a positive spin-off for the key financial role players (usually the sponsors). Accordingly, the public relations and marketing aspects are an important element of reducing financial risks. Usually a publicity plan sets out the way in which the event is to be marketed for the ultimate benefit of the sponsors. It has also been found that the larger sponsor companies can offer risk management support through their own corporate risk management personnel (Berlonghi, 1990: 86).

Effective marketing can attract the 'right' people and the 'wrong' people to an event. However, it is even more crucial to ensure that the event is supported by sufficient numbers of participants to make it a success. Perhaps the most risky aspect of any event is the fact that it only takes place after a considerable investment of time, effort and funds. Should people fail to attend, due to poor marketing, the financial losses and poor public image could seriously affect future events in the area.

Risk managers can benefit greatly from working closely with the marketing manager in order to ascertain how many people are expected to attend, the target market and the level of public awareness. Such information can be made available to the caterers, disaster management and health and safety role players in order to adequately prepare for the attendees.

Another aspect where risk can be effectively managed is with media coverage. Event organisers need to see the media as a strong support base for the event. As a result, a lot of effort needs to be made to prepare suitable accommodation for all media representatives (newspapers, journals, television and radio) in a media centre with suitable and sufficient facilities, communications technology and information.

Finally, it needs to be remembered at all times that people's opinions can be a valuable boost to marketing an event and, alternatively, negative opinions can damage an event's image irreparably. Customer care and a customer service centre which is administered professionally is essential for every event. Berlonghi (1990: 103) stresses that 'this is an excellent way of satisfying the needs and complaints of the public that might otherwise turn into claims and lawsuits'.

Such a customer service centre provides a venue where people can receive assistance, information, lodge general complaints, place telephone calls, broadcast public announcements or receive medical assistance. It is recommended that all complaints be documented and staff trained to handle public relations matters. Berlonghi (1990: 104) recommends that 'if possible Polaroid photographs of the person should be taken. This is good documentation on the exact visual conditions of the person complaining.' However, photography may inflame tempers even more and a video camera could prove less obtrusive in such situations.

Customer service centres can also offer additional services, such as banking facilities, safe deposits, a children's crèche, postal services, information technology, games arcades, gift shops, equipment rental and laundry services (Berlonghi, 1990: 105). These add-on services can be of benefit to participants and performers, but the event organisers need to be satisfied that their availability will not unnecessarily increase risk, liability, resource requirements and costs. Such sophisticated facilities would not normally be available at small, single event venues; they would, however, be expected at larger, national and international functions which have substantial sponsorship.

10.3.5 Health and safety

Price (1997: 31) defines safety as '... concerned with protecting people from injury resulting from accidents caused by their carelessness or the negligence of others. This includes helping delegates take precautions when necessary, inspecting the meeting facility to ensure that basic safety programmes are in place, and identifying sources of medical assistance that can be called in the event of an accident.'

The health and safety of performers and participants in an event should be of the greatest importance to the organisers. Berlonghi (1990: 107) describes the key areas of health and safety which he terms part of a 'loss prevention program':

- 'facility survey
- fire safety
- fireworks and pyrotechnics
- firearms
- medical services
- drug testing
- concessions and food services
- sanitation and maintenance
- equipment and decorations
- animals'.

In broad terms a survey of the venue and all facilities should be conducted in order to ascertain any likely hazards or problems which could cause injury (for example: slippery floors, unsafe walls, objects jutting out from structures, adequate entrances and exits, suitable scaffolding for light and sound equipment, adequate ventilation, sound, stage and seating facilities). The safety of a particular venue from a fire point of view requires inspection by the local authority fire officer and the necessary fire emergency requirements must accordingly be satisfied.

The difference between fireworks and pyrotechnics is that fireworks are used outdoors and pyrotechnics indoors. Once again, the safety precautions associated with such activities need to be determined by specialist personnel and the local fire officer.

Risk management of firearms is most easily achieved by not allowing these to be carried into the event premises. Should certain events require that performers have the use of firearms, designated procedures for their use, the storage of ammunition and security between events must be established (Berlonghi, 1990: 127).

Paramedical support services are widely available in South Africa. It is, however, essential to link up with the designated local authority responsible for medical services (either the City or District Council) and also to seek the support of voluntary medical groups, such as the Red Cross and St John's Ambulance services. There are several specialist planning areas for medical services which can be covered by the medical coordinator, including:

- emergency access routes;
- ambulance services;
- helicopter backup;
- training of volunteers;

- coordination with security personnel;
- mass capacity procedures.

The growing problem of alcohol abuse and the use of drugs is necessitating greater attention to these areas of safety. Drug testing is a specialist area which needs to be administered by expert medical personnel. According to Getz (1997: 246), 'reasonable care must be taken to ensure that, among other potential risks:
- no-one is served a potentially dangerous amount of alcohol;
- no-one under the legal age gets served;
- alcohol is not brought into the venue or consumed outside approved areas;
- drinking does not lead to crowd behaviour problems;
- hazards are not created (such as broken glasses);
- drinkers do not drive automobiles away from the event;
- drinkers leave the grounds safely.'

With regard to concessions and food services, the event organisers need to be satisfied that all food health regulations and standards will be complied with, cleanliness is maintained and clean-up/maintenance is acceptable. Contingency plans need to be in place to ensure adequate serving personnel to cope with long queues or peak demand periods. Similarly, maintenance of the event venue, equipment, decorations collection and disposal of litter and solid waste needs to be effectively organised to prevent hazardous conditions, pollution or an unsatisfactory event image.

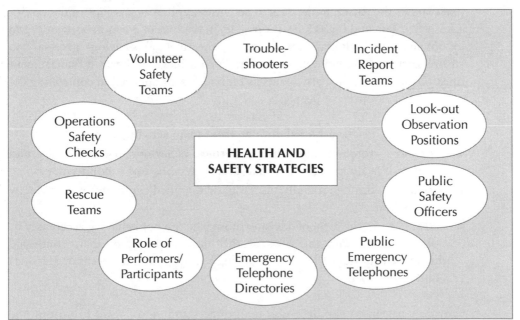

FIGURE 10.7 *Loss prevention strategies (adapted from Berlonghi, 1990: 111)*

Berlonghi (1990: 153) advises that 'under most circumstances the owners and/or keepers (those who have care, custody and control) of animals are responsible for injuries these animals might inflict'. However, it is recommended that adequate planning be conducted to prepare for animals at or within an event. Such planning needs to take into account matters such as additional costs due to special accommodation, staff and resources, security measures, containment facilities, provision of medical veterinarian services, potential damage to property and contingency plans in the event of something going wrong.

The loss prevention programme can use certain key strategies to ensure that the health and safety of personnel are taken care of (Berlonghi, 1990: 109). These strategies are shown in figure 10.7.

The details of these strategies are relatively simple and straightforward in that they are governed by common sense. All strategies employed work on the basis of preparedness, training and awareness for any eventuality. Berlonghi (1990: 109) emphasises that the success of a loss prevention programme depends on the ability of all role players to share the responsibility for preventing losses.

10.3.6 Crowd management

Crowd management enables participants at an event to enjoy the experience without feeling that they are being forced or controlled by the event managers. The overriding objective of any event is for people to enjoy the experience and Rutley (1997: 75) suggests that this can be achieved 'in creating an environment that exposes the patron to the desired activities as often as possible, in the case of a festival or fair, and for as long as possible, in the case of a concert or game, and by obtaining the voluntary compliance to the rules of behaviour necessary to ensure safety and an enjoyable experience'. To achieve this, crowd management must be focused on the participants as individuals, as opposed to controlling the entire crowd as a mass of people.

Crowd management is achieved through three main activities:
- *assistance* – through information on rules, behaviour, the availability and position of facilities, signage, public address systems and announcements;
- *persuasion* – through friendly, pleasant and dignified communication styles by officials, and
- *deterrence* – in the form of advising those who are not behaving acceptably or not complying with the rules of the likely outcome of their continued disruptive behaviour (for example, being removed from the event or arrested) (Rutley, 1997: 76).

Crowd management also depends on an understanding of crowd behaviour, the reason why panic suddenly takes hold, and different types of crowds. There are different management techniques related to crowd movement, seating arrangements, controversial issues, crowd stimuli and noise control.

- At some events the crowds are continually moving and rarely seated (such as at exhibitions) and at other events (such as concerts) the audience needs to be ushered to their seats prior to the event starting.
- Different stimuli can cause crowds to become emotional. These range from the event being cancelled, starting late or the performers failing to appear as promised; to the performer stirring up the crowd, the spectators becoming agitated or throwing objects; to racial tensions, rivalry between groups, and even heat, humidity, rainfall, lack of ventilation and smoke.
- Finally, where excessive noise can affect adjacent neighbourhoods, noise can be too loud for too long and noise can become disruptive to the enjoyment of the audience (Berlonghi, 1990: 128, 159 & 184).

In crowd management, both Rutley and Berlonghi stress the need for good, clear signage and effective public address systems. Consideration also needs to be given to access, amenities and seating for the disabled (physically challenged) and senior citizens who will attend the event.

10.3.7 Security and disaster management

Security is perhaps the most crucial component of risk management: 'security helps create an environment that offers something that the patron wants and allows them to feel safe and non-threatened while at the event' (Rutley, 1997: 75). In a more concise definition, security is said to be 'concerned with protecting people and property from injury or loss resulting from criminal activity' (Price, 1997: 32).

According to Berlonghi (1990: 197), 'event security has several basic functions:

- To provide a safe and secure environment for everyone present during the event and at event-related activities.
- To prevent crime.
- To control the orderly behaviour of spectators.
- To protect people and property.
- To monitor all admissions and access policies and procedures.
- To implement emergency services when they are required: bomb threats, evacuations, hostage situations, defections, etc.
- To request help when needed from local, regional and federal law enforcement agencies.'

In this regard, several strategies are suggested to achieve effective security (Bach, 1997: 32):

- effective locks and fencing;
- lighting of all pedestrian areas and parking zones;

- security patrols;
- surveillance cameras;
- safe storage for valuables;
- education for delegates;
- special security checks for international meetings.

Additional measures are required for security at large arenas, auditoriums and stadiums: 'overcrowding' is often a problem due to a tendency to try to attract as large a crowd as possible to ensure the event's success. Additional measures would include the provision of fencing or barriers to define the area and control the entrance and exit; adequate personnel to manage the situation; and controlling and directing the flow of crowds according to the carrying capacity of the venue/s (Rutley, 1997: 78).

Case study 10.1: 2000 Olympic Games in Sydney, Australia

The *Daily Dispatch* (Wednesday, 28 July 1999) reported that in the case of the Olympic Games preparations in Australia, the Australian Army is already engaged in anti-terrorist training. An example is given of an Australian army Blackhawk helicopter flying around the Stadium Australia recently. Training includes the army special forces who will be operating in and around the stadium during the two-week run of the games.

It is also recommended that every event should have a security plan in document form. This plan should set out all the actions to be taken in circumstances relating to security, including human resource requirements and the financial resources needed. Berlonghi (1990: 197) highlights an additional benefit of a security plan, namely having a document which could be used in the event of a claim of security negligence, either in the case of insurance assessment or a court hearing.

A security plan needs to deal with the working arrangements, roles and responsibilities of local authority police and the South African Police Services. Most event organisers hire private security companies to maintain the security operations at their event. It is advisable to enter into contracts with reputable companies having a good record. The local police commander in the town or city would normally be a suitable source of recommendation regarding available security companies. Event organisers can also call for proposals from private companies and require suitable references and records of experience to be submitted with their bids.

Some event organisers prefer to establish a volunteer security team due to budgetary constraints. Setting up a volunteer security team would require careful recruitment and selection of personnel. The various requirements for selecting personnel should include a check on the record of applicants, their ability to work in a team, working with people, ability in crowd control, professional training in first aid and assisting people (McCreedy, 1992: 16). All volunteer security personnel would need orientation as to the nature of the event and their particular roles and responsibilities.

McCreedy (1992: 19) provides the following example of a typical job description for security personnel: 'As a member of the Security Team you will have to:
- be the eyes and ears for the local police department;
- be a deterrent to potential and real problems;
- identify and react to potential and real problems,
- intercept restricted items for possible seizure by the police;
- identify and react to medical emergencies;
- assure the verification of patrons, VIPs and participants;
- provide security to patrons, VIPs and participants;
- prevent theft, damage, vandalism, personal injury and misbehaviour;
- assist with the provision of crowd control, and
- provide special assistance as needed to patrons, VIPs and participants.'

It is necessary to establish a strong working relationship with the local municipality, local police force, fire department, ambulance and service departments (electricity, water, telephone and sewerage). McCreedy (1992: 22) adds: 'To give your festival every chance of success it is an absolute must that you build security into every level of the planning process. By bringing the security issue forward at the very beginning, and by bringing the various agencies into the planning process at the beginning, you will have taken the largest, and most positive step, towards a successful event. Festivals are fun for everyone! But a few can spoil it for all!'

Case study 10.2: Woodstock 1999

'Summer of love ends in looting, arson
GRIFFISS AIR FORCE BASE – Hundreds of revelers at Woodstock '99 went on a burning and looting spree in a violent finale to the three-day concert, CNN reported yesterday.

Concert-goers set fire to 12 tractor trailers, looted booths and toppled stage lights and speakers late on Sunday as the festival wound down, the network said, quoting state police.

Riot police were called in to contain the chaos, pushing the vandals into a camping area. By early yesterday the situation had been stabilised, police said.

Many concert-goers described it as terrifying. "It was very confused, very chaotic," one reveler told local television station WIXT.

"As people were coming out, they started blowing up gas tanks or propane tanks or something," said another concert-goer.

Early in the weekend, organisers congratulated themselves on how smoothly things were going, but by the end of the music fest officials were far less forthcoming with information about incidents of arrests and injuries and it became clear the event that had been billed as a reprise of the summer of love had deteriorated.

Some 60 acts, including Alanis Morisette, Sheryl Crow, Red Hot Chili Peppers, Willie Nelson, Elvis Costello, Our Lady Peace and Metallica, performed over three days here.

The low point came on Saturday night while rock group Limp Bizkit held stage. A mob of some 200 people threw bottles at the stage, injuring a young woman.

When she sought treatment for head injuries she found the medical tent had been closed because of concern for workers' security.

Limp Bizkit singer Fred Durst tried to restore calm, but had found the sound system had been rendered inoperable.

Even members of hard rock group Rage Against the Machine – generally viewed as no strangers to raucous revelry – hesitated to take the stage, organisers admitted.

Organisers dodged all questions about drugs, omnipresent even to casual observers.

One particular popular drug on the scene apparently was "Special K", an anesthetic used by veterinarians, which has become the rage in dance clubs.

"We sold between 175 000 and 200 000 tickets," an organiser said, adding that promotional tickets probably increased that to around 225 000.

"I don't think we're disappointed" – Sapa-AFP.'

(*Daily Dispatch*, 27 July 1999)

10.3.8 Parking and transport

Risk management also extends to the parking and transport sectors of the event for several reasons.

- In most instances the event will attract the attendance of people using private and public transport.
- The success of the event could be determined by the accessibility of the venue and its parking capacity (or arrangements).
- Most events result in travel by performers, VIPs and key people. Event programmes need to be geared to air, rail and road transport to allow for rehearsal and recuperation.
- Depending on the size of the event, the support of the local authority, and even government, may be necessary to assist in augmenting the transportation system to meet the anticipated flow of guests. (An example of this type of partnership occurred during the 1994 World Cup Rugby Tournament when the South African Airways schedules had to be adjusted to suit the match itinerary and local park-'n-ride facilities had to be provided to reduce congestion outside the sporting venues.)

According to Berlonghi (1990: 259), event parking should be a concern of risk managers for the following reasons:

■ parking is usually the place where the spectator has a first impression of the event;
■ accidents and crimes often take place in the parking areas, and
■ parking can generate revenue if a safe and secure facility is made available.

In addition, in South Africa the emergence of 'car guards' has resulted in a small enterprise job creation opportunity, which can benefit local entrepreneurs and build community goodwill.

Should the event be large enough to require the assembly of a vehicle fleet, the risks associated with vehicle abuse accidents and theft need to be taken into account. There are a number of vehicle hire and fleet management companies in South Africa which can assist in this specialist operational area.

A further aspect of transportation risk could relate to traffic management: 'traffic congestion causes tempers to rise and is conducive to accidents … if the domino effect takes over this can cause serious problems in controlling fans and in the honouring of contracts' (Berlonghi, 1990: 275). Measures which could be taken to manage traffic include:

■ consulting the responsible traffic management authorities;
■ obtaining permits for road closures;
■ arranging police point duty officers for potential congestion at intersections;
■ allocating special bus lanes;
■ establishing loading/offloading areas for public transport and taxis;
■ setting up appropriate barricades, lights and pedestrian safety areas;
■ arranging police escorts for parades through public streets;
■ positing special signs to direct traffic.

Unusual circumstances could be associated with a major event: for example, a motorcade bearing a head of state or dignitary may have to be included in the risk management plan. While this specific transport operation will be managed by the South African Police Services and the local authority traffic police, the event organisers will invariably be required to make special arrangements to allow the motorcade special access. This will also result in the crowd management arrangements being geared to security for the VIPs involved. Berlonghi (1990: 285) recommends several measures to reduce risks in the event of a motorcade: the use of one-way streets, varying times, routes and methods of transport, having breakdown/tow vehicles along the route and making sure that all vehicles have sufficient fuel and backup spare wheels.

Case study 10.3: Grahamstown National Arts Festival 1999

Crime normal in festival city

Police in Grahamstown reported yesterday afternoon that there had been no escalation of crime as the city slowly gets into its annual festival swing.

Sgt. Milanda Coetzer said police were satisfied that the 20 crimes reported in the first three days of the festival were receiving necessary attention. They represent no more than is usual at this time of a month. She said, however, that police will increase their vigilance – presumably as numbers attending the festival increase. Sgt. Coetzer also urged festinos and local residents to report all crimes for investigation. She even gave the telephone number of Capt. Riaan Kemp for anyone who was not satisfied with the police services.

The first criminal fruits of 1999's special festival include: the theft of two cellular phones in High Street; three cases of possession of suspected stolen property in Cowie Street, Holland Close and High Street; six thefts from motor vehicles in Anglo-African, Grey, Bathurst, Market and Livingstone Streets; two thefts of motor vehicles in Queen and High Streets; a robbery in Beaufort Street; three housebreakings in New, Rose and Willeton Streets; two assaults in Church Square; a theft in High Street and a fraud in Village Green.

Sgt. Coetzer offered specific advice: secure mobile phones when not using them, and do not leave them on tables or anything else convenient; avoid leaving things in sight in a locked car, park cars in well-lit places, if possible; and don't walk alone after 8pm, or in deserted places.

She has other advice which we will publish later.

(*Grocott's Mail*, 130(52), Friday 2 July 1999)

Browse these Internet sites

http://www.davislogic.com/event_management.htm
http://www.efanational.com/content/attachments/riskmagt/3_Sample_Event_Risk_Management_Plan.pdf
http://www.fireservicecollege.ac.uk/library/PDF/Risk%20Management.doc
http://www.ourcommunity.com.au/files/event_management.pdf
http://www.personal.usyd.edu.au/~wotoole/epmspage1.html
http://www.sa2010bid.co.za/default.asp?cId=8511
http://www.srq.qld.gov.au/legal_issues___risk_management.cfm

QUESTIONS FOR SELF-EVALUATION

1. Provide a definition of risk and describe the four types of risk.

2. Discuss the various factors which have a bearing on risk and indicate the distinction between those that can be managed and those that are a natural phenomenon.

3. What are the six principal causes of loss?

4. Describe how we analyse risk and explain the steps involved.

5. What, in your opinion, is the benefit of creating fields of risk?

6. There are six broad strategies which can be used to manage risk; discuss these.

7. Risk management involves six sectors; explain what these are.

8. Discuss the legal arrangements to reduce risk.

9. Financial loss is one of the principal risks faced by all event organisations; discuss the measures which can be taken to manage this risk.

10. Security is one of the most important components of risk management. Describe the ten strategies to prevent loss through safety and security.

CHAPTER 11

Event Marketing

Nimish Shukla and Nancy Nuntsu

AIM OF THE CHAPTER

The aim of this chapter is to study issues relating to event marketing.

LEARNING OBJECTIVES

After having studied this chapter, you should be able to:

- define event marketing;
- explain the importance of customer care;
- describe the three Es of event marketing;
- illustrate the five Ps of event marketing;
- identify the five Ws of event marketing;
- conduct market research and list the principles of marketing research for events;
- appreciate the role of public relations in event marketing;
- identify the elements of a press release and a press kit;
- develop an electronic event marketing strategy;
- identify factors that may affect marketing strategy;
- perform a SWOT analysis;
- devise a promotional plan for an event;
- employ the full communications mix to effectively promote the event and establish and maintain relationships;
- list event marketing problems and strategies.

11.1 INTRODUCTION

This chapter is to some extent based on Rossouw (2000: 263–290).

When planning an event, the mechanical things must be done, but the risk of failure is significant if you don't think about what you are doing, why you are doing it, and for whom you are doing it. Event marketing is critical in ensuring the event's success.

To successfully market an event, you need to be sure that you have an event that people will attend. You need to evaluate your obstacles, i.e. is there enough to properly market the programme? Are there scheduling conflicts, such as university graduations or annual meetings or conventions that your potential attendees routinely attend? The point is, if attendees are really the most critical ingredients, then consider them in the beginning. It is dangerous to market your event based on your organisation's needs rather than on customers' needs. Event marketing needs to be *creative, centralised, focused* and *leveraged* to create the maximum return on event.

11.2 EVENT MARKETING DEFINED

Event marketing is the function of event management that can keep in touch the event's participants and visitors (consumers), read their needs and motivations, develop products that meet these needs, and build a communication programme which expresses the event's purpose and objectives' (Hall, 1992, as quoted by Watt, 1998: 61). It is the process of employing the marketing mix to attain organisational goals through creating value for clients and customers. The organisation must adopt a marketing orientation that stresses the building of mutually beneficial relationships and the maintenance of competitive advantages (Getz, 1997: 250).

Event marketing is always undertaken in the context of fulfilling the event's mandate and goals, whether it be public service or profit. The more comprehensive its goals, the more challenging marketing events become. In summary, event marketing involves: customer care; selling; influencing trends and attitudes; creating experiences; research; segmentation to appropriate areas; targeting; entry strategy explaining which level or group to challenge first; and marketing mix (product, price, promotion and place).

11.3 THE THREE Es OF EVENT MARKETING

Whether you are marketing a complete convention or a stand-alone awards banquet, all of the 3 Es of event marketing are critical to the continuing success of any event (Hoyle, 2002: 2).

Entertainment, for example, is available everywhere in our society. Years ago, people had to make a special effort to leave their homes to attend the theatre or a sporting event to enjoy entertainment. They are now saturated with convenient home entertainment options on television, CDs and DVDs, computers, and videos. Key to your marketing success is the need to provide entertainment that will once again compel your audience to leave home to experience something they will not find there, because what you are offering is different, unique, and designed just for them.

Excitement may seem intangible, but it is real. It is key to making an event memorable. Excitement may be generated by entertainment that 'blows the doors off the place': the great band, the dazzling magician, the fabulous party staged in the atrium lobby of a resort hotel. But entertainment may have nothing to do with the excitement promised by an event marketer. Many marketers miss the opportunity to promise excitement in other critical features of their meetings and events. The point is that it should always be considered as part of an effective marketing plan. For example, the greatest excitement for an attendee may be the eye-opening revelations of that special educational programme that advances knowledge and career opportunities and changes lives forever, or it may be the impact of that keynote speaker whose motivational message will become a lasting asset, and cherished memory, for the listener.

Enterprise is defined in *Merriam-Webster Online Dictionary* as, among other things, '*a project or undertaking that is especially difficult, complicated and risky*'.
If there is any characteristic that defines the pioneers in event marketing, it is that. The willingness to stretch the bounds of reason, to sail into uncharted waters, drove marketing's original landscapers into the imagination and conscience of the publics that they sought to attract. They understood the natural inclination of people to experience something new; to be the first to be able to describe those new experiences to their friends, and to become part of the inner sanctum of the new enterprise. They wanted to 'blow the doors off the place' and dared to ask questions.

11.4 THE SIX Ps OF EVENT MARKETING (MARKETING MIX)

The effective event manager will balance the six Ps (product, price, place, public relations, press releases, positioning) to produce a good marketing mix.

11.4.1 Product

Richards (1992: 4) indicates that the event marketer should ask him/herself the following questions:

- Will what we are doing appeal to the identified markets?
- Will there be enough for them to see/do in relationship to the proposed pricing structure?
- How can we change or add to the present product to attract more visitors and/or new market sectors?

The successful event marketer is at first the consummate student of his or her product. *The product* is the end result – the event, the tournament, exhibition, seminar or show. It also involves all the ancillary contributions like programmes, presentation, quality production and customer care. It may be an educational programme, a country fair, or a full-fledged convention. It may be a reunion for a fraternal organisation or a corporate product launch. If you are marketing the event, there are essential elements that you must know and questions you must ask of the event sponsor (Hoyle, 2002: 12–13).

What is the history of the event? Many veteran event marketers will attract participation because they can sell the celebratory essence of the event. 'The 29th National Arts Festival held in Grahamstown, South Africa' proclaims the success and venerability of an organisation, as well as the pride that goes with being part of it. But even if there is no history, there is the opportunity to be historical. For example, ' The 1st Annual Conference' will have no history but can be portrayed as an opportunity to get involved in the initial stage of a 'happening' that participants can infer will be an ongoing event, turning into a tradition, and developing long-term loyalty. The greatest part of event marketing is the opportunity to create history, by attracting people into a synergistic activity that can define the organisation and its goals. The celebration of history is a fabulous promotional asset in whatever way the event marketer wishes to interpret it for the audience.

Case study 11.1: The year the Arts Festival crossed over

After 28 years of evolving, the National Arts Festival finally and irreversibly crossed the line and became a part of South Africa's new socio-political order.

Acceptance of the festival as an asset in black-majority ruled South Africa came from Eastern Cape Premier, Makhenkesi Stofile, who opened the event last week with an open-arms welcome to international and national visitors. He encouraged them to open themselves up to the arts and culture on display from the province.

His government was footing a healthy portion of the R8m bill for the first time ever this year. Earlier this year, Finance MEC Enoch Godongwana announced that more than R7m would be spent on the event over the next three years.

The Grahamstown festival – which started out as a Shakespearian tea-drinking junket for elderly white women in the 1970s – was then taken over as a strident platform for the anti-apartheid struggle in the 1980s, and became one huge celebratory party for the liberated SA in the mid-1990s.

In the last two years, with Standard Bank giving notice that they would be withdrawing as the umbrella sponsor, the entire event's future looked decidedly uncertain up until two months ago when the Eastern Cape government confirmed that it was prepared to take up some of the gap. At last week's festival almost the entire provincial executive were seen at the shows, especially the epic theatre pieces with their all-black SA stars and the ever-cool jazz festival.

(Source: Loewe, 2002: 8)

What is the Value of the Product? Marketing an event requires that the message emphasise the manner in which the participant will benefit. The promise of increasing productivity, maximising profitability or simply having a great time can be legitimate benefits that can persuade a person to buy the product or attend the event. Designing an event with that research in hand and effectively describing how that event will fulfil those needs are keys to effective marketing.

What makes the product unique? What makes this event different from others? Why should one choose to invest time and money in this event, as opposed to the competition that surrounds it? Marketers that can identify the return on investment (ROI) that will be offered, and the added value of attendance are those who will successfully market the event. This will require research into the event market and into the objectives of the client or organisation. Only then can the uniqueness of the product be identified and described in all of the marketing media utilised.

11.4.2 Price

Richards (1992: 4) states that the marketer should ask him or herself the following questions:
Has the product been priced to match the visitor perception of good value? Will the projected income cover all fixed and variable overheads, depreciation, future capital investment and all marketing costs to yield a profit?

Other questions might include: Can the event be provided at a price acceptable to customers? Can price packages be put together to support group attendance or tourist rates?

Primary among the responsibilities of the event marketer is an understanding of the financial goals of the sponsoring organisation. Once this is determined, market research will illustrate the competition's pricing patterns: Who is offering a similar product, to whom, and at what price? Equally important are the considerations such as the level of demand for the product and economic indicators such as the relative health of the economy in a particular city or region or, to an increasing extent, globally. Price may be secondary to perceived value. It is in this area that the event marketer can play a major role. In marketing events, consider these issues of pricing (Hoyle, 2002: 13–15):

What is the corporate financial philosophy? Some events are designed to make money, pure and simple. Others are strategically developed to break even financially. And there are some that are positioned as 'loss leaders', expected to lose money in an effort to gain greater assets elsewhere, such as membership development or community goodwill. Corporate meetings are typically expensed not as profit centres but rather as 'costs of doing business' in order to build employee loyalty and pride and to learn how better to sell products and services. The event marketer must clearly understand the financial mission and designs a strategy to accommodate those goals.

What is the cost of doing business? Price must reflect the total costs of goods and services, including the cost of marketing itself. Marketing is often relegated to a secondary role in event production because the costs of printing, postage, advertising, public relations, and other basic marketing expenses may not be considered part of the event budget. Instead, marketing costs may be treated as part of the organisation's general overhead and operating expenses. The marketer will be considered an integral part of event production when that event's budget provides for marketing as a primary event function and income–expense centre.

What are the financial demographics of the target audience? Analyse your market's ability to pay. This sounds simple, but it is critical to the marketing effort. An event designed for executives who have access to corporate credit cards and can charge their participation as business expenses will likely be priced at a higher level than an event designed for those who must pay from their own personal wallets. Market research will help determine the ability and willingness of attendees to pay ticket prices at various levels, and, therefore, influence the planning of the event itself.

11.4.3 Place

In the real estate industry, the old saying about ascertaining the value of a property is 'location, location, location'. The same is said in the hospitality industry when planners decide where to buy or build new facilities. It is no less true when marketing an event. The location of your event can dictate not just the attendance, but the character and personality of the event as well. This is a consideration for the earliest part of the planning stages. For example, for an event being held at a plush resort, the setting for the event should be a key part of the marketing strategy. The event site may even be the major draw featured in brochures and advertising. An awards dinner at a new public facility in your town should emphasise the opportunity to experience the facility as an exciting highlight of the event itself. On the other hand, an educational seminar at an airport hotel would not necessarily feature the attractiveness of the site but rather could emphasise the convenience and functionality of the location as the major asset for the attendee. Place should be marketed with a number of important elements in mind, for example (Hoyle, 2002: 15):

1. proximity to the potential attendees and ease of travel;
2. availability of parking for a commuter audience;
3. ambience and originality of the site;
4. logistical practicality of staging a particular event;
5. surrounding attractions/infrastructure for ancillary activities;
6. existence of related audiences, organisations;
7. degree to which the location fits the character of the event;
8. safety, security of event attendees;
9. availability of public transportation (airport and city);
10. availability of overflow space (sleeping and meeting rooms).

Watts (1998: 66–67) has a similar opinion in this regard. He maintains that 'place' has several aspects: venue, transport, accommodation, emergency access, ancillary facilities, host town, signposting, region, maps, country, car parking, environmental conditions, catering location, geographic location, etc.

The decision to choose a location is based on more than the appearance of the facility. Selection must be made with the audience and its profile in mind.

11.4.4 Public relations

The public handling and public image of the organising group are pivotal components of a project's success. Public relations policy effectively combines all the relevant issues like advertising, image, logo and media relations with the foremost factors of customer relations and customer care.

The Public Relations Institute of Southern Africa (PRISA) states that public relations is the management through communication, of perceptions and strategic relationships between an organisation and its internal and external stakeholders (Skinner, Von Essen & Mesham, 2001: 04). These authors state that public relations helps an organisation and its publics adapt mutually to each other. It is an organisation's efforts to win the cooperation of groups of people. Thus, whatever individuals and organisations may think, their image is in the marketplace, the public's perceptions of them are all-important, whether based on fact or fiction. Public relations has a key role to play in developing understanding and support for a particular event.

Public relations is a major part of the marketing mix. You can advertise anything you want; that is, what you say about your organisation and your event. Public relations (PR) can determine how others perceive you and your mission. The PR exercise may be as bold as a team of press agents distributing releases to newspapers or staging press conferences to extol the virtues of your event. Or it may be as subtle as a trade publication interview with a leader of your organisation, when the interview includes references to your event and its benefits.

Public relations is the promotional discipline of forming what your audience thinks or feels about the value of your enterprise and, even more importantly, about your organisation as a whole. It is a broader, more time-consuming approach to building continuing allegiance to your cause and participation in your events.

You need not be a PR professional to practise effective public relations. A media release, feature article, or simply a phone call to the editor of a trade publication can result in invaluable publicity for your event. Most industry publications and newspapers welcome such information or material, which they use as 'fillers,' or even as news articles.

Getting a positive image is a high priority for many PR projects. By their very nature, events are often designed to achieve an increased awareness of the activity involved and to create a focal point for interest. Effective public relations is best achieved by influencing people through the influencers. This can be done by using the mass media and by obtaining the support of leading experts in the relevant field. Many people in the arts consider the views of the critics as the deciding factor in gauging success. This may or may not be true, but a recommendation on radio or television can be pivotal to a project's progress. And a celebrity endorsement is often influential.

The information you provide to a news source must reflect a news style rather than an advertising tone. For example, if you approach a publication with the fact that you are holding an industry conference, you will probably be told to 'buy an ad.' But if your message is that major new economic and legislative initiatives will be developed during your general session, the results of which may change the direction of the industry, your chances of getting 'ink' are much greater. You may be asked to submit an article or provide more details. You may also find a reporter in the general session to write a follow-up article or editorial covering the proceedings.

The effective event marketer will seize on every opportunity to plant the seeds of credibility and positive response. For example, the American Society of Association Executives stages a community project as an ancillary activity during its convention. Wherever the association convenes, volunteer attendees are enlisted to go into the community; grab paint cans, hammers and nails, rakes and brooms; and rehabilitate a playground or a building. Not only is this attractive to local newspapers and television and radio stations, but pictures and stories of this goodwill effort appear throughout professional journals. The positive results are priceless. The convention becomes a platform for expanded credibility, goodwill, publicity, and far-fetching recognition of the association.

Public relations requires careful analysis of the project's purposes, audiences, benefits, and the media available to deliver the appropriate message.

TABLE 11.1 *Public relations requirements (Source: Hoyle, 2002: 48)*

Always ask! Do I need media? If so, why? Media coverage is a means, not an end. Stay focused on your overall goal.
Define your goals. What specifically are you trying to achieve?
Target your Audience. Are you trying to attract students? Lawyers? Bricklayers? Men? Women? Cat owners?
Select your media. Focus on the media that will best reach your defined target market.
Define your message. Stay focused on your message throughout the campaign. Be crisp, clear, and consistent.
Find your news angle. Look for the unique and unusual news about your event.

Look for the story that will define your message. Ask yourself two key questions: What's the story here? And why do we care?

TABLE 11.2 *A summary of tools for communicating an event (Source: Hoyle, 2002: 50; Getz, 1997: 312–313)*

Tool	Purpose or Use
The media kit (*photographs, biographies, press releases*)	Provides basic information and positive features
Videos	Supplement media kits with videos for broadcast media. Get sponsors to prepare and distribute videos; sell them. Videos can have multiple uses: general broadcast, news items, recruiting and thanking sponsors, appealing to volunteers, trade show exhibits, direct sales to tour companies
Press releases	Timely, concise messages for general media use (for example, announcement of the event programme and its features, summary of the event's successes and impacts)
News conferences	Bring media together for major announcements. Usually combined with a special event to attract maximum media presence and foster more personal relationships
News reporting	Foster good relations with reporters
Calendar listings	Get into all the event listings
Posters and banners	Not just at the event
Audiovisual material (*borrowing and sales*)	Slide library, videos, tapes of musicians
VIP visits and	To attract media coverage and obtain explicit or implicit *celebrities* endorsement
Hospitality	At the event, news conferences, or other. To foster personal relationships: with writers, broadcasters, other stakeholders
Speeches	Managers or volunteer spokespersons spread the message
Ambassadors	Many events have competitions to appoint official ambassadors, often in combination with the wearing of costumes or entertainment
Appreciation rewards	Formal thanks to volunteers, media, other stakeholders
Familiarisation tours	Invite travel writers of other media to event and/or destination, leading to feature stories. Commission writers/photographers to do features
Newsletters	Keep everyone informed regularly
Charitable donations	Get publicity for all worthwhile deeds

Personal calls	Telephone three key contacts every day
Formal briefings	To financial stakeholders and sponsors. To lobby governments and officials
Publicity stunts	Often event performers can arrange a stunt prior to or at the event to attract extra attention

11.4.5 Press releases

Every press release should be designed according to the following format and with all the information outlined in this order:

- Organisational letterhead or news release form
- Name, address, phone number, fax number, and e-mail address
- Flush left: a date for release to the public, or
- The boldfaced phrase: 'FOR IMMEDIATE RELEASE'
- Flush right: (for more information: name of contact person and phone number)
- Short headline in bold capital letters
- Leading the first paragraph, begin with release date and location (city) of release. The first paragraph should clearly define the five Ws (see para 11.4.8) of the event, with additional background and information in subsequent paragraphs
- Information should be double-spaced (so editors may make notes) and printed on one side only
- If the release is more than one page, signify by writing -MORE- at the bottom of the page. Begin the next page with the page number and the identification of the event or organisation and continue with each succeeding page.

Alert the reader that the release is concluded by writing 'End' or '# # #' at the close of the last page.

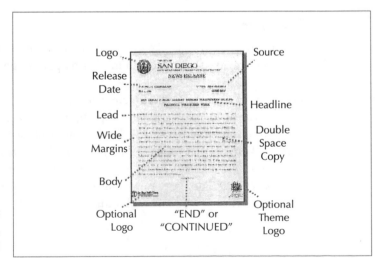

FIGURE 11.1 *Sample press release (Source: Prebyl, 1995: Internet)*

Content of the release should lead with the most important information, with additional details offered in descending order of importance

11.4.5.1 Press kits

A press kit is a more comprehensive tool used to relay as much information about an event and its purpose as possible, packaged in an attractive folder or portfolio imprinted with the name of the sponsoring organisation, the event, a logo, and other pertinent information. Typically, press kits may contain: press releases, photos, media alerts, requests for coverage, press conference announcements and invitations, speeches, background news stories, videotapes, CDs or DVDs, organisational information, biographies, folders, brochures, postcards and advertising speciality items

There are certain principles of public relations that will be employed. The first step should be to examine previous public relations efforts and their relative effectiveness in promoting greater participation or in mitigating challenges. Were the responses positive or negative? Attitude surveys, focus groups, and analysis of attendance trends are helpful in this examination. Public relations has become much more of a sophisticated marketing tool than the old days, when press agents tried to grab the lapels of newspaper reporters and gain a few column inches of coverage. Today, public relations professionals consider virtually all communications outlets in order to disseminate the message. Newspapers remain a staple outlet, as do radio and television broadcasters, magazines, newsletters, the Internet, and other online services. Related associations and corporations must also be considered as public relations resources, especially for their support of the event and their understanding of its purpose and their potential roles and mutual benefits. One of the greatest rewards of a positive public relations campaign is the discovery of partner marketers who will support your efforts in return for your support of theirs.

11.4.6 Positioning

The marketing plan will likely be the instrument that determines success or failure. And the key to a successful marketing plan is 'positioning'.

Positioning is the strategy of determining, through intuition, research, and evaluation, those areas of consumer need that your event can fulfil. What types of events is the competition offering? What level of investment are they requiring of their attendees? Who is attending, and who is not? In other words: what niche are we trying to fill? What makes us different and how can we seize upon our unique qualities to market our events? The event-marketing executive who can answer these questions has the greatest opportunity of fulfilling expectations.

Here are some key considerations when positioning an event (Hoyle, 2002: 18–20):

Proper positioning: Event marketing relies on the proper positioning of the product. No event can be effectively sold until a marketing plan is developed. Each event should have its own marketing plan that includes items such as: event aims and objectives; marketing objectives; marketing strategy; environmental and demographic factors; competition; and specific action through the Ps of the marketing mix.

Location: In selecting location for an event it is important to concentrate on issues such as: Which area is more suitable? Is a regional event in the habit of serving the city constituencies while disenfranchising those in the rural areas? Do we always meet in a hotel ballroom, when a change-of-pace venue such as a museum or amusement park may attract new interest and attendance? Issue of location must be continuously evaluated, because interests of the markets change constantly.

Attention span: People forget quickly. Studies have shown that people are bombarded with some 2 700 messages daily. In the midst of all that information, establishing the position of an event is a daunting task. Marketing materials must constantly emphasise the needs the event will satisfy and the benefits it will provide, because potential attendees will likely be thinking about a thousand other things.

Competitive costs: When positioning an event, a prime consideration is the cost of admission. What level of registration fee is the competition charging? What level of success are they experiencing? Positioning strategies must consider the economic level and flexibility of the audience being sought, and meet that expectation. Some organisations hold events where admission is free (because of limited resources of the attendees) and the costs are covered by exhibitors, sponsors, and supporters. Others may set the cost of participation exceedingly high in order to attract only the market niche represented by big spenders and industry leaders. There is no one definitive answer, other than that registration/participation fee issues are a significant part of correctly positioning the event and an integral cog in the marketing plan.

Programme: What can you offer in your event programme that no one else is offering and, consequently, market the uniqueness? You may find an opportunity to honour an industry or community leader. There may be an educational segment that can be featured or an 'open forum' debate designed to explore the future of the group or industry. Uniqueness in programming is essential to marketing success; 'sameness' is lethal in the long run.

Keep it simple: The more complex the positioning considerations, the more complex the marketing plan will likely be. The more daunting the marketing plan, the less likely you will be able to follow it faithfully. The plan should simply spell out, as briefly as feasible, the objectives, the strengths and weaknesses of your organisation and event, the needs of your potential market niche, economic considerations, and elements that will make the enterprise unique from others. Short and sweet. And easy to track.

11.4.7 Promotion (the communication mix)

Richards (1992: 4) states that the marketer should ask him/herself the following questions:

- What are we going to tell our target markets about our product?
- What is unique about our proposition or product?
- How will our messages reach the target markets?

Promotion could be defined as the striving up of interest in your enterprise (Hoyle, 2002: 41).

Regardless of the nature of your event, its success will largely depend on promotion. Promotion is vital in creating awareness of the event, a desire to participate, and a feeling by the potential participant that the investment of time and money validate the benefits the event offers. This has several aspects: advertising, pamphlets, media relations, posters, publicity, logo, merchandising and displays (Watt, 1998: 66–67). Getz (1997: 304–305) states that although many managers use the term 'promotion', it is but one of several forms of communications. The *communications mix* consists of all the methods by which the event communicates with its various constituencies and markets, including advertising, cross-promotions, street promotions, stunts, sales promotions and public relations (Hoyle, 2002: 41). Sponsorship is also considered to be an arm of communications, from the sponsor's perspective. Hoyle (2002: 41) maintains that the promotional campaign may include a wide range of marketing tools, or as few as one, depending on your products and your needs.

A marketing strategy must include the communications tasks necessary to influence the consumer-buying process: informing, educating, persuading, reminding. Public relations has the added function of fostering community support and sponsorships, but that too is part of ensuring demand for the event.

All communications must be coordinated to achieve marketing goals. Event managers have a number of special challenges to consider.

- There is often a need for intense, short-term promotion of the upcoming event.
- One-time events must manage communications very carefully to achieve early awareness and ensure a peaking of demand as the event nears.
- During long events, such as world fairs, communications can continue during the event and partially make up for earlier weaknesses.
- The communications budget is often inadequate, being of secondary importance to getting the event produced.
- Many constituencies must be involved (for example, grant-givers, sponsors, suppliers, participants, politicians, target markets, volunteers) in event communications.

- Sponsorship has the potential to greatly enhance the quality and extend the scope of communications.
- Events are often very attractive to the media, especially television.
- Many events are mostly media-oriented, with the explicit goal of generating substantial coverage and image enhancement for organisers and destinations.
- Maintaining good public relations within the host community can be essential to the long-term development of the event.

11.4.7.1 Logo

An appropriate logo can be a crucial part of any image. It is important to give it careful thought and to consult relevant agencies and authorities before finalising the design. Its impact on merchandising and souvenirs can have a sizeable effect on income. It used to be common to look for relatively simple logos using a single colour, but now multicoloured and often multi-image logos are used for international manifestations. This is to maximise colour combinations and possibilities, so maximising sales. For larger events this can be a gold mine, but smaller events should be wary of buying in too much stock of items they may not sell. A good logo should reflect the event; portray an event image; pass on what it is about; give relevant messages; be attractive and eye-catching; be colourful (preferably) (Watt, 1998: 68).

11.4.7.2 Mascot

Also related to image, any event of any size should have its own mascot, as long as it can afford one. A mascot can help to promote the event in various ways, especially with certain target groups (compare the mascots that were used for the Olympic Games and the All Africa Games). The mascot must be closely identified with the event; it should be appropriate, relevant and attractive; it should portray the project image and it should be saleable (Watt, 1998: 68).

There are many tools to be considered for use in a promotional campaign, among them (Hoyle, 2002: 42):

11.4.7.3 Sales promotions

A sales promotion is a non-recurrent action intended to generate sales or increase attendance. A sales promotion seeks to add value to the decision to purchase or attend, and to convey a sense of excitement and urgency. It can also stimulate a first visit, encourage repeat visits, and generate positive word-of-mouth discussion. Sponsors can be found to create the promotions or participate in those invented by the event marketer (Getz, 1997: 310).

All staff involved in the event have a 'selling' job to do. They need to sell participation in the event as worthwhile to everyone they come in contact with. This means a positive selling approach from the telephones and the chief executive, as well as everywhere in between. Take every opportunity to interest potential visitors and participants in the project. Everyone in the team becomes a sales representative (personal selling of events).

Another aspect to selling takes place at and around the event: merchandising, souvenir sales, franchising and trading. These are the direct financial sales which can make measurable sums of money and contribute massively to event income. For some of the bigger events, franchising (selling all or part sales rights for a fee or percentage) is the most convenient way to produce sales returns without significant work by the organising committee. It is not likely to yield the highest possible return, except in events like the Olympic Games. The franchisee gets a share of the profit, partly at the expense of the event organisers (Watt, 1998: 73).

Most often franchised are catering and souvenirs. It may be more appropriate for the organisers to merchandise the goods themselves, realising all possible profits by undertaking all sales. Event souvenirs and other related sales can be lucrative for any event. They must be carefully considered because the choice of the wrong logo, image or souvenirs can cause a severe financial loss. At all levels, these sales are absolutely vital to financial viability and must be carefully deliberated. Rash decisions can be permanently regretted. It will take courage to venture perhaps limited money on buying goods to resell, but the profits are often a financial lifeline. These sales can also help in conveying an event image for present and future events. A good range of souvenirs will certainly be appreciated; they will remind visitors of an enjoyable experience and encourage them to return. A worthwhile investment.

11.4.8 The five Ws of event marketing

Regardless of the nature of promotion you use for promoting your event, whether it includes advertising, press releases, speeches, stunts or brochures, the critical elements of 'why, who, when, where, and what' must be emphasised up front – in the first paragraph of your press release, on the cover of the brochure, or in whatever medium of promotion you are using. It constitutes the first axiom of journalism and promotion.

Hoyle (2002: 33–41) explains the five Ws of event marketing as follows:

WHY?

The opening message of virtually all promotional materials should feature the 'why?' Why should someone take the time and spend the money to come to your event? To answer that question, the marketing and management team for the event must determine the overriding reasons for the event itself. When defined, those reasons must be addressed in hard-hitting and in *second person terms* to those being sold on the idea of attending. Instead of the mundane call to attend your event with a simple 'You're invited' - *tell them why!*

WHO?

To whom are we marketing the event? Your target audience may vary, depending on the nature of the product being promoted. For example, a national convention may be aimed at the entire membership, past and potential exhibitors, past and potential sponsors, and related organisations. A training programme may be aimed primarily at those individuals whose disciplines and interests fall within the narrowly defined scope of the educational programme being offered. The target marketing would avoid those whose educational needs are not consistent with the purpose of the programme. A vigilant analysis of the audience to be attracted is essential to target marketing, economy of printing, postage, list maintenance, and staff time.

WHEN?

Timing is everything! The enlightened management team should make the marketing function an integral part of the planning process in order to maximise the value of timing of an event. Strategies in planning the timing of an event are integral to the challenges faced in the marketing process. And timing should also be carefully weighed in light of the schedules, patterns, and needs of the market being served. Scheduling conflicts with attendees present natural impediments to attendance. The marketer must consider several elements such as time of day; day of week; time of year (Seasonality) and local, ethnic, and religious holidays.

WHERE?

Location can be a key asset in promoting an event. A banquet event in a city arena may be emphasised because of the availability of public transportation or valet parking. A company meeting held at Inkwenkwezi Game Reserve rather than a hotel or convention centre is positioned by an event planner as a unique opportunity to enjoy an event 'on a game reserve', close to nature with a spectacular view of game such as rhino, giraffe, etc. In other words, the location of the event can be a critical element in driving sales. Among the assets you should look for as benefits to promote are:

- In urban areas, the availability of public transportation, valet parking, convenience, and efficiency of travel.
- In rural areas, a chance to enjoy panoramic views and pastoral scenery.
- In shopping malls, an opportunity for centralised activities, ease of parking, and ancillary shopping and entertainment features to enjoy.
- At resorts, the ambience of pools, golf, upscale shopping, beaches, and gourmet dining.
- At airport hotels, the inherent efficiency of getting the work done with minimum travel and commuting time because of the fly-in, fly-out design of the location.

WHAT?

Every event is unique unto itself, or at least the marketing executives should present it as such. It may offer an opportunity to discover a new concept, a look into the future of the industry or trade, or a chance to view an innovative line of products and ideas. Regardless of the content you have identified, every event should be presented as refreshing and exciting. Most events provide a combination of the benefits listed here, as well as others more specific to the sponsoring organisation.

TABLE 11.3 *Purpose and benefits of the event (Source: Hoyle, 2002: 40)*

Purpose of an Event	Benefits
Education and training	Attendees will learn how to face tomorrow's issues
Networking business alliances	Attendees will meet new friends and establish profitable
Entertainment banquet	Attendees will be mesmerised by the magic of our closing
'Choose your topic' Roundtable sessions	Attendees will pick a topic and discuss it over coffee with colleagues
'Support your charter School system'	Attendees will have an opportunity at our awards dinner to financially support our efforts for improved educational options for elementary school students in our community

11.5 CUSTOMER CARE IN EVENTS

However one defines marketing and event marketing, the starting point is always the customer. People are the crucial factor in delivering a good event, especially proper customer care and effective teamwork. Well-trained and capable people are a major marketing tool. Many commentators have stressed that developing a customer orientation is the heart of marketing. A *customer orientation* can be defined as: *the process of continuously identifying and meeting the needs and wants of potential and existing customers and clients* (Getz, 1997: 250).

The fundamental principle is that the customer is all-important. Everything from conception to conclusion must be performed with customers (all of them) in mind. Marketing has traditionally been applied to products, but it has recently become a recognised tool of the service industries. In event management we do produce a product, but the important factor is how it is produced, the process – and even the end product is less about tangible objects than about feelings and experiences.

Events are like services; they are distinctly different from industrial products. Here are some of their special features (Watt, 1998: 61):

Intangibility. Customers feel the benefit and the enjoyment, but they can't touch the event.

Perishability. The fun is transitory; it is rare to have lasting evidence of the event.

Inseparability. Customers associate one event with the next; they identify with the organising agency's reputation for quality.

Consistency. Customers demand consistency and it is important to achieve it.

Lack of ownership. Events don't belong to anyone but they are temporarily enjoyed by many.

Event customers are going to be very enthusiastic about how they are treated and what facilities and services are laid on; they are not content to see an art exhibition or a sporting contest in the most basic of conditions. Over recent years many providers of large spectacles have had to radically improve the level and quality of facilities and services available to patrons. Ageing theatres and football grounds are no longer adequate for their clients, who now have much more sophisticated expectations. The element, customer care, is what singles out the service sector from manufacturing industries. And it is vital to events. True quality in this area must be the constant target for all event organisers.

Customer care is a buzz-phrase across all businesses now; particularly service industries like the hospitality trade. It is a major and vital part of event management. Careful consideration needs to be given to all event customers. If they enjoy the event, they will come back and maybe invite their friends to the next part of the programme or a future event planned by the same agency (Watt, 1998: 61).

Customer care must begin as soon as the customer reaches the event, or starts travelling towards the event. The directions, the car park, the reception areas, the premises and all the facilities involved must be of the highest possible standard and ready for the customer's arrival and use. Customer care is best achieved by putting oneself in the customer's shoes and observing the event from their point of view. What is it that you want or that you need? If *you* need something, so will the customer.

Customer care must be seen as something that concerns everyone involved in the organising body, from top manager to car park attendant. Without customers, the whole event will be futile, so everyone must believe in serving the customer. Some members of the organising group may be serving the players in a football tournament; other members may be serving the spectators, the referees, the VIPs or the sponsors (Watt, 1998: 61).

Each section will have its own specific customers, but it is just as important for all groups to create a positive image and impression with each other's customers.

They must try to do everything possible for their specific customers and ultimately for everyone who attends the event. The attitude must be: let's do all we can to avoid anything upsetting our customers or spoiling their enjoyment of the event; we are all in the business of maximising their pleasure. We must try to give our customers more than they expected.

Customer care involves the very basics of looking clean, tidy and presentable; wearing the uniform or badge of the event; making quite clear who you are and what you are there to do; and learning a few basic phrases in foreign languages to make your customer feel more welcome at the event. Some visitors may be making their first trip to the country or region. Remember that 'the customer is king'. Be reverent to the king!

The most important consequence of adhering to a customer orientation is the constant development of the event to satisfy target markets. But many event producers will object to this orientation if it is carried to an extreme. Many events are service-oriented and based on the knowledge or assumption that the event does good. In this context it is common to think of the audience as clients, and the community at large as the beneficiary. Nevertheless, event managers who ignore audience development and marketing risk serious problems.

11.6 SITUATIONAL ANALYSIS TECHNIQUES

11.6.1 Market analysis

Marketers must understand the needs, motives and expectations of potential customers to influence decisions and satisfy patrons. Many event organisers do not undertake thorough customer-oriented research, believing in their own ability to know what their customers want, or lacking the resources to do it (Getz, 1997: 272).

To make any marketing work, it must be quite clear at whom it is aimed. For many promotions the audience may be quite varied: old and young, fit and unfit, academic and artisan. But some events will target a more specific group: a venture may be aimed specifically at women or the 50+ age group or the local business community, etc. This will be one of the questions answered by good market research. Whatever the group, it must be clearly identified and targeted (Watt, 1998: 65).

For events, the targets may be different for different aspects. It may be necessary to identify targets – potential participants, potential spectators, potential sponsors and potential staff – all from different areas and requiring differing marketing to obtain their support. Market research and careful use of previous knowledge will identify the groups relevant to particular events. The next step is to ascertain each group's needs and to devise a plan to meet them. This will greatly assist with overall event planning, but especially the marketing strategy; indeed, more than one strategy may be used to target the identified groups. (For a more extensive review, see Getz, 1997: 264–270.)

11.6.2 Market research

This involves determining:

- market segmentation (what group is interested in your event?)
- trends and demographics
- competition evaluation
- opportunities to identify new markets for your events.

Market research is concerned with the measurement and analysis of markets. A suitable definition is as follows: *the objective gathering, recording, and analysing of all facts relating to the provision of services for the appropriate consumer* (Watt, 1998: 63).

Extensive research before an event can help to answer some questions:
Is it serving a useful purpose?
Will people be interested in it?
Will people attend and/or participate?
Will it be financially viable?
Will it be favourably received by the business community?
Will it be favourably received by the media?
Will it be appropriate to the targeted group?

This general information, perhaps coupled with more specific details, will help to decide whether the event is relevant, interesting and viable. There is little point in proceeding with a project if the research results are negative. Good research is vital and must not be ignored once obtained. No event should proceed without some market research; the complexity of the event will determine how much and what kind. The cost of market research needs to be examined, and existing information should be checked to see what is already available. Extensive research before the East London Jazz Festival proved it to be viable. Denials over sponsorship, however, clouded the festival (*Daily Dispatch*, 15 November 1999: 9).

Market research can help to reduce uncertainty and therefore the risk of failure; it can also help to plan an effective marketing strategy and to analyse how successful it may be.

11.6.2.1 Principles of marketing research for events

1. Marketers must understand the needs and motives of potential and existing event customers. The consumer decision-making process should be used as a guide to improved marketing.
2. Events can be managed and marketed to help meet all the basic human needs: physical, social and psychological.

3. Escapism and social benefits seem to dominate among event-goers. Events should therefore be produced as a vehicle for facilitating group activities, people-watching and interactions, within a unique, enjoyable atmosphere.

4. Long-distance tourists are generally quite interested in cultural events, but often lack the information or means to attend. Event tourism strategies must make local events more accessible to the short-duration visitor.

5. Marketers should appeal to the cultural tourist's interest in authentic local experiences. Cultural tourists are more likely to be mature, female and upper income.

6. Sport tourists are more likely to be young males and focused on the sport activity. Targeted sponsorship works well with this market segment.

7. Conduct qualitative research as well as visitor and market area surveys. Do not ignore the non-customer.

8. Attractiveness of events has been found to relate to their uniqueness, perceived quality and atmosphere.

9. Visitor surveys should be customised to specific settings and needs. Random or systematic sampling is crucial to obtaining valid and reliable results. Intercept, log book and telephone survey techniques can be employed.

10. Accurate attendance counts are vital for economic impact assessments.

11. Psychographic research into attitudes, lifestyles, etc., can help target events better, but the identified segments must reveal distinct differences to be useful. (Getz, 1997: 303)

(For more information on marketing planning and measuring potential, see Getz, 1997: 254–264.)

11.6.3 Strengths, Weaknesses, Opportunities and Threats (Swot) analysis

Fundamental to any marketing project is a situational analysis – past, present and future – and how the venture will fit into it. SWOT analysis helps with realistic planning for the whole enterprise, but especially with the marketing strategy.

Situational analysis is best undertaken by SWOT (Watt, 1998: 64–65):
Strengths – the internal strengths of the organisation
Weaknesses – the internal weaknesses of the organisation
Opportunities – the external opportunities which may arise
Threats – the external threats facing the organisation

Event marketing managers should appraise each strength, weakness, opportunity and threat before marketing the event and communicating it to the public. A SWOT analysis in not inherently productive or unproductive; it is rather the way in which it is used that will determine whether it yield benefits for the marketing planning process for an event.

Some of the examples of potential SWOT are listed below:

TABLE 11.4 *Potential SWOT (Source: Du Plessis et al, 2001: 364)*

POTENTIAL STRENGTHS	POTENTIAL OPPORTUNITIES*
Abundant financial resources	Rapid market growth
Any distinctive competence	Rival firms are complacent
Well known as the market leader	Changing customer needs/tastes
Economies of scale	Opening of foreign market
Proprietary technology	Mishap of a rival firm
Patented processes	New uses of a product discovered
Lower costs	Economic boom
Good market image	Deregulation
Superior management talent	New technology
Better marketing skills	Demographic shifts
Outstanding product quality	Other firms seeking alliances
Partnerships with other firms	High brand switching
Good distribution skills	Sales decline for a substitute
Committed employees	New distribution methods
POTENTIAL WEAKNESSES	**POTENTIAL THREATS***
Lack of strategic direction of the company	Entry of foreign competition
Weak spending on research and development (R&D)	Introduction of new substitutes
Very narrow product line	Product life cycle in decline
Limited distribution	Changing customer needs/tastes
Higher costs	Rival firm adopts new strategies
Out of date products	Increased regulation
Internal operating problems	Recession
Weak market image	New technology
Poor marketing skills	Demographic shifts
Limited management skills	Foreign trade barriers
Under-trained employees	Poor performance of ally firm
* Some of the threats can also be classified as potential opportunities and vice versa.	

11.7 EVENT ADVERTISING (Watt, 1998: 68–70)

The essence of event advertising is not just that it usually costs money, but that specific messages are delivered in a predictable, often repetitive manner over (usually) mass media. The messages are one-way, can be visual, verbal, written or auditory (Getz, 1997: 304).

Well-targeted, cost-effective advertising can make the difference between success and failure. But most advertising is expensive, so it has to be done with specific objectives in mind and at a level which suits the event. It is often possible to get editorial coverage as an alternative to newspaper advertising, and pick up other space by way of low-key sponsorship from bus companies or billboard firms.
But despite its cost, successful advertising is invaluable, and the most appropriate sites should be chosen from a list of possible locations. Yet again, simple questions are among the most important:

Why?	When?
Who for?	How much?
What exactly?	Who judges the response?
Which media?	How is it evaluated?
Where?	

A successful advertising campaign:

- promotes awareness of the event;
- passes on knowledge of relevant details;
- encourages the desire to participate in or attend the event;
- promotes the conviction that the event is worthwhile;
- aims to establish attendance patterns in the long term for future events;
- encourages the decision that turns the interest into attendance or participation;
- promotes the event image and logo;
- is positive and interesting to attract attention.

Local press and radio advertising are not cheap but may well be cost-effective, especially for young people and commercial radio. Television advertising is expensive but can be very effective in reaching mass audiences. Cost is obviously a determining factor but the chosen medium should also reflect the target audience. Certain newspapers are read by certain groups and local commercial radio is said to have close contact with a younger audience, that is, under 30. Targeted advertising is necessary and should prove effective.

Hoyle (2002: 43–46) wrote the following about event advertising, psychographic data (11.7.1) and specialty advertising (11.7.2):

One of the most predominant and traditional event promotion techniques is advertising. While most think of advertising in print form, involving newspapers or magazines, it may come in many forms that we see every day. Advances in electronic and broadcast technologies provide a platform for advertising on television and radio, over the Internet through 'banner' advertisements and other inserts, and even on the big screen in movie theatres.

Marketers must be circumspect in selecting advertising media, because some may be controversial. Billboards are considered an intrusion on the environment by many, as are promotional posters attached to power poles, lining community streets, or stuffed into mailboxes. Even Internet advertising has come under severe scrutiny. Its greatest weakness may be what was initially proclaimed as its greatest strength: the ability to precisely track the number of viewers and those who were interested enough to buy the product. For many, this was cutting-edge technology and an exciting approach to marketing products and services.

But, in many cases, Web surfers did not respond as predicted (they were more casual in their surfing habits than advertisers anticipated as they eagerly used the new electronic frontier). Even online companies themselves, which were expected to advertise their services on the Internet, have become much more selective in their advertising media selections. The results have been the failure of hundreds of dot-com enterprises whose advertisers could quickly and precisely conduct their own evaluations and research, enabling them to analyse the exact numbers of 'hits' they were receiving or, even more critically, not receiving for their investment. The dollar volume of sales resulting directly from Internet advertising vis-à-vis the expenditures to advertise became an easy comparison to track.

Print advertising pervades our daily lives. As we have observed in the previous section, the images of event advertising come to us on the sides of buses, in our newspapers and magazines, on posters stapled to telephone poles, and on roadside signs, ranging from small neighbourhood notices about a yard sale to huge billboards along our highways.

Association membership directories are often financed through advertising, as are community news organs, school yearbooks, association meeting brochures, and even church and synagogue bulletins. Event marketers should analyse the audience of any publication in order to determine the potential effectiveness of that investment. The Institution of Food Technologies (IFT) realised substantial gains by creating new advertising opportunities for exhibitors and other supporters. Its programme book was 400 pages long, which constituted a huge expense item in the budget. In a short period of time, IFT was able to recover the cost of the programme book and generate a 40% profit through the sale of advertisements to exhibitors, sponsors, and supporting organisations.

How do you decide on the right advertising instrument for your event needs? First, identify the audience you wish to attract. Then investigate the demographics reached by the advertising media you wish to consider. For example, marketing executives for larger events may consider broadcast media, which may reach a regional or even a national or international audience. More localised events will likely be promoted through community newspapers, local flyers or brochures, posters, and co-promotion with supporting groups and facilities. The primary consideration is the reach, or total impressions, of the group being sought, even before considering the demographic audience of the media being utilised. Media sales representatives are equipped to demonstrate the demographics of their readers, listeners, and viewers. You should ask if the demographic data have been verified by an independent auditing firm. Ask when that audit was performed, and investigate the following criteria, among others of particular interest to you: age, income range, trade or profession, gender, geographic location, race, marital status and family size.

11.7.1 *Psychographic data*

Event marketers should analyse the psychographic profiles of their audience, namely, the values, attitudes, and lifestyles of the target market. An effective method for determining attitudes is through an attitude survey. This instrument will ask respondents to indicate preferences for a range of issues, from personal interest to educational needs to locations and timing of events. Attitudes surveys may be conducted with quantitative or qualitative strategies or a combination of both. The purpose of the attitude survey is to gain an open and objective insight into the feelings of past, present, and potential attendees. You will want to construct the questions to address only those issues that are pertinent to your marketing efforts, inasmuch as the length of the survey will impact the number of responses (the longer the survey instrument, the fewer responses you may expect to receive).

A typical attitude survey will include questions such as the following:

- Have you attended our event in the past? Please check the years (list years).
- How many kilometres did you travel to attend?
- How would you rate the event? (indicate Excellent, Good, Fair, Poor, or a numerical scale for rating).
- Are you a member of the association?
- Did you register in advance or on site?
- Do you feel the registration fee is commensurate with the value of the event?
- Did you attend as a single participant, or with spouse, friend, or family? If not with family, why not?
- Please list the five educational programmes you felt were most valuable (list sessions by name, with checkboxes).

■ Are the spring dates convenient for you? If not, please indicate which month fits your schedule best.

Obviously, the questions are as open ended as your need to know for the particular event you are marketing. Bear in mind, however, that while many commercially oriented surveys are off-putting to many, opinion and attitude surveys are more warmly received. People often enjoy having their opinions queried, and heard. You may not like the answers, but you can be assured they will guide a much more effective marketing campaign in the future.

11.7.2 Specialty advertising

Creative marketers will find that advertising is not limited to magazines, newsletters and brochures, but rather to virtually any item that will accept print. We all have coffee mugs, refrigerator magnets, calendars, and note pads with advertising messages that the user sees daily. We even buy (often at inflated prices) shirts, caps and other apparel bearing the logos and slogans of the manufacturer or a sports team. We pay for the privilege of becoming walking billboards!

At the event itself, many opportunities exist for the marketing of the event and its sponsoring organisation, creating not just a helpful item but also a memento of the event for the attendee to enjoy far beyond the final gavel. Tote bags may be imprinted with the name of the event and the sponsoring advertiser. This is an effective cross-promotion, which is often granted not just for an advertising fee but also to cover the cost of producing the bags themselves.

Directional and identification signs may carry the logo and name of the sign sponsor. Key rings, golf balls, alarm clocks, badges, stickers, playing cards, and specially designed chocolate bars – the vehicles of specialty advertising are limited only by the imagination. Many specialty advertising production companies exist, with catalogues of pre-produced advertising products designed to be imprinted with your logo, organisation name, and a short message or slogan. The per-unit cost of these imprinted specialty items will decrease as the quantity of your order increases.

Advertising approaches should be tested in advance for effectiveness. Many professionals use a 'split approach', mailing a limited amount of advertising pieces featuring different colours, design, and paper weight to two control groups and then evaluating the response. Focus groups are also an effective way to judge messages, design, and positive acceptance.

11.8 EVENT PRESENTATION

There are two critical aspects (Watt, 1998: 73–74): the promotional presentation and the event presentation itself.

The promotional presentation is for sponsors, backers, spectators, media and participants. Public expectations are now very high: consumers are used to sophisticated provision by the mass media and most providers in the leisure field. Every effort will have to be made to ensure professional and effective presentation of both aspects.

The self-respecting event organiser needs to make a good job of presenting a project to a prospective sponsor or potential participants. This can range from an attractive document, perhaps desktop published, to a high-cost multimedia or audiovisual production. To excite interest, any presentation will need to be accurate, thorough and error-free. Here are some guidelines.

■ Rehearse the presentation.
■ Be well prepared.
■ Double-check all audiovisual equipment, and carry all necessary spares.
■ Ensure that written communication is of the highest order.
■ Double-check all materials for factual inaccuracies.
■ Ensure that all information is totally correct (for example, no typing errors).
■ If possible, check out the venue beforehand.
■ Reconfirm the time and place within 24 hours.

Paid or unpaid, only such a professional approach is going to have any chance of succeeding, such are the expectations of the customer. The same meticulous thinking must also be applied to the presentation of the whole event, from beginning to end. This should be an all-encompassing concept. It involves conspicuous items like logos, advertisements, mascots and decor.

Other less obvious elements must also reflect an overall slickness of presentation. If the venture is to be taken seriously by the consumer, then high quality must be the hallmark of everything undertaken and all the event staff who do the work. The project must be accomplished in the correct manner to the highest achievable level, not just completed. An awareness of how things can appear to the customer should be developed in all staff and volunteers involved. The verbal presentation of guides, officials and speakers will influence how the event is perceived, as will the physical appearance of the venue, its facilities and equipment (Watt, 1998: 73–74).

Most important will be how the event personnel treat the participants – that is, customer care. A pleasant, positive, caring manner in all dealings will be the most significant aspect of public presentation. (For a review on developing and communicating a positive image, see Getz, 1997: 317–325).

11.9   MEDIA RELATIONS AND PUBLICITY (Watt, 1998: 69)

Media relations and publicity should be given a lot of attention. A well-planned publicity campaign should run alongside any advertising campaign. Ideally this drive should be spread over a period of months, building up to a peak shortly before the event. Early warning allows potential participants and spectators to book the event into their diaries and prevents potential clashes with rival attractions.

Some publicity will have to be paid for, but there are ways of obtaining a good deal for little or no cost. The secret is imagination and attention to detail. The Internet is one way to obtain a significant amount of publicity relatively cheaply and easily. Early contact with the media is essential. Think about a catch phrase, as well as a logo, to identify your event. Try to get a public figure involved or to open the event. This should help to get local publicity. Other media outlets that can be contacted are national and regional newspapers, trade and professional magazines, radio, television, teletext and Internet Web sites. There are also opportunities through direct mail, hoardings, national agency events lists, car stickers and word of mouth. Don't be shy about contacting the media. They rely on people telling them what's happening, especially when there's not much sport or political news.

To support South Africa's bid for FIFA World Cup 2010, the *Sunday Times* tried to obtain 1 000 000 signatures and the original petition went on to claim over 2 000 online signatures and just under 8 000 paper signatures. An event supported by a celebrity has better chances to be successful, e.g. the former president and one of the world's highly respected statesmen, Nelson Mandela, supported the FIFA Soccer World Cup 2010 Bid for South Africa, which was highly successful.

Here is a list of some general points to remember when dealing with the media (Watt, 1998: 69):

- The media need you as much as you need them.
- You know more about the technicalities of your subject than they do.
- Be confident during an interview; the cooler you appear, the easier the hot seat becomes.
- With a little imagination, it is quite possible to get thousands of rands worth of free publicity.

11.9.1 Some guidelines on getting media attention
(Watt, 1998: 69–70)

A catchy headline on a press release will attract attention and create good images in the editor's mind. A press release must have an interesting angle, and it must be placed very near the start. All press releases should be targeted for local or national consumption.

Always be *positive* about the event. Do not allow news to be twisted so it becomes negative. Journalists may be more interested in bad news than good, and may try to adjust what is happening. Be prepared for this and resist it as much as possible; seize any opportunity to convey positive information.

With the correct *emphasis,* a local story can quickly become national. Perhaps it is a national first or something totally unique.

A number of publications give *addresses and telephone numbers* for the editors of relevant newspapers, magazines, television and radio stations, etc. It is very important to get the name of an individual if you want them to respond. A general letter to the editor or sub-editor is not going to be as successful as a letter to a specific reporter, particularly one who specialises in your subject area.

Organisations like the National Sports Council may also be able to give a detailed list of specialists who may be worth contacting about a particular event. Think long and hard about *who* may be interested in what you are doing. Do not be afraid to *approach* people.

E-mail or fax are now often the preferred method, but conversation on the telephone can often arouse interest which no press release, no matter how well written, can achieve. A day's phoning will often set up more publicity for your event, and much more quickly, than two or three days' writing and sending press releases.

Spending *time with a journalist* or *editor* can be well worthwhile in setting up coverage of the event; a good working lunch can be a sound investment.

11.9.2 Golden rules of media liaison

- When dealing with the media, it is always better to be proactive rather than reactive.
- Always find a named contact; writing 'to whom it may concern' usually ends up in the bin.
- Try to think in headlines, especially when writing a press release. This may catch the eye.

- When talking to journalists, it is safest to assume that nothing is off the record.
- Find the best spokesperson for the event or promotion and appoint him or her as the media contact. This ensures that a consistent line is issued from the organisation. Having different people speak to the press is a recipe for disaster.
- Retain copies of all radio, television or other media coverage. This is important for the event and will help to keep sponsors happy. It may also help individual media contacts to hone their performance. Press cuttings agencies tend to be expensive, so they may not be financially viable except for major events (Watt, 1998: 70–71).

11.9.3 Press conferences

Holding a press conference can be a very quick and effective way of getting significant press coverage and briefing several journalists at a time. But it does require careful consideration because a press conference can be extremely risky. If nothing arouses press interest, the turnout could be poor, and a damp squib may be embarrassing.

Here are some good reasons for holding a press conference (Watt, 1998: 71):
- to launch your event or conference;
- there is genuine news to impart about someone taking part in the event who is really noteworthy;
- to explain a controversial rumour that has been circulating about the event – media speculation can be enormous and damaging;
- to reveal a major exclusive, for example that the president of Athletics South Africa will be the main speaker at the conference.

If a written statement will be adequate, use a press release. To justify a press conference, something has to benefit from further expansion and the appointed spokesperson must be adequately prepared to answer any questions accurately and confidently. Find an easily accessible venue that can provide appropriate hospitality, for example performers or artists for a photocall.

Be sure that your press conference avoids other important public events and does not clash with major sporting fixtures or art promotions. Detailed investigation will pay dividends when choosing a date and time. But there is always the danger that a major news story will steal the limelight, and perhaps no one will appear.
It is essential to phone around to remind editors of the invitation already issued and any accompanying information. Try to emphasise that certain people will appear, there will be opportunities for coherent radio and television interviews, and photo opportunities with some novel or unusual performance. Consider who is going to appear in front of the media. A sponsor will often be keen. The chairman of the organising committee or the relevant spokesperson must appear and they must be well briefed.

The venue is very important; hold it somewhere easily covered by journalists. Assemble the audiovisual aids required for the presentation; a good video or slide show really adds interest. Ensure that invitations go out to journalists well in advance and are followed up by phone calls to individuals who may be interested. Prepare a detailed agenda for the press conference and stick to it, although questions can go on a little longer if the interest exists.

It is also worthwhile to lay on hospitality for journalists and others after the formal part of the press conference. This will allow for informal contact and a slightly different sort of questioning; both can be good for developing relationships. (Watt, 1998: 71)

11.9.4 Photo opportunities

It is very important to create a visual as well as a verbal impression. Words are cheap and not necessarily eye-catching, even if they do find space in a newspaper. Yet photographs can attract a great deal of attention. They do take a bit more setting up and a little more imagination, but they can be much more worthwhile. They often generate a greater awareness of your event, so they help to satisfy a sponsor's desire for publicity.

11.9.5 Relevant media

It is essential to involve all the media, not just some. Local radio is an excellent and often forgotten medium. It offers the possibility of announcing events and interviews with organisers. It is also possible to persuade a local radio station to set up its own stand within the event, providing live publicity. Major provincial newspapers or indeed locals can be very important; don't just target the national media. Internet functions are evolving, and with the introduction of interactive capabilities there is great scope for innovation (Getz, 1997: 307).

Your audience's age, interest and likely reading or listening habits will determine which media you particularly want to cultivate. Always remember the special interest press; the South African market is vast. Coverage in an appropriate magazine will be invaluable for ensuring audience support, finding participants and giving nationwide publicity.

A promotional competition (for entry tickets), a discount scheme for bulk attendance or some other type of incentive can be a way to attract interest. Direct marketing through mail or telephone is an extremely effective, if a little intrusive, way of getting the message over to prospective customers. Even for localised events, such word-of-mouth promotion can be a leading influence in obtaining support (Watt, 1998: 72).

11.10 ELECTRONIC EVENT MARKETING STRATEGIES

The art of estimating how many people are online throughout the world is an inexact one at best. Surveys abound, using all sorts of measurement parameters. However, from observing many of the published surveys over the last two years, an 'educated guess' as to how many are online worldwide as of September 2002 is 605,60 million. In South Africa, about 3,07 million people were online as of December 2001 (NUA, 2004: Internet).

The Internet is quickly becoming known as the fourth medium of advertising, next to radio and TV broadcast and print media. With its ease of use and initial low cost, marketers are quickly turning to the Internet as the wave of the future. Note that although the online community is large, the reach of the Internet is far less than TV, radio and other advertising media. This means that although the Internet has a massive audience, it does not by any means reach the entire world. With this in mind, electronic marketing, in the beginning, should only be used as a supplement to any other promotion and/or advertising you do.

Because of the dynamics of the Internet as an ever-changing and growing medium, there are a variety of reasons for its use as the ideal marketing tool. It can reach millions of people, while also being used to target marketing at a smaller group of individuals. The 24-hours, 7-days-a-week availability is appealing. And there are no geographic boundaries. Traditional marketing is often more expensive than online marketing, which makes using the Internet more cost-effective. In addition, receiving instant results is very appealing. This not only allows immediate statistics, it also allows the marketer to review and adjust his or her campaign on a timely basis (Price, 1998)

11.10.1 Advantages of Web marketing

Unlike traditional marketing, electronic marketing deals with 'real time.' Customers experience the most up-to-date information. By keeping your Web site up to date, you will keep customers coming back over and over again. Following are the advantages of Web marketing (US Web & Bruner, 1998: 262):

- *Brand building*. Establishes an instantly recognisable brand by raising awareness of your site.
- *Direct marketing*. Eliminates the costs associated with printing and mailing. The Web gives you the ability to constantly make appropriate changes to target your audience. Allows individualised messages to specialised audiences.
- *Online sales*. Immediate order processing in an interactive environment.
- *Customer support*. Easy access to frequently asked questions.
- *Marketing research*. Provides valuable information about your customers. You can use demographics to tailor your site.

- *Content publishing services.* Makes information on your organisation available to a wider Internet audience.

11.10.2 Developing an electronic marketing strategy

When beginning to develop your electronic marketing strategy, John Fuhr, director of business development at Cvent.com, advises that the event marketers take the traditional methods of marketing and find their online counterparts. In other words, use all the strategies you would during a direct mail campaign and apply them to the Internet. For example, instead of sending a paper brochure, you would develop an online brochure (Hoyle, 2002: 56).

The Unofficial Guide to Marketing Your Business Online (Rich & Rich, 2000) suggests doing one of the following to begin your online marketing plan:

1. Use Web-based tool. Visit: http://www.bplans.com to download and edit sample business plans.
2. Buy a business planning software. Palo Alto Software products (http://www.paloaltosoftware.com) offer easy-to-use packages which will help you create a business plan.
3. Follow an online outline. Instead of creating your own, you may feel more comfortable following an existing plan. The Small Business Association (SBA) has a template for individuals to follow. Visit http://www.sba.gov/starting/indexbusplan.html.
4. Hire someone to write your plan. If writing your own plan is not your bailiwick, you can always hire someone else to do it for you. If you don't know someone, check out http://www.guru.com, which is an online forum that links independent contractors with projects.

11.10.3 Define your business

Prior to marketing your event online, you need to clearly define your event and know your goals and target audience. It's important to perform the following:
- Determine clear and concise objectives and goals of the event.
- Establish the best way to position the event in the marketplace.
- Ascertain the strengths and weaknesses of the event.
- Identify the customer, to include demographics and consumer behaviour.
- Define the competition.
- Differentiate this event from the competition.
- Evaluate the financial resources.
- Conduct comprehensive market research.
- Decide how best to reach the customer.
- Follow a detailed business plan.

11.10.4 Establish the electronic marketing plan

In establishing an electronic marketing plan, the main options are use of your organisation's Web site, online advertising and e-mail campaigns. There are a lot of options when deciding on what electronic methods to use for your marketing plans. A variety of these will be discussed.

Kevin Dolan (Dolan, Kerrins & Kasofsky, 2000), e-business development manager of Microsoft Corporation, has taken the five Ps of traditional marketing (product, price, place, public relations, and positioning) a step further for Web marketing. He recommends following these Ps to help establish a great Web marketing campaign:

- *Presence*. Having a placeholder on the Web is the first step. The main goal of your entire electronic marketing campaign will be to drive the traffic there.
- *Pleasing*. Make it pleasing to the eye.
- *Personalised*. Develop a relationship through personalisation.
- *Purchase*. Through e-commerce, buy or sell products or services.
- *Process*. Integrate your Internet site with core business systems.
- *Partnership*. Being connected with partners, suppliers, customers, and competitors expand your reach.
- *Programmable*. The Web can be easily changed to tailor your marketing message.

11.10.5 Event Web page development

The development of an event Web site takes as much time, thought and consideration as developing your overall marketing strategy. The design should ensure easy navigation and should be designed to serve your customers' needs. Jud Ashman (Ashman & Ashman, 1999) recommends these key points when creating an event e-site:

- structure
- ease of navigation
- style
- technical requirements
- consistency
- personalisation.

Choosing your event domain name is very important. Web site addresses live and die by their ability to be recognised, according to *Net-Marketing: Your Guide to Profit and Success on the Net* (Judson, 1996). In South Africa, domain names for an event can be registered with a domain company, CyberFace, at http://www.domain-names.co.za. At the time of writing, the costs (excluding VAT) of registering a new domain are as follows:

TABLE 11.5 *Prices of new domain (Source: Mansfield, 2001: Internet)*

	.co.za One year	.co.za Two years	.com One year	.com Two years
CyberFace	R250	R400	R250	R400

CyberFace creates a FREE, temporary, hosting account (essential for co.za) where you can 'park' your domain names until you decide whether to host with CyberFace, or elsewhere.

The process takes a few days. If at all possible, your domain name should incorporate some of the key words in your event title so customers can easily find your site.

According to CyberFace:

- Domain names should be as short as possible; example: www.abc.com
- Include the name of your event or company; example: *www.worldcup2010southafrica.com*
- Domain names should be easy to remember or guess; example: www.http://www.sa2010blog.com/
- Be easy to be understood when spoken aloud; example: manny.co.za might be heard as many.co.za
- Include your most important keywords; example: www. www.safootball.co.za

11.11 SUCCESS IN EVENT MARKETING

The success of each event marketing effort can be measured through the following measurements (*Card News*, 1998: 2);
http://www.smartcard.co.uk/dailynews/events.html):

- gross application volume which highlights the sales skills of the customer service representatives, and the amount of inaccurate or incomplete applications they submit
- approval rate percentage
- activation rate
- attrition rate
- balances
- losses.

Success in the event marketing process is directly related to the time spent on the continuous and disciplined asking of questions that when answered will justify and qualify the activity undertaken.

11.11.1 Monitoring marketing success

- Did we achieve the objectives/targets set?
- Were the customers satisfied?
- Would they come again? If not, why not?
- What would we change to ensure that more visitors come more frequently in the future and spend more money?
- Was the target number of visitors met? How are the visitor numbers going to be counted or assessed, especially if admission is free, or if many visitors use a form of season ticket?
- What was the incidence of repeat visitors? Percentages of repeat visits are a good indication of visitor satisfaction and allow more realistic assessments of visitor spending per head to be calculated.
- What was the visitor profile? Into which age groupings can the visitors be divided? It is particularly important to make an assessment of the numbers of children and their age grouping, bearing in mind their influence upon adults/parents
- How did they arrive? Car park observation can play a vital role: arriving numbers of visitors per car, overflow parking use, number of coaches, origin of coach and type of passenger.
- Which individual events/features were most/least popular and at what hour/s of the day? If there is no physical entrance at which counts can be made, observation using a form of prepared grid reference to obtain rough counts can be substituted.
- How satisfied were the visitors? Satisfaction surveys can only be credibly undertaken in questionnaire form as comparability and consistency are vital. They may be administered either as on-the-spot interviews or postal questionnaires. (Richards, 1992: 114)

11.11.2 Ten steps to selecting an event marketer

Selecting an event marketer is a time-consuming process. People from all these areas of the organisation should be present to ask questions of the applicants:

1. Focus on the detail in the event marketer's application processing. Review with prospective event marketers their application completion and quality process. How are they going to ensure that each application is filled out in full? Also, review coding processes with the prospective event marketer to make sure they can accommodate your way of doing things.
2. Research how much experience the company has in marketing to consumers in the credit card industry. Do they have a history of tabling at bank card events? If they do, ask for pictures of the booth set-up and a report of past results, Whitham suggests.

3. Discuss the creditworthiness of past events. What percentage of applicants at a past event was approved for a credit card?

4. Perform full due diligence. 'You will want to check all their references,' Whitham says. 'Not just those that are card-related, but all the companies (the event marketers) do business with.' Due diligence also involves sending someone to visit the event marketer's regional office to see what the facility looks like, and what happens when the applications come in. Whitham also suggests issuers go to other events the marketers operate to see them in action.

5. Judge the company on its presentation. The better its presentation is to you, the more professional that organisation is at event marketing.

6. Ask about the people staffing the table. What is the employee turnover rate and what are the prospective event marketing companies doing about it? Are the employees full-time or part-time? Who is doing the training? And how often are people re-trained or given a refresher course? Additionally, inquire about the appearance and skill sets of employees. Does the company ensure employees' attire is appropriate to the event? If the table is set up at an airport, and the target market is business travellers, employees should be dressed in business attire. However, if the booth is set at a state fair or golf tournament, the staff should be dressed in attire that is more casual.

7. Make a determination on how many customer service representatives should be available. 'You will want to have representatives available when you need to increase the volume of applications you want to bring in,' Whitham says. Depending on the size of the programme, some vendors might offer a dedicated team that just does marketing, and those reps will become experts in your business.

8. Ensure the event marketer has the ability to accommodate partner requests. For example, Firstar Bank has an airline rewards programme with Midwest Express. When the bank sets up a table at the airport and is marketing the card to business travellers, the marketing company's employees have to be ready to demonstrate Midwest Express' commitment to service. 'What that means is if someone comes up to the table and asks what their points balance is on their account, the reps pick up one cell phone and call customer service and get that information to the customer,' Whitham says. Staff must be ready to field all kinds of questions, including 'what time does my flight leave?'.

9. Set the goals for that campaign, including the minimum number of applications, acquired accounts and costs per account required. Consider the size of the event and the season of the year. Research the demographics of the event to estimate approval rates and the number of new accounts you can expect to gain. A booth during the first week of classes at a small private college, for example, may present a better demographic than a large state school, but are the smaller numbers worth the time and money spent on event marketing?

10. Review potential events. Determine the demographic you wish to reach, and review a list of events submitted by the event marketing company. Attempt to determine the proper size and creditworthiness of the event through research. Use sources like Barron's school codes, for example. On campuses, attempt to schedule the marketing campaign around special events such as freshman orientation or buy-back week at the campus bookstore. Be sure to ask about the booth or table location at each event. And remain flexible during the schedule–development phase. Monitor the schedule weekly, but if a change needs to be made, such as a special event arises at the site, adjust the marketing plan accordingly.

11.12 FACTORS TO CONSIDER IN EVENT MARKETING

Marketing can be affected by a number of issues, some controllable, some not, but organisers must be aware of them.

- *Location*. Consider the attractiveness and accessibility of the location as well as environmental factors such as traffic and scenery. (Are you still familiar with the location of the All Africa Games and all the associated traffic problems?)
- *Social factors*. The attitude of friends and colleagues will affect people's attitudes as to what is appropriate.
- *Cultural influences*. Different groups in society – for example ethnic origin, social class, part of the country – will see different events in different ways. (Cultural influences are very important in South Africa – compare the different venues for soccer with those of rugby.)
- *Fashion*. During certain periods in history, certain types of project will be in vogue and will attract large attendances (for example the Olympic Games).
- *Political factors*. Local and central government will pursue areas for support that fit with their beliefs.
- *Economic factors*. Assess how much money is available at a corporate level and an individual level; consider exchange rates and similar economic factors (these played an important role in the staging of the All Africa Games).
- *Philosophy*. The beliefs and attitudes of groups, individuals and other agencies will affect the range of events provided.

(Watt, 1998: 62; see also Getz, 1997: 250–253)

TABLE 11.6 *Event communication mix problems and strategies (Source: Price, 1998: 56–59)*

Problems	Strategies	
It takes so long to get the programme portion of the brochure together that we have time for only one mailing, and that scarcely gives attendees time to respond.	Strategy 1:	Market your meeting throughout the year. Include articles in your newsletter, add a tag line to your letterhead announcing the dates, location, and theme; send a 'save the dates' mailing focused on the preliminary details.
	Strategy 2:	Prepare the brochure as best you can, leaving conspicuous 'holes' in the programme, and pass it around to in-house people. Maybe you can shame the delinquent people into action.
	Strategy 3:	Set your deadlines back several weeks or months.
	Strategy 4:	Call weekly meetings for progress reports.
	Strategy 5:	Talk to your boss about the problems and try to get a memo or stronger commitment. Unfortunately, the culprits are often top managers, people who typically have other priorities beside your brochure.
	Strategy 6:	Within reason, let the delinquent individuals set their own deadlines, then ask them about their progress every day.
Editing of the brochure is minimal until the final typeset version comes back; then the changes are so major it's like starting over, and it wrecks our budget.	Strategy 1:	To many people, the printed word looks different, even reads different, from the typed draft. If you have this problem, typeset your copy and have people edit that instead of typed drafts. That will add dollars to that budget area, but it may save time. Also, if you keep good records, you can show the costs of copy changes after typesetting.
	Strategy 2:	Ask your best writer to clean up the copy before you take it to the typesetter.
	Strategy 3:	Don't let your programme people write copy. It usually isn't sales copy anyway, which is what your Promotional materials should be. If you have a highly technical audience that may be acceptable, but think of your audience first, then assign writing.
My brochure always looks home-made. What can I do?	Strategy 1:	Spend some money on a graphic design. A good designer can create a professional-looking promotion piece that is not necessarily expensive to print. You may increase your design costs, but you'll reduce your printing costs.
	Strategy 2:	Do a 'quick-printer.' Such photocopy shops are inexpensive, and most can do two-colour offset printing with borders and headlines. Many can professionally machine-fold the brochure too.

	Strategy 3:	Explore other options, such as do-it-yourself typesetting companies and proven desktop publishing software systems.
	Strategy 4:	Take a good look at other brochures and incorporate the elements you like.
Our mailing lists are never up-to-date, by the time we get the undeliverable pieces back, it's too late to mail a new one.	Strategy 1:	If you are marketing more than once a year, your undeliverables should be corrected immediately. Don't wait for your major conference mailing.
	Strategy 2:	Send a postcard asking individuals if they want to continue to be on your mailing list, especially if they have not participated in several years.
	Strategy 3:	Tie your computer system to your mailing lists so registration information is used to automatically update old files.
	Strategy 4:	Hire a service. This is too important to let fall by the wayside.
We never get press coverage for our meeting/event, despite our efforts to get the word out.	Strategy 1:	Invite a reporter to sit in on one of your panels or to moderate one of your sessions. That will get the press involved and interested.
	Strategy 2:	Carefully review newspapers for at least a week, evaluating their general announcement areas. Most papers have a section devoted to meetings, usually a simple listing with the phone numbers of contact people. Call the paper and ask what you have to do to have your meeting listed and when your announcement must be in.
	Strategy 3:	Take a critical look at your topics and speakers. If you can't find anything 'newsworthy', your press release will probably be tossed. Politics, the economy, famous people, and the downtrodden (such as homeless people) are areas likely to capture the interest of the press.
	Strategy 4:	Call newspapers and try to set up an appointment to discuss each one's criteria, decision-making process, deadlines, slow news days, and so on. There are generic deadlines for writing an effective press release, but the best advice is to develop a personal contact within a paper's structure.
	Strategy 5:	For non-profit organisations, explore radio and TV public service announcements. Regulations require that a certain amount of airtime be given in these areas. Public services announcements are rarely aired during prime time, but they are free. Give local cable talk shows a call and ask the same questions you asked the newspapers.

	Strategy 6:	Talk to the local convention and visitors' bureau – it exists to help you. Bureau staff members are usually active in the community, and they should know the people to contact and the type of coverage given to meetings.
We are on a tight budget. How can we inexpensively produce a good-quality, professional brochure?	Strategy 1:	You can save on mailing costs by utilising the less expensive bulk mail. This requires a permit fee and you must adhere to very specific regulations imposed by the US Postal Service. The real cost of bulk mail is that it takes up to three weeks for delivery.
	Strategy 2:	If you need faster delivery and will be sending brochures out by first-class mail, be sure each piece can be mailed for 32 cents, or within your budget allocation. Even a few cents more can play havoc with your budget, especially if you have a large mailing list.
	Strategy 3:	Use free or low-cost items from the local convention and visitors' bureau. Those organisations usually have quality promotional pieces on the local area that you can include in your mailing.
	Strategy 4:	If you typeset your brochure, save money by reducing changes after typesetting. Changes can end up costing more than the original typeset charges.
	Strategy 5:	Check paper costs, not only in actual price but for 'hidden' costs; some paper types must be scored before folding, which is an additional cost.
	Strategy 6:	Use standard ink colours. A black-and-white piece can be very dramatic if you spend a little extra on design.
	Strategy 7:	Send only what you must to promote the meeting. Save information regarding weather, dress, and so on for registrants only.
From year to year, our attendance is either stable or dropping. What can we do to build attendance?	Strategy 1:	Promote the meeting/event all year long in regular mailings, newsletters.
	Strategy 2:	Exploit the special aspects of your meeting, such as spouse and child programmes, themes, speakers.
	Strategy 3:	The best tactic is to evaluate your registration list over the past four to five years and survey the dropouts. A simple but well-worded and well-designed questionnaire should give you some information. You might even do a telephone survey to increase the response rate and to learn more. People will often tell you more in a personal conversation than on a sheet of paper.

	Strategy 4:	Look at your competition and possible date conflicts. Also look at the economy generally and in your industry and compare against the costs of attending your meeting. Sometimes the answers are obvious with a little research and a little critical thinking.
	Strategy 5:	You may be in a rut with your programme and speakers. If your programme isn't current, interesting and fun, freshen it up and promote your 'new look' in your mailings.
	Strategy 6:	Have you cut the costs of your promotional materials so much that they are ineffective? Re-evaluate your budget priorities and your promotional pieces and activities.

11.13 A MARKETING CHECKLIST (Watt, 1998: 62–63)

1. Know your organisation thoroughly and be able to identify potential market segments and target groups.
2. Know your event goals; draw up a budget and a strategic plan to achieve them.
3. Know you consumer; talk to relevant groups, visit related establishments and learn from the ideas of others.
4. Know your competitors; find out what they have to offer, their facilities and their programmes.
5. Keep in touch with others in the same business; use public relations and hospitality to make friends with the press.
6. Identify possible gaps in the market for your event; test for preliminary ideas and think through the process very carefully.
7. Look at ways to increase the size and status of the event, and make the most of any merchandising opportunities.
8. Measure the profits made in the event.
9. Create your own image for the event; begin with an efficient reception, avoid queues, and employ smart and appropriate staff at all levels.
10. Be innovative, accept original concepts and risk; be flexible to accentuate all possibilities.
11. To get publicity be original; firsts are important and always remembered.
12. Changing circumstances always mean new opportunities for promotion and publicity; take every opportunity that occurs.
13. Motivate people; make the staff part of a team that is willing to identify with the event and publicise it.
14. Make sure that every aspect of the event is designed specifically for the people who will come to it; be customer orientated.

15. Remember that 'freebies' are important, everybody likes something for nothing; a sticker or badge will help people to remember the event, before, during and after; it will also remind them of last time's positive experiences and it could persuade them to attend the next one.
16. Make the rules of the event fair and appropriate for everyone.
17. Make the facilities attractive and clean; create a quality image.
18. Make the facilities accessible with appropriate maps, signposting, parking, etc.
19. Work hard to let everyone, internal and external, know exactly what's happening at all times; lack of information is the worst type of publicity.
20. 'Sell' the event to everyone: staff, financiers, sponsors and customers.

Consider most or all of these aspects for each event. A great deal of effort will have to be expended on a true marketing approach. Support and enthusiasm for marketing your project will not simply appear: it needs to be cultivated. Marketing concepts are widely applicable commercially and are also relevant to events. Market research, self-analysis, targeting and marketing mix are all useful to help get the ideas just right. (Watt, 1998: 62–63)

Browse these Internet sites
http://www.capetown.gov.za/econdev/downloads/events_JMI.pdf
http://www.esrc.ac.uk/commstoolkit/events/marketing.asp
http://www.fleamarketguide.co.za/articles.html
http://www.mrs.org.uk/
http://www.saarf.co.za
http://www.waterfront.co.za/play/host/
http://www.whalefestival.co.za/

QUESTIONS FOR SELF-EVALUATION

1 Identify 4 Ps from the suggested list, which you feel to be the most important; state the reasons for your choice.
2 Take the four Ps you have identified in question 1 and consider them in relation to an actual event. Suggest how they affect the event you have chosen and how they would be 'mixed' by the skilled organiser to ensure a quality event.
3 Choice of media, media relations and advertising are all important. Apply them to a local pop concert and give reasons for the choices you have made and the actions taken.
4 Undertake a situational analysis of a sports federation of your choice.
5 Marketing can be affected by a number of issues. Briefly discuss seven.
6 What are the benefits of a marketing checklist?
7 Discuss the importance of customer care.

8 Briefly list the principles of marketing research for events.

9 List six golden rules of media liaison.

10 Give a brief summary of public relations and communications tools for events.

11 What items may you include in your press kit?

12 What details must you include in your press release?

13 Design your event Web page(s) and select a high-impact domain name.

14 Design an electronic event marketing strategy for an event of your choice.

CHAPTER 12

Catering Management for Events

Jürgen Gasche

AIM OF THE CHAPTER

The aim of this chapter is to examine the fundamentals involved in organising the food and beverages for events. The chapter covers both controlled and uncontrolled events. In addition, it analyses the harmonisation of entertainment, such as dancing, and other components into the catering function of a controlled event.

LEARNING OBJECTIVES

After having studied this chapter, you should be able to:

- explain food and beverage planning for events, with particular reference to fundamental planning principles and relevant case studies;
- use the case studies to determine the level of service and staff requirements for specific events, as well as how to plan appropriate menus;
- describe the working relationship with the caterer and the need to take into account religious and cultural requirements when planning meals;
- understand how to identify costs and profits at the catered event;
- identify the basic health and safety regulations as well as liquor liabilities;
- evaluate the catered event and keep accurate records;
- incorporate entertainment and other elements into the catering function to ensure a seamless event.

12.1 INTRODUCTION

The organisation and planning of events (no matter the type and size) will involve fundamental planning principles, but as each event remains a special case it will impact on certain project areas that form part of the organisation and planning strategy.

One of these areas involves food and beverage catering for an event. The type of event to be organised will determine the catering. The food choices that are made will be influenced by many interacting factors. For most persons and in ordinary circumstances, food must be palatable or have appetite appeal. The basic challenge for the organiser is to satisfy everyone's taste – for a controlled event, such as a national or international conference, this could be anything from 500 to 5 000 people. The task becomes rather daunting in an uncontrolled event such as the Standard Bank National Arts Festival in Grahamstown, where up to 20 000 people a day could call for a certain variety of nourishment.

This chapter focuses on the controlled (limited access) and uncontrolled, unlimited access event. The biggest challenge undoubtedly lies in the uncontrolled event. Circumstances beyond one's control could ruin all efforts. While the controlled event is mainly in a composed environment, the challenge lies more in the total satisfaction of all guests. Here too things can go wrong; an extended speech can ruin the perfectly baked supreme of salmon or an unexpected speaker just before dessert can destroy the flame grilled crème brûlée.

No matter the size of the event or the number of guests that are to be catered for, be it 10 or 100 000 people, the same fundamental and detailed planning has to occur. It is never easy to orchestrate an event from beginning to end and even if most of the work is contracted to professional services, the overall coordination of all contracted services lies with the event organiser.

Record-keeping is yet another factor that is discussed in this chapter. This function is essential – not only for tax purposes but also for future events. From the very day that a catering business is established, every caterer should keep records of the type of functions, food consumed, drinks served and customers catered for. In addition, a record of entertainment (music band, DJ, etc.) used will be helpful for future reference. The catering for a function can be of the best, but this could be spoilt by bad entertainment, which could reflect negatively on the caterer.

12.2 THE WORKING RELATIONSHIP WITH THE CATERER

Food, beverage and celebration are inextricably connected. From social life-cycle events to mega events such as the Olympic Games, the relationship between food and frivolity has been a close one. This is not to suggest that it is not serious business as well (Goldblatt, 1997: 153).

When a potential client approaches a caterer for the organisation of a controlled, limited access function, then it is the caterer's duty to collect as much information as possible from this client through an informal interview. This first meeting should include general questions to give the caterer a fairly good idea of the client's vision of the function. Here are a few points that should be included in a first client meeting.

- **Estimated attendance.** This needs to be finalised to an accurate number before pricing the catered event.
- **Meal service requirements.** Sit-down menu or buffet style, this factor will determine the amount of staff needed for the function. The sit-down meal will require more waiting and cooking staff than the buffet.
- **Ceremonies performed during meals.** Speeches, prize giving, special announcements, and so on during the meal service will have to be co-ordinated.

- **Religious meal requests.** Kosher meals have to be bought in; provisions have to be made for other religious requisitions.
- **Special diets.** The caterer has to be informed of allergies (shellfish allergy is fairly common) and illnesses (diabetes).
- **Client's budget.** This usually determines the extravaganza of the meal or catered event.
- **Security Measures.** Catering for dignitaries from public life, such as politicians, sports or film stars can pose difficulties for the caterer. Ever since 11 September 2001 security has been stepped up. Often whole areas are being sealed off, making it difficult for last minute supplies to reach the caterer.

After this first meeting the caterer should have a fairly good idea about the client's vision of the event. The success of a catered event depends often on the ability of the caterer to make the client's imagination a reality. This is especially true when catering for weddings or for the birthdays of elderly people where usually two to three generations of the same family are participating.

In addition to the above, the caterer can make suggestions about the meals served by providing the client with dated menus and an updated price list. This practice is often found when dealing with conference organisers. Appendix 12.1 provides examples of both buffet and served dinner suggestions.

In her book, *Planning Successful Meetings and Events,* Ann J Boehme gives a food and beverage checklist for organisers of events. The caterer can use the following abridged form of this checklist in order to determine the client's prerequisites (Boehme, 1999: 74–75):

- make dated menus available.
- ascertain the client's food and beverage budget.
- chef to meet with client.
- discuss event style and options with client.
- finalise menu.

After this first meeting the caterer now has a very good understanding of the client's needs. The caterer must now secure supplies and enquire about prices and the availability of certain products. The identification of appropriate suppliers that can handle the caterer's needs adequately is next on the list. A long-lasting and good relationship with main suppliers will have a positive impact on the overall outcome of the event. Often new suppliers promise clients the impossible, just to get their foot into the door; this can become detrimental to the outcome of the event (Shock & Stefanelli, 1992: 340). Here are some techniques that could be followed to control product costs and ensure supply of requested goods:

- Seek long-term competitive bids from suppliers and maximise purchase power.

- Qualify for purchase-price discounts, such as volume discounts.
- Make use of stock discontinuation sales.
- Seek out new-on-the-market convenience products, to benefit from introductory prices.
- Use raw food products rather than pre-manufactured products.
- Always have a contingency or emergency plan on hand, that is, a second supplier.

Food and beverage sales are an essential service at most events, and can generate a targeted profit. Whether planning the catering for an uncontrolled or a controlled event, Getz (1997) suggests a number of key principles that must be considered. The types of food to be served, the number of meals to be served, the size of meals and product availability need to be planned in harmony with revenue goals, theming and the ability of staff to do the job. Suppliers can sometimes provide information or advise on what volume of food and beverages is desirable. Monitoring sales and keeping records will help the caterer next time around when a similar event is to be catered for (Getz, 1997: 209). Appendix 12.2 (on the web site) shows examples of data-capturing sheets used for this purpose.

The cost of sales is an important calculation; it usually consists of direct costs (production costs) and indirect costs (overheads). In order to generate revenue and keep customers happy, the caterer has to carefully calculate his or her expenses and profit margin. The outcome should be a price that will satisfy both the caterer and the client. To give value for money is important.

Now that a menu has been drafted, supplies are secured and the event has been priced, it is time to have a second meeting with the client. Usually clients make minor changes and are happy with the choices presented by the caterer. However, when catering for extravagant events of leading companies, the caterer sometimes has to deal with more than one function co-ordinator or even top management wants to get involved in the planning. In this case, which can be nerve-wracking, insist on written instructions from the official function co-ordinator and, if possible, have all interested parties at the same table when having a planning meeting. Always make sure that you talk to the right person

EXAMPLE 12.1: *14 hit by food poisoning at popular restaurant*
Plettenberg Bay – At least 14 people suffered food poisoning after dining at a popular Plettenberg Bay restaurant over the New Year, forcing it to temporarily suspend operations. Samples from both the restaurant and the supplier have been sent to the National Health Laboratories in Cape Town to ascertain the break in the 'cold chain' which led to the appearance of the bacteria.
(Source: *The Herald*, 7 January 2003)

EXAMPLE 12.2: *Boy, 5, dies from food poisoning*
East London – A five-year-old boy has died and seven people are still in hospital after being admitted to hospital with food poisoning over the weekend. An estimated 100 people were admitted to hospital with food poisoning on Sunday and Monday. They are thought to have drunk contaminated ginger beer or eaten contaminated meat.

(Source: *Daily Dispatch*, 7 August 2003)

Health and safety can be detrimental to the caterer in two ways. Society is becoming increasingly health-conscious and the demand for light and healthy meals is on the increase. More and more people are declining to eat fatty food such as deep-fried fish and chips. The caterer needs to be aware of the latest food fashions and fads. In addition to the above, the caterer has to carefully observe health laws. Occasionally, newspapers report of mishaps which have occurred at large catering events. Although meals can be prepared in large numbers in advance, hygiene becomes an all-important factor in the production of large-scale food operations. If food is prepared in advance, it must be stored in almost sterile conditions and under the correct temperatures. The suspected food poisoning of 14 diners at a popular Plettenberg Bay restaurant (illustrated in example 12.1)) was in fact a direct result of a break in the cold chain. The culprit was a bacteria-generated poison called scombrotoxin, which itself generates histamines. The bacteria typically appears when fish is frozen and allowed to thaw before being frozen again. Many factors can lead to the spoilage of pre-cooked food: an unsanitised storage container, mixing hot and cold foods together, and the storage of food in a warm environment. The caterer and catering staff must understand how food poisoning develops and be able to eliminate these dangers. Literature is available that deals with these issues.

The food poising case at Nyoka Village in the Eastern Cape (illustrated in example 12.2) is an example of poor food hygiene. Sanitation and safety procedures are of paramount importance to caterers. The safety of customers and staff must always come first (Hansen, 1995: 258). Sanitary conditions apply to food handlers as well as to waiting staff. Poor personal hygiene could be the cause of sanitation problems within the catering firm.

A challenge for the caterer is always a sporting event. Depending on the level of event, be it a soccer match, cycling tour or the Olympic Games, a carefully balanced nutritional menu has to be presented. This is when a catering firm should seek the experience of a qualified nutritionist. The athletes participating in the Comrades Marathon require a different diet from that of a defender in a soccer squad. While the marathon runner will have a carbo-loaded breakfast at midnight, the soccer player will indulge in a regular breakfast at a regular time. The planning of such meals is best left to nutritionists, since they have a better insight into the nutritional requirements of sportsmen and women. In addition, digestion time plays a vital role in the meal intake of competing sportsmen. Imagine the 23 000 starters at the annual Comrades Marathon being fed a breakfast one hour before the start. Within two hours of the start, these runners would desperately need toilets!

The menu should always be the focal point of the caterer for a controlled event. A menu which is well-presented and which meets the client's highest expectations will be the deciding factor in granting the caterer the contract for a function. The caterer for an uncontrolled event – be it a food-stall at a festival or the catering for a sporting event – must ensure that his or her menu is suitable for the event.

Generally, in order to ensure success, whether catering for an event with controlled access or uncontrolled access, every caterer should prepare a checklist around the topics listed below:

- **Menu planning.** The menu should determine the following: food to be purchased, staffing, equipment, layout and space utilisation for off-premise catering, décor for buffets or food stalls, food production plan and beverages.
- **Menu categories.** The various categories include seated or served meals (in general breakfasts, luncheons, dinners and gala dinners); buffets (including breakfast, themed lunches or dinner buffets). Food stations are used when a variety of food is offered or at an uncontrolled event. Cocktail parties are always a stand-up affair where hors d'oeuvre are customarily served.
- **Planning guidelines.** Usually there are no rules for planning off-premise-catering menus. The client's request for innovation should never be ignored. Planning also depends largely on the capabilities of the caterer and his or her staff.
- **Food trends.** Popular foods, food that is in fashion and even food garnishes are not to be overlooked (Hansen, 1995: 34–55).

When catering for a controlled event, the caterer must also take into account the level of activity delegates have during the day. If a delegation has a team-building exercise during the day filled with a number of physical activities, then these guests will be much hungrier at dinner time than those who have been inactive the whole day. So, how much food should be prepared? A few factors have to be considered before ordering foods:

- **Cultural background.** Are the guests from a modern suburban environment or from rural areas? The suburbanite has greater access to health food than the rural person does.
- **Buffet style or sit-down menu.** People consume more food if eating at a buffet. However, if the room is crowded, guests will eat less since it will be difficult for them to reach the food tables. It is far easier to calculate a sit-down menu.
- **Type of menu.** Explain the type or style of a menu to the organiser. Often coordinators request a cocktail menu for lunch or a dinner on the first day of

an event to save money on catering. Guests will be disappointed with this choice especially after a long day travelling to the event.

Once again, record-keeping becomes imperative. If a record is available, the caterer can calculate the portion sizes and quantities to be ordered far more precisely. Literature on the calculation of food portions and the costing thereof to achieve a profit is available. A rule of thumb is given by Hansen and this can also be used for the local market. The smaller the number of guests, the higher the percentage of overordering, as shown below:

Attending guests	Overorder %	Order for
20	20	24
100	10	110
200	7,5	215
400	5	420

(Hansen, 1994: 49)

The caterer should also consider the loss through cooking. Depending on how well cooked the meat has to be, the caterer should calculate up to 20% loss for cooking into the portion yield. This percentage could increase to 50% if the caterer has to trim the meat. Suppliers usually deliver portioned meat, poultry or fish; however, the caterer must still be aware of the loss through cooking. Large pieces of meat that have to be cooked for buffets and are usually served well done can lose up to 20% of their weight through cooking.

> *Remember, too, that no one became a chef in a day, or stopped learning. The fun of cooking is adapting, developing, experimenting.*
> Jean-Christophe Novelli, Entrepreneur and Chef

The beverage service for a controlled event also needs to be considered. The caterer must comply with the law of the land. In South Africa, no person under the age of 18 is to be served alcoholic beverages. Employees of the caterer who serve guests with food and beverages must be made aware of this, since the caterer can be held liable if alcoholic beverages are sold to minors. Here are some pointers on controlling the sale of alcoholic beverages at a controlled event (Hansen, 1995: 58–59):

- **Encourage short cocktail hours.** Shorten the length of pre-dinner drinks or the cocktail hour before a gala dinner.
- **Serve attractive hors d'oeuvre.** Cheese, fried foods and food with a high fat content reduce the absorption of alcohol.
- **Serve attractive non-alcoholic beverages.** These include freshly squeezed fruit juices, waters and tropical punches.

- **Pour wine.** Pouring wine, as opposed to leaving wine on the table, helps to control the rate of consumption.
- **Close of bars.** It is best to close the bar one hour before the event is over.
- **Coffee service.** Serve plenty of coffees, espressos or cappuccinos towards the end of the event. This may slow down the consumption of alcoholic beverages.
- **Religious restrictions.** Although non-alcoholic beer and wine are available, the consumption thereof must be cleared with the organiser of the event. Special beverages are available for certain religions.

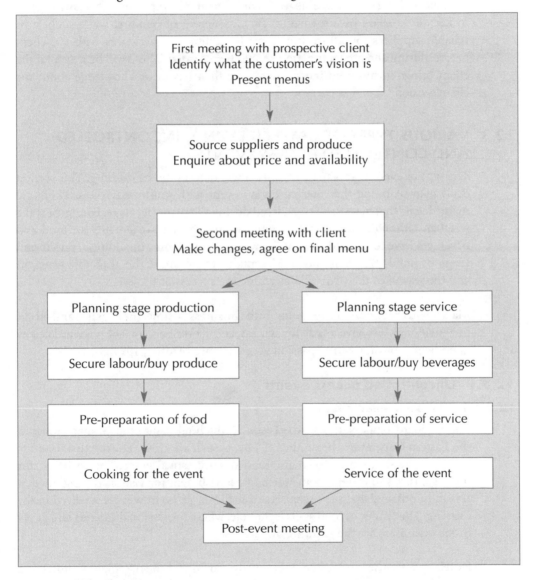

FIGURE 12.1 *The planning stages*

Small businesses are forever hunting for ways to distinguish themselves from competitors. A sure-fire way to separate yourself from the crowd is to touch your customers with kind, thoughtful gestures as often as possible. Not only will you feel better, but your patrons will notice too (Trotter, 1999: 186).

Figure 12.1 provides a planning structure that can be used for both the unlimited access event and the controlled event. The first three stages of this structure have been discussed above. The remaining stages will be elaborated on in the sections to come. During all of these stages, record-keeping is important. It is always good to keep a database of information such as names of banquet waiters, chefs or reliable suppliers for future functions. In addition, experiences with the client before, during and after a function should be recorded. These will be helpful if the client brings in more business; the caterer then has prior knowledge about the client's vision.

12.3 VARIOUS TYPES OF CATERED EVENT: UNCONTROLLED AND CONTROLLED ACCESS EVENTS

The type of event that is to be organised will determine the catering. This section deals with planning the catering for an event with unlimited access. There are many details that have to be considered during the planning stage. Foremost is the weather. Although the organiser cannot influence it, arrangements for food and beverages have to be made to suit the weather conditions. In addition, public and religious holidays, major sporting events in the vicinity, the academic calendar and the season of the year will determine the success of the event.

Many entrepreneurs have gone into business using their wits and their imagination. Most have a taste for success, and scores have a viable vision. The key ingredient is passion – true passion for excellence (Trotter, 1999: 3).

12.3.1 Uncontrolled access events

12.3.1.1 The un-themed event

The Standard Bank National Arts Festival, which takes place in Grahamstown in the Eastern Cape at the beginning of July, is such an event. During this time the streets of the sleepy little town are flooded with festival-goers. The challenge for the organiser is to provide some form of nourishment for visitors during the day. It is most unlikely that the organisers of such a large event will get involved in the catering. The tender of food stalls is the rule, where professional caterers will apply to the organisers for the granting of permits.

Hotels, guesthouses and restaurants usually provide for the overnight visitor. Food stalls at the craft market, pubs and meals at restaurants and hotels usually cater for the day visitor.

While overnight customers are predictable with their regular meal intakes, it is the day visitors that have a great impact on the food stalls as well as on the restaurants in the town. The food stalls are found in the streets of Grahamstown or are confined to one area at the craft market. The latter arrangement, which is derived from the food markets of Asia and is becoming increasingly popular with large events, can also be seen in Southern African shopping malls, where a variety of different tastes in food are found in a section of the mall. Grahamstown offers a variety of foods to suit the different tastes of various cultures visiting the festival. The multitude of food outlets ranges from German to Chinese and from Italian to Middle Eastern cuisine.

As a caterer for such an event it is important to forecast the number of people who will most likely visit. Always research how competitors performed in previous years before accepting a tender. This information can be obtained from the organisers. A good contact at the Weather Bureau might prove invaluable. Weather forecasts and the weather patterns of previous years can be obtained from the South African Weather Bureau. The biggest enemy of any food business during an uncontrolled outdoor event is the weather. Since the meal plan cannot always be changed to suit the weather, it is important that the meals provided accommodate the weather or season. Provision should also be made for sudden weather changes, such as shelter for rain or against hot sun. The caterer must be flexible and should easily adapt to these changes; after all, he or she is there to make a profit.

Factors that are often forgotten or ignored when planning the catering for a large uncontrolled event such as a festival are ablution and waste control as well as easy access to the food stall. Often the owner of a stall encounters shortages of certain ingredients. It is time-consuming and nerve-wracking having to wind your way through thousands of visitors.

A layout of the event premises should be made available to each tender of a food stall. This will enable the professional caterer to plan the shortest route to his or her outlet. The disposal of waste will have to take place unseen and preferably without coming into contact with event visitors. Running water must be available for reasons of hygiene and toilets should not be placed in close proximity to food vendors.

What does it take to successfully organise the catering for an event such as the Grahamstown Arts Festival? Prior experience in organising a large event will positively impact on the overall outcome. In addition, the following factors should be taken into account:

- *Location.* The catering grounds must be easily accessible to visitors, caterers and the municipality. Ensure that there is easy access to parking and loading space close to the grounds.

- *Visitors.* Public holidays or school holidays falling during the event could increase the number of guests unexpectedly.
- *Sporting events.* An international one-day cricket match in a neighbouring city could decrease the number of projected visitors for that day.
- *Season.* The menu should complement the season. Salads and light meals are less popular during cold winter months, but essential when catering for hot summer days.
- *Weather.* Obtain weather forecasts to predict the type of menu that should be served at the event.
- *Equipment.* The availability of natural resources (gas or electricity) for cooking equipment has to be defined before transport of such equipment to the event.
- *Menu.* The menu must be easy to prepare at the location. Baking should be avoided, as the baked goods become unstable in the oven. Frying in deep oil should also be avoided because of the odours.

Case study 12.1: Planning to operate a food stall at the Grahamstown National Arts Festival

The caterer should immediately start with the planning of the event on issue of the permit to operate a food stall at the Grahamstown National Arts Festival, which is 90 days prior to the event. It is always extremely difficult to plan for an unthemed event like this. An important issue is the location of the food stall. Will it be in the streets of Grahamstown or at the craft market on the village green? This information is usually obtained from the municipality office granting the permits or from the organiser. With it will come a layout of the location, indicating water supply, electricity, access roads, etc.

The caterer now needs to know what the surrounding stall owners will be serving to avoid duplication and also how many competitors there will be. This information is also obtained from the organisers of the event.

Researching previous years when the event was held is the biggest task now facing the caterer. Obtaining information about competitors' performance in previous years and calculating the number of expected guests for the next event are crucial to the overall success of the caterer. One way to investigate competitors' performance is to ask them. Even if they keep records and are willing to share their knowledge, you have to get a second opinion: competition sometimes leads to exaggeration. Second opinions can usually be obtained from a supplier; find out who supplied a competitor with goods during the previous festival. Suppliers or their representatives usually provide this kind of information in the hope that they will obtain more business. The event organiser might be able to give figures of guests, turnover, etc.

The calculation of expected guests is usually done in two ways. Obtain statistics from previous festival years regarding the number of people who attended and the number of people who had been served during the festival. The organisers of an event will usually make these figures available. A number of statistics can also be obtained from organisers and organisations involved in the festival. Numbers of expected visitors will be available from tourist offices and from the organisers. Although these figures are speculative, they provide the caterer with a guideline in respect of expected customers. Another way of calculating the number of expected visitors is to take the average increase in visitors to past festivals over a period of time and to use this to calculate the number of expected visitors for the next festival.

The caterer now has most of the necessary information to plan the venture. The caterer already knows that his or her stall will be at the craft market and that a German and an Italian stall will flank it. Competitors and suppliers have revealed that they sold on average 900 meals per day on Saturdays and Sundays, and 550 meals per day on weekdays. A visitor increase of 6% over the 120 000 of the previous year is expected and two new competitors have been added to the existing eight stall owners. The caterer has decided to operate an American type stall with a variety of ten hot dogs and hamburgers being the main meals to be served. The caterer's calculations should be as follows:

Expected meals during weekends are

$$\frac{900 \text{ meals} \times 8 \text{ old competitors}}{10 \text{ new competitors}} = 720 \text{ meals} \times 6\% = 763 \text{ meals per day}$$

Expected meals during weekdays are

$$\frac{550 \text{ meals} \times 8 \text{ old competitors}}{10 \text{ new competitors}} = 440 \text{ meals} \times 6\% = 466 \text{ meals per day}$$

Since the caterer has ten items on the menu, he or she should estimate to sell 76 items per weekend day or 46 items per weekday. The festival is open for 11 days, including 4 weekend days. Therefore, the caterer will sell 3 052 (763 × 4) items on the weekend days and 3 262 (466 × 7) items on the weekdays. Planning therefore should revolve around the selling of 6 314 items from his or her menu for the duration of the festival.

However, as said earlier in this chapter, planning is not all that easy. Factors beyond your control can have a drastic impact on the success of a venture. Although very unlikely, a long period of rain during the festival could change the predicted increase in visitors. In addition, an international rugby match in neighbouring Port Elizabeth could bring the expected number of sales down. On the other hand, a public holiday falling on a Friday could drastically increase the sales for that day since more people will be able to attend.

12.3.1.2 Catering for events with specific themes

The organisation of fun days will be explained here. Red Nose Day used to draw thousands of people with their families to hotels and showgrounds on Saturdays and Sundays. Supermarkets hold food and wine festivals and even public organisations such as Rotary and Lions have their regular flea markets. Recently flea markets for children, sponsored and organised by KTV, have become a national event, held in every major city in South Africa.

Organisational talent is needed to make these events a success. Since the purpose of these activities is to attract entire families, the catering must be geared to satisfy both adult and young consumers. This means that the caterer must ensure that his or her menu pleases both types of customer. Unless seating is provided near the food stall, the caterer's menu should revolve around fast-food items and pre-prepared dishes rather than cook-to-order food items. Light desserts or sweets could be included in the menu to accommodate children. The success of any catering venture depends largely on the ability of the caterer to predict what types of food visitors to the event are most likely to consume. The theme of the event will give a clue. In the case of Red Nose Day or KTV's Market Day the entire event is geared towards children; therefore the menus should cater primarily for children. A parent will most likely be directed by a child to a stall that offers child-appealing food.

As with all off-premises catering, it is vital that controls be in place to minimise loss. Lists of every item that enters the event premises should be made. Recipes should be simple, with only a few ingredients, so that control is easy.

If catering for an uncontrolled event (as described in the example below) is envisaged, the caterer should pay attention to the following check list of fundamental principles to ensure success:

- **Event theme.** It is important to determine for whom the event is largely intended to cater, such as children, beer or wine consumers, browsing families, in order to draw up a suitable menu.
- **Duration of event.** A street Christmas market that only operates on a certain day of the week for limited hours requires quick setup and breakdown of food stalls.
- **Research.** It is best to research previous or similar events and to gauge their success. Information is available from organisers and the Internet.
- **Pricing.** This should be fair and items should be neither over- nor underpriced.
- **Controls.** Control must be exercised not only over liquid assets such as cash but also over inventories.
- **Personnel.** In both cases, catering personnel should always appear friendly and professional. Family-oriented catering in particular can quickly take a plunge due to word-of-mouth bad publicity about service.

Often the success of catering for a themed event does not only depend on the above information. First-time caterers in particular should make use of the following additional guidelines when planning a themed event with unlimited access:

- **Research**. The recipe for success starts with research. Obtain as much information as possible about the existing event or contact organisers of similar events. This will help in the shaping of contingency plans. Research should also include the occurrence of other events in the vicinity, as this could impact on the turnover.
- **Location**. Plans of event premises must be available in order to plan equipment placement and a layout of the food stall. Staff members need to be informed about the exact location.
- **Visitors and duration**. An event is likely to draw a large number of visitors if it takes place during school holidays, after hours, on weekends or public holidays. The caterer's task is to ensure a steady supply of food during the entire period of the event.
- **Weather and season**. Information can be obtained from the Weather Bureau. Flexibility is essential when it comes to sudden weather changes. Menus usually complement the season.
- **Menu and pricing**. Most catering companies work on a tight budget; this does not, however, mean that the customers should be overcharged. Prices should be fair and in line with competitors. Competition with others should be reasonable.
- **Controls**. It is in the interest of the caterer to prevent theft of equipment and food stock. Control sheets and systems have to be implemented and explained to all staff members.
- **Personnel**. As stated before, the catering personnel should always appear friendly and professional. This does not exclude the management of the catering firm. Each member of the front-of-house team should have been trained in customer relations.

Case study 12.2: Planning a food stall at a beer festival

In this case the caterer is one of four other stall owners participating in an *Oktober Fest*. The duration of the festivities is over four days, starting on a Thursday with the finale on Sunday. The event opens on Thursday and Friday at 17:00 and on Saturday and Sunday at 12:00. Closing on all four days is at midnight. Since this is the first time that this event is being held, the caterer has no means of gathering information on turnover from suppliers or competitors. However, these figures are required in order to plan for the event. An estimate could be made by making enquiries with the tourist office and organisers of similar events in the region. If the event is a continuation of previous festivities, the same calculation as in the previous example can be used.

The caterer also has only limited knowledge about German food and its preparation and therefore needs to improve this knowledge. Purchasing books on the subject, visiting a library or consulting a specialist could assist in this regard. Although the *Oktober Fest* is a German invention, menu items could include even local specialities. It is also important to know what competitors will be offering at their stalls.

The planning of the menu should take into account the preferred taste of the customers most likely to visit the event, but should at the same time be in line with the overall theme of the event. Since traditional German cooking involves mostly fatty foods, it is not advisable to prepare this type of food in hot conditions. However, traditional German cooking also includes the preparation of sausages, which is also a favourite dish among local patrons. The caterer, with this newly gained knowledge on German food, can adapt traditional German food to local requirements such as 'boerewors' (alternatively known as 'barbecue sausage') in a roll, apple pie instead of *apfelstrudel*, and cheeseboards using local cheeses with German bread.

The caterer must make provision for the preparation of the food items on the menu as well. Peak periods of sale will most likely be between 12:00 and 15:00 during the day and 18:00 to 22:00 in the evening; it is also likely that when visitors start to get intoxicated the sales of food will increase! Cold-meat platters, cheese boards and apple pies can be pre-prepared away from the event and pre-plated. An item such as boerewors can be prepared slightly ahead of time and kept warm on the side of the grill or can be prepared by order. It is important for the caterer to keep a record of sales, especially if no previous sales numbers were available.

The caterer's research has revealed the following information: at a similar event in the region 250 people were served during the first day at all stalls during the lunch period. This number increased by 20% on each other day. The sales per stall during the evening started on Thursday with 350 meals per stall but only increased by 10% for the following evenings. In addition, sales during the off-peak period (15:00 to 18:00) started with 80 served meals on Thursday but increased by only 6% until Sunday. A total of 3 317 people were served meals during the entire event. That event drew a total of 15 000 visitors over the same period. This indicates that 22% of all visitors made use of the food stalls. The caterer should now plan his or her menu and preparation around these figures.

12.3.2 The controlled event

A controlled or limited access event is somewhat easier to organise than an uncontrolled event. Such an event could range from a cocktail party to a lavish wedding or presidential inauguration. However, if the caterer is not careful, mistakes can easily be made. How elaborate the catering will be depends entirely on the budget of the client and the professionalism of the caterer. Planning the catering for any event will require that you have a basic knowledge and understanding of foods.

There are a number of companies in South Africa that specialise in the organisation and operation of large events. Beauty pageants, national and international conferences, sporting events and presidential inaugurations are undoubtedly the highlights of such firms. Appendix 12.5 (see the web site) presents an African theme for a banquet. The target market for such a lavish undertaking is mainly the overseas conference organiser. Set in Sun City's Superbowl, this event calls for the coordination of various departments, such as the kitchen, bar services, decorators, dancers and banqueting. The caterer is expected to make this an unforgettable meal. A gala banquet or elaborate dinner is usually the finale to a conference. Delegates will leave a venue with pleasant memories of a superb meal and a well-organised function.

Catering for any controlled event such as a gala banquet, conference luncheon, tea break or working breakfast is more predictable than catering for an uncontrolled event. The advantage is that the number of clients to be catered for is already known to the caterer, be it through limitations of seating space at the venue or the number of attendees provided by the organiser. As already mentioned, the budget of the client and the professionalism of the caterer will determine how elaborate the catering is to be. The caterer will obviously require a basic knowledge and understanding of food. Ingredients will have to be sourced from reliable suppliers; the seasonal availability of certain foodstuffs has to be followed up. Often a client demands an ingredient, for example strawberries, that is not available all year round. If the caterer is not fully aware of the availability of these ingredients at local markets, he or she will end up paying a high price, thus resulting in less profit. Banqueting menus should be based on foods that are obtainable throughout the year. Menus should also be drawn up to appeal to the client; a variety of banquet menus, cocktail function, lunch and dinner menus are usually available. But this should not prevent the caterer from accommodating certain of the client's specific requests, such as vegetarian or religious meals. Professionalism is shown when a client's expectations and wishes are included in a menu, rather than denied because of logistic or personnel problems. This becomes especially important when the function to be catered for is a wedding.

The organisation of such an event begins at the first meeting with the client. It is important for the caterer to learn about the delegates or participants who will attend the function. Gathering as much information as possible will help in compiling a group analysis or history of the client. The points listed below should be considered when meeting the client (Hildreth, 1990: 20–31):

- *Age and gender of delegates.* This will give the caterer an idea of portion size as well as the degree of health food requirements.
- *Food and beverage preferences.* The food for tea/coffee breaks and luncheons during a conference should be kept light; alcoholic beverages are usually served only at dinners.

- **General preferences**. These can be broken down into the preferences of the delegates or the organiser's preferences.
- **Origin of delegates**. Knowledge of the country, province or city from which delegates originate can provide indications of cultural affiliation.
- **Organisation data**. This includes information on previous conferences the client has held.

This data can be obtained through questionnaires, computer searches or evaluation data stored from previous events with the client. The best way of obtaining necessary information from a client is undoubtedly a personal interview. The most frequently used method, however, is the questionnaire. Questionnaires are usually sent out to prospective delegates at the beginning of the planning phase of the event. Most event organisers incorporate this specific information with their registration forms, to be completed by the prospective delegates. Catering remains the focal point of any event, be it a refreshment break, a set menu, or any food and beverage provision. It is commonly accepted that if the catering was good the event was a success. No matter how beautifully the event was decorated and how wonderful and how smooth the service was, it is the food that most influences the perception of the delegates.

Case study 12.3: Planning a wedding reception

A family would like to organise a wedding reception at their house. The caterer has a first meeting with the family and investigates the estimated attendance, the meal service requirements, ceremonies that are planned during the meal service, and the client's budget. Since the caterer is catering for the entire event, he or she will need to know about all festivities on the premises and the timing of them. In the case of a wedding, menus are usually drawn up completely to the client's specification, since it is a special occasion.

The caterer now has a fairly good idea what the client expects; he or she also knows that there will be 150 guests attending the outdoor wedding ceremony, which will have a cocktail party prior to commencement. In addition, the main function, a sit-down wedding dinner, will be held in the evening for 100 invited guests only. Fortunately for the caterer there is a fairly large budget to work from. However, the caterer is only involved in the food and beverage planning of the function. This means that he or she has to liaise closely with the company that is involved with the decoration and set-up of the entire function. The planning of the event after the first meeting should be organised as follows.

- **Produce menu for cocktail party**. This should be up-market, for 150 people, served by waiters, and should consist of hot and cold snacks. It begins with the arrival of the first guest and continues until the wedding ceremony starts.
- **Produce cocktail list for cocktail party**. This should also be up-market, for 150 people, and should consist of light alcoholic and non-alcoholic beverages.

- *Produce menu for wedding dinner*. This should be a four-course menu; it is for 100 people and is a sit-down dinner.
- *Produce beverage menu for dinner*. This must complement the four courses of the menu; all beverages will be served and should include coffee.

This is the time for the caterer to call upon his or her suppliers to investigate the availability of certain foods and beverages. The supply of these products should preferably be secured. The menu should now be priced and a second meeting with the organiser should be held. During this final meeting, the caterer will clarify if there are any speeches during the dinner service and how long they will take. In addition the caterer should investigate the equipment that is at his or her disposal for the preparation of both meals. This is needed for the planning of the cooking stage.

Once the menu has been agreed upon, the caterer has to meet with the decorator and investigate table plans, entrances for waiters, as well as areas for the washing-up and collection of used plates and glassware. After this the caterer will plan the production of the food and the service of both meals. Appendix 12.3 (see the web site) is an example of a menu and a wine list that could be served for such an event. The caterer now has to break down each item on the menu into production units. The production unit for the starter would look like this:

12.3.3 Planning of food production

Smoked breast of duck
Smoked duck breast – pre-portioned from supplier; slicing and plating at event premises.
Oak leaf lettuce – pre-packed from supplier; washing and plating at event premises.
Raspberry vinaigrette – production at caterer's premises; pre-produce, bottle and store.
Plate garnishes – production at caterer's premises on day of event.

Appendix 12.4 (see the web site) shows a typical production sheet that can be used for the preparation of certain dishes for an event such as the wedding in this example.

After the production has been planned and supplies have been secured, the caterer now has to secure the necessary labour. This labour can be hired from a local hotel school or, if the caterer has a database of names of reliable workers, the workers can be drawn from there. According to the planning schedule, certain foods can be pre-prepared. Considerations of hygiene have top priority during the pre-preparation of food. The storage of food has to be monitored carefully. Staff not only has to be made aware of correct food handling and safe food production but also of the implications that personal hygiene can have on food production.

The final planning stage is the actual cooking for the event. In the above example the caterer has already set times for speeches with the organiser and made it clear what implications unexpected speeches can have on the outcome of the cooked meal. Certain items still have to be cooked and prepared at the event premises; however, the caterer has prepared a menu that has not only satisfied the client but is also easy to prepare.

Case study 12.4: Catering to satisfy religious and cultural requirements

The presidential inauguration dinner in April 2004 was a blend of African produce and modern production, while the buffet for the same event in 1994 was a lavish Southern African affair including items such as mopane worms, tsing and other cultural specialities. The diversity of a country's population often requires the caterer to provide meals for religious minorities.

Sometimes the caterer cannot provide for specific religious requirements because of strict regulations. One example is the Jewish faith, where meals can only be prepared in a certain kitchen under the auspices of Jewish clergy. However, food for delegates of this faith can be obtained in sealed containers from specialised companies. Catering for other religions requires the caterer to have a basic knowledge of the food requirements of any religion.

Cultural catering is very similar – the same basic knowledge of food production is required as for religious catering. When assessing food and beverage requirements with the organisers, the following aspects need to be considered:

- *Number of people attending.* It is important to have an exact number of attendees. An indication of the number of vegetarian or religious meals required should also be obtained at this stage.
- *Available budget.* This will always determine the extravagance of a function. If the budget for a conference is tight, meals during the day should be inexpensive, but dinners should be memorable and rather lavish.
- *Religious restrictions of delegates.* This is important because some require longer notification periods as specially prepared food has to be obtained.
- *Break times.* This allows the caterer to set up just in time. If times are adhered to, absolute freshness of food is guaranteed.
- *Speeches during main meals.* This is a nightmare for every caterer: the beef fillet is at its best waiting to be served and the host gets up to give an unscheduled speech! Organisers must be made aware of the implications of unexpected speeches during the meal service.

These are the basic determining factors for food and beverage provision. The most important aspect when planning the catering for an event is the type of delegates attending the event. Every delegate or attendee needs to be considered – being insensitive to their needs will lead to an unprofessional event. An organiser should never forget who pays the bills; every effort should be made to attend to the special needs of the delegates. The provision of standard menus by organisers and caterers is acceptable, but provision needs to be made for special requests.

Imagine that three guests of the Jewish faith are attending the wedding in example 12.2, in addition to three Hindus and eight Muslims. Five people are strict vegetarians and one has a diabetes problem. In order to cater for these people too, the caterer needs to have a basic knowledge of the faith and beliefs of these religions and groups. For example, the food for the guests of Jewish faith would have to be ordered in from a company that specialises in the production of kosher meals. The Hindus would not be able to eat the beef and the main course would have to be substituted with lamb or pork. The latter choice would, however, not be suitable for the eight Muslims, who are not allowed to consume pork; their meat would also have to be slaughtered in the Halaal fashion. Absolutely no meat, fish or poultry products are suitable for strict vegetarians; this includes butter or cream. A sugar substitute has to be provided for the diabetes sufferer. These are only a few examples of the challenges a caterer could be faced with during the planning of an event.

Browse these Internet sites
http://www.cateringbydeangelos.com/
http://www.caterware.com/
http://www.cooken.com/
http://www.efficient-frontiers.com/products/catering_event.html
http://www.enablez.com/html/enablez-otherproducts.html
http://www.nfs-hospitality.com/rendezvous.htm
http://www.redcliffe.com/event_management_services.asp?event_management.asp-mainFrame
http://www.spectrumconcessions.com/catering-services.cfm
http://www.synergy-intl.com/
http://www.unlv.edu/Tourism/catbib.html

QUESTIONS FOR SELF-EVALUATION

1 Why is it important for the caterer to know if there are to be speeches in between meals at a sit-down dinner or buffet dinner for 500 people?

2 The meat supplier you chose for a wedding function has failed to deliver the correct amount of portioned meat for the main course. What would your immediate response be and what long-term action should you take?

3 Your kitchen workers are preparing a chicken stew for 800 people that is to be used for a buffet dinner in two days' time. Is this kind of pre-preparation acceptable? Are there any other factors that have to be observed by the workers?

4 A client would like to entertain 150 guests for dinner, but has a very limited budget. Which type of menu would you suggest he or she choose and why?

5   You are the caterer at a function for rural municipality workers. There are 200 people attending this function. The only meat on the buffet menu is well-done topside of beef. How would you calculate your meat order, to avoid running out of meat during the function or having too much left over?

6   In the finalising stages of a meeting for a function your client mentions that he or she would like to have a cash bar, as opposed to waiters freely serving alcoholic beverages, since his or her guests have to attend an important conference the following day. You happily accept since this could generate additional revenue. Would you encourage your waiters to offer speciality coffees such as Dom Pedro after the main meal?

Note: Appendices 12.1 to 12.5 can be found on the Juta Academic web site: www.jutaacademic.co.za

Appendix 12.1   *Examples of served dinner and buffet lunch menus (Source: Sandton Convention Centre, Johannesburg)*

Appendix 12.2   *Data-capturing sheets (Source: Sun International, Sun City Entertainment Centre)*

Appendix 12.3   *An example of a wedding menu and wine list*

Appendix 12.4   *A typical production sheet*

Appendix 12.5   *African theme banquet (Source: Sun International, Sun City Entertainment Centre)*

Part C

CHAPTER 13

Mega-event Management

Kamilla Swart

AIM OF THE CHAPTER

The aim of this chapter is to demonstrate the complexities of bidding for and hosting a both sport and non-sport mega-events through the experience of bidding for and hosting of the 2004 Olympic Games and the World Summit on Sustainable Development (WSSD), respectively. It aims to alert the reader to a range of considerations to which any bidding entity, especially in a developing context, should give attention. Furthermore, consideration is also given to key aspects of hosting a mega-event to demonstrate some of the management challenges South Africa faces in hosting a successful Soccer World Cup in 2010.

LEARNING OBJECTIVES

After having studied this chapter, you should be able to:

- define what characterises a mega-event;
- understand the process of event bidding;
- understand what appropriate planning is required;
- understand the key success criteria in bidding for mega-events;
- grasp the elements of how to manage the hosting of a mega-event;
- understand the importance of evaluating the impacts of the mega-event.

13.1 INTRODUCTION

The bidding for mega-events takes place in an increasingly complex international arena that is extremely contested. A city or country's ability to succeed in the arena of hosting mega-events heralds international recognition in relation to its economic, social and political capacity; hence the increasing competition to bid for these events. A noticeable trend is that once a county is able to break into the international arena of hosting mega-events, it creates a ripple effect of attracting more and oftentimes bigger mega-events (Swart & Bob, in press). This is clearly visible in South Africa. This chapter describes the approach developed and lessons learned by the Cape Town 2004 Bid – why we bid, what was our approach, where we were successful, where we failed – important issues for other cities in developing contexts. Reference is also made to WSSD as an example of a non-sport mega-event. Key success criteria for the bidding of sport mega-events are also reviewed. Next, the experiences of Athens 2004, as a bid city that progressed to host city, are outlined. Key management services are described to illustrate the complexity of hosting the Olympic Games – the ultimate sport mega-event. It also draws upon lessons learnt from WSSD and best practice from the Sydney 2000 Olympics.

Westerbeek, Turner and Ingerson (2002: 304) note that a mega-event is characterised by its size which can be operationalised in four different ways:

- conspicuous involvement of national and regional government authorities;
- the domestic and/or international media, and the associated selling of broadcast rights;
- the superior technical competencies required – this includes the technical standards set by International Sport Federations (IFs) for competition and non-competition infrastructure as well as personnel issues, and
- the broad support required by the city from both direct and indirect stakeholders such as the general public, government, target markets and other business sectors.

In 1995 South Africa won the right to host the Rugby World Cup, and this event signified the return of South Africa to the hosting of major international events. This mega-event involved the use of venues and infrastructure in cities throughout the country. In 1997 Cape Town came third in its bid to host the 2004 Olympic Games as will be described in detail below. South Africa hosted the 7th All Africa Games, and Johannesburg was the host city for this event. South Africa came third in the race to host the 2006 Soccer World Cup and won the right to host the 2010 Soccer World Cup in 2004. Although all these events are extremely large in scale, and the bidding process for each is very similar, it is important to distinguish their respective sizes and complexities (Lloyd, 2000: 329). She adds that the rugby and soccer World Cup events occur in various venues throughout the country and do not necessarily demand the construction of new venues and infrastructure. However, the Olympic Games and All Africa Games, although different in size, occur in one city and require a high level of infrastructure (Lloyd, 2000: 329). The WSSD is similar in scope to the Olympics Games as all the activities are centralised in one city – in the case of South Africa WSSD took place in Johannesburg in 2002. However, there were many parallel events that were hosted all around the country.

The Games of the Olympiad (commonly referred to as the Summer Olympics) is considered to be the ultimate mega-event and takes place in a different city every four years. The games are recognised to be the largest peace-time event and are essentially the simultaneous organisation of 28 world championship events, involving over 16 000 athletes and officials and 20 000 media personnel (Lloyd, 2000: 329). 'The organisation of the Olympic Games does not only affect the sports world. Organisation on such a scale is essential for a country seeking to progress, to show the world what it is really like' (Mitjans, in Moragas & Botella, 1995: 262).

13.2 THE INTERNATIONAL OLYMPIC COMMITTEE (IOC) AND THE OLYMPIC BIDDING PROCESS

The IOC, the event owner, is a non-governmental, non-profit organisation with its headquarters in Lausanne, Switzerland (IOC, 1996: 24). It holds all rights to the Olympic Games which consist of the Games of the Summer Olympics and the Olympic Winter Games. The Olympic Movement consists of the IOC members and staff, representatives of the various International Sport Federations (IFs) and the National Olympic Committees (NOCs) of all the countries and regions recognised by the IOC, the bidding and organising committee as well as any other organisations recognised by the IOC (IOC, 1996: 11–12).

The bid process is initiated by the IOC who forwards letters to all the NOCs about nine years prior to the given Olympic Games indicating that they would like to be presented with prospective host cities within six months (Turco, Riley & Swart, 2002: 82). Only one city from a country can be nominated by its NOC. For a country with more than one city eager to host the Games, an internal bid is used to decide which city would go forward as the country's representative city. In regard to the South African 2004 Olympic bid process, Cape Town was selected as the candidate city by the National Olympic Committee of South Africa (NOCSA) in January 1994 ahead of Johannesburg and Durban. The city's candidature becomes official when the city officials and the NOC present themselves as candidate to host the Olympic Games. An informational meeting is then held by the IOC for all the Olympic candidate cities. As the bidding process has been strongly criticised over the years, the IOC published the *Manual for Cities Bidding for the Olympic Games* in order to streamline the bidding process (Pike Masteralexis, Barr & Hums, 1998: 223). These regulations were enforced in February 1992, hence the Sydney 2000 Olympic Games was the first bid according to these guidelines. These regulations were subsequently amended by the IOC in December 1999, whereby a two-phased procedure was introduced (see case study 13.1 below) (IOC, 2003a: 1). Swart and Bob (in press) note that these questions aid the IOC to screen potential bidders as well as provide a framework for the city itself to determine whether the baseline capacity and competence exist to bid for (and ultimately) host the Games.

Based upon the manual, the candidate cities have to respond to a questionnaire covering a number of themes which is presented in the candidature file or bid book. Turco *et al* (2002) noted that the Cape Town 2004 bid book included the following 19 themes:

- national, regional, and candidate city characteristics
- legal aspects
- customs and immigration formalities
- environmental protection
- meteorological and environmental conditions

- security
- medical services
- programme
- general sports organisation
- sport
- Olympism and culture
- Olympic village
- accommodation
- transport
- technology
- media
- finance
- marketing
- guarantees.

The bid book is then submitted to the IOC and an Evaluation Commission visits each city on behalf of the IOC to evaluate the merits of each bid. Based upon a report, the number of cities is narrowed down to the potentially four or five best Olympic cities. Cape Town was competing against ten other cities in the race to host the 2004 Games. For the first time there were many developing cities participating in the bid, namely Buenos Aires, Cape Town, Istanbul and Rio de Janeiro. The finalist cities for the 2004 Games were Athens, Buenos Aires, Cape Town, Rome and Stockholm. Seville, St Petersburg, Rio de Janeiro, San Juan and Istanbul were eliminated. The Evaluation Commission's report is forwarded to each IOC member (107 at the time of the Cape Town bid) for examination. At the time of the 2004 bid, IOC members had the chance to visit these cities before the final vote was taken. The point of the city's bidding campaign is to gain as many votes as possible from the IOC members. About 80% of the IOC members visited Cape Town. Event lobbying was a significant aspect of the 2004 bidding process, and it is not unexpected that (given allegations of bribery) as part of the IOC policy reform in 1999, IOC members are no longer allowed to make formal or informal visits to candidate cities (Turco *et al*, 2002: 84).

The final step of the bidding process is the candidate presentation at the IOC session at which the Olympic host city will be selected. Each city is given an hour to present its bid and to answer questions posed to them by the IOC members. Once the cities have presented, the IOC Evaluation Commission presents its findings from the visits to the candidate cities and invites questions. Subsequently, voting commences by secret ballot and the process continues until the city with a simple majority wins. This generally takes several rounds with the city obtaining the lowest number of votes dropping out during each round. IOC voting is dominated by Europe (40%); Africa and Asia combined account for another 40%;

South America has 15% of the votes and North America makes up for 5% of the votes (Duncan, 1996: Internet). Swart and Bob (in press) contend that it is this balance of power which affects the final outcome of the votes. Cape Town and Buenos Aires, the two non-European cities as well as the two cities that had not previously hosted the games, were tied at the bottom after the first round of voting (16 votes each). In each of the consequent rounds of voting, Athens and Rome were the clear leaders. Stockholm was eliminated in the third round, while Cape Town was eliminated in the following round. Athens beat Rome in the fifth and final round by 61 to 44. Athens won the right to host the 2004 Games by a margin of 25 votes.

Case study 13.1: Candidate Acceptance Procedure
(Source: IOC, 2003a, Internet)

In December 1999 at the 110th IOC Session a two-phase procedure was introduced in relation to the election of the Host City for the Olympic Games.

1. Phase 1: Candidate Acceptance Procedure
No city is considered a 'Candidate City' until it is accepted as such by the IOC Executive Board. All cities are considered 'Applicant Cities' during this period. For the 2012 bid process, the phase will end in mid-June 2004. Applicant cities are required to answer a questionnaire which provides the IOC with an overview of each city's project to host the Olympic Games. Applications are then assessed by a working group comprised of external experts and IOC administration members to determine the cities' potential to organise the games. This assessment includes a number of technical criteria including government support, public opinion, general infrastructure, security, venues, accommodation and transport. Based upon the Candidate Acceptance Procedures, the IOC Executive Board will determine which cities are to be accepted as 'Candidate Cities'.

2. Phase 2: Candidature Phase
Cities accepted as 'Candidate Cities' will go through a second phase where they are required to submit a Candidature File to the IOC. An Evaluation Commission, comprised of, members representing the IFs, NOCs, IOC members, representative of the Athletes' Commission and the International Paralympic Committee as well as IOC experts, examine the city's candidature and prepare an evaluation report, which is then used as a basis to select the Candidate Cities to be submitted to the IOC Session for election. Throughout the entire bid process close co-operation between the NOC and the city is required.

13.2.1 Other bidding processes

Similar to the changes adopted by the IOC, FIFA, the world governing body for international football, introduced a rotation system following South Africa's dramatic loss to Germany for the 2006 World Cup (FIFA World Cup 2006, 2003:

Internet). Africa was awarded the right to host the 2010 World Cup, and South Africa won the rights to host this event when they beat Morocco in the first round of voting by 14 votes to 10. As a result of these policy changes, the World Cup will be coming to Africa for the first time. FIFA's flagship event will be held in South America in 2014 (FIFA, 2004: Internet).

Similar to sport mega-event bidding, cities and countries also bid for conferences. They too have to demonstrate that they have the capacity to host these events successfully. During the United Nations General Assembly 55th session it was decided that a major summit would be held during 2002 in order to assess and continue the ground-breaking work of the United Nations Conference on Environment and Development (UNCED) which was held in Rio de Janeiro, Brazil 1992 (United Nations, 2000). The United Nations WSSD is considered to be the largest conference to be held anywhere in the world (South Africa, Republic of, 2002: Internet). South Africa and Johannesburg specifically won the bid in December 2000 to host WSSD 2002. This event is also known as the Johannesburg Summit and brought together tens of thousands of participants, including heads of state and government, national delegates and leaders from non-governmental organisations (NGOs), businesses and other major groups to focus the world's attention and direct action toward meeting difficult challenges, such as improving people's lives and conserving our natural resources in a world that is growing in population, with ever-increasing demands for food, water, shelter, sanitation, energy, health services and economic security (JOWSCO. 2002a: Internet).

13.3 THE IMPORTANCE OF APPROPRIATE PLANNING

This section outlines the key elements identified by Lloyd (2000: 331–333) that are critical to a successful bid. She asserts that appropriate planning is a prerequisite and it should comprise and integrate all the requirements of preparing a bid, and the impact and the legacies of the event on the city. Thus it is necessary to link spatial planning to financial planning and budgeting; to communication and broadcasting; to operational planning and community involvement.

The 2004 Olympic Games had the potential to act as a catalyst of economic growth and of urban management in Cape Town. The infrastructural requirements for the games needed to be planned during the bidding process to fit into Cape Town's contexts and future development plans should the bid be successful – political, economic, social, environmental, physical – so that it maximised the benefits, and minimised the possible costs and risks. Cape Town's bid had to reconcile the philosophical and technical needs of the IOC while ensuring that whatever was planned and implemented left a positive legacy that would help to meet the requirements of the metropolitan area of Cape Town. Ideally, any city bidding for a mega-event should have developed a vision for its future and, as a part of this, a comprehensive, long-term strategy for the hosting of mega and other events. The Cape Town Olympic Bid Company's (CTOBC) vision was that 'the Olympic process (from bidding to hosting to the post-event phases) must contribute to improving the quality of life of people of the city, region and nation in a manner that is environmentally, socially and economically sustainable'.

Cape Town was fortunate in having both national and metropolitan visions, which still guide the future development of the city – the Reconstruction and Development Programme (RDP) and Growth, Employment and Redistribution strategy (GEAR) at the national level and the Metropolitan Spatial Development Framework (MSDF) at the metro level. The MSDF represented the approved and supported vision for guiding and managing the future growth of the metropolitan area and formed the planning starting point. The facilities plan for the 2004 Olympics ensured that proposals derived from and supported these frameworks. In fact, the energy unleashed by the bidding process contributed greatly to moving these visions closer to their actual implementation.

Spatial planning for the Olympic Games was necessarily undertaken as a dynamic and strategic process by the CTOBC to guide, give direction to, and manage growth over a long period of time. The procedure used had been developed in Cape Town and tested in South Africa over the past decade. The 'Package of Plans' procedure was first developed by Peter de Tolly (1992: 23) for the City of Cape Town. It creates a set of tools by which land may be strategically developed and managed over time and provides the basis for obtaining the necessary approvals for site and project development. It is a multi-tiered and integrated procedure consisting of an interrelated set of hierarchical policies, plans and action programmes.

The 'Package of Plans' procedure comprises the following features:

- *A contextual framework.* This provides the link to broader frameworks and sets down public sector intentions for an area surrounding a particular site. In Cape Town the RDP and MSDF provided this context and guided the formation of principles to inform the location and provision of Olympic facilities throughout the metro area.
- *A development framework.* This provides the basic physical organisation for the proposed development of a site. These were prepared for each of the larger proposed Olympic sites.
- *A precinct plan.* This provides a guide to the form and shape of future development parcels on a site and urban design guidelines for these.
- *A site development plan.* Each precinct plan is divided into these smaller development parcels. Plans are prepared for groups of buildings.
- *A building plan.* This is the individual plan relating to a particular building.

'The conclusion is that while the object of the pageantry and spectacle associated with the Olympics is to sell the city to the world at large, the pursuit of this goal must ensure that the pageant also serves the interest of the locals. More

© Juta & Co Ltd

particularly, it must be seen to serve the interests of those groups who are least able to participate in the spectacle or to benefit from the more evident economic and financial gains' (Cox, 1994: 19).

13.4 MANAGING THE BIDDING PROCESS

13.4.1 Management systems

The bidding process for a mega-event is usually tight, extremely demanding, conducted by individuals from a wide range of backgrounds/professions and does not allow for anything less than getting it right the first time round (Lloyd, 2000: 333). The complex and time-limited nature of the process (especially for a first-time bid) will almost certainly require bidding entities to cope with crisis management. Lloyd (2000: 333) contends that in the early phases of the bid, energy should be spent on establishing and instituting processes and systems which are correct, simple and effective. The bidding process in Cape Town for the Olympic Games required prioritising specific areas of work at different stages of the bid in order to allocate very scarce resources. Financial management systems were established at the outset. Cost monitoring will be a constant activity and, for most bids, cost saving will be a constant priority. Planning to prepare the event plan and local community involvement should be important in the early stages. Later, moving into implementation, marketing and international communication become a more urgent priority.

13.4.2 Structuring the bidding organisation

Lloyd (2000: 333) contends that Cape Town set up a relatively flat, flexible, fast-reacting and productive organisational structure, which required minimal prescriptive management for the 2004 Olympic Games Bid. The performance of the bid could be severely compromised by inadequacies of structure, resource support or systems. The structure of the CTOBC was derived from the questions in the *Manual for Bidding Cities* provided by the IOC. Cape Town, however, employed international expertise to prepare its work schedule, which presented unique problems as the scheduling did not take into account local dynamics in setting its unrealistic timetables.

The structure of the organisation must suit the broad areas of work necessary, ensuring that areas of responsibility are clearly defined, leaving no opportunity for confusion or overlap and allowing total accountability for completing each task. The broad blocks of activity will change as the bidding process evolves: from plan preparation to document submission and then to the lobbying of the individuals who will make the ultimate choice. The structure of the bidding entity should be designed as an adaptable team so that it may respond to and evolve as a result of these changing work or activity sequences through the bidding process. The structure of the bidding entity should:

- represent the spectrum of stakeholders through a responsive, active and effective board of directors;
- allow for the participation of interested parties though the structure, and other committees established (if it is not possible to establish these types of bodies in the bidding phase, they will become very important in the hosting stages of a mega-event);
- be led by a charismatic leader, and
- allow him or her freedom to establish and run the company to win the bid.

At the director (that is, senior manager) level, multiple responsibility for single activities must be avoided. Accountabilities and responsibilities between different directorates and key authorities at all levels must be clearly defined. The CTOBC succeeded in this to a degree, but grey areas between the responsibilities of different directorates inevitably led to some confusion and delays while responsibilities were defined more specifically. A project as complex as bidding for an Olympic Games requires the input of many specialists and stakeholders outside of the bidding entity. The CTOBC understood well which relevant national and local institutions and structures already existed and established 13 specialist committees (task teams). In the sense that these provided the opportunity for inclusive participation, they succeeded. The degree to which they were constructive and incisive varied considerably.

13.4.3 Staffing

This section outlines the significance of staffing the bid company appropriately as identified by Lloyd (2000: 336–338). A bid for a mega-event will stand or fall on the quality of its personnel asserts Lloyd (2000: 334). 'Projects that demand such superhuman dedication are only bearable if the fascination is greater than the brutality of the stress. And the fascination is produced by an almost chemical combination of two factors: people and objectives' (Josep Miquel Abad, in Moragas & Botella, 1995: 15).

Staffing is critical as the ultimate aim is the creation of a high-performance team made up of people whose personalities complement one another, and who are mutually supportive. In resourcing the organisation, two broad choices may be available. The first would be to recruit staff from a central point and to concentrate all staff management and human resource responsibilities within one clearly identified area. An alternative option would be to delegate all staff recruitment and management to each director. It is difficult to determine which of these options is the most effective and this would be influenced by individual circumstances. The CTOBC relied on the latter option which ensured that each director had the utmost confidence in his or her staff. In each case, however, while the pressure and circumstances of a bid are unique, there will be a need and responsibility to recruit staff who are both expert and robust, and who can excel in these crisis-laden environments. To ensure that the activities of each directorate are continuously and clearly targeted towards achieving a common objective, it may be necessary to employ a general manager who is able to direct the work objectively, unencumbered by direct responsibilities for planning, lobbying, etc. This frees the CEO (and to some extent the directors) to play the creative role that will be required by the demands of the bid. The CTOBC did not employ a managing director and suffered as a result.

In structuring the organisation it should be remembered that although the life span of the organisation may be short- term, this does not negate the need for human resources skills, whether available as a dedicated service or from each individual director. The appropriateness of independent staffing as against line management structures must be carefully considered. Staff will be working under extraordinary circumstances – impossible deadlines, flattened conventional hierarchies, outrageous working hours and stress, and politics, etc. It is debatable whether the directors, pressurised and overworked themselves, will have either the time or ability to provide the human resource management successfully. A mechanism that provides for people's development is essential, if personal and economic empowerment is to result from the process. The CTOBC did not consider human resource management a priority and employed no such skills, leaving all responsibility to each director. Staff issues arose which demanded these skills which were then outsourced – not the ideal situation; all attention was focused only on winning the bid.

13.5 COMMUNICATIONS STRATEGY FOR A MEGA-EVENT

Lloyd (2000: 338–339) highlights the importance of a well-organised communication strategy. Effective communication should be at the core of a successful bid. Without it a bid will fail, irrespective of its other merits. Communicating with authorities, interest groups and communities will involve everyone in the organisation. Bidding for a mega-event involves two related activities: technical preparation and lobbying. Lobbying consists of presentations and visits locally and abroad to sell the technical proposals and the credibility and capacity of the city and country bidding.

A coordinated, integrated communication strategy must be designed at the start of a bidding process to ensure that:

- everything the bid entity does has maximum impact;
- a simple, strong and winning message is communicated;
- the energy and resources expended on international communication balances with that on local initiatives (the challenge of winning hearts and minds locally can be termed a form of lobbying);
- speakers of all relevant languages are considered;
- different interest groups are reached, and
- the information imparted by bid entity staff is consistently presented so that no mixed or conflicting messages are communicated.

This will require integrating the activities of the media, public relations, marketing and public involvement departments. A lesson learnt from Cape Town 2004 is that these areas of work should not be seen as independent entities. They should rather be grouped into one unit so that the ultimate products are strategically targeted and appear part of a related family of products designed for effective communication – written, graphic, verbal, computer-based, radio and television. The combined products must simultaneously target the key demands of the event owners who make the final decision and the local communities who need to be kept informed of proposals which affect them – authorities, private sector and the publics, who can make or break a bid.

A coordinated communications unit will form one of the heaviest cost centres of the bid organisation and must be adequately funded if the bid is to have any hope of success. There is little point in developing an excellent event plan and programme if it cannot be communicated appropriately both locally and internationally. For Cape Town, the coordination of an integrated communications plan was impossible – differences in message, image and style abounded – and the bid never succeeded in producing adequate responses to the key concerns of those who opposed the bid, and communicating them. The communication approach in Cape Town involved primarily the media and marketing directorates. The media strategy involved coordinating both internal and external information flows. It was vitally important to create and monitor external flows of information, to inform and assist local journalists, feed information to the event owners and brief international journalists. The marketing strategy included the production of newsletters, promotional magazines, exhibitions, videos and TV commercials.

For future bids, a group of products will need to be produced which should be conceptualised early in terms of the key messages to be communicated. Seen together, they should form a family of products, with each immediately recognisable as part of a greater body of information. It is equally important that the information produced, in whatever form, is distributed to international organisations, placed in local libraries and is accessible to the local population. The CTOBC attempted – and to a certain extent succeeded – in creating a strong corporate identity in all the material prepared by it or by its consultants. However, the nature of the work includes very severe time frames and a large number of people or groups working on different (often apparently unrelated) aspects of the project. In this context it is an almost impossible task to coordinate the look of the final products, unless considerable thought has gone into it beforehand, and is directed on a continuous basis. It is therefore critical that a professional art director be given the responsibility of designing and coordinating the image of the bid and its products from the very beginning. For Cape Town, it was difficult to ensure that the approaches and products emanating from the different directorates communicated a common style, image and content. From a technical point of view, to achieve a common graphics approach to the production of the Olympic Plan as a whole was not possible.

Technical and financial people often do not have an appreciation for the amount of effort and thought required in the design process or the skills that the designers must have. Unfortunately, it is usually these very people who control the budgets and the outputs of the company. The appointment of an art director is, therefore, not something that will be forthcoming from any management team, unless someone with vision fights for it. The vast number of products included the bidding document, designing an Internet Web site, media inserts in local newspapers, radio and TV broadcasts, video material, clothing, merchandise and gifts, monthly fact sheets and updates on progress, technical documents made user-friendly, presentation material on slide or computer, and exhibition material.

13.5.1 Communicating locally

Lloyd (2000: 338) notes that communicating locally is as important as communicating with the international community, as outlined below. Each member of the bidding organisation should know what is required in terms of bidding, in order to be convincing of the approach adopted in the event plan and be able to describe where proposals will be implemented. Staff who will bear the brunt of the many public presentations should be trained early in the process to ensure that they are able to communicate the required level of information. If staff have not been trained and primed in the communications process, what will ensue is a mixed and difficult-to-understand message being delivered unconvincingly. The time pressures for Cape Town necessitated that the directors and senior staff make almost nightly presentations to interested and affected parties. There was no time for preparation and staff often had to present and answer questions on issues outside their fields of expertise. For instance, staff from the planning directorate had to communicate financial, sporting, environmental, and technological and transportation aspects of the bid. Recognising that time and resources are scarce, it will be imperative to ensure that those who will engage with the publics are sufficiently competent to do so.

An open and honest approach to engaging with community groupings at presentations is essential. Consideration should be given to making presentations in people's home languages or making translation facilities available. The community's input should be viewed as a valuable contribution to the process. A defensive attitude conveys the impression that the public's constructive criticism and contribution are not really valued. Constructive communications training should be instituted to help people to overcome an inherent shyness, to be more approachable and personable.

13.5.2 Communicating with the international community

As noted by Lloyd (2000: 338) above, a communication strategy has to target both the local and international communities. This section will focus on the international community. Communicating with the international community, particularly when lobbying the individuals who will make the choice of city to host the event, requires a high level of diplomacy, fluency in the relevant language, a knowledge of the person's country and culture in order to be able to converse freely and offer efficient hospitality services. The CTOBC established an International Relations Directorate to coordinate all communication with the international community. If it is recognised that the bidding process will require a large amount of international communication, it will be important to identify those who will be involved and to provide them with the necessary training early in the process. Members of the board of the bidding entity, technical staff, politicians from the local mayor to national government ministers and people with experience in the hospitality industry must be trained to make foreign presentations and to host international visitors comfortably, professionally and in a friendly manner. Professional interpreters and translators may be necessary and they too will have to be trained. Documentation sent to individuals overseas should be produced in the home language of that person. This is all far more achievable if the need is identified early enough.

13.6 MANAGING THE POST-DECISION PHASE

Lloyd (2000: 339–342) provided the following insights as a result of her experience in the Olympic Bid announcement. The transition from the bidding phase to that of securing and hosting an event will involve a change in organisation and, to a certain extent, a change in manpower. To successfully create a lasting legacy for the city, it will be vital to ensure that mechanisms are put in place to guarantee a continuation of skills development and empowerment and the bidding phase policy direction. The vision and policies formulated during the bidding phase should be implemented in the organising phase and not jeopardised by the focus on organising the event.

Every bid for a mega-event will face its final decision day, when it either is relegated to the trashcan of failed bids or takes its place in the pantheon of successful ones. It needs to plan and prepare for either eventuality well before the decision date, and to have the agreement of its board and other key stakeholders as to its proposed plan of action. This will entail a number of activities, which either will be common to both success and failure, or singular to one or the other. After the decision of which bid is to become host city, irrespective of whether the bid is successful or unsuccessful, the bidding organisation may have to be closed within a defined time period. In the case of the Olympic Games, that period is eight months, during which time the Organising Committee for the Games

(OCOG) must be established. Because closure will always be difficult, its requirements need to be thought through well before the decision date. This will not be easy because so much of the energy of the bid will be focused on the final lobbying and presentation to win the bid.

Another difficulty is the climate surrounding the closure after the decision. The mood surrounding the bid will be profoundly different – everyone loves a winner! The bid owners will be concerned to secure as much continuity as possible from bidding to hosting so as to minimise time wastage and to secure as much knowledge as possible for the hosting phase. They will also wish to work with the people in the bid whom they have come to trust and like.

Provisions should be made for the timing of the release of contract staff. These should be discussed with staff and agreed to with them before being implemented. This will save a lot of friction (and money) and should ensure that closure of the company takes place in a spirit of friendliness and acceptance. This is particularly important if the bid fails, because people will be feeling absolutely shattered. Counselling and placement of staff may be required. Budgeting in the months just prior to the decision should make provision for severance arrangements to provide staff with an incentive to remain until the decision is made. Some staff will have been seconded from their organisations. Their time away from these organisations will impact on their long-term careers and they should be assisted in their negotiations to return to their organisations (with, for example, prevention of pay decreases). Some staff (such as finance and accounting staff) will be required after the decision to close down the company. The reasons for extending their contracts while other staffs are asked to leave need to be explained so that staff leaving understand and accept. Equally, provision will have to be made for the possibility of success and with it the retention of key people who should go through to the organising committee. This will not be easy; in some instances, it may not be possible because people cannot afford not to secure their futures before the decision, while in others the politics surrounding the bid may be so arcane that no immediate succession planning is possible. The CTOBC lost a number of key staff during the last weeks of the bid to organisations which could offer them a secure future. Had the bid been successful, it would have been difficult to secure these key people.

Bid material will need to be archived for forwarding to the next host authority. What this entails will need to be determined and initiated before the final decision. It is the kind of activity that nobody except, perhaps, a librarian wants to do. If left too late – that is, after the decision – it may never happen. The material will need to be separated from what may be called 'intellectual property'. This technical work and its documentation have value for the bid. To capitalise on it will need forethought and preparation. The work will have to be properly packaged and a method of disposal decided on. The documentation pertaining to the developmental planning approach forms an important legacy for local planning authorities. The archiving of material should ensure the accessibility and usefulness of this information.

It bears repeating that in the lead up to the final decision, the politics surrounding the bid are likely to be at their most complex. Faced with the imminent prospect of success and all of the glory and wealth (actual or putative) that accompanies becoming the hosting city, politicians and other power brokers become highly attentive to the bid and its management. Indeed, the bid may well find itself facing attempted takeovers of its role and function. Politics will impact on the bid's planning for closure.

13.6.1 The need for a media strategy that provides for success or for failure

In the period before the final decision, the focus of CTOBC's media efforts was largely on influencing the IOC to vote in our favour. The bid was the subject of intense media scrutiny, both local and international, and that scrutiny was a marvellous marketing opportunity. The problem with all the attention and publicity was that it raised false expectations in public and political circles that the bid was destined to win. Failure could not be conceived of.

For whatever reasons, as decision day approached for 2004 on 5 September 1997, the Cape Town and South African media, politicians and the public had convinced themselves that Cape Town would and should win. Celebrations were arranged in Cape Town on the city's largest square – 500 000 people gathered in full anticipation of engendering on themselves the mother and father of hangovers. Their utter disbelief that Cape Town had failed was visible all over the world as celebration turned into wake. Insufficient work had gone into a positive plan B, and blame and finger pointing began.

The problem with bidding for a mega-event is that there is only one winner. A media strategy must be designed that prepares people for the eventuality of failure. One might term this an 'exit strategy'. Central to this exit strategy will be ensuring that the legacies of the bidding phase have been properly drawn out of all the technical work that has been done, across the bid. People need to be reminded that the bid was entered into in the full knowledge that it could fail and that it was planned from the outset to be as much of a win–win effort as possible.

Case study 13.2: Reasons for a failed Cape Town Bid

(Source: de Lange, 2001: 160–224; Lloyd, 2000: 343–345 and Swart & Bob (in press))

The experience of Cape Town's Bid for the Olympic Games 2004 offers a number of lessons for future bidding cities. They provide some suggested preconditions for the successful bidding and hosting of a mega-event. Cape Town's bid failed for a number of reasons as outlined below:

- Strategic faults displayed by NOCSA – the ousting of the original bidding committee led to the loss of services of experienced international consultants and left the new team with little time to prepare;
- the late decision to bid without the established support of the Cape Town residents;
- the extremely tight time frames within which to prepare the candidature file;
- the other development challenges facing the city in providing for the sustainable future of its residents, the context of local government transition and the resultant limited capacity to extend municipal responsibility to supporting the Bid Company;
- very late commitment from national government to the bid, followed by excessive political interference in the lobbying process;
- poor communication techniques and limited resources to address local and international communities, leading to mistrust and scepticism ;
- lack of experience in bidding for mega-events;
- scepticism of our ability to deliver and manage such a large event – Cape Town's ability to deliver the required accommodation stock and transportation infrastructure as well as the capacity to handle the 28 sport world championships that would occur simultaneously;
- limited exposure to hosting international sporting events at the time, particularly in relation to Olympic sports, and in terms of a sport mega-event strategy – interesting to note that only recently have Cape Town and South Africa embarked on processes to develop and articulate clear event strategies and policies;
- insufficient lobbying with IOC members in general, and African IOC members in particular;
- the benefits of economic development and national unity which were expected to flow from the Olympics were overemphasised at the expense of the benefits that would accrue to the Olympic Movement itself;
- perceived high risk internationally in terms of crime, safety and security – an important aspect of the issue of crime in South Africa is related to perceptions and the way in which the international media portrays criminal activities and rates, and
- political pressure to award the Centennial Games to Athens in lieu of awarding the games to Atlanta in 1996.

13.7 KEY SUCCESS CRITERIA IN BIDDING FOR SPORT MEGA-EVENTS

Westerbeek *et al* (2002: 311) developed a survey instrument to identify key success factors of bidding for sport mega-events. They report that respondents ranged from those who had extensive experience in the bidding process, to event owners as well those who wanted to organise an event. The Olympic Games was one of the organisations represented. Respondents resided in 21 different countries, with the majority of respondents (42%) coming from Australia, followed by the US and UK (11% each) and Canada and Switzerland (8% each). It is important to note that countries from the developing world were under-represented. Westerbeek *et al* (2002: 314) assert that this could be as consequence of language barriers or the fact that mega-events are organised mainly in North America and Europe, and to a lesser extent Australia. They add that this research is exploratory and nor confirmatory. The eight key success factors that emerged from the findings of Westerbeek *et al* (2002: 313–319) are illustrated in the table below.

TABLE 13.1 *Key success factors in bidding for sport mega-events (Source: Westerbeek et al, 2003: 313–319)*

Success Factors	
Description	
1. Accountability	• the capacity the bid team and the city have to deliver high quality services to the event promoter and the community stakeholders • must have an established presence in the bidding marketplace • must have a reputation as a city for hosting successful sport events • must be able to showcase a variety of excellent facilities through the hosting of previous mega-events
2. Political support	• increased government involvement in the process of bidding • government involvement enhances the value of the event to the event owner
3. Relationship marketing	• the power of the bid committee to influence key decision • makers • effective lobbying is critical • built up with experience at bidding and hosting
4. Ability	• organisation and event management skills, including sport-specific technical skills and all the basic requirements to host an event • a solid track record in hosting similar events is critical

5. Infrastructure	• the city must have the necessary infrastructure to host a successful event • includes the ability to deliver services, accommodation, transportation as well as community support
6. Bid team composition	• a mix of talent on the team is essential to the way the team is perceived by the key decision-makers as well as to the success of the operation
7. Communication and exposure	• the strength of a city's brand image is critical to attracting tourists • communication and IT systems in place to ensure global coverage of the games
8. Existing facilities	• existence of critical event facilities at the time of the bid • relates to quality facilities provided by the hosting of previous mega-events

Westerbeek *et al* (2002: 319) reported that these factors could be further grouped in terms of importance. They assert that the ability to organise an event was the most important factor, followed by a group of factors, namely political support, infrastructure and existing facilities. A second group of factors are at the next level of importance: communication and exposure, accountability and bid team composition. The final factor, relationship marketing, was considered to be least important and perhaps influenced by the controversial status of relationship marketing tools. It is evident that most bidding cities are technically competent in terms of the operational aspects of hosting the games. Nevertheless, as pointed out by Westerbeek *et al* (2002: 320), the second group of factors or supporting factors, may well provide the distinctive edge that cities require to be successful. This kind of reasoning seems to fit the case of the failed Cape Town bid – technically competent but did not have the established relationships with power brokers (Swart & Bob, in press). It is contended that these criteria provide useful guidelines for cities intending to bid for mega-event.

13.8 FROM BID CITY TO CANDIDATE CITY

The organisation of the Olympic Games is assigned by the IOC to the NOC of the country of the host city as well as to the host city itself (IOC, 2003b: Internet). An Organising Committee for the Olympic Games (OCOG) is then formed, and communicates directly with the IOC, from which it receives instructions. The OCOG executive body includes: the IOC member or members in the country; the President and Secretary General of the NOC; and at least one member representing, and designated by, the host city (IOC, 2003b: Internet). It also generally includes representatives of the public authorities and other leading figures.

OCOG is governed by various policies and documents such as the Olympic Charter, the contract entered into between the IOC, the National Olympic Committee and the host city (Host City Contract) and the instructions of the IOC Executive Board. In recent years, these organising committees have turned into huge administrative entities employing hundreds of people (see Athens 2004 organogram in the annexure to this chapter). The work of the OCOG usually starts with a period of planning followed by a period of organisation which culminates in the implementation or operational phase (IOC, 2003b: Internet). Some of the aspects of the OCOG's work identified by the IOC (2003b: Internet) are highlighted below:

- to give equal handling to every sport on the programme and ensure that competitions are held according to the rules of the respective IFs;
- to ensure that no political demonstration is held in the Olympic City or its surroundings;
- to choose and, if required, create the necessary installations: competition sites, stadiums and training venues and organise the required equipment;
- to accommodate the athletes, their associates, and the officials;
- to arrange medical services;
- to solve transportation problems;
- to meet the requirements of the mass media to allow for the best possible information on the games to the public;
- to organise cultural events that are an important element of the celebration of the Olympic Games, and
- to write the Final Report on the games and distribute it within two years after the completion of the games.

Case study 13.3: Candidate Bid to Host City – Athens 2004
(Source: Athens 2004a, 2004, internet)

On the 5 September 1997 Athens was selected as the host city of the 2004 Olympic Games in Lausanne, Switzerland, and the Host City Contract for the Games of the XXVIII Olympiad was signed. These events marked the beginning of a unique journey in the history of Olympism and culminated in Greece from 13 to 29 August 2004. The games have returned home to the country which staged the first modern Olympic Games in 1896.

The ATHENS 2004 Organising Committee for the Olympic Games was the body responsible for organising and hosting both the 2004 Olympic and Paralympic Games. To realise its mission and to ensure flawless performance and functioning of all operational areas during the games, ATHENS 2004 combined forces with the Greek Government as well as with local authorities all over the country. ATHENS 2004 co-operated closely with the IOC on all organisational matters and was in constant contact with International and National Sports Federations, as well as, with non-governmental organisations and other entities involved in the preparation of the games.

ATHENS 2004 was governed by a 17-member Board of Directors, which under its full session comprised of the President, the Vice President, the Managing Director, 3 Executive Directors and 11 members. It mission was to:

- organise a technically excellent Olympic Games;
- provide a unique Olympic experience to the athletes, spectators, viewers and volunteers;
- display the Olympic ideals in a modern-day setting through their traditional Greek symbols;
- promote and implement the Olympic Truce through the Torch Relay;
- control the commercial aspect of the Olympic Games;
- promote the cultural and natural heritage of Greece;
- protect and enhance the natural environment and promote environmental awareness; and
- promote the benefits of the games throughout the country.

The process of proceeding from a bid city to a host city for sport mega-events is very similar for non-sport mega-events. In April 2001, the Johannesburg World Summit Company (JOWSCO), a Section 21 company, was established by the South African Government as a special-purpose vehicle with the sole mandate to coordinate and manage the operations and logistics for WSSD 2002 (JOWSCO, 2002b: Internet). It soon became evident that JOWSCO was faced with a major logistical challenge within the limited time available as per the case study 13.4 below. Similar challenges will be faced by the World Cup 2010 Organising Committee, and hence appropriate planning and implementation will be required.

Case study 13.4: Bid City to Host City – WSSD
(Source: JOWSCO, 2002b, internet)

A Host Country Agreement was signed with the United Nations in New York. The United Nations projected attendance of WSSD 2002 by more than 100 heads of state. It was estimated that up to 65 000 delegates, media and suppliers would have to be accredited for WSSD 2002 and its parallel events. Few venues were fully geared to host WSSD 2002. In addition, accommodation would have to be sourced throughout the province, adding to the complexity of the transport system. To meet this challenge, Jowsco was structured into logical components, with a Chief Executive Officer and executive managers heading up each of the main business units: Finance and Administration, Public Affairs, Operations and Logistics, Marketing, Communications and Technology. These units were further broken down into specialised portfolios.

Several fora were also established to ensure participation of major stakeholders, including:

- A Management Committee consisting of the Jowsco executives and representatives from the City of Johannesburg and the Gauteng Department of Agriculture, Conservation, Environment and Land Affairs provided strategic direction and assisted with high-level decision-making.

- A National Logistics Committee consisting of Jowsco managers and representatives from relevant departments of all government levels reviewed all logistical preparations and provided necessary leadership and guidance.
- A Memorandum of Understanding detailing the roles and responsibilities of national, provincial and local government was drafted.

An additional challenge for Jowsco was the decision by the United Nations to move the summit dates forward a week (from 2–11 September 2002 to 26 August – 4 September 2002) to avoid a clash with the first anniversary of the September 11 disaster in New York.

13.8.1 Operational Management of the Games

As highlighted above, the management of the Olympic Games is highly complex. The key operations will be outlined in this section. A broad range of management skills is required in the following areas, and are illustrated in the table below. It is evident that in addition to the general management skills such as people and communication skills, mega-event management in particular requires the ability to manage diversity; managing technology, awareness of organisational politics and managing change. It will be necessary for mega-event managers to learn, understand and respect cultural differences when dealing with the international sport and non-sport domains. While it is beyond the scope of this chapter to give attention to all these areas, it is hoped that this list provides an illustration of the complexity of managing a mega-event. The next section will describe some pertinent management areas in greater depth by providing case studies from Athens 2004. While a sport mega-event is depicted, non-sport mega-events require very similar management focus areas.

TABLE 13.1: *Key management focus areas for sport mega-events (Source: Athens 2004, 2004b: Internet)*

Management focus area	Description
Venue operations	• Competition venues • Non-competition venues • Olympic Village • Accreditation • Food Services • Health Services • Security
Sports	• Doping Control • Games Planning • Competition • Sports Services • Paralympic Games
Marketing	• Opening and Closing Ceremonies • Sponsorship

	• Licensing • Ticketing • Torch Relay • Spectator Services
Technology	• Information Technology • Communications
Volunteers	• Recruitment • Selection • Orientation
International Relations	• NOC Relations • IOC Relations • Translation Services
Broadcasting	• Main Press Centre • Venue Media Centres • International Broadcast Centre
Environment	• Environmental Programmes • Environmental Awareness
Transportation	• Traffic and Transport Authorities Coordination • Bus Network Services
Financial Services	• Financial Planning and Budget • Procurement • Value-in-kind control • Logistics
Administration Services	• Personnel • Education and Training • Public Administration and Local Authorities

13.8.2 Environmental management

The environment has become one of the most significant aspects of any bid to host the Olympic Games, as the IOC needs to ensure that the games are held in a manner which demonstrates a responsible concern for environmental issues (Athens 2004, 2004c: Internet). The aim is not only to ensure that holding the Games has no negative impact on the environment, but also to try to leave behind a positive 'green' legacy. In order to do this, Athens 2004 initiated the following environmental programmes:

- The Olympic Green Spaces Programme
- Environmental Awareness and Performance Initiatives
- Waste Management and Recycling Initiatives
- Environmental Friendly Transportation
- Sponsors and Licensees Environmental Performance
- Environmental Coordination and Networking
- Biodiversity Initiatives (Athens 2004, 2004c: Internet).

In addition, Athens 2004 promoted environmentally friendly construction materials, new energy technologies and the comprehensive protection of natural resources.

Case study 13.5: Athens 2004 Sponsors and Licensees Environmental Performance
(Source: Athens 2004, 2004d, internet)

The mission of Athens 2004 was the enhancement of the environmental performance of sponsors and licensees before, during, and after the games. This involved improving the corporate image of sponsors and licensees, by considerably changing their approach towards environmental issues, and educating the general public.

In order to achieve this, Athens 2004 implemented the following:

- assisted in developing products or installations in compliance with recognised environmental certification systems;
- financially supported events and environmental activities as signature events;
- submitted tenders for sponsoring and licensing to address environmental considerations in relation to product manufacture, use, and disposal;
- cooperated with its sponsors to develop responsible waste management policies, and
- positively influenced its corporate partners' public image concerning the environment.

To further capitalise on the industry's contribution to the environmentally friendly performance of the games, the committee established the Sponsors Network for the Environment and worked to ensure that, wherever possible, the design and packaging of products included educational messages about the environment.

13.8.3 Security

With increasing threats of terrorist attacks at large-scale global events, security is a key issue for host cities of any type of mega-event. Security was a top priority for Athens 2004. In order to host a safe and secure games, the Athens OCOG worked in close partnership with the Hellenic Police, the Greek Government and international security experts (Athens 2004, 2004e: Internet). The Olympic Games Security Division (OGSD) – a special police unit created for the 2004 Games – was responsible for Olympic security. OGSD reported directly to the Chief of the Hellenic Police and was staffed by police, coast guard, fire brigade and defence forces personnel. OGSD was responsible for the planning of all security and public order measures required during the preparation and the hosting of the Games, the implementation of all security operational plans and the coordination of all organisations and agencies involved in Olympic security (Athens 2004, 2004e: Internet). It is further noted that in order to coordinate and integrate the plans of OGSD with those of the functional areas of Athens 2004, the Athens 2004 Security

Division was set up. This division also acted as a liaison between the Olympic Movement agencies and OGSD, outlining all requirements that the Olympic agencies set and informing them on the progress of OGSD operations. An Olympic Advisory Group (OAG), a seven-nation task force with extensive experience in the security planning of sport mega-events, also worked closely with Athens 2004 and OGSD (Athens 2004, 2004e: Internet). In addition, a specially trained security force of over 41 000 personnel worked tirelessly to ensure the security of the games.

13.8.4 Catering

The task of planning and providing high quality food services was the concern of the Food Services Department (Athens 2004, 2004: Internet). Furthermore, their services were enhanced by experienced food service companies that were selected via international competitive bids. About 17 000 staff were employed to fulfil the programme's goals. Consideration was also given to ethnic preferences and dietary requirements such as halaal (food preparation according to Islamic customs), kosher (food preparation according to Jewish customs) and iodine intolerance (Athens 2004, 2004: Internet). In addition, the catering provided an opportunity to taste Greek cuisine and products. To manage the issue of food safety, the Food Services Department worked closely with the Hellenic Food Authority and the OGSD (Athens 2004, 2004f: Internet).

Case study 13.6: Athens 2004 Olympic Village Catering
Requirements (Source: Athens 2004, 2004f, internet)

Athens 2004 provided about 12 million meals to athletes, team officials, Olympic and Paralympic Family, workforce, technical officials, accredited media, sponsors and spectators. At the Olympic Village, meals were prepared for about 22 000 persons on a 24-hour basis; 50 000 meals were served on a daily basis from 1 500 international recipes, utilising 100 tons of food daily and created 55 tons of waste. Within the Olympic Village, the following supplies were required to prepare 6 000 meals per hour:

- 15 000 litres of milk;
- 2 500 dozen eggs;
- 300 tons of fruits and vegetables;
- 120 tons of meats;
- 85 tons of seafood;
- 25 000 loafs of bread;
- 750 litres of tomato sauce;
- 2 million litres of bottled water, and
- 3 million refreshments.

By planning and preparing a great variety of meals, Greek companies were trained to meet the increased demand and particular requirements of the 2004 Games. With this new experience and knowledge, the Greek catering industry was transformed.

13.8.5 Logistics

The Logistics Department aimed at providing the Olympic and Paralympic Family, and the functional areas of Athens 2004, with the best possible logistics services in order to ensure the best possible support of the games within the existing budget (Athens 2004, 2004g: Internet). Prior to the games, the Logistics Department was responsible for the receipt, the storage, the distribution, the installation (in some cases), the tracking of the assets, and the handling of the equipment and material required for the implementation of all the programmes of Athens 2004.

During the games, this department was responsible for the scheduling of deliveries to the venues through the management of the Master Delivery Schedule, for providing assistance to all the functional areas through the work orders, for the asset tracking management of the equipment of the venues, in addition to the management of the procurement in the venue (Athens 2004, 2004g: Internet). Post-games, the Logistics Department was responsible for getting back all Athens 2004 property from the venues, while supervising and coordinating the procedures that ensured the protection of the materials and the minimisation of the losses. Warehousing and Distribution, Olympic Family Freight Forwarding and Venue Logistics were some of the responsibilities that fell within the sphere of the logistics department.

Case study 13.7: Athens 2004 Entrance and Circulation of Delivery Vehicles in Competition and Non-Competition Venues (Source: Athens 2004, 2004h, 9)

Each delivery to the Olympic venues was scheduled through the Mastery Delivery Schedule (MSD). The delivery programme was scheduled per venue, per vehicle and per kind of delivery. The period of application extended from the start of the bump-in period until the end of the bump-out period. The Central Team of the MSD and the Venue Logistics Manager (VLM) of each venue were responsible for the delivery schedule. The procedure covered all vehicles arriving at the venue for delivery/ collection of material and equipment, food supply, cleaning of venue, etc. More specifically, it concerned the following:
- delivery vehicles coming from the Olympics Logistics Centre;
- suppliers'/ vendors' vehicles;
- waste and cleaning vehicles, and
- venues' catering vehicles.

The adherence to the time schedule occured at the venues' checkpoints where the time were verified in accordance with the MDS. The MDS were communicated to the Security and Transportation Departments the day prior to the Logistics Department. The MDS procedures were distinguished according to pre-games procedures and procedures during the games. A separate procedure existed for dealing with emergency and/ or non-scheduled deliveries.

13.8.6 Broadcasting

One of the largest operational programmes relates to the broadcasting coverage of the Olympic Games. The rights to broadcast the games were granted to radio and TV stations globally by the IOC through a tripartite agreement between the IOC, Athens 2004 and the Rights Holding Broadcasters. The revenues of the agreements were determined by the IOC, 49% of which was received by Athens 2004. Olympic Broadcasting is governed by the Olympic Charter, the Host City Contract and the Radio and TV Agreements (Athens 2004, 2004i: Internet). Athens Olympic Broadcasting (AOB) was established as the Host Broadcaster of the Games. Its central role was to produce the International Television and Radio official signal of the games and to deliver it to the venues and the International Broadcast Centre (IBC). AOB also provided the required broadcasting services and equipment to the Rights Holding Broadcasters. The IBC was the 'heart' of broadcasting operations.

For Athens 2004, the following provisions were made for the coverage of the games:
- about 3 800 hours of live signal broadcasting;
- 3 700 AOB staff during the games;
- more than 1 500 commentator positions;
- 1000 cameras, and
- 100 AOB and Rights Holding Broadcasters Mobile Units (Athens 2004, 2004i: Internet).

13.8.7 Volunteers Programme

The Volunteers Programme is an often overlooked yet criticall aspect of any mega-event. In fact, without volunteers, these events would probably not be able to take place on the scale that they do. The process of volunteering usually takes place during the bidding phase. For the 2010 Winter Games in Vancouver, the Vancouver 2010 Bid Corporation collected more than 50 000 names of those who were interested in volunteering for the Olympic and Paralympic Winter Games in 2010 (Vancouver 2010, 2004: Internet). This database has been turned over to the Organising Committee of the Olympic Games. The Games Organising Committee will develop a formal volunteer recruitment and training programme which will probably be initiated in 2008. The Winter Games will need about 25 000 volunteers, whereas the Summer Games require substantially more volunteers as indicated in case study 13.9 below. The 2006 Soccer World Cup in Germany will require 12 000 volunteers (FIFA World Cup 2006, 2003: Internet). Volunteer opportunities cover a broad spectrum, from stewarding through to accompanying a national squad throughout the tournament, with length of service varying between five days and six months.

Torino 2006, the hosts of the XX Winter Olympics, have utilised a volunteer application form that addresses the following areas:

- personal data
- experience and training (previous experience as a volunteer)
- skills (languages, sport event organisation, medical qualifications, etc.)
- preferences (area of activity, days available, etc.) (Torino 2006, 2002: Internet).

In view of the 2010 World Cup, it would be critical for South Africa to encourage volunteerism at the many events and festivals that take place nation-wide. In addition, South Africa should capitalise on using those volunteers who worked at WSSD and the Cricket World Cup (refer to chapter 16 for further information on the volunteer database that was set up as a result of the Cricket World Cup).

Case study 13.8: Athens 2004 Volunteer Programme
(Source: Beijing 2008, 2004, internet)

The number of Official Volunteer applications for the Athens Olympics reached 150 360 at the end of February, six months prior to the Olympic Games. To meet the requirements of the 2004 Olympic and Paralympic Games, about 45 000 and 15 000 volunteers were required respectively. Of the volunteer applications received, 65,4% of candidate volunteers live in Greece, while 34,6% live abroad. Of these volunteers who live abroad, 25,15% are foreigners and 9,45% are Greeks abroad. By the end of February 2004, 67 950 attended an interview in Greece, while more than 45 000 candidate volunteers living abroad were interviewed by means of a special questionnaire. The number of candidate volunteers to whom an Offer of Voluntary Employment exceed 15 000 According to the applications submitted, 68% of the candidates indicated their availability of working for more than 15 days. Fifty-six percent of candidate volunteers were women and 44% are men. Volunteers' selection and placement in specific positions phase was launched in 2003. Volunteers who accepted the offers made to them were invited to attend training programmes. These programmes were specially designed to address the requirements of the games, but also provided participants with broader knowledge and practical experience, which they will be able to exploit in the post-Olympic period.

13.8.8 Legacy

One of the most significant reasons for cities and governments to bid and host mega-events are the legacies they are purported to leave behind. For Greece, the legacy of the 2004 Games included the economic benefits of investing in upgrades to the transportation infrastructure, telecommunications system, and the environment (Athens 2004, 2004: Internet). These benefits comprise the following:

- 65 000 new permanent jobs;
- 120 kilometres of new road;

- 290 000 new trees and 11 million new shrubs;
- a new International Airport;
- an upgraded metro system;
- a new, ultra-modern Traffic Management Centre;
- an increase in tourism;
- a boost in public sector revenues (€1,22 billion), and
- 35% improvement of the quality of the environment.

Furthermore, the skills, expertise and training of the Greek workforce across every sector have been improved. The new skills and expertise gained from managing a large-scale, complex project such as the Olympics are valuable assets that will last beyond the completion of the games. Renewed civic pride and the upsurge in volunteerism have also contributed to a positive legacy for Greece (Athens 2004, 2004j: Internet).

Even a failed bid can leave behind important legacies, as evidenced by the Cape Town 2004 case. Cape Town went beyond the use of major event facilities for local sports development, as the underlying philosophy of the bid was 'developmental' as outlined in the planning section (paragraph 13.3) of this chapter. In the history of the games, it was the first bid that sought to promote the ideal of human development as the fourth pillar of Olympism; the other pillars being sport, culture and the environment. The aim of Cape Town's bid was to use the Olympic Games as a platform to improve the lives of all its citizens, especially those who were disadvantaged by apartheid, and to redesign the structure of the apartheid city (Olympics Assessment Team, 1997: Internet). Hiller (2000: 445–450) reported that there were nine main ways in which the bid was 'developmental'. While it is beyond the scope of this chapter to describe each of these elements in detail, suffice it to note that it included an Olympic plan that would serve as a transformational catalyst accelerating change, the construction of facilities in disadvantaged areas and the use of facilities as 'kick-start' initiatives for local businesses in disadvantaged areas. In order to show government's commitment to development, R86 million was dedicated to the construction of the eight priority projects, of which seven facilities were in disadvantaged areas (Cape Town Olympic Bid, 1997: 19).

13.8.9 Measuring the impacts of mega-events

Despite the purported benefits of mega-events, very little research has been conducted into the actual impacts of the events. However, it is necessary to evaluate whether the huge costs entailed in bidding and hosting mega-events pay off in the long term. The Department of Canadian Heritage's Sport Hosting Program has undertaken a comprehensive evaluation of events supported (PCH, 2004: Internet). They report that major sports events meet a number of the economic, cultural, and social objectives because many bids include strong community economic impact and legacies components. A number of events have been evaluated by the Canadian Heritage Program to ascertain whether expected results have been achieved, using the evaluations and final reports submitted after the events. Table 13.3 below illustrates this approach by utilising reports of the 8th International Amateur Athletic Federation (IAAF) World Championships in Edmonton, Alberta in 2001. It compares the projected impacts (original intended impacts) to the actual (reported) impacts, and provides some important lessons in terms of the hosting of mega-events.

TABLE 13.3: *Original and intended impacts of the 8th IAAF World Championships in Athletics – Edmonton 2001 (Source: PCH, 2004: Internet)*

Benefits	Original intended impacts	Reported impacts
Opportunities for coaches, athletes and officials	Opportunities to participate in a national multi-sport games	• 206 federations, 1 766 athletes and 1 413 officials participated • Increased number of skilled and experienced athletics officials • Increased number of Canadians competing
International profile	Enhance international profile – specific objectives not stated	• Canada enhanced its reputation to host international sporting events • City called 'Deadmonton' by a British journalist due to low spectator numbers; positive and negative media coverage of the city and event
Sport development	• Enhance sport performance • Increased sport development opportunities for athletes, coaches and officials	• Canadian athletes performed better at this event than in Sydney 2000 • School programmes emerged as a result of hosting the event • No measurable increase in the awareness/appreciation for sport
Access and equity	• Gender participation to be more balanced • Participation to be more inclusive – physical disabilities, non-traditional groups	• Slightly more men than women on Canadian team; only one female coach • Gave wheelchair, visually impaired and amputee athletes opportunity to compete • More could have been done for those of a visible minority or aboriginal descent

Social and cultural outcomes	• Implement a youth strategy • Positive effects on the community • Increase public awareness	• Have a youth strategy to ensure there is a youth voice on relevant issues • Closed local public wading pool; had negative impact on public during hot weather • 4 billion viewers saw IAAF championships; 1 643 broadcast media from 86 countries • One-quarter of Canadians watched at least some of the championships
Economic impact on community	Positive economic impact on community and province	• 400 000 people attended the Championships • Visitors spent over CAD$23 million on food, accommodation and travel in Edmonton • Total economic impact of the expenditures estimated at CAD$183,4 million in Canada • Ticket sales generated CAD$12,6 million with a CAD$3 million surplus • Games created 3 854 person years of employment • Direct increase in business activity, direct capital expenditures, and tourism
Economic impacts – legacies	• Establish legacies • Increase volunteer capacity	• Legacy fund of CAD$8 million created for training, coaching, education and research • 10 000 volunteers participated
Best practices and expertise		• Less funding restrictions put on the local organising committee by the international association • Federal Hosting Policy monitored and enforced continually • Federal involvement from the beginning • Legacy planning committee should be developed from the beginning • Conduct social impact assessment to reduce/offset negative local impacts • Provide template and a systematic database to compile historic data on events • Multi-party negotiations completed early and involve federal and provincial funds

13.8.10 Lessons learnt and best practice

In this section, some of the key lessons learnt during implementation of WSSD 2002 will be reviewed in order to ensure better planning for similar events in the future. In addition, best practice from Sydney 2000 will be presented as it is considered to be most successful Olympics of all time.

Case study 13.8: Lessons Learnt – WSSD 2002
(Source: South Africa, Republic of, 2004, internet).

Some of the crucial lessons learnt by South Africa from hosting WSSD 2002 include the following:

- Ensure that channels of communication are open so that the implementation phase of the event/s is dealt with in such a manner as to address any issue if and when they arise.
- If all the reservations can be controlled by one organisation, it would ensure that there is detailed information available about the location of the delegates; this would also ensure that transport problems could be addressed.
- Ensure that a record is kept of all contractual agreements that were established relating to the events, and also to ensure that these agreements are abided by.
- Ensure that all people involved in the event/s are informed with regard to the transport plan.
- Tour packages should be evenly spread across the host country in order to ensure that the business tourists receive maximum exposure to what the country has to offer.
- It is necessary that the government of the host country provide sufficient support to the additional events in order to provide credibility.
- It is important that the expectations that are created amongst business and the pubic be met because this will have a direct influence on people's attitudes.
- Procedures that have to be followed in order to meet the organisational requirements should be explained in a detailed manner in order to ensure that no-one is exclude from the process, it is however important to inform people about the high standards that are set for those that do want to become involved in the event.
- If alternative plans with regard to dealing with the weather are not put in place, many of the people involved in the event/s will not experience benefit from their involvement.
- Accreditation is undertaken to provide certain measure against uncontrolled protest and violence that is experienced during events similar to the WSSD, and therefore it is important that one organisation is responsible for managing the process in its entirety.
- It is important to ensure that the correct infrastructure is put in place in order to deal with the increased pressure that an event similar to the WSSD is going to place on the existing infrastructure network.

- Due to the high political profile of an event such as the WSSD and the stature of the people attending it is very important to ensure safety as to promote the image of the host country.
- The impression created by an event such as WSSD with the national general public will have a greater impact in the future if they are considered in the planning for such an event.

Michael Payne, Director of Marketing for the IOC, commented that 'Australia is the first Olympic host nation to take full advantage of the Games to vigorously pursue tourism for the benefit of the whole country. It's something we've never seen take place on this level before, and it's a model that we would like to see carried forward to future Olympic Games in Athens and beyond.' (ATC, 2001: Internet). The Sydney 2000 Olympic Games Strategy will be reviewed to ascertain how they were able to maximise the potential of hosting mega-events.

Case study: 13.9 Best Practice – Sydney 2000 Olympic Games
(Source: ATC, 2001, internet).

Evolution of the Programme

In September 1993, Sydney was awarded the right to host the 2000 Summer Olympic Games. Back in the early 1990s Australia was rarely on the world stage. With this in mind, Australia's tourism authorities led by the Australian Tourism Commission (ATC) formed a powerful partnership to ensure the whole of Australia benefited from the games. Their strategy was unique in that no other host country had taken the opportunity to use the games to promote the whole country's tourism image. No other host country has worked so closely with the Olympic partners to develop mutual benefits from linking the tourism brand with their products and services. And no other country has developed such an extensive media relations programme to ensure that every possible publicity opportunity was maximised.

Strategy

The tourism strategy was aimed at enhancing Australia's international image and to increase long-term economic and social benefits for Australia through increased export earnings, employment, visitor arrivals and visitor dispersal.

The strategy was implemented in several key steps:
- Formulating the Olympics strategy and establishing a specialist unit. The formulation of the strategy examined lessons learned by previous host cities of the Olympics and other mega-events.
- Educating the ATC internally on the strategy and gaining ownership on a world-wide basis.
- Obtaining the support of the local tourism industry for a co-ordinated approach.
- Obtaining the support of the Sydney OCOG.

- Obtaining government policy support and funding to implement the programme.
- Establishing relationships with the Olympic Family – the IOC and local sponsors, the media, broadcast rights holders, NOCs and their tour operators and the sport federations.

Olympic Games Liaison Business Unit (OGLBU)
The OGLBU was established in 1995, with the principal function of identifying opportunities, co-ordinating activities and managing relationships resulting from Australia hosting the Olympic Games, Paralympic Games and the Olympic Arts Festival. The unit, in conjunction with other stakeholders, worked toward identifying Olympic-related tourism opportunities that offered extraordinary leverage to the ATC's marketing efforts, both within Australia and overseas.

Australia 2000 Fun and Games Campaign
The Australia 2000 fun and games campaign commenced in September 1999. ATC announced that it would spend US$34 million over 12 months to ensure Australia achieved growth of around 10% in visitor numbers in 2000. The campaign comprised consumer and trade advertising designed to motivate consumers to travel to Australia in 2000. Work was undertaken with industry partners to promote special packages and deals to Australia throughout the period. The ATC established a dedicated web site, www.2000.australia.com, that was an information base of everything that was happening in Australia in 2000. The ATC also organised a National Forum to finalise tactics for the tourism industry's busiest year ever.

Brand Australia
Central to the thinking of the ATC's Olympic Tourism Strategy was to use the games to add depth and dimension to Brand Australia by promoting more than just the typical tourism images and themes in the lead up to and during the games. This was done by bringing together Brand Australia, the Olympic Brand and the brands of the Olympic partners (sponsors, broadcasters and the Olympic Family). ATC aimed to make the Olympics a two-week documentary on all of Australia for a global audience of 3,7 billion people over 36 billion viewer hours. Underlying the strategy was the need to continue the relationships well after the games had concluded.

ATC's Olympic Media Strategy
ATC undertook the biggest media relations programme by any country for the Olympic Games or any other single event in the world to boost a nation's tourism profile. The ATC's Olympic Media Strategy included:
- Hosting more that 2000 international journalists to Australia in 1999 and 2000 through the Visiting Journalists Programme
- Servicing more that 50 000 international media inquiries;

- Providing a specialist web site for the international media;
- Bringing international broadcasters to Australia before the games;
- Working with international television and radio broadcasters to provide story leads, production assistance and quality sound and vision resources of all parts of Australia;
- Assisting international newspapers and magazines with story leads and photography of all regions of Australia;
- Assisting communities around Australia to maximise media relations opportunities of the Olympic torch relay;
- Bringing together Australia's top tourism media and public relations professionals to assist with the world's media during the games period, and
- Working with the Department of Foreign Affairs and Trade, Tourism New South Wales, the Sydney Harbour Foreshore Authority and New South Wales Department of State and Regional Development on the provision of a non-accredited media centre in Sydney City in 2000.

During the Olympics, ATC's activities were primarily confined to hosting international tourism VIPs under the Business Development Programme, assisting the media at the Main Press Centre and Sydney Media Centre and informing the Australian public via the media on the tourism benefits of the games and how Australia was being reported internationally.

ATC's Post-Games Strategy
The post-games strategy included four key elements that were specifically aimed at capitalising on Australia's post-games popularity. The four key elements included:
- Over 90 joint tactical advertising campaigns promoting holiday deals launched immediately following the games. The joint campaigns involved more than 200 industry partners, and were worth more than US$25 million.
- An aggressive US$3 million direct marketing campaign including the re-development of the ATC's web site, australia.com. Research was undertaken on how the Olympic exposure had shifted Australia's image internationally.
- The building of the lucrative MICE sector, through Team Australia, a coalition of MICE bodies led by ATC. New Century. New World. Australia 2001 Campaign
- A major MICE (meeting, conference, exhibition and incentives) campaign was developed to maintain the momentum of the Olympic Games in 2000. The New Century, New World, Australia 2001 Campaign aimed to attract additional business travel to Australia.

Key Results
The Olympic Games remains the most significant beneficial event in the history of Australian inbound tourism. Over the course of four years, well over 1 000 individual projects were implemented of which the majority occurred in 2000.

The most significant results were:

- An additional 1,6 million visitors spending US$3,5 billion
- Accelerated development of Brand Australia by 10 years
- Media relations and publicity programmes generating US$2,1 billion
- Olympic sponsors spending US$170 million promoting Australia
- Australia 2000 – fun and games campaign generating 11% increase in visitor arrivals in 2000
- Increased likelihood of visitation because Australia has hosted the games
- A 700% increase in traffic to australia.com
- Australia improving its standings in the meetings market
- Post-games tactical campaigns generating significant business

The 2000 Olympic Games in Sydney have left a lasting legacy for ATC, the Australian tourism industry and Australia as a whole:

- The amount of exposure and interest that the games have generated is unrivalled.
- The world's view of Australia has changed forever with greater consumer knowledge of everything that Australia has to offer.
- Visitor numbers have increased significantly injecting billions into Australia's economy – creating jobs and opportunities for Australians.
- For the ATC, the games have created many new opportunities and opened many doors in business, government and the media, both in Australia and overseas.
- Australia achieved celebrity status, national pride skyrocketed and the country has entered the new millennium with a renewed confidence.

John Morse, ATC Managing Director, noted "We were delighted when the IOC declared the ATC's strategy as a role model for future host countries. But what is even more important is that we, as the ATC, take what we have learned through working with the Olympics and use it in the future. A smarter ATC is a great legacy of the Olympic Games."

Browse these Internet sites:
2006 FIFA World Cup Germany fifaworldcup.yahoo.com/06/en
Athens 2004 www.athens2004.com
Beijing 2008 en.beijing-2008.org/
Federation Internationale de Football Association www.fifa.com/en/index.html
International Olympic Committee (IOC) www.ioc.org
National Olympic Committee of South Africa (NOCSA) www.nocsa.co.za/
South African Football Association (SAFA) www.safagoal.net/
Vancouver 2012 www.vancouver2010.com
World Summit on Sustainable Development
www.http://www.environment.gov.za/sustdev/jowsco/jowsco_index.html

QUESTIONS FOR SELF-EVALUATION

1 What are the characteristics of a mega-event? Describe the various types.
2 Why is appropriate planning crucial in preparing to host a mega-event?
3 What are the important elements of managing a bidding process?
4 What are the key elements of a successful bid?
5 What are the key management areas that should be considered for hosting the 2010 Soccer World Cup in South Africa?
6 Why is it important to evaluate the actual impacts of a mega-event and what are the critical aspects to be measured?
7 Review some of the lessons learnt from the hosting of previous mega-events and develop a mega-event strategy for the 2010 Soccer World Cup. Have a group discussion.

Note: Appendix 13.1 can be found on the Juta Academic web site: www.jutaacademic.co.za
Appendix 13.1 *Athens 2004 Organisation Chart (Source: Athens 2004, 2004: Internet)*

CHAPTER 14

Meeting Management

Debbie Johnson

AIM OF THE CHAPTER

The aim of this chapter is to examine the aspects involved in professional meeting management.

LEARNING OBJECTIVES

After having studied this chapter, you should be able to:

- explain the concept of *meetings*;
- explain and understand the purpose of effective meeting management;
- differentiate between the various activities which form part of the meeting programme;
- explain and understand the techniques of professional meeting management;
- understand the legal requirements within the context of professional meeting management;
- explain the importance of effective staff relations;
- recognise the importance of technology as part of professional meeting management.

14.1 INTRODUCTION

South Africa today is regarded as one of the fastest growing tourist destinations in the world. South Africa as a destination offers affordable experiences linked to good weather year-round. The tourism market of South Africa can be divided into two distinct categories, that of *leisure tourism* and *business tourism*.

Business tourism contributes significantly to tourism in general as businesspersons travel to meetings representing their companies. This phenomenon has created a lucrative and growing market, namely meeting organising and management. The reason for the creation of a lucrative and growing market is due to the spending capacity of conference delegates. They are generally higher spenders than the average tourist (Mosia, 2004: Internet).

Meeting organising has been described as an art in itself, focusing on competencies such as identifying suitable venues, negotiating rebated accommodation rates, pricing and quoting delegate fees, lining up keynote speakers, finding sponsors, and many more. The complexities of arranging any event on behalf of other people can be very challenging. What is required is stamina, a positive frame of mind at all times, as well as a practical approach. Most importantly, you need to be a good administrator.

What do you need to survive as a professional conference organiser (PCO) in this very challenging world of today? The following will serve as a personal survival kit to face all the challenges this industry will bring to your door.

Today, much emphasis is placed on values – in service, time, our resources, in the way we conduct our business, even in the way we look and feel every day. To be the best PCO, you will need to make some sacrifices during your career; you require knowledge to stay ahead in the industry; you need to focus on hard work; and you need to have a very positive attitude. Four simple but very necessary areas to enforce in your career as a PCO. Which one of the four would be the most important and would really need attention all the time? Well, surprise. It all comes back to us as individuals; our ATTITUDE. Our attitude will win us a contract or can make us lose a contract. Our attitude can earn us a good reputation in the industry or make us disappear from the industry. Even when times are difficult, always remember to keep a good and positive attitude and, combined with sacrifice, knowledge and hard work you are bound for success (Hudson, 2004: Interview). Remember, as the PCO, you can make a choice about the attitude you will adopt and that will influence your career in the event industry.

Besides our four key areas to personal success the following are critical to the way you will conduct your activities when organising an event:

- Develop a system for tasks and activities.
- Use a system and work according to it.
- Without planning failure will occur.
- Be responsible for the financial implications of the event.
- Call in the assistance of professionals when needed.
- Expect the unexpected – be prepared for a challenge and always have a contingency plan.
- Always be cooperative and professional.

The purpose of this chapter is to provide some fundamental principles and techniques to enable you to organise meetings in a professional manner.

14.2 CONFERENCING IN SOUTH AFRICA

Research recently commissioned by SA Tourism provided evidence that more than 110 000 foreign MICE (meetings, incentives, conferences and exhibitions) participants visit South African annually.

This research further indicated that 41 000 of these delegates attend approximately 860 annual international conference events where at least 40% of the participation is foreign. Researchers conclude that the balance, which is 70 000, attend the many national and local events where less than 40% of the participation is foreign. According to SA Tourism, these international conference delegates spend on average 4,2 days at the conference event and a further 1,8 days at the conference destination. A further 39% of international conference delegates visit another part of South Africa during their stay, which constitutes another 3,3 days in the destination. Bongi Mosia of SA Tourism's Convention Bureau is quoted as saying: 'Although this indicates that our average conference delegates is staying only 9,3 days, in the country, compared to the 17 days for the average tourist, they are high spenders during that period. On average, during the conference they spend R1 450 per day and before/after the event, R916 per day. This compares very favourably to the R834 per day spend by South Africa's average international visitor (travelling by air). Indeed, the South African conference delegate spends R1 450 that is in line with the amounts spent in other countries by conference delegates – R1 540 in the UK and R1 600 in Australia. Another important element of the international conference industry is that 19% of delegates bring an accompanying person, making the total number of foreign tourists visiting for international conferences and conventions almost 50 000' (Mosia, 2004).

It is evident that the meeting industry is a contributor to the economy and is therefore an important component of the tourism industry. Benefits generically include foreign income, employment creation, networking, building bridges, improved communication between institutions, and investment. The value-added spin-offs that meetings generate, nationally or internationally, can be grouped into economic spin-offs, public relations and tourist value.

14.2.1 Economic spin-offs

Meetings held in conjunction with an exhibition ensure that products are brought to the attention of the delegates and add income for that meeting and destination as a whole. These types of events are known as *confexes*. Exhibitions on their own contribute greatly to tourism and in today's industry an exhibition plays a vital role in meetings. Many meetings have an exhibition running for the duration of the meeting, making it worthwhile for business people to visit. For the meeting organiser the exhibition is an important source of income which will assist in covering certain costs; for the exhibitor the meeting delegates are seen as potential customers and, of course, for the delegate it is both entertaining and educational. The type of meeting will determine the type of exhibition required. The meeting organiser can organise the exhibition, but a word of advice gained from experience – to preserve your sanity, hire in the services of professional exhibition coordinators. You can negotiate a fee with them for services rendered or contract it (hire it) out.

The research commissioned by SA Tourism states that more than half a billion rand (R547 million) is spent in South Africa (excluding airfares) by the foreign delegates and their accompanying people. This is worth approximately R922 million in total contribution to the GDP (Gross Domestic Product) and represents some 11500 jobs. Further, the local and international MICE industry is estimated at 101 000 events attended by 11 million participants, which represents approximately 15 million days. The MICE industry generates more than 200 000 job opportunities in total and makes a 2,7% contribution to the GDP, compared to the 8,5% contribution of the total tourism industry to the GDP (Saunders, 2004).

14.2.2 Public relations spin-offs

A professionally organised meeting effectively builds the image of the host destination. Delegates who have had a positive experience will go home as goodwill ambassadors and will motivate their colleagues to host their meeting at that destination.

Examples of some events organised professionally, namely the World Summit on Sustainable Development, the World Road Transport Conference, the World Parks Conferences, the prestigious President's Cup golf tournament and the International Cape Wine Expo have lead to the industry gaining tremendous confidence in South Africa as a MICE destination. Together with the increase in world-class international conference venues and growing authentic travel experiences, the opportunity to bid for international events has increased.

14.2.3 Tourist value spin-offs

Meetings stimulate the tourism industry in many ways – through pre- and post-tours, as well as by patronising well-known areas and visiting lesser-known areas on professional tours. The delegates gain insight into the diversity and impact of the destination and could often return later with friends and families for a holiday. Examples of some of the tours that delegates can experience include exciting and imaginative incentive offerings such as white-river rafting, horseback safaris, sophisticated wine routes and many more.

Meetings support the tourism infrastructure with special reference to hotels, guest houses, bed-and-breakfast establishments, self-catering facilities, youth hostels, organised coach tours, tour operators, tourist guides, restaurants, airlines, travel agents, translators, car rental firms, resorts and meeting venues.

14.3 TYPES OF MEETING

The Meetings Industry Association of the United Kingdom provides the following definition of a *meeting*:

A meeting is 'An event involving ten or more people for a minimum of four hours during one day or more, frequently held outside the company's own premises' (Meetings Industry Association, 1996: 1).

To date in the South African context the word conference has been used as a generic term to describe various types of meetings. However, for the purpose of studying events, we propose that we follow Meeting Planners International's definition of meetings. Here is a list of the various types of meetings.

- **Convention.** A convention generally consists of informative sessions with a specific theme or topic and can be an annual gathering of members of an organisation.
- **Conference.** Conferences can be used as an appropriate tool by any organisational group, private or public body, corporation, trade association, scientific or cultural society wishing to confer, exchange views and consequently convey a message, open a debate or give publicity to some area of opinion on a specific issue. They are usually of short duration with specific objectives and are generally on a smaller scale than a congress.
- **Congress.** A congress is a gathering held at regular intervals for a formal exchange of views and information; attendance is generally large and the purpose is often to resolve current issues or problems.
- **Colloquium.** This is an academic meeting where one or more academics present lectures on specific topics and then answer questions.
- **Forum.** This is a gathering of participants to discuss matters of public importance.
- **Symposium.** This refers to a large gathering at which the audience is addressed by panellists who are experts in their specific fields.
- **Seminar.** This involves a group of up to 30 people, plus a leader or an expert in a shared field, working through problems and joint experiences.
- **Workshop.** In a workshop the participants are divided into small groups, working face to face, teaching each other new skills and gaining insight into common problems (McCusker, 1996. Telephonic interview, 25 June).

These typically can be regarded as business or educational events. These events take place on international level and on a domestic (national level).

14.3.1 Why are meetings held?

In South Africa meetings can be held for a variety of reasons; these could include any of the following:

- to provide a forum for the generation and exchange of information and ideas;
- to share knowledge;
- to enhance communication;
- to generate unity and cooperation;

- to afford opportunities to define and promote the aims of an organisation;
- to obtain commitment to decisions;
- to enable delegates to network, thus enhancing the exchange of information;
- to provide an opportunity to explore hidden agendas;
- to provide educational opportunities (to learn something);
- to train;
- to plan and solve problems;
- to generate revenue.

14.3.2 Who holds meetings?

In South Africa the meeting business can be grouped into two specific areas – the *corporate market* and the *association market*. Corporates refer to companies which have identified the need to hold a meeting for any of the above-mentioned reasons. The majority of corporate meetings are the responsibility of a manager or secretary to organise. As a result of the downsizing of companies and the concomitant increased responsibilities of staff members, contracting out activities has become standard practice; nowadays meeting organising is being contracted out to professional meeting organisers. Organising a meeting requires undivided attention and responsibility; it is therefore advantageous for a company to hire the services of a professional meeting organiser to take the hassle and 'worry' out of meeting organising. The company can focus on business while the meeting organiser focuses on providing a professional service.

The association market also plays an important role. The difference between the association market and corporate market is that of profit-making. The association business is nonprofit-oriented, while the corporate market focuses entirely on making a profit out of their meetings. Some associations are managed by paid staff, unpaid volunteers, the government and quasi-government organisations. This market is extremely diverse and is almost impossible to classify. In South Africa these associations can be grouped into two categories, namely *professional* and *voluntary*.

Professional associations can include trade associations, scientific associations, technical associations, military associations, industrial bodies, government, trade unions and political unions.

Voluntary associations can include Rotary Clubs, alumni societies, sports clubs, craft clubs, hobby clubs, women's associations, student bodies, lobbying groups, youth groups, charitable associations and religious groups. For a more detailed discussion, refer to chapter 2.

Although meetings can be very costly to organise, they play a vital role in fostering education and training, as well as providing a platform for the corporate and association market to deal with issues of mutual interest. A few examples are provided below:

- SAACI (Southern African Association for the Conference Industry) is a trade association which holds an annual congress to provide members and the tourism/hospitality/events industry with the latest information on current issues and trends. The association provides an educational and information platform for the industry.
- WOSA (Wines of South Africa) is a trade association that represents South African wine farms on the international wine market. The association provides a platform to educate the international buyer and promoter of wine to the products of South Africa by means of an exhibition with meetings which is hosted every two years in South Africa. For more detail on this event, refer to the case study 17.1 in chapter 17.
- Corporates such as car dealers (Toyota, Volkswagen) organise regular training workshops for staff. Focus areas include service excellence, communication, new trends in technology, market research, marketing, training of mechanics, and so on. They provide a training platform for their staff.

For a more comprehensive discussion on this topic, refer to chapter 2.

14.4 FUNDAMENTALS OF ORGANISING A PROFESSIONAL MEETING

The following section examines all the aspects of professional meeting management. Topics covered include meeting planning; the meeting programme; selection of destination and site; liaison with other site services; marketing strategies; selection and training of staff; evaluation of meetings; legal requirements; and use of technology. These principles apply to both national and international meetings.

14.4.1 Meeting planning

No meeting will ever be successful without thorough planning – planning is the cornerstone of success. Planning will provide an appropriate time frame to follow and result in the setting of specific goals and objectives for the meeting. Meeting planning is the foundation of professional meeting management.

The need for a meeting will be identified by the corporate and/or the association market. Either an in-house meeting organiser will organise the event or the services of a professional on the outside will be hired. In either case the same amount of work and planning will be involved. Each meeting is unique but all require proper planning and administration.

Organising a conference or any meeting is a process. The process must be integrated and is usually quite complex. There are so many issues to consider and to remember. As the PCO, it is your responsibility to identify, determine and examine the many factors that will shape the design and the production of the meeting. This will be applicable to any type and size of event. Some of the factors to keep in mind will be the needs of the stakeholders, the practicality of the logistics, the availability of the resources, the vision, mission, goals and objectives of the meeting. Every detail of putting the event together will have an impact on the total event. Decision-making is thus a vital skill that must be developed. A decision that you make will affect how the actual resources are allocated. Every event that you will deal with will have positive features and negative features to overcome. The secret lies in being systematic in what you do. Follow a logical sequence of planning and putting your event together. According to Goldblatt (2002: 16), there is a process to follow when creating and producing a professional event. This process includes five specific phases namely:

- concept of the event
- researching the event
- planning the event
- coordinating the event
- evaluating the event.

As mentioned in the introduction to this chapter, it is an art to put together an event; you become the architect. Approach your event, be it a meeting or conference, in a creative manner. The world is your STAGE and you will be playing a very large role in the production you mount, to ensure that your event is memorable for the client, stakeholders and the participants:

S	satisfy the needs
T	tantalise the senses
A	analyse the site
G	guide guest impressions
E	establish the atmosphere

Remember that the nature of the event will inspire the design and theme of the event. The best option to begin with would be to have a brainstorming session. Brainstorming is the process of sharing creative ideas and concepts without criticism. Brainstorming produces IDEAS:

I	include your ideas
D	develop exercises
E	encourage creativity
A	accept all suggestions
S	select the best components

(Goldblatt, 2000)

PHASES IN ORGANISING A SUCCESSFUL MEETING

1
Association/corporate market identifies the need to hold a meeting

15
Post-meeting evaluation

2
Initial enquiries regarding the proposed meeting, identification of meeting organiser and very basic discussions regarding the budget

14
Actual meeting

3
Initial discussions with meeting organiser and decision is made to go ahead with the meeting

13
Time frame running up to the meeting

4
Establish local organising committee; roles and responsibilities are delegated under supervision of the chairperson and meeting organiser; discussions regarding the budget

12
Finalise relationships with other role players

5
Determine destination and venue

11
Determine marketing strategy, media and public relations

6
Determine time and date to hold the meeting

7
Establish the theme, goals and objectives

10
Gather delegate information/ delegate history analysis

8
Determine the budget and in-kind sponsorship

9
Determine the meeting programme and speakers

FIGURE 14.1 *Phases to be followed in organising a successful meeting (adapted from Hildreth, 1990: 11)*

It is also advisable to have a basic toolkit from which to work. An implementation toolkit can include generic areas of event management which can be applied to each event that you will be involved in organising. According to Van Der Wagen (2001: 258), such a generic toolkit can include the following crucial elements:

- *Event description* generally refers to the name of the event, the type of event, the location, the date, the actual duration and the overview of the event, which involves determining the vision, mission goals and objectives.
- *Event management* involves identifying the key responsibilities and accountabilities of the management function; it is really about who does what and who manages what. As the key organiser you could have coordinators working under you managing certain responsibilities but as the key person you will remain accountable for every aspect of the event.
- *Approvals and consultation* focuses on from whom you obtain approval for certain areas of your event such as safety/security issues, the venue approval, insurances, health issues, permission from authorities and copyright issues.
- *Marketing* of your event, to whom, and how, needs must be met. How will you advertise and promote the event and who will be responsible for the public relations of the event.
- *Financial control* of the event is vital. These issues will involve funding requirements, the fees, the costs, the control system, taxations, profit-and-loss statements, the cash-flow analysis and sponsorship.
- *Risk management* will assist you in identifying potential problems and hazards.
- *Event staging* is more aimed at the actual event when it starts and will include aspects such as theme, services, décor, catering and waste management.
- *Staffing* generally refers to the selection of those who will work with you, and would involve rosters, training and briefings.
- *Safety and security* ensures that all possible measures are in place to ensure a very pleasant (hopefully hassle-free event). Issues to consider would be the safety of the main players, delegates, on-site security and general health and safety.
- *Operational plans* refers to all the logistical issues of your event such as dealing with complaints, managing crowds, setting performance standards and having backup plans.
- *Evaluation* is having a briefing once the meeting has been completed to determine the success and areas for improvement.

Based on the abovementioned, it is evident that there are a variety of tasks and activities that need to be carried out in order to achieve a successful event; these must be performed timeously and accurately. In order to achieve this, it is wise to follow a *critical path analysis,* which means following a specific project plan to organise your meeting. All the fundamentals you will follow to organise the meeting are known as the *project areas.* Remember to brainstorm and to evaluate your generic toolkit, then ask yourself the following questions (Cloete, 2004: Interview).

- *What* tasks need to be accomplished?
- *When* do these tasks need to be completed?
- *Why* do these tasks need to be done?
- *Who* will be responsible for performing these tasks?
- *How* will these form part of the big picture?
- *Which* alternatives need to be considered along the way?

What kinds of tasks will the meeting organiser be faced with? A great variety – the most fundamental areas being those outlined below. (Remember that each meeting is a special case and must be approached in such a manner. By using the generic toolkit as a guideline, you will be able to establish the fundamental areas for the meeting you are organising).

- **Event description**. This means deciding on the name, title and objective of your meeting.
- **Destination, location and venue**. A decision must be made regarding where the meeting will take place: the destination, specific area at the destination, and the actual meeting facility.
- **Public relations**. This involves promoting the meeting, obtaining media exposure, getting the message out.
- **Marketing**. This involves identifying the event market segments and devising strategies to attract the most lucrative ones.
- **Coordination**. Coordination of all the tasks is necessary to achieve a successful meeting.
- **Resources**. This refers to all that is necessary to organise the meeting and can include human resources, physical resources such as equipment, and more.
- **Role players**. These are all the people directly or indirectly linked to organising the event.
- **Participants/delegates**. This involves deciding who the target market is, who must attend the meeting.
- **Sponsors and donors**. This refers to those 'angels' in the industry who give/donate towards the meeting. This could include financial sponsors, sponsoring of meals, transport, and many more aspects of the meeting.
- **Finance**. This means the cash required to cover the costs of the meeting.
- **Speakers**. These people form part of the meeting programme and the whole event is organised around the type and quality of speakers who are invited.
- **Entertainment, for example social activities and recreation**. Meetings are not just serious, boring events. There is a lighter side to everything. To provide the ultimate experience, serious programmes should be balanced with social activities such as special dinners and tours. This provides the participant or delegate with the opportunity of learning and having a good time.

- **Services provided.** These are the other services relied on to get the job done, for example: travel arrangements, transport, technical visits, special equipment hiring, catering, and so on.
- **Liabilities and insurance.** Murphy's law has taught everyone that 'what can go wrong, will go wrong'. There are no exceptions. As an entrepreneur, ensure that care is taken; for example: if the meeting is cancelled just prior to commencement or the client is dissatisfied with the service, who provides cover if financial losses are incurred?
- **Contingencies.** This means planning for the 'unforeseen' when organising events: for example, escalating costs and perhaps those extras not budgeted for such as extra printing.

14.4.1.1 Date charts and checklists

Once you have identified the project areas of your event, how do you manage them? A simple manner would be to follow a date chart and checklists, as shown in examples 14.1 and 14.2 below.

EXAMPLE 14.1 *Example of a date chart (Cloete, 2004: Interview)*

ITEM DESCRIPTION	MEETING TIMETABLE				
	JAN	FEB	MARCH	APRIL	MAY *
	1 2 3 4	1 2 3 4	1 2 3 4	1 2 3 4	1 2 3 4**
Transport					
■ Finalise transport contributor					
■ Plan logistics of movements					

The *date chart* is almost like a year planner: it is a physical reminder of the time frame available to complete tasks. Being able to see at a glance the time available to perform the various tasks helps you to be better organised and relieves some of the stress involved with meeting organising.

As mentioned before, each meeting/event is a special case and thus will require its own unique *checklist*. No list can be exhaustive and you will learn to draw up checklists as you gain experience in the industry and are exposed to different events.

A checklist is vital. You can have it with you all the time to show what tasks have been identified, what tasks have been completed in a given time frame, and who was responsible. Your checklist can be computerised or you can carry it around manually. An example of a very basic checklist is provided below (see example 14.2); this can be adapted to suit your particular needs. It follows a blank format; you can write your project areas in, instead of setting up a predetermined list.

EXAMPLE 14.2 *Example of a checklist*

		COMPLETION DATE			
ALL-PURPOSE CHECK LIST FOR MEETINGS/EVENTS:					
....					
....					
....					
ACTIONS	RESPONSIBLE PERSON	Anticipated date	True date	COMPLETED	COMMENTS

EXAMPLE 14.3 *Example of a meeting checklist (Cloete, 2004: Interview)*

MEETING CHECK LIST					COMMENTS

NAME OF EVENT _____

NAME OF CLIENT _____

Street address _____ Suburb/Town _____

Full postal address _____ Suburb/Town _____

Telephone no _____ Postal code _____

E-mail address _____ Fax number _____

PHYSICAL DETAILS FOR EVENT

Name of venue _____

Full postal address _____ Suburb/Town _____

Fax number _____ Postal code _____

E-mail address _____

Telephone numbers _____

Full street address _____

Function space _____

General information _____

Accessibility:

Location map	Supplied	Drawn	Attached	To be mailed
Road approach				

COMMUNICATIONS

Banqueting/Catering — (Name) _____

— (Name) _____

Accommodation — (Name) _____

— (Name) _____

Public Relations — (Name) _____

— (Name) _____

Other — (Name) _____

— (Name) _____

Nearest airport _____ Transport options _____

Nearest station _____ Transport options _____

Car parking potential _____ No of bays _____

Parking for coaches and large vehicles _____

Distance from venue _____Charge per day _____per night _____

General information _____

MEETING VENUE   Room name _____
(Separate form per room)

SPACE UTILISATION

Conference (school/room)   Max no _____   Rental _____

Conference (cinema)   Max no _____   Rental _____

Reception (cocktail/buffet, etc)   Max no _____   Rental _____

Sit-down meal   Max no _____   Rental _____

Display/Exhibition/Registration   Max no _____   Rental _____

Boardroom/syndicate   Max no _____   Rental _____

GENERAL INFORMATION

Table formation/number of chairs per table, etc (on above) _____

_____

Ceiling height (from lowest ceiling fixture to floor) _____

No of doors (to access outer areas) _____

No of doors (to service areas) _____

No of other doors _____

Fire regulations _____

Access route (from main foyer to meeting venue)

Steps _____

Escalators _____ No _____

Facilities for physically challenged _____

Lifts _____ No _____ Size _____

Loading capacity _____

* Here you can add in information regarding your participants

SYSTEMS

Lighting:

Main _____

Spots _____

Dimmers _____

Flood _____

Fixed _____

Moveable _____

Blackout:

Curtains _____ Individual _____ Cord/pull/motor _____ Other _____

Natural light _____

Screen: Fixed size _____   Type _____

Sound system/PA _____   Microphone _____

Built-in projection equipment _____

	COMMENTS
Overhead projector and screen _____	_____
Flipchart _____	_____
White boards _____	_____
Electrical voltage Load _____ Power _____ Amps _____ Plug/points _____	_____
Ventilation Air conditioning _____ Heating _____	_____
Noise level _____	_____
Decor Walls _____ Floor _____ Ceiling_____	_____
Toilet facilities Male _____ No _____ Female _____ No _____	_____
Secretarial support services _____	_____
Other _____	_____
	_____
ASK TO HEAR AND SEE ALL EQUIPMENT AND SYSTEMS FUNCTIONING	_____
Set-up time allowance _____	_____
Will the following be supplied? (tick where applicable):	_____
Ashtrays _____	_____
Peppermints _____	_____
Ice water jugs and glasses _____	_____
Note pads _____	_____
Pens _____	_____
Platforms _____	_____
Lectern _____	_____
Podium _____	_____
Pointer _____	_____
Felt pens _____	_____
Table cloths _____	_____
Green baize _____	_____
Set-up and cleaning personnel _____	_____
Type and size of tables _____	_____
Type and size of chairs _____	_____
Photographs taken/supplied _____ No _____	_____

These checklists are simply examples. It is advisable to design a checklist to suit the requirements of the particular event. The information contained in the checklist (depending on the nature of the event) could include:

- first meeting with client and what is discussed at this meeting (client discussion checklist);
- event description;
- destination, location and venue;
- budget/finance;
- public relations and media;
- marketing;

- resources;
- role players;
- sponsors and donors;
- speakers;
- delegates;
- entertainment;
- services provided;
- liabilities and insurance;
- contingencies.

14.4.1.2 Personnel involved in planning: organising committees

As meeting organiser you will work with many types of people. The selection of the best personnel to plan and implement the necessary fundamentals is important. Once the organiser receives confirmation of the event, it is important to establish who does what and to whom the different responsibilities are to be delegated. The organisation which initiates the meeting usually has a discussion to outline the basic issues. They are the main organisers of the event and they normally appoint an internal meeting organiser or hire the services of an outside professional to do the actual work. It is normally at this point that the organising committee is established and the first meeting held. Example 14.4 shows the proposed agenda for such a meeting and example 14.5 the composition of the organising committee. These are just examples and yours could look quite different when you organise a meeting. As mentioned before, each meeting is a special event and will be organised differently, but the fundamentals and approach remain the same. (These examples were kindly provided by the South African Association for the Meeting Industry, SAACI.)

EXAMPLE 14.4 *Example of an agenda (Information: Courtesy of SAACI, 1996)*

**PROPOSED AGENDA FOR FIRST MEETING
OF THE MAIN ORGANISING COMMITTEE**

1. Introduction and background information
2. Identify the main organisers and others associating or collaborating
3. Members of the Organising Committee
4. Date and venue
5. Title, theme and objective
6. Organisational structure for congress
7. Provisional technical programme — scope and topics

© Juta & Co Ltd

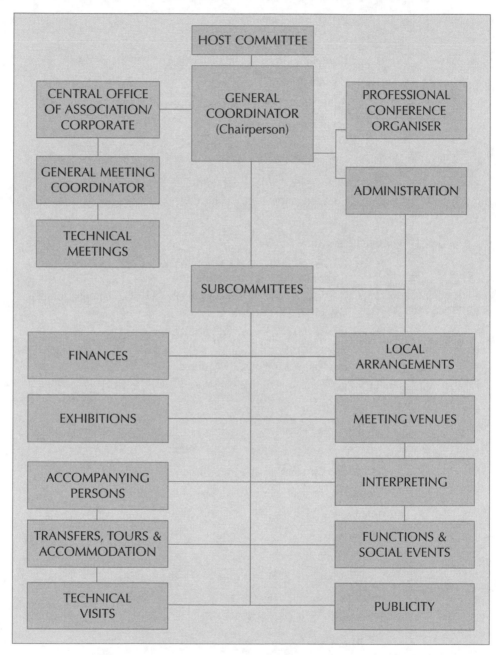

Depending on the size of your event, this structure could change and could become less technical, as shown in example 14.6.

EXAMPLE 14.6 *Example of simple organisational structure*

(Based on the organisational structure of the 18th International Conference on Yeast Genetics and Molecular Biology, organised by Mrs Deidré Cloete, Conferences Et Al.)

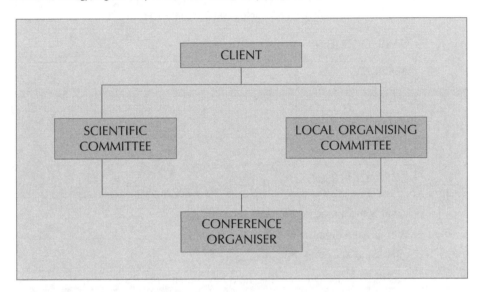

The meeting organiser will be responsible for organising the event and could delegate responsibilities to staff such as booking of venues, obtaining quotes, and so on. The client will instruct the meeting organiser what must be done, working through the scientific committee and local organising committee. The subcommittee functions (as in the previous example) in this case will thus become the full responsibility of the meeting organiser.

In the case of major events (over 500 delegates), it is advisable to form subcommittees with designated responsibilities to assist with general organising. The meeting organiser will be the manager and can check if tasks are being performed. Timing is vital and preparatory steps should take place prior to the meeting – each meeting is a special case and you will adapt the timing of each meeting as you go along. Consider using a client discussion sheet: it will assist you in planning your meeting.

EXAMPLE 14.7 *Client discussion sheet (Input: Cloete, 2004: Interview)*

WESTERN CAPE MEETING CONSULTING SERVICES CC
(in small letters your address, tel, fax, e-mail)

CLIENT DISCUSSION SHEET/FORM	
NAME OF CLIENT	
ADDRESS	
TEL/FAX	
E-MAIL	
CELL	
CONTACT PERSON	

What is the theme of the meeting?..

Who are the organisers? ....

Others involved with the organisation? ....

Has the organising committee held any meetings to date?

When? ....

What commitments have been made/discussed?.........................

How many main organising committee meetings do you

envisage holding? ....

How many members on the organising committee?.....................

Have firm dates been decided for the meeting? ....

Have the site and venue been decided? ....

Is it a national or international meeting? ....

How many delegates to attend? ....

Fixed ideas on the format of the meeting? ....

Will there be an exhibition complementing the meeting? ....

Will there be a technical programme coordinator/committee

and will the services of a meeting organiser be required? ....

Are presenters being invited? ....

Will presenters be offered perks? ....

Are you going to call for papers, select presenters and edit papers?...........

Will you publish proceedings? ....

Will VIPs and government or others be involved?.....................................

Will you require interpreters? ....

Are social/entertainment events to be offered? ....

Will a separate 'partners' programme' be offered?

(selecting a DMC for this)..

Child-care programmes?..

How many announcements do you envisage?...

Will you want a separate printed programme? ....

Will pre- and post-tours be offered? ....

Will technical excursions be part of the meeting? ....

Who will be responsible for the finances?

Is basic support funding available? ....

Will you be seeking sponsors? ....

Who will manage the finances? ....

Who handles registration? ....

Housing arrangements for delegates..

Transportation ....

Audiovisual aids...

Legal issues considered ....

Space use and set-up design ....

On-site communications ....

Meeting wrap up..

The questions can be adapted to suit any particular event.

14.4.2 The meeting programme (For more detailed information, refer to chapter 9.)

The meeting programme encompasses a great deal and involves a number of important phases, including:

- establishment of the theme, goals and objectives;
- budgeting;
- producing a meeting plan;
- meeting proceedings;
- social programme, extramural activities.

14.4.2.1 Establishment of the theme, goals and objectives

Establishing the title and theme of the meeting makes the planning of the meeting easier – there is something to work towards. An example is provided below (example 14.8).

EXAMPLE 14.8 *Meeting theme and objectives*

Title: Studying Tourism – Where to From Here?
Theme: Education, skills and tourism
Objective: To highlight the challenges facing graduates when completing a tourism management programme

The goals and objectives of the meeting will be determined by the client and the meeting organiser who is planning the meeting. They are crucial to the success of the meeting as they can assist with:

- coordination;
- teamwork;
- determining the contribution of people's ideas;
- defining key responsible areas and tasks;
- providing a platform for the process of achieving results, and
- providing guidelines for the delegation of tasks to staff.

Goals tend to be aimed at long-term achievement and objectives at the short term. To determine the goals and objectives of the event, compile a questionnaire to be completed during the first meeting with the prospective client (refer to the client discussion sheet).

14.4.2.2 Budgeting (For more detailed information, refer to chapter 8.)

Meetings are costly and it is the responsibility of the meeting organiser to negotiate the best deal where possible – this will have a definite impact on the meeting programme.

Just as each meeting is different, so is each meeting budget. There are, however, some basic budgeting principles to be followed. A meeting should not drain the resources of the association/corporation which is organising it. In some instances it is possible to make a profit. Income is normally obtained from the registration fees, exhibitors and sponsors. The important aspect to remember is to establish a budget to cover initial costs before income is generated. There are certain important questions to ask and bear in mind; a budget can only be prepared once the actual objective of the meeting has been established as this determines what the meeting is all about and what is hoped to be achieved. Questions to be asked could include those listed below (Cloete, 2004: Interview):

- Is it expected to make a profit?

- Does finance need to be raised?
- Who pays for what?
- Who will monitor the expenses?
- Who authorises expenses?
- Who makes the decisions regarding expenses and obtains sample signatures?
- Who is responsible for 'auditing' the final accounts?
- Do you have a contingency worked into the budget (20% of total costs)?

Control of finance is vital – this involves constant bookkeeping of all details of income and expenditure. The minimum could be a cash book (basic financial records), but most clients require audit (accountant to analyse the books) services. The following is an example of what you could budget for, this can however, be adapted to suit any specific function.

EXAMPLE 14.9 *Budgeting for a conference (adapted from Meeting Division Budget Form: SATOUR, 1996)*

EXPENSES	Cost per item	Quantity	Total
VENUE Auditorium and break-away rooms Audiovisual services Additional hire charges for other services Additional equipment, eg interpreting booths, microphones, audiovisual Flowers			
OFFICIAL FUNCTIONS Meet and greet, refreshments Welcome cocktail Official opening banquet/dinner Mayoral function Entertainment			
CATERING Tea/coffee at registration Mid-morning tea/coffee and scones Lunch Afternoon tea/coffee and biscuits Dinner/Braai/Theme evening			
TRANSPORT Buses between hotel and venue Technical visits/inspection tours Social functions			
COMPANIONS' PROGRAMME Strongly recommended that you obtain assistance and quotes from Tour Operator/DMC or organise the companions' programme			

SUBSISTENCE AND TRAVEL			
Airfare for speaker/s			
Accommodation, S & T for speaker/s			
Honorarium, speakers' fees			
Airfare for Council members			
S & T for Council members			
Travelling expenses for committee members and/or congress coordinators			
PRINTING			
Official meeting letterhead			
First announcement			
Tear sheet/reply card			
Second announcement/call for papers			
Third/final announcement			
Official meeting programme			
Media releases/flyers			
Presenters' papers and post-meeting copies			
Meeting folders			
Invitation cards, menu cards, etc			
Photocopying			
STATIONERY REQUIREMENTS AND POSTAGE			
Files, printer cartridge, printing paper, labels			
Envelopes (various sizes)			
Notepads and pens/pencils			
Delegate nametags/lapel badges			
Briefbags/delegates' kits			
Postage costs			
Telephone and cellphone calls			
Faxing costs			
GENERAL			
Translation costs			
Recording of proceedings			
Transcription costs			
Media coverage			
Advertising costs			
Flowers			
Gifts to speaker/s			
Give-aways to delegates			
Signage/boards to indicate venue			
Honorariums			
INCOME			
Delegates' registration fees			
Government grant			
Sale of exhibition space			
Advertising in meeting programme			
Sales: of papers, curios, etc			
Financial sponsorship			
Sponsorship for: airtickets, briefbags, teas/coffees, lunches, dinners, give-aways/mementoes			

IF THE CONFERENCE IS MARKETED OVER A PERIOD OF TWO/THREE YEARS, REMEMBER TO
ENVISAGE AN ESCALATION IN COST DURING THIS TIME

Sponsorship, or in-kind sponsorship, is important to consider for any meeting. Most meetings in South Africa work on a sponsorship basis as meetings are *very expensive* to organise. As meeting organiser it is your responsibility to arrange and search for sponsorships. What gets sponsored? Many aspects of the meeting can in fact be sponsored; let us use a hypothetical example.

For such a meeting sponsors can be generated for: financial support, catering, accommodation for speakers, transport for speakers, printing and stationery requirements. You can even try to get everything sponsored.

How do you go about getting sponsors? This involves research and you should allow ample time to work on the research. Meetings are organised from one to five years in advance as they require plenty of work. One of the most time-consuming aspects is sponsorship which is a lengthy process. Here is a suggested sponsorship plan.

Sponsorship research must be done and possible sponsors or donors must be identified. Make sure that they are capable of giving and are interested in the actual cause of the client.

Information must be collected and stored in a data bank and should include the funding guidelines of the sponsor, what their vested interest would be; contact person and details such as address, telephone number, fax number, e-mail and cell phone number; listing of directors and involvement of other parties (executives, partners, and so on). When trying to raise sponsors, you will also need certain tools to assist you; these include a predetermined budget, letter of appeal and a proposal. Most sponsors require these documents to evaluate your appeal. What should you include in your proposal? Information on the meeting (theme and title), overall goals of the meeting, brief history of the corporation/association; what needs will be met, and who will benefit. Why is it important to raise sponsors? Sponsorship leads to increased income and can assist in building new contracts. What does the sponsor get out of it? The sponsor can get quite a lot in return such as recognition, giving something back, identifying with a cause, compassion, increased sales, advertising, public relations, vested interest and tax benefits. All in all, everyone gains.

When the meeting is over, it is advisable that you provide your sponsors with a detailed report of the results of the meeting, delegate participation, if the goals were met, future planning and financial statements. Of course, a thank-you letter should be included (Cloete, 2004: Interview).

For a more comprehensive discussion on this topic, refer to chapter 8.

7th International Symposium on Adjuvants for Agrochemicals

8 to 12 November 2004
Cape Town , South Africa

EXCURSIONS

The organisers will also offer several exciting day and half day excursions for accompanying persons. These tours will definitely include a trip up the famous Table Mountain with the aerial cable car, a visit to the Cape Peninsula to see some of South Africa's most spectacular coastline and a visit to the Winelands, to taste some of South Africa's award winning wines.

For more details please visit our website: www.ISAA2004.com

GENERAL TRAVEL INFORMATION ON SOUTH AFRICA

Climate
The Western Cape has a Mediterranean climate and November is considered as early summer with warm sunny days. The temperature ranges between 18 °C and 23 °C during this month.

Airlines
Many international carriers operate direct flights into Cape Town International Airport from Europe and the USA. Alternatively participants may travel via Johannesburg to Cape Town.

Pre and post tours
South Africa is regarded as 'A world in one country' that offers the conference delegate a variety of options to consider for pre and post conference tours. Tour itineraries range from the Garden Route (South/East Coastline)-experiencing the spectacular coastline and seaside resorts, to the Highveld, to experience the African Bushveld and wildlife.

CONTACT DETAILS

Conference Secretariat: Deidre Cloete
Conferences et al
P O Box 452
STELLENBOSCH, 7599 SOUTH AFRICA
Tel: 27 21 8864496
Fax: 27 21 883 8177
e-mail: deidre@iafrica.com

CONFERENCES
■ ET ■ AL

Photographs kindly supplied by SA Tourism, University of Stellenbosch: Agronomy and Deciduous Fruit Producers' Trust

---

"The fairest cape that I have seen in the whole circumference of the earth."
(Sir Francis Drake sailed around the Southern most tip of Africa in 1577)

The beautiful Mother City of Cape Town will host the Seventh International Symposium on Adjuvants for Agrochemicals (ISAA 2004) from 8 to 12 November 2004. The ISAA will be held in the newly built International Convention Centre in the heart of the city and at the entrance to the popular Victoria and Alfred Waterfront with its many hotels, restaurants, boat cruises and entertainment.

Cape Town owes its popularity with tourists to its cultural mixture of African, European and Asian influences and yet is within easy access to the delights of the dark continent's charm. Cape Town is one of South Africa's as well as Africa's top business locations. This combination and the excellent infrastructure makes Cape Town a very attractive destination.

OBJECTIVES

The 7th International Symposium will be concerned with the role of adjuvants in agrochemicals. The adjuvant industry is facing increasing pressure for 'greener' products while the agrochemical industry needs to reduce contamination levels. How is the adjuvant industry facing up to these challenges?

The objectives of the symposium will be:

■ To educate through transfer of knowledge
■ To exchange ideas, information and common problems
■ To promote the awareness of the role of adjuvants in agriculture
■ To promote an understanding of the need for research

SYMPOSIUM PROGRAMME

The symposium will be organised by the ISAA 2004 Organising Committee in collaboration with an international scientific committee. The organisers will ensure that there is an attractive mixture of science, commercial opportunities and cultural events. Individuals and companies are cordially invited to attend and to contribute to ISAA 2004. The Symposium will include plenary sessions, workshops, a trade exhibition and poster sessions.

Topics presented will be under the broadly defined concepts below;

■ Regulatory and environmental challenges
■ Biological performance
■ Trends in metrology and chemistry
■ Drift and vapour management
■ Wetting and uptake

REGISTRATION FEES

The registration fees to attend the ISAA 2004 have not yet been finalised but the organisers expect the fees to be approximately 600 US$.

SECOND ANNOUNCEMENT

Further details of the symposium arrangements, including the deadlines for submission of abstracts and papers and registration requirements will be included in the Second Announcement to be issued in July 2003.

A copy of the Second Announcement will also be placed on the ISAA 2004 website (www.ISAA2004.com). The site will also include all details regarding the symposium and include information on hotel accommodation, places of interest and registration.

Please contact the Conference Secretariat with your postal and e-mail details to ensure that you receive a copy of the second announcement.

EXHIBITIONS AND SPONSORSHIPS

As in the past, companies will be invited to exhibit equipment and products for the duration of the symposium and will also be offered sponsorship opportunities.

Attendance at previous symposia varied from 300 to over 400 delegates from all over the world. Sponsorship therefore offers exposure to a wide audience.

Delegates attending ISAA represent a diverse range of interests and include the Chemical retailing companies, Chemical manufacturing companies, Agricultural Researchers, Chemists & Biochemists.

■ Special mention will be made during the symposium and at the banquet of any sponsorship. Details of the sponsorship will be published on the website and in the proceedings.
■ Sponsoring of the symposium will benefit the company depending on the amount of money donated.

Categories of sponsorship
■ Diamond (Undisclosed Euro amount above Platinum)
■ Platinum (20 000 Euro)
■ Gold (10 000 Euro)
■ Silver (5000 Euro)
■ Bronze (2500 Euro)

14.4.2.3 Producing a meeting plan

The meeting plan contains all the details of what you aim to do and could include the following:

- arrival and departure times of meeting staff;
- arrival and departure times of speakers and VIPs;
- arrival and departure of delegates;
- meeting pattern;
- programme (schedule, delegates, speakers, meeting venue, equipment required);
- registration (setup and procedure);
- exhibit space and arrangements;
- catering (food and beverage);
- accounting;
- storage of equipment;
- letters of agreement;
- staff responsibilities;
- accommodation;
- transportation.

A critical path analysis is advisable to assist with the planning of the meeting.

14.4.2.4 Meeting pattern or proceedings

The meeting pattern or proceedings involves each activity from arrival to departure. It involves check-in, hospitality, catering, recreation, entertainment, and break-away sessions. Before the meeting pattern is in place, the *meeting agenda* should be developed. The agenda is the actual programme for the duration of the meeting – it is the focus of the meeting, and comprises the opening and welcome, speakers, slots, meals, breakaways and entertainment. The agenda needs to be structured; being aware of objectives prior to setting the agenda will prove useful and assist in determining what will form general and smaller sessions/presentations. Take note of the following guidelines on preparing the meeting agenda.

- Place the most difficult material between 09:30 and 12:00 or between 14:00 and 17:00.
- Incorporate a discussion session so that material can be used in a 'hands-on situation'.
- Determine, a policy on speakers, welcoming speaker, opening address, keynote address, other speakers, closing address.
- Decide on a chairperson, discussion leaders, recorders (taping the event, audio and visual).
- Allocate adequate tea breaks and a lunch break (tea ± 15 to 30 minutes and lunch 60–90 minutes).
- Ensure that delegates are kept interested to the end of the meeting; have some good and entertaining speakers at the beginning and the end of the meeting (Hildreth, 1990: 83–94).

14.4.2.5 Social programme and extramural activities

Social events are just as crucial to the success of a meeting. As meeting organiser you should ensure a balance between the technical and social programmes.

The social programme is a vital part of the meeting as it provides opportunities for delegates to relax. It can relieve the stress of sitting still for long periods while listening to speakers and can generate excitement, something to look forward to. One excellent spin-off of a social function is that it allows for social interaction, meeting and networking with other delegates which leads to the generation of goodwill.

What kind of activities could be included in a social programme? One idea is a special meet-and-greet function; this is normally held on the first evening of the meeting to put everyone at ease. Other ideas include special dinners, cocktail parties, banquets, and perhaps a free evening where delegates can do their own thing. Let the creative side take over when organising social programmes.

Another approach would be to include pre- and post- special interest tours for delegates and, if required, for spouses as well. Make sure that a professional tour operator takes care of organising the tours. These tours should include visiting special sites that acquaint delegates with the destination.

14.4.3 Selection of destination and site

This is a decision for the local organising committee and meeting organiser. The destination must have some kind of attraction, a sort of 'exotic' feeling. Figure 14.2 illustrates destination appeal. Some other aspects to be considered are discussed in the sections which follow.

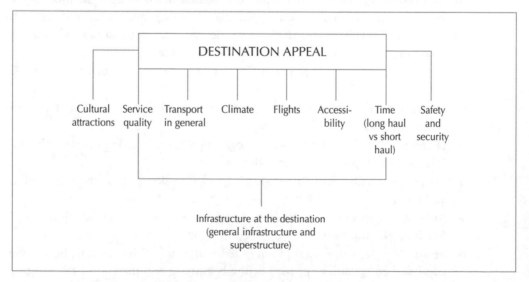

FIGURE 14.2 *Destination appeal*

© Juta & Co Ltd

14.4.3.1 Date

When should the event take place? Consider factors that could influence the attendance of the event, such as public, religious and tertiary/school holidays.

14.4.3.2 Number of delegates

Never overestimate; always be realistic about delegate numbers. It is important to take into account whether there will be accompanying persons, as this could influence the financial situation of the meeting. It is advisable to do some research. By doing research you can formulate a group history and analysis that can assist in planning effectively for the meeting. Such information can indicate the demographics of your delegates such as male/female, age, cultural differences, special needs, and so on. These vital statistics assist with the organising of the event as you will know *who* and *what* to plan for.

14.4.3.3 Venue selection

The type of meeting will determine the type of venue. The location is important, accessibility being the principal consideration. Other aspects to be taken into account are convenience and attributes. When selecting a venue, you must identify the meeting objectives, the format and the physical requirements. The actual meeting room must provide the necessary comfort: the room should never be cramped, delegates must be comfortable at all times. Should the programme include break-away discussions, ensure that the venue can provide rooms for this purpose. To recap: adequate space, comfortable seating and good lighting are important. It is advisable to have a technician present to deal with technical requirements (assistance with equipment). Separate lighting at the stage and podium are necessary. Another consideration is the way the rooms are set up – the way the tables and chairs are arranged. The type of meeting will determine these setups. Figure 14.3 illustrates just a few examples of room setups that you could consider.

FIGURE 14. 3 *Meeting room setups (adapted from Pain, 1979: 41–43)*

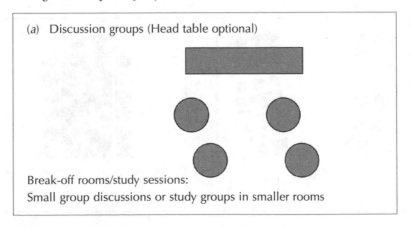

(a) Discussion groups (Head table optional)

Break-off rooms/study sessions:
Small group discussions or study groups in smaller rooms

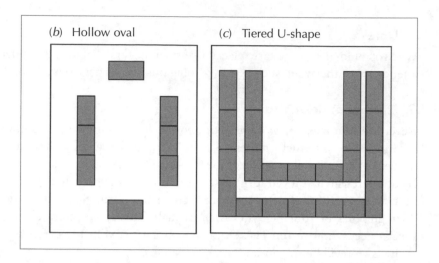

FIGURE 14.4 *Meeting venue setups (adapted from Pain, 1979: 41–43)*

(*a*) Theatre arrangement

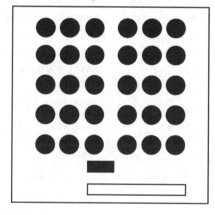

(*b*) Amphitheatre arrangement

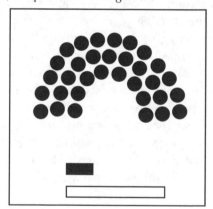

(*c*) Classroom arrangement

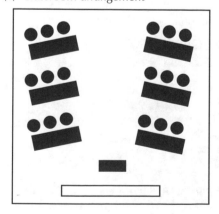

(*d*) Centre table arrangement

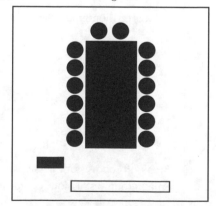

(e) U-shaped table arrangement

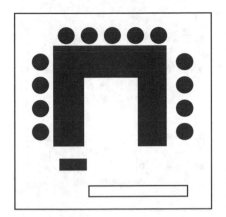

(f) Hollow square arrangement

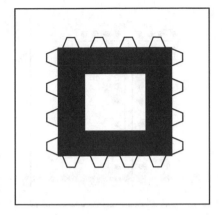

(g) Herringbone arrangement

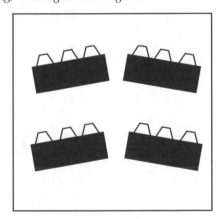

(h) V-shaped classroom arrangement

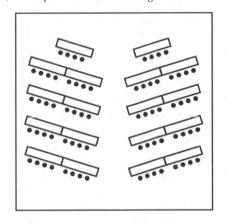

(i) Reception arrangement

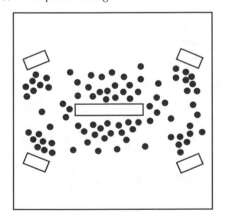

(j) E-shaped arrangement

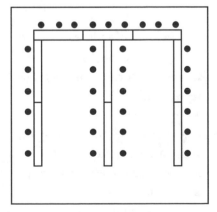

(k) T-shaped arrangement

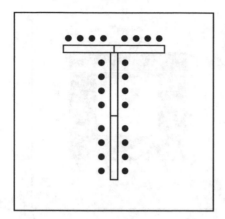

(l) Banquet arrangement

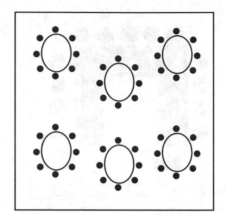

(m) Board of directors arrangement

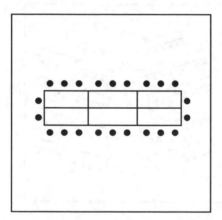

14.4.3.4 Technical facilities/audiovisual equipment

The following should be available in the meeting room:

- public address system with back-up;
- aisle microphone;
- lapel microphones;
- microphones for main tables;
- projection screens;
- overhead projector with a spare lamp, transparencies and pens;
- slide projectors;
- laptop and data projectors;
- laser pointer.

© Juta & Co Ltd

This is the basic equipment that should be available in the meeting room. Other visual equipment can be hired, depending on the nature of the meeting. It is always advisable to have technical experts present should something go wrong. Some tips: have all the equipment demonstrated in its working position the day before and check it the morning of the meeting; brief the users of equipment beforehand – even have a trial run if time allows.

14.4.3.5 Catering

It is very challenging to offer exciting meals. Presentation is extremely important and it is advisable to build up a good relationship with your caterer or chef. Always be aware of the dietary requirements of your guests. Refer to chapter 12 for more detailed information.

14.4.3.6 Registration

First impressions are lasting impressions. A welcoming atmosphere and organised facility should be created at the registration desk. Alphabetical registering by delegate name speeds up the process. Registration sheets should be kept at the registration area and could be used as a checklist. An area should also be available for brief bags and documentation. This must be marked in advance with the names of the delegates. A finance section (where delegates can pay registration fees), tours and airline desk, banking and postal facilities (mailing), luggage storage, telephone services and general office facilities should be made available – depending on the nature of the meeting. Freedom of movement outside the meeting room is vital, with casual seating. Exhibition and poster board space may be required; this again is determined by the nature of the meeting.

14.4.4 Liaison with other site services (working with others)

(For more detailed information, refer to chapter 2.)
This involves all the site services (people, businesses and institutions) that will have a role to play in assuring the ultimate success of the meeting. These services could include:

- transportation services;
- tourism authorities;
- convention bureaux;
- producers of products;
- travel agents;
- tour operators;
- venue services;
- interpreters.

- **Transportation services.** Transportation needs are identified as the planning of the meeting takes place. It is necessary to do a needs analysis of the types of transport required. Transport to the destination is usually required and in most cases this will be done by a particular airline. Other transportation needs include transport from airports to accommodation and venue, to social events, pre- and post-tours, technical (special) visits, courtesy transport and spouses' transport. A tip to remember: always evaluate the parking facilities at a venue and prearrange parking.

- *Tourism authorities*. National, regional and local tourism authorities could be possible sponsors for the meeting in terms of tourism brochures and materials to put into the delegate packs. They could also be sponsors for other aspects of the meeting, for example banners, wine, a lunch, dinner, and so on.
- *Convention bureaux*. These provide general assistance in the form of information regarding the services available in the meeting industry to assist you: for example, entertainment, decorating companies, caterers, audiovisual equipment, part-time assistance, union rules, and so on. Convention bureaux also assist South African organisations in bidding for international conferences to be held in South Africa. Other services include helping to make conferences more professional and organising pre- and post-tours.
- *Producers of products*. This refers to all the general services and companies you could call on to supply services for your meeting. These could include restaurants, auditors, lawyers, and so on. Remember that the nature of your meeting will determine what other services and facilities could be used.
- *Travel agents*. Travel agents are there to assist meeting organisers. It is advisable to appoint a reputable travel agent in the beginning stages to take care of all travel arrangements related to the meeting.
- *Tour operators*. Tour operators are just as important to the meeting organiser. Appoint an experienced operator to handle all the transport arrangements and tours for the duration of the meeting.
- *Public relations/banqueting manager*. The first person the meeting organiser will encounter at the venue is the public relations manager or banqueting manager. Build up a good relationship from the start. This person will serve as liaison and assist with everything you might want arranged for the particular meeting. This person can also assist with site inspections and familiarisation trips. It is advisable to book block accommodation in advance to secure accommodation requirements for the meeting. Understand the contracts of particular venues, always read the small print, and be aware of regulations with regard to deposits.
- *Interpreters*. Interpreting is a very specialised activity and should be conducted by professionals. Should you require these services for a meeting, book or contact the interpreters immediately. To assist the interpreter it is advisable to obtain all the copies of papers and notes to be presented by the speakers so that the interpreter can become familiar with the concepts and terms utilised. A tip: during the meeting it is vital that the speaker does not present his or her speech too fast. Organise a meeting between the speakers and interpreters and check the equipment before and on the day of the meeting.

14.4.5 Marketing strategies (For more detailed information, refer to chapter 11.)

Promotion and publicity should be undertaken right from the start and every possible source should be utilised. This can be regarded as a specialised skill and it could require some expertise to manage. The first question to ask: who is the market? The delegates, of course. Delegates can be divided into two specific categories, namely:

- *external market:* potential delegates;
- *internal market:* a specific market to invite (customers, members).

Public relations is important as it enhances the image of the meeting and the organisation which initiated the meeting.

The mailing list refers to prospective delegates you wish to attract to the meeting. Their names will be stored in a data bank and all the information regarding the meeting (such as announcements) will be mailed to them. Information on prospective delegates can be obtained from the main organisers of the event, associated societies and institutes. National tourism organisations and embassies/consular offices could be approached to distribute information regarding your meeting.

Documentation refers to all 'paperwork' concerned with the meeting. The focus area for documentation includes:

- announcements;
- papers and proceedings;
- the printed programme;
- list of delegates;
- invitation cards;
- social event programmes;
- menus;
- question cards;
- guide for speakers;
- brief bags;
- nametags;
- photographs.

It is important to remember the scheduling of your marketing promotion strategy. Meeting planning can start anything from one to five years in advance. Hypothetically speaking, should you start organising a year in advance, your first mailing should occur at least 12 to 14 months prior to the event. The first mailing is normally what is called a *first announcement.* A first announcement contains very basic information about the event and is used to elicit interest. Nine months before the meeting the first media releases can be mailed to prospective participants/organisations; seven months before your advertisements should be placed in publications relevant to the 'theme' of the meeting and your second announcement should be mailed to potential delegates; five months before send a reminder (third announcement) to potential delegates; three months before send a final announcement to potential delegates and eight weeks before send a final programme to potential delegates (Hildreth, 1990: 125–126).

(*Note:* a second announcement is similar to the first announcement and will include more information about the meeting than your first mailing.)

14.4.6 Selection and training of staff

It is most important to select enthusiastic staff and to provide training for maximum performance – after all, your image is on the line and first impressions are created by the way your staff handle themselves.

As a meeting organiser you need to gain maximum performance from staff; you need to be fair and a good leader. You must have effective communication skills and must be assertive, determined, able to negotiate, to sell yourself, to delegate effectively and manage time. Most importantly, you must inspire them. You will have to determine the need for staff in particular areas. Prior to the meeting, touch base regularly to ensure that they know what is expected of them at all times. If necessary, you must provide basic training if skills are lacking. Your relationship with staff is ongoing and will last even after the meeting is over. If you treated them fairly, they will be there for the next one. Some tips to keep in mind:

- set specific time frames indicating when tasks need to be completed;
- adhere to deadlines;
- provide staff with job descriptions (clearly indicate their particular role and responsibility).

For a more comprehensive discussion on this topic, refer to chapter 6.

14.4.7 Evaluation of meeting

Evaluation is most important as it will provide three essential areas of information regarding your meeting:

- how the meeting compared to previous meetings;
- what the delegates thought of the session, presenters and meeting as a whole;
- how well the meeting accomplished the set objectives.

EXAMPLE 14.11 *Example of evaluation questionnaire*

CAPE TECHNIKON TOURISM DEPARTMENT in association with
DEPARTMENT OF ECONOMIC DEVELOPMENT & TOURISM
presents

TOURISM success

QUESTIONNAIRE

Thank you for taking the time to fill in our questionnaire. This will help us determine which aspects of the conference you enjoyed and which were less successful. Once you have completed the questionnaire, drop it into one of the boxes placed near the exit.

Mark and **X** in the appropriate block for each question.

1. How did you hear about our conference?
   □ First or final announcement   □ Lecturer/teacher
   □ Word of mouth
   Other

2. Please rate the professionalism and appearance of the student organisers.
   □ Excellent   □ Good   □ Average   □ Poor

3. Please rate the registration process.
   □ Excellent   □ Good   □ Average   □ Poor

4. Please rate the physical layout of the event, for example, the exhibitions.
   □ Excellent   □ Good   □ Average   □ Poor

5. Please rate the signage of the event.
   □ Excellent   □ Good   □ Average   □ Poor

6. Please rate the quality of all printed communication, for example, announcements, forms and posters.
   □ Excellent   □ Good   □ Average   □ Poor

7. Please rate the refreshments and lunch served at the conference.
   □ Excellent   □ Good   □ Average   □ Poor

8. Were the topics covered during the course of the conference useful to you?
   □ Excellent   □ Good   □ Average   □ Poor

9. Please indicate how well the conference met your overall expectations.
   □ Excellent   □ Good   □ Average   □ Poor

10. Any comments or suggestions for future conferences?

Thank you very much for completing our questionnaire.
The organisers

Key focus areas in the evaluation process include:
■ what to actually evaluate;
■ when to evaluate;
■ how to evaluate (Cloete, 2004: Interview).

Besides the evaluation, there are seven follow-up actions any meeting organiser should try to undertake after the event:

- write to all concerned;
- have the necessary bills paid;
- compile a report on the event;
- prepare and hold feedback meetings with the stakeholders;
- file away all relevant documentation;
- check media for press cuttings on the event;
- hold a special meeting/function to thank your team (Whale, 1997: 91).

For a more comprehensive discussion on this topic, refer to chapter 9.

14.4.8 Legal requirements

As the meeting organiser, you may be held responsible for the behaviour of the delegates, damage caused by the delegates, violation of certain laws, cancellation of a meeting, and damage to property. (For a more comprehensive discussion on this topic, refer to chapter 10.)

South African law is complex and every meeting organiser should have a professional lawyer. Services are expensive but not as expensive as being sued – not good for business and image. According to Neethling, Potgieter and Visser (1989: 3), 'the purpose of law is to regulate relations between individuals in a community'.

As this is a very diverse topic, every meeting organiser should become acquainted with the following types of information:

- municipal bylaws (local authorities);
- the Basic Conditions of Employment Amendment Act 11 of 2002;
- the Occupational Health and Safety Amendment Act 181 of 1993 and regulations;
- law of delict/liability;
- criminal procedure;
- the Liquor Amendment Act 57 of 1995;
- the White Paper on the National Disability Strategy.
- Setting up the business
    - the sole proprietorship
    - the partnership
    - the company
    - the close corporation
    - the business trust
    - expenses
    - operating requirements (further reference, chapter 6)

- Taking on staff
  - finding the right person
  - drawing up a contract
  - duties of employees
  - dismissing an employee
  - trade unions (further reference, chapter 6)
- Running the business
  - responsibility to employees
  - hours (further reference, chapter 6)
- Providing services
  - dangers of misleading advertising
  - contracts of sale
  - complaints about service provided
  - fees (further reference, chapter 6)
- Insuring against business hazards
  - policies
  - special insurances
  - keeping insurance up to date
  - claiming
  - other risks (further reference, chapter 10)
- Protecting commercial ideas
  - what to do
  - registering of a design
  - copyright
  - protection of copyrights
  - trademark (further reference, chapter 10)
- Taxcs and VAT
- Business names

(*Reader's Digest,* 1984: 533–570)

It is advisable to obtain relevant information on these issues. Information can be obtained from South African law books and the relevant Acts. Most of all, have a good relationship with a lawyer.

14.4.9 Use of technology

International industry experts have predicted that technology will completely alter the planning of meetings. The focus is on the meeting and what the client needs. It can be difficult finding solutions that work for the South African industry.

What is required is state-of-the-art equipment, high-resolution equipment. Equipment needs to be matched to its application. Instead of purchasing expensive equipment, equipment should be hired.

Delegates also rely on technology as they use Internet and e-mail to stay in contact with their businesses. They are not on holiday: they are working while attending meetings. Another important aspect is that each venue/site should provide staff with the necessary technological expertise during meetings – it just gives that professional touch and, should something go wrong, they are there to assist. Meetings are serious business and must deliver the goods – and this includes the use of state-of-the-art technology (*Meeting, Exhibition & Incentive Guide*, 1998: 7).

Selby (2004: 22) says the days of speakers arriving on site with a 3,5 floppy disk and trying at the 11th hour to borrow a notebook for their presentation have gone. Selby SA is excited to announce a new network facility which will become a virtual wireless network. According to Selby, this network will enable the data and information to be accessed and transferred to required venues in a matter of split seconds. Such a wireless networking service enables the client to use the facility in any venue, non-dependent on any existing or non-existing infrastructure.
It is advised that PCOs keep an eye on the developments regarding technology in this industry and to familiarise themselves with latest developments to enrich the services they provide to the industry.

14.4.10 Some general tips when organising a meeting

- Think through the entire process; cover all your possible areas.
- The most obvious is always forgotten and taken for granted; nothing is to small to cover.
- Keep minutes/records of every meeting (formal/informal) and ensure that everyone involved receives a copy; confirms and agrees.
- Connect any arrangements with your budget (careful for hidden costs).
- Ensure that you draw up contracts for every aspect of your meeting; your contract content will be guided by the nature of your meeting and remember to have the dates of delivery clearly stipulated.
- Ensure that clear communication is focused on, keep all informed all the time.
- Have lots of patience and endurance and remember to be tolerant.

Case study 14.1: Student Tourism Conference, 2–3 October 2002, Cape Technikon, Cape Town

The senior students enrolled in the Tourism Management Programme of the Cape Technikon were challenged with the task of organising a conference for tourism students. The conference was aimed at assembling tourism students to exchange information, to debate and to discuss issues related to tourism education and training. The conference provided these tourism students with the opportunity to apply the relevant event management skills to a real event. The task areas of this conference included:

- event administration
- event budget
- event catering
- event coordination
- event description, programme, social programme
- event exhibition
- event media and public relations
- event speakers
- event sponsorship
- event travel, tours and accommodation.

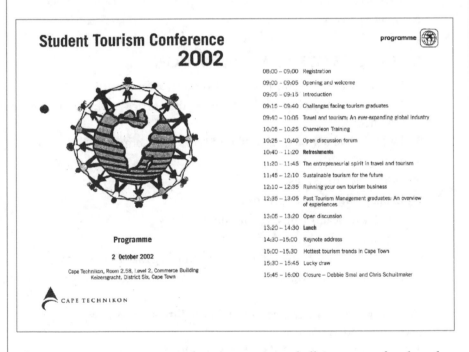

The event was a great success; however, various challenges were faced, such as working with first-time meeting organisers, limited time and restricted resources. Relevant input from industry stakeholders such as SAACI, Western Cape Tourism, Cape Town Convention Bureau and various others assisted the first-time meeting organisers to overcome these challenges by providing professional guidance and sponsorships. The post-tour included was also a great success. The event attracted many delegates from communities around South Africa, as the fee was affordable. It made tourism accessible to many young students who could never attend events because of the high costs. A total of 200 delegates attended the event. A post-evaluation was conducted and the results were very encouraging: 52% of the total delegates rated the event excellent and 48% rated the event very good. Some of the comments received included: 'Keep it up, it was hot'; 'Very professional, looking forward to the next one'; 'Excellent and professional'. The success of this event can be ascribed to the Attitude of those involved. The team was committed from the beginning and worked together as a team.

Browse these Internet sites

- www.conventionbureau@capetown.gov.za
- www.worldofevents.net
- www.saaci.co.za
- www.iccaworld.com
- www.iapco.org

QUESTIONS FOR SELF-EVALUATION

1 Why is meeting organising regarded as 'an art in itself'?
2 Explain the meetings industry in South Africa with specific reference to benefits.
3 Differentiate between the different types of meetings.
4 Why are meetings held?
5 Who holds meetings?
6 Explain why planning is essential.
7 What is a local organising committee?
8 Explain why budgeting is important.
9 What other role players does the meeting organiser network with?
10 Explain how you would go about raising sponsorships for your meeting.

Note: Appendix 14.1 can be found on the Juta Academic web site: www.jutaacademic.co.za
Appendix 14.1 *Examples of meetings organised*

CHAPTER 15

Organising a Carnival

Wren Dry and Greg Damster

AIM OF THE CHAPTER

The aim of this chapter is to enable a person (or group) to stage and organise a carnival.

LEARNING OBJECTIVES

After having studied this chapter, you should be able to:

- understand operational issues and infrastructure;
- outline the factors relevant to the target market;
- explain the importance of theming and programme/event format;
- describe marketing and advertising;
- discuss finance;
- describe risk management, security, alcohol management;
- understand and apply for all permits required for staging a carnival.

15.1 INTRODUCTION

This chapter is based on the Community Chest Maynardville Carnival (better known as The Community Chest Carnival), which is an annual event with trading over a four-day period. Each year the carnival raises in excess of one million rand and attracts more than 100 000 guests. However, bear in mind when staging your own carnival that the Community Chest has been running this carnival for the past 53 years. In 1951 the carnival started out as a Theatrical Garden Party and has grown into the biggest fundraising event on the Community Chest Calendar. It is driven by a small administrative team employed by the Community Chest and is run by more than 9 000 volunteers from service clubs, the international communities and individuals.

15.2 TARGET MARKET

15.2.1 Date and site (Refer to appendix 15.1. on the web site)

Check the Community Calendar for your area and decide on a date and venue.

Where the event is to be held is critical to its success. Determine the target market and ensure that the area is conducive to that market. (*It is no use having a boat race in a desert.*) Remember that whatever you decide on it must be in line with your mission statement.

- **Large town.** A large town offers a complete spectrum of income brackets – from the rich to the poor, evenly spread. This, however, creates a greater demand for diverse entertainment to ensure that all guests enjoy the event.
- **Rural Village.** The inhabitants of a rural village will come mainly from the lower income bracket, with only a small group of wealthy folk.

- Consider public and religious holidays, major sporting and political events, and school/university vacations.
- If your event is to be held outdoors, take the weather and seasons into consideration.
- Remember set-up and clean-up times; if these fall on public holidays, costs could increase unless previously negotiated or the availability of services could be a major cost factor.
- Allow for sufficient time to book the venue. If your event is not date-sensitive or weather dependent, an out-of-season booking will probably be cheaper.

15.2.2 Appropriate entertainment

If your event is aimed at the family (including senior citizens), remember to have a full mix of entertainment, food and attractions that will appeal to all members. There should be adequate seating so that the elderly and parents with young children can rest. When choosing the entertainment there must be something for everyone, for example a tea garden for the older folk, a beer garden for the adult sector, an alcohol-free youth area for the teenager, a fun fair for both the very young and teenagers. Remember that if you are going to have music, noise levels must be taken into consideration and an application for exemption in terms of regulation 7(2) of the Noise Control Regulations P.N.627/1998 must be obtained from your local administration. Please note that these regulations and requirements could vary from administration to administration. (Refer to Appendix 15.2 (on the web site) for an example of a Noise Permit.)

In order to obtain this exemption, all surrounding neighbours (business or residential) must be notified of the event and trading times. Each neighbour must provide written permission for you to proceed with the anticipated sound factor of the event. These letters together with the application for exemption and a full entertainment programme providing times and types of entertainment being provided must then be submitted to the Community Services Health Directorate. Food and beverage outlets should also be selected for the variety of their cuisine (catering for vegetarians and those who do not enjoy hamburgers and chips). Please note that the permission to host from a health permit aspect is obtained from the same local authority.

Always ensure that your venue provides access for the disabled. If the event is being held indoors, ensure that there are ramps and toilet facilities for

© Juta & Co Ltd

wheelchairs. If the event is outdoors, remember that uneven ground can be tricky for wheelchairs, prams and the elderly.

15.2.3 Theme and programme/event format

A theme is essential for any event as it creates cohesion. To avoid any confusion at the actual event, determine how the event is to be run then create a full programme/event format with all the essential events dated and timed. This will prevent being sidetracked and possibly forgetting specific items.

The main attraction of your event must be in line with your theme. This must be the pivotal point with the programme and smaller vents revolving around this. The Community Chest Maynardville Carnival has an international cuisine theme. Volunteers have been sourced from the relevant international communities. The embassies and consuls are committed to the carnival and help with importing the foods relevant to their countries. This guarantees a genuine international flavour and can also reduce importation costs. Most of the foodstuffs imported are donations solicited by the consuls from their countries. The carnival offers the international community a platform to share their culture and cuisine with the communities of this country.

Be aware of your communities' dietary needs, for example kosher, halaal, etc.

15.3 MARKETING AND ADVERTISING

The success of any event depends on a comprehensive marketing and advertising plan. In other words, if people don't know about your event, they won't know they can attend.

15.3.1 Publicity and advertising (Also refer to chapter 8.)

Publicity can make or break your event. Paid media advertising is extremely expensive, so try to enter into a partnership with your local media. Take advantage of free advertising space in your local paper (use the *What's On guide*), radio and television stations. Remember that advertising has the most impact two weeks prior to an event. If your advertising campaign starts earlier it might have the opposite affect. People have short memories and most people don't decide where to go too far in advance. Don't forget to send press releases to all print media agencies; however, there is no guarantee of publication and only if space allows will yours be printed. Your press release must be exciting and have appeal or it will be discarded in favour of one that will appeal to the readership of that publication. A good way to draw media interest is to run a phone-in or SMS competition. Prizes offered can be entry tickets to the event.

Posters and flyers are a great inexpensive tool for advertising your event. Each municipality has rules for the placing of street posters. Printing of posters and flyers can become an expensive exercise try to have one colour (for example black print on red) to reduce costs. Posters and flyers must be bold, concise and to the point. Too much information becomes boring and difficult to read. Recognise that motorists driving by read street posters – use simple and bold writing stating where and when.

Celebrities are a great way of enticing people to your event. By announcing their participation you are automatically advertising your event. If you are staging a charity event, most celebrities will either appear free of charge or have a reduced rate. If you choose a celebrity who is sympathetic to your cause, you have a greater chance that he or she will appear free of charge.

15.3.2 Sponsorship (Also refer to chapter 11.)

Corporate sponsorship is crucial to the financial success of any event. Review previous similar events and the sponsorship of these events. Prepare a written proposal that includes an overview of the event and the number of guests expected to attend. Set up meetings to present your proposal – make sure that you list the benefits for the sponsor. Without benefits to the company you are approaching, you will not receive the sponsor's product if you sponsor accepts, remember to get the acceptance in writing with all the conditions agreed to and the relevant action.

Remember the 'What's in it for me?' rule.

A good way of ensuring that the sponsor knows what is and what can be expected of them is to have a sponsors' manual. The manual should contain other sponsors and the degree of sponsorship, as well as a briefing for the sponsor. Remember to have deadlines for all actions and to indicate who is responsible for such actions. Use the barter system: offer advertising opportunities in return for product/services. Take into account that your organisation's identity needs to be protected. For example, never give full naming rights to the sponsor as the event then becomes synonymous with the sponsor and your organisation, as the event organiser, is forgotten.

Should your event be volunteer-driven, be careful of over branding of sponsors, as the event could be perceived as just another commercial venture.

After the event, don't forget to send written thanks and to follow up on whether the sponsor's expectations were met. Follow through on all commitments and promises to the sponsor and make sure that all financial obligations are finalised. A post-mortem should be held with the organising committee and the sponsors.

If your event is linked to one radio or television station, you will lose the support of rival stations. Should you award sole broadcasting rights, make sure that the station you choose reaches your prescribed target market.

15.4 FINANCE (Also refer to chapter 7.)
15.4.1 Budgets

A finance committee should be appointed. Develop a budget according to necessity, and then add extras that will enhance your event (the *nice to haves but not necessities*). Balance your income with your anticipated expenses, but always keep your financial goal in sight. If your sponsorship does not cover upfront costs, a fundraising drive may be necessary. This should all be taken into account when planning the event.

Some of the expenses you will need to consider before your event will be: publicity, printing and postage, food and beverage, site fees, licences and permits, labour costs, insurance, deposits (rental, entertainers, etc.), decorations, prizes (if no sponsor is found for this).

15.4.2 Yield Management

- *Admission fees*. Research is imperative in this instance. In the case of a fundraising event, the more visitors have to spend on admission, the less they have to spend in the grounds. The Community Chest Carnival has a wide range of admission fees to encourage attendance. Bear in mind that if your entrance fee is too low, it may attract an unwanted element. A good idea is to offer free admission at specified times, for example for an hour on a particularly slow day such as during the week.
- A concession for families is a big draw card to lure guests to an event.
- The complimentary ticket is an invaluable way of saying thank you to sponsors, donors, etc.
- The complimentary ticket is also a way of increasing guest attendance on perceived slow days.
- *Donated goods*. The donation of an item or ingredient does not mean that the selling price should be unrealistically low. The estimated purchase price of a donated product must be taken into account (see case study 15.2 below).
- *Imported goods*. When setting the price for specially imported foods and liquor, the import duty (if applicable), local and international transport costs, VAT, bond store costs and local storage costs (if applicable) must be included when determining the actual cost price.
- *Food outlet prices*. The basic outside market selling price should be a factor when pricing the product (see case study 15.1).
- *Purchasing*. Negotiate a sale or return deal for any product where possible. If you are unable to get this, try for a buy-one-get-one-free deal. Companies may

donate part of the consignment in exchange for branding at the outlet. Always shop around for the best prices and tell suppliers that you can get a better deal at a different place – this often prompts them to conclude a better deal to ensure they get the order.

If your event has trading times that fall outside your suppliers' usual trading hours, check that they can accept and deliver orders after hours. This will prevent loss of income and chaos should you run out of supplies.

Case study 15.1: The Community Chest Maynardville Carnival Formula

The simple formula: the Community Chest applies the following formula for the carnival when determining the selling price of an item:

Cost of ingredient (including wrapping, plate, plastic glass, etc)	R 2,00
Labour cost (your donation) (+ 50%)	1,00
	R 3,00
Mark-up (+ 100%)	R 3,00
SELLING PRICE	R 6,00

Case study 15.2: The example of the 'potato story'

If you are going to use vast quantities of hot potato chips, bear the following in mind when ordering.

The yield from 10 kilos of potatoes when peeled by machine is $7\frac{1}{2}$ kilos compared with the yield of $6\frac{1}{2}$ kilos obtained when the potatoes are peeled by hand. Therefore, unless these potatoes are a donation or obtained at an excellent price, it may be more cost-effective to buy peeled and pre-cut potatoes for chips. They also have a longer shelf life and require less oil when frying. Unopened packs can also be returned to the supplier if stored correctly.

15.5 RISK MANAGEMENT (Also refer to chapter 11.)

Ascertain the areas of risk pertinent to your event.

15.5.1 Public liability

Public liability insurance is essential, but each event will dictate the requirements.

Check with your insurance agent for the cover you will need. Remember that if a member of the public is injured while visiting your venue, you will be held responsible for his or her treatment and this could run into millions — so check what you will be liable for.

15.5.2 Medical services

Consult your local administration about the requirements for the necessary medical services as there are regulations governing public events. Your local St John's First Aid division can be helpful here and a possible cost saver. Alternatively, approach a private hospital/clinic and offer advertising and branding space in return for free medical services during your event. Take into account the possibility of charges being levied for medical services. Always ensure that a first-aid service is available during set-up and dismantling of the event.

15.5.3 Venue Operational Control Centre (VOCC)

This is a centrally situated control centre that is the hub of all security/safety issues and must embody members of the event organisation, disaster management, fire and safety services, the South African Police Services, private security (if applicable) and medical services.

15.5.4 Scaffold and marquee compliance

When erecting marquees/scaffolding ensure the necessary certificates of compliance are obtained from the supplier.

If you are selling alcohol at your event, it is a good idea to have a 'recovery' tent available for those who may have overindulged. This unfortunately has the downside of having to be manned and it is a good idea to approach your local army depot for extra volunteer manpower for this facility.

15.6 OPERATIONAL AND ORGANISATIONAL ISSUES

15.6.1 Permission to host a Public Event

- *Population participation.* Prior to hosting a public event, permission must be obtained from the Building Survey division of your local authority. (Appendix 15.1 — on the web site — illustrates a layout plan.) In order to obtain this, plans must be submitted detailing the following:
- Size of venue
- Ablution facilities
- Public entrances and exits
- Emergency exits
- Vehicular access

- Staging facilities and temporary grandstands
- Marquees– size must be clearly indicated
- Gas facilities and equipment to be used
- Gas bulk storage facility
- Storage facilities
- Medical facilities
- VOCC
- *Population Certificate.* Check with your local administration whether a Population Certificate is required to host your event. Should this be necessary, the following information will be required: square meterage of usable public area; erf no.; number of floors (for indoor event) and name of landowner.
- *Smoking.* In compliance with the smoking regulations, smoking in a marquee is prohibited. Clear and visible signage must be displayed to indicate smoking and non-smoking areas. These areas must be monitored at all times.

15.6.2 Parking and traffic controls

- *Parking/public transport.* One of the biggest frustrations for guests at any event is the lack of adequate parking. When choosing a venue, make sure that there is adequate parking available and also remember to secure this area. The venue should also have an adequate public transport infrastructure close by. An option might be a ferry system from the parking area or public transport depot, but take into consideration that this will push up costs. If guests can't get to your venue, you might have no guests!
- *Traffic control.* The laws governing residential, public and private roads are varied and complex. At any event emergency services must have clear access to and from the venue. The local traffic/fire and ambulance services must be consulted on these issues when any large event is planned. Please note that this service can attract an exceptionally large bill. Negotiate upfront with your local traffic division for reduction in costs and ensure you get a written response.

15.6.3 Power supply

Ascertain prior to the event what power supplies are available at the chosen venue and also what supply all the participants will need. Bear in mind that if you have to have electricity supplied to your venue, there will be connection costs.

- *Electricity.* If you as the organiser are supplying the necessary electrical facilities, a qualified electrician must be appointed and available at all times. Determine the basic electrical services to be supplied, for example power points, light fittings, etc. Power supply of electrical equipment used by exhibitors/stallholders must be conveyed to the electrician, for example 3 phase, 15 amp, etc. This all helps to prevent power failures during trading times when the power output is at its highest. A suspension of power results in a loss of income, breach of security and a safety hazard to all. A good idea is to have a dress rehearsal when all your stallholders/exhibitors can check the power supplies and this also gives the electrician a chance to iron out any problems prior to paying guests entering the venue. A generator might be needed to either supplement the power supply or to be used as a back-up system.

- **Power installation.** Once the power installation has been completed a compliance certificate must be obtained from the accredited person (the installation electrician) confirming that the installation has taken place in compliance with the Occupational Health and Safety Act 85 of 1993.

- **Gas.** Prior to trading, an application must be lodged with the local administration for a Flammable Substance Certificate. Without this certificate your event will be shut down. (Appendix 15.4 — on the web site — illustrates an application for a flammable certificate.) The following steps must be adhered to in order to obtain a Flammable Substance Certificate:
  - A full layout plan of the venue indicating all gas usage areas, gas storage areas, fire extinguishers and medical assistance
  - A layout plan of the stall indicating where the gas will be used, the relevant overhead cover and distances between gas users, equipment and neighbouring stalls
  - A layout plan of the gas storage area (Appendix 15.3 — on the web site — illustrates a plan of a gas storage area)
  - The size of gas bottles to be used must also be indicated (19 kg maximum).

When using gas equipment on wooden tables, always make sure that non-combustible/heat-resistant material (for example asbestos) is placed between the burner and table to prevent burning or damaging the wood.

- **Open Fire.** All safety rules apply. Ascertain if your venue is in a *smoke-free zone* before deciding on this option.

  Note: *Fire extinguishers and the necessary information and warning signage must be visibly displayed.*

Plastic aprons are always hazardous in a heat-generating environment.

15.6.4 Sanitation (Also refer to chapter 6.)

Ascertain the facilities available at the chosen venue and complement these with adequate temporary services. Guests may be deterred from attending an event if there are insufficient toilet facilities.

- **Toilet facilities.** First ascertain the availability of temporary toilet facilities from your local council or municipality and building industry as this could reduce costs. Where supplementing is needed, negotiate for sponsorship or donations with local suppliers of temporary/mobile facilities. An attendant in these facilities is advisable to ensure that sufficient supplies of toilet paper and soap are available at all times. The temporary facilities must be serviced regularly during your event to avoid possible overflowing.

- **Plumbing.** If there is an insufficient permanent water supply, temporary facilities must be installed. This applies mainly to an event where food is prepared and consumed, as running water must be available at these outlets in order to comply with health regulations.
- **Hygiene.** The health requirements dictated by your local authority must be you guideline here.
- **Refuse.** Adequate refuse collection services must be employed and sufficient refuse bins must be strategically placed throughout the venue to ensure a clean and hygienic environment for your guests.

 Recycling waste products such as tins, cardboard, etc is an invaluable source of extra income. If you are unable to manage the collection for recycling, contact a local organisation (for example a school, church, welfare agency, etc) to offer them the opportunity. This also serves to confirm your commitment to the community.

15.6.5 Security (Also refer to chapter 10.)

No event should be held without being properly secured. Ensuring the safety of ideas, guests, organisers and assets is of paramount importance. In today's climate of indiscriminate violence in South Africa, security at any public event is extremely important.

Security services must be arranged in conjunction with the South African Police Services, where necessary the South African Defence Force and with private security companies. Bear in mind that an excessive visibility of South African Police Services in uniform can have a negative effect.

Security can incur enormous costs and eat away at any budget; however, a private company registered with the South African National Security Association or the Security Officers Board is advisable because of their credibility. Many security companies will say that they are able to deal with all situations or that they have a large enough force to handle the event, yet they may not have the necessary experience or qualifications.

Whichever security company you choose to have at your event, take into account screening and obtaining references from a wide spectrum of clients can reduce the risk of possibly choosing the wrong company. Security personnel are highly visible and therefore act as public relations officers for your event; they should be forceful but polite at all times.

15.6.6 Venue security

In the case of an outdoor venue, ensure that the site is properly secured, for example fencing, walls, gates, etc. An insecure perimeter is an open invitation to the more adventurous at heart that will attempt to enter without paying.

Security should be strategically deployed to prevent unscrupulous people from entering with the intention of selling products that are in direct competition with stallholders, not paying an entrance fee and possibly bringing in illegal substances. This will also be a deterrent for individuals who have the intention of illegally removing goods from the venue.

15.6.7 Gate security (Also refer to chapter 6.)

- *Vehicle access*. All vehicles entering or exiting the premises must be searched. It is a good idea to minimise vehicle access to the main public area, both form a security and safety point of view. Restricted hours of access of vehicles to public areas are imperative to control the movement of goods and to ensure the safety of guests.

A central drop-off zone for deliveries will ensure the control of distribution and collection of goods. An internal delivery system must be in place if this option is used.

- *Guest entrances*. Signage must be prominently displayed, informing the guests of the rules of the venue, for example right of admission reserved, no firearms, no dangerous weapons, no alcohol may be brought onto the premises, etc. A safe for the safe storage of firearms should be provided as a courtesy to guests.

Signage must include the following: **Failure to comply with the rules could result in access to the venue being denied the guest.**

- *Wristbands*. Using wristbands as an entry ticket, whilst more expensive than a printed ticket, has numerous benefits. Two colours can be used — to identify guests over 18 and those under 18 years old. This is of immediate assistance to liquor stallholders and the security force in enabling them to identify under-18s who try to buy alcohol for their own consumption.

  If your event is being held over a few days, different coloured wristbands can be used for each day so that guests cannot use the same 'ticket' to gain entrance on a different day. Security can quickly locate guests who haven't paid if their wristband is not being worn or if it is the wrong colour.

  A way of minimising costs is to use only one colour of wristband for either over- or under-18s; however, this could result in a loss of entrance income by guests gaining access without paying the entrance fee.

- *Random searches of person and baggage/apparel*. These must be conducted in a manner prescribed by the law. High visibility of signage warning of these searches is imperative and must be placed at all entrances and exits.
- *Celebrity guests*. All high-profile guests (mayors, parliamentarians, entertainers, etc.) must have adequate security. These requirements must be negotiated with the in-house security team.
- *Security of money*. Every event involving the exchange of money or goods will attract a criminal element. Checks and balances must be put in place for the handling of cash in any situation. This particularly applies to events where volunteers are used who may not necessarily be au fait with issues around the handling of money in public areas.
- *Movement of money*. Strict security measures must be in place for the movement of money coming into and leaving the venue, being transported within the venue and at any ATM facility within the venue. The professional security personnel appointed will advise on these needs.

15.6.8 Identification badges

- *Workers*. It is necessary to identify all persons who are working on site. Such badges should be spit into various categories with different colours for quick identification, for example volunteers, cleaning crew, entertainers, stall holders, etc.

 At a volunteer-driven event always boldly print VOLUNTEER on the badge as this is a form of recognition for their time and effort.

- *Vehicles*. A deliver sticker must always be displayed to gain access to the site. This must be on every vehicle (private or commercial) that needs access. Security of the grounds is very important and the drop-off zone here will help contain the number of vehicles on the grounds. This will also help to prevent the unauthorised removal of goods from the grounds. Security cannot always check everything going in and coming out of the site, so to ensure maximum security it is advisable to limit access to the stalls. Random checks of all vehicles are a good deterrent for people trying to remove goods from the grounds.
- *Parking*. This sticker identifies who is entitled to park in designated areas, for example Celebrities Park closer to the venue and workers should have secure parking that is for their use only and not available to the general public. These arrangements should not be in breach of your security procedure. Event workers are first to arrive and last to leave, therefore secure parking facilities should be available and can be regarded as a perk at your event

Ensure that al the above badges/stickers cannot be simply reproduced – for example, use a recorded number system to prevent photocopying and do not use a ticket available for sale at commercial outlets such as stationers. Two colours are advisable, but be aware that this will push up printing costs.

15.6.9 Alcohol management

Whenever alcohol is introduced, the occurrences of public disorder rise. It is very important that your organisation is clear about how it will manage alcoholic products available at the event. It is also the responsibility of the licence holder to ensure the safety of all guests. A policy should be drawn up on alcohol management at your event; this should include the following:

- purchasing;
- terms of sale;
- hours of salc;
- transportation;
- distribution;
- licensing;
- storage;
- closure and distribution.

If you need assistance with drawing up this policy, talk to your local law enforcement agency, your insurance agents and the Liquor Board.

- **Liquor licence.** Whenever alcohol is dispensed at an event, the necessary temporary liquor licence must be obtained in advance. Written approval from the landowner/landlord must accompany your application for a liquor licence.
- **Rules.** All the legal rules and regulations must be displayed at the alcohol outlets – for example, signage stating that no alcohol may be sold to under-18. It is advisable to get the convenor of the liquor outlet to sign an undertaking to ensure that the rules of the liquor licence are adhered to. Appendix 15.5 (on the web site) illustrates such an undertaking, which should help to reduce alcohol abuse at your venue. When alcohol is sold, there should be a minimum of a 100% mark-up on the selling price.

It is always a good idea to up the age limit in order to prevent alcohol abuse by youngsters. Always put up clear signage stating the age that one needs to be in order to purchase alcohol. Take into consideration that you are the licence holder and can set the age limit. The bad publicity received because of the youth who abuse alcohol will be far more damaging that the few complaints you will receive from those who are unable to purchase alcohol. This is especially the case if you have a sponsor and/or your event is charity-related.

15.7 OPERATIONS SCHEDULING PLAN (Also refer to Chapters 5, 6 & 9.)

To ensure the success of any event or function, draw up a scheduling plan of all the tasks that need to be done to avoid any last-minute panic situations. Appendix 15.6 (on the web site) illustrates a basic scheduling plan.

At the initial planning meetings draw up a list of all the key duties and write these in the space provided. A champion is needed to ensure that these duties are completed on time. Several subgroups may be needed to complete the tasks. There must always be someone who is held accountable to ensure that the job is done.

There should be a minimum of two deadline dates that coincide with meeting dates. Should any problems arise in completing the tasks, they can be sorted out at the first deadline date. Depending on the timing available before the event, there should be as many meetings as possible to ensure that all the tasks are completed. All agreements entered into should always be confirmed in writing and have a penalty clause that can cover any financial losses incurred.

15.8 THANKS/ACCREDITATION (Also refer to Chapter 11.)

Thanking sponsors, donors, volunteers, etc as soon as possible after the event is imperative to ensure their continued support. In the thank you letters state the net amount and whether the target was achieved. If you did not achieve your target, end on a positive note for the success of the next event. If your target was achieved, state the next target (which should be larger) and extend an invitation to them to join in the success of the next event.

A Certificate of Appreciation could be used and presented. These are easily drawn up with a computer and a scanner for the logos. Try to avoid giving gifts as a token of thanks, especially if it is a charity event and you are thanking donors. This could have a negative affect, such as 'they have too much money if they can afford to give away things', unless these are donated. If this is the case say so.

Case study 15.3: The history of the Community Chest Carnival

The carnival started out in 1951 as 'The Theatrical Garden Party' and was held in De Waal Park, Cape Town. In 1962 it moved to Maynardville Park, Wynberg, Cape Town (where it has remained ever since) and became known as the 'Community Chest Carnival'.

It is the major annual fundraising and public relations event on the Community Chest Calendar. Over the four-day carnival trading period, 9 000 volunteer workers from across the social and professional spectrum are to be seen lending a hand at the many tasks involved in running a carnival of this magnitude.

The construction of the carnival village takes five weeks; some 5 000 kilometres of coloured lighting are used; 26 400 rolls are consumed over the carnival period; a ton of calamari and half a ton of boerewors are eaten! The carnival sells 45 000 drinks of Coca-Cola products (this entire quantity is a donation by Peninsula Beverage) and Premier Milling donates one and a half tons of flour used in the preparation of the various dishes sold at the carnival. These are but two of the many sponsors that donate either a product or a service (whichever may be required) to ensure the cost-effectiveness and smooth running of the carnival.

The 'national stalls' are a major attraction of the carnival. Mainly members of the international community run these stalls, with strong local resident backing as well as from the Consular Corp representing their home nation or country. Many consuls are found working alongside their fellow nationals and the major nations also provide entertainment to reinforce the cultural experience that this 'window' to their country provides.

These national stalls are complemented by the many smaller stalls which play a vital role in providing a diverse range of products and attractions ... these guarantee that there is something for everyone at the carnival.

The function of the main open-air arena stage – sited as it is in the centre of the carnival village – is to entertain patrons between their visits to the stalls. The arena events are also a draw card to the public via a well-publicised programme of events both before and during the carnival. The carnival now attracts more than 100 000 people over the four-day period.

It would be difficult to find another event anywhere in the world where so many work together for the same cause at no personal financial gain to themselves. The whole experience of being involved adds up to something magical and many of our volunteers come back year after year.

It is always a source of amusement that every year at the end of the carnival when tired helpers are packing the carnival back 'into its box', they are heard to say – 'Definitely, never again' and in the same breath – 'we must remember to do this that way next year ...'

15.9 SUMMARY

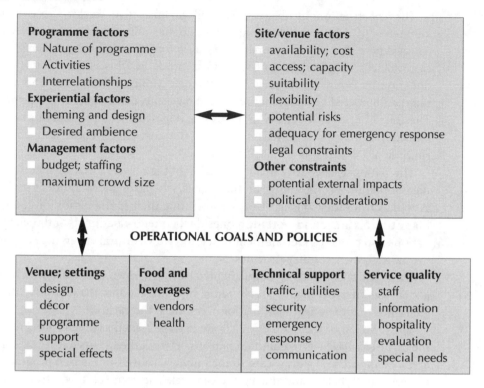

Programme factors
- Nature of programme
- Activities
- Interrelationships

Experiential factors
- theming and design
- Desired ambience

Management factors
- budget; staffing
- maximum crowd size

Site/venue factors
- availability; cost
- access; capacity
- suitability
- flexibility
- potential risks
- adequacy for emergency response
- legal constraints

Other constraints
- potential external impacts
- political considerations

OPERATIONAL GOALS AND POLICIES

Venue; settings
- design
- décor
- programme support
- special effects

Food and beverages
- vendors
- health

Technical support
- traffic, utilities
- security
- emergency response
- communication

Service quality
- staff
- information
- hospitality
- evaluation
- special needs

Browse these Internet sites:

http://iafrica.com/highlife/goodlife/gourmetfestival/224978.htm
http://www.festivals.com/
http://www.ipanema.com/carnival/home.htm
http://www.nationalcherryblossomfestival.org/

www.capetownevents.org
www.cheesefestival.co.za
www.comchest.org.za

QUESTIONS FOR SELF-EVALUATION

1 Name the factors relevant to your target market.
2 Name the important factors in yield management.
3 Name and explain the operation and organisational issues that must be taken into consideration when planning a carnival.
4 Describe the permits necessary for staging a carnival.

Note: Appendices 15.1 to 15.6 can be found on the Juta Academic web site: www.jutaacademic.co.za

Appendix 15.1 *A full layout plan of grounds: an example*
Appendix 15.2 *An application for noise control permit: an example*
Appendix 15.3 *Gas storage layout: an example*
Appendix 15.4 *Flammable Substance Certificate Application: an example*
Appendix 15.5 *Undertaking to be signed by the convenor of a liquor outlet: an example*
Appendix 15.6 *Basic scheduling plan: an example*

CHAPTER 16

Sports Event Management

Kamilla Swart

AIM OF THE CHAPTER

This chapter looks at the management of sports events from a practical perspective.

LEARNING OBJECTIVE

After having studied this chapter, you should be able to:

- adopt a practical approach to sports event management.

16.1 SPORTS EVENT MANAGEMENT: A PRACTICAL APPROACH

Nb

In order to stage a sports event, you must be able to:

- effectively plan the event;
- ensure and facilitate the involvement and participation of all the possible role players;
- coordinate the entire process leading up to the actual event as well as post-event;
- understand the needs of your customer and ensure that the event attracts players and spectators alike and satisfies their needs as well as the needs of the sponsor;
- ensure that the event is organised in such a manner that it meets the requirements of the game, players, spectators and sponsors, thus ensuring that they all look forward to the next game;
- function effectively under pressure;
- continuously monitor and evaluate the event and make the required adjustments to solve problem areas.

In order to successfully manage a sports event, the sports event manager or the event management team should have the following qualities:

- Meticulous – attention to detail is of paramount importance
- Creative and innovative – open to change
- Energetic and enthusiastic
- Diplomatic but also persuasive and forceful
- Diligent, committed and hardworking
- Positive – a 'can do' attitude is necessary
- Preferably experienced in event management.

Can you add any other ability/skill to this list?

Irrespective of size, all events require a high degree of planning, a range of skills and a lot of energy (Parks and Recreation New Zealand, 2002: 2). Careful and detailed planning is highly significant in order to avoid and/or to resolve potential problems. The next sections (16.1.1–16.1.3), as outlined by Rossouw (2000: 413–419), provide guidelines as to how you should plan and what to consider in your attempts to effectively organise the sports event, be it a local derby (Ajax CT vs. Santos), a tournament (SA Tennis Open) or a prestigious marathon (Old Mutual Two Oceans Marathon).

16.1.1 Before the event: can we really organise the event?

It has often happened that attempts to organise a sports event have failed because the organiser chose the wrong event to promote, had too many other things to do, or was unable to organise the event due to lack of knowledge, skills, etc.

You must be completely confident that you are able to organise the specific event in mind, before embarking upon it.

The sports event manager will have to organise:
- ordinary games – for instance league games from week to week, or
- special events – for instance a one-day or week-long tournament. On a local level, these events are usually organised to generate funds, market the team or club, and/or to create community involvement. On a national or international level, these events are generally organised to meet the same type of requirements but for more professional reasons. Events have become big business, thus the value of the event from a sponsor's perspective is increasingly important.

Before you attempt to organise a specific game/special event, take note of the following key factors:
- Is this event a good idea?
- Do we have the right skills available?
- Will the community accept this game – who are the role players?
- Who will participate/be a spectator? What class of athletes?
- Do we have the right infrastructure (for example facilities, equipment, emergency services)?
- Where will it be held?
- Will we be able to attract players and spectators?
- Will we attract media support?
- Who will support us (sponsors, etc.)?
- If there are costs involved, will we be able to cover them?

In this section the importance of making sure of your ability to organise a game was identified. It is essential to consult the guidelines listed before deciding to organise a game.

16.1.2 Planning

As stated earlier, the success of an event/game is to a large extent determined by how well and how thorough planning has been undertaken by the organiser and the committee. Preparation is the key to any successful event.

16.1.2.1 Guidelines for planning

Step 1: Forming an organising committee

- It is important for the sports event manager not to attempt to do everything. The involvement of other players, officials, parents or friends is important. Here is the perfect opportunity to involve them by forming an organising committee. The key players should have a mix of the following skills: financial, marketing, operational and legal. Through the delegation of tasks it will be easier to complete the arrangements in time. This is of particular importance with special events. The organising committee should be set up well in advance of the event.
- Terms of reference for the organising committee should be set up, for example who are they responsible to, duties they are to undertake, specific reporting dates, etc.
- It is necessary to list the names and addresses of the committee members and to have regular status meetings. The progress of various event organisational aspects will be tracked during these meetings.
- It is necessary to appoint a sport event manager who will be responsible for the overall planning, coordination and evaluation of the event. The sports event manager should liaise with the organising committee, the community and the officials. Depending on the level of the event, a professional event management company may be employed to organise the event.

Step 2: Setting the objective of the game

An objective is something you want to achieve in the future.

- Before you can host any game, you must be certain of what you want to achieve. It could be only to provide exercise for your players, to promote goodwill between different teams or, in the case of special events, to promote the club, to generate funds or increase brand awareness and drive sales for the sponsors.

Step 3: Selecting an event

- Identify who your target market for the event will be. This is a significant factor in determining all the other elements of the event. If your audience is not reached by all aspects of your event, it could fail miserably.

- Allow sufficient time to organise the event. Generally, two to four months is required for a community event, while larger events require planning for more than a year.
- In terms of timing of the event, avoid clashes with other tournaments and fixtures and try to ensure that it fits into the school, provincial, regional and/or national calendar. One would also need to consider clashes with non-sports events in your community, for example a Youth Day celebration as well as clashes with an event television broadcast, for example Kaizer Chiefs vs. Orlando Pirates. Stipulate or estimate the number of entrants or teams and allocate enough time to complete the event, allowing for unforeseen problems such as adverse weather conditions. It is also necessary to consider set-up and breakdown times required, the event schedule of the participating sports federation and the arrival and departure times of participants.
- Venue capacity, location, facilities and 'fit' all influence the choice of the venue for the event. The venue size should be appropriate to the necessary accommodation of the technical requirements of the competition. The venue should be accessible to the public from a transportation perspective and should also have facilities relevant to the scale of the event being staged, e.g. ablution facilities, disability access, catering facilities, etc. Finally, the venue has to fit the profile of the event being staged, i.e. fit with the sponsor's brand and objectives.

Step 4: Setting up a checklist
- This checklist should contain *all* the activities that need to be completed in order for the game to be hosted. The checklist should also contain a space for the person responsible, as well as a D-day for that specific activity. Remember to continuously monitor the checklist to ensure that assignments are carried out (see section 16.4).

16.1.2.2 General tips
- Use a checklist when organising your game and modify this checklist to suit your specific needs (for example, book the stadium according to the number of participants and spectators you anticipate will attend).
- Try to involve all the important role players in your community in the event. This is particularly significant in the organising of a special event. Be sure not to offend any individual or group in your community (religious, political, interest or cultural).
- The invitations, notifications and entry forms for the event and the participants should be sent out long before the game to ensure that you can plan for the number of people attending.
- If it is necessary and possible, try to attract the local media, for example the local community newspaper, radio, etc. to promote your event.

- Market the event through applying advertising, personal selling, sales promotion and publicity creation techniques.
- If you are not sure how successful your proposed event will be, try the following:
  - consult another area where such an event has taken place;
  - find out how successful it was;
  - ask about the problems;
  - check the costs and profits if any;
  - ask if you would have the same problems in your region.
- Try to get assistance from your local sporting bodies and code to help you with equipment and planning, especially when it is the first event you organise.
- Set up a sound budget of all possible income and expenses.
- Conduct a study on how the event will benefit your community economically and socially, and take steps to minimise the risks. Put an environmental management plan in place, for example the allocation of rubbish bins for litter, acceptable levels of sound, etc.
- Third party contracting is an essential part of sports event management as one particular company does not supply all the elements to make an event happen. The most common third-party contracts include the following:
  - catering
  - scaffolding
  - sound equipment
  - sport-specific technical equipment (beach volleyball area, boxing ring, etc.)
  - stage and lighting
- Always make sure that you have contingency plans as backup for original plans that do not work (for example, have a referee on stand-by if the assigned referee does not show up).

From this section it should be clear that proper planning can ensure that the organisation of your sports event runs smoothly, without your having to deal with surprises and mishaps.

16.1.3 The day of the game

If you have planned properly according to the checklist, everything should be in place for the day of the game.

Here is a list of important factors to be considered on the day of the game:

- *Format of the competition*. The event format looks at the duration of the event, and the schedule that will be used during that time. Is it a normal game or, in the case of special events, a tournament in the form of a round robin or knockout?

- **_Honorary guests_**. Honorary guests like sponsors and local leaders are very important and special attention should be paid to the care of these persons (VIPs). It is important that the person assigned to take care of these people is aware of who the dignitaries are in order to prevent embarrassment. The designated incumbent should also be sufficiently skilled in terms of protocol, for example the manner in which the invitations are addressed, seating arrangements, etc.
- **_Players_**. Players should be made as comfortable as possible (for example, change rooms should be clean and transport should have been arranged if necessary).
- **_Refreshments_**.
  - For honoured guests and players – involve club- and/or family members with preparations for local events. Ensure that dietary requirements are met, vegetarian, halaal, kosher, etc.
  - For spectators – ensure that sufficient products are available to sell to raise funds for the club as well as sufficient variety to meet the needs of spectators.
- **_Merchandising_**. Merchandising involves the selling of official goods (caps, T-shirts, balls, etc.).

Before deciding on the purchase of products to sell at the game, you must ensure that you will obtain the best quality for your money and that there would be enough buyers to merit such a venture.

- **_Liability_**. What happens if a player or spectator gets injured at your match and the wrong treatment is administered? Turco, Riley and Swart (2002: 121) caution that, while the sport event manager does not have to protect the participant or spectator from every conceivable risk, reasonable care must be taken to protect them from the most serious potential hazards. Thus the sports event manager must be equipped to deal with emergency medical or security problems that may occur in a large public gathering.
- **_Letters of consent and indemnity_**. Consent must be obtained from parents or guardians of under-aged children participating and indemnity forms from adult participants. Clear notices must be placed at the entrances to the stadium indicating the indemnity from expenses arising from injuries and loss or damage to property of spectators and players. This assists in indemnifying the organisers from claims resulting from the above.
- **_Safety and security_**. Try to involve the local services (for example the SA Police Services and ambulance services) to assist with these matters. A safety and security representative could serve on the organising committee to ensure efficiency with regard to emergency matters. A disaster management plan should also be put in place, with a spokesperson appointed to deal with the media in the event of a major disaster occurring at your event.

- *Closing-down.*
  - Arrange for a closing ceremony to acknowledge the performance of the teams/participants.
  - All sponsors and other VIPs involved must be thanked by means of written or verbal communication on or as soon as possible after the day.
- *Post-match evaluation.*
  - Consult your planning checklist to ascertain which tasks were performed incorrectly or not at all and try to rectify for future reference.
  - Try to establish from players and spectators which aspects can be improved upon, so that you can do better when organising future games.
  - Keep a record of all incidents, both good and bad, in order to formulate a comprehensive evaluation report. An official impact study conducted by an independent party can also assist in organisational improvement of future events. This report is important for sponsors, federations and all role players, as the report can confirm the success or failure of the event.
  - Sponsors often insist on these evaluations and they should be done as a matter of course.

This section indicated the importance of devoting attention to the finer details to ensure success on the day of the game.

Case study 16.1 provides an example of some of the results of a socio-economic impact study conducted by an independent research agency on behalf of the City of Durban. The 2003 Commonwealth Stillwater Championships was held in Durban from the 2–5 July 2003 at the Kings Park swimming pool and the last day was held at North Beach. The event attracted 11 participating countries including Botswana, Swaziland, Lesotho, Indonesia, Sri Lanka, Northern Ireland, Ireland, England, Canada, Australia and New Zealand.

16.1.4 Final aspects for consideration

- Don't ever overlook details.
- Don't ever count on the availability of a venue until everything is in writing.
- Don't forget to have written contracts with all third party suppliers.
- Don't try to organise an event you don't know anything about.
- Don't forget to involve all role players.
- Don't forget the importance of financial planning if money is involved.
- Don't underestimate the value of volunteers.
- Don't underestimate the importance of planning.

Case study 16.1: Socio-economic Impact Study of the 2003 Commonwealth Stillwater Championships

(Source: Durban Events Corporation, 2003, 1–7)

Economic evaluation

The volume attendance at the events was 3 425. Most of the respondents (69%) attending the event indicated that they spent money (Table 28, Appendix 1). Purchases were on food and refreshments (65%), photos of event (5%) and clothes (1%). The average daily expenditure of people attending the event was calculated to be R42. As stated earlier, 69% of the total number of spectators attending the event purchased items. This would imply that 2 364 persons spent an average of R42 at the event. This translates into R99 288 being generated for the Durban economy in terms of peoples' daily expenditure at the event. In terms of the accommodation industry, 55% of the respondents were tourists. Of this 14,5% stayed in luxury hotels, 5,5% in holiday flats, 38,2% in family hotels, 25,5% in bed and breakfast establishments, 1,8% in holiday homes and 14,5% with friends and family. The average number of days spent in paid accommodation was 6,6 nights. The average rate per hotel room during the event period was calculated to be R350. Since 9,2% of the tourists staying in paid accommodation indicated that they came specifically for the lifesaving event or scheduled their visits to Durban to coincide with the event, the direct economic impact of the accommodation industry on the Durban Unicity was R202 096. From the above estimations, it can be deduced that the total revenue generated in terms of peoples' daily expenditure (R99 288) and from the accommodation industry (R202 096) that can be attributed directly to the event is R301 384.

Demographic profile of spectators

Forty-nine percent of the respondents were males and 51% were females. In terms of historical race classification (Table 39, Appendix 1), the event attracted Whites (58%), Coloureds (15%), Indians (14%) and Africans (13%). Respondents interviewed ranged in ages from less than 20 years to 70 years. The average age of respondents was calculated to be 38 years. Residents from the Durban Unicity (40%) were dominant amongst respondents. The visitors from other South African provinces came from Gauteng (15%), Western Cape (8%) and Eastern Cape (2%). International visitors came from New Zealand (4%), Lesotho (2%), Mozambique (1%), Scotland (1%), Sri Lanka (1%), Australia (3%), Namibia (1%), Botswana (1%), Britain (3%) and Canada (1%).

Factors influencing decision to attend the event

The following were the main influencing agents:

- Word of mouth   83%
- Participants   31%
- Newspaper ads   2%
- Television   1%

Sponsor identification and perception

An important component of the study was the identification of sponsors by respondents. All the respondents were able to identify at least one sponsor of the event. Twelve sponsors were identified in total. The main sponsors identified are listed below:

- Barclays   51%
- Suncoast Casino   26%
- SA Lifesaving   7%
- Commonwealth   5%

Perception of/attitudes toward the event and the Durban Unicity

The respondents rated their event experience in the following way:

- Excellent   19%
- Good   63%
- Okay   18%

This section indicated that, when a game is successful, the benefits can be much more than a healthy profit. A well-staged game can put a community 'on the map' and provide a community or region with a sense of pride and confidence. This is one of the best ways to bind communities and take people's minds off the differences and difficulties of everyday life (Rossouw, 2000: 417).

16.1.5 Generating volunteers

Most events rely on volunteers to create a successful event (Turco *et al*, 2002: 112). They add that volunteers may be committed to the event but they may not necessarily have the required qualifications to perform the job successfully. Hence recruiting, training and maintaining the volunteer base is critical.

The first step will be to break down the operation plan into tasks required so that one can determine the number of volunteers, with the appropriate skills and abilities, required to host the event (Turco *et al*, 2002: 112). The next phase will be recruitment. Wilkinson (1988, cited by Turco *et al*, 2002: 112) notes that various organisations such as schools, community organisations and related government departments can be contacted for volunteer recruitment. Furthermore, educational institutions are an important source of volunteers as projects and internships can be tailored to include students in the event (Getz, 1997: 189).

Volunteers can be recruited in several ways, ranging from personal contact to various advertising modes, for example public service announcements (PSAs), bulletin boards and flyers. Catherwood and Van Kirk (1992: 96) note that the PSAs, which run anywhere from 30 to 60 seconds when read, usually have a telephone number at the end of the message so that the volunteer will know who and where to call. The spots may be aired by local radio and TV stations. News releases with the same slant should be sent to local print media, as well as any publications that may be published by civic groups or the local chamber of commerce. The event itself can be an influential medium of recruitment as a stall with information on how to volunteer can be assembled (Turco *et al.*, 2002: 113). They add that pertinent information relevant to the potential volunteer such as the name, address, phone number, skills, interest, time availability and prior experience should be filed.

Orientation and training of volunteers are critical in ensuring that the volunteers fulfil their responsibilities, grow within the organisation, and develop their potential (Getz, 1997: 199). Support and recognition are essential in promoting a sense of belonging and commitment to the event. Material recognition often includes uniforms, pins, free admission, etc. However, it is important to stress that the genuine reward is in the task itself. It is evident that volunteers play a crucial role in the success of your event, and it is advisable that sport event managers acknowledge the significance of the volunteer workforce.

Case study 16.2: Volunteer Programme of the ICC CWC
(Source: South African Sports Commission, 2003: Internet)

Two thousand seven hundred and ten volunteers were utilised for the ICC Cricket World Cup 2003 (ICC CWC 2003) hosted by South Africa. The volunteer database contains the details of every individual that volunteered for, and participated in, the ICC CWC 2003. A fulltime Volunteer Manager, along with a national committee, was responsible for the overseeing of the project, including:

- the development of the event-specific unit standards;
- the setting of criteria for the day-to-day management of the volunteers at the respective stadiums;
- the development of the recruitment criteria for volunteers;
- the development of the curriculum and training schedule for the training of volunteers, and
- the selection of training facilitators.

The national committee comprised representatives from within the sporting fraternity, THETA (the hospitality and education training authority), and other relevant bodies.

Volunteers were selected countrywide to act, amongst others, as ushers, car park attendants, information kiosk attendants, VIP assistants, media and media accreditation assistants; queue busters and magnetometer attendants. The scale of the ICC CWC 2003 demanded a thorough training programme. Topics such as Functioning in a Team, Organising Oneself in a Workplace, Occupational Health and Safety and, most significantly, Customer Care all formed part of the curriculum.

In addition, the volunteers were exposed to cricket matches at various venues around the country, for practical, hands-on experience. In so doing, the volunteers not only had an opportunity to implement the theory learnt, but it also provided them with the occasion to familiarise themselves with the venue where each would be stationed. It further allowed them to assess their readiness for the actual World Cup, and to improve on areas that still required further training and development.

'We specifically designed the programme to include customer care because of the anticipated numbers of international guests and tourists that would flock to South Africa for the Cricket World Cup. As South Africa's ambassadors, we acknowledged the key role that our volunteers would play, and thus believed that it was our responsibility to sufficiently empower them so that they would reflect our country's robust hospitality, and showcase our ability to host international events of this magnitude,' said Dr Bacher (Director of the ICC CWC 2003).

16.1.6 Safety, security and risk management implications

Risk management is becoming increasingly important for the success and survival of any event (Turco *et al*, 2002: 122). It includes the process of anticipating, preventing or minimising the potential costs, losses or problems for the event. No matter how big or small your event, the attention given to risk management, loss prevention and safety is of crucial concern when prospective insurance underwriters, investors, sponsors and spectators evaluate the benefit of their participation (Rossouw, 2000: 418).

Levine (1988, cited by Turco *et al*, 2002: 122–123) notes that a comprehensive risk management plan will take the following into consideration:

- Identify all areas of potential risk (risk analysis).
- Exclude or reduce risk by conducting training programmes, safety programmes and inspection procedures.
- Establish protective funds for risks that cannot be eliminated.
- Implement a risk management plan.

Rossouw (2002: 418) reports that the plan will involve not only those who plan the methods that help to ensure a safe sports event but also will include comments from the beneficiaries of your planning: the participants and spectators as well as sponsors and other guests. Involve these key groups in your planning to make certain that you have considered as many safety hazards as possible and that your final plan is practical and can be easily used by the participants and spectators. Your internal planning team may select a seemingly perfect location for your first-aid station, only to find out that neither the participants nor the spectators elected to use it because of its inconvenience. Their input is essential in creating a workable safety plan.

The following general pointers provided by Rossouw (2000: 419) should be considered when dealing with the risk management plan:

- Use a focus group comprised of event staff to help you identify a wide range of potential threats and plan for their efficient management.
- Provide effective oral, visual and physical communications so that employees, spectators and participants will know what to do in an emergency. Use one central control centre for emergency medical services (EMS) so that miscommunication will not occur and radio lines are left open. Write a report after each incident for litigation and evaluation purposes.
- Select an insurance broker knowledgeable in the sports event field who can advise you wisely about the amount and type of coverage you need.
- Involve external groups such as athletes and spectators in the safety review process to ensure overall acceptance and usage.

Crowd management strategies are critical to a smooth-running event. Preventative measures such as clearly marked exits, staff training with regard to alcohol policies, etc. should be in place. It is important to recognise that the risk management plan does not exonerate the sports event manager from all responsibility and liability regarding the event (Turco *et al,* 2002: 123). If the sports event manager does not organise the event in a safe and responsible manner, he or she may be liable for any injuries or problems that may arise (Pike Masteralexis, Barr & Humms, 1998: 334). These authors conclude that the sports event manager should acknowledge the importance of addressing risk management concerns related to the event in order to confine the legal liability of the event.

Case study 16.3: The 2001 Ellis Park Stadium soccer disaster
(Source: South Africa, Republic of, 2002: Internet)

A Commission of Inquiry into the Ellis Park Soccer Stadium disaster was released in 2002. The report chronicles South Africa's worst sporting crowd disaster. On 11 April 2001, at a high profile match, Kaizer Chiefs and Orlando Pirates, 43 people were killed and more than 150 were injured at Ellis Park. Fourteen factors were identified as contributing to crowd crush tragedy and mismanagement:

1. Poor forecast of match attendance
2. Failure to learn from the lessons of the past
3. Failure by the role players to clearly identify and designate areas of responsibility
4. Absence of overall command of the Joint Operation Centre
5. The inappropriate and untimely announcement that tickets were sold out
6. Failure to adhere to FIFA (international controlling body) and SAFA (national controlling body) guidelines

7. Unbecoming spectator behaviour
8. Sale of tickets at the venue and unreserved seating
9. The use of teargas or a similar substance
10. Corruption on the part of certain members of security personnel
11. Dereliction of duty
12. Failure to use the big screen
13. Inadequate public address system
14. Failure by the Public Order Police Unit to react timeously and effectively.

While it is beyond the scope of this case study to list all the recommendations, the following guidelines were highlighted as minimum security enforcement facilities for stadiums:

- Facilities to carry out a continuous counting of admitted spectators from the opening of the gates
- Crowd monitoring facilities, both inside and outside the stadium
- An effective public address system
- Effective communication system between all the security enforcement agencies
- Effective evacuation arrangements
- Mechanisms, such as the provision of multiple entrances, to avoid the concentration of spectators in one particular area
- Proper lighting inside and outside the stadium
- Emergency, medical and related facilities
- The calculation of stadium capacity
- Seat numbering or identification (coding)
- The demarcation of standing areas where applicable
- Demarcated areas for family, children and disabled persons
- Proper signage.

It is evident that an effective crowd management system could have prevented or lessened the Ellis Park crowd safety breakdown. In the section below, a case study (16.4) is provided which underscores the role of technology in effective security planning.

16.1.7 The use of technology in sports event management

Technology is evolving rapidly every day and sports event managers have to be aware of how technology affects how they run their daily business operations (Pike Masteralexis *et al*, 1998: 31). One area in which technology impacts on event organisation to a significant extent is that of media relations. Email, the World Wide Web, fax-on-demand and fax back have contributed to almost instantaneous information regarding the particular sporting event. It is important for home pages to be updated continuously so that media have the most current material.

News releases are now made available via the Web site or fax-on-demand. Turco *et al.* (2002: 136) add that communication via the Internet has become an ever more popular means of advertising and providing information about one's event. Have a look at the following examples which provides online registration, travel packages, and other pertinent event information.

- www.cycletour.org.za
- www.midmarmile.co.za
- www.twooceansmarathon.org.za

Another technological development that has an impact on sports event management is that of transportation. Turco *et al* (2002: 243) note the ease of transportation will enable participants and spectators to engage in non-native sports as effortlessly as sports in their own areas. They add that major sports will become more globalised, and professional leagues will spread across continents. A case in point is the Super Twelve Rugby league which takes place in Australia, South African and New Zealand.

A third way in which technological innovations affect event organisation is that of security. Case study 16.4 details some of the state-of-the-art security measures that were implemented for the ICC Cricket World Cup in South Africa.

Case study 16.4: Safety and Security at the ICC Cricket World Cup in South Africa
(Source: Blick South Africa, 2003: Internet)

One of the fundamental components which underscored the success of safety and security delivery during the tournament was the countrywide host venue deployment of metal detectors and highly sophisticated digital CCTV installations. The installation design called for no less than 53 PTZ Dome Cameras, integrated with remote control units, system controllers, 14-inch colour monitors, 24-hour time lapse VCRs, input digital recorders and matrix switchers. The equipment was installed at all 12 local host cricket grounds. Pilot tests were mostly conducted during the Sri Lankan and Pakistan tours between October 2002 and January 2003. The technicians were present at every pilot and Cricket World Cup match to confirm 100% performance. Upon reviewing the tournament at its completion, Bacher (Director of the ICC CWC 2003) said, 'When I first proposed the comprehensive safety and security measures recommended by the Security Directorate, incorporating the use of state-of-the-art electronic security measures, many people felt I was way over the top. But so successful did our measures prove to be that I would be very surprised if the International Cricket Council does not make them mandatory for future

Cricket World Cup tournaments as well as all One-Day International matches. Such a development would be yet another first for South Africa.'

In this section we have reviewed technological development in three areas of event organisation, namely media relations, transportation and safety and security. It is evident that the successful sports event manager will have to keep abreast of technological changes in all aspects of event organisation, particularly with regard to how these developments impact daily operations.

16.2 A CHECKLIST FOR OPERATIONS

The following checklist for operations is adapted from Getz (1997: 89–91).

Accessibility and flow:

- Number and arrangement of entrances and exits; gate control.
- Directional signage.
- Parking: number of spaces for cars, buses, trucks, bicycles; loading zones; reserved spots; special needs; emergency vehicles; parking permits or fees, collection and control personnel, directional signage; vehicle repair and emergency services; barriers; appropriate legislation checked; overflow and other contingency plans; entrance and exit segregation; avoiding congestion.
- Shuttles and public transit (special or extra services; schedules posted).
- Special needs (wheelchair access; others).
- Crowd-control devices (barricades, signs).
- Fire regulations; capacity (persons, vehicles, etc.).
- On-site vehicles for staff (and identification thereof).

Accreditation:

- For media, VIPs, staff and volunteers, officials (police, fire, etc.), research fieldworkers.
- Types: badges; tickets; uniforms; wrist bands.
- Authority to issue: controls (e.g. pre-approved lists, photo ID).

Activity requirements, setting types:

- Stages and assembly; dressing rooms; trailers; rehearsal area; special technicians; seating arrangements; viewing quality; acoustics.
- Processions parade marshals; crowd controls; seating; staging and activity area requirements; viewing.
- Open spaces; path versus free movement.
- Exhibition and sales; optimal site arrangement for viewing and line-ups (floor plan).
- Theming, decorations, design elements.

- Permission and special provision for fireworks, loud music, lasers, balloon releases, oversize balloons or equipment.
- Special provisions for animals.

Cancellation or venue change procedures:
- Weather forecasting and monitoring.
- Crowd and vehicle counts; observation to identify problems.
- Ways of instantly communicating changes (e.g. loudspeaker system; signs).
- Policy and procedures for reissuing tickets, rain checks, etc.

Command and operations facilities:
- Office and communications centre.
- Visibility in and out.
- Centrality and accessibility.
- Links to staff, emergency response teams.
- Refreshments and rest areas for staff, volunteers, participants.

Communications:
- Needs assessment (users, types of use, especially security, media suppliers).
- Types: telephones; radios; computers; pagers; photocopiers; signs; notice boards; maps; audiovisual.
- Special needs (e.g. telecommunications device for the deaf).
- Emergencies.
- Translation services.

Equipment, tools and supplies:
- Ticketing and financial control.
- Merchandising, food and beverage.
- Command and communications functions.
- Programme activities.
- Suppliers and participants.
- Customer services and information.
- Volunteers.

Hospitality:
- VIP, sponsors, officials and performers' facilities.
- Separation from other activities.
- Special viewing requirements.
- Special transport to, from and on site.
- Protocol for VIPs.

- Food, beverage, gifts.
- Hosts/servers; any tour guides required.

Infrastructure:
- Power needs (generators and dedicated lines; amperage for special equipment; protection from weather; outlets; heat or air conditioning; lighting and sound systems; backup and contingency plans); consultations with suppliers; need for electricians or permits; covers to protect people and lines.
- Water: for drinking; food and beverage preparation; washrooms; participants; check legislation; backup supply.
- Sewerage: existing lines and capacity: toilet requirements.
- Gas availability.

Merchandising and financial control:
- Special equipment (booths, cash registers, computers, kitchens, ice, refrigeration, storage, cars, canopies, seating, etc.).
- Security guards and vehicles; special accessibility and identification.
- Supervision or electronic monitoring.
- Safe money counting, storage and removal.
- Deposit slips and receipts.
- Foreign exchange rates posted and accounted for.
- Credit card validation machines and computer linkups; validation slips.
- Alarms and emergency signals.
- Bonding of key personnel.
- Cashiers and cash registers.

Quality control, supervision and evaluation:
- Rehearsals.
- Supervision.
- Evaluation.

Safety, security, comfort and health:
- First aid; lost children; lost and found.
- Emergency response and accessibility; evacuation procedures.
- Comfort stations; toilets; water; sewerage.
- Shelters from weather.
- Police or security presence.
- Waste disposal and recycling; green solutions; hazardous substances and the law.
- Safe storage spaces.

Storage and movement:

- Tools, equipment and vehicle storage.
- On-site movement.
- Structures needed (permanent or temporary).

Technicians required (and related equipment):

- Electrical; lasers and special effects.
- Sound systems.
- Fireworks.
- Plumbing (water and gas).
- Audiovisual equipment.
- Communications equipment.
- Computing.
- Video and photo; audio recording.
- Broadcasting.
- Timing and scoring.
- Registration and ticketing.
- Emergency response; police; fire; ambulance; first aid; medical/dental.
- Vending machines.
- Cooking/heating.
- Mechanics.

16.3 COMPONENTS OF A COMPREHENSIVE BUSINESS PLAN FOR EVENT ORGANISATIONS

The following components of a comprehensive business plan are adapted from Getz (1997: 92–93).

Format and size:

- Business plans are usually short – up to 35 pages long plus appendices.
- A professional and user-friendly format should be used.
- Detailed contents should be provided, as well as an executive summary and useful support material (viability and feasibility).
- Clearly define the intended use(s) and distribution of the plan. For example, is it confidential?

Background on the organisation and event:

- The origin and development achievements should be briefly stated.
- The organisation should be described as a legal entity.
- Provide an organisational chart with descriptions of the management team; profiles of role players and key staff; specify volunteer support; highlight the partners and sponsors.

- Clearly define the existence of a strategic or marketing plan; state the mission, vision, key goals; comment briefly on the existence of human resource or operations plans, strategic and site plans.
- Provide solid indications of sound management support.
- A fact sheet with relevant contact names and addresses should be attached.

The event:
- Provide an explanation of the event's purpose, programme and its benefits; if relevant, highlight its uniqueness and tourist appeal.
- Briefly name any competitors.
- Plans for developing and improving the event should be fully described.
- Highlight quality control measures.
- Add photographs as evidence of attendance and growth.

Marketing:
- The marketing and communications goals and objectives should be stated.
- Clearly define the marketing budget and new changes arising.
- The relation to revenue generation of positioning and marketing mix strategies should be briefly and concisely presented.
- Profile the audience and define the research efforts and results of past market research.
- Estimate the attendance in respect of demand/growth.
- Key target market segments should be highlighted as well as their financial importance to the event (e.g. income levels and willingness to pay).
- Explain combined marketing with sponsors.
- Indicate tourist-oriented promotions and packaging; briefly name the distribution system (e.g. of tickets, merchandising, etc.).

Financial management:
- Fully describe the efforts and successes of cost and revenue management.
- The financial control systems should be explained.
- Briefly state the cash-flow issues.
- Provide information on the organisation's assets and available collateral.
- Provide financial forecasts and risks.
- The current budget, cash-flow statement, income–loss statement, balance sheet (assets and liabilities) and key performance ratios should be given.
- Give the financial requirements.
- Plans and methods for repayment of any requested loan should be explained.

Summary:
- Request financial assistance if required.

Appendices:

- Highlight successes and uniqueness by supplying photos and other tangible evidence of the event and the organisation.
- Clearly define the main points of research.
- Provide an organisational chart.
- Give examples of any media coverage (or summarise the value thereof).
- Give endorsements and testimonials.
- Supply resumés of key leaders and staff.

16.4 CHECKLIST FOR CHAMPIONSHIPS, TOURNAMENTS AND COURSES

TABLE 16.1 *Sport Event Checklist (Source, Getz, 1997: 92–93)*

1	Type of sport ....
2	Name of organising official ....
3	Type of competition/championship ....
4	Venue ....
5	Amount granted by committee
6	First organising committee meeting
	Place .... Date .... Time ....
7	Members of organising committee
	Chairman: .... Tel (w) .... (h) ....
	Secretary: .... Tel (w) .... (h) ....
	Treasurer: .... Tel (w) .... (h) ....
	Tel (w) .... (h) ....
	Tel (w) .... (h) ....
8	Meetings held to control the organisation
	Date .... Place .... Time ....
	Date .... Place .... Time ....
	Date .... Place .... Time ....
	Date .... Place .... Time ....

16.5 CONTROL STATE

The following checklist is adapted from Rossouw (2000: 427–431) and Sport and Recreation New Zealand (2002: 12–15). It can be further adapted or modified for your specific event. This is the most important document in a sports event manager's life, and should someone else have to take over the project, the checklist should be so detailed that this process occurs smoothly.

TABLE 16.2 *Control Checklist (Source: Rossouw, 2000: 427–431; Sport and Recreation New Zealand, 2002, 12–15)*

ASSIGNMENT	ASSIGNED TO	CONTROL	COMPLETED
1. Admission control VIPs, ticket holders Ticket sales point/outlets Guards at gates Printed tickets Specific prices Etc.			
2. Communications Major sponsor Co-sponsors General public, e.g. lost property/people Advertising Programmes PR Ambush Trouble-shooting Etc.			
3. Décor Banners Flags Flagpole Plants Small flags Etc.			
4. Equipment A. General Time-keeping equipment Rostrum Tables/chairs Writing material Umbrellas Scoreboards Bells/whistles Computer Tape recorder/music Pistol Etc.			

B. Specific sports equipment Obtain a full list from sport organisations			
5. Facilities Book venue Preparation of field Cleaning services Venue for reception Control of seating arrangements Toilet facilities Keys for admission to all facilities First aid Etc.			
6. Finances Budget Banking facilities Signing authority Auditing Collection of funds raised			
7. First aid First-aid service (e.g. Red Cross) Hospital service Ambulance service Doctor on duty or stand-by Etc.			
8. Guests of honour and invitations List of honorary guests Invitations Reception of guests of honour Seating of VIPs Serving of refreshments Parking for VIPs Etc.			
9. Hospitality Sponsor Media VIPs Location Set up Catering, drinks Passes, parking Hosting Etc.			
10. Legal Contracts Licensees Local body/Council approvals Venue approvals Contingency Etc.			

11. Lighting Organise switching on/off Electrician available Lights for warming up Light for ticket sales points Test lights beforehand			
12. Medals/certificates/trophies Pressing of medals Printing of certificates Ribbon for medals Trophy (sponsors) Engraving Table for exhibition Cushions for medals Presentation Etc.			
13. Media Media registration Press kits Press releases Press/photos/sketches Film Media room Interview area Television facilities Telephone/fax/workstations Posters Banners Etc.			
14. Merchandising Range Quality Sales-pricing Displays Advertising Signs Licences Etc.			
15. Opening/closing Ceremony March on/off Positions Band Anthem Etc.			
16. Parking and traffic regulations Traffic departments Parking facilities Signboards			

Parking for ambulance			
Etc.			
17. Participants/competitors			
Standards			
Name lists			
Participants' official			
18. Personnel/Services			
Announcer			
Cleaners			
Caretaker/toilets			
Caterer			
Programme sellers			
Typist			
Officials			
Signage/Marquee maintenance			
Power			
Water			
First aid			
Translators			
Volunteers			
Venue operations			
Etc.			
19. Printing work			
Programme			
Invitation cards			
Entrance tickets			
Service tickets			
Official tickets			
Participants' tickets			
Entry forms			
Complimentary tickets			
Press tickets			
Parking stickers			
Posters			
Information booklet			
Etc.			
20. Refreshments			
Public/officials/participants			
Guests of honour/press			
Refreshment stalls and kitchen section			
Reception			
Refreshment personnel			
Etc.			
21. Seating reservations			
Advance bookings			
Seating and booking plans			
22. Security			
Risk management plan			
Police during meeting/match/game			

Security police			
Venue			
Hospitality			
Cash			
Etc.			
23. Signage			
Production			
Delivery			
Erection			
Quantity			
Tear down			
Storage			
Etc.			
24. Sponsors			
Find sponsors			
Sponsor contracts			
Fulfil sponsors' requirements			
Advertising in programme			
Announcements over loudspeakers			
Banners			
Collect adverts for programme			
Ambush marketing control plan			
25. Technical			
Power source			
Phones			
Faxes			
TV/videos			
Mobile phones			
Pagers			
Two-way radios			
PA System			
Loudspeakers			
Microphone			
Scoring			
Music			
Etc.			
26. Transport			
Arrival and departure times			
Schedules (also for practice)			
Arrange buses according to schedule			
Permits			
Transport of equipment			
Etc.			
27. Travel and boarding			
Travel agent			
Hotel arrangements			
Permits			
Information brochures			
Street map			

Etc.			
28. After project has finished Tidying up Return borrowed equipment Thanks Accounts Report and auditing Debriefing Recommendations and reports			

Browse these Internet sites

International Events Group, Inc (IEG) www.sponsorship.com

International Festival and Events Association (IFEA) www.ifea.com

Travel and Tourism Research Association (TTRA) www.ttra.com

SPRIG Promoting Information in Leisure Tourism and Sport
http://www.sprig.org.uk

Leisure Information Network www.lin.ca

Recreation Management http://leoisaac.com/sportman/

International Olympic Committee (IOC) www.ioc.org

South African Football Association (SAFA) www.safagoal.net/

Supersport www.supersport.co.za

QUESTIONS FOR SELF-EVALUATION

1 Identify the problems you experienced in your region when organising or attending a game.

2 Take an example of a game in your community that was not very successful:
   – identify the problems;
   – identify the possible causes of the problems.
   Have a group discussion.

3 Take a game hosted in your community and draw up a checklist of all the activities that have to be planned for.
   Have a group discussion.

4 Take a game hosted in your community and draw up a risk management plan based upon the requirements of the game.
   – identify the possible risks;
   – identify ways to reduce the risks;
   – have a group discussion.

5 Take a game hosted in your community and devise a volunteer management plan based upon the requirements of the game:
   Have a group discussion.

CHAPTER 17

Exhibition/Exposition/Trade Show Management

Howard Pell and John Knocker

AIM OF THE CHAPTER

The aim of this chapter is to describe the development of the exhibition industry from inception, with particular reference to South Africa. It also aims to provide an insight into the various techniques that can be used for the successful planning, organisation and management of exhibitions.

LEARNING OBJECTIVES

After having studied this chapter, you should be able to:

- understand the various types of exhibitions;
- demonstrate the importance of carrying out thorough research before launching a new exhibition;
- demonstrate which aspects have to be taken into consideration when planning and organising an exhibition;
- demonstrate how to realise an exhibition once the decision has been taken to proceed;
- indicate ways to enable the visitor to obtain the maximum benefit from visiting an exhibition.

17.1 INTRODUCTION

While it is difficult to give an exact date for the start of exhibition activity it is certain that trade fairs were held in Biblical times and an international fair was held regularly at Tyre in Palestine.

During the Middle Ages large fairs were held at regular intervals in different parts of Europe and one of the earliest was the Leipzig Fair which started in 1165. Industrial exhibitions commenced in the sixteenth century when first-such events were held in Nuremberg in 1569. By the nineteenth century exhibitions were taking place on a regular basis in many of the leading cities in Europe.

A landmark event was the Great Exhibition that was held in the Crystal Palace in Hyde Park, London, England in 1851. This displayed to the world the achievements of British manufacturers and illustrated the industrial predominance of Great Britain at that time. The exhibition remained open for five months and attracted in excess of six million visitors (Alles, 1988: 1–2).

Following on from the Crystal Palace event was an era of great industrial exhibitions and world fairs. These contributed to changes in our environment and have influenced styles and fashions of buildings, furniture and articles in everyday use.

Since 1945, exhibition activity has expanded at a tremendous rate throughout the world and currently there are in excess of 5 000 major events per year and every continent has exhibition halls of high quality.

17.2 SOUTH AFRICA

The start of the exhibition business in South Africa can be traced back to the agricultural shows that took place from time to time in various parts of the country. Whilst many areas claim to be 'the first' it seems that the first event to take place on a regular basis was the Royal Show at Pietermaritzburg in 1851. The Port Elizabeth Show followed this shortly afterwards in 1864 and the Rand Show organised by the Witwatersrand Agricultural Society in 1894.

The Rand Show, which took place annually, was initially built around livestock, agricultural produce and farmers' requirements. Gradually, with the industrial expansion of the country, it became a showplace for industrial products and later for consumer goods.

The Milner Park Showgrounds in Johannesburg, which were owned by the Witwatersrand Agricultural Society, was the only suitable venue for holding large-scale exhibitions. The society, understandably, resisted letting any other organisation use the showgrounds for exhibition use as this could be detrimental to the Rand Show. However, in 1954 the Office Appliance Association persuaded the society to let one of the halls for running a Business Efficiency Exhibition.

From this point on Milner Park, and subsequently the society's new showgrounds at NASREC, were increasingly used for the expanding calendar of trade and industrial exhibitions.

Due to the ever-increasing demand for exhibition space a number of other venues came on stream in Johannesburg and the other main centres in South Africa. The country now has an excellent range of exhibition halls that are able to accommodate the events that take place on a regular basis.

Venue	Location exhibition	Year of first	Total m² gross	Inside	Outside
Cape Town International Convention Centre	Cape Town	2003	9 705	9 705	Nil
Durban Exhibition Centre	Durban	1986	21 000	10 000	11 000
Expo Centre	Johannesburg	1985	120 000	40 000	80 000
Feather Market Hall	Port Elizabeth	1991	2 560	2 560	Nil
Gallagher Estates	Midrand	1994	24 000	24 000	Nil
Good Hope Centre	Cape Town	1987	11 500	10 000	1 500
Heritage Conference	Johannesburg	1994	1 735	1 735	Nil
International Convention Centre	Durban	1997	5 370	5 370	Nil
Khayalami Exhibition Centre	Johannesburg	1992	14 600	7 300	7 300
MTN Sundome	Johannesburg	1997	16 000	16 000	Nil
Pretoria Showgrounds	Pretoria	1939	102 000	42 000	60 000
Sandton Convention Centre	Johannesburg	2000	22 000	22 000	Nil
Sun City Complex	Pilansberg	1986	1 250	1 250	Nil
Technikon S.A. Conference Centre	Johannesburg	1998	4 000	4 000	Nil
Volkswagen Convention Centre	Midrand	1990	6 052	1 052	5 000

Table 17.1 illustrates the development of available exhibition space, especially since 1990. As can be seen from the number of venues available, these would not have been established without a need, *and have resulted* from the growth in exhibitions.

In 2001, the Exhibition Association of Southern Africa (EXSA) commissioned Research Services (RS) Johannesburg, to undertake research on 201 known exhibitions organised by 102 EXSA members. The purpose of the research was to establish the size and growth of the traditional exhibition industry. A further objective was to determine whether there was growth in the number of visitors to exhibitions. The research covered the larger stand-alone exhibitions (average size 4 018m²), but excluded purely agricultural shows. Some of these exhibitions are run every second or third year, whilst others are run on an annual basis. With the apparent increase in the overall number of events, both large and small, it had become difficult to know whether the traditional aspect of the industry was increasing.

The research revealed that exhibitions were growing in the number of exhibitors and visitors, even though some had not grown in size. In effect, the size of stands had become smaller. The choice in the number of exhibitions had become greater and more exhibitions were available, giving exhibitors a greater choice. Further, where this was the case, exhibitors could chose to exhibit more frequently and /or on smaller stands.

Venue	Location	Year of first exhibition	Total m² gross	Inside	Outside
Cape Town Convention Centre	Cape Town	2003	9 705	9 705	Nil
Durban Exhibition Centre	Durban	1986	21 000	10 000	11 000
Expo Centre	Johannesburg	1985	120 000	40 000	80 000
Feather Market Hall	Port Elizabeth	1991	2 560	2 560	Nil
Gallagher Estates	Midrand	1994	24 000	24 000	Nil
Good Hope Centre	Cape Town	1987	11 500	10 000	1 500
Heritage Conference Centre	Johannesburg	1994	1 735	1 735	Nil
International Convention Centre	Durban	1997	5 370	5 370	Nil
Kyalami Exhibition Centre	Johannesburg	1992	14 600	7 300	7 300
MTN Sundome	Johannesburg	1997	16 000	16 000	Nil
Pretoria Showgrounds	Pretoria	1939	102 000	42 000	60 000
Sandton Convention Centre	Johannesburg	2000	22 000	22 000	Nil
Sun City Complex	Pilansberg	1986	1 250	1 250	Nil
Technikon SA Conference Centre	Johannesburg	1998	4 000	4 000	Nil
Volkswagen Convention Centre	Midrand	1990	6 052	1 052	5 000

FIGURE 17.1 *Annual number of EXSA affiliated exhibitions since 1994 (Source: EXSA)*

Some associated industry exhibitions have been consolidated into larger events to make them more effective for exhibitors, visitors and organisers. Consequently, statistics have been skewed in this regard, as there has been consolidation of exhibitions in the industry, namely larger EXSA events. This in no way presupposes a decrease in the total *number* of exhibitions being organised. On the contrary, there has been an increase in the number of (non-EXSA) events with many smaller niche shows being run as free-standing events (many as Confexes), but not necessarily by EXSA members.

A growing sector in the exhibition industry has been the introduction of Confex events. They are conferences within an industry or profession with a small number of exhibition stands included – and are generally erected in the foyer area of the conference. In the 1990s Confexes were small sections of other exhibitions.

Trade and other associations or interest groups, which are not members of EXSA, often staged Confex events (these were also excluded from the research). There are cases where an exhibition had developed from a portion/sector of a larger event into a reasonably sized, stand-alone, exhibition.

The Exhibition Industry is made up of the following sections:
- venue owners;
- exhibition organisers, who research, develop and put on shows;
- service providers such as stand constructors, carpet contractors, furniture hirers, electrical contractors, security companies, caterers (for further information refer to section 17.7.6).

The controlling body for the industry is the Exhibition Association of Southern Africa (EXSA) which endeavours to set standards and provides liaison between the different sectors of the industry.

17.3 DEFINITION OF AN EXHIBITION

Exhibitions, also known as expositions, trade fairs, trade shows and so forth are an increasingly important part of sales promotion activity. The simplest definition of this activity is:

The bringing together in one place for a set period of time of buyers and sellers where products can be viewed, handled and demonstrated.

17.3.1 Exhibitions can be divided into two main categories:
- *Trade/Industrial*. Visitors to such events are investigating/purchasing goods for use in a business organisation. Generally visitors do not pay to enter the exhibitions; they come by invitation or are given free access on production of their business card.
- *Consumer*. These are concerned with promoting/selling goods which the purchaser will use in his or her private capacity. Normally visitors are charged an entrance fee at such events.

These divisions are not arbitrary and there will be occasions when one exhibition is for both trade/industrial and consumer visitors. An example of this is the Rand Easter Show that combines the traditional agricultural show with a consumer goods and entertainment event.

17.4 EXHIBITION OBJECTIVES

Having defined an exhibition, it is necessary to consider what it is designed to achieve – what is its purpose. Quantifiable objectives set before an exhibition enable you to measure the success of the event afterwards. The purpose of an exhibition is best described by listing the various objectives that can be achieved by taking part in an exhibition:

- To write orders on the stand.
- To obtain enquiries which can be followed up after the show and developed into orders.
- To launch a new product or service.
- To open a new market – this may be in another city which has not been covered before or another country. In both cases an exhibition is an ideal method to develop the new market.
- To service existing customers – an exhibition enables executives to meet customers who usually only have contact with the firm's representatives.
- To reactivate former customers who visit the stand.
- To develop new prospective customers who visit the stand.
- To make use of an excellent opportunity for technical and administrative staff to make contact with customers.
- To make contact with prospective dealers/agents. This can be particularly useful when the exhibition is being used to penetrate a new market.
- To conduct market research – to obtain feedback on new products and/or new uses for existing products.
- To obtain industry information.
- To acquire more information about competitors.
- To make use of the occasion for sales training – an exhibition is an opportunity for sales management to observe sales staff in action.
- To arouse the interest of potential staff who will be visiting the exhibition – by means of an attractive and well-designed stand.
- To promote a favourable image of the company.

17.5 PRIOR RESEARCH

17.5.1 Market research

Before commencing any new business activity it is normal practice to carry out market research to ensure that there are potential customers for the product or service proposed. Exhibitions are no exception and the reason for an event failing to live up to expectations can often be attributed to lack of adequate market research beforehand.

There are two main areas where research is essential – numbers of potential exhibitors and visitors. To take an example, one can consider the first specialised trade exhibition held in South Africa, the Business Efficiency Exhibition. In the case of potential exhibitors there were numerous companies supplying typewriters, adding machines and other office machines, office furniture, stationery, intercom systems, copying machines, etc., so there were numerous companies who would be interested in exhibiting. In the same way, every commercial and industrial organisation, professional bodies, government and municipal departments, etc., use such equipment and would be potential visitors. On the other hand, to take an absurd example, while almost everybody in the country uses matches, if there is only one company manufacturing matches, there would be not much scope for a match exhibition!

17.5.2 Areas which should be investigated

The responsibility for carrying out prior research to establish the viability of a proposed exhibition rests with the exhibition organiser and the following paragraphs indicate the areas which should be investigated.

17.5.2.1 Potential exhibitors

There are numerous sources for finding out the names, addresses, etc. of companies manufacturing particular product(s) or product groups:

- trade directories;
- trade associations;
- advertisements in trade publications serving the industry;
- if similar exhibitions have been held previously, the exhibition catalogue can be a fruitful source;
- there may well be a professional body serving the particular industry and a list of members would be a useful source.

All the information obtained from these sources must be systematically recorded as this will form the basis for the prospect list to be used by representatives when the campaign to sell exhibition space to potential exhibitors commences.

17.5.2.2 Potential visitors

To assess the viability of the event it is necessary to form as accurate a figure as possible of the number of potential visitors who could visit the exhibition. It must be remembered that the reason companies take a stand is to meet potential customers.

There are a number of sources that can be used to arrive at this figure:

- There may well be professional people who would visit. For example, in the case of a building products exhibition, architects, quantity surveyors and consulting engineers would all be prospects and their numbers can be obtained from the appropriate professional bodies.

- Every industry is served by a number of trade and technical publications. The number of readers for such publications can be regarded as potential visitors.
- An approach to some of the more prominent potential exhibitors who are *au fait* with the industry can be used to obtain an indication as to the number of customers for the industry.
- In certain cases the retail outlets for the products being displayed would also be potential visitors. An approach to the relative trade association would be valuable.

Once an overall total of potential visitors has been calculated, it will be necessary to make an estimate of the percentage who will attend the exhibition.

After the first event has taken place, it will be easier to arrive at the expected number of visitors for future exhibitions as the number attending the first event can form the basis.

17.5.2.3 Professional/trade organisations

Apart from providing useful information in regard to potential exhibitors and visitors, it is important during the research stage to establish a good working relationship with such bodies. The approval and support from the appropriate organisations can be very helpful in getting a new exhibition 'off the deck'. Through such contacts, the organisation should be encouraged to hold a conference alongside the exhibition. Such an event adds to the prestige of the exhibition, ensures visits from high-calibre individuals, and is a useful publicity platform.

17.5.2.4 Overseas events

During the research stage it is important to find out if any similar events have taken place in other countries. If an exhibition of this sort has not been staged before, it will be necessary to find out why. This may indicate that the proposed exhibition would not be viable.

On the other hand, if similar events have been held before, this is a positive sign and it would be important to find out as much information as possible about the overseas exhibitions. If it can be arranged and if time allows it would be very worthwhile to arrange a visit to such an event.

As discussed below on the subject of timing for the exhibition (section 17.6.2), it is essential to avoid clashing with overseas events of a similar nature so early knowledge on this aspect is important.

17.6 FUNDAMENTALS

17.6.1 Objectives

A hackneyed but true saying is *'If you don't know where you're going, you're very unlikely to get there'*. This applies to the exhibition business, whether one is looking from the point of view of the organiser, exhibitor or the visitor.

In so far as the organiser is concerned, the basic objective is to plan and mount a successful and profitable event which can become a regular feature of the exhibition calendar.

With regard to exhibitors, in section 17.4 above a list of possible objectives has been given and the exhibitor must select those which will apply to participation at a particular exhibition and ensure that all staff members are aware that these are the company targets.

Case study 17.1: Cape Wine 2004 (Source: Cloete, 2004: Interview)

A highly reputable conference organiser, *Conferences Et Al* was appointed to organise the Cape Wine Expo, 2004 during January 2003. The client was WOSA, Wines of South Africa.

Purpose of the event

The event was organised on behalf of the South African Wine Industry. It was the third biennial wine trade event, which was held at the Cape Town International Convention Centre, 30 March to 2 April 2004. The purpose was to bring the international wine buyer and media into contact with South African wine producers.

About the event

Cape Wine 2004 was South Africa's biggest-ever wine trade exhibition, and covered 256 wineries, exhibiting 4 000 wines over four days to more than 1 200 international delegates.

This event provided many challenges to the organiser, Conferences Et Al. The event was extremely professionally organised. The organising of this event started a year prior to its staging and involved extensive consultation with the client, WOSA. The event was a trade exhibition and also involved separate seminars every day focusing on wine issues in the South African industry. The attending delegates were also treated to social events, meetings with the industry and pre and post tours. To ensure the successful staging of the event the organiser made use of service providers to the event industry. The service providers provided services such as:

- venue
- accommodation
- tour operating services
- audiovisual
- printing
- webmaster designing
- graphic artist
- exhibition contractor
- exhibition designer
- speakers
- company providing glasses for the tastings
- travel arrangements.

The delegates also attended a charity wine auction that raised over R40 000 in aid of Dopstop and the Makukhanye Choir of Nkquebela in Robertson.

17.6.2 Timing

Under this heading there are three main aspects to consider.

17.6.2.1 Frequency

On the assumption that it is intended for the exhibition to be a regular event, it is necessary to decide if it should take place annually, biennially or at longer intervals. In this connection an important factor to take into consideration is the frequency of technological change which applies to the products being displayed. In the case of computers, where the change is very rapid, an annual event is called for as applies to the Computer Faire in South Africa.

However, in the machine tool industry change is less rapid and for this reason the local exhibition usually takes place on a longer cycle. In this instance the very heavy costs involved in setting up the equipment also detract from more frequent exhibitions.

17.6.2.2 Time of the year

In South Africa, account must be taken of the holiday period of December/January. Particularly in the case of trade/industrial events, many potential visitors will be away over this period and this will detract from the all-important visitor attendance. To a lesser extent the other school holiday periods can be a factor.

As already mentioned above, it is important to avoid clashing with a major overseas event in the same industry. An example is the printing industry where the DRUPA exhibition in Germany attracts all the major buyers from around the world; obviously it would not make sense to hold a printing equipment exhibition in South Africa at the same time.

When considering dates for a proposed exhibition, it is essential to consult both overseas and local exhibition calendars to avoid clashing with competing events.

17.6.2.3 Duration

The advantages and disadvantages of short versus long periods are difficult to evaluate. For exhibitors duration periods of more than five to six days are very tiring and except in exceptional circumstances should be avoided. The general pattern is tending towards events of a three- to four-day duration.

17.6.3 Selection of venue

In recent years the number of exhibition sites in South Africa has increased substantially and now there is a very wide choice of suitable venues. While the majority of sites are located in Gauteng Province, all other major cities have at least one exhibition hall and additional facilities are coming on stream in the future.

The first decision is in which city the exhibition will take place. As Gauteng at present is the main commercial/industrial centre, the majority of the larger events take place here, although an increasing number of regional shows are now coming on stream.

There will be cases where the industry being served will dictate the location of the exhibition. In the case of an event for the fishing industry, the obvious choice would be Cape Town.

Once the geographical situation has been settled, if there are several venues available a number of factors come into play. The following are some of the main points to consider:

- *The age of the exhibition hall.* A newer building will probably have better facilities.
- *The physical location of the building.* Ease of access for potential visitors could affect attendance.

- *Parking facilities.* What parking facilities exist for visitors, and for exhibitors during build-up and breakdown.
- *Floor loading capacity.* Particularly important if heavy equipment or vehicles are to be featured.
- *Supply of electricity, water, compressed air. etc.* Is there an adequate supply.
- *Catering facilities.* What type is available.
- *Availability of conference facilities.* If it is planned to have a conference running concurrently with the exhibition, is the conference facility adequate.

17.6.4 Prospective exhibitor list

This point has been mentioned previously in section 17.5 (Prior research) and it must be emphasised that without an accurate and comprehensive list of prospective exhibitors there is no chance of making a success of the exhibition. As the selling period may well run over two or more years, it is necessary to be constantly on the lookout for new companies coming into the market who could be prospective exhibitors.

Apart from organisations located in South Africa, attention must be paid to companies domiciled overseas who could be interested in taking part in the exhibition. Contacts should be maintained with local trade consuls who can assist in locating suitable potential exhibitors. Examination of catalogues from overseas exhibitions in the same field is a good source of finding exhibitors. Appointing an overseas agent in the appropriate countries can also assist, although this can be an expensive process with no guarantee of results.

17.6.5 Visitor profile

It is necessary to draw up an accurate profile of the potential visitors (PV), as this will be a valuable guide when the visitor promotion programme is being drawn up. The following is an indication of the points that need be considered.
- In which categories of business/profession/etc does the PV work?
- Which professional bodies would the PV belong to?
- Which professional/trade/technical publication would the PV read?
- A meeting with some of the leading potential exhibitors will be useful to establish the categories of visitor in which they would be interested.

17.6.6 Liaison with trade/professional bodies and relevant publications

This aspect was touched on above in section 17.5. Once the decision has been made to proceed with the exhibition, it is important to establish formal or semi-formal relationships with such organisations. Some of the more necessary aspects are as follows.
- *Sponsorship.* If there is a leading trade or professional body that is associated with the trade/industry around which the exhibition has been built it is

valuable to persuade them to act as sponsors to the exhibition. Such official backing will be most helpful in attracting visitors to the event. In some cases it may be necessary to make a payment to the body in question, possibly based on the number of visitors coming to the exhibition.

- *Publicity*. The bodies mentioned in the preceding paragraph usually have an official publication and if a good relationship has been established it should be possible to obtain editorial mention about the exhibition, both during the build-up period and immediately before the exhibition takes place.

- *Conferences*. A substantial number of trade/professional bodies hold conferences on a regular basis and to have such an event taking place at the same time as the exhibition will be beneficial for both parties.

- *Publications*. These play an important role in the promotion of exhibitions, both to exhibitors and visitors. Editorial publicity is an obvious benefit and often the publication can assist in the distribution of visitor admission tickets before the exhibition opens.

- *Catalogues*. This is a vital aspect of an exhibition but its compilation and production is an onerous and time-consuming task, most of which has to be carried out just before opening day when the organisers' staff are under maximum pressure. For these reasons it is often advisable to outsource the publication of the catalogue to a publication, preferably the most influential one in that industry.

- *Radio or newspapers*. The sponsorship support of one or both of these media is invaluable in publicising an exhibition and attracting an audience. This type of media is used to get to the public to attend consumer and public events.

17.7 ORGANISING AND COORDINATION

17.7.1 Hall plans

As indicated above, one of the fundamental decisions which has to be taken at an early stage is selecting the venue where the exhibition will take place. The next step is to have a set of hall plans prepared which will show the position of the stands that will be occupied by exhibitors. Sales representatives will use these plans when calling on prospective exhibitors to decide which stand/s will be occupied. Various aspects must be taken into account when drawing up the plans.

- *Aisles, entrance features, service areas, etc*. Provision must be made for such areas and as a rough rule of thumb they will use up 40 to 45% of the total space available in the hall. The smaller the space used for such purposes the more space available for sales and the higher the income that can be achieved.

- *Services such as electricity, water, compressed air, etc*. These will usually be available via ducts under the floor of the hall in more modern structures but some older halls may provide these from overhead. Stand allocation must take the position of ducting into account.

17.7.5 Visitor promotion (VP)

It must always be remembered that the reason exhibitors sign up for a stand is to see the *maximum* number of the *right* people and it is the organiser's responsibility to produce this audience.

Failure to adequately promote an exhibition is the main reason for failure of an event, causing major dissatisfaction with exhibitors.

It will be the organiser's decision as to whether the VP campaign will be planned and carried out 'in-house' or whether an outside agency will be used. It must be remembered that the majority of advertising agencies are concerned with the promotion of consumer goods where the principle media used are daily press, radio and TV – all of which are expensive. For an exhibition substantial use is made of 'below-the-line' methods which are less expensive and often more effective for industrial products.

The following is a list of the various media that should be brought into the VP campaign:

- **Distribution of complimentary tickets.** This is probably the most effective means of bringing in visitors. Tickets can be distributed in the following ways:
  - by exhibitors – they have the best idea of who they want to see at the exhibition and can distribute tickets in various ways – their own mailing list, included with monthly statements, handed out by their own representatives, through agents;
  - trade/technical publications – either by including the ticket as an insert in the publication before the show takes place or the publication may provide the organiser with a subscriber list;
  - professional bodies – those organisations who are associated with the industry featured at the exhibition may agree to distribute tickets to their members.
- **Adverts and editorials in appropriate trade/technical journals.**
- **Adverts in the daily press.** These are best placed just before and during the show. It must be remembered that press advertising is expensive. A special supplement' about the exhibition is good publicity and often exhibitors can be persuaded to take adverts in the supplement.
- **Posters.** These are a useful 'reminder' to potential visitors that the exhibition is taking place. It is important to keep the design of the poster simple. The name of the exhibition, venue and dates are all that is required.
- **Radio.** This is also an excellent 'reminder' and the best time is when potential visitors are driving to or from work.
- **Television.** This type of advertising is expensive and is generally only worthwhile for a consumer exhibition.

17.7.6 Appointment of contractors

Once the exhibitor has booked the stand there are numerous activities that have to take place, mostly shortly before the exhibition opens, to ensure that the show is a success. Most of this work is carried out by outside contractors and the organiser must make certain that the contractors appointed are suitable for the work. The following is a list of the main areas that have to be covered.

■ *Stand construction*. All the exhibitor gets from the organiser is a specified amount of many square metres of floor space in the hall. To make an effective display it is necessary to have a stand constructed. For smaller stands use can be made of a shell scheme which generally consists of back and side walls, a fascia board to feature the exhibitor's name and stand number and, possibly, some form of ceiling. The organiser appoints a contractor to provide shell scheme to the exhibitors who require this form of stand.

For larger and more distinctive stands a special design is needed and there are specialist stand constructors who carry out this work. The organiser may appoint such a contractor or the exhibitor may appoint his or her own.

■ *Electrical fittings*. All stands require light and power points and there are specialist electrical contractors who carry out this work. It is usually preferable to use the services of a single contractor.

■ *Carpets.* The majority of stands will require carpeting and the organiser will appoint a contractor to carry out this work.

■ *Plumbing*. Some stands may require a water supply and a plumbing contractor will be appointed to make the necessary connections.

■ *Furniture*. Most exhibitors will need to hire furniture of various kinds for the duration of the exhibition and contractors are available for this purpose.

■ *Security*. This is essential at all exhibitions. In some cases the venue owners may provide the service in others the organiser will appoint a security company.

■ *Catering*. This is one of the areas which often causes problems. Many complaints are received by organisers that the standard was poor and the prices excessive. Here again some venue owners provide the catering facilities; if not, the organiser has to appoint a catering company and it is important to keep a constant check on this aspect of the show.

■ *Forwarding agents*. Particularly when exhibitors are domiciled overseas or in other areas of South Africa than where the exhibition is taking place, it will be necessary for materials to be transported and delivered to the exhibition hall. To avoid problems and confusion it is advisable for the organiser to appoint a reputable company to carry out this work.

17.7.7 Catalogue

The exhibition catalogue is a vital element in the information aspect of the show and in the case of major events it acts as a reference book with an effective life span of one or more years. The responsibility for the production of the catalogue rests with the organiser although this may be passed over to a trade publisher.

The catalogue generally contains the following information:

- message from the organiser
- hall plans
- alphabetical listing of exhibitors with brief details of their exhibits
- a product cross-index
- advertisements.

The biggest problem in the compilation of the catalogue is obtaining the necessary information from exhibitors about their company and product/s.

The usual method is by means of a form contained in the Exhibitor Manual which exhibitors use to order their services. Constant 'chasing' is required to ensure that this information is received in time to meet print deadlines.

17.7.8 Conferences

As indicated previously, a conference is a valuable addition to an exhibition from the viewpoints of prestige and quality visitor attendance.

From the organisers standpoint it is highly desirable that the venue for the conference is adjacent to the exhibition hall/s as this will make it easy for delegates to attend the exhibition. It should be arranged for conference delegates to receive with their conference manual complimentary tickets for admission to the show. It is a worthwhile gesture to allocate reserved parking for conference delegates and this can help to cement the relationship with the organisers of the conference.

17.7.9 Training of exhibitors' staff

It is astounding that companies will spend very large sums on their stand at an exhibition but fail to give any specialised training to the staff that are going 'to man' the stand to ensure that they are able to take full advantage of the selling/promotional opportunities which will be available.

The first step is for the company to clearly define what the objectives are that they are setting out to achieve by participating in the event. These objectives should preferably be quantified so that it is possible to measure the degree of success after the exhibition is over.

Next, a stand manager should be appointed with the necessary skills and ability to ensure that the exhibiting company's objectives are attained. Stand managers must also be given the necessary authority to take whatever actions are needed. It is advisable to draw up a job description with the managers, covering their objectives, functions, responsibilities and authority.

The persons who are going to staff the stand during the exhibition need to be thoroughly briefed as to their duties. It has to be clearly understood that selling from an exhibition stand is very different from the normal selling activity.

In many cases the company and their staff are unaware of what is needed to make a success of their participation at the exhibition and unless steps are taken to deal with this situation, the company may well come to the conclusion that exhibiting is a waste of time and will not take part in future exhibitions.

It is for these reasons that in many instances the organiser arranges training sessions for the exhibitors' staff to ensure that they are prepared for the different circumstances which they will encounter at the show and can maximise the selling/promotional opportunities. There are some excellent training films covering selling at exhibitions that can be used with effect at such training sessions.

17.7.10 Finance

Apart from normal financial controls and practices, it is important to exercise stringent credit control over payment of stand rentals by exhibitors. It is usual to take a deposit from an exhibitor when the space contract is signed; alternatively, a portion is paid at an agreed time well before the show opens and the balance about three months before opening.

Any exhibitor who has not paid the full amount for stand rental before the opening of the show must not be allowed to take part.

17.8 EXHIBITION ACTIVITIES, PERSONNEL AND PREPARATION

17.8.1 Stand construction

- The first requirement is to mark out the hall/s indicating the position of the stands. It is essential to ensure that the layout conforms to the final, agreed hall plan (see section 17.7.1 above).
- The stands will either be of the standard shell scheme supplied by the contractor appointed by the organiser or will be individually designed and constructed by contractors used by exhibitors – this will usually be in the case of larger stands.

■ The contractors are experienced in this work and provided there is sufficient time can generally be relied upon to have the stands completed by opening day. The organisers need to keep an eye on their work to ensure that everything is running smoothly.

17.8.2 Build-up and breakdown activities

The organiser has rented the hall/s for a set period into which must be fitted the build-up, exhibition opening and breakdown periods. It must be remembered that the longer the rental period, the higher the cost involved.

All contractors must be made aware, well in advance, of the times which are available for the different activities and the organiser must exercise strict supervision to ensure that there is no overlap.

FIGURE 17.2 *An example of a 2 m × 2 m booth (Source: Cape Wine, 2004: 2)*

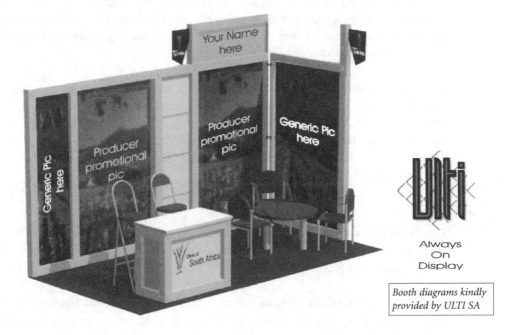

Always
On
Display

Booth diagrams kindly
provided by ULTI SA

FIGURE 17.3 *An example of a 2 m × 3 m booth (Source: Cape Wine, 2004: 3)*

17.8.3 Venue facilities

The organiser needs to check that the following facilities are available and in order when taking over the hall/s.

17.8.3.1 Parking

This has to be allocated amongst exhibitors, visitors, press, conference delegates, VIPs and organiser's staff. Clear signage is necessary to indicate the different areas and during the exhibition it is advisable to have parking attendants to avoid any confusion.

During the build-up and breakdown periods provision must be made for the various contractors.

17.8.3.2 Vehicle access

This is mainly of concern during the build-up period when contractors and exhibitors are bringing material into the hall/s and care must be taken to avoid aisles and entrances being blocked.

17.8.3.3 Catering

The hall owner generally provides the basic facilities in the way of preparation areas, tables and chairs, etc. In some cases the hall owner has given the catering concession to a caterer and in this case the organiser is concerned with the type of refreshments to be served, prices, opening and closing times, etc. and these will be agreed with the caterer. If there is no 'on-site' caterer, the organiser must appoint an organisation to provide the necessary facilities.

More complaints are received from exhibitors and visitors about catering at exhibitions than any other aspect. Any such complaints are detrimental to the organiser's reputation. For this reason it is essential to have a firm understanding with the caterer before the show opens about all details pertaining to this side of the show. It is advisable to check constantly during the exhibition that the standards agreed to are being maintained.

17.8.3.4 Toilets

This is another area where complaints can arise. When taking over the hall/s the organiser should inspect the toilet facilities with the hall owner to ensure that these are up to an acceptable standard.

During the period of the exhibition these areas must be cleaned regularly and a check kept that supplies of towels, soap, toilet paper, etc. are always on hand. Here again a member of the organiser's staff must be made responsible for carrying out daily checks on the facilities.

17.8.3.5 Electricity, water, compressed air facilities, etc.

At the time of taking over the hall/s the organiser must check with the hall owner that these aspects are of an acceptable standard. It is wise to establish what remedial action to take if there is a power failure at any time; for example, are stand-by generators available.

17.8.3.6 Fire protection

It is necessary to check with the hall owner that the required standard of fire protection equipment is in place. Have available the telephone number of the nearest fire brigade station. Ensure that an evacuation procedure in the event of fire has been given to all exhibitors and the organiser's staff are fully aware of the action they have to take in such an eventuality.

17.8.3.7 Signage

Insufficient signage can often be an irritation to visitors. One must put oneself in the position of a person who is coming for the first time to the city where the exhibition is taking place. He or she has probably had a great deal of difficulty in finding the exhibition venue so is not in the best frame of mind. It is up to the organiser to make certain that the signage in the exhibition (including the parking area) is clear and prominently displayed.

Exhibition halls, catering facilities, toilets, conference venue, banking and postal points, the way to the exit, etc. must all be well signposted.

Once the visitor has reached the exhibition hall, he or she must be able to find the location of any particular stand without difficulty. Both at the entrance to the hall and in prominent positions in the hall, it is helpful to have display boards indicating the position of all stands within the hall.

17.8.3.8 Visitor reception area

The speedy and efficient registration of visitors is the mark of a professional organiser. At a trade/industrial exhibition the majority of visitors will probably already be in possession of a complimentary ticket. However there will be visitors who do not fall into this category but qualify for free entrance. Provision must be made for such people to be able to complete tickets without any difficulty.

Nowadays most organisers make provision for speedily recording visitor details on a computer system, a by-product of which will be a visitor badge. Within the visitor reception area there should be booths for the selling of the exhibition catalogues.

If the reception area also contains the exit point, provision should be made for the research staff who will be conducting exit interviews with a predetermined percentage of visitors.

17.8.4 Security

Worldwide, security is a problem at exhibitions and similar events where large numbers of people are gathered together. Organisers must be aware of this situation and take the necessary measures to protect exhibitors and visitors against potential risks. There are two aspects to this problem:

- *Overall security at the exhibition.* This entails guarding the parking areas, reception, catering and halls. This is the responsibility of the organisers and entails employing a company which specialises in this type of work. The selected company must be given a clear brief as to their responsibilities that must be agreed on and implemented. During the course of the exhibition the organiser must carry out regular checks to make certain that the work is being carried out.
- *Exhibitors' responsibilities.* The security of exhibitors' stands and equipment is the responsibility of the exhibitors themselves and this point must be made quite clear right from the beginning. The company appointed by the organisers will be available to provide security on individual stands; alternatively, exhibitors may appoint their own security company. In such cases it is important that there is close liaison between the different organisations. It must be made quite clear that in the case of any clash or disagreement between separate companies, the organisers will make the final decision.

Exhibitors are responsible for arranging their own insurance for the products on their stands as well as for the stand construction, where a specially constructed stand is erected.

The period when the most problems occur is during breakdown when the hall/s are filled with exhibitors and contractors all intent on moving out their equipment as rapidly as possible. This is the time when thefts are most likely to occur and the utmost vigilance is needed.

17.8.5 Visitor/exhibitor research

The organiser has the responsibility for carrying out research on the attitudes and opinions of both exhibitors and visitors to a show. The basic reasons for this are to highlight any problems that occurred during the event so as to avoid a recurrence in the future and to obtain information that can be used to sell the next exhibition.

17.8.5.1 Exhibitors

The close of the show is not the ideal time to ask exhibitors to fill in a questionnaire. These can be distributed with the request that they be returned to the organiser when completed. Alternatively they can be posted to exhibitors shortly after the end of the show.

The information to be asked for covers the exhibitor's views on the facilities at the show, i.e. venue, length of exhibition, opening and closing times, services provided by contractors, parking, catering, toilets, etc. At the same time the exhibitor should be asked for views on the visitors, i.e. numbers, categories, enquiries and orders obtained.

Exhibitors should also be asked whether they will take part in the next exhibition. It is desirable to obtain a completed questionnaire from every exhibitor attending the show.

17.8.5.2 Visitors

Information about a visitor's attitudes and views are usually obtained by means of an exit interview. The questionnaire used should not be too lengthy as the visitor has probably spent several hours at the exhibition, is tired and wants to get home! The questions asked should cover such aspects as the visitor's name, employer, position, professional qualifications, views on the venue and facilities, products on display, attitude of exhibitor's staff, were any orders placed at the exhibition, are orders likely to be placed in the future, how did the visitor come to hear about the exhibition and whether he or she is likely to visit the next exhibition.

In some cases it can be worth sending a follow-up questionnaire to selected visitors to gather additional information after the show is over.

It is usual to employ a professional market research company to carry out the visitor research – such companies will decide how many interviews need to be carried out to obtain a statistically accurate result.

17.8.6 Exhibitor manual

This is published by the organiser and is issued to all exhibitors well in advance of the exhibition. It contains information of a general nature such as any restrictions imposed by the hall owner which could affect stand construction, dates and times when the halls will be open for build-up and breakdown. There will be forms by means of which the exhibitor can order requirements for shell scheme, furniture, carpets, stand cleaning, electrics, telephones, etc. The manual will also contain a section dealing with the exhibition catalogue so that the exhibitor can indicate the information to appear about his or her company and, if required, place an order for advertisements in the catalogue.

In some instances the organisers may issue a set of rules and regulations covering the exhibition.

17.8.7 Banking and postal facilities

At some of the larger venues these facilities are provided and it is worthwhile having them available in the case of larger exhibitions.

17.8.8 Follow-up activities by exhibitors

It is astounding that exhibitors, having spent very large sums on their participation at the show and used their staff to man the stand, often fail to follow up on the enquiries received at the show. This point should be brought to exhibitors' attention at the training sessions referred to above (section 17.7.9) and a reminder sent in the follow-up communication after the show.

17.9 VISITING EXHIBITIONS

In order to obtain the maximum benefit from their visit to an exhibition, visitors need to plan in advance.

- Set objectives – a visitor should be clear why he or she is visiting an exhibition. This may be to look for a particular product or service, to catch up on the latest developments in the industry, to meet suppliers who are exhibiting, to look for alternative suppliers, etc. In many cases the relative trade publication/s will publish a preview of the exhibition in the issue before the exhibition opens; alternatively, it may be possible to obtain an advance copy of the catalogue or ask the organisers for a list of exhibitors. This will enable the visitor to plan am economical tour of the show.
- Going around an exhibition is a tiring process and it is often better to make two visits on successive days rather than try to cover the whole show in a single day

- The majority of exhibitors will have available brochures, pamphlets and technical literature about their products that the visitor will want to collect. It is advisable to have some sort of bag or container to hold brochures and samples, although often it will be possible to obtain a suitable bag at the exhibition.

17.10 CODE OF ETHICS

EXSA requires its members to subscribe to and apply the Code of Ethics which has been established. This is designed to ensure that organisers deal with visitors and exhibitors with professionalism, integrity and courtesy. A lack of such treatment should be brought to the attention of EXSA for the matter to be investigated and dealt with speedily and professionally. The following is the Code of Ethics applicable to EXSA members.

Code of Ethics

The purpose of the EXSA Code of Ethics is to foster mutual respect and trust amongst individuals and organisations within the exhibition industry with regard to business dealings as members with other members, clients and the public in general.

Industry relationships and partnerships form an integral part of the provision of services and are critical to the success of exhibitions. This Code of Ethics has as its guidelines the principles of:

Honesty
- Integrity
- Fair Dealing
- Professionalism
- Accountability

Member companies and their representatives shall:
- Conduct business in accordance with accepted principles of honesty and shall speak truthfully in all business practices to pursue their client's legitimate objectives.
- Strictly adhere to and comply with current laws, regulations and legislation pertaining to the exhibition industry and in business operations.
- Bring credit to the association and the exhibition industry by displaying a high standard of professional behaviour to maintain accepted standards and quality of service.
- Endeavour to understand and fairly represent their own scope of knowledge and ability in performing services.

> ■ Undertake to treat all knowledge of a client's intentions or business organisation as confidential, until and with permission of the source to disclose it.
>
> ■ Display integrity and fair dealing with clients, competitors and vendors to foster healthy competition and the creation of value.
>
> ■ Be accountable and responsible for business dealings by using all reasonable effort to resolve any disputes or impropriety with members, suppliers, clients or any other party.

FIGURE 17.4 *EXSA Code of Ethics (Source: EXSA)*

Browse these Internet sites

http://www.exsa.co.za

http://www.aeo.org/

http://www.ceir.org/

http://www.iaem.org/

http://www.auma.de/

http://www.tradeshowweek.com/

http://www.international-confex.com/

QUESTIONS FOR SELF-EVALUATION

1 Discuss the purpose an exhibition is supposed to achieve.

2 Describe what research a prospective organiser should undertake prior to launching an exhibition.

3 What role does timing play in organising an exhibition?

4 Indicate the relevance of building prospective exhibitor lists when organising such an event.

5 When organising an exhibition hall plan, the budget and sales promotion activities need to be considered. Explain.

6 Indicate the role the appointment of outside contractors can play in organising an exhibition.

7 Explain what facilities an exhibition organiser must ensure are available at an exhibition venue.

8 What important elements should be contained in an exhibitors' manual?

9 Describe ways an exhibition organiser can ensure that the event provides visitors with maximum benefit from visiting an exhibition.

10 Indicate what research an exhibition organiser should undertake during the show. What is the relevance of this?

CHAPTER 18

Managing Political Events

Jo-Ansie van Wyk

AIM OF THE CHAPTER

The aim of this chapter is to enable the planning, management and evaluation of political, government and civic events.

LEARNING OBJECTIVES

After having studied this chapter, you should be able to:

- define and identify political, government and civic events;
- explain the objectives of political events;
- discuss the tourism potential of political events;
- elaborate on celebrity endorsement of political events;
- establish a process of planning, decision-making, implementing and managing;
- identify major stakeholders and other participants;
- determine fundraising and sponsorship needs;
- identify the potential security threats to a political event;
- be equipped to plan, manage, host and evaluate political events;
- research and promote historically significant events as tourism attractions.

18.1 INTRODUCTION

Since 1997, a number of national and international political events were held at the International Convention Centre (ICC) in Durban. Some of these include the Conference of the Non-Alignment Movement (NAM) in 1998, the Democratic Party Congress (1999), the World Conference Against Racism, Discrimination, Xenophobia and Related Intolerances (2001) and the World Movement for Democracy (2003 and 2004) (ICC, 2004a: 1–7). Furthermore, South Africa hosted the delegates of the peace negotiations at Sun City, the World Summit on Sustainable Development (WSSD), three presidential inaugurations, political party conferences, civil society events such as marches on HIV/Aids-related issues, hosting meetings of the Pan-African Parliament (PAP), the inaugural meeting of the African Union (AU) and events related to the twinning agreements signed between South African provinces and those abroad (see DFA, Undated: 1–30 and Van Wyk, 1998: 21–59).

This chapter focuses on various aspects related to managing and staging events with a political nature in order to achieve various political objectives such as those outlined in the next section. Furthermore, we introduce you to political events, and their significance and objectives; discuss their tourism potential; elaborate on the benefits of celebrity endorsement for such events; establish a process of planning, decision making, implementing and managing; identify major stakeholders and other participants; determine fundraising and sponsorship needs; identify the potential security threats of events; plan, and equip you to research, plan, manage and promote events celebrating historically significant political events as tourism attractions.

Staging a political event flawlessly offers noteworthy rewards to the event manager. Some of these awards are financial, others are more opportunities and greater prestige. Top political event managers/organisers take a strategic and comprehensive approach by building a solid organisational structure, facilitating collaboration between all stakeholders, managing suppliers, sponsors and donors effectively, communicating often and tracking all potential security and other risks, their potential impact and develop contingency plans (Kearney, 2002: 1 – Internet).

The main focus of this chapter is on the celebrations related to South Africa's decade of democracy as well as the presidential inauguration of 2004. Most political events can be described in terms of the phases of such an event. Often the planning, managing, hosting and concluding of a political event, whether it is sport or cultural or goes through a generic process, such as the generic process outlined in this section. For our purposes, Thabo Mbeki's inauguration in 2004 for his second term in office as State President, which coincided with the 10th celebration of South Africa's inclusive democracy is presented as a case study as it includes political, cultural, sports and other types of events as well. Both events are significant political events and were staged in various phases inside South Africa as well as abroad. The South African cabinet agreed to link all national holidays as well as Africa Day celebrations to the 10th-year celebrations. Not only did representatives from over 80 countries, 6 000 invited guests and 45 000 South Africans attend it, but was it celebrated widely across South Africa as well as at South African embassies abroad. Furthermore, celebrations at the Union Buildings included the performance of some of South Africa's top artists, 12 background singers, two 10-piece bands, traditional horn players, 12 traditional drummers, a 14-piece strong brass band and a mass choir.

18. 2 POLITICAL EVENTS: DEFINITION, OBJECTIVES AND EXAMPLES

What constitutes *politics*, or the *political* or *a political event*? Harold Laswell, an American political scientist, defined politics as the process of 'who gets what, when, where and how.' This definition assumes the presence of decision-makers (stakeholders), some form of authority (people with a mandate, planners and managers) (*who*), objectives (see below), position, interests or power to be achieved (*what*), a time frame (*when*), events, policies or campaigns (*how*), and at what venue and level, be it governmental, provincial, local (*where*). Whenever there is competition (*get*) in any society for scarce resources (be it water, land, jobs, contracts, power or a political appointment) this competition can be defined as *political*. For the purposes of our discussion, we define a political event as outlined below.

We can define a political event as a carefully planned, organised, managed and implemented/hosted event by political office bearers in either government, interest groups, civil society members or outsourced to event managers. Furthermore, this event has a political or public nature with a political purpose and message, with the intention to reach as many people as possible by a variety of means such as hosting an event, marketing and the media, and the intention to reach a specific objective or a number of objectives.

Further examples of political events are cited in figure 18.1.

The Constitution of the Republic of South Africa Act 108 of 1996, in sections 16, 17 and 18 of the Bill of Rights, guarantees all South Africans freedom of speech, association, assembly and expression. The importance and significance of political events (see figure 18.1 for some examples) lie in expressing these freedoms, having a number of political objectives it wants to achieve, having some tourism potential, creating employment and generating business opportunities.

As Tiffany (2001: 1 – Internet) indicates, some of the objectives/purposes of a political event are:

- To promote public policy or to harness public support for a new direction in government policy. Since 1994, for example, the South African government embarked on the process of introducing a new water and sanitation policy. Various events were organised by the national Department of Water Affairs and Forestry and non-governmental organisations (NGOs) in the water sector to consult and educate South Africans on the new policy. These culminated in the promulgation of a new water and sanitation policy in 1998 (see, for example, Van Wyk, 2000a).
- To increase political power and influence by, *inter alia*, winning an election, be it on national, provincial or local level. Political parties canvass for votes and campaign once again, as was evident in South Africa's general election in April 2004. These campaigns, for example, included a number of events such as political party rallies at the FNB Stadium in Soweto, various public meetings, and advertisements on the Internet, in newspapers and on the radio.

- To celebrate an event of historical significance such as an election victory, the funeral of Saartjie Baardman in 2003, and a decade of democracy in South Africa at the Freedom Park and Union Buildings in Pretoria during 2004.
- To celebrate and commemorate public holidays with historical political significance such as Human Rights Day (21 March), Freedom Day (27 April), Workers Day (1 May), National Women's Day (9 August), Heritage Day (24 September) and the Day of Reconciliation (16 December) as determined by the South African Public Holidays Act 36 of 1994.
- To conclude agreements as outlined in the document, *Practical guide and procedures for the conclusion of agreements*. Drafted by the Office of the Chief State Law Adviser (International Law), this document contains detailed procedures and processes for managing such events (DFA, Undated: 1–30).
- To communicate, to create awareness of and educate about an issue of public or international importance in order to influence government(s) to address the issue. This can include events to campaign to reinstate the death penalty in South Africa, or a march by business people to protest against crime or to create awareness of child abuse, or a government *imbizo*.

Political party and nongovernmental organisation (NGO) canvassing and/or campaign events

Fundraising activities for political parties, interest groups and NGOs

Political party conventions

Government *lekgotla's* and *zimbizos* (Zulu for 'open gathering') of which 410 were held in October 2003 across the country

General elections

Distribution of flyers during election or awareness campaigns

Protest marches

Political party rallies

Public speeches or statements by official office holder

Lobbying

Inaugurations and commemorations

Public holiday events

Political road shows

Campaign management and communication

Issue management

Fundraising

Public opinion surveys

Investment and UN conferences

Nelson Mandela's 85th birthday party

FIGURE 18.1 *Selected examples of politically related events (adapted from Attorney General, 2000: 1–3; Swindell, 2002: 1–6; and GCIS, 2003a: 1)*

18.3 GOVERNMENT, POLITICAL EVENTS AND TOURISM

The commemoration of historically significant political events has major tourism potential – especially when held at historically important venues. A tourist can be described as a person visiting or invited to an area for business, family affairs, political activities, celebrations, education, sport or holiday away from his/her hometown as well as spending money in a location other than the one where he/she earns it. Events held at, for example, Robben Island (where Nelson Mandela and others were imprisoned) off Cape Town, Ulundi (the seat of the Zulu king), the Voortrekker Monument (commemorating The Great Trek) and the Union Buildings (official seat of government) in Pretoria, parliament in Cape Town, and Soweto (where, for example, the 1976 uprisings took place) are well known to attract domestic and international tourists to the venue and area where it takes place (see figure 18.2). Think of the thousands of invited guests and members of the public who attended the 1999 and 2004 presidential inaugurations on the lawns of the Union Buildings or those who assembled outside Victor Verster Prison to watch Nelson Mandela's release from prison after 27 years. The 1998–2000 centennial commemorations of the South African War (also sometimes referred to as the Anglo-Boer War) is another illustration of the tourism potential of historical events. Various initiatives such as the Diamond Fields National Battlefield Route in the Northern Cape along the N12 highway between Hopetown and Kimberley, theme exhibitions, walking trails, and battlefield tours focusing on the Siege of Kimberley and Magersfontein attract domestic and international tourists.

---

5 000 (including 30 heads of state) international and local dignitaries attended the 1999 presidential inauguration

50 000 people attended the abovementioned event

700 local and international journalists and camera crews covered the event

45 foreign heads of state and governments attended President Mbeki's second inauguration in 2004

45 000 South Africans attended the 2004 presidential inauguration

---

FIGURE 18.2 *Some statistics relating to political events held in Pretoria at the Union Buildings (Sources: Van Wyk, 2000b: 460–482; News24.com, 2004a: Internet)*

Furthermore, tourism's economic and political dimensions have implications for the allocation of and competition for power (and hence decision-making) and resources, and access to these resources (such as budgets) within host communities, cultural representation, socialisation and the income of a particular community or province. By their nature, governments and their decision-makers have the power to decide, and, to return to Laswell's definition, 'who gets what, where, when and how' in the development of tourism. This is illustrated in the establishment of a Ministry of Environmental Affairs and Tourism in 1994 and the South African government's decision to market and develop the country as a major tourist attraction and world-class venue for staging international events.

Governments issue passports to their citizens to travel, governments institute visa requirements, and governments regulate procedures for the conclusion of international agreements (see DFA, Undated; 1–30) and foreign exchange transactions. In undemocratic countries, the government even issues travel documents for its citizens to travel from one of its regions to another as free movement of people is strictly regulated to, *inter alia*, prevent political events from taking place. It is also often governments that warn their citizens not to pay a visit to a particular unstable state or region. The US and UK governments, for example, regularly issue statements to discourage their citizens from visiting the Middle East – especially since the war in Iraq in March 2003. Statements issued by the British Foreign and Commonwealth Office (FCO) advising British and other citizens about the advisability or otherwise of travelling to a particular region are often available on its Web site at www.fco.uk.

Targeting tourists is sometimes used as a political tool by radical anti-government groups to gain national and international recognition for their cause. The killing of tourists aboard the cruise liner *Achillo Lauro* in the Mediterranean Sea, the Lockerbie air disaster in Scotland, the kidnapping of German tourists in North Africa and some Latin American states are cases in point. As we elaborate on later, the potential security risks of political events have become more significant since the attacks of 11 September 2001 in the US, the bomb explosion in a Bali nightclub in October 2002 where a number of Australian tourists were killed, and the subsequent global alerts issued by governments warning against possible terrorism attacks.

18.4 CELEBRITY ENDORSEMENT OF A POLITICAL EVENT OR CAUSE

As Chen and Henneberg (2004: 4–5) and Pringle (2004: 7) indicate, commercial companies, political parties and interest groups often use celebrities extensively to increase the support for their ideas and policies, and appeal and promotion of their products and/or services. Pringle (2004: 7) cites *Forbes'* rating of the top 100 celebrities endorsing products and services. These include, amongst others, Tiger Woods, Oprah Winfrey, Steven Spielberg, Jennifer Lopez, Will Smith, Eddy Murphy, Michael Jordan and Michael Schumacher. Celebrity endorsement done by sports personalities, actors, figures in the entertainment industry, and leading church and business figures in the society is increasingly becoming a powerful business, political, advertising and communication instrument. A celebrity or public figure's status, prestige, legitimacy and credibility can by his or her political endorsement create 'positive effects' in the minds of supporters, donors, sponsors, tourists, voters, tax payers and consumers. As case study 18.1 indicates, a celebrity can act as spokesperson, campaigner and/or endorser (supporter) for a specific political event or cause. In 2003, the Hollywood actor and producer Arnold Schwarzennegger was elected as California's governor having been an endorser/supporter of the Republican Party earlier. Pringle's (2004: 7) conclusion about celebrity endorsements is simply 'celebrity sells'.

Case study 18.1: An example of celebrity endorsement
(Source: BBC News, 2004b: Internet)

Stars prepare for war charity gig

Nineteen years ago, Quincy Jones produced charity hit *We Are The World* to help raise money for Ethiopian famine victims.

On Sunday he is doing it again, this time in Rome, which will be the setting for a huge star-studded concert.

Stars such as Alicia Keys, Norah Jones, Naomi Campbell and Angelina Jolie will be there to launch Jones' new project We Are The Future.

The concert will help children living in war-torn cities across the globe.

Jones, arguably the most famous record producer in the world, is known as the man behind Michael Jackson's best-selling albums during the 1980s.

He is also the driving force behind this new project, which is designed to help children in conflict zones around the world by setting up child centres in Rwanda, Afghanistan, Ethiopia, Eritrea, Palestine and Sierra Leone, the first of which is already open.

'You have to care about the other people now, and especially the plight of the children who are going to be the future.' Quincy Jones

Despite the many successes of his career to date, Quincy Jones is evidently very excited to see his project coming together.

He told the BBC: 'Two weeks ago the mayor of Kigali in Rwanda announced the opening of the first We Are The Future centre.

'It's open! The kids are playing in it right now! But the only way we can secure their future is to create a common destiny.

'We can't say, "Our kids are okay, they've got clean clothes, they've got education, food every day, I don't care what happens with the rest."

'That's over, that's over believe me.'

Jones is by no means a music industry guru who organises things from his office.

In June he was in Baghdad trying to get children in need of medical treatment to hospital in Washington.

Health is one of the ways in which We Are The Future aims to help, as Jones explained.

'It will adopt six of the most in crisis cities in the world and systematically implement them with a system of support, though the World Bank, through water purification, through agriculture and the World Food Programme, through sports with FIFA, through technology,' he said.

The concert on Sunday evening will take place at Circo Massimo, at the heart of ancient Rome.

It is free and will be broadcast around the world by MTV, to raise the profile of the project and attract future funding. A charity record will also be produced. Artists from the countries We Are The Future aims to help, such as Noa from Israel, will perform alongside Carlos Santana, Italian singer Zucchero and host of others, while leading figures like Oprah Winfrey, tennis star Serena Williams and Italian footballer Francesco Totti will help present the show.

The concert was first announced last year at a conference organised by the Rome-based Glocal Forum.

'Charity fatigue'

As part of this different unifying events were held, including football matches with Israelis and Palestinians playing against Tutsis and Hutus, and children from Sarajevo and Belgrade singing *We are the World* together.

For Jones this was a kind of test, to see whether the concert would work, and he left convinced it would: 'It just clicked as a family, something magical happened.

'It was meant to be and we decided that the concert like We Are The World would be the great launch, like the exclamation point that launches it all.'

The world has seen lots of charity concerts, but Jones rejects any idea of charity fatigue, believing now it is more important than ever to do all you can.

'You think you can get away with it because you've got a nice big house, a barbecue pit and all of that but it's not true.

'You have to care about the other people now, and especially the plight of the children who are going to be the future. This situation can only get worse if you don't care.'

Chen and Henneberg (2004: 19–25) also cite how celebrity political endorsement was applied during the campaign for the Taipei City Councillor election in 2002. Here celebrities participated in political party meetings and door-to-door canvassing for an election, political event or cause, political leafleting and bill boards (where the celebrity is figured supporting a campaign, event or person).

About Entertainment, a South African events management company, books South African celebrities and artists such as, *inter alia*, Vicky Sampson, The Soweto String Quartet, Barry Hilton, Basetsane Kumalo, Vuyo Mbuli and Bayete for similar and artistic events. Celebrity endorsement of the democracy celebrations in 2004 were illustrated by, for example, the appearance of 200 celebrities and artists such as Hugh Masekela, Danny Kay, Sibongile Khumalo, Miriam Makeba, Vusi Mahlasela at the concert staged at the Union Buildings (Biz-Community, 2004: Internet; News24.com, 2004a: Internet).

18.5 SECURITY, RISKS AND POLITICAL EVENTS

Recent protest marches, bomb threats and explosions at politically related events included the disruption of several annual meetings of the World Bank, the World Trade Organisation (WTO) and International Monetary Fund (IMF) as well as the postponement of an international trade fair in Baghdad, Iraq, in April 2004 (Forbes, 2004: 1).

Event security risks can be defined as any event, action or individual that could disrupt the managing and staging of an event, pose safety and security hazards, or cause reputation damage. Event risk management entails an analysis of crowd management systems, command and control assessments, contingency plans, incident management training of all relevant staff, emergency evacuation, risk assessment before, during and after an event, security procedure development, site safety, access control, and a comprehensive search of venue prior to an event (Control Risks Group, 2003: 1).

Security and risks are some of the main concerns on the part of the client and the event managers that needs to be addressed early in event management process as well as during the planning and hosting process. In the wake of 11 September 2001, a greater awareness exists with regard to the potential risks for attacks on major public and/or international venues and meetings with historical and/or political significance. Even prior to 2001, evidence illustrates the political and security risks and concerns associated with such events and venues.

In the past a number of Olympic Games were used for political purposes, for example, in 1936 Nazi Germany under Adolf Hitler staged the Olympic Games in Berlin in such a way as to glorify his ideas about national socialism. The 1972 Olympic Games in Munich, Germany, the first to be held in Germany since the 1936 Games and the Second World War, is alas also often remembered for the killing of Israeli athletes. In 1980, the US boycotted the Moscow Olympic Games, followed in 1984 when the then USSR boycotted the Los Angeles Olympic Games – both states using it as a political instrument against one another during the height of the Cold War. In the build-up to the Athens Games in 2004, concerns were once again expressed about a 'high degree of probability' for violent attacks during the course of the games (BBC News, 2004a: Internet).

Perpetrators of violence or those posing a risk to political events often target public events in order 'to achieve maximum publicity for explicit aims' (Whittaker, 2004: 50). Violence or attacks at political events are often premeditated, politically motivated and are applied to threaten and/or intimidate government or the general public. Whittaker (2004: 92) concludes 'violence makes the headlines' – especially if it happens at a politically significant event.

© Juta & Co Ltd

Four broad areas with regard to security management of a political event need to be considered and implemented. These are:

- professional security management;
- threat assessment;
- security objectives and plan, and
- post-event assessment and critique.

When appointing an events security company, confirm the credentials of the company. Threat assessment includes the assessment of safety risks associated with a particular event, venue, and/or person. An assessment of the venue, the significance of the event, the event theme, the expected attendees/audience are factors to consider. Most often political events necessitate the involvement of metropolitan police, the South African Police Services (SAPS) and the South African National Defence Force (SANDF). Once a security firm has been appointed, security objectives can be identified and a security plan and protocol developed. This should be done in consultation with the event management team. Security deployment should include security inspections at entrances, explosive detection dogs and equipment, metal detection technology, uniformed and undercover guard placement, searches, radio equipment, vendor accreditation and crowd control plans. Security services should already be operational during the event set up phase. Service providers as well as guest accreditation, clearance and ticketing should be done during this phase. Lastly, security services offered during an event should be assessed after the event by both the security company as well as event managers (Buser, 2004: 1–5; McGuire, 2004: 6–7).

18.6 EVENTS TECHNOLOGY

During the 2004 US presidential campaign, a number of candidates cited the major role played by the Internet in their campaign. Political event managers were quick to harness the power of technology. Furthermore, computer software programs such as those developed by Vocus enabled event managers to distribute information as well as execute management functions electronically. Examples of these include automated invitations to and attendance of political events, surveying the benefits and costs from attending and managing a particular event, as well as conducting online public opinion polls on issues such as those offered by Netpulse Real-Time Online Polls (PoliticsOnline, 2004a: Internet). The political event manager can also programme this package to address the specific needs of a client. By entering information about your client, his or her competitors and the relevant issues, this computer program can determine whether it is useful to attend a particular political event or support a cause (Vocus, 2004: Internet).

Similar services are offered by, e.g., K-Praxis (2004: 1), *Campaign Organizer* (advertised as 'political campaign management software'), PoliticsOnline (2004b:

Internet) and Cubistix's (2004: Internet) *Political Opsware* software which, inter *alia*, tracks political risk management. *Database Systems Corp.* applies call-centre technology in managing political events and uses its PACER political message dialling system through which it broadcasts and markets upcoming political events, as well as party positions on issues and related news to targeted audiences. Event managers use this system, for example, to play a particular political message, introduce candidates and/or issues, promote an upcoming political event, conduct political surveys and touch-phone responses and political fundraising. Lastly, this software has the ability to generate real-time reports, graphs and statistics, an important evaluating service to measure the effectiveness and impact of the political event or campaign (*Database Systems Corp*, 2004: Internet).

18.7 GENERIC PHASES OF A POLITICAL EVENT

Political players, as clients, often outsource the planning, implementation and management of political events to professional event management companies and/or consultants with a proven track record, such as the example in figure 18.3. Politicians simply either do not have the skills nor the time to plan and manage an event. Political event consultancy firms, such as the Australian-based *Political Solutions* (2004: Internet), the US-based *Urban Strategies* (2004: Internet) and *RedZone Communications Inc.* (2004: Internet) advertise themselves as offering the following political event management services:

- briefings for political stakeholders;
- briefings on government tender processes;
- issue management;
- government relations;
- grass roots organising;
- political fundraising;
- financial management and reporting;
- planning, implementing and managing an event with a specific purpose;
- lobbying;
- training seminars;
- public meetings and conferences;
- acting as political power brokers and creating access to key decision makers;
- managing election campaigns and election contribution campaigns;
- organising high level conferences, commemorations, inaugurations and celebrations;
- organising celebrity endorsement of a political event;
- facilitating the attendance of key government official at major events;
- finding and managing the venue;
- arranging accommodation for participants, and
- conducting evaluations of the event.

Inaugural celebrations of various US presidents and governors
Over 100 memorial ceremonies including the Vietnam War Memorial and Korean War Memorial
Eight presidential inaugurals
Special Events Director for US Government General Services Administration
Pope John II's visit to the US
Economic summits such as the Pacific Rim Economic Summit and the International Joint Economic Summit
Republican Party National Committee Annual Gala – a tribute to Ronald Reagan
Desert Storm National Victory Celebration Parade
Washington DC Bicentennial Celebrations
Martin Luther King Junior Birthday Celebrations
Earth Day celebrations

FIGURE 18.3 *Political events planned, implemented and managed by special political events consultant, Jim Arthur (Source: Westward Connections, 2004: Internet)*

Most political events can be described in terms of the phases of such an event. Often the planning of an event, whether it is political or cultural, goes through a generic process; such a generic process is outlined in this section. As indicated in the introduction, this process will be applied by referring to the events of April 27, 2004. Figure 18.4 outlines an operations checklist followed in the planning of this and related events.

■ ***Identification of need.*** The need for a political event (such as those mentioned above) is identified by a political player (the client) who either approaches an events manager, an event management company or institutes a bidding/tendering process. During this phase the client identifies the type of event required to be arranged as well as the purpose it aims to achieve. In our case study (18.2a), the need was to commence the organisation of celebrations for the 10th year of democracy as well as the inauguration of the president after the April 2004 elections. The proposed special political event is researched, budgeted and presented to the highest political authority for consideration. The goal is to receive approval for the organisation to participate or produce the event with a political impact. Next the assignment of an event manager, committee as well as which departments or sectors will participate in and coordinate the event occurred. This was identified by, *inter alia*, Government Communications and Information Services (GCIS) and the ANC. Former ANC MP and former South African Ambassador to The Netherlands, Carl Niehaus, was appointed as project manager. Event planning started in September 2003 (News24.com, 2004e: Internet). 'Celebrating ten years of freedom: a people united for a better South Africa and a better world' was chosen as the theme for these celebrations (GCIS, 2003b: 1). Towards the end of 2003 a document, 'A strategic framework for marking ten years of freedom', was released outlining the purpose, challenges, structures, processes, phases and themes for these events. The Department of Foreign Affairs (DFA) also released a document, 'Ten years celebrations of freedom. The international programme', outlining events to be celebrated abroad (DFA, 2003: 1–43).

- **Bidding/tendering process.** Whether a bidding process is required or not, the event manager (in this case GCIS as well as registered service providers) was expected to present preliminary models to the organising committee. This process could include a SWOT analysis (see figure 18.4) by the event manager of various event options, his or her company's ability to plan, manage and host such an event, research into the background to the event and the identification of the client's needs and requirements, as well as a preliminary budget. A SWOT (Strengths, Weaknesses, Opportunities and Threats) analysis is just one way of establishing the potential security risks of an event; or an event manager's potential to manage and stage an event. Once these are achieved, the proposal is submitted to the client. In our case study (18.2a), cabinet approved all the main events.

Strengths	Weaknesses
Opportunities	Threats

FIGURE 18.4 *Elements of a SWOT analysis (Source: Quickmba, 2004: Internet)*

- **Evaluation and approval of proposal(s).** Once the organising committee has evaluated the proposal, consultations with the event manager take place in order to reach agreement on matters such as the scope, impact, budget and nature of the event. Approval of the proposal means that the event manager can now plan the event in greater detail.
- **Defining overall management structure, appointment of staff and responsibilities assigned.** During this phase, personnel are appointed or assigned by advertising, screening, appointing, training (if needed). Other members of the planning team such as those responsible for finances, marketing, logistics, client relations, operations and legal matters are appointed.

  A task team appointed by cabinet, consisting of ministers and directors-general of government departments were responsible for supervising the planning for the anniversary celebrations and the presidential inauguration. Secondly, the task team was responsible for leadership to structures and institutions such as the Government Communication and Information Service (GCIS), the Department of Foreign Affairs (DFA), The Presidency, the International Marketing Council, the Proudly South African campaign, SA

Tourism, and all government and provincial departments planning the event. Furthermore, planning, preparation and coordination structures included a Project Team and Steering Committee assisted by various teams (GCIS, 2003c: 4).

- **Planning.** This is the most important phase and is presented in a number of sub-phases discussed below. Five phases (see table 18.1) were identified and followed by the organisers for these celebrations.

TABLE 18.1: *Phases in the planning of celebrations for South Africa's decade of democracy (Source: DFA, 2003: 1–43; GCIS, 2003c: 1–5)*

Phase 1: Pre-communication phase
Started at President Mbeki's State of the Nation address to Parliament in February 2003 and lasted until Freedom Day in April 2003.
This initiated an early awareness campaign of event planning and preparation
Phase 2: The tenth year of freedom begins
Freedom Day, 27 April 2003 initiated this phase which lasted until President Mbeki's State of the Nation address in February 2004. 
Freedom Day marked the 10th year of democracy in 2004 and national days such as Heritage Day and government activities were linked to this. Consultations started with various stakeholders. Events were planned for celebrations in the US, UK, Africa and Asia. South African National Orders were newly branded. (National Orders are awards offered by the government to individuals as a recognition of their contribution in any field in South Africa.)
By September 2003, election campaigns for April 2004's election started.

Phase 3: State of the Nation address (From April 2004 and including elections)
The State of the Nation address included a Ten Year Review, events structured for Freedom Park, the 10th anniversary of the SANDF and public service, consultations, state visits, South African events at the United Nations and African Union.
Phase 4: From the first decade of freedom to the next: celebrations on Freedom Day and presidential inauguration
This period included local and international celebratory events as well as the presidential inauguration.
Phase 5: Sustaining the platform created through the celebrations for some time after the celebrations
For the remainder of 2004, all national public holidays and other related events were branded accordingly.

One important aspect of managing a political event is regular consultations with various stakeholders. Due to the nature of politics, various interests are at stake. When stakeholders and their interests are not taken into account, the success of an event can be jeopardised. In August 2003, for example, Deputy President Jacob Zuma met with political parties represented in parliament to brief them as well as receiving their input on proposals for the celebrations of South Africa's 10th year of democracy (The Presidency, 2004: 1). Similar consultations were held with representatives of civil society sectors such as organised labour, business, academia, the media, agriculture, religious groups, the South African Local Government Association (SALGA), parastatals, South African missions abroad and education. These representatives were required to consult with their constituencies and give feedback at subsequent meetings of this nature (GCIS, 2003b: 1; 2003c: 1–5).

- *Securing funds, sponsors and donors*: The benefits for companies that sponsor an event include contributions to the event programme, marketing, networking opportunities and privileged access to main stakeholders of the event. Securing funds for any political event often determines the scope of the event. In order to address this need, sponsors and donors are often approached. Once funds are secured, stakeholder management becomes more important. The South African government budgeted R60m for the inauguration and R30m for the 10th anniversary of democracy celebration. One of the sponsors of the event was The Coca-Cola Company (News24.com, 2004f: Internet).

- *Venue identification*: Political events are sometimes staged at historically significant venues, buildings or areas. A venue should be able to house the expected number of people from a logistical point of view. Venues such as Mary Fitzgerald Square in Newtown, Johannesburg, St George's Park Stadium in Port Elizabeth, V&A Waterfront in Cape Town and the Peter Mokhaba

Stadium in Polokwane were previously used for some or other political event. Since 1994, South African presidents have been inaugurated in the Amphitheatre at the Union Buildings in Pretoria followed by a mass outdoor concert on the lawns of the complex. When deciding on a venue, a number of important aspects related to the smooth running of the event are important to consider. Some of these can be illustrated by the services offered by the International Convention Centre (ICC) in Durban, as well as those that needed to be in place for the inauguration and celebrations:

- access to airports, bus and railway stations, taxi stands;
- access to accommodation facilities (if required);
- a business centre with telephones, fax, postal, Internet and courier services;
- facilities for physically challenged persons;
- a computerised message service;
- catering facilities;
- medical services;
- secure parking;
- suites for private meetings;
- security teams and surveillance cameras;
- automatic fire detection and sprinkler systems;
- banking and foreign exchange facilities (ICC: 2004a: Internet).

- **Information technology and sound systems.** During this phase, the scope of technology available and determining what is required, are identified. Furthermore, event support systems, computer hardware and software programs, media information systems, Internet, ticketing/access should be determined as well as contingency plans.

- **Marketing.** Once the abovementioned aspects have been clarified, a Web site of the event should be constructed as well as a media and marketing campaign initiated. Media operations such as accreditation, a media centre, licensing of broadcast rights, as well as regular press statements and conferences about the event should be organised during this phase. In the run-up to the main events, the Department of Foreign Affairs marketed South Africa abroad and staged events in foreign countries where South Africa is represented (DFA, 2003: 1–43).

- **Set up of event.** This phase initiates the period just before the event takes place and includes attending to and setting up of all the physical requirements such as audiovisual equipment, seating arrangements, signs and table settings. Furthermore, as case study 18.2a indicates, various other issues need to be taken into account – an operations checklist that can be applied to most events is included in the case study.

- **Rehearsing.** In order to pre-empt any unwanted events hijacking the main day, rehearsing the day or event is of major importance. The outdoor concert staged on April 27, 2004 and organised by Joe Chakela was rehearsed during the weekend prior to the inauguration (News24.com, 2004e: Internet).

- **Arrival of foreign guests.** See case study below and the discussion above.

Case study 18.2a:
A summarised operations checklist for the presidential inauguration which coincided with the main event at the Union Building on April 27, 2004 (Adapted from: Kearney, 2002: 1–12; Getz, 1997: 89-2-93)

What is the purpose of the event? The celebrations for South Africa's decade of democracy were aimed at 'uniting the country in marking the achievements of South Africa and the consolidation of democracy since 27 April 1994. The celebrations also provide an opportunity to consolidate the emergence of our national identity as well as for international positioning of the country' (The Presidency, 2003: 1).

Who will be involved in the planning, management and staging of the event? This is discussed above.

What is the programme for the event? For President Mbeki's inauguration, the ceremony started with songs and a film on the apartheid struggle broadcast on giant television screens at the foot of the Union Buildings (News24.com, 2004a: Internet). One hundred big screen televisions were placed at venues around the country (*Mail & Guardian* Online, 2004: Internet. See also table 18.1 and case study 18.2b). Major events as planned by DFA and outlined in 'Ten years celebrations of freedom. The international programme staged abroad' (DFA, 2003: 1–43).

What are the requirements pertaining to the management of this event?

Where will the event take place? What locations were identified? Refer to case study 18.2c.

What are the requirements for ticketing, sales and access of the event? The domestic as well as the global market should be considered. What are the requirements for merchandise sales?

Will any procession, parades, crowd control, seating and staging of an activity be required?

Should open spaces be left to allow for the free movement of people?

What decorations and/or décor (such as flags, banners and posters) will be required and allowed?

Should any special provision be made for animals (dogs and/or horses) for crowd control, or facilities for use by disabled persons?

What assistance is provided for disabled individuals?

What are the infrastructure and transport requirements for the event? What provision should be made for infrastructure? Who will manage and set these up? The area around the Union Buildings was cordoned off, as were streets near the Caledonian Sports Grounds, Supersport Stadium in Centurion and the State Theatre in the city centre. Public transport bused people from points in Pretoria, Johannesburg and Ekurhuleni. VIPs were transported to the Amphitheatre from Bryntirion, the parliamentary village in Pretoria. Other

VIPs such as Nelson Mandela and FW de Klerk arrived by motorcade and journalists were transported from Supersport Stadium in Centurion (News24.com, 2004g: Internet).

What power needs exist? Should power generators, phone lines and computer access be organised?

What special equipment is required for, for example, medical emergencies, access control, security and vehicles? Who will supply these? Although security was tight at the inauguration and the concert that followed it, a stampede of 200 people injured at least 15 people during the concert when more than 20 000 people broke through security fences at the start of the concert. This caused the concert to be interrupted to bring the situation under control. A number of local and foreign journalists were also robbed in the process (News24.com, 2004b: Internet; 2004c: Internet). Injured people were taken to the nearby Pretoria Academic Hospital, which also needed to be included with other medical services in the planning phase (News24.com, 2004b: internet).

What equipment, tools and supplies are needed during the planning process as well as on the event day? This is discussed below.

What security risks may arise? What type of access control will be followed? Special security measures were in place by 27 April 2004 as many foreign representatives, South African dignitaries and ordinary people were attending the event. Police and other security force members from all over the country arrived in Pretoria the week prior to the inauguration. Their duties included regular explosives sweeps of hotels hosting VIPs as well as the Union Building complex, visible policing along main routes into Pretoria, emergency drills as well as crime prevention operations. Security services included the SAPS' VIP protection unit, the bomb disposal unit, the crack squad and hostage negotiations units as well as Tshwane Metropolitan Emergency and Security Services. Health services were also on standby and disaster management experts assessed fire hazards and crowd control. Furthermore, a no-fly zone was enforced around the Union Building (*Mail & Guardian* Online, 2004: Internet; *Business Day*, 2004: Internet).

What command and communications functions should be catered for? Who is responsible for specific functions on the day of the event? This is discussed above.

What programmes and activities should be planned for and compiled? Refer to case study 18.2c.

Are volunteers going to assist in the event? If so, advertising, screening, appointing, training, clothing and scheduling of staff will be required. Furthermore, identification and access control should be arranged for.

What directions, parking, loading zones and signage are needed?

With regard to transportation infrastructure, the following should be considered: adequate and secure parking, access control with clear directions and seating arrangements, public transportation, transportation of event organisers, general public, VIPs and equipment, as well as the transportation of materials needed. Arrangements should also be made for the transportation of materials after the event.

What guidelines should be followed during accreditation? Who should be accredited? How should accreditation be indicated?

What arrangements should be made for safety, security and medical needs during the event? These arrangements should include first-aid, emergency response and accessibility, comfort stations such as ablution facilities, shelters from the weather, security force presence and waste disposal. For example, 400 portable toilets were erected on the lawns of the Union Buildings (News24.com, 2004g: Internet).

What provision should be made for hospitality and refreshments? A fast-food outlet distributed 40 000 food parcels and Coca-Cola provided free cool drinks and water. Catering, as with so many aspects of an event, can easily go wrong such as on the day of the inauguration when the caterers arrived late with beverages for hundreds of journalists and workers who had been working since 3.00 a.m. Tight security was one of the reasons why the caterers failed to deliver on time as this aspect of the event was not taken into account. Furthermore, the caterers failed to set up their canteen before the noon deadline on the day before the event (News24.com, 2004i: Internet).

What protocol should be followed? This was done in consultation with the Department of Foreign Affairs (DFA).

What command and operations facilities should be in place?

How are communications managed before, during and after the event?

Will any celebrities and artists be appearing? Refer to case studies 18.2b and 18.2c.

What kind of technical facilities are needed? These could include electricity, communications systems, media liaison, sound systems, public address systems, video screens, computer screens, audiovisual equipment and those relating to broadcasting. Furthermore, determine capacity requirements such as cables and power sources, an event network, network equipment and cabling, public announcement system, telephones and fax machines, and wireless systems (such as walkie-talkies and cell phones). By applying various instruments and types of technology, the event manager can provide high volume contacts and notifications, extend business hours, cut costs, provide multilingual support, and efficiently plan, market and manage a political event. The main event of 27 April 2004 was relayed to the nearby Caledonian Sports Grounds in Pretoria where the whole programme was broadcast on big screens.

What contingency plans are in place? Has insurance been taken out?

■ *Event day. 27 April 2004* celebrated the exact 10th commemoration of democracy in South Africa. Case studies 18.2b and 18.2c include details of the main event in Pretoria as well as other events countrywide and abroad.

Case study 18.2b:
A brief review of the event (Sources: News24.com, 2004e; 2004f; 2004g; 2004h: Internet)

Sunday, 25 April
VIPs arriving at Johannesburg International and Waterkloof Air Force Base

Monday, 26 April

02:00	Guests and accredited journalists arrived at Supersport Park, Centurion to be bussed to the Union Buildings at 05:00
06:00–23:00	Live broadcast of day's events on SABC2
07:00	Start of entertainment on lawns of Union Buildings
08:30	Arrival of first invited guests
10:00	Prayers by representatives of several faiths and induction and inauguration of president by Chief Justice Arthur Chaskalson.
10:45	President Mbeki addressed the nation
11:00–12:00	SANDF military salute, air display and national salute
12:00–13:00	Hour long respective play depicting South Africa since 1994
13:00–14:00	Lunch for invited guests in marquees
14:00–19:00	Mass outdoor concert featuring 200 artists produced by Billy Domingo. Performance of, *inter alia*, songs composed especially for inauguration by group called Creative Collectors. Performing artists included Wanda Baloyi, Bongo Maffin, Danny K, Fohloza, Jennifer Jones, Jabu Khanyile, Mafikizolo, Arthur Mafokate, Busi Mhlongo, Joe Nina, PJ Powers, Karen Zoid, Dolly Ratebe, Abigail Kunheka, Lundi and Ishmael.
Evening	Gala event for 1 300 VIPs at State Theatre where some top South African artists such as Semenya, Hugh Masekela, Letta Mbulu, Sibongile Khumalo, Judith Sephuma, Vicky Sampson, Abdullah Ibrahim, Gwangwa, etc. performed. Event relayed to big screens on Church Square and broadcast on SABC2 TV.

> **Case study 18.2c:**
> **A selection of some of the special local and international events staged to celebrate South Africa's 10th year of democracy** (Sources: DFA, 2003: 1–43; News24.com, 2004d; 2004h: Internet)
>
> Ten-day celebrations in Belgium and Luxembourg including a film festival showing *Amandla*, *Promised Land* and *Malunde*, expos of all nine South Africa's provinces, photo exhibitions, Manneken Pis dressed as Nelson Mandela
>
> Music festivals around the country featuring Stimela, Jabu Hlongwane, Sipho Makhabane in Nelspruit
>
> Birthday parties for children born on 27 April 1994
>
> Songs especially composed for event by Creative Collectors
>
> Sports events, theatre productions
>
> Unveiling of sculptures of South Africa's Nobel Peace Prize laureates such as Chief Albert Luthuli, Archbishop Desmond Tutu, FW de Klerk and Nelson Mandela
>
> Events in, for example, Algeria, Nigeria, The Netherlands, Egypt, Sweden, Russia, Germany, Spain, France, Hungary, the UK and Italy
>
> Briefings to the diplomatic corps
>
> Annual International Fair at the Union Buildings
>
> Outreach Programme of DFA
>
> Lecture/seminar programme with local and international intellectuals and academics

- **Tear down.** All items set up before the event are taken down. This phase also involves finalising insurance and legal claims, final accounting and media communications. During this phase all items and temporary structures set up for the event are taken down. Before the South African elections of April 2004, political parties put up campaign posters. The tear-down phase for their political events in some cases was neglected causing some parties to be fined for not removing their posters as agreed (*The Cape Argus*, 2004: Internet).

- **Post-event management and evaluation:**
  - **Follow-up.** After the conclusion of the event, all action and follow-up items are completed
  - **Debriefing and evaluation.** After the debriefing, the event manager and event coordinators evaluate the event and ascertain whether objectives were achieved. A report is compiled and distributed to decision-makers. The event manager, coordinators, staff and outside consultants meet to determine the degree of success of the event. Refer to table 18.2.

TABLE 18.2: *Venue debriefing questionnaire (Source: Catherwood & Van Kirk , 1992: 188)*

Venue location: ....

Name of event: ....

Date: ....

Timing of event: ....

Provide descriptive details of any of the following occurrences.

Accidents:..

Injuries: ....

Security problems: ....

Event interruptions: ....

Thefts:..

Construction failures:..

Threatened claims of litigation:..

Other accidents: ....

Suggestions for improvements: ....

Browse these Internet sites

www.gov.za South African government
www.gcis.gov.za Government Communication and Information System (GCIS)
www.dfa.gov.za South African Department of Foreign Affairs (DFA)
www.10years.gov.za South Africa's 10th year of democracy celebrations
www.saconference.co.za and www.biz-community.com
Direct Access – *The conference handbook.*
www.mbizo.co.za *ABC of Event Management and ABC of Event Success.*
www.gov.za/sa overview/holidays.htm Origins and significance of South African
public holidays
The March 2004 edition of *Event Solutions* is a special edition on suitable
technology for events. Access www.event-solutions.com/articles/mar04/ for more
information.

QUESTIONS FOR SELF-EVALUATION

1 Define the concept *political event*.
2 Summarise the generic phases of a political event. Cite relevant examples.
3 Compile an operations checklist for a political event of your choice.
4 Explain the tourism benefits of a political event.
5 The South African Public Holidays Act 36 of 1994 cites the annual official public holidays in South Africa. Some of these holidays are religious holidays while others have a historical political significance. As an events manager you will sometimes be expected to research the origins and relevance of a particular public holiday in order to plan and implement a political event. Choose any two official South African public holidays of historical significance and write notes on the background of the public holiday and draft a plan for a political event to commemorate the day. Apply the generic phases of a political event mentioned in this chapter.
6 Your events management company was awarded a contract to stage an event to celebrate the historical significance of Robben Island. Your client requested the details as outlined in table 18.3. Compile these details.

Some useful information may be available on the Robben Island Museum's Web site at www.robben-island.org.za

TABLE 18.3: *Research requested to manage and stage an event (Based on: GCIS, 2004: 1–5; Goldblatt, 2004a, 2004b)*

Client information and contact details
Research proposal, problem and background
Main aim and objectives of research
Event stakeholders
Title of research or event
Branding of event
Preliminary programme and entertainment
Target group/audience
Vendor contracts
Marketing strategy
Celebrity endorsement
Identify resources
Budget and funding required
Communication of results (Internet, media statements)
Briefings (by whom, to whom?)
Time frames for event planning and event day
Details of project leader

References

Alles, A. 1988. *Exhibitions: A Key to Effective Marketing.* London: Cassel Educational Ltd.

Argus, The. 1999. Tourism boom for Durban. 31 March: 10.

Ashman, SG & Ashman, J. 1999. *Introduction to Event Information Systems.* Washington, DC: George Washington University.

ATC. 2001. *Australian Tourist Commission Olympic Games Strategy.* Available at: http://www.australia2001.com/news/olympic/olympicreview.pdf [accessed on 29 June 2002].

Athens 2004. 2004. *Sponsors.* Available at: www.athens2004.com/athens2004 [accessed on 20 April 2004].

Athens 2004. 2004a. Bid city to host city. In *Athens 2004.* Available at: http://www.athens2004.com/athens2004/page/legacy?lang=en&cid=ffe8b002e4d89f00VgnVCMServer28130b0aRCRD&oid=9aa850c2c3f69f00VgnVCMServer28130b0aRCRD [accessed on 22 June 2004].

Athens 2004. 2004b. Company Structure. In *Athens 2004.* Available at: http://www.athens2004.com/athens2004/page/legacy?lang=en&cid=3358470429149f00VgnVCMServer28130b0aRCRD [accessed on 22 June 2004].

Athens 2004. 2004c. *Environment.* In *Athens 2004.* Available at: http://www.athens2004.com/athens2004/page/nochildren?lang=en&cid=ab08470429149f00VgnVCMServer28130b0aRCRD [accessed on 22 June 2004].

Athens 2004. 2004d. *Sponsors and Licensees.* In *Athens 2004.* Available at: http://www.athens2004.com/athens2004/page/legacy?lang=en&cid=0418470429149f00VgnVCMServer28130b0aRCRD [accessed on 22 June 2004].

Athens 2004. 2004e. *Security.* In *Athens 2004.* Available at: http://www.athens2004.com/athens2004/page/legacy?lang=en&cid=5088470429149f00VgnVCMServer28130b0aRCRD [accessed on 22 June 2004].

Athens 2004. 2004f. *Catering.* In *Athens 2004.* Available at: http://www.athens2004.com/athens2004/page/legacy?lang=en&cid=2d1a470429149f00VgnVCMServer28130b0aRCRD [accessed on 22 June 2004].

Athens 2004. 2004g. *Logistics.* In *Athens 2004.* Available at: http://www.athens2004.com/athens2004/page/legacy?lang=en&cid=dd08470429149f00VgnVCMServer28130b0aRCRD [accessed on 22 June 2004].

Athens 2004. 2004h. *Master Delivery Schedule Procedure, 1-45.* In *Athens 2004.* Available at: http://www.athens2004.com/files/files/Logistics/mds_en.pdf [accessed on 22 June 2004].

Athens 2004. 2004i. *Broadcasting.* In *Athens 2004.* Available at: http://www.athens2004.com/athens2004/page/legacy?lang=en&cid=d9e850c2c3f69f00VgnVCMServer28130b0aRCRD [accessed on 22 June 2004].

Attorney General. 2000. *Memorandum for all Department of Justice non-career employees.* Washington: Office of the Attorney General. Available at: www.usdoj.gov/jmd/ethics/docs/agpolactpol.htm [accessed on 16 April 2004].

Author Unknown. 1998. Technology: how it is impacting on the meetings industry. *SA Conference & Exhibition Guide,* 18 (11/12), 7.

Bach, SA. 1997. Planning meetings with safety and security in mind. In *The Complete Guide to Professional Meeting and Event Co-ordination,* ed C Price. Washington: George Washington University.

BBC News. 2004a. *Spitz raises Olympic fear.* Available at: http://newsvote.bbc.co.uk [accessed on 28 April 2004].

BBC News. 2004b. *Quincy Jones plans charity gig.* Available at: www.newsvote.bbc.co.uk [accessed on 23 April 2004].

BBC Sport. 2003. *Mandela Calls for British support.* Available at: http://news.bbc.co.uk/sport2/hi/football/internationals/england/3045945.stm [accessed on 26 May 2004].

Bell, RA & Vazquez-Illa, J. 1996. Planning for competitive strategy in declining industry. In *Practising Responsible Tourism*, eds LC Harrison & W Husbands. New York: John Wiley & Sons.

Berlonghi, A. 1990. *The Special Event Risk Manual.* Mansfield: Bookmasters Inc.

Bett, D. 1996. Conference industry deserves better recognition. *SAACI Western Cape Newsletter*, 2, 1.

Biz-Community. 2004. *At About Entertainment we are proud to celebrate South Africa's 10 years of democracy.* Available at: www.biz-community.com [accessed on 20 April 2004].

Blick South Africa (2003). Surveillance a success at sporting event. *Technews.* http://securitysa.com/article.asp?pklArticleid=2405&pklIssueID=325&pklCategoryID=3 [12 May 2004].

Boehme, AJ. 1999. *Planning Successful Meetings and Events.* New York: American Management Association.

Bruner, RE. 1998. *Net Results: Web Marketing That Works.* New York: Hayden Book Company.

Buser, B. 2004. Security: adapting for the future. *Event Solutions.* Available at: www.event-solutions.com/articles/sep03/ [accessed on 23 April 2004].

Business Day. 1999. Survey: Arts sponsorship awards. 25 May, 29–31.

Business Day. 2004. Multi-million dollar inaugural bash looms. Available at: www.bday.co.za/bday/content/direct/ [accessed on 26 April 2004].

Cameron, N. 2002. *Measuring Sponsorship's Return.* Avalilable at http://www.sponsorshipinsights.com.au/Docs/Measuring Sponsorship's Return.pdf [accessed on 28 June 2004].

Cape Town Olympic Bid Company, Task Team One. 1997. Managing the Cape Town 2004 Olympics – A study of event and construction Management in Atlanta and Sydney.

Cape Wine. 2004. *Exhibitors Manual.* Wines of South Africa: Conferences Et Al.

Catherwood, DW & Van Kirk, RL. 1992. *The Complete Guide to Special Event Management.* New York: John Wiley & Sons.

Chen, YL & Henneberg, SCM. 2004. *Political pulling power: celebrity political endorsement and campaign management for the Taipei City councillor election 2002.* Bath: University of Bath School of Management Working Paper Series 2004.02. Available at: www.bath.ac.uk/management/research/papers.htm [accessed on 16 April 2004].

Citrine, K. 1997. Site planning for events. In *Event Operations.* Washington: International Festivals and Events Association (IFEA).

Cleland, DT. 1999. *Project Management,* 3 ed. New York: McGraw-Hill.

Cloete, D. 1999. Telephonic interview, 23 March. Conferences Et Al, Stellenbosch.

Cloete, D. 2004. Personal interview: 25 May. Conferences Et Al, Stellenbosch.

Contact Publications. 1998. *1998–2007 SA Conference & Exhibition Calendar.* Durban.

Contact Publications. 1999. *1999–2008 SA Conference & Exhibition Calendar.* Durban.

Contact Publications. 2000. *2000–2009 SA Conference & Exhibition Calendar.* Durban.

Contact Publications. 2001. *2001–2009 SA Conference & Exhibition Calendar*. Durban.

Contact Publications. 2002. *2002–2010 SA Conference & Exhibition Calendar*. Durban.

Contact Publications. 2003. *2003–2011 SA Conference & Exhibition Calendar*. Durban.

Contact Publications. 2004. *2004–2012 SA Conference & Exhibition Calendar*. Durban.

Control Risks Group. 2003. *Event security*. Available at: www.crg.com [accessed on 11 November 2003].

Cooper, C, Fletcher, J, Gilbert, D, Shepherd, R & Wanhill, S. 1999. *Tourism: Principles and Practice*, 2 ed. Essex: Addison Wesley Longman Ltd.

Copeland, R & Frisby, W. 1996. Understanding the sport sponsorship process from a corporate perspective. *Journal of Sport Management*, 10, 32–48.

Coughlan, D & Mules T, 2001. Sponsorship awareness and recognition at Canberra's Floriade Festival. In *Event Management*, vol. 7, (1–9).

Cox, G. 1994. *The Olympics and Housing*. Sydney: University of Western Sydney.

Crayton, C. 1997. Managing volunteers. In *Event Operations*. Washington: IFEA.

DAC. 2004. *Celebrating 10 Years of Democracy*. Available at: www.dac.gov.za/home.htm. [accessed on 18 June 2004]. Pretoria: SA Government (Department of Arts and Culture).

Daly, J. 1996. Design and decor. In *ISES Gold*, 2 ed. Arlington, Virginia: International Special Events Society (Educational Services Institute).

Database Systems Corp. 2004. *Political Phone Campaigns*. Available at: www.databasesystemscorp.com/pspolitics.htm [accessed on 16 April 2004].

DEAT. 2003. *Responsible Tourism Handbook*. Pretoria: SA Government (Department of Environmental Affairs and Tourism).

De Kock, R. 1996. Conference industry deserves better recognition. *SAACI Western Cape Newsletter*, 2, 1.

De Tolly, P. 1992. Cape Town's Central Waterfront. *Architecture SA*, May–June, 23–26.

Department of Economic Affairs and Tourism. 1998. *Guideline Document – Environmental Impact Management* (EIA Regulations). Pretoria: DEAT.

Department of Environmental Affairs and Tourism. 1997. Regulations under Act 73 as promulgated in *Government Gazette* 18261 of 5 September 1997 (Government Notice R1182) as amended by *Government Gazette* 18783 of 27 March 1998 (Government Notice R448), and by *Government Gazette* 23401 of 10 May 2002 (Government Notice R670).

Department of Housing and Local Government. 1998. *Planning Handbook*. Bisho, South Africa: Eastern Cape Provincial Government.

DFA (Department of Foreign Affairs). 2003. *Ten Years Celebrations of Freedom. The International Programme*. Pretoria: DFA.

DFA. Undated. *Practical Guide and Procedures for the Conclusion of Agreements*. Pretoria: DFA. Office of the Chief State Law Adviser (International Law). Also available at: www.dfa.gov.za

Dickey, J. 1975. *Metropolitan Transport Planning*. Washington, DC: Scripta Book Company.

Dolan, K, Kerrins, D & Kasofsky, G. 2000. *Internet Event Marketing*. Washington, DC: George Washington University.

Du Plessis, PJ, Jooste, CJ & Strydom, JW. 2001. *Applied strategic marketing*. Johannesburg: Heinemann Publishers.

Durban Events Corporation. 2003. A socio-economic impact study of the 2003 Commonwealth Stillwater Championships. Unpublished report.

FIFA World Cup 2006. 2003. *Volunteers.* Available at: http://fifaworldcup. yahoo.com/06/en/o/octeam/volunteers.html [accessed on 27 June 2004].

FIFA. 2004. *Host Nation of 2010 FIFA World Cup – South Africa.* Available at: http://www.fifa.com/en/media/index/0,1369,101476,00.html?comp=WF&year=2010&articleid= 101476 [accessed on 22 June 2004].

GCIS (Government Communications and Information System). 2003a. *Imbizo* – A new approach to governance. *BuaNews Online.* 28 October. Available at: www.gcis.gov.za/buanews/ [accessed on 20 April 2004].

GCIS. 2003b. Outcome of government briefing to stakeholders on plans to celebrate ten years of freedom. Statement issued by GCIS on 23 September. Available at: www.10years.gov.za/ celebrate/statements/23sept03.htm [accessed on 19 April 2004].

GCIS. 2003c. A strategic framework for marking ten years of freedom. Available at: www.10years.gov.za/celebrate/docs/framework/ [accessed on 19 April 2004].

George, R. 2002. *Marketing South African Tourism and Hospitality,* 2 ed. Cape Town: Oxford University Press.

Getz, D. 1991. Special events. In *Managing Tourism,* ed S Medelik. Oxford: Butterworth-Heinemann.

Getz, D. 1994a. Event tourism and the authenticity dilemma. In *Global Tourism – The Next Decade,* ed WF Theobald. Oxford: Butterworth-Heinemann.

Getz, D. 1994b. Event tourism: evaluating the impacts. In *Travel, Tourism and Hospitality Research – A Handbook for Managers and Professionals,* eds JR Brent Ritchie & CR Goeldner, 2 ed. New York: John Wiley & Sons.

Getz, D. 1997. *Event Management & Event Tourism.* New York: Cognizant Communication Corporation.

Goldblatt, JJ. 1997. *Special Events: Best Practices in Modern Event Management.* UK: John Wiley & Sons.

Goldblatt, JJ. 2004a. Special events. Best practices in modern event management. Taken from advertisement available at: www.entertainoz.com.au/article/ Special_Events.html [accessed on 23 April 2004].

Goldblatt, JJ. 2004b. Special events: global event management in the 21st century. 3 ed. Taken from advertisement available at: www.entertainoz.com.au/article/ Special_Events.html [accessed on 23 April 2004].

Goldman, J. 1996. Inflatable sculpture. In *ISES Gold,* 2 ed. Arlington, Virginia: International Special Events Society (Educational Services Institute).

Hall, CM. 1992a. Adventure, sport and health tourism. In *Special Interest Tourism,* eds B Weiler & CM Hall, London: Belhaven Press.

Hansen, B. 1995. *Off Premises Catering Management.* New York: John Wiley.

Harris, EJ. 1998. *Advanced Project Management: MS Project.* Bisho: Fort Hare Institute of Government, Information Technology and Management Centre.

Hildreth, RA. 1990. *The Essentials of Meeting Management.* Englewood Cliffs: Prentice-Hall.

Hiller, HH. 1998. Assessing the impact of mega-events: the linkage model. *Current Issues in Tourism,* 1(1), 47–57.

Hiller, HH. 2000. Mega-events, urban boosterism and growth strategies: An analysis of the objectives and legitimations of the Cape Town 2004 Olympic Bid. *International Journal of Urban and Regional Research,* 24(2), 439–458.

Hoyle, LH. 2002. *Event Marketing, how to successfully promote events, festivals, conventions, and expositions.* New York: John Wiley and Sons.

Hudson, P. 2004. Personal interview on motivation. Full Gospel Church of God, Bellville: 2 May.

Huffadine, M. 1993. *Project Management in Hotel and Resort Development.* New York: McGraw-Hill.

ICC (International Convention Centre). 2004a. *Booked Events.* Available at: www.icc.co.za/about/pastevents.asp [accessed on 20 April 2004].

ICC (International Convention Centre). 2004b. *Services.* Available at: www.icc.co.za/about/services.htm [accessed on 20 April 2004].

IEG. 1996. *Complete Guide to Sponsorship – every thing you need to know about sports, arts, event, entertainment and cause marketing.* Illinois: IEG Inc.

IFEA. 1997a. *Event Operations.* Washington: IFEA.

IFEA. 1997b. *Official Guide to Sponsorship.* Washington: International Festivals and Events Association.

International Cricket Council (ICC) Development International Ltd. 2002. *ICC's 'Deep Concern' with Samsung Ambush Marketing.* Available at: http://ind.cricinfo.com /link_to_database/ARCHIVE/CRICKET_NEWS/2003/FEB/140262_ICC_14FEB2003.html [accessed on 24 June 2004].

IOC. 1996. *Olympic Charter.* Lausanne: IOC.

IOC. 2003a. *Candidate Acceptance Procedure Games of the XXX Olympiad 2012.* Available at: http://multimedia.olympic.org/pdf/en_report_711.pdf [accessed on 22 June 2004].

IOC 2003b. *The Organising Committees of the Olympic Games.* Available at: http://www.olympic.org/uk/organisation/ocog/index_uk.asp [accessed on 22 June 2004].

ISES. 1996. *ISES Gold,* 2 ed. Arlington: Educational Services Institute.

Jackson, R. 1997. *Making Special Events Fit in the 21st Century.* Champaign: Sagamore.

Jago, LK & Shaw, RN. 1998. Special events: a conceptual and definitional framework. *Festival Management & Event Tourism,* 5, (1/2), 21–33.

JOWSCO. 2002a. *What is the World Summit on Sustainable Development?* In Department of Environmental Affairs and Tourism South Africa. Available at: http://www.environment.gov.za/sustdev/jowsco/jowsco_index.html [accessed on 27 June 2004].

JOWSCO. 2002b. Annual Report for the period ended 31 March 2002. In Department of Environmental Affairs and Tourism South Africa. Available at: http://www.environment.gov.za/sustdev/jowsco/jowsco_index.html [accessed on 27 June 2004].

Judson, B. 1996. *Net Marketing – Your Guide to Profit and Success on the Net.* New York: Wolff New Media. [Information from: http://www.atsf.co.uk/manmult/ ch_118_index.html accessed on 26 October 2004].

Kearney, AT. 2002. *The Main Event. Best Practices for Managing Mega-sports Events.* Available at: www.atkearney.com [accessed on 20 April 2004].

Kerzner, H. 1998. *Project Management,* 6 ed. New York: John Wiley & Sons.

King, G. 1998a. Growth curve continues. *SA Conferences, Exhibitions & Incentives Guide,* 18(5), 4.

King, G. 1998b. SA growth curve continues as international conference destination. *SA Conferences, Exhibitions & Incentives Guide,* 18(9), 5.

King, G. 1999. South Africa moves to capture more of the international market. *SA Conference & Exhibition Guide,* 19(5), 7.

Koenderman, T. 2000. Event management: sponsors are queuing up for winners. Available at: http://secure.financialmail.co.za/report/adfocus2000/amarket.htm [accessed on 24 June 2004].

K-Praxis. 2004. Political risk analysis and unstructured information management. Available at: www.k-praxis.com/archives/000054.html [accessed on 16 April 2004].

Leibold, M. 1990. *Tourism Marketing and Publicity.* Cape Town: SAPTO.

Light, D. 1996. Characteristics of the audience for 'events' at a heritage site. *Tourism Management,* 17(3), 183–190.

Lloyd, N. 2000. Mega-event management. In *Event Management: A Professional and Developmental Approach,* ed D Tassiopoulos, 1 ed. Cape Town: Juta Education.

Loewe, M. 2002. The year the Arts festival crossed over. *Daily Dispatch,* 16 July, 8.

Mack, RW. 1999, Event Sponsorship: an exploratory study of small business objectives, practice and perceptions. *Journal of Small Business Management,* 37(33), 25–30.

Mail & Guardian Online. 2004. Pretoria ready for Mbeki's R90m bash. Available at: www.mg.co.za/Content/ [accessed on 26 April 2004].

Mansfield, P. 2001. Cyberface domain registration. Available from http://www.domain-names.co.za/index.html [accessed on 22 June 2004].

Martin, EL. 1992. *Festival & Sponsorship Legal Issues.* Washington: IFEA.

Masberg, BA. 1998. Defining the tourist: is it possible? *Journal of Travel Research,* 37, August, 67–70.

McCarville, RE, Flood, CM & Froats, TA. 1998. The effectiveness of selected promotions on spectators' assessment of a non-profit sporting event sponsor. *Journal of Sport Management,* 12, 51–62.

McCreedy, G. 1992. *Safe & Sound – A Public Security Handbook.* British Columbia: Association of Festivals & Events.

McGuire, W. 2004. The event. Safe, secure, successful. In *Event Solutions.* Available at: www.event-solutions.com/articles/sep03/ [accessed on 23 April 2004].

Meetings Industry Association. 1996. *UK Conference Market Survey.*

Moragas, M & Botella, M. 1995. *The Key to Success: The Social, Sporting, Economic and Communication Impact of Barcelona 1992.* Lasusanne: Centre d'Estudies Olympics del'Esport. (Documents of the Museum)

Mosia, B. 2004. *Meeting Statistics.* Available from http://www/saaci/co.za/Meeting Statistics.htm [accessed on 23 April 2004].

Moxley, J. 1995. *Advanced Co-ordination Manual.* Boulder, Colorado: Zone Interactive.

Mummaw, D. 1996. CAD applications for special events. In *ISES Gold*, 2 ed. Arlington, Virginia: International Special Events Society (Educational Services Institute).

News24.com. 2004a. Eclectic mix for SA freedom. Available at: www.news24.com/News24/ South_Africa/Decade_of_Freedom/ [accessed on 28 April 2004].

News24.com. 2004b. Stampede mars democracy party. Available at: www.news24.com/News24/ South_Africa/News/ [accessed on 28 April 2004].

News24.com. 2004c. Tshwane plays down stampede. Available at: www.news24.com/ News24/ South_Africa/Decade_of_Freedom/ [accessed on 28 April 2004].

News24.com. 2004d. Mopani worms and morogo. Available at: www.news24.com/ News24/ South_Africa/Decade_of_Freedom/ [accessed on 26 April 2004].

News24.com. 2004e. R90m 'party for the people'. Available at: www.news24.com/ News24/South_Africa/Decade_of_Freedom/ [accessed on 26 April 2004].

News24.com. 2004f. Union Buildings bustle with activity. Available at: www.news24.com/ News24/South_Africa/Decade_of_Freedom/ [accessed on 28 April 2004].

News24.com. 2004g. All set for inauguration. Available at: www.news24.com/ News24/South_Africa/Decade_of_Freedom/ [accessed on 26 April 2004].

News24.com. 2004h. Mbeki's inauguration to rock. Available at: www.news24.com/ News24/South_Africa/Elections2004/ [accessed on 26 April 2004].

News24.com. 2004i. Bring on the coffee. Available at: www.news24.com/ News24/South_Africa/Decade_of_Freedom/ [accessed on 28 April 2004].

Nickle, N. 1989. *Parade Management*. Pasadena: Neil Nickle (IFEA).

Nicolson, D. 2004. Copyright in South Africa. E-mail received on 25 May 2004. Available at: Nicholson.D@Library.wits.ac.za.

NUA 2004. Jupitermedia Corpoation. [Online]. Available at: http://www.nua.net/surveys/ how_many_online/index/html [accessed on 25 October 2004].

Olympics Assessment Team. 1997. *Strategic Environmental Assessment of the Cape Town 2004 Olympic Bid*, vol. 1–3, Cape Town.

Pain, JH. 1979. *An Introduction to Hong Kong's Conference and Meetings Potential*. Hong Kong: Hong Kong Tourist Association.

Parks and Recreation New Zealand. 2002. *Running Sport: Event Management*. http://www.sparc.org.nz/sports_admin/rs1.php [10 May 2004].

PCH. 2004. *Summative Evaluation of the Department of Canadian Heritage's Sport Hosting Program*. Available at: http://pch.gc.ca/progs/em-cr/eval/2004/2004_02/ 5_e.cfm [accessed on 17 June 2004].

Pearce, PL. 1991. Towards the better management of tourist queues. In *Managing Tourism*, ed S Medelik. Oxford: Butterworth-Heinemann.

Perry, M, Foley, P & Rumpf, P. 1996. Event management: an emerging challenge in Australian higher education. *Festival Management & Event Tourism*, 4, (3/4), 84–95.

Pike Masteralexis, L, Barr, CA & Hums, MA. (1998). *Principles and Practice of Sport Management*. Gaithersburg, MD: Aspen.

PoliticsOnline. 2004a. Online polls and opinions. Available at www.aol-politicsonline.com/entryway/onlinepolls.asp [accessed on 16 April 2004].

PoliticsOnline. 2004b. Fundraising & Internet tools for politics. Available at: www.politicsonline.com [accessed on 16 April 2004].

Polivka, EG. 1998. *Professional Meeting Management,* 7 ed. Alabama: PCMA.

Polonsky, MJ & Speed, R. 2001, Linking sponsorship and cause related marketing. *European Journal of Marketing*, vol. 35, no. 11/12, 1361–1385.

Prebyl, J. 1995. *The anatomy of a Press Release*. Available at: http://www.ssdesign.com/librarypr/content/f4spr.html [accessed on 26 May 2004].

Price, CH. 1997. *The Complete Guide to Professional Meeting and Event Co-ordination.* Washington, DC: George Washington University Event Management Programme (ISBN 0966340000).

Pringle, H. 2004. *Celebrity Sells.* New York: John Wiley & Sons.

Quickmba. 2004. *SWOT Analysis.* Available at: www.quickmba.com/strategy/swot/ [accessed on 28 June 2004].

Rae, M. 1999. Parade coverage in festivals. In *The How-to of Festivals and Events.* Port Angeles, Atlanta: IFEA.

Reader's Digest. 1984. *Family Guide to the Law in South Africa.* Cape Town: Reader's Digest.

RedZone Communications Inc. 2004. *Services.* Available at www.redzonecommunications.com/services.html [accessed on 16 April 2004].

Render, B & Heizer, J. 1997. *Principles of Operations Management*, 2 ed. New Jersey: Prentice-Hall.

Render, B & Stair, RM. 1982. *Quantitative Analysis for Management.* Boston: Allyn & Bacon.

Rich, J & Rich, JR. 2000. *Unofficial Guide to Marketing Your Business Online.* New Jersey: John Wiley & Sons Inc.

Richards, B. 1992. *How to Market Tourist Attractions, Festivals and Special Events.* Essex: Longman.

Ritchie, BW. 1996. How special are special events? The economic impact and strategic development of the New Zealand Masters Game. *Festival Management & Event Tourism*, 4, 117–126.

Roaf, V, Van Deventer, K & Houston, C. 1996. *The Olympics and Development: Lessons and Suggestions.* Cape Town: Development Action Group (DAG).

Rogers, T. 1998. *Conferences – A 21st Century Industry.* Harlow: Addison Wesley.

Rosenberg, Michael R, Woods, Kimberley, P. 1995. Event sponsorship can bring kudos and recognition. *Bank Marketing*, vol. 27, no. 5, 13–18.

Rossouw, J. 2000. Event sponsorship; Event marketing and communication; Sports event management. In *Event Management: a professional and developmental approach*, ed D Tassiopoulos, 1 ed. Cape Town: Juta: 185–207; 263–290; 412–432.

Rutherford Silvers, J. 2004. Speaking of events ... Available at: www.juliasilvers.com/ embok/ [accessed on 15 June 2004].

Rutley, JA. 1997. *Security in Event Operations.* Washington: International Festivals and Event Association.

Ryan, C, Smee, A, Murphy, S & Getz, D. 1998. New Zealand: a temporal and regional analysis. *Festival Management & Event Tourism*, 5, (1/2), 71–85.

SA Tourism & DEAT. 2002. *Towards a National Event Strategy for South Africa: Final Report (October)*. Pretoria: SA Government (Department of Environmental Affairs and Tourism and South African Tourism).

SA Tourism. 2001. *Calendar of Events.* Johannesburg: SA Tourism database (paper).

SA Tourism. 2002. *Calendar of Events.* Johannesburg: SA Tourism database (paper).

SA Tourism. 2003. *Calendar of Events.* Johannesburg: SA Tourism Web site.

SA Tourism. 2004. *Calendar of Events.* Johannesburg: SA Tourism Web site.

SA Tourism. 2004. South Africa – conference and incentives. Johannesburg: unpublished information document.

Saunders, G. 2004. *Meeting Statistics.* Available from http://www/saaci/co.za/Meeting Statistics.htm [accessed on 23 April 2004].

Schaaf, P. 1995. *Sports Marketing.* New York: Prometheus Books.

Schmader, SW & Jackson, R. 1997. *Special Events: Inside and Out*, 2 ed. Champaign, Il: Sagamore Publishing.

Selby, R. 2004. Computer Network Technology facilitates the AV running of a conference. *Conference, Exhibition & Events Guide*, 10 (2), 22.

Sheldon, P. 1997. *Tourism Information Technology*. Oxon: CABI.

Shock, PJ & Stefanelli, JM. 1992. *Hotel Catering.* New York: John Wiley & Sons.

Sivek, R. 1996. Working with unions at facilities. In *ISES Gold*, 2 ed. Arlington, Virginia: International Special Events Society (Educational Services Institute).

Skinner, JC, Von Essen, L & Mersham, GM. 2001. *Handbook of Public Relations*, 6 ed. Cape Town: Oxford University Press.

South African Sports Commission. 2003. *Bidding To Host Sport and Recreation Events in South Africa*. Centurion: South African Sports Commission

South African Sports Commission. 2003. *News – Volunteer database finds new home* (26 May 2003). Available at: http://www.sasc.org.za/News.asp?ID=19 [12 May 2004].

Southern Africa Conference, Exhibition & Events Guide. 2004. *SAFCC – raising SA's Profile*, vol. 24, no. 3.

Spilling, OR. 1998. Beyond intermezzo? On the long-term industrial impacts of mega-events: the case of Lillehammer 1994. *Festival Management & Event Tourism*, 5, 101–122.

Sportsmatch, 2004. Sponsorship Evaluation: How and why to evaluate your own sponsored project. Available at: http://www.sports-sponsorship.co.uk/sponsorship.htm#evaluating [accessed on 28 June 2004].

SRS Consulting. 2001. *Sponsorship and Event Program Guidelines.* Available at: www.communitybuilders.nsw.gov.au/download/SydneyWater_Sponsorship.pdf [accessed on 26 June 2004].

Sturken, C. 1997. Planners portfolio – checklist. *Meetings and Conventions*, 39, March, 48.

Sunday Times. 1999. Business Times Survey – Conferences & Exhibitions. 28 February, 16–18.

Swart, K & Bob U. No date (in press). Major sport event bidding in the global arena: A case study of the Cape Town 2004, Olympic Bid. *Third World Quarterly*.

Swindell, EM. 2002. *Political Activities Training Module 2002*. Washington: Office of the General Counsel (Ethics Division), Department of Health and Human Services.

The Cape Argus. 2004. Clean up – or be fined R25 for a poster. April 21, p. 2.

The Presidency. 2003. Deputy President Zuma discusses celebration of 10-year anniversary with political parties. Statement issued on 18 August 2003. Available at: www.10years.gov.za/celebrate/statements/18aug03.htm [accessed on 19 April 2004].

Torino 2006. 2002. Volunteers. Available at: http://www.torino2006.org/passione/content.php?idm=100385 [accessed on 27 June 2004].

Trigg, P. 1995. *Leisure and Tourism GNVQ: Intermediate.* Oxford: Butterworth-Heinemann.

Trotter, C. 1999. *Lessons in Excellence.* Berkley: Ten Speed Press.

Turco, DM, Riley, R & Swart, K. 2002. *Sport Tourism.* Morgantown, WV: Fitness Information Technology.

UKSport. 2003. *Major Sports Events: The Guide.* Available at: http://www.uksport.gov.uk/images/uploaded/msetgMajor_Events_Guide.pdf [accessed on 12 May 2004].United Nations. 2000. Press Release ENV/DEV/557 PI/1318. United Nations to hold 2002 World Summit on Sustainable Development in Johannesburg, South Africa. 21 December 2000.

Urban Strategies. 2004. *Political Management.* Available at: http://urbanspin.tripod.com/id15_m.htm [accessed on 16 April 2004].

US Web and Bruner, RE. 1998. *Net Results: Web Marketing That Works.* Indianapolis: Hayden Books.

Vancouver 2010. 2004. *Volunteer Opportunities.* Available at: http://www.vancouver2010.com/GettingInvolved/VolunteerOpportunities/Default.htm [accessed on 27 June 2004].

Van Aardt, I & Van Aardt, C. 1997. *Entrepreneurship and New Venture Management.* Johannesburg: International Thomson Publishing.

Van der Merwe, D. 2004. BC in line for Cup stadium. In *Daily Dispatch*: 20 May. Available at: http://www.dispatch.co.za/2004/05/20/Easterncape/aalead.html [accessed on 27 May 2004].

Van Der Wagen, L. 2001. *Event Management for Tourism, Cultural, Business and Sporting Events.* Melbourne: Hospitality Press.

Van Meter, D. 1999. *Peace of Mind in Festivals. The How-to of Festivals and Events.* Port Angeles: IFEA.

Van Wyk, JK. 1998. The external relations of selected South African sub-national governments: a preliminary assessment. *South African Journal of International Affairs*, 5(2), 21–59.

Van Wyk, JK. 2000a. *Aspekte van die openbare beleidsproses in Suid-Afrika met spesiale verwysing na waterbeleid* (1994–1999). Unpublished MA dissertation. Stellenbosch: University of Stellenbosch.

Van Wyk, JK. 2000b. Political, civic and governmental event management. In *Event management. A professional and developmental approach*, ed D Tassiopoulos, 1 ed. Cape Town: Juta.

Vocus. 2004. *Event Management.* Available at: www.vocus.com [accessed on 16 April 2004].

Watt, DC. 1998. *Event Management in Leisure and Tourism,* New York: Addison Wesley Longman.

Westerbeek, HM, Turner, P & Ingerson, L. 2002. Key success factors in bidding for hallmark sporting events. *International Marketing Review*, 19(3), 303–322.

Westward Communications. 2004. *Jim Arthur.* Available at www.westward.com/people/jdarthur.htm [accessed on 16 April 2004].

Whale, M. 1997. *ABC of Event Management.* Bedfordview: Dictum Publishers.

Whittaker, DJ. 2004. *Terrorists and Terrorism in the Contemporary World.* London: Routledge.

Wright, RA. 1988. *The Meeting Spectrum.* San Diego: Rockwood Enterprises.

Wycoff, J. 1991. *Mindmapping: Your Personal Guide to Exploring Creativity and Problem Solving.* New York: Berkley Books.

Yaffe, J. 1999. Balloons: decorating and effects. In *ISES Gold,* 2 ed. Arlington, Virginia: International Special Events Society (Educational Services Institute).

Youell, R. 1995. *Leisure & Tourism – Advanced GNVQ,* 2 ed Harlow: Longman.

Index